A. Thompson
Cardiff 1996

# Modernity

# Modernity
# An Introduction to Modern Societies

Edited by Stuart Hall, David Held,
Don Hubert, and Kenneth Thompson

Polity Press

Copyright © The Open University 1995

First published in 1995 by Polity Press
in association with Blackwell Publishers Ltd.

*Editorial office:*
Polity Press
65 Bridge Street
Cambridge CB2 1UR, UK

*Marketing and production:*
Blackwell Publishers Ltd
108 Cowley Road
Oxford OX4 1JF, UK

ISBN 0-7456-1614-3 (pbk)

A CIP catalogue record for this book is available from the British Library.


Typeset in 10 on 12 pt Melior
by Best-set Typesetter Ltd., Hong Kong
Printed and bound in Great Britain by
Hartnolls Limited, Bodmin, Cornwall
This book is printed on acid-free paper.

# Contents

List of Contributors    ix
Preface    x
Acknowledgments    xii

**Part I    Formations of Modernity**    1

Introduction    3
*Stuart Hall*

1    The Enlightenment and the Birth of Social Science    19
*Peter Hamilton*

Introduction    20
What was the Enlightenment?    24
Enlightenment as the Pursuit of Modernity    35
Revolution and Reformation    44
The Birth of Sociology: Saint-Simon and Comte    48
Conclusion    51

2    The Development of the Modern State    55
*David Held*

Introduction    56
A Brief History and Geography of European States    58
Why did Nation-States Become Supreme?    73
Conclusion    84

3    The Emergence of the Economy    90
*Vivienne Brown*

Introduction: The Economic Formation of Modernity    91
A Modern Economy in the Making?    93
The Beginnings of Modern Economics    107
A Modern Economics?    114
Conclusion: Signposting the Future?    118

4    Changing Social Structures: Class and Gender    122
*Harriet Bradley*

Introduction    123
Pre-Industrial Society    124
Class, Gender, and Industrialization    133
Industrial Society and the Growth of Feminism    143
Conclusion    146

5    The Cultural Formations of Modern Society    149
*Robert Bocock*

Introduction    150
Defining Culture    151

|  | Analyzing Culture | 154 |
|  | Culture and Social Change | 163 |
|  | The Costs of Civilization | 171 |
|  | Conclusion | 181 |

| 6 | The West and the Rest: Discourse and Power | 184 |
|  | *Stuart Hall* |  |

|  | Introduction | 185 |
|  | Europe Breaks Out | 189 |
|  | Discourse and Power | 201 |
|  | Representing "the Other" | 205 |
|  | "In the Beginning All the World was America" | 216 |
|  | From "the West and the Rest" to Modern Sociology | 221 |
|  | Conclusion | 224 |

| **Part II** | **Structures and Processes of Modernity** | 229 |
|  | Introduction | 231 |
|  | *Don Hubert and Kenneth Thompson* |  |

| 7 | The State in Advanced Capitalist Societies | 239 |
|  | *Anthony McGrew* |  |

|  | Introduction | 240 |
|  | The Advanced Capitalist State: Diversity and Uniformity | 242 |
|  | The Formation of the Advanced Capitalist State | 249 |
|  | Putting the Advanced Capitalist State in Perspective | 261 |
|  | Putting the Advanced Capitalist State in its Place | 272 |
|  | The ACS: A Review | 275 |

| 8 | Fordism and Modern Industry | 280 |
|  | *John Allen* |  |

|  | Introduction | 281 |
|  | Ford, Fordism, and Modern Industry | 282 |
|  | Progress and Modern Industry | 297 |
|  | Conclusion: Globalization and Industry | 304 |

| 9 | Divisions of Labor | 307 |
|  | *Peter Braham* |  |

|  | Introduction | 308 |
|  | From a Manufacturing to a Service Economy? | 309 |
|  | Labor Market Segmentation | 312 |
|  | Gender and Labor Market Segmentation | 317 |
|  | Migrant Workers and Divisions of Labor | 321 |
|  | A New International Division of Labor? | 327 |
|  | The Division of Labor and Flexible Specialization | 332 |
|  | Conclusion | 337 |

| 10 | Women and the Domestic Sphere | 343 |
|  | *Helen Crowley* |  |

Introduction                                                                344
Women and the Family: Some Theoretical Issues                               348
Conclusion                                                                  360

11      The Body and Sexuality                                              363
        *Jeffrey Weeks*

        What do we Mean when we Talk about the Body and
            Sexuality?                                                      364
        Sexuality and Sexual Norms                                         372
        Sexuality and Power                                                375
        Sexual Identities                                                  380
        Sexuality and Politics                                            388

12      Religion, Values, and Ideology                                     395
        *Kenneth Thompson*

        Introduction                                                       396
        Enlightenment: The Dilemmas of Modernity                          398
        Secularization and Community                                      403
        Foucault: Integration through Discourses                          407
        Gramsci: The Struggle for Ideological Hegemony                     410
        Ideological Community                                             412
        Conclusion                                                         420

**Part III   Modernity and its Futures**                                   423

        Introduction                                                       425
        *Stuart Hall, David Held, and Gregor McLennan*

13      The 1989 Revolutions and the Triumph of Liberalism                 436
        *David Held*

        Introduction                                                       437
        The Triumph of Liberalism?                                        442
        The Necessity of Marxism?                                         447
        From Modernity to Post-Modernity?                                 452
        The Story So Far, and the Question of the Political Good           457
        Democracy: Between State and Civil Society?                       459
        Conclusion                                                         463

14      A Global Society?                                                   466
        *Anthony McGrew*

        Introduction                                                       467
        Modernity and Globalization                                       469
        Mapping the Dimensions of Globalization                           473
        A Global Society?                                                  480
        Globalization and the Future Political Community                  488
        Globalization and a Universal Sociology                           497

15      Environmental Challenges                                           504
        *Steven Yearley*

Introduction                                                         505
Ecological Threats to Modern Society: An Overview                    507
Developing a Green Political Ideology                                514
Growth, Capitalism, and Green Consumerism                           523
Conclusion: Environmental Challenges and the
  Enlightenment                                                     529

16    Post-Industrialism/Post-Fordism                               533
      *John Allen*

Introduction: The Economy in Transition                             534
From Industrialism to Post-Industrialism and Beyond                 536
From Fordism to Post-Fordism                                        546
Assessing Economic Transitions                                      555
Conclusion: Beyond the Modern Economy?                              560

17    Social Pluralism and Post-Modernity                           564
      *Kenneth Thompson*

Introduction                                                         565
Post-Modernism                                                       569
Post-Modernism as the Cultural Logic of Late Capitalism             572
Rejections of Post-Modernism                                         578
Reconstructions in Post-Modernity or New Times                      580
Post-Modernity: Consumption and Appearances                         583
New Connections of Constructive Post-Modernism                      586
Conclusion                                                           591

18    The Question of Cultural Identity                             595
      *Stuart Hall*

Introduction: Identity in Question                                  596
The Birth and Death of the Modern Subject                           601
National Cultures as "Imagined Communities"                         611
Globalization                                                        618
The Global, the Local, and the Return of Ethnicity                  623
Fundamentalism, Diaspora, and Hybridity                             629

19    The Enlightenment Project Revisited                           635
      *Gregor McLennan*

Introduction: The Post-Modern Condition                             636
A Debate: Post-Modernity versus Enlightenment                       638
Lyotard: Abandoning the Metanarratives of Modernity                 639
Habermas: Defending Modernity and Enlightenment                     642
A Problem with Post-Modernism: Its Relativism                       644
A Problem with Enlightenment: Its Hubris                            648
Post-Modernity as "Reflexivity"                                     651
Overview                                                             654
Conclusion                                                           661

Index                                                                664

# Contributors

| | |
|---|---|
| John Allen | Senior Lecturer in Economic Geography, Open University |
| Robert Bocock | Senior Lecturer in Sociology, Open University |
| Harriet Bradley | Lecturer in Sociology, University of Bristol |
| Peter Braham | Lecturer in Sociology, Open University |
| Vivienne Brown | Senior Lecturer in Economics, Open University |
| Helen Crowley | Senior Lecturer in Women's Studies, North London University |
| Stuart Hall | Professor of Sociology, Open University |
| Peter Hamilton | Lecturer in Sociology, Open University |
| David Held | Professor of Politics and Sociology, Open University |
| Don Hubert | Post-graduate Researcher, University of Cambridge |
| Anthony McGrew | Senior Lecturer in Politics, Open University |
| Gregor McLennan | Professor of Sociology, Massey University, NZ |
| Kenneth Thompson | Professor of Sociology, Open University |
| Jeffrey Weeks | Professor of Sociology, South Bank University |
| Steven Yearley | Professor of Sociology, Queen's University, Belfast |

# Preface

*Understanding Modern Societies* is a new sociology textbook which aims to provide a comprehensive and stimulating introduction to the history, sociology, and ideas of modern society. It has been written for students and readers who have no prior knowledge of sociology, and is designed to be used in a variety of social science courses in universities and colleges.

The volume is divided into three parts, corresponding to the formation, consolidation, and prospects of modernity. Within each part, care has been taken to provide a balanced, multi-dimensional account, covering not only political and economic factors but social and cultural ones as well.

Part I, "Formations of Modernity," introduces the central themes of the volume. It is concerned not only with the historical development of the modern state, the capitalist economy, and the Industrial Revolution, but also with the simultaneous emergence of the Enlightenment and the social sciences. By broadening their focus beyond political and economic transformations, these chapters argue that social and cultural processes are not merely manifestations of political and economic forces, but are in fact central to the constitution of modernity. These cultural claims are developed further through an examination of the relationship between Europe as the birthplace of modernity, and its expansion into the rest of the world on both historic and discursive levels.

Part II, "Structures and Processes of Modernity," explores the formalization or consolidation of these emergent trends, particularly in the twentieth century. Central themes here are the expansion of the state, particularly in the provision of welfare, the emergence of mass production industry, and changing divisions in the labor market. Several chapters in this section focus on the constructed nature of gender relations which affect both the domestic sphere and the regulation of the body and sexuality. The section closes with an examination of the important and changing roles of religion and ideology in western societies.

Part III, "Modernity and its Futures," explores the various directions in which western societies, and the Enlightenment project, appear to be headed. These chapters are concerned with the notions of change and continuity in each of the four constitutive processes. With respect to the political sphere, part III grapples with the status of liberalism and socialism at the end of the Cold War, and with the explosive dynamics of globalization. In the realm of economics the debates around post-industrialism and post-Fordism are explored, while for society more generally the chapters debate the significance of the post-modernist challenge and the unstable nature of identity. In conclusion the question of social science as an enterprise is reevaluated. The post-modern themes of doubt and uncertainty, in contrast to the

Enlightenment focus on truth and control, have raised doubts about many foundational assumptions of the social sciences which necessitate a widespread reappraisal.

The volume places considerable emphasis on theoretical and conceptual issues while providing authoritative empirical data to substantiate its claims. Although originally targeted towards a British audience, there is substantial comparative analysis, with several sections explicitly international or global in scope. Each of the three parts begins with a substantial introduction highlighting the philosophical and theoretical perspective adopted, the central themes developed, and a brief chapter outline. Each chapter also includes a bibliography which gives references for citations within the chapter, and provides an entry point for further inquiry into the relevant literature.

The chapters in this book have been selected and abridged from a four-volume series entitled *Understanding Modern Societies*, which was developed as the primary text for an Open University course of the same name. These chapters are therefore the result of a collaborative effort by a course team consisting of academic authors and consultants, an external academic assessor, and secretaries. We would like to thank the following individuals for their contributions: Margaret Allott, David Boswell, Dianne Cook, Robert Cookson, James Donald, Molly Freeman, Paul du Gay, Paul Lewis, Celia Lury, Denise Riley, Graeme Salaman, Alan Scott, David Scott-Macnab, Keith Stribley, Bryan Turner, Pauline Turner, Diane Watson, Geoffrey Whitty, David Wilson, and Chris Wooldridge.

*Stuart Hall, David Held, Don Hubert, and Kenneth Thompson*

# Acknowledgments

The authors and publishers wish to thank the copyright holders for permission to reprint the following copyrighted material.

**Chapter 1**  Bonnie Anderson and Judith Zinsser, excerpts from *A History of Their Own, Vol. II*, pp. 106–9, 112–15, 118–20. Copyright © 1988 by Bonnie Anderson and Judith Zinsser. Reprinted by permission of HarperCollins Publishers, Inc., New York.

**Chapter 2**  Figure 2.1, Colin McEvedy, Europe in AD 406 from *The Penguin Atlas of Medieval History*. Copyright © 1961. Reprinted by permission of Penguin Books Ltd., London. Figure 2.2 Colin McEvedy, Europe in AD 998 from *The Penguin Atlas of Medieval History*. Copyright © 1961. Reprinted by permission of Penguin Books Ltd., London. Figure 2.3 Colin McEvedy, Europe in AD 1478 from *The Penguin Atlas of Medieval History*. Copyright © 1961. Reprinted by permission of Penguin Books Ltd., London. Figure 2.4 Colin McEvedy, Europe in AD 1980 from *The Penguin Atlas of Recent History*. Copyright © 1982. Reprinted by permission of Penguin Books Ltd., London. Figure 2.6 M. Mann, British state expenditure, 1695–1820 from *The Sources of Social Power*, p. 484. Copyright © 1986. Reprinted by permission of Cambridge University Press, Cambridge England. Table 2.2 M. Mann, Austrian state expenditure, 1795–1817 (in percent) from *The Sources of Social Power*, p. 487. Copyright © 1986. Reprinted by permission of Cambridge University Press, Cambridge, England.

**Chapter 3**  R. Porter, excerpt from *English Society in the Eighteenth Century*, second edition, pp. 190, 193–6. Copyright © 1990. Reproduced by permission of Penguin Books Ltd., London. Table 3.1 R.V. Jackson, Annual growth rates of output, population, and output per head in eighteenth-century Britain from "Government expenditure and economic growth in the eighteenth century," *Economic History Review*, XLIII, 1990, pp. 219, 225. Copyright © 1990. Cambridge, MA: Blackwell Publishers. Reprinted by permission of Blackwell Publishers Ltd., Oxford, England. Table 3.2 Eurostat. Annual rates of growth or gross domestic product per head of total populations, 1983–8 from *Basic Statistics of the Community*, 1990, 27th edition, pp. 40. Copyright © 1990. Reprinted by permission of Eurostat, Luxembourg. Table 3.3 R.V. Jackson, Annual growth rates for different sectors in eighteenth-century Britain (excluding government) from "Government expenditure and economic growth in the eighteenth century," *Economic History Review*, XLIII, 1990, p. 232. Reprinted by permission of Blackwell Publishers Ltd., Oxford, England. Table 3.4 R. Cole, Proportion of national output produced by the agricultural and industrial/commercial sectors in the eighteenth century (England and Wales) from "Factors in demand 1700–1800" in R. Floud and D. McCloskey (eds.), *Economic History of Britain Since 1700, Vol. I, 1700–1800*, p. 64. Copyright © 1981. Reprinted by permission of Cambridge University Press, Cambridge, England. Table 3.5 Composition of output in the UK, W. Germany,

France, the USA, and Japan, 1987 from *Basic Statistics of the Community*, 1990, 27th edition, p. 41. Copyright © 1987. Reprinted by permission of Eurostat, Luxembourg.

**Chapter 4**  E.P. Thompson, excerpt from *The Making of the English Working Class*, pp. 9–11. Copyright © 1963 by E.P. Thompson. Harmondsworth, England: Penguin Books Ltd. Reprinted by permission of Pantheon Books, a division of Random House, Inc., New York. Table 4.1 L. Holcombe, Total working population in England and Wales, 1861–1911 from *Victorian Ladies at Work*, p. 213. Copyright © 1973. Reprinted by permission of David and Charles Publishers, Newton Abbot, Devon, England.

**Chapter 5**  M. Weber, excerpt from *The Protestant Ethic and the Spirit of Capitalism*, 1971, pp. 181–3. Copyright © 1958, Talcott Parsons, translator. Reprinted by permission of Prentice-Hall, Inc., Upper Saddle River, New Jersey. Sigmund Frend, excerpt from *Civilizations and Its Discontents*, translated from the German by James Strachey with the permission of W.W. Norton & Company, Inc., pp. 24–5. Copyright © 1961 by James Strachey, renewed 1989 by Alix Strachey. Reprinted by permission of W.W. Norton & Company, Inc., New York.

**Chapter 6**  M. Mann, excerpt from "European development: approaching a historical explanation" in J. Baechler et al. (eds.), *Europe and the Rise of Capital*, pp. 10–15. Copyright © 1988. Reprinted by permission of Blackwell Publishers Ltd., Oxford, England. J.M. Roberts, excerpt from *The Triumph of the West*, British Broadcasting Corporation, 1985, pp. 194–202. Copyright © 1985 by J.M. Roberts. Reprinted by permission of Little, Brown and Company, Boston. Figure 6.3 Jan van der Straet. *Europe Encounters America*, c. 1600. Copyright © British Museum. Reprinted by permission of the British Museum. Figure 6.4 Theodore de Bry. Columbus being greeted by the Indians, 1590. Reprinted by permission of The British Library, London.

**Chapter 7**  Jens Albert. Excerpt from "Continuities and changes in the idea of the welfare state," from *Politics and Society*, 16:4, 1988, pp. 451–68. Copyright © 1988. Reprinted by permission of Sage Publications, Inc., Thousand Oaks, CA. Table 7.1 R. Rose, The growth in central government departments, 1849–1982 from *Big Government*, p. 157. Copyright © 1984. Reprinted by permission of Sage Publications, Inc., London. Table 7.2 J. Berger, Public expenditure in fifteen OECD countries as % of GDP from "Market and state in advanced capitalist societies" in A. Martinelli and N. Smelser, *Economy and Society*, p. 117. Copyright © 1990. Reprinted by permission of Sage Publications, Inc., London. Table 7.3 C. Tilly, Military expenditure as a percentage of state budgets 1850–1975 from *Coercion Capital and European States*, p. 124. Copyright © 1990. Reprinted by permission of Blackwell Publishers Ltd., Oxford, England. Table 7.5 P. Kennedy, War expenditure and total mobilized forces, 1914–19 from *The Rise and Fall of the Great Powers*, p. 274. Copyright © 1987 by Paul Kennedy. New York: Alfred A. Knopf. Reprinted by permission of Random House Inc., New York. Table 7.6 P. Kennedy, Armaments production of the powers, 1940–3 (billions of 1944 dollars) from *The Rise and Fall of the Great Powers*, p. 355. Copyright © 1987 by Paul Kennedy. New York: Alfred A. Knopf. Reprinted by permission of Random House Inc., New York. Table 7.8 C. Lehmbruch, A cumulative scale of corporation from J. Goldthorpe, *Order and Conflict in Contemporary Capitalism*, p. 66. Copyright © 1984. Oxford: Clarendon Press. Reprinted by permission of Oxford University Press, Oxford, England.

**Chapter 8**   Figure 8.1 P. Armstrong et al., Output, capital stock, productivity, and employment in the advanced industrial economics, 1952–70 from *Capitalism Since 1945*, p. 118. Copyright © 1991. Reprinted by permission of Blackwell Publishers Ltd., Oxford, England.

**Chapter 9**   F. Frobel et al., excerpt from *The New International Division of Labour*, pp. 12–15. Copyright © 1980. New York: Cambridge University Press. Reprinted by permission of Cambridge University Press, Cambridge, England. Figure 9.1 N. Abercrombie, A. Warde, et al., Approximate proportions of workers in different economic sectors, 1801–1986 from *Contemporary British Society*, p. 84. Copyright © 1988. Oxford: Polity Press. Reprinted by permission of Blackwell Publishers Ltd., Oxford, England. Figure 9.2 R. Loveridge, Organizational and firm-specific labour markets from "Labour market segmentation and the firm," in J. Edwards et al. (eds.), *Manpower Planning: Strategy and Techniques in an Organizational Context*, Fig. 7.1, p. 159. Copyright © 1983. Reprinted by permission of John Wiley & Sons Ltd., West Sussex, England.

**Chapter 11**   Carole Vance, excerpt from "Social construction theory," in A. van Kooten Niekerk and T. van der Meer (eds.), *Homosexuality, Which Homosexuality?*, pp. 18–19. Copyright © 1989. Reprinted by permission of GMP Publishers, London.

**Chapter 12**   M. Foucault, excerpt from *The History of Sexuality, Vol. I*, pp. 58–63. New York: Vintage Books, 1980. Copyright © 1976 by Editions Gallimard. Reprinted by permission of Georges Borchardt, Inc.

**Chapter 13**   Photo, G. Pinkhassov, The Removal of the statue of Felix Edmundovitch Dzerzhinsky, founder of the KGB, from Moscow on 22 August, 1991. Reprinted by permission of Magum Photos, Inc., New York. H.V. Perlmutter, excerpt from *Human Relations*, 44:9, September 1991, pp. 898, 902–6. Reprinted by permission of Plenum Publishing Corporation, New York.

**Chapter 14**   Photo, George P. Windham, The UN takes on a vital role in the "new world order" following the end of the cold war. Reprinted by permission of Associated Press, New York.

**Chapter 15**   Andrew Dobson, excerpt from *Green Political Thought*, 1990, pp. 7–10. London: Unwin Hyman. Reprinted by permission of Routledge, London.

**Chapter 17**   F. Jameson, excerpt from *Postmodernism or the Cultural Logic of Late Capitalism*, pp. 319, 326, 331. Copyright © 1991. Reprinted by permission of Verso, London. D. Hebdige, excerpt from "After the Masses," in S. Hall and M. Jaques (eds.), *New Times*, pp. 90–1. Copyright © 1989, Verso. London: Lawrence and Wishart. Reprinted by permission of Verso, New York.

**Chapter 18**   K. Robins, excerpt from "Tradition and Translation," in

J. Coroner and S. Harvey, *Enterprise and Heritage*, pp. 25, 28–31, 33–6, 41. Copyright © 1991. Reprinted by permission of Routledge, London. D. Massey, excerpt from "A global sense of place," *Marxism Today*, June 1991, pp. 25–6. Copyright © Democratic Left. Reprinted by permission of Democratic Left, London.

**Chapter 19** J.-F. Lyotard, excerpt, from *The Postmodern Condition: A Report on Knowledge*, 1984, pp. xxii–xxv, 3–11. Reprinted by permission of Manchester University Press, Manchester, England. Z. Bauman, excerpt from *Legislators and Interpreters: On Modernity, Post Modernity, and Intellectuals*, 1988, pp. 140–4. New York: Cornell University Press, 1988. Copyright © Zygmunt Bauman, 1987. Used by permission of Cornell University Press.

# Part I
# Formations of Modernity

# Introduction

Stuart Hall

"Formations of Modernity," as the title suggests, is concerned with the process of formation which led to the emergence of modern societies, and which stamped them with their distinctive character. The following chapters address a number of questions which have proved to be of fundamental importance throughout the history of the social sciences. When, how, and why did modern societies first emerge? Why did they assume the forms and structures which they did? What were the key processes which shaped their development? Traditionally, modern societies have been identified with the onset of industrialization in the nineteenth century. "Formations" breaks with this tradition, tracing modern societies back to their origins in the rapid and extensive social and economic development which followed the decline of feudalism in Western Europe. It sees modern societies now as a global phenomenon and the modern world as the unexpected and unpredicted outcome of, not one, but a series of major historical transitions.

The six chapters which comprise part I not only map this historical process of formation, but attempt to provide an explanatory framework for this development. The common-sense term "modern" – meaning recent, up-to-date – is useful in locating these societies chronologically, but it lacks a theoretical or analytic rationale. "Formations of Modernity," however, analyzes the passage to modernity in terms of a theoretical model based on the interaction of a number of "deeply structured processes of change taking place over long periods," as David Held puts it in chapter 2. It does not collapse these into a single process (e.g. "modernization"), but treats them as different processes, working according to different historical time-scales, whose interaction led to variable and contingent outcomes. As Held observes, "the stress is on *processes, factors* and *causal patterns* . . . there is no mono-causal explanation – no single phenomenon or set of phenomena – which fully explains [their] rise . . . It is in a combination of factors that the beginnings of an explanation . . . can be found." We return to the implications of this multi-causal approach later in this introduction.

The four major social processes which "Formations" identifies are: the political, the economic, the social, and the cultural. They form the basis of the four central chapters in part I, and organize the narrative or "story-line" of the rest of the volume. In part II, "Structures and Processes of Modernity," these four processes provide the framework for an analysis of what developed industrial societies look like and how they work. In the final part, "Modernity and its Futures," they provide the basis for identifying the emergent social forces and contradictory processes which are radically reshaping modern societies today.

"Formations of Modernity" is divided into six chapters. In chapter 1, "The Enlightenment and the Birth of Social Science," Peter Hamilton examines the explosion of intellectual energy in eighteenth-century Western Europe which became known as "the Enlightenment." This movement gave definition to the very idea of "modernity" and is often described as the original matrix of the modern social sciences. Of course, in one sense, the study of society was not new. Writers had been making observations about social life for millennia. But the idea of "the social" as a separate and distinct form of reality, which could be analyzed in entirely "this-worldly," material terms and laid out for rational investigation and explanation, is a distinctly modern idea which only finally crystallized in the discourses of the Enlightenment. The "birth of the social" as an object of knowledge made possible for the first time the systematic analysis and the practices of investigation we call "the social sciences."

Chapter 1 examines the historical and geographical context of the European Enlightenment, and the vision of intellectual emancipation which seized its principal figures – the *philosophes* – including such major precursors of modern social theory as Montesquieu, Diderot, Voltaire, Rousseau, and the luminaries of the "Scottish Enlightenment" such as David Hume, Adam Smith, and Adam Ferguson. It discusses the Enlightenment critique of traditional authority and examines some of its leading ideas – progress, science, reason, and nature. These gave shape to the "promise" of the Enlightenment – the prospect which it opened up of an unending era of material progress and prosperity, the abolition of prejudice and superstition and the mastery of the forces of nature based on the expansion of human knowledge and understanding. The chapter takes the story forward, through the Romantic movement and the French Revolution to those major theorists of nineteenth-century social science – Saint-Simon and Comte. It looks forward to that later moment, at the end of the nineteenth century, when the social sciences were once again reorganized.

This second moment in the development of the social sciences – between 1890 and 1920 – was the time of what are now known as the "founding figures" of sociology: Durkheim, Weber, Simmel, and Tönnies. Thereafter the social sciences became more compartmentalized into their separate disciplines, more specialized and empirical, more "scientific" (positivistic) and more closely engaged with application to the "real world" through social engineering. Nevertheless, these classical figures of modern sociology also undertook a major examination of the formation of the modern world and its "laws of development," not unlike that which the Enlightenment *philosophes* had inaugurated. These Enlightenment concerns continue to underpin the social sciences today. Indeed, in recent years, there has been a remarkable revival in historical sociology, which is concerned with these questions of long-term transformation and development; and, interestingly, they are being pursued in a more interdisciplinary way, drawing together the researches of sociologists, economic and social historians, political theorists, and philosophers. It is as if these profound questions about the origin and destiny of the modern world are surfacing again at the very moment when modernity itself – its promise and its vicissitudes – is being put in question. This book draws on much of that new work in historical sociology and reflects these emerging concerns and debates.

The second chapter, "The Development of the Modern State," opens by examining the formation of the modern state. David Held sees the modern state emerging at the intersection of the national and international systems. He traces the state's development through a variety of historical forms – from the classical European empires, the divided authority of the feudal states (Papacy and Holy Roman Empire), the estates system and the absolutisms of the early modern period, to the emergence of the forms of political authority, secular power, legitimacy, and sovereignty characteristic of the modern *nation-state*. The chapter considers the roles of warfare, militarism, and capitalism in underpinning the supremacy of this nation-state form. It discusses the system of nation-states as the foundation of the modern international order and looks forward to the emergence of liberal democracy as the privileged twentieth-century state-form of modern societies in the West.

In chapter 3, "The Emergence of the Economy," Vivienne Brown examines the formation of a distinct sphere of economic life, governed by new economic relations, and regulated and represented by new economic ideas. She describes the spread of commerce and trade, the expansion of markets, the new division of labor, and the growth of material wealth and consumption – "opulence" – in eighteenth-century British society, consequent upon the rise of capitalism in Europe and the gradual transformation of the traditional economy. European economic development began early – some date it as early as the fifteenth century – and the expansion of trade and the market was at the center of the process. But for a long time, capitalism developed under the protective shadow of state monopolies at home and mercantilism overseas. By the eighteenth century, however, *laissez-faire* and the market forces of the private economy were beginning to unleash the productive energies of the capitalist system. Vivienne Brown reminds us that the engines of this development were the commercial and agrarian revolutions. The economic model in the mind of Adam Smith when he wrote *The Wealth of Nations* – that bible of capitalist development – was agrarian and commercial capitalism, not the industrial smokestacks and factory-hands of Marx and Engels. The chapter weaves together an account of the formation of the modern economy and the new ways of speaking and thinking about economic life – the new economic discourse – which emerged in the eighteenth century. It provides a re-reading of Adam Smith's classic work, which became such a landmark text of the modern age, and sets its ideas in their proper historical and moral contexts.

In chapter 4, "Changing Social Structures: Class and Gender," Harriet Bradley takes the story forwards from the agrarian and commercial revolutions of the eighteenth century to the upheavals of the Industrial Revolution of the nineteenth. She also shifts the focus from economic processes to the changing social relations and the new type of social structure characteristic of industrial capitalist society. Her chapter is concerned with the emergence of new social and sexual divisions of labor. She contrasts the class and gender formations of pre-industrial, rural society with the rise of the new social classes, organized around capital and waged labor; the work patterns associated with the new forms of industrial production; and the new relations between men and women, organized around the shifting distinctions between the public and the private, work and home, the public world and the family and household.

The chapter discusses some of the major sociological theories and models of class formation. It also deploys the concepts of gender, patriarchy, and family which feminist social theorists have advanced in the social science agenda and which are increasingly problematizing "class" as the master (sic) explanatory category. Harriet Bradley analyzes the social structure of industrial society in terms of the deep interpenetration of class *and* gender. The chapter points forward to how these class and gender structures evolved and were complicated by questions of race and ethnicity in the twentieth century.

In chapter 5, "The Cultural Formations of Modern Society," Robert Bocock looks at the increasing importance given to the analysis of culture, meaning, language, and the symbolic structures of social life in contemporary social theory – what the anthropologist, Lévi-Strauss, identified as "the study of the life of signs at the heart of social life." The chapter then turns to a discussion of three key cultural themes in the transition to modernity; first, the shift from a religious to a secular world-view, and from a "sacred" to a "profane" foundation for social and moral values, which characterizes the passage from traditional society to modern society; second, the role which religion played in the formation of the "spirit of capitalism" – a discussion of Max Weber's thesis about "the Protestant ethic"; third, the growing awareness among western philosophers and social theorists of the costs of modern culture – what Freud called civilization's "discontents," and Weber saw as the consequences of the increasing rationalization and disenchantment of the modern world. This final theme points forward to recent critiques of the "promise" of the Enlightenment, which are taken up in subsequent chapters of the book. It shows that a pessimistic assessment of enlightenment and modernity has in fact been part of Enlightenment reason – its "dark shadow" – from its very inception.

Finally, in chapter 6, "The West and the Rest: Discourse and Power," Stuart Hall places the early Europe-centered – and Euro-centric – account of the evolution of modern societies and modernity in the West in a wider global context. The gradual integration of Western Europe, its take-off into sustained economic growth, the emergence of the system of powerful nation-states, and other features of the formation of modern societies is often told as a purely *internal* story – as if Europe provided all the conditions, materials, and dynamic necessary for its own development from within itself. This view is challenged at several places in this book and chapter 6 reminds us, once again, that the process also had *external* and global conditions of existence. The particular form of "globalization" which is undermining and transforming modernity today (the internationalization of production, consumption, markets, and investment), is only the latest phase in a very long story; it is not a new phenomenon. The early expansion of the European maritime empires in the fifteenth century, the exploration of new worlds, the encounter with new peoples and civilizations very different from those of Europe, and the harnessing of them to the dynamic development of Europe through commerce, conquest, and colonization are *key* episodes (but often neglected ones) in the formation of modern societies and the modern age.

Chapter 6 argues that the integration of Western Europe also involved the construction of a new sense of cultural identity. Europe only discovered and produced this new identity in the course of representing itself as a distinct, unique, and triumphant civilization, and at the same time marking its difference from other cultures, peoples, and civilizations. These "Others" were incorporated into the West's image of itself – into its language, its systems of representation, its forms of knowledge, its visual imagery, even its conception of what sorts of people did and did not have access to reason itself. This encounter with difference and the construction of "otherness" is sketched in relation to the European exploration and conquest of the Americas, Asia, Africa, and the Pacific between the fifteenth and nineteenth centuries. The chapter analyzes the formation of these discourses of "self" and "otherness," through which the West came to represent itself and imagine its *difference* from "the Rest." It looks forward, across the centuries, to the way these images of the West and "the Rest" resurface in contemporary discourses of race and ethnicity, at a time when "the Other" is beginning to question and contest the "centeredness" of the West, which western civilization (and western social science) has for so long taken for granted.

We can now turn to consider in greater detail some of the themes and approaches in part I. As noted earlier, the account of the formation of modern societies is organized principally in terms of four major processes – the political, the economic, the social, and the cultural. The transition to modernity is explained in terms of the interaction between these four processes. It could not have occurred without them. No one process, on its own, provides an adequate explanation of the formation of modern societies. Consequently, no one process is accorded explanatory priority in the analysis. Analytically, we treat each process as distinct – an approach which has certain consequences to which we shall return in a moment. However, it must be borne in mind that, in "real" historical time, they interacted with one another. The evolution of the modern state, for example, has a different history from that of the modern economy. Nevertheless the nation-state provided the institutional framework and shared legal and political norms which facilitated the expansion of the national economy. Modernity, then, was the outcome, not of a single process, but of the condensation of a number of different processes and histories.

How does this relate to the definition of a society as "modern"? What characteristics must it have to merit that description?

What we mean by "modern" is that each process led to the emergence of certain distinctive features or social characteristics, and it is these features which, taken together, provide us with our definition of "modernity." In this sense, the term "modern" does not mean simply that the phenomenon is of recent origin. It carries a certain analytic and theoretical value, because it is related to a conceptual model. What are these defining features or characteristics of modern societies?

1   The dominance of secular forms of political power and authority and conceptions of sovereignty and legitimacy, operating within defined territorial boundaries, which are characteristic of the large, complex structures of the modern nation-state.

2   A monetarized exchange economy, based on the large-scale production and consumption of commodities for the market, extensive ownership of private property and the accumulation of capital on a systematic, long-term basis. (The economies of Eastern European communist states were an exception to some of these features, though they were based on the large-scale industrial production and consumption of goods.)

3   The decline of the traditional social order, with its fixed social hierarchies and overlapping allegiances, and the appearance of a dynamic social and sexual division of labor. In modern capitalist societies, this was characterized by new class formations, and distinctive patriarchal relations between men and women.

4   The decline of the religious world-view typical of traditional societies and the rise of a secular and materialist culture, exhibiting those individualistic, rationalist, and instrumental impulses now so familiar to us.

There are two other aspects of our definition of modernity which should be loosely included under the rubric of "the cultural." The first refers to ways of producing and classifying knowledge. The emergence of modern societies was marked by the birth of a new intellectual and cognitive world, which gradually emerged with the Reformation, the Renaissance, the scientific revolution of the seventeenth century, and the Enlightenment of the eighteenth century. This shift in Europe's intellectual and moral universe was dramatic, and as constitutive for the formation of modern societies as early capitalism or the rise of the nation-state. Second, "Formations of Modernity" follows modern social analysis in the emphasis it gives to the construction of cultural and social identities as part of the formation process. By this we mean the construction of a sense of belonging which draws people together into an "imagined community" and the construction of symbolic boundaries which define who does *not* belong or is excluded from it. For many centuries, being "Christian" or "Catholic" was the only common identity shared by the peoples of Western Europe. "European" was an identity which only slowly emerged. So the formation of modern societies in Europe had to include the construction of the language, the images, and symbols which defined these societies as "communities" and set them apart, in their represented differences, from others.

The importance given to major historical processes helps to explain the significance of the term "formations" in our title. The political, economic, social and cultural processes were the "motors" of the formation process. They worked on and transformed traditional societies into modern ones. They shaped modern society across a long historical time-span. We speak of processes rather than practices because, although processes are made up of the activities of individual and collective social agents, they operate across extended time-scales, and seem at times to work on their own, in performing the work of social transformation. One effect of the operation of these processes is to give modern societies a distinctive shape and form, making them not simply "societies" (a loose ensemble of social activities) but *social formations* (societies with a definite structure and a well-defined set of social relations). One particular feature of modern social formations is that they became articulated into distinct, clearly demarcated zones of activity or social practice. We call these domains – corresponding to the processes which produced them – the polity, the economy, the social structure, and the cultural sphere. These spheres are the "formations" of modern societies. "Formations," then, in our title refers to *both* the activities of emergence, and their outcomes or results: both process *and* structure.

The next aspect which deserves discussion is the role of history. As we noted earlier, "Formations of Modernity" adopts a historical perspective on the emergence of modern societies. The relation between history and the social sciences has often been a troubled one. Our aim is to map long-term historical trends and changing social patterns. There is an extensive use of historical evidence; a number of summary histories are embedded in the chapters, which provide a historical context and chronological framework for different aspects of the formation process; and there are several comparative historical case studies. We also use simple contrasts (e.g. feudalism vs capitalism), summarizing concepts (e.g. traditional vs modern society), and rough-and-ready chronologies (e.g. towards the end of the fifteenth century).

However, there is no attempt to match the detail and specificity which is the hallmark of modern historical scholarship. By contrast, these accounts make extensive use of *historical generalizations*. Generalizations always abstract from the rich detail of complex events – that is their function. There is nothing wrong with this: all serious intellectual work involves abstraction. The point, however, is always to bear in mind the *level of abstraction* at which the generalizations are working. Each level has its strengths (i.e. it is good for highlighting some aspects) and its limitations (it is obliged to leave out much of importance).

"Formations of Modernity" works with historical generalizations, because its purpose is not only to describe when and how modern society developed, but to explain *why* it happened. However, describing a process and providing an explanation are more closely related than is sometimes assumed. The sociologist Michael Mann has remarked that "the greatest contribution of the historian to the methodology of the social sciences is the date," by which he meant that careful periodization is an essential part of explaining the development of any social phenomenon. As he went on to say, ". . . when things happened is essential to establishing causality" (Mann, 1988, p. 6). In "Formations," care is taken to establish, as far as possible, when things happened. This includes simple things like giving the dates of major figures, key events, or important texts. The point is not to oblige readers to memorize dates but to help them develop a sense of historical time, context, and sequence. However, readers will notice that there is no attempt to provide a precise date when modern societies began. There are at least several reasons for this reluctance.

First, the formation processes operated across several centuries and in a slow, uneven way, so it is difficult to identify a clear starting point. For example, when exactly does trade and commerce cease to be the economic basis of a few European cities – Venice, Florence, Bruges – and become the dominant economic form of western societies as a whole? Another reason is that there is no convenient cut-off point between what emerged and what went before. The processes we have identified as necessary to modern formation worked on and transformed already-existing societies. Those "traditional" societies were the "raw materials," the preconditions of modernity – the cloth out of which its shapes were cut. Modern capitalism sprang up in the interstices of the feudal economy. The modern nation-state was carved out of the old feudal and absolutist systems. So where does modern history really start – since it seems to have been always-already in process? This is an old problem in historical explanation – what is sometimes known as the danger of infinite regress, which, if we aren't careful, will transport us back to the beginning of time! Of course, this does not mean that history just seamlessly unfolded. That would be to hold an evolutionary model of historical development. In fact, as we show, as well as continuities connecting one historical phase or period to another, history is also full of *discontinuities* – breaks, ruptures, reversals. The focus on "transitions" in this book is designed precisely to emphasize these significant breaks in historical development.

Another reason for avoiding a simple date when modern societies began is that, as we noted earlier, the processes which form the main explanatory framework of the book had different time-scales. They began at different times, followed different trajectories, had different turning-points and seem to exhibit different tempos of development. This is reflected in the different periodizations used in each chapter. Chapter 2 takes the history of the modern state back to the Greek and Roman empires. Chapter 3 on the economy is mainly an eighteenth-century story. Chapter 4, on the industrial social structure, focuses on the nineteenth century. Chapter 5 begins with the Protestant Reformation in the sixteenth century. And the last chapter begins with Portuguese explorations in the fifteenth century.

Therefore, it does not make much sense to say that modern societies started at the same moment and developed uniformly within a single historical "time." The modern state, for example, has a very different "history" and "time" from the capitalist economy. Thus you will find that, although the various chapters cross-refer to different processes, they do not chart the formation of modern societies as a single historical process. The book has been written in the aftermath of the break-up of a more uniform conception of history which tended to dominate nineteenth-century evolutionary social theories; that is to say, in the wake of a certain relativization of historical time. The use of the plural – histories, societies, formations, conditions, causes, etc. – is one way of recognizing and marking these differential times of "history," avoiding what some theorists have called "homogeneous time" (Benjamin, 1970; Anderson, 1986).

Closely related to this idea of a single historical time-scale is the view that modernity is really *one* thing, towards which every society is inevitably moving, though at different rates of development. Some social scientists not only conceptualized history as one process, working to a unified time-scale, but saw it as unfolding according to some necessary law or logic towards a prescribed and inevitable end. This was true not only of certain kinds of classical Marxist historical analysis but also of those theorists who, while not accepting the Marxist model, did assume some form of western-style modernity to be the inevitable destiny of all societies. This assumption of an inevitable progress along a single path of development may have made it easier to read the meaning of history, since – despite much evidence to the contrary – it seemed to give it direction and we knew in advance the end of the story. But it did not square very easily with the great diversity of actual forms of historical development. Critics now call this one-track view a "teleological" conception of history – moving towards a preordained end or goal. Modern social theorists have become increasingly aware of the limitations of this position in all its variants. It seems more and more implausible to see history as unfolding according to one logic. Increasingly, different temporalities, different outcomes seem to be involved. Many events seem to follow no rational logic but to be more the contingent effects of unintended consequences – outcomes no one ever intended, which are contrary to, and often the direct opposite of, what seemed to be the dominant thrust of events. Of course, the processes of formation were not autonomous and separate from one another. There were connections between them – they were articulated with one another. But they weren't inevitably harnessed together, all moving or changing in tandem.

One major weakness of the teleological view of history is that it tended to assume that there is only one path of social development – the one taken by western societies – and that this is a universal model which all societies must follow and which leads sooner or later, through a fixed series of stages, to the same end. Thus, tribal society would inevitably lead to the nation-state, feudalism to capitalism, rural society to industrialization, and so on. In one version, this was called "modernization theory," a perspective which became very popular in the 1950s, particularly in the writings of Walter Rostow (Rostow, 1971). This formed the basis of much western policy in the Third World, which was directed at bringing into existence as rapidly as possible what modernization theorists identified as the necessary conditions for western-style development and growth. Modernization theory also assumed that there *was* one principal motor propelling societies up this ladder of development – the economy. The laws of capitalist industrialism – capital accumulation, supply and demand, rapid industrialization, market forces – were the principal engines of growth. Paradoxically, though they took a very different view of the nature and consequences of capitalism, modernization theorists tended to agree with Marxists in attributing social development ultimately to one, principal cause: the economic. This belief that all societies could be laid out at different points along the same evolutionary scale (with, of course, the West at the top!) was a very Enlightenment conception and one can see why many non-European societies now regard both these versions as very Euro-centric stories.

Few would now deny the link between capitalism and modernity. But in general these chapters break with this kind of one-track modernization theory and with the economic reductionism which was a key feature of it. In general, they adopt a more multi-causal explanation of how modern development in Western Europe occurred. They note that few modern societies are or even look the same. Think of the US, the UK, France, and Japan. Each took a radically different path to modernity. In each, that evolution depended on not one, but a number of determining conditions. In general, though economic organization is a massive, shaping historical force, the economy alone cannot function outside of specific social, political, and cultural conditions, let alone produce sustainable development. Modern societies certainly display no singular logic of development. The formation processes combine, in each instance, in very different ways. Japan, for example, combines a fiercely modern, high-tech economy with a strikingly traditional culture. Dictatorship was as much the engine of industrialization in Germany, Japan, and the Soviet Union as democracy. Force, violence, and coercion have played as decisive a historical role in the evolution of capitalism as peaceful economic competition. One of the purposes of comparative analysis is to highlight differences as well as similarities, and thus to underline the necessity of a break with mono-causal or reductionist explanations of social development.

In fact, even the idea of a necessary forward movement or progressive impetus towards "development" built into history may be open to question. Development has indeed become the goal of many societies. But not all societies are in fact "developing." And the under-development of some appears to be systematically linked to the over-development of others. So the "law" of historical development keeps missing its way or failing to deliver. Development itself turns out, on inspection, to be a highly contradictory phenomenon, a two-edged sword.

Many social theorists now see unevenness and difference as an even more powerful historical logic than evenness, similarity, and uniformity. Gradually, therefore, a more plural conception of the historical process of formation has emerged in the social sciences. It lays more stress on varied paths to development, diverse outcomes, ideas of difference, unevenness, contradiction, contingency (rather than necessity), and so on. However, it should be noted that giving greater weight to contingency in the accounts of social development does not mean that history is simply the outcome of a series of purely random events. But it does imply that in history everything does not seamlessly unfold according to some internal logic or inevitable law.

These are contentious issues in social science, and the questions they raise are far from settled. The six chapters in part I, for instance, take different positions on these questions. But the critique briefly outlined above is now widely accepted. The contributors still hold to the view that there *are* processes of formation which have shaped western societies, that these can be identified, mapped, and analyzed, and that explanations for some of their directions can be provided. That is to say, these chapters remain committed to what may be described as a qualified version of the Enlightenment belief that social development *is* amenable to rational analysis and explanation. But unlike many earlier sociological accounts, which tended to privilege class as the "master" category, they do not adopt a clear hierarchy or priority of causes, and are generally critical of economic reductionism, in which the economic base is assumed to be the determining force in history "in the last instance," as Friedrich Engels once put it. As one social theorist, the French philosopher Louis Althusser, remarked, the trouble is that "the last instance never comes." Instead, these chapters analyze different, interdependent "organizational clusters" – the polity, the economy, the social, and the cultural – whose "original association in western Europe," as Perry Anderson puts it, "was fortuitous" (Anderson, 1990, p. 53). In general, the contributors adopt a weaker notion of formation and causality and a pluralization of key concepts, as we noted earlier.

We have suggested why the history of modern societies had no absolute beginning or predetermined goal. However, it is almost impossible to describe the process of formation without using the language of "origins," "development," and, at least implicitly, "ends." Organizing the account of the formation of modern societies as a "story" seems to carry its own narrative logic. A story-line imposes a form on what may be otherwise a formless and chaotic series of events. Narrative gives a chapter a certain impetus, flow, and coherence, moving it smoothly from a "beginning" to "the sense of an ending" (as all good stories do). This imposes a certain order or meaning on events which they may have lacked at the time. Increasingly, historians and philosophers have been puzzling over this impact of language, narrative, and the literary devices which we use when constructing accounts, on the content and logic of an argument (White, 1987; Derrida, 1981). Some "deconstructive" philosophers, for example, go so far as to argue that the persuasiveness of philosophical argument often depends more on its rhetorical form and its metaphors than its rational logic. And they point to the fact that, in addition to imposing one meaning on events, narrative lends an account a certain unchallengeable authority or "truth."

The contributors have tried to build up the accounts they offer on the basis of a careful sifting of evidence and arguments which make their underlying theoretical assumptions clear. Nevertheless, you may also notice the impact of a greater reflexivity and self-consciousness about language, writing, and the forms which explanations take in the way the chapters in this book are written. Authors are constantly aware that it is *they* who impose a shape on events; that all accounts, however carefully tested and supportod, are in the end "authored." All social science explanations reflect to some degree the point of view of the author who is trying to make sense of things. They do not carry the impersonal guarantee of inevitability and truth. Consequently, arguments and positions are advanced here in a more tentative and provisional way. It is more a choice between convincing accounts, which deal persuasively with all the evidence, even the part which does not fit the theory, than a simple choice between "right" and "wrong" explanations. Readers should recognize that arguments advanced are open to debate, not variants of the Authorized Version.

Of course, being sensitive to language, meaning, and the effect of narrative does not imply that social science simply produces a series of "good stories," none better than the other. This would be an extreme form of relativism which would undermine the whole project of social science. There are criteria of assessment which help us to judge the relative weight and explanatory power of different accounts. Most social analysts are still committed to providing systematic, rigorous, coherent, comprehensive, conceptually clear, well-evidenced accounts, which make their underlying theoretical structure and value assumptions clear to readers, and thus accessible to argument and criticism. But the greater degree of awareness of one's own practices of producing meaning, of writing, even while doing it, means that we cannot deny the ultimately interpretative character of the social science enterprise.

This greater reflexivity – the attention to language, and the plural character of "meanings" – is not, of course, entirely novel. Many earlier traditions which have influenced social science practice have raised similar issues – for example, linguistic philosophy, hermeneutics, phenomenology, interpretative sociology – though they pointed to different philosophical conclusions. However, the return of these issues to the center of social theory in recent years reflects what some social theorists now call the "discursive turn" in social theory (Norris, 1983; Young, 1990). This implies a new – or renewed – awareness in theory and analysis of the importance of language (discourse) and how it is used (what is sometimes called "discursive practice") to produce meaning. Meaning is recognized to be *contextual* – dependent on specific historical contexts, rather than valid for all time. You will find this "discursive turn" reflected, to different degrees, throughout this volume. The "discursive turn" in modern philosophy is more fully debated in Gregor McLennan's final chapter in part III.

The "discursive turn" affects not only how some chapters are written but what they are about. The processes of economic, political, and social development seem to have a clear, objective, material character. They altered material and social organization in the "real world" – how people actually behaved – in ways which can be clearly identified and described. But cultural processes are rather different. They deal with less tangible things – meanings, values, symbols, ideas, knowledge, language, ideology: what cultural theorists call the symbolic dimensions of social life. Hitherto (and not only in Marxist types of analysis), these have been accorded a somewhat secondary status in the explanatory hierarchy of the social sciences. The cultural or ideological dimensions of social life were considered by some to be "superstructural," dependent on and merely reflecting the primary status of the material base.

These chapters give much greater prominence and weight to cultural and symbolic processes in the formation of modern societies. Chapters 1, 5, and 6 all deal directly with broadly cultural aspects. More significantly, culture is accorded a higher explanatory status than is customary. It is considered to be, not reflective of, but *constitutive* of the formation of the modern world: as constitutive as economic, political, or social processes of change. What is more, economic, political, and social processes do not operate outside of cultural and ideological conditions. The distinction between "material" and "ideational" factors in sociological analysis is thus considerably weakened, if not invalidated altogether. Language is seen to be "material" because it is the result of social practice and has real effects in shaping and regulating social behavior. Similarly, material processes – like the economy or politics – depend on "meaning" for their effects and have cultural or ideological conditions of existence. The modern market economy, for example, requires new conceptions of economic life, a new economic discourse, as well as new organizational forms. It may not be helpful to draw hard-and-fast distinctions between these two aspects of social development – the material and the discursive.

Max Weber argued that social practices are always "meaningful practices" and that this is what distinguishes them from mere biological reflexes, like an involuntary jerk following a tap on the knee. What Weber meant was not that practices have only one, true meaning, but that all social practices are embedded in meaning and are in that sense cultural. In order to conduct a social practice, human beings must give it a certain meaning, have a conception of it, be able to think meaningfully about it. Marx (to many people's surprise) said something rather similar when he observed that "the worst of architects is better than the best of bees." What he meant was that bees build hives by instinct whereas even the worst architects are obliged to use a conceptual model of the buildings they are constructing. The production of social meanings is therefore a necessary condition for the functioning of all social practices. And since meanings cannot be fixed but constantly change and are always contested, an account of the discursive conditions of social practices must form part of the sociological explanation of how they work. This explains why, in general, "Formations of Modernity" gives greater weight to the discursive aspect of social processes than is conventional.

Nothing demonstrates better the importance of social meanings than the word which both features in the title of part I and occurs regularly throughout its argument: the term "modern." Is it as innocently descriptive a concept as it seems, or is it more "loaded"? Raymond Williams argues that the word "modern" first appeared in English in the sixteenth century, referring to the argument between two schools of thought – the Ancients and the Moderns (a long-running dispute between those following classical literary models and those wanting to update them). "The majority of pre-nineteenth century uses," he notes, "were unfavourable." Claiming things to be "modern" – up-to-date, breaking with tradition – was, on the whole, held to be a bad thing, a dangerous idea, which required justification. It is only in the nineteenth century and "very markedly in the twentieth century" that there is a strong movement the other way, "until 'modern' becomes virtually equivalent to 'improved'" (Williams, 1976, p. 174).

This suggests that the discourse of "the modern," which we slip into without thinking, has never been purely descriptive, but has a more contested discursive history. Historians sometimes call the period of European history which begins in the late fifteenth century the "early modern' period. They are using the term to mark the break with the old, the collapse of older structures, models, and ways of life and the rise of new conceptions, new structures. As Harold Laski wrote:

> By 1600 we may say definitely that men [sic] are living and working in a new moral world. . . . There is a new social discipline which finds its sanctions independently of the religious ideal. There is a self-sufficient state. There is an intellectual temper aware . . . that a limitation to the right of speculation is also a limitation to the right to material power. There is a new physical world, both in the geographical sense and the ideological. The content of experience being new also, new postulates are needed for its interpretation. Their character is already defined in the realm of social theory no less than in those of science and philosophy. This content is material and of this world, instead of being spiritual and of the next. It is expansive, utilitarian, self-confident. It sets before itself the ideal of power over nature for the sake of the ease and comfort this power will confer. In its essence, it is the outlook of a new class which, given authority, is convinced that it can remould more adequately than in the past, the destinies of man.
> (Laski, 1962, pp. 57–8)

This is the moment of "the modern," albeit in its very early stages. This book begins with this moment and what follows from it. But, as we noted, "modernity" has a long and complex history. Each succeeding age – the Renaissance, the Enlightenment, the nineteenth century (the age of revolutions), the twentieth century – has a sense of itself as representing the culminating point of history, and each has tried to clinch this capture of history by claiming the epithet "modern" for itself. Yet in each age the claim has proved illusory. Each age succumbed to the fantasy that *it* was the last word in advanced living, in material development, in knowledge and enlightenment. Each time that "modern" was superseded by something even more up to date! The whole idea of modernity received an enormous impetus towards the end of the nineteenth century, when industrialization was rapidly transforming social and economic life, not only in Western Europe but elsewhere, and the globalization of the world economy and of western ways of life rapidly reshaped world history. This is the period of the new avant-garde intellectual and artistic movements in the arts, literature, architecture, science, and philosophy, sometimes called "Modernism," which aggressively embraced "the new" – novelty for its own sake – and revelled in challenging and overthrowing the old forms, traditions, theories, institutions, and authorities.

Today, "post-modernism" is challenging the old "modernisms." The closure of history keeps advancing into the future. It sometimes seems that what is quintessentially "modern" is not so much any one period or any particular form of social organization so much as the fact that a society becomes seized with and pervaded by this idea of ceaseless development, progress, and dynamic change; by the restless forward movement of time and history; by what some theorists call the compression of time and space (Giddens, 1984; Harvey, 1989). Essential to the idea of modernity is the belief that everything is destined to be speeded up, dissolved, displaced, transformed, reshaped. It is the shift – materially and culturally – into this new conception of social life which is the real transition to modernity. Marx caught this spirit of modernity in his prophetic epigram – "All that is solid melts into air."

However, this idea of "the modern" as a roller coaster of change and progress contains a paradox. At the very moment when "the modern" comes into its own, its ambiguities also become evident. Modernity becomes more troubled the more heroic, unstoppable, and Promethean it seems. The more it assumes itself to be the summit of human achievement, the more its dark side appears. The pollution of the environment and wastage of the earth's resources turns out to be the reverse side of "development." As many recent writers have noted, the Holocaust, which ravaged European Jewry, was perpetrated by a society which regarded itself as the summit of civilization and culture. The troubled thought surfaces that modernity's triumphs and successes are rooted, not simply in progress and enlightenment, but also in violence, oppression, and exclusion, in the archaic, the violent, the untransformed, the repressed aspects of social life. Its restlessness – a key feature of the modern experience – becomes increasingly unsettling. Time and change, which propel it forward, threaten to engulf it. It is little wonder that modern societies are increasingly haunted by what Bryan Turner calls a pervasive nostalgia for past times – for lost community, for the "good old days": always day-before-yesterday, always just over the horizon in an ever-receding image (Turner, 1990). The logic of modernity turns out to be a deeply contradictory logic – both constructive and destructive: its victims are as numerous as its beneficiaries. This Janus-face of modernity was inscribed in its earliest moments, and many of its subsequent twists and turns are laid out for inspection and analysis in this exploration of the modern story.

## References

Anderson, B. (1986) *Imagined Communities*, London, Verso.

Anderson, P.A. (1990) "A culture in contraflow," *New Left Review*, no. 180, March/April.

Benjamin, W. (1970) "Theses on the philosophy of history," in *Illuminations*, London, Cape.

Derrida, J. (1981) *Writing and Difference*, London, Routledge.

Giddens, A. (1984) *The Constitution of Society*, Cambridge, England, Polity Press.

Harvey, D. (1989) *The Condition of Postmodernity*, Oxford, Basil Blackwell.

Laski, H. (1962) *The Rise of European Liberalism*, London, Unwin.

Mann, M. (1988) "European development: approaching a historical explanation," in Baechler, J. et al. (eds) *Europe and the Rise of Capitalism*, Oxford, Basil Blackwell.

Norris, C. (1983) *The Deconstructive Turn*, London, Methuen.

Rostow, W. (1971) *The Stages of Economic Growth*, London, Cambridge University Press.

Turner, B. (1990) *Theories of Modernity and Post-modernity*, London, Sage.

White, H. (1987) *The Content of the Form: Narrative, Discourse and Historical Representation*, Baltimore, Johns Hopkins University Press.

Williams, R. (1976) *Keywords*, London, Fontana.

Young, R. (1990) *White Mythologies: Writing, History and the West*, London, Routledge.

# 1 The Enlightenment and the Birth of Social Science

Peter Hamilton

## Contents

| 1 | Introduction | 20 |
|---|---|---|
| 2 | What was the Enlightenment? | 24 |
| 2.1 | The social, historical, and geographical location of the Enlightenment | 25 |
| 2.2 | The *Encyclopédie* | 27 |
| 2.3 | Tradition and modernity | 30 |
| 2.4 | Social orders and social structure | 31 |
| 2.5 | Women and the Enlightenment: the salon | 33 |
| 3 | Enlightenment as the Pursuit of Modernity | 35 |
| 3.1 | Enlightenment, science, and progress | 37 |
| 3.2 | The communication of Enlightenment | 38 |
| 3.3 | Enlightenment and social science | 40 |
| 4 | Revolution and Reformation | 44 |
| 5 | The Birth of Sociology: Saint-Simon and Comte | 48 |
| 5.1 | Saint-Simon | 48 |
| 5.2 | Comte | 49 |
| 6 | Conclusion | 51 |
| References | | 54 |

# 1  Introduction

> Know then thyself, presume not God to scan,
> The proper study of Mankind is Man.
>
> > Alexander Pope, Epistle ii, *An Essay on Man*

This chapter sets out to do the following:

- provide a critical, analytical introduction to the key ideas of the body of writers and writings known as the Enlightenment;
- demonstrate the centrality of *the social* in Enlightenment thought, and to indicate the relative lack of intellectual boundaries between disciplinary domains;
- analyze and present the key ideas of Enlightenment sociology and social science;
- indicate how some key ideas of Enlightenment sociology and social science were incorporated within the characteristic features of nineteenth-century sociology and social thought;
- present and contextualize the thesis that the Enlightenment represents a watershed in human thought about society – that it produced a qualitatively new way of thinking concerned with the application of reason, experience, and experiment to the natural and the social world.

In the chapter I set out to examine critically the emergence of sociology – and the social sciences generally – as a distinctive form of thought about modern society. My argument is that one of the formative moments in this process came about in the eighteenth century, in the work of a key group of thinkers: the Enlightenment philosophers and their successors.

My main task is to trace the development of distinctively "modern" forms of thought about society and the realm of the social. Although their roots are evident as early as the sixteenth and seventeenth centuries in the works of such figures as Bacon, Hobbes, and Locke, these ideas received their most effective expression in the mid-eighteenth century, in the writings of a number of Enlightenment thinkers. These thinkers include men (there are almost no prominent women among them, for reasons to which we shall return) such as the Baron de Montesquieu (1689–1755), whose *De l'Esprit des Lois* (The Spirit of the Laws) is the starting point for a modern understanding of the relationship between the sociology of politics and the structure of society; Voltaire (1694–1788), whose writings on science, freedom of thought, and justice express so well the excitement generated by the critical rationalism and secularism which characterizes the Enlightenment; David Hume (1711–76), who formulated a theory of human nature which sets the tone for modern empirical research in psychology and sociology; and Adam Ferguson (1723–1816), whose writings on "civil society" prefigure modern comparative sociology.

My task is also to trace how certain elements of the central mode of thinking about modern society established by the Enlightenment are carried into nineteenth-century "classical sociology" in the writings of Henri de Saint-Simon (1760–1825) and Auguste Comte (1798–1857), and underpin the emergence of a distinctively modern sociology.

In a special sense, *Understanding Modern Societies* is all about the formation – the *invention* and the *reproduction* – of a *modern* way of thinking about society. This theme finds its way into all the chapters in a more or less explicit way. And this form of reflection upon *society* – which is after all a less than tangible entity – is one of the characteristic features of *modern* in contrast with earlier forms of thought. Such a reflection allows us to conceive of society itself as something over and above the individual – as the early sociologist Émile Durkheim (1858–1917) said, as something unique, society as a social fact, "*sui generis.*" We are concerned with the emergence of a *new group of ideas* about society and the realm of the social. These ideas provided a reflection of a changing and evolving society, and in turn helped people to think about society in a different way, as something open to change and transformation. This new way of thinking about society appeared shortly before certain very significant changes began in the ways in which western societies were organized – symbolized by the American and French Revolutions on the one hand, and the Agrarian and Industrial Revolutions on the other.

Before going further I should point out one difficulty with the attempt to present – even in outline – a history of the sources of sociology. No history is innocent of the purposes of its author. So you should always bear in mind that, in trying to make connections between a discipline as it is practiced in the last decade of the nineteenth century and the writings of a group of European intellectuals of the eighteenth century, I shall be looking to make exactly those connections which allow me to present a coherent history; that is, an account which does indeed draw connections between the ideas of now and then. I attempt to control the distorting possibilities of this approach by relating my account as accurately as I can to the context of the time, and connecting what was written then to the environment in which it was written and the audiences to whom it was directed. As you will see when you come to chapter 3, the use of the writings of Adam Smith as a precursor of modern economics is a particularly apt example of how distorting it can be to treat an eighteenth-century text in the intellectual context of contemporary issues in political economy.

When the American historian Crane Brinton said that "There seem to be good reasons for believing that in the latter part of the eighteenth century more intellectual energy was spent on the problems of man in society, in proportion to other possible concerns of the human mind, than at any other time in history" (Brinton, 1930, p. 129), he may have been exaggerating a little: but the argument that this period of intense concentration on the social produced an emergent "science of society" seems incontrovertible. Indeed, Crane Brinton even argued, quite convincingly, that the term "*philosophe,*" which was used to describe the main figures of the Enlightenment, would nowadays be rendered as "sociologist," given the term's usage at the time. I shall use this term to refer to the central figures of the Enlightenment throughout the chapter; its meaning will be explored in more detail in section 2.1.

In order to understand the impact of the Enlightenment on modern sociology and the emergent social sciences, my thesis is that we must also examine the carry-through of Enlightenment ideas into the nineteenth century. Perhaps the most significant example of this is the project originally undertaken by Henri de Saint-Simon, and later more fully extended by his follower, Auguste Comte, to construct a "positive science" of society, or in other words a *sociology* – the very word Comte coined to name this entirely now science. The sociology of Comte and Saint-Simon is not, as some have argued (e.g. Robert Nisbet, 1967), just a mirror image of the Enlightenment program – a sort of nineteenth-century conservative inversion of what the *philosophes* tried to do. It is similarly hard to see it as a radical break or jump from one mode of thinking about society to another. In a very real sense, the Comtean project of a positive sociology is the Enlightenment's *continuation*. It prepared the way for the emergence of a professionalized discipline of sociology in France, Germany, and America at the end of the nineteenth century. But that is to anticipate my account, which returns to this issue in section 5.

The concerns and interests of Saint-Simon and Comte prefigure those of modern sociology, principally (though not exclusively) via Émile Durkheim; but they are also deeply rooted in the Enlightenment's preoccupations with a particular mode of thought. It is convenient to call this mode of thought *critical rationalism*, for it combines the application of reason to social, political, and economic issues with a concern with progress, emancipation, and improvement, and is consequently *critical* of the status quo. The critical rationalism of the Enlightenment is the precursor of the "positivism" of Saint-Simon and Comte, understood as the striving for a *universal* science which, through the application of a reason tempered by experience and experiment, would eliminate prejudice, ignorance, superstition, and intolerance. At the same time it would be hard to understand the work of Marx, particularly in what is called his Young Hegelian period up to about 1850 (and one so important for certain central concepts of sociology, such as alienation and ideology), without drawing a connection between his version of critical rationalism and that of the Enlightenment *philosophes*, for the latter informs and underpins his early writings too. We shall not examine Marx's work in this chapter, but it is important to bear in mind that many of the ideas that he developed as a young student and philosopher in Germany prior to 1845 were directly influenced by the central ideas of the Enlightenment.

Before looking at the content and context of the key ideas of the Enlightenment, let us set them out in a concise form here. They make up what sociologists call a "paradigm," a set of interconnected ideas, values, principles, and facts which provide both an image of the natural and social world, and a way of thinking about it. The "paradigm" of the

Enlightenment – its "philosophy" and approach to key questions – is a combination of a number of ideas, bound together in a tight cluster. It includes some elements which may even appear to be inconsistent – probably because, like many intellectual movements, it united people whose ideas had many threads in common but differed on questions of detail. As a minimum, however, all the *philosophes* would have agreed on the following list:

1   *Reason* – the *philosophes* stressed the primacy of *reason* and rationality as ways of organizing knowledge, tempered by experience and experiment. In this they took over the "rationalist" concept of reason as the process of rational thought, based upon clear, innate ideas independent of experience, which can be demonstrated to any thinking person, and which had been set out by Descartes and Pascal in the seventeenth century. However, the *philosophes* allied their version of rationalism with *empiricism*.

2   *Empiricism* – the idea that all thought and knowledge about the natural and social world is based on empirical facts, things that all human beings can apprehend through their sense organs.

3   *Science* – the notion that scientific knowledge, based on the experimental method as developed in the scientific revolution of the seventeenth century, was the key to expanding *all* human knowledge.

4   *Universalism* – the concept that reason and science could be applied to any and every situation, and that their principles were the same in every situation. Science in particular produces general laws which govern the entire universe, without exception.

5   *Progress* – the idea that the natural and social condition of human beings could be improved, by the application of science and reason, and would result in an ever-increasing level of happiness and well-being.

6   *Individualism* – the concept that the individual is the starting point for all knowledge and action, and that individual reason cannot be subjected to a higher authority. Society is thus the sum or product of the thought and action of a large number of individuals.

7   *Toleration* – the notion that all human beings are essentially the same, despite their religious or moral convictions, and that the beliefs of other races or civilizations are not inherently inferior to those of European Christianity.

8   *Freedom* – an opposition to feudal and traditional constraints on beliefs, trade, communication, social interaction, sexuality, and ownership of property (although as we shall see the extension of freedom to women and the lower classes was problematic for the *philosophes*).

9   *Uniformity of human nature* – the belief that the principal characteristics of human nature were always and everywhere the same.

10 *Secularism* – an ethic most frequently seen in the form of virulent anti-clericalism. The *philosophes'* opposition to traditional religious authority stressed the need for secular knowledge free of religious orthodoxies.

It would be possible to add other ideas to this list or to discuss the relative importance of each. However, the above list provides a good starting point for understanding this complex movement, and for making connections between its characteristic concerns and the emergence of sociology. Each of these central ideas weaves its way through the account that follows, and all form part of the new social sciences which emerged in the nineteenth century.

## 2　What was the Enlightenment?

A simple answer to this question would separate out at least eight meanings of the Enlightenment:

1　A characteristic bundle of ideas (as in the list at the end of section 1).

2　An intellectual movement.

3　A communicating group or network of intellectuals.

4　A set of institutional centers where intellectuals clustered – Paris, Edinburgh, Glasgow, London, etc.

5　A publishing industry, and an audience for its output.

6　An intellectual fashion.

7　A belief-system, world-view, or *Zeitgeist* (spirit of the age).

8　A history and a geography.

All of these are overlapping aspects of the same general phenomenon, and they remind us that it is ultimately futile to try to pin down a single definitive group, set of ideas, or cluster of outcomes and consequences, which can serve as *the* Enlightenment. There were many aspects of the Enlightenment, and many *philosophes*, so what you will find here is an attempt to map out some broad outlines, to set some central ideas in their context, and to indicate some important consequences.

In its simplest sense the Enlightenment was the creation of a new framework of ideas about man, society, and nature, which challenged existing conceptions rooted in a traditional world-view, dominated by Christianity. The key domain in which Enlightenment intellectuals challenged the clergy, who were the main group involved in supporting existing conceptions of the world, concerned the traditional view of nature, man, and society which was sustained by the Church's authority and its monopoly over the information media of the time.

These new ideas were accompanied by and influenced in their turn many cultural innovations in writing, printing, painting, music, sculpture, architecture, and gardening, as well as the other arts. Technological innovations in agriculture and manufactures, as well as in ways of making war, also frame the social theories of the Enlightenment. We have no space to explore such matters here, except to point out that the whole idea of a professionalized discipline based on any of these intellectual or cultural pursuits was only slowly emerging, and that as a consequence educated persons of the eighteenth-century Enlightenment saw themselves as able to take up any or all of them which caught their interest. The notion that Enlightenment knowledge could be strictly compartmentalized into bounded domains, each the province of certificated "experts," would have been completely foreign to Enlightenment thinkers. The "universalism" which thus characterized the emergence of these ideas and their cultural counterparts assumed that any educated person could in principle know everything. Paradoxically, the Enlightenment heralded the very process – the creation of specialized disciplines presided over by certificated experts – which appears to negate its aim of universalized human knowledge. Such a "closing-off" of knowledge by disciplinary boundaries occurred earlier than anywhere else in the natural sciences, those models of enlightened knowledge so beloved of the *philosophes*. The main reason for this was that science produced specialist languages and terminologies, and relied in particular upon an increasingly complex mathematical language, inaccessible to even the enlightened gentleman-*philosophe*. Denis Diderot (1713–84), a key figure in the movement, noted perceptively in 1756 that the mathematical language of Newton's *Principia Mathematica* is "the veil" which scientists "are pleased to draw between the people and nature" (quoted in Gay, 1973b, p. 158).

However much they might have wanted to extend the benefits of enlightened knowledge, the *philosophes* helped the process by which secular intellectual life became the province of a socially and economically defined group. They were the first people in western society outside of the Church to make a living (or more properly a *vocation*) out of knowledge and writing. As Roy Porter has put it, "the Enlightenment was the era which saw the emergence of a secular intelligentsia large enough and powerful enough for the first time to challenge the clergy" (Porter, 1990, p. 73).

In the next section, I want to locate the Enlightenment in its social, historical, and geographical context.

## 2.1   The social, historical, and geographical location of the Enlightenment

When we use the term "the Enlightenment" it is generally accepted that we refer to a period in European intellectual history which spans the time from roughly the first quarter to the last quarter of the eighteenth century. Geographically centered in France, but with important outposts in most of the major European states, "the Enlightenment" is composed of the ideas and writings of a fairly heterogeneous group, who are often called by their French name *philosophes*. It does not exactly correspond to our modern "philosopher," and is perhaps best translated as "a man of letters who is also a freethinker." The *philosophes* saw themselves as cosmopolitans, citizens of an enlightened intellectual world who valued the interest of mankind above that of country or clan. As the French *philosophe* Diderot wrote to Hume in 1768: "My dear David, you belong to all nations, and you'll never ask an unhappy man for his birth-certificate. I flatter myself that I am, like you, citizen of the great city of the world" (quoted in Gay, 1973a, p. 13). The historian Edward Gibbon (1737–94) stressed the strongly European or "Euro-centric" nature of this *universalistic* cosmopolitanism: "it is the duty of a patriot to prefer and promote the exclusive interest and glory of his native country; but a philosopher may be permitted to enlarge his views, and to consider Europe as a great republic, whose various inhabitants have attained almost the same level of politeness and cultivation" (quoted in Gay, 1973a, p. 13). Gibbon even composed some of his writings in French, because he felt that the ideas with which he wanted to work were better expressed in that language than in his own.

The Enlightenment was the work of three overlapping and closely linked generations of *philosophes*. The first, typified by Voltaire (1694–1778) and Charles de Secondat, known as Montesquieu (1689–1755), were born in the last quarter of the seventeenth century: their ideas were strongly influenced by the writings of the English political philosopher John Locke (1632–1704) and the scientist Isaac Newton (1642–1727), whose work was fresh and controversial while both *philosophes* were still young men. The second generation includes men like David Hume (1711–76), Jean-Jacques Rousseau (1712–78), Denis Diderot (1713–84), and Jean d'Alembert (1717–83), who combined the fashionable anti-clericalism and the interest in scientific method of their predecessors into what Gay calls "a coherent modern view of the world." The third generation is represented by Immanuel Kant (1724–1804), Adam Smith (1723–90), Anne Robert Turgot (1727–81), the Marquis de Condorcet (1743–94), and Adam Ferguson (1723–1816), and its achievement is the further development of the Enlightenment world-view into a series of more specialized proto-disciplines: epistemology, economics, sociology, political economy, legal reform. It is to Kant that we owe the slogan of the Enlightenment – *sapere aude* ("dare to know") – which sums up its essentially secular intellectual character.

Of course there is a danger in applying the term "the Enlightenment" too loosely or broadly to the whole of intellectual life in eighteenth-century Europe, as if the movement was one which touched every society and every intellectual elite of this period equally. As Roy Porter emphasizes in an excellent short study of recent work on the Enlightenment, the Enlightenment is an amorphous, hard-to-pin-down and constantly shifting entity (Porter, 1990). It is commonplace for the whole period to be referred to as an "Age of Enlightenment," a term which implies a general process of society awakening from the dark slumbers of superstition and ignorance, and a notion certainly encouraged by the *philosophes* themselves, although it is one which perhaps poses more questions than it resolves. Kant wrote an essay

"*Was ist Aufklärung?*" (What is Enlightenment?), which actually says "if someone says 'are we living in an enlightened age today?' the answer would be, 'No: but . . . we *are* living in an Age of Enlightenment'." The French *philosophes* referred to their time as "*le siècle des lumières*" (the century of the enlightened), and both Scottish and English writers of the time talked about "Enlightened" thinking.

Certainly the metaphor of the "light of reason," shining brightly into all the dark recesses of ignorance and superstition, was a powerful one at the time: but did the process of Enlightenment always and everywhere have the same meaning? One recent historical study of Europe in the eighteenth century has suggested that the Enlightenment is more "a tendency towards critical inquiry and the application of reason" than a coherent intellectual movement (Black, 1990, p. 208).

In fact, if we look at such indicators as the production and consumption of books and journals, the Enlightenment was a largely French and British (or more properly Scottish) intellectual vogue, although one whose fashionable ripples extended out to Germany, Italy, the Austro-Hungarian Empire, Russia, the Low Countries (Belgium and Holland), and the Americas. But its center was very clearly Paris, and it emerged in the France of Louis XV (1710–74), during the first quarter of the eighteenth century.

By the last quarter of the eighteenth century, Enlightenment ideas were close to having become a sort of new intellectual orthodoxy among the cultivated elites of Europe. This orthodoxy was also starting to give way to an emergent "pre-Romanticism" which placed greater emphasis on sentiment and feeling, as opposed to reason and skepticism. However, the spirit of enlightened and critical rationalism was quite an influential factor in the increasing disquiet about how *ancien régime* France was being run, which began to set in after about 1770 (Doyle, 1989, p. 58). It helped to encourage a mood of impending disaster which led inexorably towards the French Revolution of 1789, a topic to which we shall return in section 4. If we need to find a historical end to the Enlightenment, it could be said to be the French Revolution – but even that is a controversial notion.

Although the Enlightenment was in reality a sort of intellectual fashion which took hold of the minds of intellectuals throughout Europe, rather than a consciously conceived project with any institutionalized form, there is one classic example of a cooperative endeavor among the *philosophes*: the great publishing enterprise called the *Encyclopédie*.

## 2.2 The *Encyclopédie*

In order to explain the influence of this massive publication, it is worth reminding ourselves that by the mid-eighteenth century French was the language of all of educated Europe, except for England and Spain (and even in those two countries any self-respecting member of the educated elite would have had a good knowledge of the language). As a Viennese countess put it, ". . . in those days the greater part of high society in

Vienna would say: I speak French like Diderot, and German . . . like my nurse" (Doyle, 1989, p. 58).

The universality of French as the language of reason and ideas explains in part the Europe-wide popularity of the *Encyclopédie*, where the intellectual fashion for treating all aspects of human life and the natural world as open to rational study is displayed in astonishing depth.

The cooperative endeavor which produced the *Encyclopédie* parallels another distinctive feature of the Enlightenment – the learned society committed to the pursuit of knowledge, whose prototypes were the Académie française (est. 1635) and the Royal Society of London (est. 1645). Such organizations were the first modern social institutions devoted to the study of the arts and sciences. The most distinctive break with the past came about because the members of such academies believed in the grounding of knowledge in experience as opposed to secular authority, religious dogma, or mysticism.

Science was the supreme form of knowledge for the *philosophes* because it seemed to create secure truths based on observation and experiment. Their confidence in scientific method was such that they believed it was a force for enlightenment and progress: there was in principle no domain of life to which it could not be applied. They believed that a new man was being created by this scientific method, one who understands, and by his understanding masters nature.

The *Encyclopédie* represented this belief in the beneficial effects of science put into practice. It was also the product of an intellectual society – "a society of men of letters and artisans" as Denis Diderot, one of its main editors, described it. Its purpose was summed up by Kant's definition of Enlightenment: "man realising his potential through the use of his mind" (quoted in Gay, 1973a, p. 21).

The concept of the *Encyclopédie* was originally based on an English work, Ephraim Chambers's *Cyclopaedia or Universal Dictionary of Arts and Sciences* (1728). Although initially intended to be a translation of this popular and successful work, it soon became an original work in its own right, after Denis Diderot and Jean d'Alembert (a scientifically inclined *philosophe*) took over the editorship for its publisher, Le Breton. Virtually all of the major *philosophes* contributed to it, and its influence was very widespread in eighteenth-century Europe.

There are two striking characteristics of the *Encyclopédie* from our point of view. First, in creating a plan for the enterprise – a way of linking all the articles together in a coherent manner – the decision was taken to place man at the center; as Diderot said (in an entry in the *Encyclopédie* under the heading "Encyclopédie"), what he and his associates wanted for the *Encyclopédie* was a plan or design that would be "instructive and grand" – something which would order knowledge and information as "a grand and noble avenue, stretching into the distance, and along which one would find other avenues, arranged in an orderly manner and leading off to isolated and remote objects by the easiest and quickest route" (*Encyclopédie*, vol. 5, 1755). Second, the *Encyclopédie* is truly "universalistic" in its approach. Diderot and his colleagues wanted it to be the sort of work from which, should a disaster overtake civilization, all human knowledge could be reconstructed. As a result, it is a vast publication: it took over twenty years to be published, from 1751 to 1772, and amounts to seventeen volumes of text and twelve volumes of plates.

The pre-eminence in the eighteenth century of French as the language of culture and of ideas made the *Encyclopédie* a widely-known work – some 50 percent of the 25 000 copies in various editions which sold before 1789 were purchased outside of France. It is not surprising perhaps that from a modern standpoint this endeavor should seem to support the idea of an "Enlightenment project," the notion that a planned and influential intellectual movement, designed to popularize certain key notions to do with science, reason, and progress, was at work in the eighteenth century. But from the evidence available on those who purchased copies of it, the *Encyclopédie* sold more because of its critical and irreverent notoriety than for any specific program or project which it represented (Doyle, 1989, p. 52). What is more, it is clear that the term "Encyclopedism" was quite widely used at the time as a synonym for the refusal to accept anything uncritically.

Indeed, a key feature of the whole Enlightenment period is the influence of a wide range of individual writers on educated and cultivated opinion. Thinkers such as Voltaire, Montesquieu, Diderot, Hume, Smith, Ferguson, Rousseau, and Condorcet – to mention only some of the most notable – produced a large collection of novels, plays, books, pamphlets, and essays which became bestsellers among an audience which was avid for new and exciting ideas, and receptive to the notion that the application of reason to the affairs of men would encourage a general advance of civilization. This audience was not however dominated by the "new" social groups, the emergent middle classes of manufacturers and merchants, but by members of more traditional elite groups – nobles, professionals (especially lawyers), academics, and the clergy. The idea of disciplinary demarcation was foreign to such people, for whom the ideal of Renaissance Man was the archetype of cultivated knowledge – a person whose knowledge and understanding enabled him or her to pick up a book on physics, read a text of Tacitus, design a Palladian villa, paint a *Mona Lisa*, or compose a sonnet with equal facility. They had for the most part received a classical education (in French colleges of the mid-eighteenth century, for example, four hours a day were given over to the study of the classics), but also some introduction to the sciences. Men (and the much smaller number of women educated to the same level) would expect to understand and participate in the spread of knowledge about new ideas, whether in the field of moral philosophy or physical science. Yet women, though they played a major part in the development and diffusion of Enlightenment ideas, found themselves in a contradictory position in the application of such ideas to their social condition. We shall return to this in section 2.5.

## 2.3   Tradition and modernity

The *philosophes* took a very clear position in their writings on certain
important transitions underway within European society. These
involved the move from a traditional social order and a traditional set
of beliefs about the world to new forms of social structure and ways of
thinking about the world which were distinctively modern. The
modernity of these modes of thought lay in the innovative way in
which the *philosophes* sought to demolish and replace *established*
forms of knowledge dependent on religious authority, such as the
biblical account of the creation of the world, with those new forms of
knowledge which depended on experience, experiment, and reason –
quintessentially, science.

Until the eighteenth century, what passed in Europe for knowledge
about the creation of the world, about man's place in that world, about
nature and society, and about man's duties and destiny, was dominated
by the Christian churches. Knowledge was continually referred to
scriptural sources in the Bible, and was transmitted through the
religious institutions of universities, colleges, religious orders, schools,
and churches. A typical visual representation of the traditional world-
view shows heaven and earth as physically contiguous. Even Bossuet's
*Histoire Universelle* (Universal History) of 1681 began its account of
human history over the previous 6000 years with Adam and Eve's
departure from the Garden of Eden, and did not mention the Chinese
once. Yet, as Voltaire pointed out (in his *Lettres Philosophiques*), the
Chinese could trace their civilization back through "36 recorded
eclipses of the sun to a date earlier than that which we normally
attribute to the Flood."

The astronomic discoveries of Kepler and Copernicus in the
sixteenth and seventeenth centuries about the nature of the universe,
the observations of Galileo concerning the movements of the planets,
the lessons of empirical science, and the increasingly common accounts
of distant and exotic societies available through travellers' tales,
combined to provide an effective scientific and empirical base from
which to challenge traditional cosmologies (a cosmology is an
intellectual picture or model of the universe) founded on Christian
belief, which placed the earth at the center of the universe, and
Christendom at the center of the world. This was fertile ground for the
*philosophes*, who opposed traditional religious authority and the false
knowledge which it ordained.

The particular form in which Enlightenment anti-traditionalism
appears, then, is as a debunking of outmoded, scripturally-based
concepts of the universe, the earth, and human society. Although we
must be clear that many of the *philosophes* were in fact believers in a
God, or at least a divine entity, this did not prevent much of their
writing from heaping scorn on religious teaching, and being virulently
anti-clerical. The *philosophes* challenged the traditional role of the
clergy as the keepers and transmitters of knowledge because they
wished to redefine what was socially important knowledge, to bring it
outside of the sphere of religion, and to provide it with a new meaning

and relevance. As a result, they typically presented traditional religious world-views as attempts to keep people in a condition of ignorance and superstition, and thus reserved much of the most pointed of their intellectual attacks for key elements in what they saw as the ideological window-dressing of the Church, such as miracles and revelations.

Religious ideas and knowledge also underpinned the absolute claim to power exercised by the French, Austrian, and German kings, and the Russian Czar, and were also used, in a modified form, to support the claim on the British throne of the German Hanoverians. Some of the *philosophes* were quite explicitly antithetical to "despotism" (the Enlightenment's code-word for absolutism); others were more equivocal about the virtues of a strong monarch, and both Voltaire and Diderot were virtually apologists for the absolutist regimes of Frederick the Great of Prussia, and Catherine the Great of Russia.

The ideas developed and disseminated by the *philosophes* touched critically upon nearly all aspects of the traditional societies in which they operated, and sought to question virtually all (the condition of women being, perhaps, the main exception) of the forms which that society took. One of the main sources of their approach to the critique of traditional society is found in their enthusiasm for science, and the notions of progress and reason for which it seemed to provide a guarantee. We shall return to the connection between the Enlightenment and the emergence of modern science in section 3.1.

## 2.4   Social orders and social structure

Despite their secular radicalism, the ideas of the typical *philosophes* were not as subversive of the traditional social structure in which they lived as might have been the case. There is perhaps a simple reason for this: self-interest. The English historian Edward Gibbon described himself as fortunate to have been placed by the lottery of life among a cultured and leisured elite, the "polished and enlightened orders of society," which he contrasts with the condition of the masses:

> The most numerous portion of it [society] is employed in constant and useful labour. The select few, placed by fortune above necessity, can, however, fill up their time by the pursuits of interest or glory, by the improvements of their estate or of their understanding, by the duties, the pleasures, and even the follies of social life.
> (Gibbon, 1966, p. 207)

Most of the *philosophes* came from the higher orders of society. Many were of noble birth, while some came from the gentry classes or from a professional milieu. Montesquieu, for example, was a great landowner in the Bordeaux region of France. Diderot and Rousseau came from the traditional middle class – Diderot's father was a master-cutler, Rousseau's a watchmaker.

Peter Gay describes the *philosophes* as a "solid, respectable clan of revolutionaries" (Gay, 1973a, p. 9). Most were born into a cultured elite, and in the main their works were circulated among other

members of that elite. It was not until almost the eve of the French
Revolution, in the 1780s, that a new social group emerged, concerned
with popularizing Enlightenment ideas (Darnton, 1979).

This new group was composed largely of lower-middle-class hack
journalists and other writers, who supplied the growing number of
popular newspapers with a diet of scandal mixed up with simplified
Enlightenment ideas. Their audiences were the disaffected and
propertyless lower middle classes, for whom the traditional social
structure had little to offer.

The traditional social structure of eighteenth-century Europe was
essentially based on the ownership of land and landed property. It was
a society composed of orders, rather than economically defined classes,
although class formations were beginning to appear. The great noble
landowners formed the dominant ruling order (of which a Louis XV or
a George III was simply a leading member), and although there was
considerable variation within Europe over the extent of their political
power – in France, for example, only feudal rights over land still
remained; in Russia serfdom of the peasantry was the norm – they
dominated an economy in which at least 80 percent of the population
derived their employment and income from agriculture in one form or
another.

Beneath the landed nobility there existed a stratum of "traditional"
professional orders which had changed little since the feudal period –
lawyers, clerics, state officials, etc. – and also a stratum of small
landowners or gentry-farmers. In France the latter group (the
*hobereaux*, or gentry) was quite numerous, but often possessed only
modest means. Frequently reasonably well-educated, they were the
social group from which many of the lesser figures of the
Enlightenment emerged, for an acceptable profession for this social
group was that of "writer." There was an emergent and growing "new"
middle class involved in new forms of manufacture and trade, as well
as the traditional merchant order of feudalism, which included the
quite large numbers of urban craftsmen – from the wealthy goldsmiths,
perfumiers, or tailors who worked for the nobility, through to an
assortment of printers, furniture makers, or carriage makers, down to
the modest shoemaker or mason. Below the urban middle class was to
be found a large class of domestic servants, and a small urban working
class, supplemented on a daily or seasonal basis by day laborers from
the countryside. Peasants or smallholders made up the great mass of
the population – in mid-eighteenth century France they probably
accounted for eighteen of the twenty million or so of the population.

In eighteenth-century France, these social orders were represented as
three "Estates" – Clergy, Nobility, and the "Third Estate," which
comprised everyone else, from wealthiest bourgeois to poorest peasant.
Some *philosophes* were members of the Second Estate, which perhaps
also indicates why they should be less explicitly subversive of the
traditional social order than of the traditional religious order.

For the lower orders of European eighteenth-century society, the
Enlightenment had apparently little to offer. Voltaire was fond of
describing the peasantry in terms which put them hardly above the

beasts of the field, in order to criticize the sort of social system which reduced men to such a level of ignorance and bestiality. However, he showed little interest in a levelling of social distinction. Few indeed of the *philosophes* were interested in the greater involvement of the great mass of the population in the government of society, for the most part favoring a system like that of Great Britain, where political power was extended to the propertied classes and the landed gentry, but not beyond.

The Enlightenment certainly propagated concepts of equality, (limited) democracy, and emancipation. But in the societies in which it flourished, its ultimately revolutionary implications were not grasped by (or meant to be extended to) the mass of poor and uneducated people. Nonetheless, ruling elites in particular saw the ideas of the Enlightenment as a threat to the established order. Because they discerned in it certain dangerous and revolutionary elements, both secular and religious authorities tried to control the spread of Enlightenment culture. However, the *philosophes* themselves refused to believe that they were rebels or revolutionaries: they thought that progress could come about within the existing social order by the spread of their ideas among men of influence. As Diderot once said, their aim was to "change the general way of thinking," and was revolutionary only insofar as it sought "the revolution which will take place in the minds of men" (quoted in Eliot and Stern, 1979, p. 44).

## 2.5 Women and the Enlightenment: the salon

Although there were some wealthy and powerful women manifestly involved in the propagation of its principles – Catherine the Great of Russia was one of its staunchest supporters at one stage – the Enlightenment was essentially promoted and prosecuted, at least in its public face, by a male intellectual elite. Women figured as either silent partners in the intellectual enterprises of their more famous consorts (Voltaire spent much time performing scientific experiments with the aid of his mistress Madame du Châtelet, while much of what we know of the intellectual society of the times comes from Diderot's voluminous correspondence with his mistress, Sophie Volland), or as the (frequently brilliant) hostesses of the regular salons and soirées where the *philosophes* and other members of the cultivated elites would meet.

The institution of the salon had begun in seventeenth-century Paris, the invention of the Marquise de Rambouillet in 1623, who created "a space in which talented and learned women could meet with men as intellectual equals, rather than as exceptional prodigies" (Anderson and Zinsser, 1990, vol. 2, p. 104). Anderson and Zinsser describe its development:

> One hundred and fifty years after Rambouillet's creation – in the second half of the eighteenth century – the salon achieved its greatest influence and prestige in Europe. In the leading capital cities, salons flourished, and their existence signaled an active

intellectual and cultural life. Appearing in many nations, the salon reached its apogee in eighteenth-century France. There, where women's influence in the courts – as *maîtresse-en-titre*, as queen, as courtier – increased, women's influence also flourished outside the court, in the salons. In the relatively rigid hierarchical society of pre-revolutionary France, where a person had to prove four quarters of nobility to hold many important posts, the salon allowed both women and men a social mobility which existed nowhere else. The salon mixed elements of the nobility, bourgeoisie, and intelligentsia and enabled some women to rise through both marriage and influence. . . .

Intellectually, the salon provided shelter for views or projects unwelcome in the courts: when Voltaire was *persona non grata* with Louis XV because of his critical views of monarchy, he was deluged with invitations from Parisian salonières eager to be his hostess. The great Enlightenment project of the *Encyclopédie*, which sought to categorize, define, and criticize all existing knowledge, was suppressed by the French court, but completed in secret with Mme. Geoffrin's social and financial assistance. She welcomed the Encyclopedists to her salon, and their presence was sought by other salonières as well. . . .

Rational conversation, sociability between women and men, delight in the pleasures of this world are the hallmarks of Enlightenment culture. The men who mingled with the Bluestockings and frequented the salons were the men who produced the Enlightenment. It is a tragedy for women that these men, who were aided, sponsored, and lionized by the salonières, produced – with very few exceptions – art and writing which either ignored women completely or upheld the most traditional views of womanhood. Just as there was no Renaissance or Scientific Revolution for women, in the sense that the goals and ideals of those movements were perceived as applicable only to men, so there was no Enlightenment for women. Enlightenment thinkers questioned all the traditional limits on men – and indeed challenged the validity of tradition itself. They championed the rights of commoners, the rights of citizens, the rights of slaves, Jews, Indians, and children, but not those of women. Instead, often at great cost to their own logic and rationality, they continued to reaffirm the most ancient inherited traditions about women: that they were inferior to men in the crucial faculties of reason and ethics and so should be subordinated to men. In philosophy and in art, men of the Enlightenment upheld the traditional ideal of woman: silent, obedient, subservient, modest, and chaste. The salonière – witty, independent, powerful, well-read, and sometimes libertine – was condemned and mocked. A few Enlightenment thinkers did question and even reject subordinating traditions about women. But those who argued for a larger role for women – like the Englishwoman Mary Wollstonecraft in her *Vindication of the Rights of Woman* (1791), the French Marquis de Condorcet in his *Admission of Women to*

*Civic Rights* (1790), the German Theodor von Hippel in his *On the Civic Improvement of Women* (1792), the Spaniard Josefa Amar y Borbón in her *Discourse in Defense of Women's Talent and Their Capacity for Government and Other Positions Held by Men* (1786) – prompted outrage and then were forgotten. Instead, most philosophers and writers reiterated the most limiting traditions of European culture regarding women, often in works which condemned traditional behaviour for men. . . .

By the end of the eighteenth century, the salonière was repudiated in favor of more traditional women. This change occurred very rapidly during the era of the French Revolution and the Napoleonic Wars (1789–1815). The social and political power which the salonières had wielded in pre-revolutionary France became a leading criticism of the old monarchy, and people of differing classes and political philosophies united in condemning this "female influence". "Women ruled [in the eighteenth century]", the French artist and Marie Antoinette's portraitist, Elizabeth Vigée-Lebrun remarked in her memoirs, "The Revolution dethroned them." Vigée-Lebrun exaggerated women's powers, but accurately perceived their decline in influence. The revolution unleashed a flood of criticism about women's "unnatural" usurpation of the male domain of politics. Female political activity was outlawed in 1793, and male politicians, journalists, and philosophers condemned women's political influence whether it was republican or monarchist, revolutionary or counter-revolutionary.

(Anderson and Zinsser, 1990, pp. 106–9, 112–15, 118–20)

The salon proved to be a rather double-edged sword in the expansion of women's rights. Although many of those set up in imitation of Mme de Rambouillet's were presided over by women who, like her, refused sexual liaisons so as to free themselves for a role beyond that of wife or courtesan, many salons were also the locus for affairs between talented or titled men and intellectual women, and the reputation of all *salonières* (chaste or otherwise) was affected: it was assumed that relations between men and women, however intellectual or artistic they might appear, could not remain platonic.

# 3   Enlightenment as the Pursuit of Modernity

A specifically "modern" concern with man conceived of as a social being was forged by the key figures among the *philosophes* during the mid-eighteenth century, principally in France and Scotland, but with certain important contributions from thinkers in Italy and Germany.

Taking account of the diversity of views espoused by the *philosophes*, there are broadly four main areas which distinguish the thought of the *philosophes* from that of other intellectuals of their period, and from earlier intellectual approaches:

- **Anti-clericalism**: the *philosophes* had no time for the Church (especially the Catholic Church) and its works – a perspective summed up in Voltaire's phrase "*Écrasez l'infâme*" ("crush the infamous thing," the "thing" being the authority of the Catholic Church). They were particularly opposed to religious persecution, and although some went further, denying the existence of a God altogether, most acknowledged that reason indicates the likely existence of a God, but not one who has provided a "revelation" of Himself through scripture, the life of Christ, miracles, or the Church.

- **A belief in the pre-eminence of empirical, materialist knowledge**: the model in this respect being furnished by science.

- **An enthusiasm for technological and medical progress**: scientists, inventors, and doctors were seen as the curers of society's ills.

- **A desire for legal and constitutional reform**: in the case of the French *philosophes*, this was translated into a critique of French absolutism, and an admiration for the British constitution, with its established liberties.

This qualitatively new mode of thought about man and society, which had its roots in the Scientific Revolution of the seventeenth century and the subsequent diffusion from about 1700 onwards of scientific concepts and methods, led to the creation of a small group of "moral sciences" as David Hume called them, which included what we would now call sociology. The word "sociology," as a description of a science, does not appear until the nineteenth century: but that is of little importance in the sense that characteristically *sociological* concerns about the ways in which societies are organized and developed, and about human social relationships, are clearly identifiable from the middle of the eighteenth century in the writings of a number of *philosophes*.

It is these "moral sciences" which, concerning themselves with the deeper understanding of the human condition as a prelude to the emancipation of man from the ties of superstition, ignorance, ideology, and feudal social relationships, constituted the turning point for sociology and the other social sciences, and eventually formed the basis of their professionalized disciplines in the early nineteenth century. As part of this concern with reformulating moral philosophy as "moral science," the understanding of *human nature* was regarded as the key to an objective "science of man." Indeed it was also the key to a secure foundation for *all* science, natural as well as social. As David Hume put it: "the Science of man is the only solid foundation for the other sciences" and "Human Nature is the only science of man" (Hume, 1968, pp. xx and 273).

In their aim to destroy the Christian view of man's nature and place in the world, the *philosophes* gave a particular conception of human psychology a central and strategic scientific position. Their basic assumption was that human nature possesses an essential *uniformity*, though it does exhibit a wide empirical variation. Following in part the philosopher John Locke (1632–1704), the *philosophes* took over his "empiricist" ideas that the mind of the human being at birth is, in important respects, comparable to an empty sheet of paper, and that all his or her knowledge and emotions are a product of experience. Locke may, in this regard, be looked upon as the founder of the philosophy of *empiricism*, which holds to this doctrine of knowledge proceeding only out of experience. The science of man that the *philosophes* of the Enlightenment developed was distinctly empiricist; it follows that the social sciences that they inaugurated reflected both this concern with understanding social phenomena on the basis of human experience, and a scientific approach to those phenomena.

## 3.1   Enlightenment, science, and progress

As we have seen, for the intellectuals of the Enlightenment, science was the epitome of enlightened reason. Both were vehicles which – together – would move human society onwards and upwards to a more enlightened and *progressive* state.

The founding concepts of social science were intimately bound up with the Enlightenment's concept of *progress*, the idea that through the application of reasoned and empirically based knowledge, social institutions could be created that would make men happier and free them from cruelty, injustice, and despotism. Science played an important role in this process for the men of the eighteenth century, because it seemed to offer the prospect of increasing man's control over those aspects of nature most harmful to human interests. Science could ensure a more efficient and productive agriculture, and thus the elimination of famine; it could lead to the invention of processes and machines which would convert raw materials into goods that would be of benefit to mankind; it could ensure the reduction of illness and infirmity, and hold out the prospect of a population no longer kept in "ignorance and superstition" by received wisdom about the Christian creation myth, and religious concepts of cause and effect. The discovery that smallpox could be prevented by simple inoculation was only one among a great range of scientific innovations which seemed to roll back the frontiers of a nature hitherto quite hostile to man.

The great impact of the achievements of science, and especially the work of Newton, led the *philosophes* to believe that scientific method might be applied to society, and that science could become the basis of future social values, which could be selected rationally in relation to predetermined goals. Indeed Newton himself held this view. In his *Opticks* (1663) he had written: ". . . if natural philosophy, in all its parts, by pursuing this method, shall at length be perfected, the bounds of moral philosophy will also be enlarged."

The wit, playwright, historian, novelist, and philosopher Voltaire had a good deal to do with the emergence and diffusion of the fashion for science within enlightened thought. Voltaire embraced certain ideas and principles which had impressed him during a visit to England in the 1720s: Locke's empiricism, with its notion of our psychological pliability to the impressions we receive; Bacon's ideas about the use of empirical methods; Newton's great achievements in scientific

knowledge of the universe; and the religious pluralism and tolerance
which he found in British society. He melded them in a persuasive mix
of new ideas which he published in his *Lettres Philosophiques* of 1732.
The book was immediately banned and publicly burned, naturally
becoming as a result a huge publishing success. It was largely
responsible for the rapid spread of knowledge about the new scientific
method, making both Locke and Newton household names in
cultivated circles. The well-known story about Newton discovering
gravity as a result of an apple falling on his head was actually invented
by Voltaire to help non-scientists understand the concept, and is
typical of Voltaire's urge to popularize and make more accessible the
new "natural philosophy."

Voltaire's success was due not merely to his genius as a writer: what
his work evoked in his audience was a great desire for new ideas, for
an understanding of how society could progress through an application
of the best knowledge available in the arts and sciences. This belief in
the new, in progress and change through the application of reason and
knowledge, represented a qualitative shift in the attitudes of the literate
elite (although we should be careful about assuming that literacy was
confined only to the cultured elite: by the time Louis XVI came to the
French throne in 1774, about a third of the French population could
read and write). We might characterize this shift as a new thirst for
*modernity* in all its possible forms. As Peter Gay points out in his
classic study of the Enlightenment:

> In the century of the Enlightenment, educated Europeans awoke to
> a new sense of life. They experienced an expansive sense of
> power over nature and themselves: the pitiless cycles of
> epidemics, famines, risky life and early death, devastating war and
> uneasy peace – the treadmill of human existence – seemed to be
> yielding at last to the application of critical intelligence. Fear of
> change, up to that time nearly universal, was giving way to fear of
> stagnation; the word innovation, traditionally an effective term of
> abuse, became a word of praise. The very emergence of
> conservative ideas was a tribute to the general obsession with
> improvement: a stationary society does not need conservatives.
> There seemed to be little doubt that in the struggle of man against
> nature the balance of power was shifting in favour of man.
> (Gay, 1973b, p. 3)

## 3.2   The communication of Enlightenment

As I have argued in the previous section, the emergence of prototypical
social sciences owes much to the fascination of the *philosophes* with
natural sciences, and the applications of their methods to medicine,
agriculture, and industry. The *philosophes* saw science as an ally in
their common desire to combat religious intolerance and political
injustice, and their writings are full of discussions of the way in which
science contests theological representations of the earth's history, of
man's constitution, and of divine rights.

However, the Enlightenment was not simply a set of ideas. It helped to create a new secular intelligentsia, and to give the role of the intellectual a social and cultural base independent of traditional institutions such as the Church. It also represented (perhaps more significantly) a great cultural and social change in the way in which ideas were created and disseminated, and was a truly modern intellectual movement in the sense that its propagation depended on the creation of secular and cross-cultural forms of communication. The Enlightenment forged the intellectual conditions in which the application of reason to practical affairs could flourish – principally through the invention of such modern institutions as the scientific academy, the learned journal, and the conference. It also helped establish a modern "audience" for social, political, philosophical, and scientific ideas, and thus created the circumstances in which a class of intellectuals could live from writing about them.

The case of France, center of European cultural and intellectual life, demonstrates this "explosion" of new forms of communication very well. During the eighteenth century, a welling tide of journals, concerned with literary matters, news, art, science, theology, philosophy, law, and other matters of contemporary concern, appeared and were distributed throughout Europe. Between 1715 and 1785 the number of such regularly published journals grew from twenty-two to seventy-nine (Doyle, 1989, p. 45). The boldest journals, those with the most radical or "dangerous" ideas, were published beyond the frontiers of France. Some, such as Baron Grimm's *Correspondance Littéraire*, which had a Europe-wide circulation, were extremely costly and went only to such people as rulers and monarchs anxious to keep up with the heady life of the Parisian salons, and to keep abreast of new knowledge. Although publishing was (technically) strictly supervised by a system of censorship, there were many ways in which books and journals which were contrary to the government, to morals, and to religion could be published without receiving the official "privilege," and very few were banned. From the 1770s, book and journal publishing accelerated enormously, with newspapers starting to be available as well.

The audience for this massive explosion of printed material was potentially very large. However, access to this material was greatly restricted by two things: cost (a subscription to a journal could cost 20–50 *livres* per year, when the wages of the most skilled craftsman would not exceed 30 *livres* a week, with most earning half that sum or less); and restricted availability of the cultural education necessary to understand and take part in the debates about new ideas. Access to books and journals was facilitated for the impecunious by the rapid growth, after the mid-century, of subscription libraries and reading rooms, which had membership fees of about the cost of a single journal subscription. Some of these had conversation rooms set aside, but in the main, discussion took place in a different and equally popular institution, the literary society. These also had libraries where journals could be read, but in addition they held regular public sessions where their members read their own works or debated questions of the day.

They organized essay competitions, public lectures, and other cultural events, and were popular with the educated classes in all French towns: "One sees societies of this sort in almost all the towns of the kingdom . . . such an agreeable resource for the select class of citizen in all walks of life," noted a Dijon newspaper in 1787 (Doyle, 1989, p. 47). Even more select were the academies. Their members were elected, their membership carefully restricted, their constitution recognized by royal letters-patent. Apart from the three main Parisian academies founded in the seventeenth century, there were only seven provincial academies in 1700: this number had grown to thirty-five by the 1780s, although their combined membership throughout the entire period only amounted to some 6000, of whom 37 percent were nobles. The academies were culturally pre-eminent, international bodies in the sense that they included distinguished foreign associates and correspondents on their lists (Adam Smith was a correspondent of the Academy of Toulouse, for example). Success in their regular essay competitions could launch careers – Rousseau's triumph in the Dijon Academy's competition of 1750 being a notable example (Doyle, 1989, pp. 47–8).

The consumers of this intellectual culture were mainly nobles, clerics, and the professional bourgeoisie – members of the traditional social orders. They were mostly residents of towns, and particularly those towns *least* influenced by commerce or manufacturing. The new, "modern" middle classes of merchants and manufacturers were seemingly not so interested in the world of ideas. "I do not expect you will be able to sell any here" writes a bookseller of Bar-Le-Duc, an eastern French textile manufacturing town, to the publishers promoting a new edition of the *Encyclopédie* in 1780: "Having offered them to everybody here, nobody so far has come looking for a copy. They are more avid for trade than for reading, and their education is quite neglected . . . the merchants prefer to teach their children that 5 and 4 make 9 minus 2 equals 7 than in telling them to refine their minds" (quoted in Doyle, 1989, p. 48).

In this context it is perhaps not surprising that for the *philosophes*, as for the consumers of their writings, the domain of enlightened thought was not subdivided by a barrier between the disciplines which studied natural and social worlds: the implication of this for an emergent sociology and the other social sciences is of fundamental importance. It is not until the late nineteenth century and early twentieth century that a gulf begins to emerge between natural and social sciences, exemplified particularly by the great *methodenstreit* or methodological argument which raged in Germany from the 1880s, and which turned upon the question of whether the sciences which study history, society, and culture share the same scientific methods as those which study matter.

## 3.3   Enlightenment and social science

As the *philosophes* saw it, science was the epitome of reason because it made possible objective statements which were beyond philosophical, theological, or ideological dispute. Indeed, the concern of the Enlightenment thinkers with science was not in any sense the espousal of mere principles alone, but in many cases proceeded from a very full immersion in scientific knowledge and practices. As we noted above, Voltaire, who visited England in 1726–9, produced a lucid and popular exposition of Newton's major scientific achievements. Voltaire idealized Newton as a sort of new hero; one more fitting to an age which was concerned with reason, progress, the future:

> If true greatness consists of having been endowed by heaven with powerful genius, and of using it to enlighten oneself and others, then a man like M. Newton (we scarcely find one like him in ten centuries) is truly the great man, and those politicians and conquerors (whom no century has been without) are generally nothing but celebrated villains.
> (quoted in Gay, 1973b, pp. 128–9)

The deification of Newton was in fact a common theme of the Enlightenment. Jean-Jacques Rousseau was at one point called the "Newton of the moral world" by Kant, and to be a "Newton" was just about the most flattering thing anybody could say about a *philosophe* (Gay, 1973b, p. 129).

A number of central figures of the Enlightenment (David Hume, Jean d'Alembert, Étienne de Condillac, and Immanuel Kant) made significant contributions to the philosophical understanding of science, and thus to the acceptance of scientific method as the basis for an understanding of human nature. The achievements of science were of signal importance, for they pointed to the possibility of a rational and empirically-based method for creating a form of knowledge which was not conditioned by religious dogma or superstition. The *philosophes* were concerned with moral issues, but they wished to free moral philosophy from its reliance on theology, put it on a scientific and rational base and derive objective knowledge from it. Their critical rationalism and their support of science were in certain respects a confusion of two different intellectual strands, and the progressive espousal by the sciences of what are termed *positivist* methods, which make a very rigid distinction between fact and value, ultimately caused them some philosophical problems. They wished to use science and reason to counteract the founding of social institutions on what they saw as repressive values derived from Christianity or feudalism: but they did not foresee that the separation of fact and value implicit in scientific method would make it difficult to establish a scientific basis for the societal and cultural values which they espoused. If science is indeed value-neutral, then the knowledge it creates confers no special status on any social arrangement, however "enlightened" it may appear.

Nonetheless, the long love-affair of the *philosophes* with science was important in the emergence of social science. The prototypical social sciences required two basic conditions in order to develop coherent areas of study and methods of inquiry, which they derived from the example of the natural sciences: *naturalism* and the *control of prejudice*. Naturalism, the notion that cause and effect sequences in the natural world (rather than a spiritual or metaphysical world) fully explain social phenomena, was provided by the Enlightenment emphasis on scientific method. The control of prejudice is necessary in the social sciences as a means of preventing value-judgments from unduly influencing the results of empirical study. It is arguable whether it is possible to eliminate prejudice or value-judgments completely from the selection of a topic of research, but it is clear that in the evaluation or analysis of evidence and data the social scientist must prevent his or her prejudices from influencing the results. The *philosophes* – although they were on many occasions prey to prejudice in their work (and nowhere is this clearer than in their treatment of the rights and condition of women) – wanted to let facts, rather than values, test their theories. The presence of these two conditions in the intellectual climate of the Enlightenment fertilized the growth of the social sciences, but it also created a number of major philosophical difficulties which remained essentially unresolved.

The overarching emphasis of the *philosophes* on rationalism, empiricism, and humanitarianism was largely responsible for their work in the new social sciences having two distinct characteristics:

1   the use of *scientific methods* in attempting to justify the reform of social institutions; and

2   *cultural relativism*: the realization, by many *philosophes*, that the European society in which they lived did not represent the best or most developed form of social organization.

The first of these is evidenced by the widespread belief among the *philosophes* that scientific knowledge of human affairs could be directly applied to the transformation of human institutions. Believing, as Voltaire put it, that men were corrupted by "bad models, bad education, bad laws," the *philosophes* placed a great reliance on the functions of knowledge itself as an agent of social change. Man's natural innocence and his dependence on himself as an adult would provide the material, with objective knowledge to reject corrupt influences. Diderot wrote a play *Est-il Bon? Est-il Méchant?* (Is he Good? Is he Wicked?), which aptly sums up the wholly *modern* way in which questions about human morality were to be treated by the Enlightenment: as problems to be solved by intellectual inquiry, rather than by the imposition of an external authority.

The second major characteristic of the new social sciences was their new mood of *cultural relativism*: the notion that there was no single culture, and certainly not any Christian culture, which could provide a standard of perfection by which to judge others. This mood was by no means universal among the *philosophes*, but it was a strong feature of the approach we associate with the French Enlightenment. Scottish Enlightenment figures (especially Hume, Smith, and Ferguson) were attached to a stage-model of human development, in which modern European society appeared to be the most advanced. The French *philosophes* were frequent users of the literary ruse of providing a critique of some aspect of European society with which they disagreed, by means of an account written by what would have been considered in their time as a "barbarous" non-European – Montesquieu's *Lettres Persanes*, a criticism of absolute monarchy as practiced by Louis XIV and XV, is a classic of the genre. Apparently written by a Persian traveller, it inverts the classic western assumption that despotism is only practiced in the East.

The *philosophes* were extensive if somewhat uncritical users of the reports of travellers, explorers, or even missionaries about foreign lands and other cultures (a theme explored in much more detail by Stuart Hall in chapter 6). They employed these in the service of their important contention that human nature was basically uniform, and varied only in response to certain local conditions and particular circumstances, ranging from the ecological to the political. As Montesquieu put it, the Enlightenment's maxim of cultural relativism worked like this: "one should not sit in judgement upon the ways of other people, but rather seek to understand them in the context of their circumstances, and then use one's knowledge of them to improve understanding of oneself" (Porter, 1990, p. 63). Although they were often a little credulous in their usage of some of the more dubious of these travellers' tales, the *philosophes*' passionate interest in other cultures was crucially important to the development of a basic component of social science: cross-cultural comparison. For it is a central methodological tenet of the social sciences that theories and hypotheses should be formulated in a way which allows their employment in comparative studies. It is important to separate this cultural relativism from the belief in progress – the idea that the application of science and enlightened thought to the improvement of man's lot could make the European societies in which the *philosophes* lived the most advanced in the world. And we should be aware that intellectually the key figures of the Enlightenment stood in opposition to the domination of alien cultures and civilizations, and especially to the enslavement of their populations.

It is important to observe that the treatment of other cultures is one where the contradictions and inconsistencies of the Enlightenment are most evident. Several French *philosophes* used the example of other cultures to point up the "barbarism" of the French state. Some, like Rousseau, used the example of "savage society" to demonstrate how civilization makes men subvert their natural humanity and create inequalities. His idea of the "noble savage," the notion that man is naturally good and is only made bad by society, fits well with the Enlightenment concept of the uniformity of human nature. By contrast, the Scottish Enlightenment developed several "stadial models" of the historical stages through which human society was supposed to have evolved. These models typically set up the Scottish society of the eighteenth century as the pinnacle of human development, with the "savage" or "barbarous" societies discovered by colonial exploration in the Americas and elsewhere at the other end of the scale.

Although these two ways of using other cultures in the emergent social science of the Enlightenment clearly differ, they do have one important common characteristic: the need to compare European society with that of other cultures and to understand its characteristics and history in a wider context.

# 4   Revolution and Reformation

In the emergence of distinctively modern societies, the social and political transformations which occurred in the American and French Revolutions of 1776 and 1789 appear to be intimately linked. They are widely represented as the thresholds between traditional and modern society, symbolizing the end of feudalism and absolutism, and the rise of the bourgeoisie as the dominant class in capitalist society, as well as major steps along the roads to both liberal democracy and totalitarianism. But what is the precise nature of the relationship between the Enlightenment and the French and American Revolutions? This topic has been hotly debated for the last 200 years, and we are not going to resolve it in this chapter. Our concerns are more with some of the implications of these Revolutions for the emergence of sociology and the other social sciences as institutionalized disciplines.

The American Revolution and the War of Independence which followed it (1776–83) appeared to prove that a new Republic could be created, that it could defeat a powerful monarchy, and that it could encapsulate Enlightenment ideas. A number of the central figures of the new American Republic – notably Thomas Jefferson, Benjamin Franklin, John Adams, and Alexander Hamilton – were *philosophes* in the sense of being part of the wider circle of intellectuals in touch with the key figures of the Enlightenment. The Republic's constitution enshrined a number of central precepts of the Enlightenment: the uniformity of human nature (equality), tolerance, freedom of thought and expression, the separation of powers. It owed a lot to Montesquieu's ideas about the social basis of political order, to Hume's conception of the universality of human nature, and to Voltaire's concern with freedom of thought. Yet like most products of the Enlightenment it had its dark side: slavery paradoxically remained legal (Jefferson was himself a plantation owner and a slave-master).

The success of the American Revolution – helped to no small degree by aid from the French state, as part of its long struggle with Britain for European dominance – encouraged those in France who wished to see an end to the "despotism" of absolute monarchy in Europe.

It was widely thought at the time that the French Revolution was in part at least a by-product of the dangerous ideas proposed by the *philosophes*. As Catherine the Great of Russia wrote in 1794 to the Baron Grimm:

> Do you remember that the late King of Prussia claimed to have been told by Helvétius that the aim of the *philosophes* was to overturn all thrones, and that the *Encyclopédie* was written with no other end in view than to destroy all kings and all religions? Do you also remember that you never wished to be included

among the *philosophes*? Well, you were right . . . The sole aim of
the whole movement, as experience is proving, is to destroy.

Yet, as we have noted, the *philosophes* for the most part thought that
progress could come about *within* the existing social order. As Diderot
once said, their aim was revolutionary only insofar as it sought "the
revolution which will take place in the minds of men" (quoted in Eliot
and Stern, 1979, p. 44). Indeed, Voltaire believed in the necessity of
absolute monarchs (like Louis XV, whose historiographer-royal he
became) because only they would have the power to sweep away the
institutions and outmoded laws which kept men in a state of ignorance
and superstition.

In Britain, Edmund Burke (1729–97), a political theorist of the Whig
party, put forward what was to be an influential conservative
interpretation of the Enlightenment, which saw it as an intellectual or
philosophic conspiracy, fomented by a "literary cabal," and designed to
destroy Christianity, and in the process bring down the French state. To
support his case he used the example of the Bavarian *Illuminati*. There
had been a notorious conspiracy by a group of Enlightenment-
influenced intellectuals in Bavaria – the *Illuminati* – to use freemasonry
to bring down the Church-dominated government of the German
principality in 1787.

In his widely read *Reflections on the Revolution in France* (1790),
Burke laid responsibility for the Revolution squarely at the door of the
*philosophes*. He told the French that there was nothing fundamentally
wrong with the *ancien régime*, and that they had no need to bring the
monarchy down: "You had the elements of a constitution very nearly
as good as could be wished . . . but you chose to act as if you had never
been moulded into civil society and had everything to begin anew"
(quoted in Doyle, 1989, p. 166).

Burke's ideas were vigorously contested by Thomas Paine (1737–
1809), among others. His *Rights of Man* made a strong case for the
republican argument, and one which stressed that the French were
creating a new constitution on the basis of Enlightenment thinking –
rational, equitable, based on natural law and scientific principles. The
debate between Burke and Paine was linked quite closely to a wider
political struggle over parliamentary reform in England, and continued
until about 1800. Although Paine's ideas were highly influential in
Britain, in Europe Burke's argument that societies were very unwise to
abandon heritage and established traditions struck a strong chord –
particularly among the cultivated and ruling elites who perceived that
the example of the French Revolution threatened their own vested
interests.

In one sense, the *philosophes* were a key factor in the French
Revolution. As Albert Sorel, writing a century later would say:

> The Revolutionary situation was a result of the faults of the
> Government, but the philosophes gave it leaders, cadres, a
> doctrine, direction, the temptation of illusions and the irresistible
> momentum of hope. They did not create the causes of the
> Revolution, but they made them manifest, actuated them, gave

them emotive force, multiplied them and quickened their pace.
The writings of the philosophes were not responsible for the
disintegration of the ancien régime: it was because it was
disintegrating of its own accord that their influence promoted the
Revolution.
(Sorel, 1969, pp. 238–9; first published 1885)

As Sorel and many historians since have made very clear, the
conditions for revolution existed at least as early as the reign of Louis
XV: only a certain sense of optimism that his successor would put
things right, founded in the residual legitimacy of the monarchy for
most of the French, delayed the events which finally occurred in 1789.
Despite the *philosophes'* own protestations to the contrary, the
Enlightenment was a radical force in undermining the legitimacy of the
*ancien régime*. The main factor in this was the great popularity of
Enlightenment thinking among the educated elites. We have noted the
virtual explosion in the number of books, newspapers, journals, literary
societies, and subscription libraries between 1725 and 1789. This
provoked a growth in the number of state censors, from 41 in 1720 to
148 by 1789. The expulsion of the Jesuit order in 1764 as a result of a
long dispute between the order and the French *Parlements* (which
seriously disrupted the French educational system: about a quarter of
the French *collèges* were run by Jesuits) also gave a boost to the
mounting tide of irreligion and to demands for greater religious
tolerance, largely emanating from the *philosophes*. The Church itself
tried to stem this tide by publishing refutations of philosophic
impieties, and getting pious laymen in positions of authority to
suppress dissent, but of course as a result it only succeeded in
encouraging the wider debate of central issues of Enlightenment
thought.

The French Revolution became, as the historian William Doyle has
said, "an opportunity for enlightened men to bring about a more
rational, just and humane organisation of the affairs of mankind." The
National Assembly, which launched the Revolution in 1789, included
"the cream of the country's intelligentsia, who consciously saw
themselves as the products and the instruments of the triumph of
Enlightenment. All over France men of similar background rallied to
them, inspired by the same ideals" (Doyle, 1989, p. 393). The
revolutionary constitution which that Assembly produced in 1791 was
directly based on ideas first enunciated in *De l'Esprit des Lois* by
Montesquieu, especially those relating to the separation of powers
between executive, legislature, and judiciary.

It would be misleading to see the French Revolution as no more than
the putting into practice of the intellectual principles of the
Enlightenment. As Mounier, the moderate royalist leader of 1789,
argued much later, "it was not the influence of those principles which
created the Revolution, it was on the contrary the Revolution which
created their influence" (quoted in Hampson, 1969, p. 256).

As a socio-political event, the French Revolution stands at the
threshold of the modern world, and that world is arguably

inconceivable without it, for it transformed men's outlook on the nature and organization of society. If we then look at the chief architects of that Revolution, and ask from where their own outlook was derived, we come back to the main figures of the Enlightenment – to Voltaire, Montesquieu, Diderot, Rousseau, Condorcet, Benjamin Franklin.

It is in the areas of civil law, parliamentary control of taxation, the liberties of the press and of the individual, religious tolerance, and the wholesale sweeping away of feudal laws and obligations ("privilege") that the influence of the Enlightenment on the Revolution is clearest. The *philosophes* believed that "men would live with greater happiness and dignity if their social institutions were determined by what was considered reasonable or scientific rather than regulated by prescription" (Hampson, 1969, p. 252). With this went the assumption that men had certain inalienable rights, such as unrestricted freedom of access to information, freedom of speech, freedom from arbitrary arrest, and freedom of economic activity. Taken overall, they appear as the Revolution's drive to institutionalize a greater degree of social, political, and economic equality within the state, to counter the natural inequality of man which underpinned the whole complex system of law, taxation, and local government of the *ancien régime*. Yet, at least in its early stages, the ideal of equality was a limited one, and not as radical as it might appear. What the revolutionaries of 1789–91 wanted was an opening up of French society to those men – essentially the educated, cultivated "gentlemen" who had been some of the main consumers of Enlightenment thought – then excluded from power and influence. In many ways they wanted a society like that of England, where a limited democracy was available.

The Revolution took a different turn after 1792, entering a clear second phase and becoming both more radically republican and Rousseauist in its form. The Republic was engaged in a war against numerous absolutist or monarchist states on its frontiers (Austria, Prussia, Holland, Spain, Britain) and internally against those who opposed the increasingly democratic and totalitarian directions which its institutions were taking. It had progressively less to do with the basic principles of the *philosophes*, and became closer in spirit to the ideas of Jean-Jacques Rousseau, with the Republic represented as a sort of Ideal City, and society seen as a means for reinforcing the morality of its members. The execution of Louis XVI in 1793, and the Terror unleashed against many of those who had been the main supporters of the Revolution of 1789, seemed to many outside of France to be proof that the Enlightenment had created a monster. Many European intellectuals – Kant among them – were repelled by the violence of the Revolution and the increasingly belligerent nationalism of France.

The latter history of the Revolution, and its transformation into a new form of absolutism under Napoleon, thus helped to accelerate a move away from the ideals of the Enlightenment. Only those measures which helped national efficiency (e.g. internal free trade, technical education) remained. Basic liberties, such as freedom of the press and freedom from arbitrary arrest, were suspended. The Enlightenment as a force for progress and intellectual change was effectively at an end.

Nevertheless, the intellectual principles which it had institutionalized among the cultivated elite survived, and formed the basis of a new set of reflections upon the ordering of a post-revolutionary society.

# 5   The Birth of Sociology: Saint-Simon and Comte

Although the Revolution and its aftermath carried away with it some of the "momentum of hope" engendered by the Enlightenment, the intellectual advances it brought in ways of thinking about man and society were not jettisoned in the process. Other intellectual fashions – especially, in the more conservative forms of Romanticism, a return to a belief in order and tradition – held sway, but the palpable advances of the natural sciences and their progressive institutionalization as professionalized disciplines continued to provide a model for the social sciences to follow. The social changes which the French Revolution had brought in its train – notably the emergence of an economically powerful middle class – also provided a new social force in the constitution of civil society, and with it the creation of new social theories which could make sense of the new directions in which an emergent "modern" and "industrial" society was heading.

Although a properly professionalized sociology was not to appear until the latter half of the nineteenth century, it is in the carry-over of ideas and concepts from the Enlightenment into the "classical sociology" formulated in the first decades of the nineteenth century that we can discern its roots. In the writings and activities of Saint-Simon and Comte, a theory was elaborated about the emergent "industrial society" forming itself in post-revolutionary Europe, and this constituted an agenda of interests for the new science of sociology which was still being debated by Émile Durkheim and Max Weber in the 1890s.

## 5.1   Saint-Simon

When Henri de Saint-Simon (1760–1825) set out to construct a new science of society from the wreckage of the Enlightenment, he saw himself as carrying the *philosophes'* ideas onto a new plane: "The philosophy of the eighteenth century has been critical and revolutionary; that of the nineteenth century will be inventive and constructive" (quoted in Taylor, 1975, p. 22).

Saint-Simon was a typical product of the Enlightenment. From a noble family, he received an education steeped in the classics, the new science of Newton, and the writings of the *philosophes*, typical of the second half of the eighteenth century. As he later wrote: "Our education achieved its purpose: it made us revolutionaries" (quoted in Taylor, 1975, p. 14).

Saint-Simon narrowly escaped becoming a victim of the Terror before a series of successful financial speculations made him (briefly) a rich man. He used the leisure this brought him to follow and even finance courses in the study of science and physiology, the latter because he held the view that a new science of society – a "social physiology" – would be necessary if order and stability were to become possible again. Saint-Simon came to believe that modern society was threatened by the forces of anarchy and revolution, and that society would only progress beyond this stage if science and industry were put at the service of mankind through a major social reorganization. Scientists would become the new religious leaders because, as human thought had become more enlightened since the Middle Ages, the Catholic clergy could no longer demonstrate the spiritual power required to hold society together. Saint-Simon proposed a "religion of Newton" organized on both national and international levels, with the world's most eminent scientists and artists at its head. Temporal power would belong with the property owners, representatives of the new industrial class.

Although these notions received relatively little attention, Saint-Simon's ideas about the need for a science of man and society became progressively more influential as war and social disorder engulfed Europe in the first two decades of the nineteenth century. His *Mémoire sur la Science de l'Homme* (Memoir on the Science of Man) and *Travail sur la Gravitation Universelle* (Work on Universal Gravitation), both written in 1813, received wide recognition as an appeal to found a new social science which would counteract the forces of conflict and disorder. As a result of this and later work, Saint-Simon became a key figure in the "liberal" political movements of post-Napoleonic Europe. In his journal *L'Industrie*, Saint-Simon used the term "liberal" to describe economic and political values which were in favor of greater freedom for manufacture and trade, and of a bigger say in how the country was run for those who owned factories and other businesses.

## 5.2  Comte

Auguste Comte (1798–1857) was the first person to use the term "sociology" to describe the scientific study of society. Comte's work has been presented as a synthesis of the writings of key Enlightenment figures such as Montesquieu, the physiocratic economist Turgot, Condorcet, and of his erstwhile patron and collaborator, Saint-Simon. Although the *philosophes* clearly inspired Comte, his work in defining the subject matter and methods of the new science – sociology – goes far beyond them, and offers a clear link to the professionalized discipline of the twentieth century (Thompson, 1976, p. 6).

Comte wished to create a naturalistic science of society capable of both explaining its past and predicting its future. He developed a theory which has many affinities with those of the Enlightenment *philosophes*, in that it proposed a series of stages (The Law of Human Progress or the Law of Three Stages), through which society has progressed. Unlike the stadial (staged) theories of Ferguson or Smith, however, his notion of development was based on the idea of a development of the human mind, and societal stages thus mirrored these developments in terms of social organization, types of social unit, and forms of social order. Like the *philosophes*, he saw society as developing progressively through the emancipation of the human intellect. Where he differed from them most substantially was in the notion that societies are in effect like giant biological organisms. Their evolution and development thus follow well-defined, law-like stages, much as the development of an animal follows a clear pattern.

Comte believed that sociology was the study of such patterns of societal evolution, and that it would proceed through an analysis of both *static* and *dynamic* aspects of social organization. He distinguished these two not by empirical criteria, but methodologically. Static and dynamic, order and progress are always present in an interconnected way, and thus their differentiation in any empirical context is always a matter of methodological distinction, based on theoretical concepts. It is often very hard to make a purely empirical distinction between these elements in a given situation, where the point at which progress ends and order begins becomes a matter of interpretation. Comte's insight is that these distinctions are theoretical, rather than simple observations.

Like Saint-Simon, Comte used ideas about the function of religion as a sort of social cement which binds societies together. Language also performs this function, but without some form of religion (adapted to the stage of society in which it is found) governments would possess no legitimacy, and society would be torn apart by factional violence. Comte also used a further notion, derived essentially from the Scottish Enlightenment, to explain social order – the division of labor. Men are:

> bound together by the very distribution of their occupations; and it is this distribution which causes the extent and growing complexity of the social organism.
>
> The social organization tends more and more to rest on an exact estimate of individual diversities, by so distributing employments as to appoint each one to the destination he is most fit for, from his own nature . . . from his education and his position, and, in short, from all his qualifications; so that all individual organizations, even the most vicious and imperfect . . . may finally be made use of for the general good.
> (Comte, *Cours de Philosophie Positive*, 1830–2, vol. 2; quoted in Thompson, 1976)

Many of Comte's ideas are remarkably close in spirit to the sociology developed by Émile Durkheim at the end of the nineteenth century, especially his emphasis on the clear definition of sociology's subject matter, and on the methodological principles underlying the new science – observation, experimentation, comparison. Durkheim was also concerned with the role of religion in generating social cohesion or solidarity, in the role of the division of labor within industrial societies, and in the forms of solidarity which modern societies required. Indeed, all of Durkheim's most characteristic ideas have close affinities with those of Comte and Saint-Simon, although it is also quite evident that Durkheim departed from their perspective in a number of respects. But the crucial point is that Émile Durkheim provided theories, methodologies, and subject matter for the earliest institutionalization of sociology as a university-based discipline. With Comte and Saint-Simon, then, we are at one of the crucial bridges between the ideas of the Enlightenment and those of modern sociology. They provided the conduit along which certain central principles of the Enlightenment's world-view flowed into modern sociology.

# 6   Conclusion

The Enlightenment, which its proponents saw as spreading reason like light, played a critically important part in the emergence of the social sciences. It formed the first stage in the forging of a modern conception of society as an entity open to human agency, whose workings are in principle open to our scrutiny. It created the elements from which intellectuals could begin to construct an image of society which reflected human interests. The *philosophes* certainly believed that human agency, if properly informed by enlightened self-knowledge, was perfectly capable of controlling society – for what was the latter but the aggregated wills of individual men and women? We can be skeptical about the extent to which they really wanted to change society as a result of that self-knowledge; there is little doubt that most of the major figures in the movement wished only for the end of absolutist rule, and for a political regime which extended if only in a limited way the liberties of the social orders from which they issued.

It is also clear that, like all knowledge, that of the Enlightenment spilled over from the narrow cup into which it was poured by the *philosophes*, and washed over those for whom it was not originally intended, being taken up by a wide range of popularizers and political activists of many hues. When the great rupture between traditional and modern society first took shape in the French Revolution, the jettisoning of traditional values based on Christianity and absolutism must have seemed to many people a logical outcome of the radical program of the Enlightenment – its hatred of religious orthodoxy and the clergy, its opposition to the political controls of the absolutist state, and its egalitarian ideology. Having prepared even unwittingly – the ground for revolution, it is not surprising that the Enlightenment's central ideas were tarred by the ruling elites of post-1815 Europe with the brush of sedition, subversion, and disorder. Indeed, it is a paradox of some magnitude that while the Enlightenment never developed a coherent theory or model of the society from which it issued, it produced enough elements of a *critique* of that society to help it along the way to an eventual demise.

How does the Enlightenment link to later stages in the emergence of a science of society? To begin with, we can assess its impact as an early and rather rickety sociological "paradigm" – a cluster of interconnected ideas which were influential in the ways people thought about the social world and human relationships. If we think of Kant's motto *sapere aude* – dare to know – we can capture the essence of this new approach, this new paradigm. For the first time, man could "dare to know" about the social arrangements under which he lived, rather than have them presented to him through the obscuring haze of a religious ideology. By knowing about these social arrangements, their operation would become clear, and thus open to change. Much in the same way as knowing about the cause of smallpox enabled man to devise a way of preventing it, it seemed to the *philosophes* self-evident that knowing about the cause of a social injustice, like religious persecution, would enable him to stop it occurring. Rather than a model of society, the Enlightenment had a model of how to think about social arrangements. Its practitioners were not loath to use the term "society," but rarely even approached a definition of what could be meant by the word. The nearest the *philosophes* came to achieving a modern concept of society is thus the Scottish Enlightenment's ideas about human civilization going through a series of stages, which become the progressive unveiling of the uniformity of human nature. Ferguson's concept of "civil society" thus appears as a setting in which the uniformity of human nature is finally allowed to operate as a set of arrangements for conducting the business of a nation in an enlightened fashion. It is in "civil society" that the division of labor enables human nature to work most efficiently, and without unnecessary restraint.

We must not forget that the Enlightenment also encompassed medical, scientific, technological, and other innovations, and that as a result it was widely thought of as part of a society-wide process of improving human life. It also made a big impact on education and therefore came to be part of the body of knowledge and ideas which were passed on in the process of schooling. In a general sense, once ways of thinking have been changed, they rarely go back to an earlier state. If I tell you something important which you did not already know, it will be hard for you to forget it. Those who thought and wrote about the society which emerged from the ashes of Revolutionary France, like Saint-Simon and Comte, could not escape their upbringing, which was steeped in the ideas and learning of the *philosophes*. They could not forget the Enlightenment, but they could react against it, and attempt to surpass it. The very thing that was deficient in Enlightenment thought – its inability to provide a coherent explanatory model of the society in which it existed – was precisely the thing that Saint-Simon and Comte tried to improve. They used the concept of society to describe the new combination of people, institutions, social groups, and manufacturing processes which was emerging from the wreckage of the traditional European world. But their aim was not merely to describe and understand: like the *philosophes* their objective was to change society. Saint-Simon and Comte wished to see created the "industrial society" dealt with in their writings.

By contrast, most *philosophes* stopped short of a properly worked out model of society, because they held an essentially "individualist" conception of man, and because their social theory hardly needed the explicit conception of society as an entity. Once we "know" that all men share a uniform human nature, it appears possible to construct an explanation of the behavior of a multitude of people by simply aggregating individual characteristics (as a way of explaining social behavior, this approach is known by the term "methodological individualism"). Saint-Simon and Comte went beyond this to write quite explicitly about society as an entity which can be "known" independently of individual men, as a force which can coerce and constrain individuals to behave in certain ways. Their ideas were influenced both by the traditionalism and romanticism of their time (a sort of reaction to the Enlightenment idea that man is a self-sufficient individual), and by the success of life-sciences such as biology and medicine, in which understanding the interconnections of organic processes played a crucial role. In Comte's work, man becomes subject to society once more, no longer self-sufficient but pushed and pulled by the twin forces of statics and dynamics. Comte presents society as a system which obeys certain laws – the laws which his positive sociology was established to study. His approach is often called "organicism" because it uses the idea of society as a huge organism, as something more than the sum of its parts. If we take out one unit of that society – a particular person, for instance – we can know something about him or her, but not about how the whole society operates. But in the Enlightenment model, that person is a microcosm of society: by studying him or her we can build a picture about how society as a whole will operate – there are no "laws of society" which are independent of the individual.

The history of sociology since the Enlightenment can be presented as the tension between the two approaches to society outlined above: one based in the *philosophes'* idea that society is no more than an aggregate of individuals, the other in Comte's idea that society is a super-individual entity, with a life of its own. Such a tension appears in the approaches of the central figures of nineteenth-century sociology, from J.S. Mill and Herbert Spencer to Émile Durkheim and Max Weber. Durkheim developed his own version of organicism, while Weber's approach recast the "methodological individualism" of the Enlightenment in a modern form.

The Enlightenment, then, is one of the starting points for modern sociology. Its central themes formed the threshold of modern thinking about society and the realm of the social. Perhaps of equal importance is that it signalled the appearance of the secular intellectual within western society, a figure whose role is intimately bound up with the analysis and critique of society. It is from that role that emerged, among other intellectual positions, the modern conception of the professional sociologist, based in a specific institution. It may be that we have to thank Comte for the name "sociology," but it is arguably to the Enlightenment that we should turn to see the emergence of the profession of sociologist.

# References

Anderson, B. and Zinsser, J. (1990) *A History of their Own: Women in Europe from Prehistory to the Present*, 2 vols, Harmondsworth, England, Penguin.

Black, J. (1990) *Eighteenth Century Europe 1700–1789*, London, Macmillan.

Brinton, C. (1930) "The Revolutions," *Encyclopaedia of the Social Sciences*, vol. 1, New York, Macmillan.

Darnton, R. (1979) *The Business of Enlightenment. A Publishing History of the Encyclopédie 1775–1800*, Cambridge, MA, Harvard University Press.

Doyle, W. (1989) *The Oxford History of the French Revolution*, Oxford, Clarendon Press.

Eliot, S. and Stern, B. (eds) (1979) *The Age of Enlightenment: An Anthology of Eighteenth Century Texts*, London, Ward Lock Educational.

Gay, P. (1973a) *The Enlightenment: An Interpretation. Vol. 1: The Rise of Modern Paganism*, London, Wildwood House.

Gay, P. (1973b) *The Enlightenment: An Interpretation. Vol. 2: The Science of Freedom*, London, Wildwood House.

Gibbon, E. (1966) *Memoirs of my Life* (ed. G. A. Bonnard), London, Nelson.

Hampson, N. (1969) *The Enlightenment*, Harmondsworth, England, Penguin.

Nisbet, R. (1967) *The Sociological Tradition*, London, Heinemann.

Porter, R. (1990) *The Enlightenment*, London, Macmillan.

Sorel, A. (1969) *Europe and The French Revolution: The Political Traditions of the Old Regime* (first published 1885), London, Collins.

Taylor, K. (1975) *Henri Saint-Simon 1760–1825: Selected Writings on Science, Industry and Social Organisation*, London, Croom Helm.

Thompson, K. (1976) *Auguste Comte: The Foundation of Sociology*, London, Nelson.

# 2 The Development of the Modern State

David Held

## Contents

| | | |
|---|---|---|
| 1 | Introduction | 56 |
| 1.1 | Some preliminary definitions | 56 |
| 1.2 | The structure of the chapter | 57 |
| 2 | A Brief History and Geography of European States | 58 |
| 2.1 | Empires | 62 |
| 2.2 | Systems of divided authority in medieval Europe | 63 |
| 2.3 | The polity of estates | 65 |
| 2.4 | Absolutist states | 66 |
| 2.5 | Modern states | 70 |
| 3 | Why did Nation-States Become Supreme? | 73 |
| 3.1 | War and militarism | 74 |
| 3.2 | States and capitalism | 79 |
| 4 | Conclusion | 84 |
| References | | 87 |

# 1    Introduction

This chapter has two overall purposes: first, to introduce the diversity of state forms which have existed over time and which constitute the broad historical context for understanding the nature of the modern state; second, to explore the question: Why did the nation-state become the supreme form of the modern state? These objectives are clearly wide-ranging; but by devoting attention to both I hope to shed some light on the key formative processes of the modern state and the controversies that surround it.

The prime focus of this chapter will be the making of the modern state in Europe. There are a number of important reasons for this geographic restriction. In the first instance, the story of the formation of the modern state is in part the story of the formation of Europe, and vice versa. The development of a distinctive "European" identity is closely tied to the creation of Europe by states. Moreover, the states system of Europe has had extraordinary influence in the world beyond Europe: European expansion and development has had a decisive role in shaping the political map of the modern world. Furthermore, debates about the nature of the modern state in large part derive from European intellectual traditions, notably the Enlightenment, although to recognize this is by no means to suggest that everything of importance about the state was understood and expressed in Europe alone.

## 1.1    Some preliminary definitions

It is intriguing to note that for the greater part of human history states have not existed at all. States are *historical* phenomena, constructed under particular conditions, and far from fixed or "natural" entities. In hunting-and-gathering communities, in small agrarian cultures, and in the regions wandered by semi-nomadic or nomadic peoples there has been no recognizably separate state or political organization. Today, there are still many communities which anthropologists refer to as "stateless" – communities such as the Jale people of the New Guinea highlands, the pastoral Nuer of the South Sudan, the M'dendeuili and Arusha of East Africa. "Stateless," however, should not be taken to mean the absence of any mechanisms of regulation or government through which decisions affecting the community can be made and disputes settled. A diverse array of such mechanisms has existed, from family and kinship structures to the rules and norms of custom or tradition, and to the established powers of a chief (a warrior or priest, or both), often assisted by a council or court.

Table 2.1 provides a useful starting point by juxtaposing stateless and state societies in order to bring the latter's broad characteristics into relief. Table 2.1 offers only rudimentary definitions. One reason for this is that states, like other social phenomena, have changed over time, partly in relation to the transformation of the conditions of the societies in which they arose. There have been many different state forms which have set down elements of rule in a succession of different ways. Rule

Table 2.1   Features of stateless and state societies

| Stateless societies | State societies |
| --- | --- |
| informal mechanisms of government | political apparatus or governmental institutions differentiated from other organizations in the community |
| no clear boundaries to a society | rule takes place over a specific population and territory |
| disputes and decisions settled by family or kin groups, or by larger tribal structures headed by a chief with the support of a council | legal system, backed by a capacity to use force |
| relationships and transactions significantly defined by custom | institutional divisions within government (the executive, civil service, and army, for example) are formally coordinated |

or rulership has no single "essence" or fixed quality. Examples which will be drawn upon to highlight this are empires, feudal political relations, and absolutist monarchies.

This chapter distinguishes the characteristics of stateless and state societies from those of the modern state. Several key features of the latter will be elucidated in section 2.5, but for the present it is sufficient to stress that the concept of the modern state refers to that type of state which emerged in the European states system from the sixteenth century onwards. The concept connotes an impersonal and privileged legal or constitutional order with the capability of administering and controlling a given territory; that is, a distinct form of public power, separate from both ruler and ruled, and forming the supreme political authority within certain defined boundaries (Skinner, 1978, p. 353; cf. Neumann, 1964). The "other side" of the modern state is "civil society." Civil society – like nearly all concepts in social and political analysis – has a long and complex history; but by "civil society" I will here mean those areas of social life – the domestic world, the economic sphere, cultural activities, and political interaction – which are organized by private or voluntary arrangements between individuals and groups outside the *direct* control of the state (cf. Bobbio, 1989; Pelczynski, 1985; Keane, 1988). The modern state and civil society were formed, as will be seen, through distinct but interrelated processes.

## 1.2   The structure of the chapter

This chapter has two main parts which correspond to the aims stated at the outset. The objective of the first part (section 2) is to provide a brief chronological sketch of the development of the state in Europe, and an account of its chief variants. It is not my intention here to suggest that the variants followed one another according to an evolutionary pattern through which states passed from the "primitive" to the "civilized," from the "simple" to the "complex," or from "lower" to "higher" stages – far from it! My aim is to establish a political map or set of bearings which can become a basis for asking in the next section (section 3):

What explains the movement and change among state forms, and how can one understand the rise of the nation-state? If section 2 expounds a *typology* of states, section 3 seeks to explicate the *underlying processes* or *causal patterns* which might illuminate why particular types of state have taken the form they have, and why one of these types – the modern nation-state – became the dominant form over time.

The particular emphasis of this chapter is on the active role played by the state in the making and shaping of modernity. Throughout the nineteenth and twentieth centuries most of the leading perspectives on social change emphasized that the origins of social transformation were to bo found in processes *internal* to society and, above all, in *socio-economic* factors. In many of these perspectives, the interrelations *among* states and societies were barely explored. By focusing on the war-making capacity of states, and on the role of the state in domestic *and* international affairs, this chapter sets itself against this neglect. In so doing, it aligns itself with a notable strand of recent scholarship on the history of states (much of it referred to in the pages which follow), which emphasizes the independent and autonomous part played by *political* and *military* factors in the formation of Europe and the modern world. While this story could be told from a number of different starting points, the initial focus will be a sketch of the history and geography of European states, beginning with Rome. This sketch provides a useful background to the diversity of states and their alteration over time.

# 2   A Brief History and Geography of European States

Sixteen hundred years or so ago "Europe" was dominated by the Roman Empire, albeit an empire divided and disintegrating. Theodosius I (A.D. 379–95) was the last "sole ruler" of the Roman Empire, which, after his death, split into the Western and Eastern Roman Empires. The Western Empire suffered from repeated attacks and grew weak in comparison with the East. In 410, the city of Rome was sacked by the Visigoths, a wandering Germanic people from the North-east. The fall of Rome was completed in 476, when the last Roman emperor of the West was deposed. The Eastern Empire, economically securer than its Western counterpart owing to spice and other exports, continued as the Byzantine Empire through the Middle Ages until it was successfully challenged and displaced by the Islamic Ottoman Empire in 1453.

In the centuries which succeeded the disintegration of the Roman Empire, "Europe" did not experience the rise of another imperial society, although it was chronically engaged in war and harassed from outside. A contrast has often been drawn between an essentially civilized Europe and a despotic or barbarous East. There are many reasons for distrusting this contrast (see Bernal, 1987; Springborg, 1991). Some of these reasons will be explored in chapter 6 of this volume, but two should be emphasized here. First, as recent historical

and archaeological research has shown, some of the key political
innovations, conceptual and institutional, of the putatively western
political tradition can be traced to the East; for example, the "city-state"
or *polis* society can be found in Mesopotamia long before it emerged in
the West. Second, "Europe" was the creation of many complex
processes at the intersection of "internal" and "external" forces and
relations. A thousand years ago Europe as such did not exist. The
roughly thirty million people who lived across the European landmass
did not conceive of themselves as an interconnected people, bound by
a common history, culture, and fate (Tilly, 1990, p. 38).

The larger power divisions on a map of "millennial Europe" (c. A.D.
1000) to some extent mask the area's fragmented and decentered
nature. Those who prevailed over territories – emperors, kings, princes,
dukes, bishops, and others – did so above all as military victors and
conquerors, exacting tribute and rent to support their endeavors; they
were far from being heads of state governing clearly demarcated
territories according to formal law and procedure. As the historian
Charles Tilly put it, "nothing like a centralized national state existed
anywhere in Europe" (1990, p. 40).

Yet one can talk about the beginnings of a recognizable states system
at the millennium. In the Italian peninsula, the Papacy, the Holy Roman
Empire, and the Byzantine Empire claimed most of the territory, even
though these claims intermingled and were contested routinely by many
localized powers and independent and semi-autonomous city-states.

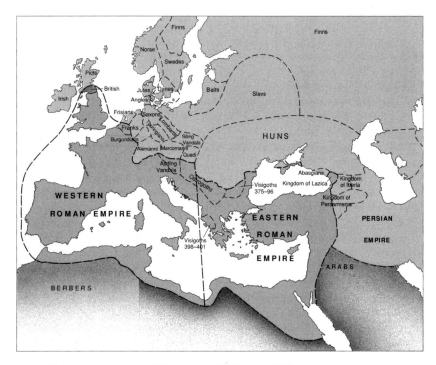

Figure 2.1   Europe in A.D. 406. Source: McEvedy, 1961.

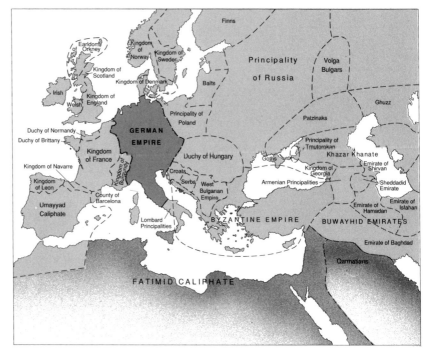

Figure 2.2   Europe in A.D. 998. Source: McEvedy, 1961.

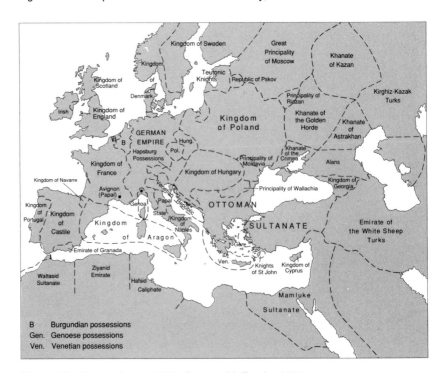

Figure 2.3   Europe in A.D. 1478. Source: McEvedy, 1961.

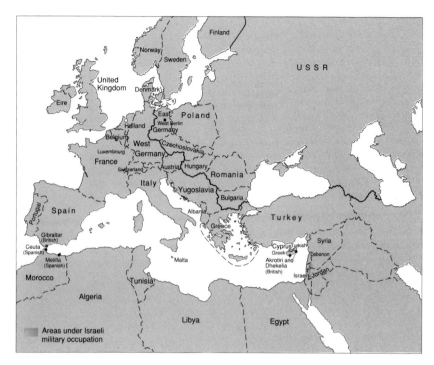

Figure 2.4   Europe in A.D. 1980. Source: McEvedy, 1982.

But the political map of Europe was to be shaped and reshaped many times. For example, the European map of the late fifteenth century included some 500 more or less independent political units, often with ill-defined boundaries. By 1900 the number had dwindled to about twenty-five (Tilly, 1975, p. 15). It took a long time for national states to dominate the political map, but the era they ushered in was to change fundamentally the nature and form of political life itself.

Since the fall of Rome, it is not just the number of states which has altered dramatically, but the forms and types of states as well. There are five main clusters of state systems which can be distinguished:

1   traditional tribute-taking empires;
2   systems of divided authority, characterized by feudal relations, city-states and urban alliances, with the Church (Papacy) playing a leading role;
3   the polity of estates;
4   absolutist states;
5   modern nation-states, with constitutional, liberal democratic, or single party polities locked progressively into a system of nation-states.

Figure 2.5 provides an approximate guide to the periods in which each type of state system could be found. For the remainder of this section, I

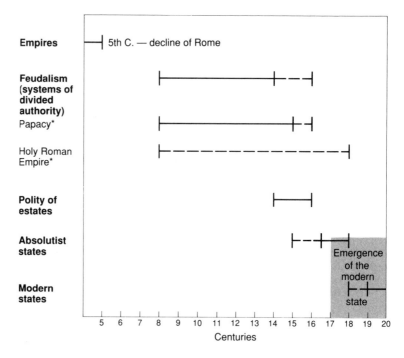

Broken lines indicate that a political system's influence was not continuous,
but rather broken from time to time.

* The Papacy and the Holy Roman Empire, while at certain stages essential
elements of the feudal system of authority, have been separated out for later
reference.

Figure 2.5   State forms and historical periods

shall examine each type in turn before pursuing the question: What
accounts for the eventual dominance of the nation-state?

## 2.1   Empires

Empires or imperial systems have dominated the history of states over
the centuries, particularly in their size and grandeur. Some, notably
Rome (and China in the East), retained identifiable institutional forms
over long periods. Empires required an accumulation and concentration
of coercive means – above all, of war-making ability – to sustain
themselves. When this ability waned, empires disintegrated. All
"traditional" empires developed as a result of expansion from initially
more restricted power-bases and confined states. Moreover, the
deployment of military strength was uppermost in the creation and
maintenance of frontiers or territorial boundaries, though the latter
were often in flux and shifted according to patterns of rebellion and
invasion. Territorial boundaries were by no means yet "fixed borders"
(Giddens, 1985, pp. 80–1).

While empires frequently were crossed by long-distance trading
routes, and indeed often engaged directly in long-distance trade

themselves, their economic requirements were largely met through the exaction of *tribute*, some of which was used to buy off threatened assaults if military power fell short. The tribute system supported the emperor, his administrative apparatus and the military. But however powerful empires might have been relative to contending power centers, they could sustain only limited administrative authority. Empires stretched over a plethora of communities and societies which were culturally diverse and heterogeneous. Empires were *ruled* but they were not *governed*; that is to say, emperors dominated a limited social and geographical space, but lacked the administrative means – the institutions, organizations, information, personnel, and so on – to provide regularized administration over the territories they claimed as their own. The polities of empires busied themselves with conflicts and intrigue within dominant groups and classes and within local urban centres; beyond that the resort to military force was the key mechanism for binding and integrating peoples and territories. Although force was frequently effective, its significance should not be exaggerated. For the size, mobility, and deployment of armies depended on the availability of water and local harvests to plunder. The military depended on the countryside and could move no more quickly than its men could march in a day, subject to the availability of foodstuffs.

## 2.2   Systems of divided authority in medieval Europe

Feudalism – a political system of overlapping and divided authority – assumed many forms between the eighth and the fourteenth centuries. But it is probably fair to say that it was distinguished in general by a network of interlocking ties and obligations, with systems of rule fragmented into many small, autonomous parts (Poggi, 1978, p. 27). Political power became more local and personal in focus, generating a "social world of overlapping claims and powers" (Anderson, 1974, p. 149). Some of these claims and powers conflicted; and no ruler or state was sovereign in the sense of being supreme over a given territory and population (Bull, 1977, p. 254). Within this system of power, tensions were rife and war was frequent.

The early roots of feudalism can be traced to left-overs of the Roman Empire and to the militaristic culture and the institutions of Germanic tribal peoples (Poggi, 1990, pp. 35–7). A concern with loyalty in war and effective leadership among these peoples led to a special relationship between a ruler or lord or king (generally acclaimed or "appointed" by his followers on the basis of his military and strategic skills) and the tribe's leading warriors, called *vassi* ("vassals"; "servants"). The warriors declared bonds of loyalty and homage to their lord in return for privileges and protection. In the late seventh century, Frankish rulers connected the idea of a vassalic bond not just to military endeavor, but to the governing of territories more generally: rulers endowed vassals with rights of land, later called *feudum* ("fief"), in the hope of securing continued loyalty, military service, and flows of income. The result, however, was rarely a simple hierarchy of lord, vassal, and peasants; rather, the hierarchy was often characterized by a great chain of relations and obligations as major vassals, "subcontracted" parts of their lands to others. At the bottom of the hierarchy was, of course, the vast majority of the population: "the object of rule . . . but never the subject of a political relationship" (Poggi, 1978, p. 23).

While feudal kings were *primus inter pares* ("first among equals"), they were locked (with certain exceptions, notably in England and northern France) into wide-ranging systems of privileges and duties which often imposed on them a requirement to consult and negotiate with the most powerful lords or barons, when taxes or armies were to be raised. Lords were expected to maintain an autonomous military capability to support their kings; but it was a capability that provided them with an independent power-base which they could be tempted to use to further their own interests. With some political forces seeking to centralize power and others seeking local autonomy, the feudal states system contained significant disintegrative tendencies.

Within medieval Europe the economy was dominated by agriculture, and any surplus generated was subject to competing claims. A successful claim constituted a basis to create and sustain political power. But the web of kingdoms, principalities, duchies, and other power centers which depended on these arrangements was complicated further by the emergence of alternative powers in the towns and cities. Cities and urban federations depended on trade and manufacture and relatively high accumulations of capital. They developed different social and political structures and frequently enjoyed independent systems of rule specified by *charters*. Among the best known were the Italian cities of Florence, Venice, and Siena, but across Europe hundreds of urban centers developed. Nowhere, however, did they (and the web of feudal relations in the countryside) alone determine the pattern of rule or political identity. For in the Middle Ages "Europe" more accurately meant "Christendom." And the Papacy and the Holy Roman Empire gave Christendom what overarching unity it had.

The Holy Roman Empire existed in some form from the eighth until the early nineteenth century. For while the Roman imperial title had lapsed in the fifth century, it was revived in 800 by Pope Leo III and conferred on Charlemagne, King of the Franks. Later, the title Holy Roman Emperor was borne by successive dynasties of German kings, although its actual significance, like that of the Empire more generally, varied considerably over time. At its height, the Holy Roman Empire represented an attempt, under the patronage of the Catholic Church, to unite and centralize the fragmented power centers of western Christendom into a politically-unified Christian empire. The countries federated under the Empire spread from Germany to Spain, and from northern France to Italy. However, the actual secular power of the Empire was always limited by the complex power structures of feudal Europe on the one hand, and the Catholic Church on the other.

The chief rival power to the medieval feudal and city networks was the Catholic Church itself. Throughout the Middle Ages the Catholic Church sought to place spiritual above secular authority. While it would be quite misleading to suggest that the rise of Christianity effectively banished secular considerations from the lives of rulers and ruled, it unquestionably shifted the source of authority and wisdom from this-worldly to other-worldly representatives. The Christian world-view transformed the rationale of political action from an earthly to a theological framework; it insisted that the Good lay in submission to God's will.

In medieval Europe there was no theoretical alternative – no alternative "political theory" – to the theocratic positions of Pope and Holy Roman Emperor. The integration of Christian Europe came to depend above all on these authorities. This order has been characterized as the order of "international Christian society" (Bull, 1977, p. 27). International Christian society was conceived as being Christian first and foremost; it looked to God for the authority to resolve disputes and conflicts; its primary political reference point was religious doctrine, and it was overlaid with assumptions about the universal nature of human community.

It was not until western Christendom was under challenge, especially from the conflicts generated by the rise of national states and by the Reformation, that the idea of the modern state was born, and the ground was created for the development of a new form of political identity – national identity.

## 2.3  The polity of estates

Some date the crisis of feudalism as early as 1300. But whether or not one accepts this date, the decay of feudalism can be detected over a substantial period as competing claims to more extensive and penetrating political power were fought out. Within this process of transformation, new understandings about political arrangements emerged. Some writers argue that these "new" concepts and ideas – for example, the claims of various social groups or "estates" (the nobility, clergy, and leading townsmen or burghers) to political prerogatives, particularly to rights of representation – were merely extensions of existing feudal relations. However, others emphasize their novel and distinctive qualities.

Those who emphasize the innovative nature of the post-feudal system of rule draw attention to a number of larger territories in which successful rulers created new kinds of political relations with various elements of society. One observer has described the arrangements thus:

> In the first place, in the polity of estates the rulers present themselves primarily not as feudal superiors, but as the holders of higher, public prerogatives of non- and often pre-feudal origins, surrounded by the halo of a higher majesty; often imparted by means of sacred ceremonies (for example, the *sacre du roi* ["consecration of a king"]).
>
> In the second place, the counterpart to the ruler is typically represented not by individuals, but by constituted bodies of various kinds: local assemblies of aristocrats, cities, ecclesiastical bodies, corporate associations. Taken singly, each of these bodies – the "estates" – represents a different collective entity: a region's

noblemen of a given rank, the residents of a town, the faithful of a parish or the practitioners of a trade. Taken together, these bodies claim to represent a wider, more abstract, territorial entity – country, *Land, terra, pays* – which, they assert, the ruler is entitled to rule only to the extent that he upholds its distinctive customs and serves its interests.

In turn, however, these interests are largely identified with those of the estates; and even the customs of the country or the region in question have as their major components the different claims of the various estates. Thus, the ruler can rule legitimately only to the extent that periodically he convenes the estates of a given region or of the whole territory into a constituted, public gathering.

(Poggi, 1990, pp. 40–1)

In these circumstances, rulers had to deal with estates and estates had to deal with rulers. Out of this emerged a variety of estates-based assemblies, parliaments, diets, and councils which sought to legitimate and enjoy autonomous faculties of rule. The "polity of estates" was characterized by a "power dualism": power was split between rulers and estates.

This "power dualism" did not endure; it was challenged by the estates seeking greater power and by monarchs hoping to subvert the assemblies in order to centralize power in their own hands. As the grip of feudal traditions and customs was loosened, the nature and limits of political authority, law, rights, and obedience emerged as a preoccupation of political thought.

## 2.4   Absolutist states

The historical changes that contributed to the transformation of medieval notions of politics were complicated. Struggles between monarchs and barons over the domain of rightful authority; peasant rebellions against the weight of excess taxation and social obligation; the spread of trade, commerce, and market relations; the flourishing of Renaissance culture with its renewed interest in classical political ideas (including Athenian democracy and Roman law); changes in technology, particularly military technology; the consolidation of national monarchies (notably in England, France, and Spain); religious strife and the challenge to the universal claims of Catholicism; the struggle between Church and State – all played a part. In the sections that follow, I shall return to discuss a number of these developments, but it is important first to clarify the notion of the "absolutist" state.

From the fifteenth to the eighteenth century two different forms of regime can be distinguished in Europe: the "absolute" monarchies of France, Prussia, Austria, Spain, Sweden, and Russia, among other places, and the "constitutional" monarchies and republics found principally in England and Holland (Mann, 1986, p. 476). There are important conceptual and institutional differences between these regime types, although in terms of the history of state/society relations some of the differences have, as we shall see, been more apparent than real. I shall discuss constitutional states shortly, but will focus in the first instance on absolutism.

Absolutism signalled the emergence of a form of state based on: the absorption of smaller and weaker political units into larger and stronger political structures; a strengthened ability to rule over a unified territorial area; a tightened system of law and order enforced throughout a territory; the application of a "more unitary, continuous, calculable, and effective" rule by a single, sovereign head; and the development of a relatively small number of states engaged in an "open-ended, competitive, and risk-laden power struggle" (Poggi, 1978, pp. 60–1). Although the actual power of absolutist rulers has often been exaggerated, these changes marked a substantial increase in "public authority" from above. Certainly, absolutist rulers claimed that they alone held the legitimate right of decision over state affairs. One of the most remarkable statements of this view has been attributed to Louis XV, king of France from 1715 to 1774:

> In my person alone resides the sovereign power, and it is from me alone that the courts hold their existence and their authority. That . . . authority can only be exercised in my name . . . For it is to me exclusively that the legislative power belongs . . . The whole public order emanates from me since I am its supreme guardian. . . . The rights and interests of the nation . . . are necessarily united with my own and can only rest in my hands. (quoted in Schama, 1989, p. 104)

The absolutist monarch claimed to be the ultimate source of human law, although it is important to note that his broad writ was understood to derive from the law of God. The king's legitimacy was based on "divine right." In this very particular sense, political authorities were regarded as being as much under the law as any other corporate institution (Benn and Peters, 1959, p. 256).

In a striking and somewhat (maliciously) humorous account of the public standing of the French monarch, perhaps the supreme example of an absolutist figure, the sociologist Gianfranco Poggi has written:

> [The] King of France was thoroughly, without residue, a "public" personage. His mother gave birth to him in public, and from that moment his existence, down to its most trivial moments, was acted out before the eyes of attendants who were holders of dignified public offices. He ate in public, went to bed in public, woke up and was clothed and groomed in public, urinated and defecated in public. He did not copulate in public; but near enough, considering the circumstances under which he was expected to deflower his august bride. He did not much bathe in public; but then, neither did he in private. When he died (in public) his body was promptly and messily chopped up in public, and its severed parts ceremoniously handed out to the more exalted among the personages who had been attending him throughout his mortal existence.
> (Poggi, 1978, pp. 68–9)

The absolutist monarch was at the apex of a new system of rule which was progressively centralized and anchored on a claim to supreme and indivisible power: *sovereign authority*. All these qualities were manifest in the routines and rituals of courtly life.

However, linked to the court there developed a new administrative apparatus involving the beginnings of a permanent, professional bureaucracy and army (Mann, 1986, p. 476). If the French monarchy of the eighteenth century represents the best example of an absolutist court, Prussia under the Hohenzollern dynasty provides the best example of the "prototypes of ministries" (Poggi, 1990, p. 48). These "prototypes" increased the state's involvement in the promotion and regulation of a hitherto unparalleled diversity of activities. Six ensuing developments were of great significance in the history of the states system:

1   the growing coincidence of territorial boundaries with a uniform system of rule;

2   the creation of new mechanisms of law-making and -enforcement;

3   the centralization of administrative power;

4   the alteration and extension of fiscal management;

5   the formalization of relations among states through the development of diplomacy and diplomatic institutions; and

6   the introduction of a standing army (see Anderson, 1974, pp. 15–42; Giddens, 1985, ch. 4).

Absolutism helped set in motion a process of state-making which began to reduce the social, economic, and cultural variation *within* states and expand the variation *among* them (Tilly, 1975, p. 19).

According to one interpretation of these changes, the expansion of state administrative power was made possible to a significant extent by the extension of the state's capacity for the surveillance of its subjects; that is, the collection and storing of information about members of society, and the related ability to supervise subject populations (Giddens, 1985, pp. 14–15). However, as the state's sovereign authority expanded and its administrative centers became more powerful, there was not simply a concentration of power at the apex. For the increase in administrative power via surveillance increased the state's dependence on cooperative forms of social relations; it was no longer possible for the state to manage its affairs and sustain its offices and activities by force alone. As a result, greater reciprocity was created between the governors and the governed, and the more reciprocity was involved, the more opportunities were generated for subordinate groups to influence their rulers (Giddens, 1985, pp. 198ff.). Absolutism, in short, created within itself a momentum towards the development of new forms and limits on state power – constitutionalism and (eventually) participation by powerful groups in the process of government itself.

Whatever the other merits of this particular interpretation, it usefully draws attention to the gulf that existed between the claims of the absolutist monarch, on the one hand, and a reality, on the other hand, which imposed on the monarch requirements of negotiation and cooperation if the state was to function effectively. This gulf has been explored further in the recent work of the sociologist Michael Mann, who distinguishes between a "strong" regime's power to effect its will over civil society, which he calls "despotism," and its power to coordinate civil society, which he refers to as "infrastructural strength" (1986, p. 477). Comparing a range of absolutist regimes, Mann argues that the absolute monarch was "no ancient emperor – he was not the sole source of law; of coinages, weights and measures; of economic monopolies . . . He could not impose compulsory cooperation. He owned only his own estates" (Mann, 1986, p. 478). Absolutist regimes, Mann concludes, had limited despotic reach; they were weak in relation to powerful groups in society, for example, the nobility, merchants, and urban bourgeoisie. But, like their constitutional counterparts, they were engaged increasingly in the coordination of the activities of these groups and in building up the state's infrastructural strength.

By the end of the seventeenth century Europe was no longer a mosaic of states. For the "consolidated independent sovereignty of each individual state . . . was at the same time part of a process of overall inter-state integration" (Giddens, 1985, p. 91). A concomitant of each and every state's claim to uncontestable authority was the recognition that such a claim gave other states an equal entitlement to autonomy and respect within their own borders. The development of state sovereignty was part of a process of mutual recognition whereby states granted each other rights of jurisdiction in their respective territories and communities. In the international context, sovereignty has involved the assertion by the state of independence; that is, of its possession of sole rights to jurisdiction over a particular people and territory. This dimension of sovereignty has, in addition, been associated with the claim that, by virtue of the very argument which establishes the sovereignty of a particular state, that state must accept that it will be one among many states with, in principle, equal rights to self-determination. In the world of relations among states, the principle of the sovereign equality of all states was to become paramount in the formal conduct of states towards one another.

The conception of international law which emerged within the new "international society of states" has been referred to by international lawyers, notably Richard Falk and Antonio Cassese, as the "Westphalian model" (after the Peace of Westphalia of 1648, which brought to an end the Eighty Years War between Spain and the Dutch and the German phase of the Thirty Years War). The model covers the period of international law from 1648 to 1945 (although some would say it still holds today). It depicts the emergence of a world community consisting of sovereign states which settle their differences privately and often by force; which engage in diplomatic relations but otherwise minimal cooperation; which seek to place their own national interest above all others; and which accept the logic of the principle of effectiveness, that is, the principle that might eventually makes right in the international world – appropriation becomes legitimation. The model of Westphalia can be summarized by the following seven points (see Cassese, 1986, pp. 396–9; Falk, 1969):

1   The world consists of, and is divided by, sovereign states which recognize no superior authority.

2   The processes of law-making, the settlement of disputes, and law-enforcement are largely in the hands of individual states subject to the logic of "the competitive struggle for power."

3   Differences among states are often settled by force: the principle of effective power holds sway. Virtually no legal fetters exist to curb the resort to force; international legal standards afford minimal protection.

4   Responsibility for cross-border wrongful acts are a private matter concerning only those affected; no collective interest in compliance with international law is recognized.

5   All states are regarded as equal before the law: legal rules do not take account of asymmetries of power.

6   International law is oriented to the establishment of minimal rules of co-existence; the creation of enduring relationships among states and peoples is an aim only to the extent that it allows military objectives to be met.

7   The minimization of impediments on state freedom is the "collective" priority.

The new international order, ushered in by the era of the absolutist state (and its constitutional counterpart, a discussion of which follows), had a lasting and paradoxical quality rich in implications: an increasingly integrated states system simultaneously endorsed the right of each state to autonomous and independent action. The upshot of this development was, as one commentator has aptly noted, that states were "not subject to international moral requirements because they represent separate and discrete political orders with no common authority among them" (Beitz, 1979, p. 25). According to this model, the world consists of separate political powers pursuing their own interests, and backed ultimately by their organization of coercive power.

## 2.5   Modern states

The proximate sources of the modern state were absolutism and the inter-state system it initiated. In condensing and concentrating political power in its own hands, and in seeking to create a central system of rule, absolutism paved the way for a secular and national system of power. Moreover, in claiming sovereign authority exclusively for itself, it threw down a challenge to all those groups and classes which had had a stake in the old order (the polity of estates), and to all those with a stake in the new developing order based on capital and the market economy. It forced all these collectivities to rethink their relationship to the state, and to re-examine their political resources. In addition, the myriad battles and wars fought out in the inter-state system altered fundamentally the boundaries of both absolutist states and the emerging modern states – the whole map of Europe changed as territorial boundaries progressively became fixed borders.

Although the transition from the absolutist to the modern state was marked by dramatic events and processes such as the English (1640–88) and French (1789) Revolutions, an exclusive focus on these hinders an understanding of the way in which the absolutist state itself was crucial in the development of modern political rule. It was the confluence of "internal" transformations in European states with shifting geopolitical relations and forces which provided a, if not *the*, key impetus to the formation of the modern state. I shall return to elements of these "macropatterns" in section 3; in the meantime, what should be understood by the term "modern state"?

All modern states are nation-states – *political apparatuses, distinct from both ruler and ruled, with supreme jurisdiction over a demarcated territorial area, backed by a claim to a monopoly of coercive power, and enjoying a minimum level of support or loyalty from their citizens* (cf. Skinner, 1978, pp. 349–58; Giddens, 1985, pp. 17–31, 116–21). Like all definitions in the social sciences, this one is controversial. But for my purposes here, this particular definition is useful because it underscores a number of the crucial innovations of the modern states system; these are:

1  *Territoriality.* While all states have made claims to territories, it is only with the modern states system that exact borders have been fixed.

2  *Control of the means of violence.* The claim to hold a monopoly on force and the means of coercion (sustained by a standing army and the police) became possible only with the "pacification" of peoples – the breaking down of rival centers of power and authority – in the nation-state. This element of the modern state was not fully present until the nineteenth century.

3  *Impersonal structure of power.* The idea of an impersonal and sovereign political order – i.e. a legally circumscribed structure of power with supreme jurisdiction over a territory – could not predominate while political rights, obligations, and duties were conceived as closely tied to property rights, religion, and the claims of traditionally privileged groups such as the nobility. This matter was still in contention in the eighteenth and nineteenth centuries.

4  *Legitimacy.* It was only when claims to "divine right" or "state right" were challenged and eroded that it became possible for human beings as "individuals" and as "peoples" to be active citizens of a new order – not merely dutiful subjects of a monarch or emperor. The loyalty of citizens became something that had to be *won* by modern states: invariably this involved a claim by the state to be legitimate because it reflected and/or represented the needs and interests of its citizens.

There is a further clarification which should be made at this juncture. The concept of the nation-state, or national state, as some prefer, ought not to be taken to imply that a state's people necessarily "share a strong linguistic, religious, and symbolic identity" (Tilly, 1990, pp. 2–3). Although some nation-states approximate to this state of affairs, many do not. It is therefore important to separate out the concepts of "nation-state" and "nationalism." Anthony Giddens has made the point succinctly: ". . . what makes the 'nation' integral to the nation-state . . . is not the existence of sentiments of nationalism but the unification of an administrative apparatus over precisely defined territorial boundaries (in a complex of other nation-states)" (Giddens, 1987, p. 172). The concept of "nationalism" – denoting the existence of symbols and beliefs which create patterns of ethnic, or religious, or linguistic commonality and political ambition – should be reserved for highlighting particular types of configuration of peoples and states.

It has been argued that the difference between absolute and modern states is not as great as conventionally thought, for two reasons (see Mann, 1986, pp. 450–99). First, absolutist states, as already noted, had less power over civil society than is frequently claimed. Second, modern states are rarely "bounded" by their constitutions and borders and, hence, have often behaved like arrogant "absolutist" states, especially in their dealings with peoples and cultures overseas. Both points carry weight and need to be borne in mind in what follows. However, neither point negates fully the conceptual and institutional innovations introduced by the modern state. In order to highlight these, it is useful to draw attention to a number of forms of the modern state itself. These are the *constitutional state*, the *liberal state*, the *liberal-democratic state*, and the *single-party polity*.

1   *Constitutionalism* or the *constitutional state* refers to implicit and/or explicit limits on political or state decision-making, limits which can be either procedural or substantive; that is, specifying how decisions and changes can be made (proceduralism), or blocking certain kinds of changes altogether (substantivism) (see Elster, 1988). Constitutionalism defines the proper forms and limits of state action, and its elaboration over time as a set of doctrines and practices helped inaugurate one of the central tenets of European liberalism: that the state exists to safeguard the rights and liberties of citizens who are ultimately the best judges of their own interests; and, accordingly, that the state must be restricted in scope and constrained in practice in order to ensure the maximum possible freedom of every citizen.

2   The *liberal state* became defined in large part by the attempt to create a private sphere independent of the state, and by a concern to reshape the state itself, i.e. by freeing civil society – personal, family, and business life – from unnecessary political interference, and simultaneously delimiting the state's authority (Held, 1987, chs 2–3). The building blocks of the liberal state became constitutionalism, private property, the competitive market economy, and the distinctively patriarchal family (see chapter 4 of this volume). But while liberalism celebrated the rights of individuals to "life, liberty, and property" (John Locke), it should be noted from the outset that it was generally the male property-owning individual who was the focus of so much attention; and the new freedoms were first and foremost for the men of the new middle classes or the bourgeoisie. The western world was liberal first, and only later, after extensive conflicts, liberal democratic;

that is, only later was a universal franchise won which in principle allowed all mature adults the chance to express their judgment about the performance of those who govern them (Macpherson, 1966, p. 6).

3 The third variant of the modern state is *liberal* or *representative democracy* itself, a system of rule embracing elected "officers" who undertake to "represent" the interests or views of citizens within the framework of the "rule of law." Representative democracy means that decisions affecting a community are not taken by its members as a whole, but by a sub-group of representatives whom "the people" have elected for this purpose. In the arena of national politics, representative democracy takes the form of elections to congresses, parliaments, or similar national bodies, and is now associated with the system of government in countries as far afield as the United States, Britain, Germany, Japan, Australia, and New Zealand.

4 Finally, there is the form of the modern state known as the *one-party* or *single-party polity*. Until recently, the former Soviet Union and many East European societies were governed by such systems, and for several Third World countries this continues to be the case. The principle underlying one-party polities is that a single party can be the legitimate expression of the overall will of the community. Voters have the opportunity to affirm the party's choice of candidate, or occasionally to choose from among different party candidates (although some may doubt whether this constitutes an opportunity for the exercise of choice at all).

Little further will be said about the single-party polity in this chapter. (For further discussion of this state form see chapter 13.) This chapter will instead attend to those elements of the first three state forms listed above which require elaboration and examination. But before turning to this task, it is important to respond to the question: What accounts for the emergence of the modern nation-state? In other words, why did national states come to predominate in the political world?

# 3 Why did Nation-States Become Supreme?

In order to address the above question, this section will examine a number of key factors, or causal patterns, in the development of the states system and of the modern state in particular. The prime focus will be on war and militarism and on the relationship between states and capitalism, although other significant factors will be touched on. Once again, it will be useful to examine deeply structured processes of change taking place over long periods. It should be noted that the stress is on *processes*, *factors*, and *causal patterns*; that is to say, this section is guided by the assumption that there is no mono-causal explanation – no single phenomenon or set of phenomena – which fully explains the rise of the modern state. States, like other collectivities and institutions, depend for their existence on broad experiences and diverse conditions. It is in a combination of factors that the beginnings of an explanation for the rise of the modern state can be found.

## 3.1  War and militarism

It has already been suggested that the nature and form of the states system crystallized at the intersection of "international" and "national" conditions and processes (the terms in quotation marks are so expressed because they did not take on their contemporary meanings until the era of fixed borders, i.e. the era of the nation-state). In fact, it is at this intersection that the "shape" of the state was largely determined – its size, external configuration, organizational structure, ethnic composition, material infrastructure, and so on (Hintze, 1975, chs 4–6, 11). At the heart of the processes involved was the ability of states to secure and strengthen their power-bases and, thereby, to order their affairs, internally and externally. What was at issue, in short, was the capacity of states to organize the means of coercion (armies, navies, and other forms of military might) and to deploy them when necessary. How important this element of state power has been to the history of states can be gleaned by examining the case of England/Britain.

From an analysis of state finances (how the state raised and spent what money it had) over several centuries, Michael Mann has shown that "the functions of the state appear overwhelmingly military and overwhelmingly geopolitical rather than economic and domestic" (Mann, 1986, p. 511; see also Mitchell and Deane, 1962; Mitchell and Jones, 1971). Mann calculates that from about the twelfth to the nineteenth century, between 70 and 90 percent of the English state's financial resources were continuously devoted to the acquisition and use of the instruments of military force, especially in international wars. For most of this period the state grew slowly and fitfully (although when it did grow it was due to warfare and related developments), and its size, measured in relation to the resources of the economy and its impact on the daily life of most people, was small. But in the seventeenth and eighteenth centuries the state's real finances grew rapidly, largely in response to the escalating costs of the means of "coercive power", in this case, the growing professional, standing armies and navies. Expenditures on non-military civil functions remained minor.

Reliable annual sets of accounts are available for central government expenditure in Britain for the period after 1688. These are presented in figure 2.6, taken from Mann (1986). Mann's comments on figure 2.6 are telling:

> Note first the upward trend in the financial size of the British state: Between 1700 and 1815 real expenditures rise fifteenfold (and the increase at current prices is thirty-fivefold!). This is easily the fastest rate of increase we have seen for any century . . . But the upward trend is not steady. The total rockets suddenly six times. It will come as no surprise that all but one of these are at the beginning of a war, and all six are due primarily to a large rise

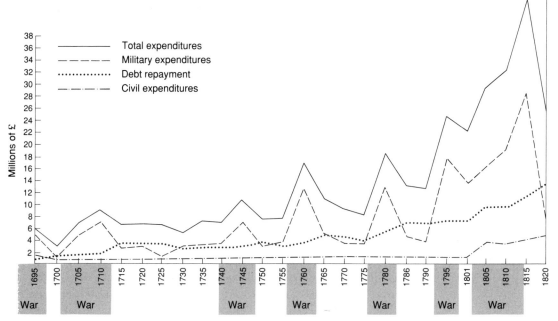

Figure 2.6   British state expenditure, 1695–1820 (at constant prices: 1690–9 = 100)
Source: Mann, 1986, p. 484

in military expenditures. Furthermore debt repayment, used exclusively to finance military needs, rises toward the end of each war and is maintained in the first years of peace. The pattern is beautifully regular . . .

These figures confirm every hypothesis made for previous centuries on the basis of sketchier data. State finances were dominated by foreign wars. As warfare developed more professional and permanent forces, so the state grew both in overall size and (probably) in terms of its size in relation to its "civil society".

(Mann, 1986, pp. 485–6)

The significance of these remarks is highlighted further if it is recalled that they bear on the activities and functions of a constitutional state. In fact, over the whole period in question, broadly the eighteenth and early nineteenth centuries, whether a state was "constitutional" or "absolutist" made little difference to the proportion of its expenditure on the military. This can be seen by comparing figure 2.6 with table 2.2, which shows Austrian state expenditure for part of the same period.

Sketchier evidence appears to confirm a similar pattern of income and costs for France, Prussia, and Russia, although each had its peculiarities.

The above material is not an argument for "military determinism"; that is, for a view which asserts that changes in war and the military

Table 2.2   Austrian state expenditure, 1795–1817 (in percent)

| Year | Military | Debt repayment | Civil | Total expenditure at current prices (in millions of guldern) |
|------|----------|----------------|-------|--------------------------------------------------------------|
| 1795 | 71 | 12 | 17 | 133.3 |
| 1800 | 67 | 22 | 11 | 143.9 |
| 1805 | 63 | 25 | 12 | 102.7 |
| 1810 | 69 | 20 | 11 | 76.1 |
| 1815 | 75 | 4 | 21 | 121.2 |
| 1817 | 53 | 8 | 38 | 98.8 |

Source: Mann, 1986, p. 487

are the exclusive source of change in the state and the states system. However, it does indicate that the development and maintenance of a coercive capability was central to the development of the state: if states wished to survive they had to fund this capability and ensure its effectiveness.

The process of state-making, and the formation of the modern states system, was to a large degree the result, as Poggi has observed, "of the strenuous efforts made by rulers, each by means of his/her apparatus of rule, to widen and secure their power base and to increase their own effectiveness and discretion in managing and mobilizing societal resources" (1990, p. 101). State-makers were locked into an open-ended and ruthless competition in which, as Tilly put it, "most contenders lost" (1975, p. 15). The successful cases of state-making such as England, France, and Spain were the "survivors."

The competition among states was driven not just by the ambitions of rulers and internal or domestic considerations, but also by the very *structure* of the international system: individual states, pursuing their own security, had to be prepared for war, a process which itself generated insecurity in other states which sought to respond in kind. In short, states armed and became militaristic partly to ensure their own safety and, in so doing, they ensured the insecurity of others who armed in turn – thus making all states less secure. (This vicious circle of mutual insecurity is often referred to as the "security dilemma" of the state.)

The ability to wage war was dependent on a successful process of *extraction*; that is, on a state's capacity to extract resources – whether these be men, weapons, foodstuffs, taxes, or income substitutes – in support of its endeavors. Few subjects, however, were willing to sacrifice their resources or lives without a struggle for some kind of return or recognition, and conflicts and rebellions against economic and political demands were rife. In response, state rulers built state structures – administrative, bureaucratic, and coercive – in order to aid the coordination and control of their subject populations. In short, direct connections can be traced between a growth in the requirement for the means of waging war, an expansion in processes of extraction, and a concomitant formation of state executive and administrative offices to organize and control these changes. The development of some of the key organizations of the modern state emerged at the intersection of warfare and the attempt to pay for it. War and its financial burdens promoted "territorial consolidation, centralization, differentiation of the instruments of government and monopolization of the means of coercion . . ." (Tilly, 1975, p. 42).

It has already been noted (in section 2) that different state forms prevailed in Europe in different eras and regions. The organizational form of the state varied too. Tilly has sought to examine this variation with reference to the ways state development was mediated by, or filtered through, the social structure of particular societies – that is, the particular constellation of social classes and groups which existed within the terrain of the state and which were either cooperative with or resistant to state-makers (Tilly, 1990, pp. 15, 27–8, 57, 117ff.). The shape of each such constellation was significantly affected by the different kinds of resource base which could be drawn upon by the various groups and classes comprising it, and the options they had for involvement (or otherwise) in state politics. As Tilly explains:

> The organization of major social classes, and their relations to the state, varied significantly from Europe's coercion-intensive regions (areas of few cities and agricultural predominance, where direct coercion played a major part in production), to its capital-intensive regions (areas of many cities and commercial predominance, where markets, exchange, and market-oriented production prevailed). The demands major classes made on the state, and their influence over the state, varied correspondingly. (Tilly, 1990, p. 15)

For example, in "capital-intensive" regions, like those found in the Dutch Republic in the seventeenth century, city-based merchants and capitalists favored, and sometimes achieved, state structures which extended representation to include their interests. By contrast, in "coercion-intensive" areas such as the Russian Empire, landlords gained greater control of the state and were able to hinder or block the development of representative councils or assemblies.

Over time it was the increasing scale of war, and particularly its growing reliance on technological change, industrialization, and specialization which, in combination with the growth of commercial, legal, and diplomatic interaction among states, gave the modern centralized nation-state its distinctive edge over other state forms. States that could mobilize and sustain standing armies and/or navies gained a war-making advantage. To quote Tilly again: ". . . states having access to a combination of large rural populations, capitalists, and relatively commercialized economies won out. They set the terms of war, and their form of state became the predominant one in Europe. Eventually European states converged on that form: the national state" (Tilly, 1990, p. 15).

The above discussion has concentrated on the relationship between warfare, state-building, and the modern state. However, the relationship between warfare, state-building, and democratic representation needs further specification. Yet, here too the role and changing form of war was important. It has been argued by a number of scholars that the more military superiority depended on the ability of a state to mobilize large numbers of soldiers, particularly large numbers of lightly-armed foot soldiers, the greater have been the prospects for representative or popular government (Dahl, 1989, p. 245; Andreski, 1968). The subject–soldier has often become, and struggled to become, a citizen–soldier (Janowitz, 1978, pp. 178–9; cf. Dahl, 1989, p. 247). As the political scientist Robert Dahl put it:

> . . . to see oneself as a member of a nation, a privilege for which one was expected to make sacrifices, could also justify one in making a more expansive claim, including a right to a fair share in governing . . . or at any rate [as] entitled to the franchise. Countries with mass armies now found that they had ushered in the Age of Democratic Revolutions. It was under these historical conditions in which military organisation and technology were more favourable to democratisation than they had been for many centuries that . . . the institutions of polyarchy ["representative government"] took root in one country after another.
> (Dahl, 1989, p. 247)

The more costly and demanding war became, the more rulers had to bargain for and win the support of their subjects. And the more people were drawn into preparations for war and war-making, the more they became aware of their membership in a political community and of the rights and obligations such membership might confer. While the nature of this emergent identity was often initially vague, it grew more definite and precise over time. The conditions for the development of citizenship varied across countries and regions (see Therborn, 1977; Mann, 1987; Turner, 1986). But the expansion of citizenship, or membership of an overall political community, was undoubtedly bound up with the military and administrative requirements of the modern state and the "politicization" of social relations and day-to-day activities which followed in its wake (cf. Giddens, 1985, ch. 8). In fact, it has been argued that the democratization of the modern nation-state was largely "a martial accomplishment" (Therborn, 1977). Whether or not this statement is fully justified, it usefully highlights the impetus received by institutions of representation and democracy from the conditions of mass mobilization and the political demands created by the modern state, although it is also important to stress that while some democracies were stimulated by processes of mass mobilization (Britain, Canada), others became democracies by defeat (Austria, Germany, Italy, and Japan; see Therborn, 1977). It would be misleading to suggest that war created any one single pattern of causation in the building of democratic institutions.

There is not scope here to focus on nationalism as such, but it is useful to add that nationalism was a critical force in the development of the democratic nation-state. The conditions involved in the creation of the modern state were also often the conditions which generated nationalism. Nationalism has been closely linked to the administrative unification of the state. For the process by which national identities were formed was often the result of both a struggle for membership in the new political communities, and a struggle by elites and governments to create a new identity to legitimize the actions of the state. In other words, the construction of national identity has been part of an attempt to bind people together within the framework of a delimited territory in order to gain or enhance state power. The requirements of political action have led to the deployment of national identity as a means of ensuring the coordination of policy, mobilization, and legitimacy (Breuilly, 1982, pp. 365ff.). However, the conditions of "state-making" and nationalism or "nation-building" never fully overlapped – and nationalism itself, especially in the late nineteenth and twentieth centuries, became a force frequently deployed to challenge existing nation-state boundaries (e.g. Northern Ireland; see Poggi, 1990, pp. 26–7).

It is a paradoxical result of the waging of war that it stimulated the formation of representative and democratic institutions. But to note this is not to claim that democracy is fully explained by the pursuit of war. The historical conditions surrounding the rise of democracy have been complex and varied (Dahl, 1989; Held, 1991). It is one thing to suggest that there is a direct connection in certain countries between, for example, the extension of the universal franchise and the emergence of modern infantry armies, but it is quite another to argue that democracy is thereby fully explained. Furthermore, if war gave democracy an impetus within particular nation-states, the rights and principles of democracy were often explicitly denied to those who were conquered, colonized, and exploited by powerful nation-states. While the expansion of Europe became the basis of the political unification of the world into a system of nation-states, the main purpose of this expansion was to further European commerce and trade; the rights of colonial subjects were a secondary matter, if a matter of concern at all.

## 3.2   States and capitalism

In the interpretation that has been offered so far about the development of the modern state, little has been said about the *economic motives* or *economic interests* of political and social actors, and about the economic conditions and limits of state action, other than to examine the issue of extraction of men, arms, income etc. (see section 3.1). The main emphasis has been on the non-economic features of the modern state; that is, on the independent and autonomous capacities of its organizations and agencies. Does the introduction of an account of economic relations, and of the impact of the development of capitalism especially, alter the view set out so far of states as competing geopolitical institutions, above all else? Did the modern state system shape and constrain the modern capitalist economy as the latter developed after A.D. 1500? Or was the formation of the capitalist economy on a progressively more international basis a, if not the, prime determinant of the scope or limits of state power? As state boundaries became more fixed, did the formal state rulers "rule the roost," or was the "roost" impinged on more and more by the rising economic classes?

In short, what was the effect on the nation-state of the development of the modern economic system; and who exactly rules the nation-state? As with previous sections, it is useful to take several steps back in time before seeking to discriminate among, and weigh up, the multifarious factors which were at play.

At about A.D. 1000 the nearest approximation to a world-wide order of politics and trade was the Moslem world. Its dominance, however, was slowly challenged: faced with Mongol invasions in the thirteenth and fourteenth centuries, on the one hand, and later outflanked by European naval expeditions, on the other, the vitality of the Islamic world declined (Modelski, 1972). Europe was to "explode outward upon the world" (Mann, 1986, p. 500). The growth of interconnections between states and societies – that is, of *globalization* – became progressively shaped by the expansion of Europe. Globalization meant western globalization. Key features of the modern states system – the centralization of political power, the expansion of administrative rule, the emergence of massed standing armies, the deployment of force – which existed in Europe in embryo in the sixteenth century were to become prevalent features of the entire global system. The chief vehicle for this was, to begin with, the European states' capacity for overseas operations by means of naval and military force capable of long-range navigation.

Among the early leaders in exploration were the Spanish and Portuguese (see chapter 6, section 2.3). If the Iberian monarchies led the first two centuries of "European globalization," their position was eroded in the seventeenth century by the Dutch and then by the English. English influence was markedly in the ascendant in the eighteenth century and quite dominant in the nineteenth. British naval and military power conjoined with London as the center of world trade and finance. However, it is doubtful whether any one single power was dominant until the nineteenth century. At least two powerful states were always contending for hegemony in Europe, and the expansion of world commerce drew in non-state actors as well (Tilly, 1990, p. 189).

The expansion of Europe across the globe enhanced the demand, as one observer has noted, "for organizations that would be capable of operating on such a scale. All the basic organization types of modern society – the modern state, modern corporate enterprise, modern science – were shaped by it and benefited greatly from it" (Modelski, 1972, p. 37). In particular, globalization itself became a major source of expansion of state activity and efficiency. Governments organized and reaped some of the fruits of the "discovery" and exploitation of non-European lands as it became essential to equip, plan, and finance exploration and manage newly acquired posts and territories. In turn, state bureaucracies and executive powers were better resourced and this enhanced their autonomy in the face of local assemblies and parliaments. Once again, those states which were able to call upon an administrative infrastructure, substantial manpower, and a wide tax base, alongside arms and shipbuilding industries, gained an advantage. In the seventeenth and eighteenth centuries this advantage was enjoyed by absolutist and constitutional governments; in the nineteenth century by the emergent leading nation-states.

If the consolidation of the modern European state was aided by globalization, this process involved great social costs: the progressive collapse of non-European civilizations, among them the Moslem, Indian, and Chinese; the disorganizing effects of western rule on a large number of small societies; and the interlinked degradation of the non-European and European worlds caused by the slave trade. The benefits and costs were not, however, just the result of the expansion of the European states system: the picture was more complicated.

The diffusion of European power occurred mainly through the medium of sea-going military and commercial endeavors; and in the process Europe became connected to a global system of trade and production relationships. At the center of the latter were newly expanding capitalistic economic mechanisms which had their origins in the sixteenth century, or in what is sometimes called the "long sixteenth century" running from about 1450 to 1640 (Braudel, 1973). One of the foremost analysts of this period is the sociologist Immanuel Wallerstein. As Wallerstein points out, "capitalism was from the beginning an affair of the world economy and not of nation-states . . . Capital has never allowed its aspirations to be determined by national boundaries" (1979, p. 19). The emergence of capitalism ushered in a quite fundamental change in the world order: for the first time genuinely global interconnections were achieved among states and societies. Capitalism has been able to penetrate the distant corners of the world.

Wallerstein makes a fundamental distinction between two types of *world-system* which have existed historically: world-empires and world-economies. World-empires were political units characterized by imperial bureaucracies. With substantial armies to exact tax and tribute from territorially dispersed populations, their capacity for success depended on political and military achievements. World-empires were not as flexible and, ultimately, as adaptable as the emerging world-economy of the sixteenth and seventeenth centuries, and they were finally displaced by the European world-economy as it expanded globally. They were displaced, Wallerstein argues, because the new world economic system was based on a process of endless accumulation of wealth. This world-economy was an economic unit which transcended the boundaries of any given political structure. If it constrained anything it was states, not the process of economic expansion.

According to this view, the modern world-system is divided into three components: the core (initially located in north-west and central Europe); the semi-periphery (the Mediterranean zone after its decline from earlier prominence); and the periphery (colonized and captured territories), although where each of these three components is located has varied over time. Each zone of the world-economy is characterized, Wallerstein maintains, by a particular type of economic activity, state structure, class formation, and mechanism of labor control. The world capitalist economy created a new world-wide division of labor. And while in the late twentieth century colonialism in its original form has practically disappeared, the world capitalist economy creates and reproduces massive imbalances of economic and political power among different component areas.

The development of the world capitalist economy initially took the form of the expansion of market relations, driven by a growing need for raw materials and other factors of production. Capitalism stimulated this drive and was stimulated by it. It is useful to make a distinction (which Wallerstein fails to do) between the expansion of capitalist market relations based on the desire to buy, sell, and accumulate mobile resources or capital, and the formation of industrial capitalism involving highly distinctive class relations – based on those who own and control the means of production and those who have only their laboring capacity to sell. "Capitalists," under the latter conditions, own factories and technology, while wage-laborers, or "wage-workers," are without ownership in the means of production (see chapter 4 for a further discussion of these issues). It is only with the development of capitalism in Europe after 1500, and in particular with the formation of the capitalist organization of production from the middle of the eighteenth century, that the activities of capitalists and the capitalist system began to converge (Tilly, 1990, pp. 17, 189; Giddens, 1985, pp. 122–47).

The development of capitalism itself can be explained as partly the result of long drawn-out changes in "European" agriculture from as early as the twelfth century: changes resulting in part from the drainage and utilization of wet soils, which increased agricultural yields and created a sustainable surplus for trade. Linked to this was the establishment of long-distance trade routes in which the northern shores of the Mediterranean were initially prominent (Mann, 1986, p. 504). Economic networks created "north–south corridors" across the European landmass, with those networks in the north-west becoming progressively more dynamic over time. It was a combination of agricultural and navigational opportunities which helped stimulate the European economic dynamic, and the continuous competition for resources, territory, and trade. Accordingly, the objectives of war gradually became more economic: military endeavor and conquest became more closely connected to the pursuit of economic advantage (Mann, 1986, p. 511). The success of military conquest and the successful pursuit of economic gain were more directly associated.

The state slowly became more embroiled with the interests of civil society in part *for its own sake*. If state rulers and personnel wished to pursue and implement policy of their own choosing, then they would require the financial wherewithal to do so; and the more successful the economic activity in their territories, the more – through customs, taxes, investments, and other revenue-generating activity – they could sustain their own strategies and interests. By the seventeenth and eighteenth centuries absolutist and constitutional states were drawn steadily into a coordinating role with respect to the activities of civil society. The trigger for this growing responsibility almost always emanated from military commitments. But beneath this lay a general and growing requirement to regulate the developing capitalist economy and the spread of competing claims to property rights, if the economic basis of the state itself was to be properly protected (Mann, 1986, p. 512). The other side of this process was, of course, the growing enmeshment of civil society with the state; for the latter's capacity in principle to stabilize and enforce law, contracts, and currencies – to provide a coordinating framework for the new emerging capitalist economy – made it a growing object of attention for the powerful groups and classes of civil society who hoped to shape state action to suit their own interests.

What was the relationship between "states" and "classes" in the era of formation of the modern state? Any full answer to this question is likely to be controversial, and would have to be qualified in important details from one country to another. However, having said this, a pattern, first depicted by the sociologist Max Weber, can be uncovered between political rulers and the rising capitalist classes. Weber spoke of an "alliance" between modern capitalism and the emergent modern state (Weber, 1923). Analyzing the nature of this alliance further, Poggi has usefully drawn a distinction between two autonomous forces whose interests converged for a distinctive period (Poggi, 1990, pp. 95–7). The forces consisted, on the one hand, of political rulers seeking to centralize political power and fiscal arrangements by disrupting and eradicating vestiges of power held by the nobility, the Church, and various estate bodies, and, on the other hand, of the rising bourgeois classes seeking to remove impediments to the expansion of market relations based on the trading arrangements established by powerful social networks, both country (aristocratic and landed power-bases) and urban (the estate and guild systems). How the "alliance" changed and crystallized over time into different constellations of class and state power is beyond the scope of this chapter. Nevertheless, it can be noted that the alliance appears to have endured up to the Industrial Revolution and aided both the expansion of commerce and the industrialization of the economy (Poggi, 1990, p. 96).

If there was an alliance between the interests of powerful political and economic groupings during the formative phase of the modern state it was not without conflicts. For the new capitalist classes sought not only to struggle against the remnants of feudal privilege, but also to ensure the progressive separation of the economy from the state so that the economy was free from any risk of arbitrary political interference. It is at this juncture that the emerging economic classes often became the reforming classes of the eighteenth and nineteenth centuries, seeking to conjoin the struggle for an independent economic sphere with the struggle for representative government. The chief connecting mechanism was the attempt to establish civil and political rights (Marshall, 1973; Giddens, 1981). For what was at issue in the establishment of these rights was the attempt to uphold "freedom of choice" in areas as diverse as personal, family, business, and political affairs. The pursuit of civil and political rights over time reconstituted the nature of both the state and the economy – driving the former towards a liberal democratic polity and the latter towards the capitalist market system. But the meaning of membership in the modern state, that is, of citizenship, remained contested – by political rulers, anxious to preserve their traditional privileges, by powerful social groups and classes, hoping to inscribe their interests into the polity, and by all those who remained excluded from political participation until well into the twentieth century: the working classes, women, and many minority groups. Moreover, as the coordinating role of the state expanded, and it became more involved in determining the conditions of civil society, the state became more intensely contested. The risk of unwanted political interference in economic affairs, and the requirement for a regulatory framework for trade and business, gave the emerging classes of capitalist society a double incentive for involvement in setting the direction of state action.

The process and outcome of the new social struggles, it should be stressed, cannot simply be understood in their own terms; for their form and dynamic were shaped and reshaped by the states system itself. Mann has put the point sharply:

> . . . by the time of the Industrial Revolution, capitalism was already contained within a civilization of competing geopolitical states . . . [while] economic interaction was largely confined within national boundaries, supported by imperial dominions. Each leading state approximated a self-contained economic network. International economic relations were authoritatively mediated by states. Class regulation and organization thus developed in each of a series of geographical areas shaped by existing geopolitical units. (Mann, 1986, p. 513)

Class conflicts were, in other words, framed in large measure by the nature and interrelations of states (cf. Tilly, 1981, pp. 44–52, 109–44).

# 4   Conclusion

The formation of the modern state has to be related to at least two overarching phenomena: the structures of political and social groups and classes, and the relations among states – "their position relative to each other, and their overall position in the world," as Hintze put it (1975, p. 183). Struggles among social collectivities at home and conflicts among states abroad have had a dramatic impact on the nature, organization, and dynamics of individual states. The modern state has a dual anchorage "in class-divided socio-economic structures and an international system of states" (Skocpol, 1979, p. 32). If this is the context in which the rise of the modern state must be understood, it remains to draw together the grounds for why it was that the modern state came to be a national or nation-state. Briefly put, this chapter has argued that nation-states became supreme because they won at war, were economically successful and, subsequently, achieved a significant degree of legitimacy in the eyes of their populations and other states.

They won at war because as warfare became more extended in scale and cost, it was larger national states which were best able to organize and fund military power; and as these states expanded overseas this ability increased (Tilly, 1990, pp. 65–6, 190). They were economically successful because the rapid growth of their economies from the late sixteenth century, and particularly after the mid-eighteenth century, sustained the process of capital accumulation: as the economic basis of the centralized state expanded, it significantly reduced the war-making ability of smaller states (often with fragmented power structures) and traditional empires (which depended above all on coercive power for their success). And they gained in legitimacy because as they extended their military, organizational, and coordinating activities, they came to depend more and more on the active cooperation, collaboration, and support of their peoples, especially well-organized civil groups. In the wake of the erosion of the authority of the Church, the legitimacy of claims to political power came to depend on the view that such claims were justified and appropriate if popular or democratic. Calls for democratic government or democratic legitimacy became irresistible in the face of the expansion of state administrative power and the growth of new political identities – nationalism, citizenship, and "public" life.

However, the rise of Europe, of the European nation-state and of the modern states system is not fully explained by these factors and processes. There was, as there always is in politics, a fair degree of "luck," "uncertainty," or "contingency." The Mongol invasions (1206–60) could have penetrated further west with significant implications for the formation of Christian Europe; the Reformation could have drawn Europe into an endless vicious circle of religious war which might have undermined future European expansion; Napoleon Bonaparte might have conquered Russia and created a more durable empire; capitalism could have taken a firm hold in the East. The point of these and dozens of other "what-ifs" is to remind one that history doesn't unfold according to one pattern, one logic, or one evolutionary scheme. History, if the above account is useful, is rather the result of the interplay of a number of causal patterns or processes which combine to produce particular trends and developmental trajectories. Moreover, these are never set in stone; they are always affected by and open to alteration by changing circumstances, and by the outcome of key historical events. In the case of the history of states these events have been wars, first and foremost, and the development of military power to back up negotiations on pressing issues.

The difficulties of coming to a judgment about the modern state are acute, especially if one examines it in relation to the history both of the states system and of the interconnections of the world economy. By way of a conclusion, however, a number of points from the chapter as a whole can be usefully brought together, and left for you to reflect on. These can be put briefly:

1   To understand the formation of the state it is necessary to grasp the intersection of national and international conditions and processes. The state faces inwards towards its subjects and citizens, and outwards towards the states system and international economy. It has an

anchorage in both the organizations and relations of socio-economic groups and in the international order.

2   The modern state became the supreme form of the state because it most successfully marshalled the means of waging war, economic resources, and claims to legitimacy. Modern states mobilized effectively for war, for the enhancement of economic activity (capitalist expansion), and for their own legitimation. It is at the intersection of these particular formative processes that the distinctive organization and form of the modern state emerged.

3   The democratization of the modern state, that is, the establishment of the universal franchise, can be related directly to the state's search for loyalty and resources when it has been most pressed (before, during and after wars), and to its claim to a distinct form of legitimacy. Unlike its predecessors, the modern state heralds its separateness from both ruler and ruled. At the center of the self-image and representation of the modern state lies its claim to be an "independent authority" or "circumscribed impartial power" accountable to its citizens. To the extent that this claim has been redeemed, the modern state has been able to enjoy an advantage against rival political forces in the battle for legitimacy in the modern world. However, the nature and meaning of this claim have been contested from the outset of the modern state to the present day. The legitimacy of the modern state remains controversial.

4   The modern state has been neither simply a detached "judge" of the affairs of civil society, nor merely an epiphenomenon. Rather, it is best understood as a system of organizations and relations which can make and shape social, political, and economic change. The state apparatus has sufficient primacy over social classes and collectivities that discrete political outcomes – constitutional forms, coalitional arrangements, particular exercises of state coercion, and so on – cannot be inferred directly from the movements and activities of those in civil society. Political life, and state action in particular, are by no means wholly determined by socio-economic life.

5   The modern state, like its predecessors, is a system of power in its own right; it has to be understood as a set of organizations and collectivities concerned with the institutionalization of political power. While the independent and autonomous capacities of state organizations and agencies have been stressed, so have the latter as sites of contestation and conflict. The history of the modern state is also the history of the way in which social struggle has been "inscribed" into, that is, embedded in, the organization, administration, and policies of the state. As states came to depend on their citizens for support and resources, their structures and policies became subject, some would say ever more subject, to political negotiation and compromise.

6   The proper locus and form of the sovereignty of the modern state have been in dispute. Conceptions of sovereignty which neither locate sovereignty exclusively in, nor reduce sovereignty to, either state or society seem compelling; yet, these are far from secure. Further, the

operation of states in the complex international system of economics and politics raises questions about the role of sovereignty – its possible nature and extent – in a world in which powerful non-state actors, like international companies, have significant influence, and in which the fate of peoples is interconnected. Sovereignty is molded and re-molded in the international world of states and societies.

7   The processes and conflicts which have centered on and crystallized around the modern state have been the result of complex interactions between political, economic, military, and social factors, among other things. These factors cannot simply be ranked in a fixed order of importance in the explanation of the rise and development of the modern state. For it is in a combination of factors that a satisfactory explanation can be found for the major trends and developments of the modern political world. While this amounts to a rejection of arguments for economic determinism, or cultural determinism, or military determinism (and other positions which advocate focusing on one set of causal factors), it allows that one or more of these factors could have causal primacy under particular conditions and circumstances. The modern state escapes the categories of deterministic theories; but economic relations, political forces, and military forces might have all been fundamental to elements of its form and dynamics.

# References

Anderson, P. (1974) *Passages from Antiquity to Feudalism*, London, New Left Books.

Andreski, S. (1968) *Military Organization and Society*, Berkeley, University of California Press.

Beitz, C. (1979) *Political Theory and International Relations*, Princeton, Princeton University Press.

Benn, S.I. and Peters, R.S. (1959) *Social Principles and the Democratic State*, London, Allen & Unwin.

Berlin, I. (1969) *Four Essays on Liberty*, Oxford, Oxford University Press.

Bernal, M. (1987) *Black Athena*, vol. 1, London, Free Association Books.

Bobbio, N. (1989) *Democracy and Dictatorship*, Cambridge, England, Polity Press.

Braudel, F. (1973) *Capitalism and Material Life*, London, Weidenfeld & Nicolson.

Breuilly, J. (1982) *Nationalism and the State*, Manchester, England, Manchester University Press.

Bull, H. (1977) *The Anarchical Society*, Cambridge, England, Macmillan.

Cassese, A. (1986) *International Law in a Divided World*, Oxford, Clarendon Press.

Dahl, R. (1989) *Democracy and its Critics*, New Haven, Yale University Press.

Dunn, J. (1969) *The Political Thought of John Locke*, Cambridge, England, Cambridge University Press.

Dunn, J. (1984) *Locke*, Oxford, Oxford University Press.

Elster, J. (1988) "Introduction," in Elster, J. and Slagstad, R. (eds) *Constitutionalism and Democracy*, Cambridge, England, Cambridge University Press.

Engels, F. (1972) *The Origins of the Family, Private Property and the State*, New York, International Publishers.

Falk, R. (1969) "The interplay of Westphalia and Charter conceptions of international law," in Black, C.A. and Falk, R. (eds) *The Future of the International Legal Order*, vol. 1, Princeton, Princeton University Press.

Giddens, A. (1981) *A Contemporary Critique of Historical Materialism*, London, Macmillan.

Giddens, A. (1985) *The Nation-State and Violence*, Cambridge, England, Polity Press.

Giddens, A. (1987) *Social Theory and Modern Society*, Cambridge, England, Polity Press.

Held, D. (1987) *Models of Democracy*, Cambridge, England, Polity Press.

Held, D. (1991) "Democracy, the nation-state and the global system," in Held, D. (ed.) *Political Theory Today*, Cambridge, England, Polity Press.

Hinsley, F.H. (1986) *Sovereignty*, 2nd edn, Cambridge, England, Cambridge University Press.

Hintze, O. (1975) *Historical Essays*, New York, Oxford University Press.

Hobbes, T. (1968) *Leviathan*, Harmondsworth, England, Penguin.

Janowitz, M. (1978) *The Last Half-Century*, Chicago, University of Chicago Press.

Keane, J. (1988) *Democracy and Civil Society*, London, Verso.

Locke, J. (1963) *Two Treatises of Government*, Cambridge, England, Cambridge University Press.

Macpherson, C.B. (1966) *The Real World of Democracy*, Oxford, Oxford University Press.

Mann, M. (1986) *The Sources of Social Power*, vol. 1, Cambridge, England, Cambridge University Press.

Mann, M. (1987) "Ruling strategies and citizenship," *Sociology*, vol. 21, no. 3.

Marshall, T.H. (1973) *Class, Citizenship and Social Development*, Westport, CT, Greenwood Press.

Marx, K. and Engels, F. (1948) *The Communist Manifesto*, New York, International Publishers.

McEvedy, C. (1961) *The Penguin Atlas of Medieval History*, Harmondsworth, England, Penguin.

McEvedy, C. (1982) *The Penguin Atlas of Recent History: Europe since 1815*, Harmondsworth, England, Penguin.

Mill, J.S. (1951) *Considerations on Representative Government*, in Acton, H.B. (ed.) *Utilitarianism, Liberty and Representative Government*, London, Dent.

Mitchell, B.R. and Deane, P. (1962) *Abstract of British Historical Statistics*, Cambridge, England, Cambridge University Press.

Mitchell, B.R. and Jones, H.G. (1971) *Second Abstract of Historical Statistics*, Cambridge, England, Cambridge University Press.

Modelski, G. (1972) *Principles of World Politics*, New York, Free Press.

Neumann, F. (1964) *The Democratic and the Authoritarian State*, New York, Free Press.

Pelczynski, Z.A. (1985) *The State and Civil Society*, Cambridge, England, Cambridge University Press.

Poggi, G. (1978) *The Development of the Modern State*, London, Hutchinson.

Poggi, G. (1990) *The State: Its Nature, Development and Prospects*, Cambridge, England, Polity Press.

Rousseau, J.-J. (1968) *The Social Contract*, Harmondsworth, England, Penguin.

Schama, S. (1989) *Citizens*, New York, Knopf.

Skinner, Q. (1978) *The Foundations of Modern Political Thought*, 2 vols, Cambridge, England, Cambridge University Press.

Skinner, Q. (1989) "The state," in Ball, T. et al. (eds) *Political Innovation and Conceptual Change*, Cambridge, England, Cambridge University Press.

Skocpol, T. (1979) *States and Revolutions*, Cambridge, England, Cambridge University Press.

Springborg, P. (1991) *Western Republicanism and the Oriental Prince*, Cambridge, England, Polity Press.

Therborn, G. (1977) "The rule of capital and the rise of democracy," *New Left Review*, vol. 103.

Tilly, C. (1975) "Reflections on the history of European state-making," in Tilly, C. (ed.) *The Formation of National States in Western Europe*, Princeton, Princeton University Press.

Tilly, C. (1981) *As Sociology Meets Men*, New York, Academic Press.

Tilly, C. (1990) *Coercion, Capital and European States, AD 990–1990*, Oxford, Basil Blackwell.

Turner, B.S. (1986) *Citizenship and Capitalism*, London, Allen & Unwin.

Wallerstein, I. (1979) *The Capitalist Economy*, Cambridge, England, Cambridge University Press.

Weber, M. (1923) *General Economic History*, London, Allen & Unwin.

Weber, M. (1972) "Politics as a vocation," in Gerth, H.H. and Mills, C.W. (eds) *From Max Weber*, New York, Oxford University Press.

# 3 The Emergence of the Economy

Vivienne Brown

## Contents

| | | |
|---|---|---|
| 1 | Introduction: The Economic Formation of Modernity | 91 |
| 2 | A Modern Economy in the Making? | 93 |
| 2.1 | A new commercial society in the eighteenth century? | 93 |
| 2.2 | Discourses on the economy | 100 |
| 2.3 | Structural change in the eighteenth century | 101 |
| 2.4 | Conclusion | 106 |
| 3 | The Beginnings of Modern Economics | 107 |
| 3.1 | Adam Smith | 107 |
| 3.2 | The operation of the free market economy | 108 |
| 3.3 | The division of labor | 110 |
| 3.4 | Self-interest | 112 |
| 3.5 | After Adam Smith | 113 |
| 3.6 | Conclusion | 114 |
| 4 | A Modern Economics? | 114 |
| 4.1 | Anticipating the modern economy? | 114 |
| 5 | Conclusion: Signposting the Future? | 118 |
| | References | 120 |

# 1 Introduction: The Economic Formation of Modernity

The "economy" as an object of interest is so much a part of our everyday lives and concerns that it is easily taken for granted. Newspaper headlines provide the latest economic forecasts and economic gurus on TV offer a stream of opinions about any and every aspect of economic performance. In this way, economic terms and economic analysis have entered into the daily media coverage of events, and most people have some working understanding of these debates even if the points of economic detail seem arcane.

Though we take this kind of economic debate for granted, it is a "modern" debate indicative of a "modern" society. Its comparative modernity may be seen in a number of different ways. First, such a debate takes for granted a certain kind of economy: a modern economy where there is a highly specialized and educated workforce organized to produce a differentiated range of goods for sale on a world-wide market. This presupposes a multinational corporate structure which is itself organized on a global scale, together with a vast network of interlinking financial, marketing, scientific, and technological agencies.

Second, such a debate is articulated within a set of economic terms and economic models that derive from a certain way of thinking about the economy; that is, from modern economic theory. Experts in the field of modern economic theory are specialists in the sense that they have undergone a lengthy period of training and are now employed in a range of specialist institutions, such as: universities, governmental and commercial organizations, and international agencies, such as the Organization for Economic Cooperation and Development and the International Monetary Fund. Although it is these professional economists who develop economic theory and conduct economic research, many of the key terms of the economic debates are understood by a wider and ever more discerning public.

Third, such an ongoing economic debate presupposes not only a literate and informed public audience, but also one which considers that it has the political right to be well-informed about the performance of the economy. This itself presupposes a political context of open democratic debate (whatever the actual restrictions may be in practice), where critical arguments may take place over the conduct of economic policy.

Living and working as we do in the midst of this "modern economy," it is easy to take it for granted. In this chapter we are going to pause to consider the emergence of the modern economy and ways of thinking about it. In line with other chapters, we shall examine the emergence of the economy as part of the more general emergence and definition of modernity that we now associate with Enlightenment thinking in the eighteenth century. As chapter 1 showed, the Enlightenment was a period of intense questioning about the nature of society and, inevitably, some of this questioning was also directed towards those parts of society that we would now designate as "economic," although this term, a modern one, was not used then.

In presenting a series of "histories" of different aspects of the formation of modern societies, these first chapters are underlining the multifaceted character and complexity of modern societies. This is an important point and one to which this book will frequently return. But these different "histories" of the emergence of modern society also contribute to another and more fundamental point: that our understanding of modern society is itself closely linked to the kind of "history" that we tell about it. The notion that there are different "histories" of modern society as opposed to a single "history" unsettles any idea that there is only one correct view either of a society or of its history. It also displaces any notion that historical time is a one-dimensional course of events or a single historical process. This means that a historical account of the formation of modernity will uncover discontinuities in the development of modernity as well as a continuous thread of progress, and that understanding any period in history entails looking backwards and sideways, as well as forwards.

By exploring the emergence of the economic formation of modernity, this chapter examines some of these issues. Section 2 compares the contours of the economy in eighteenth-century Britain with those of the modern UK economy of the twentieth century, and discusses the extent to which the rudiments of a modern economy can be discerned in the eighteenth century. Two different historical approaches to this issue are presented, thus providing two different "histories" – or "discourses" – of economic change during the period, but the overall conclusion of the section is that recent historical research has underlined the gradual nature of the economic changes taking place in the eighteenth century.

Section 3 investigates what are generally taken to be the origins of modern economic analysis in the eighteenth century. One of the reasons for the fascination of this period for those wishing to acquire an understanding of the development of modern economics is that it is regarded as the century which produced the first systematic treatise on the economy. In 1776, Adam Smith published *An Inquiry into the Nature and Causes of the Wealth of Nations*. Adam Smith is often regarded as the "father" of economics because he published the first major book on the subject at just that moment in Britain's history when signs of the modern economy seemed to be appearing. Armed with prescient insight and a commitment to objective economic analysis, Adam Smith is thought to have initiated the scientific study of economics and to have heralded the new era of the modern, industrial, profit-seeking economy. Changes in the economy in the eighteenth century are thus thought to be "mirrored" by corresponding changes in economic thinking, and both processes are seen as providing a clear overture to the later economic developments of the Industrial Revolution and beyond. This interpretation, which many historians and economists have found deeply compelling, is discussed in section 3.

Just as section 2 problematizes the notion that the eighteenth century could be understood in terms of later economic developments, section 4 questions this popular view of Adam Smith as the spokesman for the emerging capitalist market order. It presents recent research on Adam Smith which locates his writings within the broad cultural context of the eighteenth century rather than seeing him as the originator and prophet of later economic developments.

Hence, the chapter concludes that one of the interesting links between the eighteenth century and ours is not so much that the eighteenth century and its thinking signposted modernity but that, looking back into the past, modernity retrospectively reinterprets the past. According to this view, writing "histories" is also partly a process of constructing a story about society's own origins, and this process involves both self-recognition and self-reconstruction. It is also a process in which the "classic" books of the past take on a new meaning as they are reinterpreted as signposts of the future order. This concluding account of the economic formation of modernity is presented in section 5.


# 2   A Modern Economy in the Making?

## 2.1   A new commercial society in the eighteenth century?

Looking back, the eighteenth century seems to be the moment when the pace of economic life began to quicken. To those living and writing at that time, it was the age of "commerce," the apex or culmination of a long period of social development in a country's manners, laws, and government, as well as in its productive powers and patterns of consumption. The idea of a commercial society included social as well as economic considerations, with an emphasis on the polite, even polished, character of the manners of the time made possible by what was thought to be a more refined way of life and enlarged cultural horizons.

Differences in wealth and lifestyle, however, were enormous: a great nobleman might get £10000 per year, a prosperous knight £800 per year, and a poor laborer £10 per year. But the social ladder was finely graduated along its entire length and so a certain degree of social mobility could take place across adjacent rungs, more so than in other European countries where the class structure was more ossified and the rungs of the ladder were further apart. While Enlightenment thinking may have opened up the intellectual and cultural horizons of the age, life still remained wretched for many. As a correspondent in the *Northampton Mercury* wrote in 1739: "I never see lace and embroidery upon the back of a beau but my thoughts descend to the poor fingers that have wrought it . . . What would avail our large estates and great tracts of land without their labours?" (quoted in Porter, 1990, p. 87). Even so, the increasingly commercial basis of social relations did make possible new standards of consumption for many that would have been inconceivable a generation earlier, even though these standards were not achieved uniformly or for everyone. Population increased, and so did the urban areas. The population of the UK increased from about 9.4

million in 1701 to 10.5 million in 1751, and 16.0 million in 1801, with a marked increase in the proportion living in urban areas. London dominated, but Manchester, Liverpool, Birmingham, Bristol, Leeds, Glasgow, Edinburgh, and Dublin were all growth points. Urban growth was accompanied by the development of characteristic Georgian flat-fronted brick row-houses which introduced a more wholesome and spacious style of living for many. Canals and road improvements opened up the regions to the cultural influences of the metropolis and they also provided vital infrastructure for the burgeoning trade links between the rapidly growing cities. Road travelling times were slashed: the Edinburgh to London journey was reduced from 256 hours in 1700 to 60 hours in 1800, and the journey from Bath to London was reduced from 50 hours to 16 hours over the same period. As in the twentieth century, improved roads led to increased travel, congestion, and moralists decrying the obsession with speed. In 1767, the *London Magazine* reported that: "There is scarce a cobbler in the counties of York and Lancaster, but must now be conveyed to his cousin german [i.e. his first cousin] in Wapping in two days time" (quoted in Langford, 1989, p. 407).

Improved communications meant that people and goods could travel more easily; so too could fashions and trends in consumer taste. The eighteenth century has been identified by some historians as the period of the "birth of a consumer society" (McKendrick et al., 1982), when social emulation manifested itself in a fast-moving fashion-consciousness in dress and in household goods. Although some manufacturers were careful to cultivate the patronage of royalty and the aristocracy in order to promote the fashionable credentials of their wares, the consumer markets thus developed were essentially popular rather than socially exclusive. The excerpt below is an account by Roy Porter of English society at this time. It describes how the growth of shops and advertising in newspapers enabled the new fashions to be quickly transmitted from London to the provinces, thus contributing to the first national market in clothing and household goods.

> A thousand other developments expedited trade. For instance, foreigners complimented the English on their retailing. "The magnificence of the shops," wrote Von Archenholz, "is the most striking thing in London." Defoe underlined the key distributive role of shops (bright, glass-fronted and bow-windowed) in serving householders with goods from the length and breadth of the country – hangings from Kidderminster, a looking-glass from London, blankets from Witney, rugs from Westmorland. He rhapsodized over their sheer number: "I have endeavoured to make some calculation of the number of shop-keepers in this kingdom, but I find it is not to be done – we may as well count the stars" (yet the old Puritan in him begrudged the outlay lavished on their tinsel display). Advertising swelled enormously, especially in newspapers. Between 1747 and 1750 Bottely's *Bath Journal* carried 2,740 advertisements, between 1780 and 1783,

well over twice as many. Provincial newspapers especially alerted readers to metropolitan tastes. Thus a North Walsham staymaker told lady readers of the *Norwich Mercury* in 1788 "that he is just returned from Town with the newest Fashions of French and Italian Stays, Corsetts and Riding Stays . . . their Orders will be executed in an Height of Taste not inferior to the first shops in London" (who could resist?). A Newcastle-on-Tyne lady was demanding a Wedgwood dinner service with an "Arabesque Border" before her local shopkeeper had even heard of it; she insisted on that precise pattern, having discovered it was "much used in London at present", and refused to be fobbed off with substitutes. In 1777 Abigail Gawthern noted in her diary that she "used a parasol for the first time . . . the first in Nottingham". Advertising's role in puffing demand was clear to all. "Promise, large promise, is the soul of advertisement," wrote Dr Johnson, who believed "the trade of advertising is now so near perfection that it is not easy to propose any improvement". Advertising's allure whipped up demand for knick-knacks, curios and all manner of disposable items, bought upon whim, and increased turnover in fashion. Handkerchiefs were hawked with Marlborough's five great victories painted on them; other designs celebrated Dr Sacheverell or the Peace of Utrecht. The radical John Wilkes's squinting face was plastered over mugs, jugs, teapots, plaques and plates.
(Porter, 1990, p. 190)

In this extract Porter points to the development of a national market and the importance of the growth in advertising. Porter mentions the increased availability of home furnishings – wall hangings, blankets, and rugs, together with mirrors and china as well as fashion clothes. The eighteenth century was the age when Josiah Wedgwood commercialized the manufacture of china and made expensive dinner and tea services which were eagerly sought after by the rich and fashionable; it was the age when Chippendale, Hepplewhite, and Sheraton established new designs for elegant furniture; and it was the age of Georgian silverware, buckles, buttons, new fabrics, high wigs, new breeds of animals, and new species of plants. Porter also refers here to a general paraphernalia of "knick-knacks" and "curios" which were bought on whim and appealed to a newly developing sense of novelty. Note too the development of retailing, with its alluring presentation of goods, and the power of advertising in stimulating a demand for the new products of the day. London acquired a reputation as the most dazzling shopping opportunity in all Europe, with its paved and well-lit shopping streets where even the most obdurate would be unable to resist the enticement of gorgeous displays presented in glass-fronted shop windows. Reading this description of eighteenth-century advertising and retailing, it comes as no surprise to recognize why many twentieth-century shopping malls and "boutiques" are neo-Georgian in style, with bow windows and reproduction decors. Even the commercialization of commemorative cups and handkerchiefs adorned with the symbols of national events have sound historical precedents!

Porter's account provides a telling insight into some of the changes taking place in eighteenth-century society, changes which were apparent to observers at the time and which were widely commented on. These changes were also noted by visitors to Britain, who compared it in favorable terms with other European countries. Ordinary folk seemed to be better dressed, better fed, and better housed than the native peasantry in other countries or, at least, in the words of one American traveller, "the poor do not look so poor here as in other countries" (quoted in Porter, 1990, p. 86). Ordinary folk seemed cleaner too; in the 1720s a visitor remarked: "English women and men are very clean; not a day passes by without their washing their hands, arms, faces, necks and throats in cold water, and that in winter as well as in summer" (Porter, 1990, p. 221). As a mid-century commentator from Nottingham observed, imported goods such as tea, coffee, chocolate, and sugar were no longer regarded as expensive luxuries reserved for the few but had entered the national diet: ". . . not only Gentry and Wealthy Travellers drink it constantly, but almost every Seamer, Sizer and Winder will have her Tea in a morning . . . and even a common Washer woman thinks she has not had a proper Breakfast without Tea and hot buttered White Bread!" (Porter, 1990, p. 218). Entertainment, music, and the theater were also becoming commercialized and available to a growing ticket-buying audience, and this brought with it a large increase in the number of amusement parks, pubs, coffee houses, theaters, and concerts. In the middle of the century, for example, in 1749, 12000 people paid to hear Handel's *Fireworks Music* in London, and in the last decade of the century when Haydn visited London, the concert halls were packed with enthusiastic and musically literate audiences.

This description of eighteenth-century English social life is an optimistic one, in which a more refined and comfortable way of life is seen to be spreading right down the social scale. Such accounts also have a directly modern ring to them; it seems easy to bridge the historical gap of 200 years or so by imagining those eighteenth-century folk on their shopping sprees, lounging in the newly-opened amusement parks, or doing some home improvements on the side. Porter's account is written in a very engaging style too; this isn't the formal history of kings and queens and high diplomatic maneuvers, but the everyday history of ordinary folk – folk like us – going about their lives. Thus, the style that Porter uses to recount an engaging story about the new consumerism of the eighteenth century contributes to our sense that this early consumerism was not so unlike the consumerism of the 1980s and 1990s with which we are familiar.

Porter's account of eighteenth-century consumer society, and the informal style in which it is written, both contribute towards painting a distinctly "modern" picture of the eighteenth century, and it is easy to conclude that the eighteenth century really did contain an embryonic version of the modern consumer economy of today which has developed directly from it. But this style of social history is itself new. This account of the eighteenth century reflects a relatively recent interest in the everyday facets of social history, and the wealth of detail that makes Porter's descriptions so fascinating is often culled from relatively new research. What this means is that his own project in writing this kind of social history, fascinating and scholarly though it is, is itself part of a relatively new trend in writing history. Porter's interest in the consumer activities of the eighteenth century is also partly the result of a recent trend in writing social history that attempts to counter what is seen as an excessive emphasis on the production aspects of the Industrial Revolution; in this approach, the "consumer revolution" is seen as an essential precursor of the better-publicized "Industrial Revolution."

But recent scholarly interest in the new consumer activities of the eighteenth century may also be seen partly as the result of the consumer orientations of the latter part of the twentieth century. Thus, interest in the consumer society of the late twentieth century has to some degree stimulated a lot of fine research on similar tendencies in eighteenth-century society. This contributes to our sense that the eighteenth century contained the seeds of modern society, but we must remember that it was modern society that itself produced the detailed research that made such a historical understanding possible. And furthermore, the consumer orientations and ideologies of late twentieth-century society are often taken as symptomatic of a *post-modern* social order, and sociological analyses of these are often denominated as "post-modern" analyses. Thus, there is a sense in which Porter's account of eighteenth-century consumerism not only pulls that period into line with modernity, but even propels it beyond that and into line with current trends identified with post-modernity.

Porter's social history relies on anecdotal and literary evidence from a wide range of sources: from letters, journals, foreign visitors' accounts, newspapers, and private papers. Very often economic historians attempt to provide a quantitative estimate of the changes that were taking place. By collecting statistical evidence they try to answer questions such as: By how much were standards of living increasing over the period? Were trade and commerce expanding at a greater rate than agriculture during this period? The attraction of this kind of research is its generality and its precision; for example, if national output is increasing at 3 percent per year and population at 1 percent per year, then the society is able to support a rising population with an approximate 2 percent annual increase in the standard of living. The great difficulty with this approach is that the statistics become increasingly unreliable as they are projected further back in time. The margin of error may then become so wide as to make the conclusion unreliable. If, in the above example, both statistics are subject to an error of 0.5 in either direction, then the result is that output increases by between 2.5 and 3.5 percent while population increases by 0.5 to 1.5 percent. In this case the average standard of living will be increasing by somewhere between 1 percent and 3 percent per year approximately, a much less precise result. Here at least, in this example, the margin of error is known. A greater source of difficulty with historical statistics is that the degree of unreliability may also be subject only to informed guesswork.

In spite of these difficulties, research on the quantitative dimensions of the eighteenth century provides another way of understanding the changes taking place; it may not tell us what an individual family had for breakfast but it may indicate whether living standards were improving on average. This kind of historical research poses questions that are quantitative in nature and which require detailed statistical analysis in order to provide answers. Table 3.1 (from an article by the economic historian R.V. Jackson) shows the annual growth rates over two periods during the eighteenth century: from 1700–60 and from 1760–1800. The first row shows the annual percentage increase in real output, the second shows the annual percentage increase in population, and the third shows the annual percentage increase in output per head of population.

Table 3.1    Annual growth rates of output, population, and output per head in eighteenth-century Britain

|  | 1700–60 (percent per annum) | 1760–1800 |
|---|---|---|
| Output | 0.58–0.60 | 1.04–1.20 |
| Population | 0.38 | 0.83 |
| Output/head | 0.20–0.22 | 0.21–0.37 |

Source: Jackson, 1990, pp. 219, 225

The table suggests that output increased by between 0.58 and 0.60 percent each year on average in the early period, and that this rate of growth increased to between 1.04 and 1.20 percent each year on average in the later period. Taking account of population growth during the period, this means that real output per person grew at an average annual rate of between 0.20 and 0.22 percent in the early period and between 0.21 and 0.37 percent in the later period. Although highly tentative, these figures suggest that the rising output over the eighteenth century did enable a growing population to live at a rising standard of living, a standard which increased at a somewhat higher rate in the latter part of the century; but note how small these increases are. This suggests that the optimistic picture painted by Porter's account should perhaps be tempered a little by the realization that, although increased consumption was available for many members of a rising population, on average the rate of improvement was slow.

But to say that the rate of improvement was slow suggests a standard of comparison of some sort. What is the implicit standard of comparison that is being used in the previous paragraph? Compared with improvements in living standards in the seventeenth century, the figures in table 3.1 may look substantial. For those living and writing during the eighteenth century, the point of comparison would have been either backwards to an earlier period, or sideways to other countries at the same period. And clearly, from Porter's account, many contemporary observers did find the changes remarkable. But if we are comparing the eighteenth with the twentieth century, then these figures do look small. Table 3.2 provides a modern point of comparison by presenting data for the UK, West Germany (as it then was), France, the US, and Japan.

Table 3.2   Annual rates of growth of gross domestic product per head of total population, 1983–88

| | 1983–88 (percent per annum) |
| --- | --- |
| UK | 3.4 |
| W. Germany | 2.5 |
| France | 1.7 |
| US | 3.4 |
| Japan | 3.8 |

Source: *Basic Statistics of the Community*, 1990, 27th edn, Luxembourg, Eurostat, p. 40

The statistics in table 3.2 were compiled on a different basis from those in table 3.1 and so they are not directly comparable, but they are clearly of a different order of magnitude from those in table 3.1. The range of figures is from 1.7 percent for France to 3.8 percent for Japan. Thus we can say that the annual increases in output during the eighteenth century were small by present-day standards, but they were significant and observable to many of those living in the eighteenth century.

The quantitative results shown in table 3.1 may look firm and definite, giving us a clear bird's-eye view of the long term trajectory of economic change in the eighteenth century. For this reason they may appear more secure than the portrayal of contemporary life in Porter's account, especially in view of the realization that Porter's description is partly the result of modern research in social history and a recent interest in the consumer aspects of society. But Jackson's data in table 3.1 are also representative of a relatively new style of economic history, known as "cliometrics," where the statistical techniques and modelling methods of modern economic theory are applied to the past. So in Jackson's case, too, the insights provided into the course of economic development in the eighteenth century are the product of modern ways of analyzing the economy. Thus, the statistics presented in table 3.1 are the product of recent research, and reflect the belief of many economic historians that the rate of economic growth during the eighteenth century was lower than had previously been thought (see also Crafts, 1985). This new conventional wisdom suggests that there was a smaller increase in output over the course of the century, but that there was a smoother trend over the century as a whole; in particular, this implies that earlier views of the 1780s and 1790s, as marking a dramatic turning point in economic development and as heralding the onset of the "Industrial Revolution," now seem to be an exaggeration. According to the new estimates, the Industrial Revolution took place in the nineteenth century rather than the late eighteenth century, and even then it was a more gradual and piecemeal affair than had previously been thought.

Furthermore, in the article from which these statistics were taken, Jackson goes on to present revised estimates that challenge even these more circumscribed views on the eighteenth-century pattern of economic change. Jackson argues in this article that inclusion of government activities seriously distorts the national output figures for purely statistical reasons; when government activities are excluded to provide an estimate of the growth of *private* sector output growth per head, the rate of growth of output per head falls *below* the level reported in table 3.1. Jackson estimates that, on this revised basis, output growth per head was about 0.13 percent per year during the 1700–60 period and 0.19 percent per year from 1760–1800, but the article reiterates the important point that all these estimates must be regarded as highly approximate and that they are all subject to a very wide margin of error. As other economic historians readily agree, these economic statistics represent hypotheses for future research rather than final judgments about what actually happened.

## 2.2   Discourses on the economy

Just as Porter's description of eighteenth-century consumerism is a "modern" account of the eighteenth century, so are economic statistics such as those presented by Jackson. Both approaches to describing the eighteenth century are the product of modern intensive research by specialist professional historians using up-to-date resources and methods. And both accounts will surely need to be amended in the future as new historians construct new ways of formulating evidence and arguments from the archives. Thus, as more knowledge is produced about the eighteenth century, we can see how that knowledge is itself a product of modern society and would not have been available without the priorities, attitudes, perspectives, theories, and research techniques that are themselves a product of modern society.

This underlines a more general point that knowledge about the eighteenth century does not exist in a pure or absolute form, just waiting for historians to come and record it. Knowledge about the period, about any period (including our own), has to be "produced" and this process of research production necessarily takes place within the context of modern academic life. This means that the research produced will bear the marks of modern academic conventions concerning standards of scholarship, the questions which are deemed worthy of further investigation, and the institutional bases for funding research projects.

Further, as we have seen, each of these histories of the eighteenth century offers its own insights into the social and economic processes of the time: the account of eighteenth-century consumerism offers us insights into early acquisitiveness and social emulation as structured by the commercialization of fashion; the account of national economic performance offers us insights into economic growth conceived as an aggregate or economy-wide process. Whichever approach we take, our insights are both opened up and closed off by the characteristics of that account itself.

Thus, we could say that our knowledge of the economy or of society is constituted by a series of "discourses" on these topics, discourses which structure our thinking and predispose us towards specific assumptions and specific forms of inquiry. Note too that this notion of "discourse" is also comparatively recent, but it is one that is increasingly being adopted in a number of different areas in social analysis, and you will meet it again in later chapters of this book.

## 2.3  Structural change in the eighteenth century

In trying to assess the extent to which an economy is becoming "modernized," many economists and economic historians also look at changes in the structure of output; here they try to assess the relative importance of agriculture and industry as sources of employment and final output. It is generally thought that a "pre-modern" economy is one where agriculture is more important than industry, whereas a "modern" economy is one where industry is more important than agriculture. This is a very rough-and-ready rule of thumb as different economies develop according to their own particular characteristics, but it can prove a useful starting point.

If an increasing population was experiencing an increasing standard of living in the eighteenth century, where was this increased output coming from? In a second extract by Roy Porter, you will find a brief summary of some of the sources of increased industrial output.

> Until late in the century, output operated almost exclusively through small-scale crafts, cottage and workshop industry. Expansion did not hinge on revolutionary innovations in technology, but on the steady sucking of accumulated wealth into circulation, better use of labour reserves, and new techniques facilitating exchange of goods and services. The heroes of this steady, inexorable march of commercial capitalism are largely anonymous: rank-and-file distributors, hauliers, shippers, transporters, and thousands of humble waggoners, packmen, tinkers, carters and hucksters. Up to 1760, no decisive breakthroughs had occurred in mechanization, in work organization, in the scale of the workplace, in sources of industrial power. The agricultural sector remained paramount, the fluctuating price of corn still largely dictating the tempo of commercial and industrial activity. Thus when agricultural profits were low in the 1730s, turnpiking tailed off. In mid-century, two thirds of British iron was still being used for agricultural purposes.
>
> Even profit-conscious expanding trades continued to organize their labour force in traditional ways, often within guild or company rules. Such regulation after all ensured stability and rarely proved a brake upon expansion. Manufacturing typically remained in workshops, based on the work-unit of the household. Putting out was perfect for expansion in textiles. Master-clothiers supplied workers – carders, rovers, spinners, weavers – with

materials, usually a week's supply, which they worked up on their own premises, using their own or rented wheels and looms. This system was a cost-effective use of capital. The capitalist needed to freeze little fixed capital in plant, and had flexibility in hiring and firing labour. Sub-contracting remained ubiquitous as a mode of employment and industrial organization, for instance in the "butty" system used in shallow Midlands coal-mining. It shared investment risks, profits and the problems of managing the workforce. . . .

Industry remained largely labour-intensive and skill-intensive. Weaving, smithying, hat-making, the furniture and cutlery trades, metal-working and thousands more besides expanded by recruiting more hands. When demand was high it was easy to take up the slack (and especially from mid-century, population pressure made the labour market a buyers' market). Women and children in particular could easily be drafted into the labour force. . . .

Furthermore, in the first two thirds of the century, it was highly exceptional for technological innovations to revolutionize a trade. The development of the coke-smelting of iron by the Darbys of Coalbrookdale was, of course, to prove vital in facilitating mass iron-casting. But despite rising charcoal prices, this innovation made slow headway (the Darbys kept it secret). New textile machinery such as Kay's flying shuttle also came in slowly. Newcomen's steam engine was used almost solely for pumping mines, and industrial power still came from animals, hands and feet, wind and water. Improvements occurred through the piecemeal modification of existing technologies within traditional employment structures. England consolidated her skills-base. (Porter, 1990, pp. 193–6)

One of the remarkable features of the increased economic activity right up until the later part of the eighteenth century is that it was not based on major changes in technology nor on the reorganization of the workforce into factories, the features of change which characterized the Industrial Revolution of the nineteenth century. Change as Porter describes it here was on the whole small-scale and piecemeal; industry was labor-intensive and skill-intensive and was largely based on the work-unit of the household. This system economized on capital by operating on a low capital–output basis, and it was flexible in the face of unforeseeable changes in demand. With the opening up of both the domestic market and the international market, economies of scale were gradually incorporated and a host of minor improvements was made possible; in particular, the development of the canals and the turnpike system represented a considerable investment in transport which reduced transport costs and facilitated regional specialization. But industrial giants were the exception rather than the rule, and often these were linked (as is still the case) with large government defense contracts. This was to change somewhat later on, especially during the 1780s and beyond when the Lancashire cotton industry expanded as a result of the technical developments in spinning and weaving, and cotton became the single most important industry in Britain. Later on, in the nineteenth century, factory production and a factory workforce became more significant as features of industrial production but, even at this later stage, change was piecemeal and most workers were still craft workers rather than factory operatives tending the machinery of the new technology. Certainly during the eighteenth century, production remained labor-intensive and was based largely on the household and the small workshop. The main industries in the eighteenth century were the traditional ones of wool, leather, and building, although by the end of the century cotton had caught up. The goods produced were mainly items intended for personal consumption; items such as textiles and clothing, leather goods and pottery, pots and pans, and the products of the Birmingham "toy" trade such as buttons, buckles, jewelry, and a wide range of trinkets and novelties.

Again, Porter's account focuses on the kaleidoscopic details of change. If we want to get an overall picture of structural shifts in the economy, say between agriculture and manufacturing, we need to take a quantitative approach. In an economy such as the one reported by Porter, we would not expect the annual increases in industrial output to be very large, nor perhaps would we expect those increases to be much greater than for agricultural output, and this is the picture that the statistics endorse. Table 3.3 shows the growth rates for different sectors for the same periods that were shown in table 3.1.

Table 3.3 Annual growth rates for different sectors in eighteenth-century Britain (excluding government)

|  | 1700–60 | 1760–1800 |
|---|---|---|
|  | (percent per annum) |  |
| Agriculture | 0.47 | 0.43 |
| Industry | 0.71 | 1.81 |
| Commerce | 0.51 | 1.02 |
| Services | 0.38 | 0.83 |
| Total private output | 0.51 | 1.02 |
| Output per head | 0.13 | 0.19 |

Source: Jackson, 1990, p. 232

Table 3.3 suggests that it was only in the later period that the performance of the different sectors began to diverge markedly. Although lagging behind industry and commerce, agriculture was growing at just under 0.5 percent per year in the early period. This improved agricultural efficiency had its origins in the previous century; it resulted from improved husbandry and stock breeding, a more commercial approach to agricultural organization, and a keen interest in applying scientific techniques to agriculture. But in the later period agricultural growth was clearly overtaken by industrial and commercial growth, each of which exceeded 1 percent per year; here the front runner is clearly industry with an annual growth rate of about 1.81 percent.

The significance of these changes can also be seen in terms of the structure of output during the course of the eighteenth century. The statistics so far suggest an economy that was still marked by traditional features, with a small and unmodernized manufacturing sector, a large agricultural sector, and a large domestic-service sector. It is difficult to be precise about the division of employment across these sectors, as much employment combined elements of more than one sector; for example, where the family was the unit of production, the domestic servant often performed the work of the agricultural laborer as well as of the tradesman's assistant. Table 3.4 shows estimates of the proportion of national output accounted for by the agricultural sector and the industrial/commercial sector for the years 1700, 1760, and 1800.

Table 3.4   Proportion of national output produced by the agricultural and industrial/commercial sectors in the eighteenth century (England and Wales)

|  | 1700 % | 1760 % | 1800 % |
| --- | --- | --- | --- |
| Agriculture | 40 | 34 | 35 |
| Industry/commerce | 33 | 37 | 40 |
| All other sectors (including government, domestic services, and rent) | 27 | 29 | 25 |
| Total | 100 | 100 | 100 |

Source: Cole, 1981, p. 64

Even keeping in mind the reservations about the reliability of these statistics, this table clearly shows how agriculture and industry/commerce switched over in importance during the course of the eighteenth century. In the early part of the century, agricultural output was pre-eminent; it accounted for about 40 percent of national output, whereas industry and commerce together accounted for about a third. By the end of the century the position was reversed, with agriculture contributing about a third of the national product and industry/commerce contributing about 40 percent. Thus, table 3.4 illustrates the transformation that took place in the course of the eighteenth century. At the beginning of the period the economy was very largely an agricultural one, although this does not mean that it was stagnant. But by the end of the period the agricultural sector contributed a smaller share of total output than industry/commerce, and its rate of growth also fell way behind that of the industrial sector.

As the nineteenth century progressed these trends became even more marked. By the end of the nineteenth century the agricultural share fell below 10 percent, and the combined share of industry and commerce amounted to something like two-thirds of national output. This is typical of the proportionate contribution of agriculture, industry, and commerce that has often been thought to characterize the "modern" economy; most of its employment and output derive from industry and commerce, which are increasingly organized on an international basis. This has been the pattern for economies such as those of the UK and the US, and of many other advanced industrial capitalist societies, at least until the middle of the twentieth century, and it has provided a model for what is often denoted as a "modern" economy. Since that time, however, the size of the industrial sector in many countries has shrunk and that of the service sector has grown considerably. Table 3.5 shows the relevant data for the UK, West Germany as it then was, France, the US, and Japan for 1987, the most recent year available.

Table 3.5   Composition of output in the UK, W. Germany, France, the US, and Japan, 1987

|  | UK % | W. Germany % | France % | US % | Japan % |
|---|---|---|---|---|---|
| Agriculture | 1.2 | 1.5 | 3.7 | 1.9 | 2.7 |
| Industry | 36.7 | 40.3 | 31.5 | 28.5 | 39.0 |
| Services | 62.1 | 58.2 | 64.8 | 69.6 | 58.3 |
| Total | 100.0 | 100.0 | 100.0 | 100.0 | 100.0 |

Source: *Basic Statistics of the Community*, 1990, 27th edn, Luxembourg, Eurostat, p. 41

Table 3.5 shows that the movement towards a larger service sector and a smaller industrial sector can be discerned in all the countries shown. This change has led to discussions about the "deindustrialization" of the advanced capitalist countries where the manufacturing sectors fail to compete with the low-wage, newly industrializing countries of South-east Asia. This change has focused attention on new ways of organizing the industrial sector, with a renewed emphasis on flexibility and technological innovation. It has also led to discussions of a "post-industrial" society, thought to be structurally and culturally distinct from the "modern" or "industrial" society which characterized the UK for the century and a half or so from the beginning of the Industrial Revolution. It is sometimes argued that this process of "de-industrialization" is a disease peculiar to the UK, but note that table 3.5 shows that the UK comes midway in terms of the relative sizes of the industrial and service sectors; West Germany and Japan both have larger industrial sectors and smaller service sectors than the UK, while France and the US have smaller industrial sectors and larger service sectors.

So far these tables of statistics have painted a broad picture of the changing relative importance of agriculture and industry/commerce. In table 3.4, the figures for industry and commerce were combined into a single sector, but to many eighteenth-century observers it was "commerce" itself that seemed to provide the great impetus to growth. The acute contemporary observer Arthur Young estimated that commerce amounted to about 13 percent of the national product in 1770 (leaving about 24 percent for manufacture, mining, and building) (Deane and Cole, 1967, p. 156), but even by his time commerce was almost as much an international affair as a domestic one. During the course of the eighteenth century, exports increased more than fourfold, far faster than domestic output. International commerce was accompanied by an active colonial policy and a considerable amount of protective legislation intended to promote domestic interests:

> Commerce in an international setting was an acutely competitive affair, in which the full power of the States competing was exerted

> to strengthen the national economy. The struggle for raw materials
> and tropical commodities, as well as for markets and the carrying
> trade which served them, was central to international
> relations . . . Every war during this period was in essence a
> commercial war . . .
> (Langford, 1989, p. 3)

Britain had for many years encouraged trade with old allies such as
Portugal and Holland, and discouraged trade with old enemies such as
France and Spain. This resulted in a complicated system of import
tariffs to discourage imports (especially of what were seen as "luxury"
items), export bounties to promote exports, and colonial monopolies to
encourage a favorable balance of colonial trade with the mother
country. It meant that the British gentry got drunk on port (from
Portugal) rather than on claret (from France), that aspiring ladies wore
protected home-produced silk rather than French silk, and that colonial
products such as tea and sugar became mainstays of the national diet as
we saw earlier.

Thus, the state was seen to have an active role in maintaining British
interests abroad. In normal years the expenditure of the state amounted
to about 5 percent of total national expenditure, but in extraordinary
years associated with wartime, this could increase to 10–14 percent of
national expenditure. In spite of the active role of the state in pursuing
international interests, the preference of the times was generally for
fewer state restrictions at home, although this did not stop cartels from
forming when the producers thought it was in their own interest.

## 2.4   Conclusion

This section has provided a broad view of the developing economy in
the eighteenth century and has compared some of its structural
characteristics with those of modern economies of the twentieth
century. But in building up this picture we found that the canvas itself
seemed to change shape depending on how it was being painted by the
modern historians; we could say that different "discourses" on the
eighteenth century seemed to project us into different eighteenth-
century worlds. The discourse on nascent consumerism in the
eighteenth century seemed to provide a direct forerunner of twentieth-
century consumerism, and here we could see the seeds of modernity, or
even post-modernity itself. Porter's account of industrial activity,
however, seemed to betoken an economy that was largely pre-modern,
with its cottage industries and the absence of large-scale factory
production. The cliometric discourse presented another view; here the
quirks and details of the period were smoothed over to provide simple
statistics for the aggregate economy over long historical periods.

The eighteenth century also seemed to become a less unified
economic entity as we looked at it more closely, rather like an
impressionist painting when studied close at hand. Agriculture was
predominant in the early part of the century but it was gradually
superseded by industry and commerce as the century progressed.

Though the entire century became increasingly active in an economic sense, it was not until the later period that industrial output seemed to achieve a momentum of its own, but even here the introduction of new technology was slow and uneven. Descriptions of dramatic turning points in the 1780s which characterized earlier research seem now to have exaggerated the position, and current historical research is more inclined to emphasize that the acceleration in growth was a gradual affair, both for the eighteenth and the nineteenth centuries. Production was still largely organized on a household basis and this was only partially displaced by the factory system as the new century replaced the old.

An emphasis on the slow and piecemeal nature of the economic changes taking place is, however, still consistent with a recognition of the structural changes that were taking place in the eighteenth century as agriculture slowly became eclipsed by industry and commerce, a process of change that seemed to be more or less complete by the late nineteenth century. This structure then provided something of a model for modern industrial society, in spite of the variation across individual economies, but this pattern of output itself proved to be a historically transient form for advanced economies. The passage of the twentieth century in its turn has shown that the sectoral composition of output is not a final or predetermined issue; as the industrial sector declines in importance and the service sector becomes a new source of dynamism and technological innovation, a new debate has emerged about the structural features of what has come to be known as "post-industrial" society.

# 3   The Beginnings of Modern Economics

## 3.1   Adam Smith

One of the most famous books of the eighteenth century is Adam Smith's *An Inquiry into the Nature and Causes of the Wealth of Nations*. This was not Adam Smith's first book, although it is the book for which he is now largely remembered. In 1759, when still working as a professor of moral philosophy at the University of Glasgow, Smith published *The Theory of Moral Sentiments*, and it was this book that established his reputation as a major thinker and philosopher. On the basis of the reputation thus secured, Smith resigned his university appointment in 1764 to travel to France and Switzerland as tutor to a young Scottish nobleman, the Duke of Buccleuch. The strength of Smith's reputation was such that he was warmly received by the French *philosophes* and enjoyed the friendship and intellectual activities of the Parisian salons of the time. After returning from his travels, Smith received a generous pension and this enabled him to spend some considerable time working on *The Wealth of Nations*, which was eventually published in 1776, the year in which the North American colonies achieved their independence.

Writing on the eve of the Industrial Revolution, the celebrated Scottish professor who had been welcomed into the elite philosophical circles of France has seemed to epitomize the new, enlightened ways of thinking about the economy. In his account of the social history of the eighteenth century, Porter refers to Adam Smith as "that high priest of capitalism" (1990, p. 87), and an authority on Adam Smith writes that: "The *Wealth of Nations* was adopted as the ideology of early liberal capitalism and its popularity may have been due as much to the way in which it accorded with the economic and political prejudices of the emergent bourgeoisie as to its intrinsic merits as a scholarly work" (Campbell, 1971, p. 15). Thus, many commentators have read Smith's *The Wealth of Nations* as a prescient anticipation of the capitalist economy; it has seemed to be a book that extolled the benefits of the unregulated, profit-seeking market economy at a time when commercial market relations were becoming increasingly significant.

According to this view of *The Wealth of Nations*, its centerpiece is the analysis of the "invisible hand," the mechanism by which the economic activities of profit-seeking individuals result in the greatest economic good for society as a whole. As Smith wrote of the profit-seeking individual: ". . . by directing that industry in such a manner as its produce may be of the greatest value, he intends only his own gain, and he is in this, as in many other cases, led by an invisible hand to promote an end which was no part of his intention" (Smith, 1976b, vol. 1, p. 456). Although each individual is intending his own gain, it is argued that the overall effect is the promotion of the interest of society as a whole. Here is thought to lie the central core of the message of *The Wealth of Nations*: that there exists a fundamental harmony of interests between the activities of profit-seeking individuals and the general good of society as a whole. The remainder of this section will examine three aspects of the writings of Adam Smith that have achieved prominence as integral parts of this vision of the invisible hand: the competitive market (section 3.2); the division of labor (section 3.3); and the pursuit of self-interest (section 3.4). This section will also consider very briefly how economics developed after Adam Smith (section 3.5).

## 3.2　The operation of the free market economy

By emphasizing the importance of profit-seeking and self-interest, Smith is thought to have been arguing in favor of free trade and against state involvement in the economy. The market mechanism works by allocating goods and resources by the free interplay of demand and supply, and so goods are produced only if they are thought to be profitable. In this situation, it is both unnecessary and inefficient for the state to take an active economic role. Smith's analysis of competitive markets and the formation of "market price" has seemed to later economists to represent a high point in analytical precision. This analysis provides the core of Smith's "allocation analysis," showing how resources in a capitalist economy are allocated by the operation of the price mechanism.

Smith illustrated how the competitive market price is responsive to the difference between demand and supply (Smith, 1976b, vol. 1, pp. 73–4). If demand is greater than supply, then the market price will increase, and if demand is less than supply then market price falls. In the longer term, the outcome is that the market price will eventually settle down at the level of the natural price; that is, at the level of costs of production, even though short-term shortages and surpluses will push the market price either above it or below it.

The influence of this competitive market analysis has been immensely far-reaching. The notion of the invisible hand at work in the competitive market came to form a powerful basis for the nineteenth-century argument in favor of *laissez-faire*, the admonition that government should "leave well enough alone." According to this view, the capitalist competitive market harnesses the natural self-interest of every individual person in such a way that the well-being of the society as a whole is promoted. If individuals are left alone to pursue their own profit, so the argument goes, the resulting outcome will be the most beneficial one.

The economic implication of this argument in favor of *laissez-faire* capitalism coincided with the obvious political inference to be made. As the competitive market, untrammelled by burdensome restrictions, would promote both individual prosperity and national prosperity, the state would be absolved from any duty of directing the economic affairs of private individuals, and would provide only the basic infrastructure of legal order, protection of private property – the linchpin of the system – and external defense. It was accepted that there would need to be some state provision of those items that could not be secured satisfactorily through the market. These items are sometimes known as public goods – goods such as education, transportation, and health services. Vital though these goods are, they are not supplied in sufficient quantity to all who need them when they are left to the free market, and so most modern economies have designed alternative methods of provision involving the state or other community-based organizations. Furthermore, the political liberties associated with the individual citizen were now seen to be part of a wider set of liberties connected with the use of private property and participation in competitive markets. This view seemed in many ways also to be a direct descendant of the writings of John Locke, according to which certain liberties and rights in the use of private property were "natural" rights that every person had and which could not without injustice be encroached on by the state.

The consequences of this view of the "economy" as a self-regulating mechanism operating independently of the state were crucial for the future development of economic theory. Earlier concepts of the economy as an aspect of the political power of the state implied that the directing hand of the statesman was essential to the economic well-being of the state, but Smith's concept of the invisible hand seemed to make the statesman almost redundant in an economic sense. In the earlier writings of mercantilism, the statesman had performed vital functions for the economy, controlling its direction and securing a favorable balance of trade. Similarly, earlier paternalist concepts of the moral obligation of the state in ensuring a plentiful supply of provisions to the populace also seemed to become outmoded in the face of this new reliance on market provision. The new view of the competitive market as economic regulator meant that economic activities could be conceptualized independently of the role of the government in a way that had not been possible before *The Wealth of Nations*. A new understanding of the economy was thus being developed, one that enabled the "economy" to be regarded as a separate domain or area of social life that was largely distinct from the political power and moral duties of the state.

As the process of industrialization gathered momentum in the nineteenth century, and as social and economic change became more pronounced, the issue of the role of the state became more pressing. The new analysis of the economy deriving from this reading of *The Wealth of Nations* was one that placed the state largely outside the main sphere of economic operations, and this had enormous repercussions for the actual role of the state during that time of social upheaval. It is arguable that the state was always more actively involved in the nineteenth-century economy than the official opinion of the times either sought or recognized, but the prevailing views about the limited economic role of the government did have a far-reaching effect on British public opinion. It is for this reason that Campbell could argue, as we have seen, that the influence of *The Wealth of Nations* resulted not only from its intrinsic merits as a scholarly work but also from its popularity as the "ideology of early liberal capitalism." And these political effects are still providing powerful reverberations in the last decades of the twentieth century, when a number of governments in both Eastern and Western Europe have been involved in a series of disengagements from their national economies. In the UK, the Conservative governments from 1979 initiated a series of moves intended to reduce government involvement in and responsibility for the overall economic performance of the country.

## 3.3   The division of labor

Another area in which *The Wealth of Nations* has seemed to have its finger firmly on the pulse of the future is that concerning the economic advantages deriving from the "division of labor." In chapter 1, Smith argues that the division of labor had made possible an enormous increase in the productivity of labor in what he terms "opulent" countries. There are two aspects to this division of labor. First, there is the division of labor between different trades. Second, there is the division of labor within the manufacture of a single good; here Smith provides the example of pin-making, where the operation has been divided into as many as eighteen separate activities.

Smith argues that the greatest improvements in the productive powers of labor have been the result of the division of labor, and he describes how this occurs even in a trifling manufacture such as pin-making. He refers to the eighteen or so distinct operations involved, and argues that the division of labor increases a man's output from between one and twenty pins a day to about 4800 pins a day. Smith gives the particular factors that cause this increased output as: the increased dexterity arising from the repetition of simple tasks; the saving of time lost in passing from one task to another; and the invention of specialized machines which this close division of work is thought to encourage.

The effect of this division of labor for the range and quality of goods is startling, and brings to mind Roy Porter's description of the shopping possibilities that developed during the eighteenth century. A consequence of this world-wide division of labor is that even a "common artificer or day-labourer in a civilised and thriving country" has access to a wide range of commodities that represent the labor inputs of many thousands of other workers. Thus, even an ordinary workman takes for granted the extensive world-wide division of labor involved in providing his basic articles of consumption. The result of this division of labor for the workman's overall standard of living, Smith argues, is that, though the difference between his lifestyle and that of the rich in his own country might seem great, it is probably less than the difference between his own material standards and those of an "African king, the absolute master of the lives and liberties of ten thousand naked savages." Smith's acceptance of the cultural determinants of this comparison with an "African king" points to the wide interest of the time in the experiences of other societies, something which will be explored critically in chapter 6; the point to notice here is that Smith argues that even the humble day-laborer is the unknowing beneficiary of a world-wide division of labor.

The extent to which this division of labor can actually be carried out in any society depends on the extent of the market. A porter, for example, cannot find sufficient employment in a village, and in lone houses and small villages every farmer must also be butcher, baker, and brewer to his own family. In chapter 3 of *The Wealth of Nations*, Smith goes on to recognize the productive possibilities opening up in the move towards larger urban centers and the improved transportation and communications that were illustrated in section 2 above. Smith's argument also provides powerful ammunition for the opening up of markets on both a regional and international level as, the larger the market, the greater are the possibilities for an increased division of labor and further improvements in productivity.

*The Wealth of Nations* thus suggests a view of Smith's writings as endorsing the new market-oriented commerce of his own day and also presaging the later events of the Industrial Revolution. The passages on the competitive market take it for granted that any person will use his or her own property to his or her own individual advantage; in this Smith was very much following the general approach of the eighteenth century, which placed considerable importance on the right to use one's own property. Indeed, for Smith one of the social benefits of a commercial society was that the monetized relations replacing the older relations of servitude and dependence were conducive to greater liberty for all, including the lower ranks of society; but note that this independence was based on a generalized self-interest.

## 3.4   Self-interest

In *The Wealth of Nations* Smith discusses self-interest in terms of its economic effects. Smith also discusses ambition and self-interest in the context of his account of moral philosophy in *The Theory of Moral Sentiments*, first published in 1759 but extensively revised shortly before his death in 1790. In this work Smith argues that ambition is based on a person's desire to be approved by others. It is not ease but vanity, Smith argues, that promotes people to wish to better their condition. Smith says: "To be observed, to be attended to, to be taken notice of with sympathy, complacency, and approbation, are all the advantages which we can propose to derive from it. It is the vanity, not the ease, or the pleasure, which interests us" (1976a, p. 50). Smith's argument is that it is not the pursuit of riches or luxuries for their own sake that attracts people, but the effect which the possession of these items will have on other people. For this reason it is the conspicuous consumption of the rich which marks them off and guarantees the attention and approbation of other people. From an economic point of view, Smith is here referring to what modern economists refer to as "positional goods"; that is, status goods which by definition cannot be owned by a large number of people without losing something of their appeal. Thus, Smith's analysis of human ambition is not restricted to its economic dimension. He argues that people very often strive after material goods not for the sake of those goods themselves but because of the social esteem and respect that they think such wealth will bring them. In this sense, such goods are not so much an end in themselves, but a means to an end, that of social approbation.

   Adam Smith's writings on the economy formed just a part of his larger intellectual interests, which included moral philosophy, jurisprudence, history, science, rhetoric, and the study of fine writing. In spite of the comprehensiveness of Smith's interests, however, the separation between his writings on moral philosophy (in *The Theory of Moral Sentiments*) and his writings on the economy (in *The Wealth of Nations*) has set the pattern for much economic writing since which has aspired to join the scientific rather than the moral or social approach to economic analysis. This separation has reinforced the view that *The Wealth of Nations* can be read independently of Smith's other works and that it exemplifies the new Enlightenment approach to a rational and scientific study of society. It has also provided a famous precedent for the later professionalization of economics as a discipline purportedly characterized by a scientific rather than a moral approach to economic issues.

## 3.5   After Adam Smith

Adam Smith's analysis was developed by other writers in the course of the nineteenth century, although most of these later writers took a narrower approach to the economy which excluded a historical or moral dimension.

One such writer was the economist David Ricardo (1772–1823). He took a more abstract approach to economic issues, and was particularly concerned to refine what he took to be the glimmer of a labor theory of value in *The Wealth of Nations*. In developing his own labor theory of value in his book *On the Principles of Political Economy and Taxation* (1817), Ricardo put at center stage the issue of the distribution of income between the three main classes of society (landlords, capitalists, and laborers) in his analysis of the relationship between rent, profits, and wages.

Karl Marx (1818–83) challenged Smith in a number of different ways and argued that *The Wealth of Nations* was essentially an ideological defense of emerging capitalism. *Das Kapital* was published in 1867 and translated into English in 1887 under the title *Capital*; in this book Marx argued that capitalism was characterized not by an underlying harmony of interests but by an irreconcilable conflict of interest between capital and labor. Marx's analysis therefore challenged the doctrine of the invisible hand, and instead emphasized the exploitation of the working class and the revolutionary need to overthrow the capitalist system.

In the twentieth century, one of the greatest challenges to the doctrine of the invisible hand came from John Maynard Keynes (1883–1946), whose most famous book *The General Theory of Employment, Interest and Money* was published in 1936 during a period of high unemployment. The issue that Keynes addressed was not exploitation but unemployment; he argued that, contrary to the doctrine of the invisible hand, it may not always be the case that the pursuit of individual interest is consonant with the general interest. In particular, Keynes argued that the failure of "aggregate demand" is the fundamental cause of prolonged unemployment in the modern economy, and that governments should take upon themselves the responsibility for increasing aggregate demand and reducing unemployment. Keynes' analysis was intended as an answer to the socialist challenge; by making capitalism function more efficiently and more equitably, it was thought that its revolutionary overthrow would become unnecessary.

Keynes' doctrines became influential both at the level of government economic policy and at the level of popular debate, but by the late 1970s the twin problems of "stagflation" – stagnation and inflation – were associated with a new anti-Keynesianism. By the late 1970s and early 1980s, a new free-market and anti-statist approach had become dominant in many countries including the UK, and this approach explicitly looked back to the tradition of *The Wealth of Nations* for political and analytical support. Adam Smith was then popularly cited not only as the "father" of economics but as the original architect of a free-market, capitalist order in which the economic role of the state would be minimal.

## 3.6  Conclusion

Section 3 of this chapter has shown how Adam Smith's *The Wealth of Nations* has been understood as the beginning of a new kind of scientific analysis of the capitalist market economy. In particular, the section has outlined the theory of the invisible hand as an account of the capitalist market mechanism, the division of labor as an explanation of the sources of increased productiveness, and the pervasiveness and strength of the motive to "better one's condition" as a spur to individual profit-seeking behavior. In laying down this framework for the objective study of the capitalist economy, Smith's influence was also enhanced by the fact that he correctly anticipated the actual development of the UK economy. Writing before the period when the largely agricultural economy of the UK turned into the workshop of the world, Smith was able to point to just those developments that were going to prove decisive for the industrial growth of the capitalist economy during the nineteenth and twentieth centuries. The power and appeal of *The Wealth of Nations* at both the economic and the ideological level are thus thought to be a direct result of the timely nature of its analysis.

# 4   A Modern Economics?

Seeing the analysis of *The Wealth of Nations* as a direct response to changes in the economy gives a robustness to the account of its enormous influence; as a tract for the times it spoke directly to the economic interests of its own day, and in the same vein it is thought to speak directly to us today. This approach to the founding or "classic" texts of an academic discipline is a common one, but it is a view that is not well borne out by recent research. In this section I shall draw on recent research which has attempted to understand Adam Smith's writings as part of the broader context of the eighteenth-century Enlightenment, where questions of commerce and wealth were indissolubly linked with questions of history, jurisprudence, law, government, and morality (Winch, 1978; Haakonssen, 1981; Hont and Ignatieff, 1983; Teichgraeber, 1986; Brown, 1994).

## 4.1   Anticipating the modern economy?

This newer approach to Adam Smith's writings points up a number of weaknesses in the traditional interpretation presented in section 3. First, the traditional interpretation results in a process of "historical foreshortening" that overlooks the differences between the modern period and the earlier period when *The Wealth of Nations* was written. Seeing *The Wealth of Nations* as an embryonic description of "early liberal capitalism" tends to exaggerate the extent to which the eighteenth century of Smith's own day had already embarked on an irreversible process of modern economic transformation. This reduces the historical distance between *The Wealth of Nations* and our own period, thus contributing to our sense that such a book, although written over 200 years ago, may yet speak directly to us now. But as we saw in section 2 of this chapter, the process of economic change in the eighteenth century was slow and uneven. The economy of the eighteenth century was a pre-industrial economy, and it is anachronistic to think that Adam Smith could have had in mind a later modern industrial economy.

If we reconsider the division of labor in the context of the small-scale, unmodernized state of British industry at that time, a different impression is given. Smith's discussion is framed in terms of a trifling manufacture involving very little in the way of capital investment, where the production process is very labor-intensive. Smith describes how "One man draws out the wire, another straights it, a third cuts it, a fourth points it . . ." etc. (1976b, vol. 1, p. 15). In the middle of the eighteenth century, pin production was organized as a cottage industry, with a hundred or more pin "manufactories" employing a handful or so of workers each, although much of this work was located in workhouses; the little pin manufactory that Smith himself had apparently witnessed employed only ten men. It was not until the nineteenth century that machine production of pins was introduced and it was this, rather than the division of labor as such, that vastly increased labor productivity in pin production (Pratten, 1980). Thus, what is *not* included in Smith's account is the impact of machine production on the division of labor and how this affects the size of factories and the structure of industry. We should therefore be cautious about assuming that the example of the pin manufactory provides an astute anticipation of the enormous productive potential that lurked in the shadows of the Industrial Revolution of the future. In the case of the division of labor, as elsewhere, Smith's examples are typically of small-scale, low-technology industries requiring little in the way of capital equipment, industries that were more characteristic of the small-scale manufactories and cottage industries of his own time than the factories that came in the following century.

A second major problem with the traditional view of Adam Smith is that it is based on an implicit selection of those passages that seem to speak directly to an audience of modern economists and a relative neglect of those passages that fail to do so. Thus, those passages that refer to the debates that were current in the eighteenth century gradually become invisible as they become meaningless to later readers who are unfamiliar with those earlier debates. This means that many passages containing economic arguments, historical comparisons, political analyses, juristic comment, or moral assessments that relate to an eighteenth-century context, are simply ignored as irrelevant. In this way, the main thrust of the argument of the book is reconstructed retrospectively in terms of the interests and preconceptions of a later age. For example, in spite of the conventional wisdom that Adam

Smith extolled a modern manufacturing and commercial order, *The Wealth of Nations* was based on the argument that agriculture is a more beneficial activity than manufacturing, which in turn is more beneficial than commerce. This argument was part of Smith's analysis of the process of economic development – or the natural progress of opulence – which itself was part of a wider social transformation involving legal and political change. In criticizing mercantilist policies which favored the towns over the countryside, *The Wealth of Nations* was thus attacking what it saw as an "unnatural" overdevelopment of manufactures and trade. Referring back to the discussion of structural change in section 2.3 above, Smith was making the "pre-modern" argument that the agricultural sector was inherently more productive than industry and commerce.

*The Wealth of Nations* also contains passages criticizing the effects of the division of labor and the unfettered pursuit of individual self-interest. The passage on the division of labor is a very famous one; less famous is the following passage from a later chapter on the harmful effects of the division of labor:

> The man whose whole life is spent in performing a few simple operations, of which the effects too are, perhaps, always the same, or very nearly the same, has no occasion to exert his understanding, or to exercise his invention in finding out expedients for removing difficulties which never occur. He naturally loses, therefore, the habit of such exertion, and generally becomes as stupid and ignorant as it is possible for a human creature to become. The torpor of his mind renders him, not only incapable of relishing or bearing a part in any rational conversation, but of conceiving any generous, noble, or tender sentiment, and consequently of forming any just judgment concerning many even of the ordinary duties of private life. Of the great and extensive interests of his country, he is altogether incapable of judging; and unless very particular pains have been taken to render him otherwise, he is equally incapable of defending his country in war.
> (Smith, 1976b, p. 782)

Smith's condemnation here is unequivocal and contrasts strongly with an idealized picture presented later in *The Wealth of Nations* of a person's intellectual and moral capabilities in the early stages of society before the advent of commercial society. This shows that Smith's attitude towards commercial society was not one of undiluted approval. He recognized and appreciated the improved productive power arising from the division of labor, especially as this led to an improvement in the living conditions of the poor, but he clearly disapproved of what he saw as the intellectual, moral, and martial impoverishment of the "inferior ranks" of society in the commercial stage of society.

Similarly, *The Theory of Moral Sentiments* had many harsh words to say on the vanity of ambition. Wealth and greatness are described there as "mere trinkets of frivolous utility, no more adapted for procuring ease of body or tranquillity of mind than the tweezer-cases of the lover of toys" (1976a, p. 181). Similarly, power and riches are "enormous and operose machines contrived to produce a few trifling conveniences to the body" (pp. 182–3). Here we see Smith the moral philosopher inveighing against the consumerism of his own time and the futility of worldly ambition by deploying the language and argument of Stoic philosophy. In *The Theory of Moral Sentiments* there are many references to the Stoics, whose philosophy influenced Smith more deeply than any other, although he did not accept it in its entirety. According to the Stoic philosophy, a person's happiness and virtue are not dependent on material well-being; a person may be happy and virtuous in a cottage as well as in a palace, more so most likely, and Smith generally went along with this view.

A third problem with the traditional interpretation of Adam Smith is that it is blind to the textual nuances evident in Smith's writings, even in those passages that seem to speak more directly to a later time. This leads it to overlook the range of other influences at work in Smith's texts that make the meaning of even these familiar passages much more problematic than the traditional interpretation accepts.

Smith's discussion of the competitive market includes two expressions that would not be seen in a modern piece of economic writing. The first expression is that of "natural price." The traditional interpretation of *The Wealth of Nations* regards this as a reference to "long-run costs"; the passage is thus taken to mean that in a competitive market the market price will eventually settle down at the level of long-run costs, a result that is fully consonant with modern economic analysis. But the expression derives from a long tradition of "natural law" treatises where the natural price is discussed along with the market price. Indeed, Smith first used this expression in the course of his lectures on jurisprudence, law, and government, which were delivered at the University of Glasgow during the period 1752–64; these lectures were not published during Smith's lifetime but students' notes have since been published, providing modern scholars with the content of these lectures (Smith, 1978). The natural law treatises are in turn linked to the broader tradition of Stoic philosophy. Within the Stoic philosophy, a person is enjoined to live "according to nature" and so the attribute "natural" was permeated with normative and philosophical overtones. The natural law tradition is also linked to medieval discussions of the "just price," and for this reason some commentators have argued that the expression "natural price" carries with it some of the moral resonances of the earlier "just price" discussions.

The second expression that would not be seen in a modern piece of economic writing is that of the "wanton luxury" of those demanding a good, which pushes its market price above the natural price. Modern economic analysis accepts that high-income consumers have a relatively large influence on market outcomes, but the expression "wanton luxury" carries with it a set of value judgments that modern economists would normally avoid. The expression can however be located within the context of eighteenth-century mercantilist and moral debates about the effect of "luxury" (i.e. consumerism) on morals, manners, and the employment of labor. A famous contribution to this debate was Bernard Mandeville's *The Fable of the Bees* (1714), which argued that private vices (i.e. "luxury" or consumerism) lead to public benefits (i.e. increased demand for goods and hence increased employment).

Thus, recent research on Adam Smith has argued that the traditional interpretation of his writings is inadequate, and this section has suggested some of the ways in which the traditional interpretation leads to historical foreshortening, retrospective selectivity, and textual blindnesses. Different writers within the research approach outlined in this section stress different aspects of this, but what they all share is an awareness of the historical complexity of Adam Smith's writings. Drawing on the notion of "discourse" from section 2, we could say that the new approach attempts to understand Adam Smith's writings as a distinct form of discourse according to its own terms of reference and its own framework of assumptions. This means that it has to be situated with respect to other discourses of the eighteenth century in order to identify its own internal points of reference which determine its meaning. As we saw in this section, this implies that Adam Smith's discourse can be understood only with respect to other writings of the eighteenth century and earlier, writings such as the natural law discourse, the mercantilist discourse, and the Stoic discourse. It also implies that the detailed linguistic and stylistic features of Adam Smith's writings are also significant.

In contrast to this position, those parts of *The Wealth of Nations* that seem to relate most readily to modern forms of economic analysis are the parts that are emphasized in modern interpretations of Smith's work, and those parts that refer to other forgotten or neglected approaches slip gradually from view. In this way, over a period of time, the picture of *The Wealth of Nations* that has emerged is one that is made consonant with modern interests and perspectives.

# 5   Conclusion: Signposting the Future?

One reason why the Enlightenment period is so challenging is that it seems to present social science with an account of its own origins. By searching for its origins, modern social science attempts to understand the course of its own development and hence arrive at a deeper understanding of its present state of knowledge. But this chapter has argued that we have no direct entry route into the eighteenth century, into either the course of its economic development or its writings about economic development. Any intellectual process of exploring the eighteenth century and its literary products must take place within a discursive framework of one sort or another that provides us with a way of reading and understanding those eighteenth-century materials.

In the case of the economic changes taking place in the eighteenth century, we reviewed two different approaches, each of which may be seen as a different kind of historical discourse. The discourse on nascent consumerism provided us with one way of understanding changing attitudes to the acquisition and display of material goods; it provides an interpretation of diverse materials such as newspaper advertisements, fashion reports, retailing developments, and the output of satirists, within the same unifying discursive framework. The statistical analysis of the economic historians or cliometricians represents another kind of historical discourse; employing modern economic theories and statistical methods, modern estimation techniques are used to construct a unified account of the momentum of economic development from the scattered data of the eighteenth century.

Similarly, in the case of Adam Smith's writings, or Adam Smith's discourse if you like, alternative interpretative strategies were reviewed. Section 3 outlined a traditional reading of Adam Smith's discourse which located it firmly within the context of what were perceived to be immanent changes in economic activity. According to this interpretation, *The Wealth of Nations* was a signpost for the newly emerging liberal capitalist order which became pre-eminent in the nineteenth century. According to this approach, Adam Smith is also regarded as the "father" of modern economics; by this it is meant that his work laid the analytical foundations on which modern economics has been built. A sign of his own times and a sign of the future, Adam Smith's writings were seen as the fountainhead and guiding spirit for an entirely new economic order.

But section 4 of this chapter argued that Smith's own writings do not unambiguously lend support to such an interpretation. Smith's account was based not only on the traditional analysis of the competitive market, but more significantly on the natural progress of opulence from agriculture to manufactures to commerce. The guiding hand of the statesman was replaced by the invisible hand, but this still allowed scope for state involvement in the economy in a number of ways. Smith was so far from being an uncritical supporter of an economic system motivated entirely by self-interest that he frequently made harsh judgments on the activities of employers, manufacturers, and dealers; and he was so far from recommending an expansion of commerce and manufactures that he argued instead that these sectors had been overdeveloped in relation to agriculture, a more beneficial activity.

*The Wealth of Nations* has been interpreted in terms of modern discourses on the economy and in this process large sections of the book have been overlooked. The effect of this approach has been to reconstruct *The Wealth of Nations* in the image of the concerns of a later time, and thence to find in it the origins of a later course of development. An alternative account of Adam Smith's discourse might involve using a different interpretative matrix; here Adam Smith's discourse could be interpreted in terms of other discourses of the Enlightenment which account for the particular positioning and textual resonances of the arguments of *The Wealth of Nations*. For example, Smith's own moral evaluation of commercial society could be interpreted in terms of his attachment to Stoicism and his interest in jurisprudence, rather than located on a spectrum of left–right political positions which mark the ideological parameters of a later age. But note that this approach to reading *The Wealth of Nations* also embodies a view of history: one that sees it as a less deterministic process, in which *The Wealth of Nations* was not the necessary embodiment of an age that was yet to come, but the complex product of a range of political, economic, and moral discourses that were influential at the time.

Our attempt to understand the course of economic change in the eighteenth century, together with its most famous economics treatise, has resulted in the conclusion that both have been subject to a range of interpretations that may well tell us a good deal about the present as well as the past. In this process, views about the development of the economy become intermingled with views about the classic books on the economy. Thus, the interpretation of Adam Smith presented in section 3 tends to be associated with a view of the eighteenth century as the clear beginning of industrial capitalism, and also with an interpretation of the modern economy as the inevitable result of those early eighteenth-century beginnings.

An alternative view of Adam Smith would emphasize that his works can only be understood historically in terms of the other discourses of the Enlightenment period. At the same time, it would recognize that the power and the historical significance of a book is not necessarily related to this historically-situated reading, but depends precisely on the ways in which the book's arguments have been taken over by later generations and made their own. For it is one of the characteristics of a classic book – one that has been raised to canonical status – that instead of simply pointing the way to the future, it often becomes part of the process of struggle and debate out of which that future emerges. In the course of this untidy and loose-ended process of social change, the book's meaning and significance may well change along with the perceptions and political requirements of the age. In retrospect, it seems to have had the power to predict that change, but this power of prediction may well be the result of the book's canonization rather than its cause.

## References

Brown, V. (1994) *Adam Smith's Discourse: Canonicity, Commerce and Conscience*, London, Routledge.

Campbell, T.D. (1971) *Adam Smith's Science of Morals*, London, Allen & Unwin.

Cole, W.A. (1981) "Factors in demand 1700–80," in Floud, R. and McCloskey, D. (eds) *The Economic History of Britain Since 1700*, Cambridge, England, Cambridge University Press.

Crafts, N.F.R. (1985) *British Economic Growth During the Industrial Revolution*, Oxford, Clarendon Press.

Deane, P. and Cole, W.A. (1967) *British Economic Growth 1688–1959*, 2nd edn, Cambridge, England, Cambridge University Press.

Haakonssen, K. (1981) *The Science of a Legislator: The Natural Jurisprudence of David Hume and Adam Smith*, Cambridge, England, Cambridge University Press.

Hont, I. and Ignatieff, M. (eds) (1983) *Wealth and Virtue: The Shaping of Political Economy in the Scottish Enlightenment*, Cambridge, England, Cambridge University Press.

Jackson, R.V. (1990) "Government expenditure and British economic growth in the eighteenth century: some problems of measurement," *Economic History Review*, 2nd series, vol. 43, pp. 217–35.

Langford, P. (1989) *A Polite and Commercial People: England 1727–1783*, Oxford, Clarendon Press.

McKendrick, N., Brewer, J., and Plumb, J.H. (1982) *The Birth of a Consumer Society: The Commercialization of Eighteenth-Century England*, London, Europa.

Porter, R. (1990) *English Society in the Eighteenth Century*, 2nd edn, Harmondsworth, England, Penguin.

Pratten, C.F. (1980) "The manufacture of pins," *Journal of Economic Literature*, vol. 18, pp. 93–6.

Smith, A. (1976a) *The Theory of Moral Sentiments*, ed. D.D. Raphael and A.L. Macfie; vol. 1 of The Glasgow Edition of the Works and Correspondence of Adam Smith, Oxford, Oxford University Press; reprinted by Liberty Press, 1982.

Smith, A. (1976b) *An Inquiry into the Nature and Causes of the Wealth of Nations*, ed. R.H. Campbell and A.S. Skinner; vol. 2 of The Glasgow Edition of the Works and Correspondence of Adam Smith, Oxford, Oxford University Press; reprinted by Liberty Press, 1981.

Smith, A. (1978) *Lectures on Jurisprudence*, ed. R.L. Meek, D.D. Raphael, and P.G. Stein; vol. 5 of The Glasgow Edition of the Works and Correspondence of Adam Smith, Oxford, Oxford University Press; reprinted by Liberty Press, 1982.

Teichgraeber, R.F., III (1986) *Free Trade and Moral Philosophy: Rethinking the Sources of Adam Smith's "Wealth of Nations,"* Durham, NC, Duke University Press.

Winch, D. (1978) *Adam Smith's Politics: An Essay in Historiographic Revision*, Cambridge, England, Cambridge University Press.

# 4 Changing Social Structures: Class and Gender

Harriet Bradley

## Contents

| | | |
|---|---|---|
| 1 | Introduction | 123 |
| 2 | Pre-Industrial Society | 124 |
| 2.1 | "The world we have lost" | 124 |
| 2.2 | Patriarchy and male power in pre-industrial families | 125 |
| 2.3 | Classes and power in pre-industrial society | 129 |
| 2.4 | Classical theories of pre-industrial societies | 131 |
| 3 | Class, Gender, and Industrialization | 133 |
| 3.1 | Industrialization and social change | 133 |
| 3.2 | Proletariat and bourgeoisie: the new classes of industrial society | 134 |
| 3.3 | A new role for women | 139 |
| 4 | Industrial Society and the Growth of Feminism | 143 |
| 4.1 | The maturing of industrial society | 143 |
| 4.2 | Sexual segregation and the growth of feminism | 145 |
| 5 | Conclusion | 146 |
| | References | 147 |

# 1    Introduction

In most modern societies there are divisions between rich and poor, divisions of social class, divisions between regions and between the different nationalities, divisions between people of different religions and between those of different ethnic origins, or races, to use the more popular term. Although we perhaps do not think of them in quite the same way, there are also divisions between the sexes, in terms of the typical patterns of their life histories and the different positions they occupy in the family and at work. All these divisions are aspects of what sociologists call *social structure*. This concept more generally refers to regular patterns which can be discerned in the way societies are organized; the types of divisions I have listed above are regular patterns of inequality which are deeply built into our society and tend to persist over time. Nevertheless they have not remained unchanged. The structure of social divisions in pre-industrial society was very different from what it is today. This chapter, then, is concerned with how class and gender divisions evolved with the formation of a modern social structure.

People have sometimes claimed that these divisions are disappearing over time. In the 1950s and 1960s, for instance, some social scientists believed that the working classes were being absorbed into the middle classes, a process they described as "embourgeoisement." But both statistical evidence and general consensus in the 1980s suggest a deepening of some of these divisions. The gap between the top 20 percent of households and the bottom 20 percent has been steadily increasing over the past two decades, and a survey commissioned by the EEC in 1990 found that 80 percent of people in the United Kingdom agreed with the statement, "The rich get richer and the poor get poorer."

This chapter is concerned with two types of social division and the inequalities they generate: those of gender and class. It tries to help you understand why these forms of inequality are so persistent by exploring their history. The chapter considers the changes in social structure brought about by industrialization and investigates the way contemporary patterns of class and gender inequality emerged. Émile Durkheim, one of the first academic sociologists, argued in his book *The Rules of Sociological Method* that to gain a complete understanding of any social phenomenon we have to understand why it came into existence in the first place (its causes and origins) and the reason it goes on existing (its effects or functions). This chapter is especially concerned with the former.

The chapter will also discuss some of the theories and ideas of the classical sociologists, Marx and Weber. We shall be considering their work partly because of the historical interest of their influential accounts of social change and social structure, but also because, as you will see in later chapters, many of their concepts and assumptions – the tools which they developed in their search for an understanding of how

societies work – are still used by social scientists today to analyze
contemporary societies.

# 2   Pre-Industrial Society

## 2.1   "The world we have lost"

The economic and social structure of pre-industrial Britain (i.e. roughly
before 1780) was markedly different from the world we have come to
regard as "natural" today, as Peter Laslett shows in his imaginative and
influential study *The World We Have Lost*.

Laslett (1965) paints a picture of an essentially rural world.
Although there was some manufacture of goods, the central focus of the
economy was agricultural production. At the end of the seventeenth
century, about three-quarters of the population earned most of their
livelihood from some type of agricultural work, with the majority living
in villages and small towns. Gregory King's estimates of the
occupations of the English population carried out in the 1690s show
that a fairly small minority of families worked as merchants,
shopkeepers, and artisans. Possession of land was the crucial factor in
determining people's social status, with the great aristocratic estate
owners at the top of the hierarchy. Manufacture was largely carried out
in the towns and was organized through the craft guilds; they
controlled entry to a trade through the apprenticeship system and laid
down thorough regulations for the practice of each trade, providing at
least a hope for a young entrant of working up through the ranks of
journeymen and -women to become a master or mistress of a craft in
his or her own right.

But for Laslett the most significant feature of the pre-industrial
economy was that it was organized on a household basis (which is why
Gregory King organized his census in terms of families). We could say
that in the sixteenth and seventeenth centuries Britain was made up of
small family businesses. Each member of the household was expected
to make some contribution to the joint resources. It was absolutely
normal practice for women, married or single, to work, and children
started work at an early age, sometimes well before their teens.
Household members might work cooperatively on the family farm or
smallholding, or at a single trade like shoemaking: men cutting out the
leather and lasting, women sewing up the pieces of the shoe, children
threading laces and polishing. In other cases, especially in poorer
families, household members were sent out to earn; young girls, in
particular, went to work as servants in richer households.

I have used the term *household* rather than *family* to indicate that
these family enterprises often contained individuals who were not part
of the core nuclear unit (parents and dependent children) which we in
the twentieth century have come to think of as the "normal" family.
Laslett's work certainly shows that, on the whole, apart from the great
aristocratic clans, English pre-industrial families were fairly small; as a

general rule the poorer the family the smaller it was likely to be. But many households also contained members of the wider kinship group (grandparents, aunts and uncles, nephews and nieces), and others contained non-kin members (servants, apprentices, lodgers) who were integrated into the household and joined in its communal work activities.

It was common practice in the sixteenth and seventeenth centuries to send children in their teens away from their parental homes for training: boys were commonly apprenticed and girls became household or farm servants. It is estimated that some 40 to 50 percent of young people spent some time living in another household. So widespread was this practice that shocked continental observers accused the English of hating their children; an Italian diplomat attached to the court of Henry VII wrote:

> The want of affection in the English is strongly manifested towards their children; for having kept them at home till they arrive at the age of 7 or 9 years at the utmost, they put them out, both males and females, to hard service in the houses of other people, binding them generally for another 7 to 9 years . . . They like to enjoy all their comforts themselves and they are better served by strangers than they would be by their own children . . . If they had their own children at home they would be obliged to give them the same food they made use of for themselves.
> (quoted in Macfarlane, 1978, p. 174)

## 2.2 Patriarchy and male power in pre-industrial families

As the above description suggests, families (or households) were the basic social units of these societies. A key feature of the pre-industrial family or household, noted by Laslett, was that it was *patriarchal*. Patriarchy is an important concept in contemporary sociology, but there is much disagreement over its meaning. The word literally means "rule of the father" and Laslett uses it in much this sense to denote a system of family authority which is often linked to a system of inheritance in which property is transferred through the male line. The sociologist Max Weber used the term to describe what he saw as one fundamental model of social power: for Weber, patriarchy or "patriarchalism" was a system of power common in traditional societies, "where, within a group which is usually organized on both an economic and a kinship base, as a household, authority is exercised by a particular individual who is designated by a definite rule of inheritance" (Weber, 1964, p. 346). Weber saw patriarchy as closely related to the feudal system which linked a lord and his male vassals in a power relationship, so in this sense patriarchy is not just about the relations between the sexes: the patriarch uses his power over both men and women. As head of the household, he has total control over the economic activities and behavior of the other members. Laslett's work suggests that this was true for families in pre-industrial England, which displayed clear hierarchies usually linked to age and sex. The only exception would be where a widow took over management of the household, and this would usually be only until she remarried.

The concept of patriarchy has frequently been used, however, in a much more general way to denote the whole system of male dominance in society. Feminist sociologists often use the term in this way and suggest that patriarchy is not only manifested in family authority relationships but in the whole set of social arrangements which serve to ensure that men remain in control and that women are subordinate. This approach is exemplified in the following quotation from Kate Millett's *Sexual Politics*: "Our society, like all other societies is a patriarchy. The military, industry, technology, universities, science, political office, finances – in short every avenue of power within the society, including the coercive force of the police, is entirely in male hands" (Millett, 1971, p. 25). To describe pre-industrial societies as patriarchal in this sense would mean looking beyond the family – for example, at the exclusion of women from important roles in public life, particularly from political and military activity, and their allocation to inferior jobs in the occupational structure.

One trouble with Millett's definition is that it is very general and lacks the precision of Weber's approach. Critics have argued that if we use the term in this loose way it inevitably leads us to conclude that all societies are patriarchal and allow us no way of distinguishing between them. Yet it is clear that relations between men and women were very different in Tudor Britain from what they are in Britain in the 1980s, just as they are at the present time different in Britain, in India, and in Saudi Arabia. Recent feminist analysts have, therefore, tried to make the concept more precise in two ways, while retaining Millett's implication that it relates specifically to gender relations. First, they have tried to develop accounts of how structures of patriarchy have varied in different times and places. We shall be thinking more about this later in this chapter. Second, they have tried to specify the base of patriarchy – that is, to identify the particular set of social relationships in which it is founded. Unless this is achieved, they argue, the concept will remain descriptive, rather than explanatory. Just as class relationships, as we shall see, are generated by changing forms of economic relations, so, if we are to arrive at a causal explanation of patriarchy, we must find the social arrangements from which it originates.

Feminists have not, however, been able to agree on what the basis of patriarchy is. Some, such as Shulamith Firestone, see it as springing from the family, and as being rooted in the control that men have exercised over women's reproductive powers. Others, such as Heidi Hartmann, argue that it is based on men's control of women's labor power; that is, the ability men have to force women to contribute free domestic labor in the home, and the use of male authority to exploit women as cheap labor outside the home. For the moment, our concern is with patterns of power between men and women in a particular historical situation and we will return to that issue now.

On the face of it, historical evidence would suggest that pre-industrial Britain was patriarchal in both senses examined above.

However, considerable debate exists among historians about power in the family. One important contribution to this debate was an early feminist classic, Alice Clark's *Working Life of Women in the Seventeenth Century*, first published in 1919. Clark argues strongly that marriage in pre-industrial England was more egalitarian than after industrialization. Basing her theory on the undisputed fact that married women were economically active, she sees marriage as a partnership where the importance of women's economic contribution gave them comparable status to that of men and a good degree of independence. She believes that both productive and domestic work were shared among the sexes so that there was no automatic identification of a married woman with the role of housewife.

For Clark, industrialization brought a drastic decline in women's status and economic power, forcing them into dependence on men. The separation of the workplace from the family home which came with the factory system meant that women no longer learned craft and productive skills from their fathers and husbands. Aristocratic women and the wives of merchants and craftsmen gave up working altogether and either led a life of leisure or took on purely domestic housewifely tasks; laborers' wives continued to be forced to work because of family poverty, but they had, like their husbands, to "go out to work" in factories or workshops where they were paid wages of below-subsistence level, forcing them into greater dependence on their husbands. For Clark, then, the pre-industrial economy was marked by greater gender equality.

Not everybody agrees with Clark's account. One critic is Edward Shorter, who has argued that in pre-industrial society there was a clear sexual division of labor in which women were confined to a limited range of tasks, many of which were considered subsidiary to men's work. Consequently, women had a lower economic and social status than that of men and were subordinate to them in the family. These female tasks typically centered on the home, while men's work took them out into the public sphere. Shorter claims that women were responsible for what he calls "the three big Cs" – cooking, cleaning, and childcare – and that men took no part in these domestic tasks. Shorter believes, then, that pre-industrial families were patriarchal with a clearly established sexual division of labor. He states that only after industrialization did patriarchy begin to weaken; only when women were able to go out to work as wage laborers were they liberated from a purely domestic life and provided with some measure of independence from fathers and husbands. In his words: "It was in the traditional moral economy that women suffered the most serious lack of status, and it was under capitalism that working women advanced to within at least shouting distance of equality with men" (Shorter, 1976, p. 513).

Other historical research also suggests that Clark's picture of pre-industrial gender relations is too rosy. There is considerable evidence of a well-established division of labor within both agricultural and manufacturing work. Men took the tasks that were conventionally viewed as most important (such as plowing or tending horses and cattle), while women were assigned tasks seen as less responsible and skilled (such as weeding the fields or caring for poultry and pigs). Women did do some skilled work, such as dairying, brewing, sewing, and nursing, but it tended to be in areas which had been labelled "women's work" and which often had domestic associations. Although it is possible to find examples, as Clark has done, of women practicing virtually every guild craft or trade, including traditionally male skills such as masonry, carpentry, shoemaking, and metalwork, such women were in a minority and usually gained access to the guild through family connections, being wives or daughters of craftsmen. More normally, they were found clustered in jobs traditionally designated as female, like spinning and shopkooping. Yet there was also a certain flexibility in the assignment of tasks to women and men, which is reflected in the examples of female craftworkers and similar cases of women doing heavy farmwork such as plowing or shepherding. Moreover, there were marked regional variations; in Scotland and the Northeast, for example, women were more likely to be involved in the "heavier" forms of farmwork, like stock-keeping or shepherding. This makes it hard to decide finally whether Clark or Shorter is the more correct.

I think that one reason for the ambiguity of the evidence may be the variability of family arrangements. As you will know from personal experience, families are more different from one another than are, say, factories, offices, or schools. No doubt there were henpecked husbands and bossy wives in pre-industrial families, just as there are today, even if pre-industrial society gave legal and formal sanction to male domination both in the family and at work. On the other hand, married women had fewer legal rights than men and it was socially and legally acceptable for a man to use violence to force his wife and children to obey him. In theory, if not in practice, a married woman was expected to subordinate herself entirely to her husband's wish and to practice complete obedience towards him.

*For Her Own Good* by Barbara Ehrenreich and Deidre English discusses this issue and suggests a compromise position. Ehrenreich and English believe that pre-industrial England was patriarchal but that it was also *gynocentric*, by which they mean that women's traditional skills, both productive and domestic, were seen as vital to the survival of families and thus of society as a whole. Women were the pivot of family life. The authors argue that when industrialization occurred, towards the end of the eighteenth century, it broke down male control within the family as women gained independence through wage labor, but at the same time the family became less important as an economic institution, so that women's value declined. Furthermore, their traditional skills, such as baking, brewing, and preparing herbal medicine, were lost as the economy became commercialized. Women were less dominated by husbands, but became subject to the authority of male employers; and the new industrial society was reshaped in a way that ensured the dominance of male ideas and interests in the public world of work and politics. All these changes created a problem which the Victorians named "the woman question": What would be the appropriate social role for women in the new industrialized society?

Finally, in trying to judge which of these accounts is most accurate, we have to bear in mind that historical "facts" do not speak for themselves. We should note that both Clark and Shorter were committed to particular views of history which may have influenced the kind of evidence they looked for and selected to illustrate their arguments. Clark, who was born into a business family (Clarks' Shoes), idealized the small family business and favored a return to an economy based upon it. Shorter, by contrast, is associated with "modernization" theory, which sees industrial development as part of the advance of progress, inevitably leading to a better and freer society. These perspectives and commitment to the values which are associated with them inevitably tend to color people's interpretations of history. One of the tasks which face us as social scientists is the need to move perpetually between concepts and the evidence used to support them, in order to perceive the biases associated with particular standpoints and thereby to refine our concepts and work towards a more adequate reading of the "facts." This is no easy task, as you will quickly discover when you try it for yourself!

## 2.3   Classes and power in pre-industrial society

One difficulty in assessing the position of women in pre-industrial society is that it varied according to their place in the social hierarchy. The strong, independent women whom Clark so admired were typically the wives of wealthier farmers and tradesmen; the position of laboring women was less enviable. This points to the way in which gender relations and class relations link together so that it is difficult to understand one without considering the other.

Class is a notoriously difficult concept to define, both in its sociological and common-sense usages, and there is considerable disagreement between different sociologists of different theoretical perspectives over the basis of class. However, there is general agreement that classes are produced by the economic arrangements within society. Here is my own definition, which pulls together some of the common themes from the different perspectives: a class is a group whose members share a common economic position, often involving a common lifestyle, and which is differentiated from other groups in terms of power and status, and the chances its members have of succeeding or bettering themselves in material terms. Obviously, as the pre-industrial economy was so different from ours, it generated different economic groups. Indeed, the very word class was not commonly used before the nineteenth century. People tended to talk of ranks or orders, or simply of the rich and the poor. Nevertheless, society was sharply divided on an economic basis in terms of wealth, property, and how people made their living.

At the top of the hierarchy, as we noted before, were the landowning classes, ranging from the monarch and nobility to the gentry and local squires who dominated one particular small village. This group, defined by possession of land as the basis of its wealth, was a small elite. One historian, Robert Malcolmson, estimates that 75 to 80

percent of the English population at the end of the seventeenth
century were laborers (Malcolmson, 1981). Most of these were
dependent on the elite for their livelihood, renting land from them, or
hiring themselves out to them as laborers. There were many gradations
within this group, ranging from small farmers to poor cottagers to
paupers, but what they had in common was lack of any real wealth,
dependence on the rich for work or sale of their produce, and the
possibility of falling into poverty because of their limited resources.
Craftsmen and tradesmen can be seen as a kind of middle class
between the two agricultural groupings of landowners and laborers, and
different from them in that their livelihood did not depend on land.
Karl Marx saw these urban groups as the forerunners of the now
industrial society. The guild organizations, granted rights by the
monarch with legal backing, gave the artisans some degree of
independence and security, and higher status than that of the common
agricultural laborers.

These three major class groupings had been in existence right
through from the medieval period until the end of the seventeenth
century; but the eighteenth century brought important changes in the
social structure. Even before the advent of the Industrial Revolution the
economy was changing with the development of what has been called
"proto-industry." This was the beginning of large-scale industry run on
a capitalist basis – that is, organized and controlled as a profit-making
speculation by non-laboring entrepreneurs who provided the initial
investment. In what was also known as the "putting-out system," many
families continued to work in their own homes, but with raw materials
and tools provided by the entrepreneurs, who also specified what work
should be done and marketed the finished goods. This new class of
entrepreneurs emerged from many backgrounds: some were originally
merchants or master-craftsmen, some were farmers branching out into
manufacture, some rose from the ranks of the laboring poor. But their
rise to power heralded the collapse of the independent household
work-unit. At the same time, changes in methods of agriculture meant
that many peasants or farm-laboring families lost possession of their
smallholdings or tenancies, or found them no longer viable as a means
of livelihood. The enclosure of common land, on which villagers had
been able to graze livestock and which provided them with such
necessities as fuel and building materials, also made it harder for the
poor to make a living from the land. Both in manufacture and
agriculture more and more people had to work as "day" or wage
laborers.

The eighteenth century, then, saw the emergence of the two social
groups which were held by Karl Marx to be the two great classes of
industrial society: the entrepreneurial capitalists and the landless wage-
earners or *proletariat*. While a large landowning class remained, by the
beginning of the nineteenth century the possession of capital (the
money, property, and equipment needed to carry out a profit-making
business) was becoming as important a source of social and economic
power as the possession of land, and the capitalists were getting ready
to challenge the political power of the landowners.

## 2.4 Classical theories of pre-industrial societies

One of the major concerns within sociology has always been the construction of categories – what sociologists call *social typologies* – to describe different types of society. The classical sociologists Marx and Weber were concerned to distinguish and analyze different stages in social development and to identify the causes of the transition from one stage to another. They did not develop typologies as ends in themselves; rather, by comparing and contrasting different types of society, they hoped to understand why these societies had come into existence, how they worked and what were the most important features of each type, particularly the societies in which they themselves lived. This relates to what I said at the beginning of the chapter about the need to look at the history of our society and its formation if we want to understand the present.

*Karl Marx*   Marx (1818–83) developed a very powerful method of constructing such a typology. He categorized societies in terms of their *mode of production* – that is, the relationships between groups of people who combine to produce goods and services. The term "mode of production" does not refer just to techniques and methods of economic production (like steam power, or the factory system), but also to the division of labor in society and the distribution of power, wealth, and property. Another key aspect in his thinking is the idea of surplus, that is, the stock of spare goods and wealth left over after the basic subsistence needs of the laborers who produce the wealth have been met. Those who control the surplus become the dominant group in society. Each mode of production has its own characteristic pattern of class relations and in each mode of production surplus is extracted and expropriated in a distinctive way. This is what Marx meant by the term "exploitation." In the capitalist mode of production, the surplus takes the form of the value left over from the production of goods after wages and other costs of production have been subtracted.

The type of society I have been describing Marx called *feudal* because it was founded on property and landholding arrangements developed in the Middle Ages. Feudal societies were based on agricultural production, and in them power depended on the possession of land. The two major classes were the landlords and the peasants (or, in the Middle Ages, serfs). Agricultural work was carried out by the peasants in exchange for grants of land and through this arrangement the landlords were able to extract, often by brute force, the agricultural surplus from the peasants. This form of surplus extraction, based on the legal and political power of the lords and often involving the squeezing of ever greater "dues" out of the peasants, was fiercely resented. It resulted in hostility and bitterness towards the lords, in line with Marx's belief that conflict was inevitable in all societies divided by class. Indeed, for Marx, it was conflict between the various classes, arising from the structural weaknesses or "contradictions" in any mode of production, which was the "motor of history," eventually bringing about change from one mode of production to another. Conflicts between peasants and masters, such as the Peasants" Revolt led by Jack Straw and Wat Tyler in England in 1381, were signs of the instability of such a system. In addition, men fleeing from the tyranny of the landlords tended to settle in the towns and turn to manufacture for their livelihood. This provided another threat to feudalism, especially as the expansion of manufacture depended on the free availability of labor while the feudal relationship tied people to particular masters and their land. The demand for free labor was one factor in a growing competition between the landlords and the emergent class of manufacturing entrepreneurs. According to Marx, a combination of peasant unrest and the emergence of capitalist manufacture in the towns eventually led feudal societies to collapse and industrial societies to emerge.

*Max Weber*   Weber (1864–1920) shared some of Marx's ideas about the economic relationships of feudal societies and the industrial societies which succeeded them, but his interests were broader than those of Marx. He was particularly interested in human motivation and the role of ideas in bringing about change. He drew a contrast between *traditional* and *rational* motivations which were, he argued, characteristic of agrarian and industrial societies respectively. Traditional motives are based on respect for custom and acceptance of long-standing forms of behavior, often backed by religious or superstitious beliefs. People do things "because they've always been done that way." Weber argued that peasants holding traditional values, if offered an increase in daily earnings, would simply work fewer days rather than improve their living standards or start saving up the extra cash! All they wanted was to continue their normal standard of living. In *The Protestant Ethic and the Spirit of Capitalism*, Weber argued that traditional motivation was resistant to change and also to the habits of thrift, hard work, accumulation, and reinvestment of earnings, which Weber saw as the "spirit of capitalism," the typical form of behavior in industrial society. This capitalist spirit embodied the idea of rational motivation and behavior. Rational behavior implied finding the best means to a given end, the ends in this case being bettering oneself and the accumulation of profit. Protestantism had an important role to play here as it encouraged these forms of behavior rather than either the pursuit of a gentlemanly life of leisure and conspicuous consumption or, alternatively, an unworldly devotion to spiritual things, which Weber believed characteristic of traditional religions like Catholicism or Buddhism. Later on, as societies were secularized and belief in Protestant dogma died away, people would have become habituated to rational forms of behavior and to the objectives of rational capitalism, and would follow the spirit of capitalism as an end in itself. This cultural shift is discussed at greater length in the next chapter.

As perhaps you will have perceived, both these thinkers, despite their very different focuses of interest, were trying to explain the distinctiveness of traditional societies and the transition to a new capitalist social order, and saw the decline of feudal or traditional societies and the emergence of capitalist industrial ones as a progressive development. Although Marx and Weber were very aware of the negative features of capitalist society, they nevertheless believed it to be economically more productive and efficient, and to offer greater scope for individual creativity. Yet for those caught up in the switch to the new type of society the immediate result was often misery and confusion, as we shall see in the following section.

# 3 Class, Gender, and Industrialization

## 3.1 Industrialization and social change

As we have seen, early capitalist development was agrarian in form. It was the rise of manufacturing industry which completed the transition from traditional societies to the type of modern capitalist societies we know today. Industrialization in Britain was a long, slow, and uneven process. Economic historians date the beginning of what has rather misleadingly become known as the "Industrial Revolution" at about 1780, but the process of changing to a mechanized, factory-based industrial economy was not completed until 1850, or even later in the case of particular industries. Its impact on, and disruption of, existing ways of life were therefore experienced variably across the population. Yet the changes involved were so momentous that their shadow fell across the lives even of those who were not directly affected.

One of the immediate results of industrialization was the growth of the towns. In 1750 there were only two cities in Britain with a population of over 50 000 inhabitants – London and Edinburgh; by 1801 there were eight such cities and by 1851, twenty-nine (Hobsbawm, 1968). People, especially dispossessed agricultural workers, flooded into these towns for work, in much the same way as people in the developing societies are attracted today to their cities. The influx of new inhabitants to urban areas was combined with dramatic population growth over the country as a whole: between 1750 and 1850 the population of England and Wales virtually trebled, rising from about 6.5 to about 18 million. The population rose at the rate of 10 percent each decade (Mathias, 1969). These factors led to gross overcrowding in the towns and the hasty erection of cheap housing. The works of Dickens and other nineteenth-century novelists give some impression of the terrible conditions that resulted, with thousands of people living in conditions of filth, disease, and penury. For the first time masses of people in Britain experienced urban rather than rural poverty, arguably much worse, because of the isolation from village communities with the traditional forms of support for the poor, sick, and disadvantaged which had grown up within them. The provisions of the new Poor Law of 1834, notably the infamous workhouse system, were an ineffective and unacceptable substitute. In the first half of the nineteenth century the threat of the workhouse hung continually over the lives of thousands of working people.

At the same time, conditions of work were changing, although this occurred slowly and not for everyone. It is worth remembering that in 1850 there were still three times as many agricultural workers as textile workers, and it was not until the twentieth century that agriculture ceased to be the major employer of labor. Similarly, far more women worked in domestic service than in factories. In 1851 there were over a million women servants. But the new ways of work which evolved in the new factories set the pattern for working conditions for the whole of the laboring population. Even more important than the application of steam and the use of machinery was the subdivision of labor – a key feature of industrial organization based on capitalist investment. As you saw in chapter 3 on the emergence of the economy, Adam Smith in *The Wealth of Nations* described the tremendous effects of the subdivision of manufacture in terms of increased efficiency and productivity, using the example of the manufacture of a pin. He calculated that one worker carrying out all the operations to make a pin could make perhaps twenty pins in a day. Once the job had been divided up into something like eighteen separate minute operations, each performed by a different worker, the output of each worker was equivalent to 4800 pins a day.

In their search for ever greater profits many capitalists applied these principles in reorganizing their production methods. The traditional craft-based way of manufacture, whereby apprentices learned all the techniques and processes by which raw materials became a finished product, was vanishing for ever. Craftsmen who took pride in skills which had been handed down through generations were faced with the redundancy of their knowledge, as many of these new sub-divided jobs could be performed by young men and women with little or no training. Even Adam Smith, with his admiration for the efficiency of the new methods, acknowledged the stupefying effect such work could have on the laborer. Thus the worker not only lost skills and control over the task he or she was carrying out, but his or her ingenuity was destroyed, all of which served to render working people more and more powerless in the face of their employers. Although the artisans struggled for decades to maintain apprenticeship rules, to retain the old techniques and customs of their trades, and to keep out unskilled entrants, their efforts were in many cases ultimately doomed; though it should be said that at the same time the new system did create some new forms of skilled work, especially in the machine-engineering industry.

### 3.2 Proletariat and bourgeoisie: the new classes of industrial society

Marx has provided us with the most influential account of how all these changes affected the class structure. For him, industrialization consolidated the existence of the two new classes which had been developing from, or to use his own words, "maturing in the womb" of, the old feudal society. For Marx, the most important feature of the industrial society he was analyzing was that it was capitalist; that is, it was based on the private ownership of the means of production (machines, factories, raw materials) by non-laboring entrepreneurs. In his massive study *Das Kapital*, Marx stated that capitalism exists when the owner of capital meets the seller of labor in the free market. This definition gives us the three central elements of the new society: the capitalists, the wage laborers, and the market. Marx called the two new classes the *bourgeoisie* and the *proletariat*, although we might now prefer to use the terms "capitalists" and "working classes." Like many nineteenth-century commentators, Marx also used the more abstract terms *capital* and *labor*. (This reminds us that in discussing classes we are not just talking about identifiable groups of individuals, but about a structured relationship between collectivities which embody different functions within a specific method of production.)

The bourgeoisie in England became the major holders of wealth and the social surplus, and thus the economically dominant class. In the first part of the nineteenth century they also attempted to consolidate their social and political power. On the local level they established their leadership in many towns, especially in the North and the Midlands, often through acts of public philanthropy such as establishing schools and leisure facilities. On the national level they challenged the old power group, the aristocracy, through various processes of Parliamentary reform. Especially important was the overthrow of the Corn Laws which kept agricultural prices artificially high, thereby protecting the landlords from the free market and helping to ensure their wealth and power. In political terms the bourgeoisie did not so much throw out the landed classes, as come to share the governing of the country with them.

Facing the bourgeoisie was the new urban working class, dispossessed of the means of producing their own livelihood and forced to sell their only possession, their labor, in order to survive. For Marx these two groups were locked in a relationship that was both dependent and antagonistic. The laborers needed the capitalists to provide them with work, and the capitalists needed the laborers to make profits; but the relationship was also one of inherent conflict because of the exploitative nature of these economic arrangements.

Like many other nineteenth-century commentators, Marx believed that the wages paid to the working people did not represent the full value of the goods they produced. During part of their working time, laborers produced goods of a value equivalent to the costs of their own subsistence needs (which would in turn be equivalent to a minimum wage). In the rest of the time they worked, the goods they produced represented extra value. Some of this value, "surplus value" to use Marx's term, was taken by the capitalists in the form of profit. It could be argued that the capitalists deserved to take the surplus because of the risks they took in their investment and their initiative in deciding what goods were needed by the market. This is an important argument, and is used by many people today. However, Marx took the opposing view: that it was the laborers whose work had actually produced the goods by their skill and effort and that they consequently had a right to the surplus or, to use the nineteenth-century phrase, "the full fruits of their labor." However, the mechanism of the wage, apparently offering a fair reward for a fair day's work, concealed from the workers the fact that the surplus was indeed being taken from them. This was what Marx meant by *exploitation* and it was the distinctive form by which surplus was extracted in the capitalist mode of production. Moreover, it was in the interests of the capitalists to try to increase profits by raising the amount of surplus value they took from the workers, either through cutting wages or by forcing the workers to make more goods for the same wages (that is, raising productivity). This in turn would increase the tendency to subdivision which I described earlier, so that, along with exploitation, working class people would experience ever greater levels of powerlessness and meaninglessness at work, as they carried out their repetitive and mindless labor.

Marx believed that when the working people came to understand how they were being exploited, they would see the system as unjust and seek to change it. The shared experience and awareness of exploitation would be the basis for unified class action, whereby the proletariat would eventually rise up to overthrow the whole economic order of capitalism, replacing it with a more just society in which the producers, not the capitalists, would control the surplus. For Marx, then, the working class was a class of revolutionary socialist potential. Marx recognized that other classes existed in society (for example, landlords and peasants left over from feudalism, or the growing intermediate class of administrators and professionals), but they seemed to him relatively insignificant in terms of the great struggle for power described above. It was left to Weber, writing at a much later date, to grasp the social importance of these intermediate classes, which sociologists now usually refer to as the *new middle classes*. These are the various groups of white-collar workers, from clerks to teachers to managers. Weber noted how the growth of bureaucracy had led to vast increases in their numbers. Like the industrial workers, these classes were relatively powerless since they, too, did not own the means of production within the bureaucracies but had to sell their labor; nevertheless, they received higher social rewards and therefore were placed in a situation of competition and rivalry with the proletariat. Weber, like many later sociologists, believed that the growth of the new middle classes added so greatly to the complexity of the class structure that the development of the revolutionary class struggle described by Marx would be blocked.

Weber's conceptualization of classes differed from Marx's in other important ways. While he accepted that there was a major division in society between the propertied and propertyless classes, he also emphasized very strongly that there were divisions *within* these groups. Not only was there the cleavage between the middle and working classes which we have described above, there were also splits within the working classes themselves. All these divisions were generated by the market, which gives different rewards to groups with different assets to sell. Skilled manual workers, for example, will be more highly rewarded than unskilled laborers because of their training and expertise, while the middle-class groupings have various levels of qualification, education, and training to offer. The small propertied group, too, is split on the basis of different types of property held; one such division which still remains central to our economy today is that between finance capital (the city, bankers) and manufacturing capital. While Marx's theory of exploitation and class conflict led him continually to emphasize the potential for unity within the two major classes, Weber's stress on the divisive role of the market resulted in his view of a plurality of classes, or potential classes, all existing in a climate of competition and rivalry with one another; conflict was thus as great within the broader class groupings as between them.

This effect, which later sociologists have called *fragmentation* of classes, was increased, in Weber's view, because economic relations of class were further complicated by overlapping with two other sources of social division, which Weber called *status* and *party*. Status inequality refers to the differing amounts of prestige or social standing held by various groups (status groups tend to be held together by common lifestyles and patterns of consumption). Weber argued that status divisions within the working class (the old Victorian distinction between "rough" and "respectable" is one example) worked against the development of a unified class identity as envisaged by Marx. Finally, Weber believed that parties and other political organizations would often cut across class and status divisions in their membership as they sought to mobilize power to further the interests of their members. (The sale of public housing to tenants by the Conservative party in Britain is a good example of how a party traditionally identified with bourgeois and middle-class interests can also cater to working-class needs, thereby encouraging political divisions within that class.) In these ways, among others, Weber produced a model of the class structure which allowed for infinitely more complexity than Marx's polar model.

Nevertheless, when I study the history of the early nineteenth century I find myself thinking of Marx's ideas rather than Weber's. The period between 1780 and 1850 was a time of constant upheaval, as working people struggled against the new industrial system and the hardship and poverty industrialism brought in its wake. There were food riots, hundreds of strikes and demonstrations in the industrial areas, rick-burning and riots in the countryside over agricultural wage levels; the Luddite movement smashed machinery as a result of its perceived threat to the wages of skilled workers, and the great Chartist movement of the 1840s sought political reforms, including universal male suffrage, in order to gain a Parliamentary voice for working people and then use it to address their economic grievances. Thousands of ordinary men and women set up clubs, joined trade unions, marched, went on strike, demonstrated, and signed petitions. In one city alone, Nottingham, there were no fewer than thirty-nine riots between 1780 and 1850, as people sought redress for a range of social, economic, and political grievances. Many of these riots caused substantial damage to the property of the wealthy mill- and landowners, including (in 1832) the looting and burning down of Nottingham Castle. However, these movements of resistance tended to be localized and small-scale, reflecting the fact that the development of capitalist industrialism was an extremely uneven process, which took different forms and occurred with varying speed around the country. Responses were far more militant in some areas than others, as, indeed, the degree of suffering experienced by the people varied from region to region, although the two were not necessarily linked. At times, however, as in the case of Chartism, these fragmented activities of the working class threatened to become a national movement.

A wonderful account of these conflicts has been provided by E.P. Thompson in his massive study, *The Making of the English Working Class*. Thompson is sympathetic to the ideas of Marx, but believes too many Marxist sociologists use the idea of class wrongly by ignoring the dimension of people's experiences and subjective responses. He declares that class is not a "thing" that can be studied outside of the lived experience of the men and women who constitute it. Marx himself made a distinction between "class in itself" (the economic conditions under which people live whether or not they realize it) and "class for itself" (class as a politically aware and actively organized body). Thompson believes that these two aspects cannot be separated and that classes are therefore constantly changing as the people within them change their responses and behavior.

> The working class did not rise like the sun at an appointed time. It was present at its own making. . . .
>
> By class I understand a historical phenomenon, unifying a number of disparate and seemingly unconnected events, both in the raw material of experience and in consciousness. I emphasize that it is a *historical* phenomenon. I do not see class as a "structure", nor even as a "category", but as something which in fact happens (and can be shown to have happened) in human relationships.
>
> More than this, the notion of class entails the notion of historical relationship. Like any other relationship, it is a fluency which evades analysis if we attempt to stop it dead at any given moment and anatomize its structure. The finest-meshed sociological net cannot give us a pure specimen of class, any more than it can give us one of deference or of love. The relationship must always be embodied in real people and in a real context. Moreover, we cannot have two distinct classes, each with an independent being, and then bring them *into* relationship with each other. We cannot have love without lovers, nor deference without squires and labourers. And class happens when some men, as a result of common experiences (inherited or shared), feel and articulate the identity of their interests as between themselves, and as against other men whose interests are different from (and usually opposed to) theirs. The class experience is largely determined by the productive relations into which men are born – or enter involuntarily. Class-consciousness is the way in which these experiences are handled in cultural terms: embodied in traditions, value-systems, ideas, and institutional forms. If the experience appears as determined, class-consciousness does not.

We can see a *logic* in the responses of similar occupational groups undergoing similar experiences, but we cannot predicate any *law*. Consciousness of class arises in the same way in different times and places, but never in just the same way.

There is today an ever-present temptation to suppose that class is a thing. This was not Marx's meaning, in his own historical writing, yet the error vitiates much latter-day "Marxist" writing. "It", the working class, is assumed to have a real existence, which can be defined almost mathematically – so many men who stand in a certain relation to the means of production. Once this is assumed it becomes possible to deduce the class-consciousness which "it" ought to have (but seldom does have) if "it" was properly aware of its own position and real interests. (Thompson, 1968, pp. 9–11)

In his book, Thompson argues that up to 1850 the working people of England, because of shared economic suffering, developed an awareness of common interests and grievances and attempted through the activities I have described above to redress them. Although this working-class movement might not have been quite the revolutionary force that Marx looked for, Thompson demonstrates in his book that these working people were highly critical of the industrial system and perceived it as unjust. They put forward, in numerous documents and pamphlets, plans for alternative ways of organizing society. Many of them favored ideas of cooperative production, in which there would be no need for distinct classes of labor and capital and in which everybody would work collectively for the good of the community rather than for the profit of a few individuals. If we had been alive in 1840, Marx's ideas might have seemed much more pertinent than they do today.

## 3.3 A new role for women

The impact of industrialization on gender relations was less dramatic than on class relations, but just as far-reaching. Alice Clark, whose work we discussed in section 2.2, may have had too optimistic a view of pre-industrial gender relations, but I believe she was correct about the immediate effects of industrialism on women's economic lives. We need, however, to distinguish carefully between women of the different classes. Working-class women shared in the deprivation and struggles of their menfolk. Women from the higher social groupings were obviously better-off materially, but in some ways their economic position relative to men deteriorated more sharply.

The breakup of the family unit was a slow and uneven process but its effects hit women from the higher classes more quickly. Such women lost their involvement in productive work and became quite dependent on fathers and husbands. Wives of the gentry and the entrepreneurs increasingly led a life of privileged idleness, which has been described as "the gilded cage." Only women in poorer families of, say, tradesmen or professionals, who did not succeed in finding a husband would be expected to earn, and these faced an unhappy future because of the very limited range of jobs considered respectable enough for "genteel" women. Governessing was one such job, but it was ill-paid and commanded little social respect. Many such women ended up as paupers or dependent on charity. It is not surprising that the search for a husband often became the sole purpose of a young woman's life; without one the prospect was bleak.

These developments made what the Victorians called "the woman question" an important issue of the day. If married women could not be earners what social function could they fulfill? The Victorians developed a whole new set of ideas about women which has been labelled the *ideology of domesticity*. At the core of this ideology was the now-familiar proposition that women's place is in the home. The Victorians acknowledged the seamier aspects of capitalism in representing the world of work as ruthless, polluted, and dangerous. Women were seen as essentially pure, but easily led astray; if they went out to work they were considered to risk moral corruption and sexual seduction. Instead, they should devote themselves to domestic duties, restoring husbands after their return from work, raising children and setting a moral example to them, and making the home a comfortable place, either through their own housework or by managing a household of servants.

I want to emphasize again that this was largely a new view of women's role. In pre-industrial society it was seen as desirable and normal for women to be earners and contributors to the household income. But in Victorian England the only approved roles outside the home for women from wealthy families were unpaid charitable work, visiting the sick, and improving the lives and morals of their working-class sisters.

These ideas were based on the principle that women and men were naturally different – not just biologically, but in terms of inherent personality; they were believed therefore to be fitted by nature for different social roles. This was the doctrine of separate spheres. One classic and relatively sophisticated statement of this is found in John Ruskin's essay "Of Queens' Gardens":

> Their separate characters are briefly these. The man's power is active, progressive, defensive. He is eminently the doer, the creator, the discoverer, the defender. His intellect is for speculation and invention; his energy for adventure, for war and for conquest . . . But the woman's power is for rule, not for battle, and her intellect is not for invention or creation, but for a sweet ordering, arrangement and decision . . . Her great function is Praise; she enters into no contest, but infallibly adjudges the crown of contest. By her office, and place, she is protected from all danger and temptation. The man, in his rough work in the open world, must encounter all peril and trial . . . often he must be wounded or subdued . . . and always hardened. But he guards the woman from all this . . .
> (Ruskin, 1965, p. 59)

The ideology of domesticity filtered down slowly to the working classes. In the 1830s some trade unions began to campaign against the employment of women in factories. Although this was chiefly because of fear of women's competition, they also made use of the domestic ideal. In 1842 the Mines Act prohibited women from working underground, and successive Factory Acts put limitations on women's working hours along with those of children. Although this legislation was the creation of middle-class reformers it was widely supported by working men. The Acts may have protected women from some of the worse aspects of unchecked exploitation, but they also served to suggest that women were in some way different from men as workers, an attitude that would grow in the course of the century. During the first half of the nineteenth century, however, the poverty and insecurity of working-class life ensured that most wives continued as earners where jobs were available to them.

Women without jobs often fell into destitution. The majority of paupers and occupants of workhouses were women. Many thousands more were forced into prostitution, which was extensive in Victorian England, especially in the cities. But most women managed to find work on farms, in domestic service (which remained the chief source of employment for women well into the twentieth century), in factories, and in workshops and laundries. A growing problem in finding employment resulted from the separation of home and workplace, which made it hard to combine a job with the care of young children, especially before state education developed in the latter part of the century. Working-class women adopted the same range of solutions as they do today. Some continued to find work that could be done at home (such as sewing or washing); some took up casual or part-time tasks; others used relatives or other women to care for their babies. Teenage daughters, whose earning potential was lower than that of their mothers, were often required to do housework and childcare. This growing burden of domestic responsibility was an additional restraint on women's opportunities compared to those of men.

Opportunities were also restricted by the sexual division of labor. Many of the new industrial jobs were seen by employers as ideal "women's work," being repetitive and unskilled, and they preferred to employ women and children as their labor was cheaper and they were considered more docile and less likely to join trade unions. But this did not bring an end to the sexual division of labor, although there was some shifting in the labelling of jobs as men's or women's work. For example, in the pre-industrial economy spinning was a major female occupation while weaving was a traditional male skill. Mechanization took the skill from weaving which was then assigned to women, while men captured the more important and more highly-skilled machine-spinning tasks. These changes frequently provoked industrial conflict, as male workers struggled to retain their old jobs and skills, and the outcome was often a compromise with men being promised the best and most highly-paid of the reorganized tasks. The final result was that the sexual stereotyping of jobs as men's or women's work was strengthened rather than weakened. Campaigns were mounted against women, such as field workers or "colliery lasses," working in jobs considered unsuitable because they were dirty, involved heavy labor or working beside men. Male control of the best, most highly-paid jobs was an important source of continued male dominance in industrial society.

In this period the family, too, continued to be patriarchal. This was especially the case in the families of the bourgeoisie and the upper classes, where women's total financial dependence on men deprived them of any base from which to resist male control. Among the working classes, women's continued labor-market participation gave them a stronger position with regard to their husbands. Moreover, working-class families were particularly vulnerable to breakup, because of the stresses of poverty, the need to move around the country to find work and the high mortality rates. Many widows and deserted wives found themselves in charge of the family, though husbands, when present, still held greater authority, and wives and children were often subjected to brutality and violence as men reaffirmed their right to be obeyed.

The legal position of married women remained weak. They had no rights to any property or earnings of their own, even those that they had possessed before marriage. They had no rights to divorce, and men were empowered to keep any children if a couple separated, although in practice most men left that responsibility to their wives. A woman's status was totally determined by that of her husband. If he became a pauper she had to accompany him to the workhouse.

In section 2.2 we looked at the contention of Shorter, among others, that industrialization brought an end to patriarchy, or at least weakened its grip. But others, such as Sylvia Walby, have argued by contrast that Victorian society was a high point for patriarchy in Britain, as women were pressured to withdraw from economic activity and become more dependent on men. Similarly, Heidi Hartmann has argued that patriarchy did not disappear with industrial capitalism, but merely changed its form, becoming perhaps less centrally maintained by private relationships within the household, but instead being incorporated into the new capitalist relations of production. In her paper "Patriarchy, capitalism and job segregation by sex," Hartmann argues that capitalism built upon existing patriarchal traditions at work and in the home by utilizing women as a source of cheap labor and by exploiting their weaker and subordinate social position. Sex segregation of jobs became a major vehicle for the continuing social dominance of men; the low pay given for women's work forced women into dependence on men and this encouraged the identification of women as domestic workers.

The Factory Acts can be seen to exemplify the way in which patriarchy and capitalism interacted. Patriarchal impulses from middle-class reformers who wished to push women into the home lay behind the legislation which many employers opposed since they preferred to use cheaper female labor. The motives of the working men who supported the Acts seem to have been a mix of economic consideration (fear of women's competition and the undercutting of wages) and acceptance of the domestic ideal for women which helped them to maintain their authority in the home. However, as table 4.1 suggests, the end result of the Acts was not to exclude women altogether from industry, but to push them more firmly into jobs which were subsidiary to those of men. Men retained the best jobs and their economic superiority, while employers continued with their divisive tactics and exploitation of women's cheap labor. According to Hartmann, this demonstrates how patriarchy and capitalism work together to subordinate women.

Table 4.1   Total working population in England and Wales, 1861–1911

| Year | Combined total number | Men | | Women | |
|------|----------------------|-----|---|-------|---|
| | | Total number | % of total working population | Total number | % of total working population |
| 1861 | 9,818,994 | 6,469,674 | 65.9 | 3,349,320 | 34.1 |
| 1871 | 10,730,286 | 7,329,123 | 68.3 | 3,401,163 | 31.7 |
| 1881 | 11,187,564 | 7,783,646 | 69.6 | 3,403,918 | 30.4 |
| 1891 | 12,899,484 | 8,883,254 | 68.9 | 4,016,230 | 31.1 |
| 1901 | 14,328,727 | 10,156,976 | 70.9 | 4,171,751 | 29.1 |
| 1911 | 16,284,399 | 11,453,665 | 70.3 | 4,830,734 | 29.7 |

Source: Holcombe, 1973, p. 213

Patriarchy did not come to an end with industrialization. I would accept the proposition that Victorian society saw patriarchy strengthened, as women's participation in the world outside the home diminished and sexual stereotyping became more pervasive. The doctrine of separate spheres meant that men were able to keep women out of the social institutions of the public sphere, to order them in line with male interests and ideas shaped by men, and to run them on male lines, as Ehrenreich and English argued.

# 4   Industrial Society and the Growth of Feminism

## 4.1   The maturing of industrial society

In this, the final section of this chapter, I shall look briefly at changes which occurred between the mid-Victorian period and the end of World War II.

The period between 1850 and 1900 was a crucial one for stabilizing patterns of class and gender relations, which then persisted fairly unchanged until the epoch of post-war reconstruction. In these years industrial society became much more stable as it began to achieve its mature form. Relations between the classes became far more harmonious. Strikes, demonstrations, and other manifestations of conflict still occurred, but the trend was for disputes to be settled by negotiation rather than confrontation.

Although the working classes continued to fight for their right to a decent standard of living, they no longer held so strongly to their visions of an alternative way of organizing society. Much of the working class came to accept that industrial capitalism was inevitable, aspiring merely to improve their position within it.

Many factors contributed to this change. It has been argued that divisions were becoming more apparent within the working class. One example is the emergence of a *labor aristocracy*, an elite group of skilled workers, who, in return for high wages, were persuaded to abandon radical action. Such a division, if we follow Weber's thinking, would be only one of many. Perhaps the major division was that between the sexes; the exclusionary policies of trade unions which we discussed in the last section prevented working men and women from developing a common sense of identity. Another argument is that the bourgeoisie was able to use its control of social institutions, such as the education system, the churches, and later the mass media, to ensure that its own ideology became the dominant social viewpoint. Moreover, the working classes were now developing their own distinctive lifestyle, what sociologists call "traditional working-class culture": football clubs, racing and betting shops, the local pub and working-men's clubs, music halls and dance halls. Sociologists suggest that this culture fostered defensive and fatalistic attitudes, leading to a resigned acceptance of the status quo. These and other factors contributed to a "remaking of the working class," as the more politicized class described by Thompson was reshaped.

Major advances for working people were achieved in the early twentieth century with the gaining of the vote and the right to full political representation, along with the formation of a political party designed specifically to further the interests of labor. However, perhaps because of the disruptions caused by the two world wars and the international recession of the 1920s and 1930s, the working classes were unable to make use of their political muscle to improve their socio-economic position until after 1945. Nonetheless, this incorporation of the working classes into the political structure is seen by Anthony Giddens as a mark of the maturation of industrial capitalism and another factor contributing to more harmonious class relations (Giddens, 1973).

Meanwhile, the middle classes were expanding, partly as a result of significant changes in the industrial economy. Private companies, owned by a single entrepreneur, were supplanted by public ownership; mergers and takeovers resulted in the formation of large companies with a wide range of production and financial interests. This promoted the growth of bureaucracy, which Weber considered to be a core feature of capitalist development, and produced new types of jobs. Such complex organizations needed armies of clerks, technicians, marketing specialists, and managers in order to function effectively. The professions also expanded, partly as a response to the many problems thrown up by industrialization.

As we saw earlier, Weber believed that the expansion of middle-class occupations had radically transformed the class structure, with competition between the two different sorts of propertyless worker (middle-class and working-class) becoming just as important as the original split between propertied and propertyless. While Marx in some of his later works had discussed the role of the new middle classes, conceiving them as a buffer between capital and labor, he under-estimated the social and political implications of such a development.

## 4.2   Sexual segregation and the growth of feminism

The expansion of the service sector had important effects for gender relations too. It provided new "respectable" jobs for both working- and middle-class women, especially in retailing and clerical work. Teaching was another expanding area which provided many jobs for women, along with the modernized nursing service established by Florence Nightingale. However, these increased opportunities left the structure of segregation intact. Indeed, contemporary ideas about which jobs are suitable for each sex have their origins in the period between 1850 and 1900, during which the sexual division of labor stabilized into something similar to its contemporary form. Women were concentrated in light, repetitive factory work, in the caring professions, and in lower-grade service jobs, just as they are today.

By the end of the nineteenth century the ideology of domesticity had become firmly established as the dominant way of thinking about women. It was now spreading to the working classes; the trade union movement endorsed the ideal of the family wage and the non-working wife (even if not many members achieved that ideal). Victorian ideas of sexual propriety also contributed to the segregation of the sexes (female and male office workers sometimes had to use separate doors to avoid bumping into one another!). The daily experience of men and of women was sharply differentiated.

But in opposition to this arose the movement for sexual equality, initiated by upper-class and middle-class women like Florence Nightingale, who found the restrictions placed on them intolerable. The Victorian feminist movement started in the late 1850s and rapidly gained momentum and support. Its campaigns for educational, economic, and social rights for women all had some effect. Higher education was slowly opened up to women (against voluble opposition from male students and professors); professions such as medicine admitted their first female entrants; women sat on school boards and local government bodies. Frances Power Cobbe's exposé of marital violence among the working classes, which she called "wife torture," led to working-class women getting the right to legal separation in 1878, and divorce reform slowly followed. The Married Women's Property Acts of 1870 and 1882 allowed women control of their own earnings and the property they brought into marriage. Feminists also tried to improve the lot of working-class women, encouraging them to form their own trade unions. By 1900 the fight for female suffrage had become the key issue of the feminist movement and once it was achieved the movement lost its impetus, although women could then use parliamentary procedures to campaign on issues. At its height, however, the Victorian feminist movement posed an important challenge to the ideology of domesticity, although it can be argued that most of the benefits were felt by middle-class women and had little impact on working-class women's lives.

Victorian feminism represented the first major onslaught against the structures of patriarchal control, as feminists campaigned for greater equity within the family and started to push into the public sphere. However, they failed to break down the structure of gender-based job segregation which remained a key feature of the capitalist industrial system.

# 5   Conclusion

By 1900 the class and gender relations of the maturing industrial capitalist economy had consolidated themselves on a basis which would not alter much until the 1950s. Britain was still a society rigidly divided on class lines, with little contact between the classes. The material position of working people did not improve substantially. Their standard of living remained modest and the threat of destitution and the Poor Law continued. Foreign holidays, cars, and refrigerators were as yet undreamed-of luxuries for the mass of working people.

Gender hierarchies, too, remained in place. Despite the fact that the legal framework of patriarchy was being dismantled, men continued in reality to dominate in the home and at work, and male control of the public sphere was furthered by the rigidifying of the sexual division of labor. Women's contributions to the economy in World War I posed only a short-term challenge to established ideas about gender roles, with the pre-war division of labor rapidly being restored afterwards. Before World War II, the ideology of domesticity was as strong as ever, with many organizations requiring women to give up their jobs when they married. Women and men continued to inhabit separate spheres.

This chapter has traced inequalities of class and gender in Britain through from 1800 to 1945. I hope I have demonstrated to you how particular patterns of class inequality were generated by the emergence of an industrial system of production organized on a capitalist base. Gender inequalities were not produced by capitalism, as pre-industrial societies were already patriarchal. But my argument has been that male dominance at work was deepened by industrial capitalism, which produced a more rigid sexual division of labor, and that patriarchy in the family was also initially strengthened by the separation of home and work, although it began to break down at the end of the century.

The historical developments I have described are specific to Britain. In considering other societies, we would have to take into account variations caused by differing historical and cultural antecedents, differing political contexts, and degrees of state intervention in social development, as well as the fact that capitalist economic development takes place at different paces, with a different balance of sectors and a different technological trajectory, in each society. Moreover, all these differences can also operate *within* each society, leading to marked local and regional variations. Nonetheless, we can still trace out broadly similar trends in other industrial societies. They share a common history of working-class deprivation with a struggle to improve living standards, and a common patriarchal legacy, fostering gender stereotyping and segregation. These similarities arise from their shared economic system and from the way that industrial capitalism was historically founded on a pre-industrial patriarchal base.

Since 1945, the British social formation has undergone some dramatic changes. But many of the conditions which generated the inequalities I have described still exist. Industrial production is still carried out on the basis of capitalist ownership, the profit imperative, the sub-division of the work process, and the powerlessness of the laborers. Gender segregation in employment is still marked, and the domestic ideal still casts its shadow on women's lives. Although patriarchy has been greatly eroded and the class structure has been further fragmented, class and gender hierarchies remain in force; and, as individuals, our own life chances will in part be determined by the way in which those hierarchies interact. I hope this discussion of how those hierarchies originated and have shifted as societies have developed will help you towards an understanding of contemporary social formations.

# References

Clark, A. (1982) *Working Life of Women in the Seventeenth Century*, London, Routledge.

Ehrenreich, B. and English, D. (1979) *For Her Own Good*, London, Pluto.

Firestone, S. (1979) *The Dialectic of Sex*, London, Women's Press.

Giddens, A. (1973) *The Class Structure of the Advanced Societies*, London, Hutchinson.

Hall, C. (1980) "The history of the housewife," in Malos, E. (ed.) *The Politics of Housework*, London, Allison and Busby.

Hartmann, H. (1976) "Patriarchy, capitalism and job segregation by sex," *Signs*, vol. 1, no. 3, pp. 137–68.

Hartmann, H. (1981) "The unhappy marriage of Marxism and feminism," in Sargent, L. (ed.) *Women in Revolution*, London, Pluto.

Hobsbawm, E. (1968) *Industry and Empire*, Harmondsworth, England, Penguin.

Holcombe, L. (1973) *Victorian Ladies at Work*, Newton Abbot, England, David and Charles.

Laslett, P. (1965) *The World We Have Lost*, London, Methuen.

Macfarlane, A. (1978) *The Origins of English Individualism*, Oxford, Basil Blackwell.

Malcolmson, R. (1981) *Life and Labour in England, 1700–80*, London, Hutchinson.

Marx, K. (1976) *Capital*, vol. 1, Harmondsworth, England, Penguin.

Marx, K. and Engels, F. (1934) *The Communist Manifesto*, in *Selected Works*, vol. 1, London, Lawrence and Wishart.

Mathias, P. (1969) *The First Industrial Nation*, London, Methuen.

Millett, K. (1971), *Sexual Politics*, London, Sphere.

Ruskin, J. (1965) *Sesame and Lilies*, London, Dent.

Shorter, E. (1976) "Women's work: what difference did capitalism make?," *Theory and Society*, vol. 3, no. 4, pp. 513–19.

Smith, A. (1937) *The Wealth of Nations*, New York, Random House.

Thompson, E.P. (1968) *The Making of the English Working Class*, Harmondsworth, England, Penguin.

Walby, S. (1988) "The historical periodisation of patriarchy"; paper presented at the 1988 Annual Conference of the British Sociological Association.

Weber, M. (1938) *The Protestant Ethic and the Spirit of Capitalism*, London, Unwin.

Weber, M. (1964) *The Theory of Social and Economic Organization*, London, Macmillan.

# 5    The Cultural Formations of Modern Society

Robert Bocock

## Contents

| | | |
|---|---|---:|
| 1 | Introduction | 150 |
| 2 | Defining Culture | 151 |
| 3 | Analyzing Culture | 154 |
| 3.1 | Collective representations | 157 |
| 3.2 | Primitive classification | 159 |
| 3.3 | Structuralist developments | 161 |
| 4 | Culture and Social Change | 163 |
| 4.1 | Religion and the rise of capitalism | 164 |
| 4.2 | Orientations of the world religions | 167 |
| 4.3 | Western culture, science, and values | 169 |
| 5 | The Costs of Civilization | 171 |
| 5.1 | Increasing rationality | 171 |
| 5.2 | Disenchantment with the modern world | 175 |
| 5.3 | Civilization and its discontents | 178 |
| 5.4 | The Frankfurt School | 180 |
| 6 | Conclusion | 181 |
| References | | 182 |

# 1   Introduction

> Culture is one of the two or three most complicated words in the
> English language . . . This is so partly because of its intricate
> historical development, in several European languages, but mainly
> because it has now come to be used for important concepts in
> several distinct intellectual disciplines and in several distinct and
> incompatible systems of thought.
> (Williams, 1983, p. 87)

In earlier units we looked at crucial moments, processes, and ideas in
the historical development of the political, economic, and social
spheres of modern societies. This chapter examines another part of the
story – namely, the formation of modern culture. As the quotation
above indicates, "culture" is a complex term and carries particular
meanings in different disciplines. We shall start, therefore, in the next
section, by considering what the term "culture" means and examining
its use as a sociological concept.

As we shall see, in the most important sociological use of the term,
culture is understood as referring to the whole texture of a society and
the way language, symbols, meanings, beliefs, and values organize
social practices. The sociological analysis of culture in this sense has
led to the development of a distinctive "tool-kit" of concepts and forms
of classification. A number of these derive from what is called a
structuralist approach and may at first seem rather abstract and
theoretical. These concepts will be introduced and explained in section
3, which will also examine how they have been used to analyze
cultural formations and cultural phenomena in the work of Émile
Durkheim and Claude Lévi-Strauss.

The structuralist perspective has been criticized as of limited value
in addressing questions of cultural change, and therefore as being rather
different from more traditional sociological analyses of culture which
are very much concerned with questions of how cultures change.
Section 4 will consider the transition in western society from a feudal
to a capitalist culture by focusing on Max Weber's argument that it was
a distinctive form of *religious* thinking which led to the unique, and
uniquely successful, culture of capitalism which developed in the
West. Weber's approach provides a different methodology for analyzing
culture, but there are significant links with Durkheim's, notably in
according religion a central role in determining cultural formation.

Finally, we shall examine the cultural changes associated with
industrialization, urbanization, and secularization which emerged
towards the end of the nineteenth century. Analyses by Weber, Marx,
Freud, and the Frankfurt School of social scientists all point to a
growing disillusion with this scientific and rationalist culture and
further show the significance of values and beliefs as constituents of
culture. In reading about the ways in which some of the greatest of
sociologists have set about classifying societies, and explaining cultural
change, we learn something important. It is that, in attempting to

analyze a pattern of behavior in any given society, we are forced to
reflect on how individuals *think*, communicate, and attribute meaning
to things. The attempt to relate individual experience to the wider
social structure is the essence of sociology, and at its heart is the
concept of culture.

# 2   Defining Culture

The meaning of the term "culture" has changed over time, especially in
the period of the transition from traditional social formations to
modernity.

The **first** and earliest meaning of "culture" can be found in writing of
the fifteenth century, when the word was used to refer to the tending of
crops (cultivation) or looking after animals. This meaning is retained in
modern English in such words as "agriculture" and "horticulture."

The **second** meaning developed in the early sixteenth century. It
extended the idea of "cultivation" from plants and animals to more
abstract things, like the human mind. Francis Bacon, for example,
wrote of "the culture and manurance of minds" (1605) and Thomas
Hobbes of "a culture of their minds" (1651). There soon developed the
idea that only some people – certain individuals, groups, or classes –
had "cultured" or cultivated minds and manners; and that only some
nations (mainly European ones) exhibited a high standard of culture or
civilization.

By the eighteenth century, Raymond Williams observed, "culture"
had acquired distinct class overtones. Only the wealthy classes of
Europe could aspire to such a high level of refinement. The modern
meaning of the term "culture" which associates it with "the arts" is also
closely related to this definition, since it refers not only to the actual
work of artists and intellectuals, but to the general state of civilization
associated with the pursuit of the arts by a cultivated elite. Raymond
Williams commented that "this seems often now the most widespread
use: *culture* is music, literature, painting, and sculpture, theatre and
film . . . sometimes with the addition of philosophy, scholarship and
history" (Williams, 1983, p. 87).

However, the notion of culture has been extended in the twentieth
century to include the "popular culture" of the working class and the
lower middle class – a popular culture which is penetrated by, though
not the same as, the contents of the mass media (film, television, sports,
popular music, newspapers, and magazines). Rather than this popular
culture being an extension of the notion of the cultivated tastes of a
"cultured person," it is in tension with or can be said to have displaced
it. There is often a sharp distinction drawn between "high" and
"popular" culture, and the popular arts are sometimes seen as
antagonistic to the fine arts.

Note that there is an interplay here between using such words as
"cultivated" and "cultured" in a *descriptive* way (e.g. in characterizing
the arts and artistic pursuits) and using them in an *evaluative* way

which implies that some ways of life or some kinds of taste are of higher value than others. Much of what is sometimes called the "cultural debate" about standards in the arts and the debasement of high culture by mass culture, stems from this ambiguity between the descriptive and the evaluative uses of the word "culture."

A **third** definition of "culture," which has been most influential in the social sciences, stems from the Enlightenment. In the eighteenth century, writers used the word to refer to the general secular process of social development (as in "European society and culture"). The Enlightenment view, common in Europe in the eighteenth century, was that there was a process of unilinear, historical self-development of humanity, which all societies would pass through, and in which Europe played the central, universal role because it was the highest point of civilization or cultured human development.

An important qualification in this usage was introduced by the German writer Herder in his book *Ideas on the Philosophy of the History of Mankind* (1784–91). Herder criticized this Eurocentric "subjugation and domination of the four quarters of the globe." "The very thought of a superior European culture," he wrote, "is a blatant insult to the majesty of Nature."

> It is necessary, Herder argued, in a decisive innovation, to speak of "cultures" in the plural: the specific and variable cultures of social and economic groups within a nation [and between different nations]. This sense was widely developed, in the Romantic movement, as an alternative to the orthodox and dominant *"civilization"*. It was first used to emphasise national and traditional cultures, including the new concept of "folk-culture".
> (Williams, 1983, p. 89)

Herder's innovation has proved highly significant for the social sciences, especially sociology and anthropology. In this **fourth** definition, the word "cultures" (in the plural) refers to the distinctive ways of life, the shared values and meanings, common to different groups – nations, classes, subcultures (as, for example, in phrases like "working-class culture" or "bourgeois culture") – and historical periods. This is sometimes known as the "anthropological" definition of culture.

Finally, a **fifth** meaning of the word "culture" has emerged, which has had a considerable impact on all the social sciences and the humanities in general in recent years. It is derived from social anthropology, and like the fourth definition it refers to shared meanings within groups and nations. It differs in emphasis from the fourth definition, however, by concentrating more on the symbolic dimension, and on what culture *does* rather than on what culture *is*. It sees culture as a social practice rather than as a thing (the arts) or a state of being (civilization). This way of thinking about culture is grounded in the study of *language*, a practice which is seen as fundamental to the production of meaning. The anthropologist Lévi-Strauss, who did much to develop this approach, once described his own work as "the study of the life of signs at the heart of social life."

   Those who adopt this fifth definition of culture argue that language is a fundamental social practice because it enables those people who share a common language system to communicate meaningfully with one another. Society, which arises through relations between individuals, would be impossible without this capacity to communicate – to exchange meanings and thus build up a shared culture. According to this view, things and events in the natural world exist, but have no intrinsic meaning. It is language – our capacity to communicate about them, using signs and symbols (like words or pictures) – which gives them meaning. When a group shares a culture, it shares a common set of meanings which are constructed and exchanged through the practice of using language. According to this definition, then, "culture" is *the set of practices by which meanings are produced and exchanged within a group.*

   It is important not to adopt too restricted a view of language. It is not only words which operate like a language. All sign and symbol systems work in this way. By language we mean any system of communication which uses signs as a way of referencing objects in the real world and it is this process of *symbolization* which enables us to communicate meaningfully about the world. Words create meaning because they function as symbols. Thus, the word "dog" is the symbol or sign for the animal that barks. (We must not confuse the symbol for the real thing; as one linguist put it, a dog barks, but the word "dog" cannot bark!) We could also represent, or "say something meaningful" about the animal by a drawing, photograph, moving image, sculpture, cartoon, or cave painting. So, when we say that language is fundamental to culture, we are referring to *all* the symbol and sign-systems through which meaning is produced and circulated in our culture.

   Thus, even material objects can function as "signs." Two pieces of wood nailed together form the symbol of the Cross, which carries powerful meanings in Christian cultures. The crown is used as a symbol of secular or religious power and authority. Jeans and sweaters are signs of leisure and informality. There is a language of dress, of fashion, of appearance, of gestures, as there is a language for every other social activity. Each is a means of communicating meaning about this activity and the activity could not exist, as a social practice, outside of meaning. Thus every social activity has a *symbolic* dimension, and this dimension of symbolization and meaning is what we mean by "culture."

   In this fifth definition, cultural practices are meaning-producing practices, practices which use signs and symbols to "make meaning" – hence, they are often described as *signifying practices* (sign-ifying practices).

   Let us summarize. We have identified five main definitions of the term "culture":

1   Culture = cultivating the land, crops, animals.

2   Culture = the cultivation of the mind; the arts; civilization.

3   Culture = a general process of social development; culture as a universal process (the Enlightenment conception of culture).

4   Culture = the meanings, values, ways of life (cultures) shared by particular nations, groups, classes, periods (following Herder).

5   Culture = the practices which produce meaning; signifying practices.

None of these definitions has entirely disappeared. Each is still active in contemporary usage, as we shall discover as the argument of the chapter develops.

# 3   Analyzing Culture

Now that we have a better idea of what culture is, how do we go about analyzing it? This depends on which of the five definitions of "culture" we are using. Take the fourth and fifth definitions, which have had the most impact on the social sciences. According to the fourth definition, we should analyze the beliefs, values, and meanings – the powerful symbols – shared by a particular group, class, people, or nation. In section 4 of this chapter, when we discuss Weber and the transition from a religious to a secular culture, as Europe moved into the "modern" period, we shall do exactly that. But let us stay for the moment with the fifth definition – culture as "signifying practice" – in order to see what an analysis of culture using this definition looks like and how this method of analysis works.

The shift from the fourth definition (culture as shared meanings and ways of life) to the fifth definition (culture as the practices which produce meaning) marks a significant break in cultural analysis. Both definitions point to similar aspects of culture, but each focuses on very different things. The fourth concentrates on the meanings which groups share (e.g. religious beliefs); the fifth on the practices by which meanings are produced. Put another way, the fourth is concerned with the *contents* of a culture; the fifth with cultural *practices*. Also, the fourth focuses on culture as a whole way of life; the fifth concentrates on the interrelationships between the components that make up a particular cultural practice. One commentator has summed up this difference in approach as a movement "from 'what' to 'how', from the substantive attitude to the adjectival attitude" (Poole, 1969, p. 14). In looking, for example, at the totemic objects used in tribal cultures, anthropologists using the fourth definition would ask, "What is totemism?," whereas analysts using the fifth definition would ask, "How are totemic phenomena arranged?"

*Arrangement* is what the latter approach highlights. We can see what this means by taking an example. In analyzing a ritual event, such as a wedding feast or reception in traditional societies, an analysis which uses the fifth definition would begin by looking at who sits next to the bride and groom at the main table. The seating arrangement – the way parents, siblings, aunts and uncles, etc., are placed in relation to one another – has a clear pattern or *structure*. It also carries a clear meaning or message. In kinship systems where uncles rank as "closer" to children than their natural fathers, the position of honor next to the bride and groom would normally be occupied by the uncle, not the father.

This approach to the analysis of culture looks for meaning in the arrangement, the pattern, the symbolic structure of an event. That is why it became known as *structuralism*. The advent of structuralism as a methodology or approach marked an intellectual revolution in the analysis of culture. It was pioneered by the French anthropologist Claude Lévi-Strauss (b. 1908), who built upon ideas developed for the study of language by the linguist Ferdinand de Saussure (1857–1913). Lévi-Strauss was also influenced by the early founding figure of modern sociology, Émile Durkheim.

Structuralism, as we can see from the "wedding feast" example, looks at the symbolic structure of an event in order to discover its cultural meaning. However, it has been extensively criticized for being unable to deal with social change, and therefore for being ahistorical. Also, unlike more conventional approaches in social science, it does not treat culture as "reflecting" in some way the socio-economic structure of society (for example, the way the social class of the people getting married affects how much is spent on wedding receptions). In section 4 of this chapter, we shall examine the role which culture played in the great historical transition from traditional or feudal society to early modern capitalism, and this analysis of culture and historical change (based largely on the work of another of sociology's founding figures, Max Weber) will draw more directly upon conventional sociological analyses of culture. However, my general argument is that there need not be a competition between the two approaches. It is possible to combine some of the advances of both structuralism and the sociological analysis of cultural change; and a non-dogmatic structuralist approach can throw interesting light on the analysis of cultural change.

To explain how the structuralist analysis of culture emerged entails adopting what might be called a "structuralist" re-reading of a founding father of sociology, Émile Durkheim (1858–1917). I shall aim to show that Durkheim did work, and can be read, in a structuralist way. Why would anyone want to re-read Durkheim in this way? There are a number of reasons. One is that such a reading produces a reassessment of Durkheim's work. He has often been seen as having laid the foundations for a *positivistic* approach to sociology, as in his requirement (in *The Rules of Sociological Method* and in *Suicide: A Study in Sociology*) that social scientists treat "social facts as things." Seen in this light, however, it becomes difficult to place his last major text *The Elementary Forms of the Religious Life* (1912) – a text about Australian aborigines and Amer-Indian culture, not monks, nuns, or priests!

This latter text of Durkheim's would seem to be of more interest to anthropologists who study pre-literate societies than to sociologists who study modern industrial societies. However, it is the *method* Durkheim uses in this text, and his claim that cultural elements are fundamental to understanding and analyzing *all* social formations, which are important. The method and type of analysis which Durkheim used in *The Elementary Forms of the Religious Life* are ones which can be seen as in broad respects "structuralist." To see what this claim entails, I want to discuss briefly the roots of structuralism in two other authors — Ferdinand de Saussure and Claude Lévi-Strauss. Their work affects how we might read Durkheim's *The Elementary Forms of the Religious Life* now, towards the end of the twentieth century.

Saussure introduced an important distinction in the way in which language could be studied and, by extension, the ways in which culture more broadly might be approached. He distinguished between two levels of language: language as a social institution, with its own structures, independent of the individual; and language as used and spoken by an individual user. He termed the social institution of language *langue*; that is, language as a collective system, with its own grammatical structure. Language in this sense is distinct from any single individual's use of his or her own language in everyday speech or writing, which Saussure termed *parole*. Saussure made the important point that language had to be seen as a social institution and as such was not the creation of an individual speaker. The structure, or system, of a language can also be studied outside of historical changes, for although vocabulary may change as new words are introduced and old ones die away, the grammar and structure of a language remain more stable and can be distinguished from such changes. Saussure called the kind of study of language which freezes change in order to look at structure the *synchronic* study of language, and he called the historical type of study of language *diachronic*. Synchronic means "occurring at the same time"; diachronic means "across time." It is an important distinction of which to be aware in the analysis of culture as a whole, not only of language.

Lévi-Strauss argued that a culture operates "like a language." He took from Saussure the idea of language having a given structure; that is, a set of grammatical and other, deeper, rules about how to communicate, which lie below the consciousness of any individual speaker and which are not dependent on individual consciousness of them. Lévi-Strauss applied some of these ideas about language to other cultural items, such as myths, rituals, and kinship structures, as we shall see in section 3.3. There is an important methodological point or claim here — namely that the social scientist should analyze how a structure of any kind operates as a structure before he or she is in a position to know what counts as changes, or variations, *within* a structure and what counts as a change *of* a structure. (For example, a change from an elected Democratic to an elected Republican government would be a change *within* a political structure; a change to a fascist regime, with the abolition of elections, would be a change *of* the structure.)

Synchronic structuralist analysis concentrates in the first instance on change *within* a cultural system of some kind, whether it be a system of myth and ritual, of kinship, of food and cooking and eating patterns, or whatever. We shall turn to changes *of* structures (that is, *diachronic* analysis) in section 4 of this chapter. In the rest of section 3 we shall concentrate on the analysis of cultural structures, considered as operating independently of major historical changes.

The analysis which Durkheim provided in *The Elementary Forms of the Religious Life* was not explicitly structuralist – this terminology only entered the discourse of the social sciences after his death. However, the seeds of such an approach are to be found there. The common point of departure which Durkheim and the structuralists share is that both begin from the underlying framework, the classifying systems, the structures of a culture, and both start with an analysis of what Durkheim called "collective representations."

## 3.1 Collective representations

During the eighteenth and nineteenth centuries, tradesmen and missionaries sent back reports to France, Britain, Germany, and other European countries about the ways of life of other peoples in Asia, Africa, the Americas, and Australasia (see chapter 6). Many of these reports were not only descriptive accounts, but also contained the emotional and moral responses of the European travellers to these other ways of living. Social science analyses of such societies were not written until anthropologists began the more systematic approach of trying to grasp and describe a particular people's way of living in a more objective, non-judgmental, non-value-laden way.

Durkheim used these reports as a basis for his work. He did not visit the Australian aborigines or the Amer-Indian societies about which he wrote. However, the important claims which he made are not, as we shall see, dependent upon being proved right or wrong by empirical data. What his work provides are basic theoretical propositions which formed the foundations for later, more empirical, studies by other anthropologists and sociologists. The strength of Durkheim's analysis lies in the fact that he developed a whole new *approach* to the understanding of culture through his analysis of the religious beliefs and rituals in these societies.

Central to this approach was the concept of *collective representations.* By the term "representations" Durkheim meant the cultural beliefs, moral values, symbols, and ideas shared by any human group. Such cultural components serve as a way of representing the world meaningfully to members of a particular cultural group. It is not a question of asking what it is that such cultural items represent in the outside world, as though there could be true or false representations. Myths, which are literally false, have powerful meanings and real effects. Representations create a symbolic world of meanings within which a cultural group lives. For Durkheim this included such fundamental notions as the particular way time and space are perceived in a culture, as well as its moral and religious beliefs. This approach accepts that different people inhabit different cultures, or symbolic worlds of meaning. It avoids the question of how we, from our western cultural background, would judge which of a set of beliefs and ideas are "true" or "false," since this would only tell us what we find acceptable and congruent within our own cultural framework. The issue of the truth or falsehood of different cultural worlds is thus side-stepped by using the concept of "representations" in a more relativistic, descriptive way.

The cultural values, beliefs, and symbols of a group (its representations) are produced and shared *collectively* by those who are members of the group. Like a language, they are not produced by individuals as a result of their own cultural initiative, as one might say. Indeed, in both pre-literate and modern societies, individuals who produce their own values, beliefs, and symbol systems are frequently ostracized by others, treated with hostility, regarded as mad, or tolerated as interesting eccentrics. In any case, they are not treated as full members of the group, precisely because they do not share its cultural meanings. We learn our cultural group's language, values, beliefs, and symbols as we are socialized. Even the basic layers of a person's sense of identity, of who he or she is, is produced by being a member of a specific ethnic, national, or tribal group.

Durkheim's theory of culture starts from the claim that the major symbolic components of culture are *representations* which are *collectively* produced, reproduced, transmitted, and transformed. The notion of collective representations is, therefore, the foundation of both Durkheim's approach to culture and the claim, made by structuralists, that cultural symbols are central to all sociology and social anthropology. Durkheim included in his definition of collective representations even such general conceptions as time, space, personality, and number. They provide the broad frameworks within which the social cultural life, the shared language and symbolic representations of human groups, are organized. Their existence does not require reference to some abstract cause such as "reason" or "God." Durkheim argued that this insight into the necessarily *social* nature of meanings could dissolve, or resolve, the older problems which philosophy had encountered in trying to give a satisfactory account of how forms of knowledge arose.

In *The Elementary Forms of Religious Life* Durkheim claims that even the most basic categories of thought, such as ideas of time, space, number, and causation, are also collective representations – socially shared frameworks within which individual experience is classified. These social categories of thought form the backbone – the symbolic structures – of any culture. As Durkheim says: "They are like the solid frame which encloses all thought." Such frameworks have been accounted for by traditional philosophers as being *either* part of innate reason, in-built at birth, and known *a priori* or independently of experience (rationalism); *or* as something worked out by the individual from empirical observations (empiricism). Durkheim, however, argues that reason cannot be a purely individual construction, for then it could not provide a common standard of judgment. For Durkheim, the notion of "reason" implies some socially shared standards of what is to count as a good, well-reasoned argument.

Durkheim rejects both the rationalist and the empiricist accounts of our basic categories of thought. He argues that the fundamental categories we need in order to think systematically and rationally are socially – that is, collectively – produced. Society is a reality of a unique kind, what Durkheim calls a reality "*sui generis*," and this enables groups to achieve more than individuals alone are able to accomplish. Indeed, he maintains that it is necessary to assert the discontinuity between these two realms: the societal and the individual. Hence the importance of "collective representations." Collective representations enable individual people to think. But they are produced at the level of the collective. We learn them as we learn our group's language. Language is also inherently social, or collective – an idea Durkheim suggests elsewhere in *The Elementary Forms of the Religious Life*, though he did not develop it as fully as later linguistic philosophers did.

How does this idea of "collective representations" work within a culture? Durkheim's answer is that they provide the categories, the basic frameworks, into which different items of a culture are classified. Classification schemes tell us which things belong together and which things are different. They help us to "map out" or make sense of the world. Durkheim first studied this process of cultural classification in so-called "primitive" societies.

## 3.2  Primitive classification

Early in the twentieth century, anthropologists were struck by the way in which the cultures of pre-literate societies frequently contained complex systems for classifying animals, people, plants, and objects of many kinds. Within these classification systems, particular plants, animals, or objects (i.e. *totems*) were also associated with or used to represent particular groups, clans, or tribes. The classification system thus showed which totem belonged with which group, and so helped to establish a collective sense of identity among all the members of a particular clan. It also served to establish the boundary between that group and other groups, represented by different totemic objects. Totems were thus a key part of classificatory systems in many primitive, or pre-literate, cultures. Totemic systems provided a sort of classificatory map of the society.

Such cultures were socially organized around complex patterns of kinship. Indeed, kinship was their principal form of social organization. Kinship told members of these societies who was related to whom, who they could and could not marry, who should inherit property, and who their "enemies" were. Kinship in this context meant wider sets of relations than the immediate family of grandparents, parents, and children, which is how we classify kin relations in western societies. Kinship groups would certainly include not only aunts, uncles, cousins, brothers, and sisters, but also people who in the West would not count as blood relations at all, and therefore would not be regarded as part of the kinship network.

The analysis of classification systems, for Durkheim, like the analysis of symbolic structures for Lévi-Strauss, was fundamental to all cultural analysis. Lévi-Strauss argued that the process of classification replicated the way in which the human brain operates – in terms of pairs. Things arranged or divided into twos, or pairs, are easy for humans to remember. Lévi-Strauss pointed out that in pre-literate cultures, and we might add in modern cultures too, such pairs usually appear as opposed in some way to each other. Thus, we have oppositions such as the following: hot/cold; cooked/raw; sour/sweet; wet/dry; solid/liquid; earth/air; the city/the country, etc. You can see from this list how fundamental this division into "binary opposites" is to meaning. We know what "cooked" means because it is the opposite of "raw." The pairs work in relation to one another. One fundamental pair is male/female. This is fundamental in that it both operates as a basis for marriage and sexual reproduction and provides human cultures with a general model, based on sexual difference, for thinking in terms of pairs of differences. Some languages, such as French, have feminine and masculine words for objects in the world, for example.

Lévi-Strauss called this basic principle of paired oppositions which lies behind all classificatory systems *binary oppositions*. The term was derived from the basic way in which computer languages operate – either there is an electrical current flowing or there is not (which can be indicated by a plus or minus sign, or dots and dashes, long or short signals, etc.). The important point here for Lévi-Strauss is that this binary way of thinking is not only found in so-called primitive societies. What Lévi-Strauss called "the savage mind" (i.e. thinking by classifying things into binary opposites) can also be found at the heart of the culture of modern, advanced societies.

There is one very fundamental binary opposition which is found in both pre-literate societies and, in a related but different form, in modern societies. Durkheim formulated it in *The Elementary Forms of the Religious Life* as a basic classification of all culture: the division of things into "the sacred" and "the profane."

The sacred, as Durkheim defined it, is *not* based upon a belief in supernatural entities, which others had used as a definition of religion. Some sacred activities were not dependent on supernatural beliefs, he claimed, as for example in some forms of Buddhism. The central dichotomy in pre-literate cultures, Durkheim claimed, was to be understood as separating those things, times, places, persons, animals, birds, stones, trees, rivers, mountains, plants, or liquids which were *set apart* (sacred) from *routine* (profane) uses in everyday activities. The sacred, he argued, is a fundamental category in such cultures. The distinction between the sacred and the profane involves both *beliefs*, which define what is classified as sacred in a culture, and *rituals*, which actively *set apart* particular elements, times, people, or places.

The experiences people have in their rituals are not based on something unreal, Durkheim argued, but upon a real force greater than, and operating outside of, the individual. But what is this force? Given the great variety of gods or spirits in which the members of different cultures have believed, it cannot simply be that they have all contacted the same god or spirit. Durkheim argued that, since "the unanimous sentiment of the believers of all times cannot be purely illusory" (Durkheim, 1961, p. 464), therefore the objective cause of the sensations of such people is not some supernatural being but *society* itself. In summarizing his long, complex argument on this point, Durkheim concluded *The Elementary Forms of the Religious Life* with the following statement of his sociological explanation for the existence, and indeed the persistence, of religions in human societies:

> ... we have seen that this reality, which mythologies have represented under so many different forms, but which is the universal and eternal objective cause of these sensations *sui generis* out of which religious experience is made, is society. ... society cannot make its influence felt unless it is in action, and it is not in action unless the individuals who compose it are assembled together and act in common. It is by common action that it takes consciousness of itself ...
> (Durkheim, 1961, pp. 465–6)

This is how Durkheim formulates his major claim that religious experience is not based upon illusions, but upon concrete social, collective, ritual actions or practices. Participants in such rituals (a wedding ceremony, for instance) are involved in a set of practices, often including eating a ceremonial meal, which bind them together into a collective. The wider cultural group's *values* are also affirmed in such rituals – how a husband and wife should live and how they should raise their children are often explicitly, or implicitly, articulated in marriage rites in modern Christianity. The force which people feel in such circumstances is the moral pressure arising from this belongingness, or social solidarity.

Similar rituals are still found in modern industrial societies. But there is a multiplicity of ethnic groups, religious groups, and socio-economic classes in such societies who do not share a single set of meanings, values, or beliefs. These kinds of societies have had to devise other rituals at the level of the nation-state in order to try to cement these divergent groups together. In Britain, the royal family, ceremonial occasions, even national emergencies like war, are major components in performing this task of binding diverse groups together into some sense of being part of a united society – with varying degrees of success.

The distinction between the profane and the sacred was called by Durkheim an elementary form of "primitive classification." That means not only a classification which is found in pre-literate societies, but one which is fundamental, primal, basic, to all human cultures. All social formations will have some beliefs, values, symbols, and rituals which are sacred or set apart from profane, everyday life. Even communist states in the twentieth century, whose regimes were explicitly against organized religion, nevertheless surrounded themselves with flags, parades, creeds, and ceremonials – the symbols and rituals of rulers.

## 3.3 Structuralist developments

We have seen, then, how the structuralist's concern with analyzing the symbolic structure of events was rooted in Durkheim's work on

collective representations and primitive classification systems.
(Durkheim had worked with the anthropologist Marcel Mauss in a
study of *Primitive Classification* (1903).) Lévi-Strauss, the French
anthropologist, who worked in South America, applied the principle of
binary opposites as a central feature of all classifying systems to a wide
variety of cultural phenomena. He studied Kinship Structures in *The
Elementary Structures of Kinship* (1949), the totemic systems of pre-
literate societies (*Totemism*, 1962), the myths of South American
peoples (in *The Raw and the Cooked* (1970) and *Honey and Ashes*
(1973)), and a variety of other anthropological phenomena (in *The
Savage Mind* (1962) and *Structural Anthropology* (1958)). In all of these
studies he applied the basic structuralist method of analysis. The object
of analysis was, as it were, frozen in time (synchronic), so that its
symbolic structure could be analyzed. The structure was analyzed in
terms of how its different elements were classified and arranged, how
the principle of "binary opposition" (and the mediating categories
which fitted neither sides of the binary) worked. What mattered was the
*relations between* the different elements in the classifying system
(remember the positions at the wedding feast?). The *meaning* of each
pattern or structure was "read" in terms of what it told us about the
culture. The underlying "code" (e.g. the kinship system) provided the
analyst with a way of deciphering the phenomenon.

   Such a structuralist method can be applied to any cultural pattern,
regardless of the historical period in which it may be found. What we
think of as "primitive" ways of thinking may be found both among
Australian aborigines and in modern cultures. A British anthropologist,
Mary Douglas, writing in the 1960s, has used a structuralist method to
argue that there are significant *continuities* in notions of pollution,
taboo, and ritual rules, especially about food and drinks, body
substances, and clothing, between traditional and modern cultures, in
spite of the development of modern science (Douglas, 1966). The
reactions to AIDS among westerners, some newspapers labelling it the
"gay plague," illustrates that pollution ideas have not disappeared from
modern cultures.

   We have been looking at a particular method of analysis of culture.
The method can be applied to a variety of components of a culture,
from language to rituals, from cooking and types of food eaten to
fundamental categories of thought, such as space, time, and causation.
All these diverse cultural phenomena can be analyzed as structures,
which arrange and order perceptions and regulate actions among those
who share the same cultural frameworks, the same way of "classifying"
the world. The method is applicable in the broad area which may be
termed "the symbolic." According to this conception of culture, tiny
things – small differences between the way in which food is prepared
and eaten, for instance – may be used to mark or symbolize a cultural
difference between groups, between who is a member and who is an
outsider. Different dietary habits, for example, mark major differences
between national groups, and mobilize powerful feelings of solidarity
or hostility, similarity and difference.

# 4   Culture and Social Change

So far we have been looking at culture in terms of a structural
arrangement, which carries a cultural meaning or provides us with a
clue as to the cultural codes and symbolic systems of classification
which form the frameworks of meaning in a particular society.
Essentially, as we have noted, this approach is *synchronic*. History,
movement, action seem to be omitted. Thus, we know which objects in
a society are classified "sacred," which "profane." But this approach is
not so good at telling us how changes in such cultural phenomena
occur – for example, how the "sacred" might decline, or change, when
Christian missionaries arrive. On a larger canvas, it is not so good at the
sort of *diachronic* analysis which would tell us, for example, what role
culture played historically in the transition of European societies from
feudalism to early capitalism, from a traditional to a modern form of
society. And yet some of the great figures in classical sociology have
argued that, contrary to conventional opinion, what we call *culture* did
play an enormously significant role – even, perhaps, served as one of
the main causal factors – in the historical transition to modernity. It is
certainly the case that one of the principal ways of characterizing that
transition is in terms of the move from a society in which religion
pervaded every aspect of social life (a religious or "sacred" culture, we
might say) to the much more secular (or "profane") culture, dominated
by materialistic and technological values, which is to be found in
modern, advanced industrial societies today. How are we to understand
and analyze this process of *secularization* which is typical of the
formation of modern culture?

This process of cultural change has been characterized by the
German sociologist Norbert Elias (1897–1990) as *the civilizing process*
(in two volumes published just before World War II called *The
Civilizing Process* (1939)). This term takes us back to the second
definition of culture discussed in section 2. Elias attributes the process
of pacification of medieval society to the development of individual,
moral forms of restraint and control. He analyzes these by studying the
spread of social codes of behavior, such as table manners and etiquette.
Elias also points out how this process had been accompanied by the
emergence of the state as a system of social regulation. The modern
state assisted the development of *internal* peace through its monopoly
control over the means of violence. Somewhat surprisingly, Elias sees
the modern state's control over the means of violence in a given
territory as also aiding the growth of "civilization," which required a
new individual sense of, and capacity for, self-restraint. Elias was
drawing here upon the ideas of the German sociologist Max Weber
(1864–1920) in developing his view of the conditions necessary for
modern "civilization."

Max Weber had indeed emphasized the modern state's control over
the means of violence, but his more significant contribution in this
context was his extensive analysis of the role of cultural values and

religious beliefs in the development of western capitalism. Weber was writing at about the same time as Durkheim wrote *The Elementary Forms of the Religious Life*, but his approach is very different, and provides us with a different methodology for analyzing culture. Weber is much less concerned with the formal practices and rules of symbolic classification and much more concerned with the role which values play in major historical transitions. Above all, the question which preoccupied Weber was this: How did capitalism, the economic system which underpins "modernity," arise and what part did religious values play in that evolution?

## 4.1   Religion and the rise of capitalism

Weber was not a structuralist – indeed the method did not emerge in an explicit form in the social sciences in Weber's lifetime. Nevertheless, his work can also be seen to depend upon a series of binary oppositions which he used to *classify* types of capitalism and types of cultural symbols, though this has not often been remarked on by contemporary sociologists. For example, Weber distinguished between what he called "adventurer capitalism" and "rational, peaceable, bourgeois capitalism." "Adventurer" capitalism was based upon the use of conquest and violence to extract profits. This was the predominant form during the European acquisition of colonies in Africa, Asia, and Latin America and the period of slavery in the Americas.

The second type, "bourgeois capitalism," was based on rational action, and non-violent means of exploiting labor. Weber argued that this new type of capitalism had emerged from a set of cultural values based on the notion of a vocation – that is, a calling from God. This was not like God's call to the Catholic priest to *leave* the world, but a calling which influenced behavior *in* the world.

Thus, as Weber wrote:

> One of the fundamental elements of the spirit of modern capitalism, and not only of that but of all modern culture: rational conduct on the basis of the idea of the calling, was born ... from the spirit of Christian asceticism. ...
>
> The Puritan wanted to work in a calling; we are forced to do so. For when asceticism was carried out of the monastic cells into everyday life, and began to dominate worldly morality, it did its part in building the tremendous cosmos of the modern economic order.
>
> (Weber, 1971, pp. 180–1)

Why does Weber attribute the rise of capitalism to the spirit of Christian asceticism? To grasp Weber's argument, we must look, first, at the distinction he makes between these two types of capitalism, and then at the role which the concepts of "rational" and "asceticism" play in his analysis.

Capitalism, in the sense of profitable economic activity, had existed for a very long time, and in many different societies. But only in Western Europe, from about the sixteenth century, was capitalism in its rational, modern form to be found on any extended scale. Here, "capitalism is identical with the pursuit of profit, and forever *renewed* by means of continuous, rational, capitalistic enterprise" (Weber, 1971, p. 17).

What Weber called "peaceable, bourgeois capitalism" is the predominant form which this development took in Europe (though exactly how "peaceful" the transition to it was in reality has been a subject of debate among historians). It developed as conditions for peaceful trade and production, stimulated by profit, expanded. (Weber's analysis of the rise of capitalism was briefly discussed in chapter 4.)

Now, an economic system driven by self-interest, the desire to maximize profit on a regular basis, to accumulate, invest, and expand wealth, seems to require a very materialistic set of values – the very opposite of the religious culture which predated the rise of capitalism in Western Europe. Thus, we are not surprised to discover that, as capitalism developed and expanded, so cultural values became increasingly *secularized*: that is, more concerned with the material world and less with the spiritual world, more preoccupied with attaining wealth in *this* world than with salvation in the next. Religion of course remains an active cultural force in capitalist societies, but it is confined to a smaller area of social life and is more restricted in its appeal as compared with the cultural universe in the societies of feudal Europe dominated by the Catholic faith. Secularization appears to be the major process affecting culture in the transition to modern capitalist societies.

However, the paradox which Weber develops in his work (especially *The Protestant Ethic and The Spirit of Capitalism*) is that *religion* played an absolutely critical role in the formation of early capitalism. Modern rational capitalism could not have emerged, he argues, without the mediation of religious culture, especially that variant associated with the Calvinist puritan sects of the seventeenth century. It was the "Protestant ethic" which helped to produce capitalism as a *distinctive* type of profit-making involving economic action based upon *sustained, systematic capital investment*, and employing *formally free labor* (not slavery). Weber wrote:

> . . . the Occident [West] has developed capitalism both to a quantitative extent, and (carrying this quantitative development) in types, forms, and directions which have never existed elsewhere. All over the world there have been merchants, wholesale and retail, local and engaged in foreign trade. Loans of all kinds have been made, and there have been banks with the most various functions, at least comparable to ours of, say, the sixteenth century. . . . This kind of entrepreneur, the capitalistic adventurer, has existed everywhere. With the exception of trade and credit and banking transactions, their activities were predominantly of an irrational and speculative character, or directed to acquisition by force, above all the acquisition of booty . . . by exploitation of subjects.
>
> The capitalism of promoters, large-scale speculators, concession hunters, and much modern financial capitalism even in peace

time, but, above all, the capitalism especially concerned with
exploiting wars, bears this stamp even in modern Western
countries, and some, but only some, parts of large-scale
international trade are closely related to it, to-day as always.

But in modern times the Occident has developed, in addition to
this, a very different form of capitalism which has appeared
nowhere else: the rational capitalistic organization of (formally)
free labour.

(Weber, 1971, pp. 20–1)

Weber placed considerable emphasis on the role of *rationality* in the
formation of early capitalism. What characterized "bourgeois"
capitalists was that they did not spend all the profits at once in
immediate pleasures and luxurious living. Capitalists had learned the
habits of thrift, of saving over a long period, so that they could (as in
the parable of the talents in the Bible) put money to good use: in short
they learned to accumulate and to invest. They also learned how to
calculate whether their activities yielded a profit in the long run, or
were making a loss, just as they constantly "reckoned up" how well
they were doing in the pursuit of salvation. In short, the capitalist
learned to organize economic behavior (like religious life) in regular,
systematic, long-term, instrumental ways for the purpose of increasing
wealth; that is, *rationally* maximizing profit. This adaption of means (of
economic action) to secure certain ends (profits) represented, in
essence, a *rationalization* of the whole sphere of economic behavior,
without which the sober, thrifty capitalist entrepreneur and the
rationally-organized capitalist enterprise could never have come into
existence.

But how did such a figure as the "bourgeois capitalist" first arise?
What inner compulsions converted the spendthrift feudal landlord into
the sober, respectable capitalist? How were these new cultural values
formed? How was a "culture of capitalism" or "capitalist spirit"
created? Weber's surprising answer is that it was created through the
compulsions of a certain type of *religious asceticism*. His argument was
that some moral force had to compel the new capitalist entrepreneur to
forego immediate pleasures and short-term gratifications in the interests
of the *rational* pursuit of profitable enterprise in the long run. In other
words, far from capitalism emerging because of a *loss* of religious
values, the presence of a certain type of religious culture was *necessary*
*to* its formation. But which type of religious culture best provided the
seedbed for this new spirit of capitalist enterprise? Not Catholicism,
Weber believed, since it allowed men and women to pursue pleasure,
provided they confessed, repented, and sought forgiveness from the
Church. It did not create a tough enough personal inner conscience to
drive the capitalist into sober, rational, entrepreneurial activity. So
Weber turned to Protestantism.

There were basically two types of Protestantism: that which believed
that a person could work for salvation by doing good deeds in the
world; and that variant which believed that the decision as to who
would be saved and who damned was God's alone and that people had

to live their lives as spiritually as possible, watching their every action in the hope of salvation, but never knowing whether they were among God's "elect" or not. It seems obvious that Weber would have chosen the version which stressed "doing good in the world" as the seedbed of capitalist worldly activity. But in fact he chose the latter, the Calvinist Puritanism, which believed in predestination and the arbitrary will of God, as the most likely candidate. Why? Because, according to Calvinism, the individual could not depend on the Church for salvation but was constantly and directly under the stern eye of God. Not knowing whether or not "he" (for most early capitalists were men) would be saved created:

1 a powerful inner compulsion (conscience) to order "his" life in the rational pursuit of salvation; and

2 a permanent state of "unsettledness," never knowing the outcome, which kept "him" on the straight and narrow path, prevented any backsliding, and drove him forward relentlessly.

Calvinism, Weber argued, was the type of religious asceticism which helped to form the inner character of the entrepreneurs who pioneered the transition to early capitalism. This was the link which Weber constructed between "the Protestant ethic" and the "spirit of capitalism."

## 4.2 Orientations of the world religions

To understand why Weber fastened on asceticism as a key component of the Protestant ethic, we need to know something more about how he classified or built a *typology* of the different world religions and the cultures which they produced.

Weber's work on the world religions is pitched at a global and comparative level of analysis. He wrote about Chinese, Indian, and Jewish cultures as well as the culture of Western Europe. Unfortunately, he produced no full text on Islamic culture, but his writing on the Middle East is extensive. Each of these cultures was based on what he called a "world religion."

Weber argued that the major world cultures and their religions can be classified according to the main attitudes or orientations which each fosters towards three aspects of the world:

1 The world of nature – soils, animals, plants, rivers, seas, fish, trees, etc.

2 Other people – who may be seen as sub-humans, inferiors, as slightly different, or as equals.

3 The body – the human body, a person's own body, which is not just another part of nature, but is usually seen as being "special."

Here, Weber can be seen using the method of classificatory systems and binary oppositions as a way of contrasting the cultures generated by the world religions. He contrasts Oriental (eastern) religions (Confucianism, Hinduism, Taoism, and Buddhism) with Occidental (western) religions (Judaism, Christianity, and Islam). There was a major thrust in the oriental cultures (in China and India especially) towards seeking *harmony with* the natural world, other people, and the body. This set of attitudes, or value-orientations, contrasts with those found in the cultures of the "Middle East," in Persia, Palestine, Arabia, and North Africa, where the main thrust of the religious culture was towards seeking *mastery over* the world of nature, other people, and the body. The first type of orientation Weber called "mysticism" (seeking *harmony* with); the second "asceticism" (seeking *mastery* over).

Weber also made use of another "binary opposition" – that between "inner-worldly" and "other-worldly" religious orientations. What he had in mind here were the specialist types of roles which developed for leaders (or what he called the "virtuosi") in different religions – those with a special gift for practicing the meditative techniques of religion and those who carried high social esteem, honor, and prestige. Unfortunately the way Weber's terminology has been translated into English has proved very confusing. "Inner-worldly" suggests turning away from the world and becoming preoccupied with one's inner spiritual life. For Weber, it meant exactly the opposite. It meant turning *in towards* the world. It is important to bear this point in mind. "Other-worldly" refers to those roles which are removed from everyday tasks – such as the monk, nun, priest, scholar, artist, or intellectual. "Inner-worldly" refers to those roles which carry high honor and esteem *in* the world: merchant, politician, ruler, army general, or naval officer.

The two distinctions can be combined to produce four possible types of social role which may be given the highest social esteem within a specific society. The four types are shown in table 5.1.

Table 5.1   Four types of religious orientation according to Weber

| Direction of religion | Orientations of esteemed roles | |
| --- | --- | --- |
| | Inner-worldly | Other-worldly or world-rejecting |
| Mysticism | 1 | 2 |
| Asceticism | 3 | 4 |

By combining the two sets of distinctions, we can identify four positions or types of religious orientation.

*Type 1*   Inner-worldly mysticism – Hinduism; Taoism; Confucianism.

*Type 2*   Other-worldly mysticism – Buddhism; Sufism.

*Type 3*   Inner-worldly asceticism – Calvinism.

*Type 4*   Other-worldly asceticism – Catholicism; some popular forms of Islam; Orthodox Judaism.

The important example in the typology, so far as the transition to capitalism is concerned, is Type 3. "Inner-worldly ascetic" religion produced a culture whose central values were:

1   seeking mastery over the natural world;

2   seeking mastery over other people who are seen as being prone to sinfulness, wickedness, sensuality, and laziness;

3  seeking mastery over the self – by controlling impulses to the sensual enjoyment of bodily experiences arising from wearing fine clothes, make-up, or perfumes, consuming good food and wine, or other alcoholic drinks, and above all sexual pleasure, both inside and outside marriage.

Weber claimed that this set of cultural values had emerged *uniquely* from the later forms of Calvinism in the late 1500s and early 1600s, especially among Puritan groups in Britain, Holland, and New England where early capitalism took firm root. The religious culture of inner-worldly asceticism had provided the seedbed for the formation of the "rational spirit" of modern capitalism.

Weber acknowledged that other material, technological, economic, and financial conditions needed to be fulfilled for modern, rational, bourgeois capitalism to become a possibility. Many non-European civilizations had come close to producing these material factors – Chinese, Indian, and Arab civilizations, for example, were highly developed technologically and economically, long before many parts of Europe. However, these other civilizations had not developed modern forms of capitalism, although they conducted trade for profit. Weber argued that the critical feature which these other cultures lacked was the cultural values which would have enabled rational capitalism to develop.

Many of the major world religions were not compatible with the way of life which rational capitalism imposed on culture. Traditional religions were difficult or impossible to practice faithfully in the new conditions created by modern capitalism. On the other hand, Weber also became convinced that scientific and technological values, which increasingly dominated modern capitalism, could not resolve the problem of values – of *how* we ought to live.

Science and modern capitalism were both aspects of a long historical process which Weber claimed was going on in western culture. This was a process in which *rationality* – the instrumental adaptation of means to ends – came to dominate more and more areas of life in western cultures. We shall examine this process in section 4.3 of this chapter.

## 4.3   Western culture, science, and values

Other world cultures – notably Chinese, Egyptian, and Islamic cultures – had made notable scientific discoveries. But western culture was unique in that it had developed modern science to an unprecedented degree. This process had begun in earnest with the Enlightenment, as you saw in chapter 1. Weber wrote in his Introduction to *The Protestant Ethic and the Spirit of Capitalism*:

> A product of modern European civilization, studying any problem of universal history, is bound to ask himself to what combination of circumstances the fact should be attributed that in Western civilization, and in Western civilization only, cultural phenomena

have appeared which (as we like to think) lie in a line of
development having *universal* significance and value.

Only in the West does a science exist at a stage of development
which we recognize today as valid. Empirical knowledge,
reflection on problems of the cosmos and of life, philosophical
and theological wisdom of the most profound sort, are not
confined to it, though in the case of the last the full development
of a systematic theology must be credited to Christianity under the
influence of Hellenism, since there were only fragments in Islam
and in a few Indian sects.
(Weber, 1971, p. 13)

One of the major distinctive characteristics of modern western
culture, then, was its scientific character and the prestige it attached to
"the scientific." Other world cultures developed empirical knowledge,
but this is not the same thing as theoretically organized science. They
also contained complex philosophical and theological reflections,
although these, Weber claimed, reached a higher level of development
in Ancient Greece and in medieval Europe than elsewhere. Notice,
however, Weber's questioning attitude to the supposed "universal
significance and value" of science in the above extract. Here is another
formulation which Weber gave to his concerns about science:

Science has created a cosmos of natural causality and has seemed
unable to answer with certainty the question of its own ultimate
presuppositions. Nevertheless science, in the name of "intellectual
integrity", has come forward with the claim of representing the
only possible form of a reasoned view of the world . . . something
has adhered to this cultural value which was bound to depreciate
it with still greater finality, namely, senselessness . . . all "culture"
appears as man's emancipation from the organically prescribed
cycle of natural life. For this reason culture's every step forward
seems condemned to lead to an ever more devastating
senselessness. The advancement of cultural values, however,
seems to become a senseless hustle in the service of worthless,
moreover self-contradictory, and mutually antagonistic ends.
(Weber, 1970, pp. 355–7)

There is an even more questioning or pessimistic tone in this passage.
Developing scientific rationality, Weber seems to be saying, absorbing
more and more of social life into its domain, leads not to the
"emancipation" which the Enlightenment hoped for, but to "a senseless
hustle in the service of worthless, . . . self-contradictory, . . . antagonistic
ends."

During the period in which Weber was writing, this pessimistic
assessment of the Enlightenment faith in reason and science became
more widespread. The philosopher Friedrich Nietzsche (1844–1900),
and the nihilists, for example, began to argue that there were no
grounds for making claims for any moral or political values which
everyone could accept. By the late nineteenth century, many writers
came to believe that western civilization had fallen into a state of

cultural crisis. It was a "civilization" only in the sense of being technologically advanced, especially in its industrial production processes. However, in the sphere of moral philosophy and values, European "civilization" had become nihilistic – it had nothing positive to say.

This pessimistic analysis, and its implications, underpinned Weber's comparative sociology of the world cultures and their relation to political and economic change.

# 5   The Costs of Civilization

Bryan Turner has recently argued that an essential feature of Weber's view of modernity is its ambiguity: "Modernization brings with it the erosion of meaning, the endless conflict of polytheistic values, and the threat of the iron cage of bureaucracy. Rationalization makes the world orderly and reliable, but it cannot make the world meaningful" (Turner, 1990, p. 6).

## 5.1   Increasing rationality

The rise of science and technology, the growth of western capitalism as a "rational" form of economic life, and of a political culture rooted in legal-rational laws or rules and procedure all came to be seen as part of a wider process going on in western cultures: the process Weber called "the increasing rationalization of more and more areas of life" (Weber, 1970). He made no distinction here between capitalism and socialism, both of which, he believed, led to an increasingly rational ordering of work, of the economic distribution of goods and services, and of social life in general. Both were in tension with more traditional cultures, where religion was the central component which formed ordinary people's attitudes and values.

The growth of bureaucracy as a form of organization in *both* capitalism and socialism was, for Weber, another source of evidence of the growing rationalization of modern culture. Bureaucracies were established as a means of achieving, in practice, values of *justice* (law courts) and *equality* (social security, for example). So modern cultures had derived considerable gains from the increasing rationality of social organization. But there were costs here too, when one compared modern societies with more traditional ones.

One strength of traditional cultures, as Weber saw it, lay in the fact that they offered people what he called "a solution to the problem of theodicy" (Weber, 1970). That is to say, they provided ways of explaining and justifying the ways of God to man (theodicies). In particular, they provided an answer to one of the most perplexing of human dilemmas – the moral problem of suffering. Why is there so much suffering in the world? Why do children and other innocent people, who wish no harm to others, suffer? Weber argued that every culture should provide some answer to, or explanation of, such existential questions. The role of culture was to give meaning to, or help people make sense of, life (Weber's whole sociological approach was directed towards the study of action which was "meaningful," or to which meaning could be given). The persistence of traditional cultures, he thought, could be explained in this way: their religious dimension did offer some way of handling these deep questions of human existence.

In order to become established and to persist over time in a culture, theodicies had to make sense to two groups of people:

1   The intellectuals, and scholars, who could read or write in literate cultures, or who were the priests, medicine men, shamans, or witch doctors – the "keepers of tribal and religious wisdom" – in pre-literate societies.

2   The main classes and strata in the rest of society – including the main property owners, small business and trading classes, farmers, herdsmen, warriors, peasants, artisans, and the urban working class where this had emerged.

Some theodicies, developed by the intellectuals, were popularized by priests, preachers, and teachers and, in that form, were picked up by and caught on among wider groups in society. This, Weber argued, is what had happened with Calvinism in the seventeenth century. It caught on among the newly emerging bourgeoisie during early capitalism, because its teaching and doctrine had an "elective affinity" (i.e. made a neat fit) with the unique social, psychological, and cultural needs of the rising class of early entrepreneurs. The term "elective affinity" was Weber's way of explaining the "fit" between a socio-economic group, such as a class (e.g. the rising bourgeoisie), its way of life (e.g. the new type of capitalist economic activity), and a specific set of cultural beliefs and values (e.g. Puritanism). The values and beliefs of the "Protestant ethic" gave meaning to, and helped the early capitalists to make sense of, the new kinds of economic activity in which they were engaging.

One can think of other comparable historical examples. There was an "elective affinity" between the early industrial working class in British nineteenth-century capitalist society and later versions of Calvinism, like Methodism, which offered the converted a role as the "elect," the respectable, the chosen few, at a time when they were otherwise feeling excluded from society. Even today, in an advanced industrial capitalist society with a very materialist culture like the United States, about 50 percent of the population still attend a church service once a month. American culture was deeply influenced by Protestantism, and there is also a sizeable Catholic minority (a quarter to a third of all church attenders). So, one could say there is an "elective affinity" between religion and being an American.

But what about *modern* culture – increasingly secular and materialistic in its values, instrumental rather than spiritual in its outlook and, as Weber said, dominated by scientific and technological rationality? What provides meaning in *this* culture? How do people find an answer to the fundamental problems of life?

The Enlightenment thinkers (as you may recall from chapter 1) had hoped that science could *replace* religion as a basis for moral values, and thus provide the foundation for a new culture, a modern civilization. But Weber argued that the problem of meaning, of suffering and justice, *cannot* be satisfactorily addressed by science alone. However, given its relative decline, religion had ceased to provide meaningful solutions. Two areas, Weber believed, had taken on something of the function of religion in modern culture, as a source of meaning and values not yet wholly dominated by technical and scientific rationality: the spheres of the aesthetic and the erotic.

In some traditional cultures (e.g. Hinduism, Sufism, and – though Weber did not study them – many African and native American cultures) the religious, the mystical, and the erotic (especially in the form of dance and music) were deeply intertwined. However, in the West there has always been a tension between the erotic and religion – in both the Catholic and the Protestant faiths. Catholicism found aesthetic forms more acceptable, but Protestantism in general, and Puritanism in particular, have always been profoundly suspicious of *both* the erotic and the aesthetic. On the other hand, this "asceticism" (i.e. renunciation of pleasure) was precisely the element in Calvinism which had proved of value to the early capitalists. (The Puritans objected to bear-baiting, for example, not because of the pain it gave to the bear, but because of the pleasure it gave to the spectators.) It provided that taboo on "pleasure and gratification" which, Weber argued, compelled capitalists to save, accumulate, and invest, and drove them to adopt a sober and frugal rather than a spendthrift style of life. However, once the "spirit of capitalism" had developed fully, this "taboo" on the erotic and the aesthetic created problems, because art and sexuality were two of the few remaining areas of modern culture which had to some extent resisted "rationalization."

Weber wrote that :

> . . . asceticism descended like a frost on the life of "Merrie old England". And not only worldly merriment felt its effect. The Puritan's ferocious hatred of everything which smacked of superstition, of all survivals of magical and sacramental salvation, applied to the Christmas festivities and the May Pole and all spontaneous art. . . . The Theatre was obnoxious to the Puritans, and with the strict exclusion of the erotic and of nudity from the realm of toleration, a radical view of either literature or art could not exist.
> (Weber, 1971, pp. 168–9)

Sexuality and the erotic have something of the same status – both are areas of taboo, set aside from "normal" daily life, not governed by instrumental calculation, where irrational impulses surface which, many believe, threaten the even tenor of everyday life. Especially outside conventional marriage, the erotic also marks the eruption of non-rational forces – the pleasures, desires, and wishes of the body. Weber's argument, in his essay "The aesthetic and the erotic spheres" (Weber, 1970), is that intellectuals and others caught up in modern rational work processes regard the aesthetic and erotic spheres as important spaces *set aside* (remember Durkheim's notion of "the sacred"?) from "normal life" for living for a short time in the non-rational. The underside of the increasing rationalization of life at work, and in organized leisure, is the heightened role of aesthetic and erotic pleasure in industrial, urban social formations. They become privileged zones, places specially charged with emotion and value, the only cultural spaces left where people are still in touch with "natural forces," in contact with the "real" – the body, the flesh, desire – and where one can be taken out of everyday, conscious concerns and anxieties. You can see how, paradoxically, according to Weber's argument, not only have the aesthetic and erotic spheres to some extent replaced the role of religion in modern culture; they have also acquired something of the character of what both Durkheim and Weber called "the sacred."

However, they could not compensate for the overwhelming tendency of modern culture. Though the values of Puritanism had helped to bring the "spirit of capitalism" and the rational pursuit of capitalist enterprise into existence, the religious element had long since – in Weber's judgment – given way to a more secular, materialistic culture, in which the processes of rationalization exerted the dominant force. There is no mistaking the note of chilling pessimism in Weber's description of the later stages of this development:

> The Puritan wanted to work in a calling; we are forced to do so. For when asceticism was carried out of monastic cells into everyday life, and began to dominate worldly morality, it did its part in building the tremendous cosmos of the modern economic order. This order is now bound to the technical and economic conditions of machine production which today determine the lives of all the individuals who are born into this mechanism, not only those directly concerned with ecomomic acquisition, with irresistible force. Perhaps it will so determine them until the last ton of fossilized coal is burnt. In Baxter's view the care for external goods should only lie on the shoulders of the "saint like a light cloak, which can be thrown aside at any moment." But fate decreed that the cloak should become an iron cage.
>
> Since asceticism undertook to remodel the world and to work out its ideals in the world, material goods have gained an increasing and finally an inexorable power over the lives of men as at no previous period in history. Today the spirit of religious asceticism – whether finally, who knows? – has escaped from the cage. But victorious capitalism, since it rests on mechanical foundations, needs its support no longer. The rosy blush of its laughing heir, the Enlightenment, seems also to be irretrievably fading, and the idea of duty in one's calling prowls about in our lives like the ghost of dead religious beliefs. Where the fulfilment of the calling cannot directly be related to the highest spiritual and cultural values, or when, on the other hand, it need not be felt simply as economic compulsion, the individual generally

abandons the attempt to justify it at all. In the field of its highest development, in the United States, the pursuit of wealth, stripped of its religious and ethical meaning, tends to become associated with purely mundane passions, which often actually give it the character of sport.

No one knows who will live in this cage in the future, or whether at the end of this tremendous development entirely new prophets will arise, or there will be a great rebirth of old ideas and ideals, or, if neither, mechanized petrification, embellished with a sort of convulsive self-importance. For of the last stage of this cultural development, it might well be truly said: "Specialists without spirit, sensualists without heart; this nullity imagines that it has attained a level of civilization never before achieved." (Weber, 1971, pp. 181–3)

## 5.2  Disenchantment with the modern world

Weber's theme of the ever-increasing rationalization of modern life was part of a more general argument that the evolution of modern culture has not produced the increase in overall human happiness that many hoped for. The project, set in motion by the Enlightenment, of increasing progress, wealth, and happiness through the application of science and technology, first to industry and then to social life as a whole, and the weakening of the hold of custom, magic, superstition, and other supernatural taboos over which the *philosophes* rejoiced, has been put in question. In the traditional culture of Europe before the Protestant Reformation, religion provided the moral framework for everyone. Everyday life was punctuated by saints' days, fairs, pilgrimages, festivals, seasons of feasting, atonement, and celebration. The culture of ordinary people was saturated with folk customs, magical spells, rituals, and religious occasions. Springs and wells provided healing waters, the relics of saints offered safe journeys or protection to relatives and friends.

The gradual disappearance of this culture, saturated with the religious and what would now be regarded as the irrational, and the transition to a world more and more of which could only be understood and explained through the application of rational forms of explanation, mastered and controlled through the application of instrumental reason, was described by Weber as a process of *de-magification*. (The German phrase Weber used, "*Entzauberung der Welt*," is sometimes translated as "the disenchantment of the world.") Both are aspects of that long cultural shift towards modernity which many sociologists call *secularization*.

Weber was by no means the only social scientist or social critic and philosopher to take an increasingly negative or pessimistic view of the "costs," rather than the "benefits," of modern civilization. In Britain, from the Romantic poets at the end of the eighteenth century onwards, a long line of writers and critics criticized the increasingly mechanistic character of modern industrial society and culture, and the dominance of a competitive and utilitarian ethos in it. "Men," the poet Coleridge once said, railing against industrialism, "should be weighed, not counted." These critics were protesting against the habits of mind, the culture, which modern capitalism and industry had brought to the fore. Raymond Williams, who charted this tradition of cultural criticism in *Culture and Society, 1780–1950* (1958), observed that "culture" was one of the terms used to measure critically "the great historical changes which the changes in industry, democracy and class, in their own way, represent, and to which the changes in art are a closely related response" (Williams, 1981, p. 16).

The rise of capitalism and the impact of industrial work and the factory system on workers in the nineteenth century in Britain also led Karl Marx (1818–83) to develop a not dissimilar critique of industrial "civilization" and its cultural and social impact. Capitalism, Marx argued, expropriated from the worker the fruits of his/her labor for sale in the market. But in addition, the conditions of labor in the modern industrial factory robbed the worker of a sense of self and of the capacity to be creative and to recognize the things produced as the fruit of creative activity. Marx called this cultural condition a process of "estrangement," or alienation:

> What, then, constitutes the alienation of labour? First, the fact that labour is *external* to the worker, i.e., it does not belong to his essential being; that in his work, therefore, he does not affirm himself but denies himself, does not feel content but unhappy, does not develop freely his physical and mental energy but mortifies his body and ruins his mind. The worker therefore only feels himself outside his work, and in his work feels outside himself. He is at home when he is not working, and when he is working he is not at home. His labour is therefore not voluntary, but coerced; it is *forced labour.* It is therefore not the satisfaction of a need; it is merely a *means* to satisfy needs external to it. Its alien character emerges clearly in the fact that as soon as no physical or other compulsion exists, labour is shunned like the plague. External labour, labour in which man alienates himself, is a labour of self-sacrifice, of mortification. Lastly, the external character of labour for the worker appears in the fact that it is not his own, but someone else's, that it does not belong to him, that in it he belongs, not to himself, but to another. Just as in religion the spontaneous activity of the human imagination, of the human brain and the human heart, operates independently of the individual – that is, operates on him as an alien, divine or diabolical activity – in the same way the worker's activity is not his spontaneous activity. It belongs to another; it is the loss of his self.
>
> As a result, therefore, man (the worker) no longer feels himself to be freely active in any but his animal functions – eating, drinking, procreating, or at most in his dwelling and dressing-up etc.; and in his human functions he no longer feels himself to be anything but an animal. What is animal becomes human and what is human becomes animal.

> Certainly eating, drinking, procreating, etc., are also genuinely human functions. But in the abstraction which separates them from the sphere of all other human activity and turns them into sole and ultimate ends, they are animal.
> (Marx, 1959, pp. 72–3)

Marx is assuming here that working creatively on the external world, finding pleasure in working with other people, is an essential part of what it is to be "human." The labor process in industrial capitalism, he argues, destroys these relationships with other people and with nature, turning them into alienating, estranged relations. This alienation also produces an alienated form of culture, in everyday ways of living, and in religion. Alien beings seem to be dominant: in the form of an angry God who seeks obedience, and in the form of the employer who represents Capital.

Other social theorists and critics of the industrialization and urbanization processes of modern, technical "civilization" have also argued that the change from rural and agricultural to industrial social formations has had very disturbing effects upon people's moral, religious, and everyday patterns of living. Durkheim, whose ideas about collective representations were discussed in section 3 above, also believed that these changes were profoundly unsettling. He argued that they lay behind increases in rates of mental illness, drug abuse, and suicide in western societies, especially among those groups whose way of life encouraged *individual* competition, achievement, and a sense of inner isolation. Like Weber, Durkheim found that Protestants were more prone to this condition than Catholics or Jews, where a sense of collective belongingness was stronger, and that this in large part explained why their suicide rate was higher (see Durkheim, 1952).

Urbanization and industrialization broke down traditional ways of living, with their ideas and moral values about right and wrong. No new, clear set of values or norms developed in the new situation. Durkheim described this situation as one of *anomie* (meaning literally "without norms") – that is, a social condition where no clear, generally-accepted rules about how to live were shared among people. Individuals tried to invent their own ways of living, and many came unstuck in trying to do so.

We have already mentioned Nietzsche and his philosophy of "nihilism," which emerged in Germany towards the end of the nineteenth century, and whose pessimism about modern culture influenced Weber. One of Nietzsche's arguments was that the values of western civilization, often represented as aspects of Truth and Beauty and Justice, were really simply "masks" or "fictions" used in a struggle for power – the "will to power" – among the powerful, which dissolved any objective distinction between "good" and "evil." This critique propagated a cynical or "disenchanted" view of modern culture, and a cult of power and the irrational, which became increasingly influential in Western European culture during the late nineteenth and early twentieth centuries. The question of whether the values of technical and scientific reason could supply a moral center to the cultural universe became a topic of widespread philosophical speculation among such philosophers as Husserl and Heidegger. In the social sciences, there was a parallel debate about whether science could provide the model for the construction of *positive* social laws (positivism). (Durkheim and Weber occupied leading, but contrasting, positions within this debate.)

In short, by the turn of the century, the evolution of modern culture, grounded on the domination of science and technology, scientific and technological reason, was being discussed everywhere in terms of a "crisis." This cultural "crisis" occurred at the same time as, and came increasingly to be expressed in, those movements in modern culture, painting and the arts which came to be called "modernism."

Two of the most important critiques of modern, "rationalized" culture deserve special mention because they pick up directly on themes discussed earlier. The first is the critique developed by Sigmund Freud, and the second is that of the group of German social theorists and cultural critics, Adorno, Horkheimer, and Marcuse, who belonged to the "Frankfurt School."

## 5.3   Civilization and its discontents

Freud's (1856–1939) work was produced in two main periods: before 1914, when Europeans were more self-confident about their civilization, despite the wars of the nineteenth century; and after the trench warfare of World War I. Freud's work during this second period reflected the impact of war, both because some of his patients were soldiers suffering from what were called at the time "war neurosis," and because he wished to take account of the massive implications of the fact of a total and destructive war between "civilized" nations such as Germany, France, and Britain. In *Civilization and its Discontents*, first published in 1930, he wrote about the hostility people feel towards this modern civilization:

> How has it happened that so many people have come to take up this strange attitude of hostility to civilization? I believe that the basis of it was a deep and long-standing dissatisfaction with the then existing state of civilization and that on that basis a condemnation of it was built up, occasioned by certain specific historical events. I think I know what the last and the last but one of those occasions were. I am not learned enough to trace the chain of them far back enough in the history of the human species; but a factor of this kind hostile to civilization must already have been at work in the victory of Christendom over the heathen religions. For it was very closely related to the low estimation put upon earthly life by the Christian doctrine. The last but one of these occasions was when the progress of voyages of discovery led to contact with primitive peoples and races. In consequence of insufficient observation and a mistaken view of their manners and customs, they appeared to Europeans to be

leading a simple, happy life with few wants, a life such as was unattainable by their visitors with their superior civilization. Later experience has corrected some of those judgements. In many cases the observers had wrongly attributed to the absence of complicated cultural demands what was in fact due to the bounty of nature and the ease with which the major human needs were satisfied. The last occasion is especially familiar to us. It arose when people came to know about the mechanism of the neuroses, which threaten to undermine the modicum of happiness enjoyed by civilized men. It was discovered that a person becomes neurotic because he cannot tolerate the amount of frustration which society imposes on him in the service of its cultural ideals, and it was inferred from this that the abolition or reduction of those demands would result in a return to possibilities of happiness.

There is also an added factor of disappointment, During the last few generations mankind has made an extraordinary advance in the natural sciences and in their technical application and has established his control over nature in a way never before imagined. The single steps of this advance are common knowledge and it is unnecessary to enumerate them. Men are proud of those achievements, and have a right to be. But they seem to have observed that this newly-won power over space and time, this subjugation of the forces of nature, which is the fulfilment of a longing that goes back thousands of years, has not increased the amount of pleasurable satisfaction which they may expect from life and has not made them feel happier. From the recognition of this fact we ought to be content to conclude that power over nature is not the *only* precondition of human happiness, just as it is not the *only* goal of cultural endeavour; we ought not to infer from it that technical progress is without value for the economics of our happiness.
(Freud, 1963, pp. 24–5)

Freud wrestles here with the dilemma of the lack of the expected gains from technological advances in modern "civilization." Instead of increased happiness, there is an increase in neuroses – that is, forms of mental distress milder than that found in madness (psychoses) but producing unhappy states of mind or of the body. Europeans are no longer so prone to imagine that primitive peoples are as happy as they once believed, but nevertheless technological progress does not guarantee an increase in ordinary happiness. It places demands on people, which affect their everyday lives at work and in the home. There are echoes here of Marx's notion of alienation – estrangement from others and from the *self* also.

The concept of the *unconscious*, which Freud used and systematized in his writings and in his therapeutic work with the neurotics of modern urban life, captured the importance of the irrational. The two central components of unconscious desire – sexuality and destructive aggression – became important features of the work of a group of social scientists known as *the Frankfurt School*, or *critical theorists*. It is to their work that we turn briefly in the next section.

## 5.4   The Frankfurt School

The social critics and philosophers who came to be known as the Frankfurt School also addressed some of the themes rehearsed by both Weber and Freud. Of particular relevance is the work which they produced in the 1930s, in the context of the rise of fascism in Germany (from which they were all obliged to flee) and the fearful holocaust which followed in Europe. These events led the Frankfurt School critics to ask how the promise of the Enlightenment could possibly have led to such a "barbarous" result. This was especially difficult to explain in Germany, which had come to pride itself on the "civilizing process," as Norbert Elias called it – the long process of cultural refinement culminating in a high state of cultural achievement. The high standard of manners and etiquette of the French, English, and German aristocracies, Elias argued, had been imitated by the new urban bourgeoisie. Gradually, the lower-middle and the respectable working classes of Europe began to borrow and imitate these standards of behavior. The new mass circulation press, and later radio, operated as the main vehicles for the expansion of this civilizing process. What, then, had gone wrong? How had this civilizing process produced the monstrosity of fascism with its doctrines of racial purity?

The Frankfurt critics argued that, far from being a departure from the Enlightenment, these developments were its "dark side" – as much part of its project as its dream of progress and emancipation. What in the Enlightenment had given rise to this apparent contradiction of all it appeared to stand for? The answer which they gave to this question was clearly related to Weber's. It was the domination of modern society and culture by what they called "technical reason," the spread of bureaucratic and instrumental rationality to every sphere of life, producing what they called the "totally administered" society – the society of totalitarianism – which had crippled and distorted the "promise of Enlightenment." The Enlightenment could only be, as it were, saved from itself by exposing this remorseless process of "rationalization" to a ruthless philosophical critique. Such a critique would aim to show that *technical forms of reason* had subverted and eclipsed *critical* reasoning about moral and political values. This latter concept of *critical rationality* had become lost by confusing it with scientific forms of reasoning, a process which had begun in the Enlightenment. Hope lay in recovering this form of substantive reasoning, a form inaugurated in the West by the Ancient Greek philosophers, in which moral and political values were established by public, reasoned debate, not by force.

The Frankfurt School did not accept that "reason" should be restricted to scientific and technological ways of thinking, for these excluded rational reflection on social, political, cultural, and moral values. It was partly the value-neutrality of so many academics, the Frankfurt School argued, which had allowed fascism and Nazism to develop. For if academics, philosophers, and social scientists say nothing about values, in a falsely modest eschewing of value-judgments, then no one should be surprised if the moral vacuum thereby created is filled by irrational political movements. The error the modern West had made had been in thinking that science and technology could provide values, or even that societies did not need fundamental values. Since the Enlightenment, both these errors had become dominant among different elite groups in western societies. The results were nihilism, fascism, disenchantment, and unhappiness. The solution lay, the Frankfurt School thought, in reconnecting with earlier ways of thinking about society and its relations with nature – both external nature, the environment, and nature in the human body. "Reason" could and should include such *ethical* thought. Value-neutrality was a dangerous illusion, a chimera, something to be avoided, not to be treated as a guarantee of academic respectability.

# 6  Conclusion

We have travelled a considerable distance in the course of this chapter. We began by considering definitions of culture, and two emerged as being particularly important for sociology: first, culture as the meanings, values, and ways of life shared by particular nations, groups, classes, or historical periods; second, culture as the practices which produce meaning – signifying practices. The latter idea has been important in the approach called "structuralism," a method which emphasizes the *interrelations* between component parts in a wider system or *structure* of relations. Languages, not just verbal language but other sets of symbols, such as those found in pre-literate cultures (totemism) or rituals (including social practices such as marriage rules, kinship rules, and wedding feasts), can be analyzed in terms of their meaning, using a structuralist method. Durkheim's work on the elementary forms of religion was discussed in the light of such an approach.

The concepts of *collective representations* and systems of *primitive classification* were highlighted as being especially important in reading Durkheim in a structuralist way. The idea of binary oppositions (from Lévi-Strauss), and of categories which do not fit into a particular classificatory scheme, producing, in turn, notions of the eerie, the spooky, or the weird, was used in relation to Durkheim's sacred–profane distinction.

This type of structuralist analysis is *synchronic*; that is, it is concerned with the *workings* of a structure frozen in time. We moved on to consider *diachronic* changes, changes *of* structures across historical time, by examining Weber's claims about the role of religion (Calvinism) in the development of modern, rational capitalism. Weber's analysis of Calvinism was placed in the wider context of his analysis of other cultures, centered upon different orientations to the natural world, other people, and the human body from those found in

Protestantism. Weber used two binary oppositions in this work: "mysticism" and "asceticism"; and "inner-worldly" and "other-worldly." Combining these produced four possible types of religious ethic. Calvinism was *the* unique example of one of these four types: an inner-worldly ascetic ethic. This cultural value system had been the absolutely necessary, though not the sufficient, condition for the development of modern rational capitalism, according to Weber's analysis.

Finally, the *costs* of the part played by culture in the formation of modern capitalism were addressed. Weber, although explicit about the benefits of some aspects of modernity (the gains in justice and equality from modern bureaucracy), was nevertheless haunted by the costs. The loss of a sense of *shared* meaning, and the sense of disenchantment in modern culture were, perhaps, the major disadvantages in Weber's view. Others, such as Marx and Freud, saw similar costs in modern capitalism. Marx spoke of a sense of *alienation* from others, from nature, and even from self. Freud developed the ideas of loss of meaning, of estrangement, in a way which focused upon the pains and discontents of modern *individuals*. (Weber had seen individualism as another product of Protestant culture.) The ideas of Marx, Weber, and Freud provided a basis for the Frankfurt School's critique of modern culture, which they saw as dominated by a one-dimensional form of technical reason. They saw academic neutrality as having allowed fascism to develop – if reason is not used to provide collective purposes and to criticize existing assumptions then, in their view, unreason takes over.

This last point, about value-judgments, is an important one. When making a social scientific analysis of our own or other cultures, we must attempt to set aside our prejudices and preconceptions, to describe and not to judge. And yet we need to remain morally vigilant. Although value-neutrality is a necessary methodological stance for sociologists, or anthropologists, initially, it is never enough on its own. Someone must continue to think about, and write about, human life – there must be someone to weigh up questions of value and the ultimate purpose of existing values, and to debate how we ought to live and how we ought to try to arrange our collective lives together. Who else will take responsibility for this if not intellectuals?

# References

Douglas, M. (1966) *Purity and Danger: An Analysis of Concepts of Pollution and Taboo*, London, Routledge and Kegan Paul.

Durkheim, É. (1952) *Suicide: A Study in Sociology* (trans. J. Spaulding and G. Simpson), London, Routledge and Kegan Paul.

Durkheim, É. (1961) *The Elementary Forms of the Religious Life* (trans. J.W. Swain), New York, Collier Books.

Elias, N. (1978) *The Civilizing Process. Vol. 1: The History of Manners* (trans. E. Jephcott), Oxford, Basil Blackwell.

Elias, N. (1982) *The Civilizing Process. Vol. 2: State Formations and Civilization*, Oxford, Basil Blackwell.

Freud, S. (1963) *Civilization and its Discontents* (trans. J. Riviere; ed. J. Strachey), London, Hogarth Press.

Horkheimer, M. and Adorno, T. (1972) *Dialectic of Enlightenment*, New York, Herder and Herder.

Lévi-Strauss, C. (1966) *The Savage Mind*, London, Weidenfeld & Nicolson.

Lévi-Strauss, C. (1969) *Totemism*, Harmondsworth, England, Penguin.

Marx, K. (1959) *Economic and Philosophical Manuscripts of 1844*, London, Lawrence and Wishart.

Poole, R. (1969) "Introduction," in Lévi-Strauss, C., *Totemism*, Harmondsworth, England, Penguin.

Turner, B. (ed.) (1990) *Theories of Modernity and Post-Modernity*, London, Sage.

Weber, M. (1970) *From Max Weber: Essays in Sociology* (trans. and ed. H. Gerth and C.W. Mills), London, Routledge and Kegan Paul.

Weber, M. (1971) *The Protestant Ethic and the Spirit of Capitalism* (trans. T. Parsons), London, Unwin University Books.

Williams, R. (1981) *Culture and Society, 1780–1950*, London, Fontana.

Williams, R. (1983) *Keywords*, London, Fontana.

# 6    The West and the Rest: Discourse and Power

Stuart Hall

## Contents

| | | |
|---|---|---|
| 1 | Introduction | 185 |
| 1.1 | Where and what is "the West"? | 185 |
| 2 | Europe Breaks Out | 189 |
| 2.1 | When and how did expansion begin? | 189 |
| 2.2 | Five main phases | 190 |
| 2.3 | The Age of Exploration | 191 |
| 2.4 | Breaking the frame | 195 |
| 2.5 | The consequences of expansion for the idea of "the West" | 197 |
| 3 | Discourse and Power | 201 |
| 3.1 | What is a "discourse"? | 201 |
| 3.2 | Discourse and ideology | 202 |
| 3.3 | Can a discourse be "innocent"? | 203 |
| 4 | Representing "the Other" | 205 |
| 4.1 | Orientalism | 205 |
| 4.2 | The "archive" | 206 |
| 4.3 | A "regime of truth" | 208 |
| 4.4 | Idealization | 209 |
| 4.5 | Sexual fantasy | 210 |
| 4.6 | Mis-recognizing difference | 211 |
| 4.7 | Rituals of degradation | 213 |
| 4.8 | Summary: stereotypes, dualism, and "splitting" | 215 |
| 5 | "In the Beginning All the World was America" | 216 |
| 5.1 | Are they "true men"? | 216 |
| 5.2 | "Noble" vs "ignoble savages" | 217 |
| 5.3 | The history of "rude" and "refined" nations | 219 |
| 6 | From "the West and the Rest" to Modern Sociology | 221 |
| 7 | Conclusion | 224 |
| References | | 225 |

# 1    Introduction

The first five chapters of this book examine the long historical
processes through which a new type of society – advanced, developed,
and industrial – emerged. They chart in broad outline the paths by
which this society reached what is now called "modernity." This
chapter explores the role which societies *outside* Europe played in this
process. It examines how an idea of "the West and the Rest" was
constituted; how relations between western and non-western societies
came to be represented. We refer to this as the formation of the
"discourse" of "the West and the Rest."

## 1.1    Where and what is "the West"?

This question puzzled Christopher Columbus and remains puzzling
today. Nowadays, many societies aspire to become "western" – at least
in terms of achieving western standards of living. But in Columbus's
day (the end of the fifteenth century), going West was important mainly
because it was believed to be the quickest route to the fabulous wealth
of the East. Indeed, even though it should have become clear to
Columbus that the New World he had found was *not* the East, he never
ceased to believe that it was, and even spiced his reports with
outlandish claims: on his fourth voyage, he still insisted that he was
close to Quinsay (the Chinese city now called Hangchow), where the
Great Khan lived, and probably approaching the source of the Four
Rivers of Paradise! Our ideas of "East" and "West" have never been free
of myth and fantasy, and even to this day they are not primarily ideas
about place and geography.
    We have to use short-hand generalizations, like "West" and
"western," but we need to remember that they represent very complex
ideas and have no simple or single meaning. At first sight, these words
may seem to be about matters of geography and location. But even this,
on inspection, is not straightforward since we also use the same words
to refer to a type of society, a level of development, and so on. It's true
that what we call "the West," in this second sense, *did* first emerge in
Western Europe. But "the West" is no longer only in Europe, and not
all of Europe is in "the West." The historian John Roberts has remarked
that "Europeans have long been unsure about where Europe 'ends' in
the east. In the west and to the south, the sea provides a splendid
marker . . . but to the east the plains roll on and on and the horizon is
awfully remote" (Roberts, 1985, p. 149). Eastern Europe doesn't (doesn't
yet? never did?) belong properly to "the West"; whereas the United
States, which is not in Europe, definitely does. These days,
technologically speaking, Japan is "western," though on our mental
map it is about as far "East" as you can get. By comparison, much of
Latin America, which is in the western hemisphere, belongs
economically to the Third World, which is struggling – not very
successfully – to catch up with "the West." What are these different

societies "east" and "west" of, exactly? Clearly, "the West" is as much an idea as a fact of geography.

The underlying premise of this chapter is that "the West" is a *historical*, not a geographical, construct. By "western" we mean the type of society discussed in this book: a society that is developed, industrialized, urbanized, capitalist, secular, and modern. Such societies arose at a particular historical period – roughly, during the sixteenth century, after the Middle Ages and the break-up of feudalism. They were the result of a specific set of historical processes – economic, political, social, and cultural. Nowadays, any society which shares these characteristics, wherever it exists on a geographical map, can be said to belong to "the West." The meaning of this term is therefore virtually identical to that of the word "modern." Its "formations" are what we have been tracing in the earlier chapters in this book. This chapter builds on that earlier story.

"The West" is therefore also an idea, a concept – and this is what interests us most in this chapter. How did the idea, the language, of "the West" arise, and what have been its effects? What do we mean by calling it a *concept*?

The concept or idea of "the West" can be seen to function in the following ways:

First, it allows us to characterize and classify societies into different categories – i.e. "western," "non-western." It is a tool to think with. It sets a certain structure of thought and knowledge in motion.

Secondly, it is an image, or set of images. It condenses a number of different characteristics into one picture. It calls up in our mind's eye – it *represents* in verbal and visual language – a composite picture of what different societies, cultures, peoples, and places are like. It functions as part of a language, a "system of representation." (I say "system" because it doesn't stand on its own, but works in conjunction with other images and ideas with which it forms a set: for example, "western" = urban = developed; or "non-western" = non-industrial = rural = agricultural = under-developed.)

Thirdly, it provides a standard or model of comparison. It allows us to compare to what extent different societies resemble, or differ from, one another. Non-western societies can accordingly be said to be "close to" or "far away from" or "catching up with" the West. It helps to explain *difference*.

Fourthly, it provides criteria of evaluation against which other societies are ranked and around which powerful positive and negative feelings cluster. (For example, "the West" = developed = *good* = desirable; or the "non-West" = under-developed = *bad* = undesirable.) It produces a certain kind of *knowledge* about a subject and certain attitudes towards it. In short, it functions as an *ideology*.

This chapter will discuss all these aspects of the idea of "the West."

We know that the West itself was produced by certain historical processes operating in a particular place in unique (and perhaps unrepeatable) historical circumstances. Clearly, we must also think of the *idea* of "the West" as having been produced in a similar way. These two aspects are in fact deeply connected, though exactly how is one of the big puzzles in sociology. We cannot attempt to resolve here the age-old sociological debate as to which came first: the idea of "the West," or western societies. What we can say is that, as these societies emerged, so a concept and language of "the West" crystallized. And yet, we can be certain that the idea of "the West" did not simply reflect an already-established western society: rather, it was essential to the very formation of that society.

What is more, the idea of "the West," once produced, became productive in its turn. It had real effects: it enabled people to know or speak of certain things in certain ways. It produced knowledge. It became *both* the organizing factor in a system of global power relations *and* the organizing concept or term in a whole way of thinking and speaking.

The central concern of this chapter is to analyze the formation of a particular pattern of thought and language, a "system of representation," which has the concepts of "the West" and "the Rest" at its center.

The emergence of an idea of "the West" was central to the Enlightenment, which was discussed at length in chapter 1. The Enlightenment was a very European affair. European society, it assumed, was the most advanced type of society on earth, European man (*sic*) the pinnacle of human achievement. It treated the West as the result of forces largely *internal* to Europe's history and formation.

However, in this chapter we argue that the rise of the West is also a *global* story. As Roberts observes, "'Modern' history can be defined as the approach march to the age dominated by the West" (Roberts, 1985, p. 41). The West and the Rest became two sides of a single coin. What each now is, and what the terms we use to describe them mean, depend on the relations which were established between them long ago. The so-called uniqueness of the West was, in part, produced by Europe's contact and self-comparison with other, non-western, societies (the Rest), very different in their histories, ecologies, patterns of development, and cultures from the European model. The difference of these other societies and cultures from the West was the standard against which the West's achievement was measured. It is within the context of these relationships that the idea of "the West" took on shape and meaning.

The importance of such perceived difference needs itself to be understood. Some modern theorists of language have argued that *meaning* always depends on the relations that exist between the different terms or words within a meaning system (see chapter 5). Accordingly, we know what "night" means because it is different from – in fact, opposite to – "day." The French linguist who most influenced this approach to meaning, Ferdinand de Saussure (1857–1912), argued that the words "night" and "day" on their own can't mean anything; it is the *difference* between "night" and "day" which enables these words to carry meaning (to signify).

Likewise, many psychologists and psychoanalysts argue that an infant first learns to think of itself as a separate and unique "self" by recognizing its separation – its difference – from others (principally, of course, its mother). By analogy, national cultures acquire their strong sense of identity by contrasting themselves with other cultures. Thus, we argue, the West's sense of itself – its identity – was formed not only by the internal processes that gradually molded Western European countries into a distinct type of society, but also through Europe's sense of difference from other worlds – how it came to represent itself in relation to these "others." In reality, differences often shade imperceptibly into each other. (When exactly does "night" become "day"? Where exactly does "being English" end and "being Scottish" begin?) But, in order to function at all, we seem to need distinct, positive concepts, many of which are sharply polarized towards each other. As chapter 5 argues, such "binary oppositions" seem to be fundamental to all linguistic and symbolic systems and to the production of meaning itself.

This chapter, then, is about the role which "the Rest" played in the formation of the idea of "the West" and a "western" sense of identity. At a certain moment, the fates of what had been, for many centuries, separate and distinct worlds became – some would say, fatally – harnessed together in the same historical time-frame. They became related elements in the same *discourse*, or way of speaking. They became different parts of one global social, economic, and cultural system, one interdependent world, one language.

A word of warning must be entered here. In order to bring out the distinctiveness of this "West and the Rest" discourse, I have been obliged to be selective and to simplify my representation of the West, and you should bear this in mind as you read. Terms like "the West" and "the Rest" are historical and linguistic constructs whose meanings change over time. More importantly, there are many different discourses, or ways in which the West came to speak of and represent other cultures. Some, like "the West and the Rest," were very western-centered, or Eurocentric. Others, however, which I do not have space to discuss here, were much more culturally relativistic. I have elected to focus on what I call the discourse of "the West and the Rest" because it became a very common and influential discourse, helping to shape public perceptions and attitudes down to the present.

Another qualification concerns the very term "the West," which makes the West appear unified and homogeneous – essentially one place, with one view about other cultures and one way of speaking about them. Of course, this is not the case. The West has always contained many internal differences – between different nations, between Eastern and Western Europe, between the Germanic Northern and the Latin Southern cultures, between the Nordic, Iberian, and Mediterranean peoples, and so on. Attitudes towards other cultures within the West varied widely, as they still do between, for example, the British, the Spanish, the French, and the German.

It is also important to remember that, as well as treating non-European cultures as different and inferior, the West had its own *internal* "others." Jews, in particular, though close to western religious traditions, were frequently excluded and ostracized. West Europeans often regarded Eastern Europeans as "barbaric," and, throughout the West, western women were represented as inferior to western men.

The same necessary simplification is true of my references to "the Rest." This term also covers enormous historical, cultural, and economic distinctions – for example, between the Middle East, the Far East, Africa, Latin America, indigenous North America, and Australasia. It can equally encompass the simple societies of some North American Indians and the developed civilizations of China, Egypt, or Islam.

These extensive differences must be borne in mind as you study the analysis of the discourse of "the West and the Rest" in this chapter. However, we can actually use this simplification to make a point about discourse. For simplification is precisely what this discourse itself *does*. It represents things which are in fact very differentiated (the different European cultures) as homogeneous (the West). And it asserts that these different cultures are united by one thing: the fact that *they are all different from the Rest*. Similarly, the Rest, though different among themselves, are represented as the same in the sense that *they are all different from the West*. In short, the discourse, as a "system of representation," *represents* the world as divided according to a simple dichotomy – the West/the Rest. That is what makes the discourse of "the West and the Rest" so destructive – it draws crude and simplistic distinctions and constructs an over-simplified conception of "difference."

# 2 Europe Breaks Out

In what follows, you should bear in mind the evolution of the system of European nation-states discussed in chapter 2. "The voyages of discovery were the beginning of a new era, one of world-wide expansion by Europeans, leading in due course to an outright, if temporary, European . . . domination of the globe" (Roberts, 1985, p. 175). In this section we offer a broad sketch of the early stages of this process of expansion. When did it begin? What were its main phases? What did it "break out" from? Why did it occur?

## 2.1 When and how did expansion begin?

Long historical processes have no exact beginning or end, and are difficult to date precisely. You will remember the argument in chapter 2 that a particular historical pattern is the result of the interplay between a number of different causal processes. In order to describe them, we are forced to work within very rough-and-ready chronologies and to use *historical generalizations* which cover long periods and pick out the broad patterns, but leave much of the detail aside. There is nothing wrong with this – historical sociology would be impossible without it – provided we know at what level of generality our argument is working. For example, if we are answering the question, "When did Western Europe first industrialize?," it may be sufficient to say, "During the second half of the eighteenth century." However, a close study of the origins of industrialization in, say, Lancashire, would require a more refined time-scale. (For further discussion of this point, see the Introduction to part I.)

We can date the onset of the expansion process roughly in relation to two key events:

1   The early Portuguese explorations of the African coast (1430–98); and

2   Columbus's voyages to the New World (1492–1502).

Broadly speaking, European expansion coincides with the end of what we call "the Middle Ages" and the beginning of the "modern age." Feudalism was already in decline in Western Europe, while trade, commerce, and the market were expanding. The centralized monarchies of France, England, and Spain were emerging (see chapter 2). Europe was on the threshold of a long, secular boom in productivity, improving standards of living, rapid population growth, and that explosion in art, learning, science, scholarship, and knowledge known as the Renaissance. (Leonardo da Vinci had designed flying machines and submarines prior to 1519; Michelangelo started work on the Sistine Chapel in 1508; Thomas More's *Utopia* appeared in 1516.) For much of the Middle Ages, the arts of civilization had been more developed in China and the Islamic world than in Europe. Many historians would agree with Michael Mann that "the point at which Europe 'overtook' Asia must have been about 1450, the period of European naval expansion and the Galilean revolution in science"; though as Mann also argues, many of the processes which made this possible had earlier origins (Mann, 1988, p. 7). We will return to this question at the end of the section.

## 2.2   Five main phases

The process of expansion can be divided, broadly, into five main phases:

1   The period of exploration, when Europe "discovered" many of the "new worlds" for itself for the first time (they all, of course, already existed).

2   The period of early contact, conquest, settlement, and colonization, when large parts of these "new worlds" were first annexed to Europe as possessions, or harnessed through trade.

3   The time during which the shape of permanent European settlement, colonization, or exploitation was established (e.g. plantation societies in North America and the Caribbean; mining and ranching in Latin America; the rubber and tea plantations of India, Ceylon, and the East Indies). Capitalism now emerged as a global market.

4   The phase when the scramble for colonies, markets, and raw materials reached its climax. This was the "high noon of Imperialism," and led into World War I and the twentieth century.

5    The present, when much of the world is economically dependent on the West, even when formally independent and decolonized.

There are no neat divisions between these phases, which often overlapped. For example, although the main explorations of Australia occurred in our first phase, the continent's shape was not finally known until after Cook's voyages in the eighteenth century. Similarly, the Portuguese first circumnavigated Africa in the fifteenth century, yet the exploration of the African interior below the Sahara and the scramble for African colonies is really a nineteenth-century story.

Since we are focusing on "formations," this chapter concentrates on the first two phases – those involving early exploration, encounter, contact, and conquest – in order to trace how "the West and the Rest" as a "system of representation" was formed.

## 2.3   The Age of Exploration

This began with Portugal, after the Moors (the Islamic peoples who had conquered Spain) had finally been expelled from the Iberian peninsula. Prince Henry "The Navigator," the pioneer of Portuguese exploration, was himself a Crusader who fought the Moors at the battle of Ceuta (North Africa; 1415) and helped to disperse the Moorish pirates who lurked at the entrance to the Mediterranean. As Eric Newby explains:

> With the pirates under control there was a real possibility that the Portuguese might be able to take over the caravan trade – an important part of which was in gold dust – that Ceuta enjoyed with the African interior. In the event, the attempt to capture this trade failed . . . And so there emerged another purpose. This was to discover from which parts of Africa the merchandise, particularly the gold dust, emanated and, having done so, to contrive to have it re-routed . . . to stations on the Atlantic coast in which the inhabitants would already have been converted to Christianity and of which the King of Portugal would be the ruler. (Newby, 1975, p. 62)

This comment pinpoints the complex factors – economic, political, and spiritual – which motivated Portuguese expansion. Why, then, hadn't they simply sailed southwards before? One answer is that they thought their ships were not sufficiently robust to endure the fierce currents and contrary winds to be encountered around the curve of the North African coastline. Another equally powerful factor was what is called the "Great Barrier of Fear" – evident, for example, in the belief that beyond Cape Bojador lay the mouth of Hell, where the seas boiled and people turned black because of the intense heat. The late-medieval European conception of the world constituted as much of a barrier to expansion as technological and navigational factors.

In 1430, the Portuguese sailed down the west coast of Africa, hoping to find not only the sources of the African gold, ivory, spice, and slave trades, but also the legendary black Christian ruler, "Prester John." In stages (each consolidated by papal decree giving Portugal a monopoly

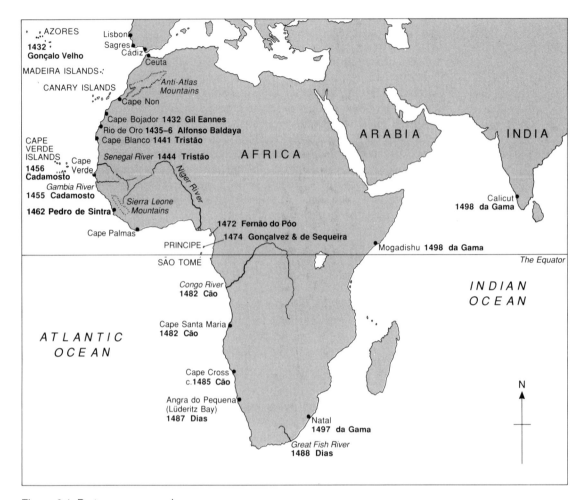

Figure 6.1 Portuguese expansion

"in the Ocean Sea . . . lying southward and eastward"), the Portuguese pushed down the African coast, and past the "Great Barrier of Fear." In 1441, the first cargo of African slaves captured by Europeans arrived in Portugal – thereby beginning a new era of slave-trading.

In 1487/8 Bartolomeo Dias rounded the Cape of Good Hope and Pedro da Covilhão, taking the caravan route overland, reached the Sudan from where he sailed to India (1488). Later, Vasco da Gama sailed around Africa and then, with the aid of a Muslim pilot, across the Indian Ocean to the city of Calicut (1497–8). Within ten years Portugal had established the foundations of a naval and commercial empire. Displacing the Arab traders who had long plied the Red Sea and Indian Ocean, they established a chain of ports to Goa, the East Indies, the Moluccas, and Timor. In 1514, a Portuguese mission reached Canton (China), and in 1542 the first contact was made with Japan.

By comparison, the exploration of the New World (America) was at first largely a Spanish affair. After long pleading, Columbus, the

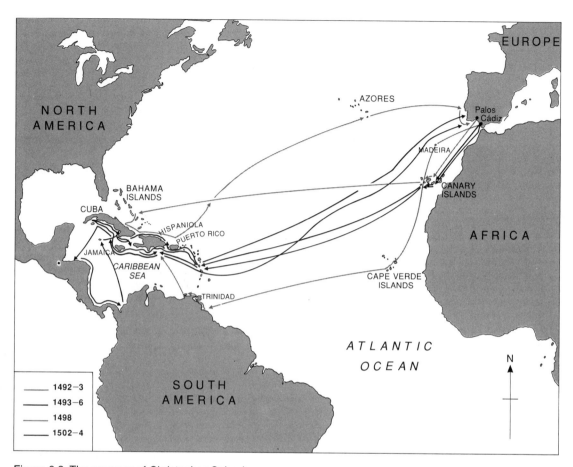

Figure 6.2 The voyages of Christopher Columbus

Genoese navigator, finally persuaded King Ferdinand and Queen
Isabella of Spain to support his "western Enterprise" to find a westerly
route to the treasures of the East. Deliberately under-estimating the
distance of Asia from Europe (he chose the shortest of a number of
guesses on offer from medieval and classical sources) he sailed into the
"Green Sea of Darkness" in 1492. In four remarkable voyages he
became the first European to land on most of the islands of the
Caribbean and on the Central American mainland. He never
relinquished his belief that "I am before Zaiton (Japan) and Quinsay
(China), a hundred leagues, a little more or less" (Columbus, 1969, p.
26). The misnamed "West Indies" are a permanent reminder that the
Old World "discovered" the New by accident. But Columbus opened
up a whole continent to Spanish expansion, founded on the drive for
gold and the Catholic dream of converting the world to the Christian
faith. Shortly afterwards, Amerigo Vespucci (to whom the American
continents owe their name) sailed north to Carolina, and south along
the coast of Brazil to Rio, Patagonia, and the Falkland Islands.

In 1500 a Portuguese called Pedro Cabral, sailing to India, was blown out into the Atlantic and landed fortuitously on the coast of Brazil, giving Portugal her first foothold in what was to become Latin America. The threatened Spanish–Portuguese rivalry was aggravated by papal decrees favoring the Spanish, but was finally settled by the Treaty of Tordesillas (1494), which divided the "unknown world" between the Spanish and the Portuguese along a line of longitude running about 1500 miles west of the Azores. This line was subsequently revised many times and other nations, like Spain's arch enemy and Protestant rival, England, greedy to partake of the riches of the New World, soon made nonsense of it with their buccaneering exploits and raids along the Spanish Main. "Nevertheless," as John Roberts observes of the treaty,

> . . . it is a landmark of great psychological and political importance: Europeans, who by then had not even gone round the globe, had decided to divide between themselves all its undiscovered and unappropriated lands and peoples. The potential implications were vast . . . The conquest of the high seas was the first and greatest of all the triumphs over natural forces which were to lead to domination by western civilisation of the whole globe. Knowledge is power, and the knowledge won by the first systematic explorers . . . had opened the way to the age of western world hegemony.
> (Roberts, 1985, p. 194)

In 1519–22, a Portuguese expedition led by Magellan circumnavigated the globe, and Sir Francis Drake repeated this feat in 1577–80.

The early Spanish explorers of the New World opened the way to that ruthless band of soldier-adventurers, the Conquistadors, who completed the conquest of Central and South America, effecting the transition from exploration to conquest and colonization.

In 1513 Balboa, having explored the northern coast of South America, crossed the Isthmus of Darien to the Pacific. And in 1519 Cortés landed in Mexico and carried through the destruction of the Aztec empire. Pizarro pushed south through Ecuador to the Andes and Peru, and destroyed the Inca empire (1531–4), after which Orellana crossed the continent by way of the Amazon (1541–4). The Conquistadors were driven by the prospect of vast, unlimited fortunes. "We Spaniards," Cortés confessed, "suffer from a disease that only gold can cure" (quoted in Hale, 1966, p. 105).

The Spanish proceeded to push up into what are now New Mexico, Arizona, Florida, and Arkansas (1528–42). Meanwhile, further north, other nations were also busy exploring. John Cabot, a Venetian sailing under English patronage, landed at Nova Scotia, Newfoundland, and New England (1497–8). In 1500–1, the Portuguese Corte Real, and in 1524 the Italian Verrazano, explored the Atlantic seaboard of North America. They were followed in 1585–7 by Sir Walter Raleigh, and a number of British colonies were soon established: Newfoundland (1583), Roanoke (1585), and Jamestown (1607).

Yet further north, British explorers such as Gilbert, Frobisher, Davis, Hudson, and Baffin (1576–1616) tried in vain to find an alternative route to the East via a north-west passage through the Arctic seas. This quest was partly responsible for the opening up of North America, and Dutch, French, and English colonies sprang up along the Atlantic seaboard. Nevertheless, the serious exploration of Canada and North America was led largely by the French: Cartier, Champlain, and their followers exploring the St Lawrence river, the Great Lakes, and the Mississippi river down to the Gulf of Mexico (1534–1682).

The Spanish and Portuguese established an early presence in the Far East, and soon the Spanish were exploring the Pacific, colonizing islands, and even commuting out of Manila in the Philippines to the west coast of America (1565–1605). But the Dutch and the English set out to flout the Spanish and Portuguese commercial monopolies. The British East India Company was founded in 1599, the Dutch East India Company in 1602. After their independence from Spain in 1584, the Dutch became one of the most powerful commercial nations, their East Indies trade laying the basis for the flourishing of Dutch *bourgeois* culture (Schama, 1977). From a base in the old spice empire, the Dutch reached Fiji, the East Indies, Polynesia, Tasmania, New Zealand, and in 1606 were the first Europeans to catch sight of Australia. Over the next thirty years they gradually pieced together the Australian jigsaw-puzzle, though the Australian coast was not completely mapped until after Cook's famous voyages (1768–79) to Tahiti, the South Pacific, and the Antarctic.

By the eighteenth century, then, the main European world-players – Portugal, Spain, England, France, and Holland – were all in place. The serious business of bringing the far-flung civilizations they had discovered into the orbit of western trade and commerce, and exploiting their wealth, land, labor, and natural resources for European development had become a major enterprise. (China and India remained closed for longer, except for trading along their coasts and the efforts of Jesuit missionaries.) Europe began to imprint its culture and customs on the new worlds. European rivalries were constantly fought out and settled in the colonial theaters. The colonies became the "jewels in the crown" of the new European empires. Through trade monopolies and the mercantilist commercial system, each of these empires tried to secure exclusive control of the flow of trade for its own enrichment. The wealth began to flow in: in 1554 America yielded 11 percent of the Spanish Crown's income; in 1590, 50 percent.

## 2.4  Breaking the frame

Towards the end of the fifteenth century, then, Europe broke out of its long confinement. What had bottled it up for so long? This is a difficult question to answer, but we can identify two sets of factors – the first, material, the second, cultural.

*Physical barriers to the East*  The Middle Ages represented an actual loss of contact with and knowledge of the outside world. Alexander the Great's conquests (336–323 B.C.) had taken the Macedonian–Greek armies as far east as the Himalayas. Only his troops' reluctance prevented him from reaching what he believed to be the limits of the inhabited world. The Roman Empire stretched from Britain to the Arabian deserts. But in the Middle Ages Europe closed in on itself. It retained some knowledge of India (especially among Venetian traders), but beyond that lay unknown territory. Though every port and trade route on the Mediterranean was mapped, the basic contours of other seas and continents were shrouded in mystery. For example, though Europe bought great quantities of Chinese silk, transported by caravan across Central Asia, it took little interest in the great civilization from which the silk came.

A key factor in this was that, after the seventh century A.D., "sea-routes and land-routes alike were barred by the meteoric rise of Islam, which interposed its iron curtain between West and East" (Latham, 1958, p. 8). It was Arab middlemen who brought eastern goods to the European sea-ports of the Mediterranean and Black Sea to sell. The Crusades (1095–1291) were the long, and for a time unsuccessful, struggle of Christian Europe to roll back this "infidel threat." But just when, at last, Europe seemed to be winning, a thunderbolt struck from a quarter unexpected by both Islam and Christendom: the invasions of the Mongol and Tartar nomads from the Central Asian steppes (1206–60), which left a trail of devastation in their wake. However, Islam suffered even more than Christendom from the Tartar invasions and, in the thirteenth century, the eastern curtain lifted briefly.

During this interval, the Venetian Marco Polo and other members of his family undertook their famous travels to the court of the Great Khan, China, and Japan (1255–95).

Marco Polo's *Travels* with its tales of the fabulous wealth of the East played a decisive role in stimulating the European imagination to search for a westerly route to the East, a search that became increasingly important. For soon the eastern opening became blocked again by the rise of a new Islamic power, the Ottoman Empire; and China, under the Ming dynasty, once more turned inwards.

This had profound effects. It stimulated expansion westwards, favoring the European powers of the Atlantic seaboard (Spain, Portugal, Britain, Holland, and France). It also tended to isolate Western from Eastern Europe – a process reinforced by the growing split between Western (Catholic) and Eastern (Orthodox) Churches. From this point onwards, the patterns of development within Western and Eastern Europe sharply diverged.

*The barriers in the mind*   A second major obstacle to the East lay in the mind – consisting not only of the sketchy knowledge that Europeans had of the outside world, but of the way they conceptualized and imagined it. To the north, they believed, there was "nothing – or worse . . . barbarian peoples who, until civilized by the church, were only a menace" (Roberts, 1985, p. 117). To the east, across the plains, there were barbarians on horseback: Huns, Mongols, and Tartars. To the south lay the shifting empires of Islam, which, despite their early tolerance of Christianity and of the Jews, had advanced deep into Europe – to Poitiers and Constantinople, across North Africa and into Spain, Portugal, and southern Italy. The cradle of European civilization and trade was the Mediterranean. In the eastern Mediterranean, there was Byzantium – a civilization which was part of Christendom. But, as we said, the Catholic and Orthodox churches were drawing farther apart as the centuries passed.

For what lay beyond, Europe relied on other sources of knowledge – classical, biblical, legendary, and mythological. Asia remained largely a world of elephants and other wonders almost as remote as sub-Saharan Africa. There were four continents – Europe, Africa, Asia, and "Terra Australis Incognita" ("The Unknown Southern Land") – the way to the latter being judged impassable. On medieval maps, the land mass crowded out the oceans: there was no Pacific and the Atlantic was a narrow, and extremely dangerous, waterway. The world was often represented as a wheel, superimposed on the body of Christ, with Jerusalem at its hub. This conception of the world did not encourage free and wide-ranging travel.

## 2.5 The consequences of expansion for the idea of "the West"

Gradually, despite their many internal differences, the countries of Western Europe began to conceive of themselves as part of a single family or civilization – "the West." The challenge from Islam was an important factor in hammering Western Europe and the idea of "the West" into shape. Roberts notes that "The word 'Europeans' seems to appear for the first time in an eighth-century reference to Charles Martel's victory [over Islamic forces] at Tours. All collectivities become more self-aware in the presence of an external challenge, and self-awareness promotes cohesiveness" (Roberts, 1985, p. 122). And Hulme speaks of ". . . the consolidation of an ideological identity through the testing of [Europe's] Eastern frontiers prior to the adventure of Atlantic exploration. . . . A symbolic end to that process could be considered Pius III's 1458 identification of Europe with Christendom" (Hulme, 1986, p. 84).

But in the Age of Exploration and Conquest, Europe began to define itself in relation to a new idea – the existence of many new "worlds," profoundly different from itself. The two processes – growing internal cohesion and the conflicts and contrasts with external worlds – reinforced each other, helping to forge that new sense of identity that we call "the West." In the following extract Michael Mann offers an explanation of European development by making a series of historical generalizations about long-term socio-economic and religious factors:

> Why is "Europe" to be regarded as a continent in the first place? This is not an ecological but a social fact. It had not been a continent hitherto: it was now created by the fusion of the Germanic barbarians and the north-western parts of the Roman Empire, and the blocking presence of Islam to the south and east. Its continental identity was primarily Christian, for its name was Christendom more often than it was Europe.

Europe was undoubtedly a place where competition flourished, but why? It is not "natural." . . . In fact, competition presupposes two further forms of social organization. First, autonomous actors must be empowered to dispose of privately owned resources without hindrance from anyone else. These actors need not be individuals, or even individual households, enjoying what in capitalist societies we call "private property." . . . But collective institutions also qualify, as long as they have a responsible authority structure empowered to dispose of its resources for economic advantage, without interference from others, or from custom – then the laws of neoclassical economics can begin to operate. . . .

Second, competition among actors on a market [basis] requires normative regulation. They must trust one another to honour their word. They must also trust each other's essential rationality. These normative understandings must apply not only in direct interaction but right across complex, continental chains of production, distribution and exchange. . . .

European social structure supplied these requirements. The social structure which stabilized in Europe after the ending of the barbarian migrations and invasions (that is, by AD 1000) was a multiple acephalous federation. Europe had no head, no centre, yet it was an entity composed of a number of small, cross-cutting interaction networks. These, based on economic, military and ideological power, each differed in their geographical and social space and none was itself unitary in nature. Consequently no single power agency controlled a clear-cut territory or the people within it. As a result most social relationships were extremely localized, intensely focused upon one or more of a number of cell-like communities – the monastery, the village, the manor, the castle, the town, the guild, the brotherhood and so on. These collectivities had a power autonomy guaranteed by law or custom, an exclusivity of control over "their" resources. They qualify, therefore, as "private" property owners. . . .

Whatever this extraordinary multiple, acephalous federation would achieve, it was unlikely to be organized stagnation. Historians over and over again use the word *restless* to characterize the essence of medieval culture. As McNeill puts it, "it is not any particular set of institutions, ideas or technologies that mark out the West but its inability to come to a rest. No other civilized society has ever approached such restless instability. . . . In this . . . lies the true uniqueness of Western civilization" (McNeill, 1963, p. 539). But such a spirit need not induce social development. Might it not induce other forms of stagnation: anarchy, the Hobbesian war of all against all, or *anomie* where the absence of social control and direction leads to aimlessness and despair? We can marry the insights of two great sociologists to guess why social development, not anarchy or *anomie*, may have resulted.

First Max Weber, who in noting the peculiar restlessness of
Europe, always added another word: *rational*. "Rational
restlessness" was the psychological make-up of Europe, the
opposite of what he found in the main religions of Asia . . .
Weber located rational restlessness especially in Puritanism.
But Puritanism emphasized strands of the Christian psyche
which had been traditionally present. . . . Christianity encouraged
a drive for moral and social improvement even against worldly
authority. Though much of medieval Christianity was piously
masking brutal repression, its currents of dissatisfaction
always ran strong. We can read an enormous literature of social
criticism, visionary, moralistic, satirical, cynical. Some is
laboured and repetitious, but its peak includes some of the
greatest works of the age – in English: Langland and Chaucer.
It is pervaded by the kind of psychological quality identified by
Weber.

But to put this rational restlessness in the service of social
improvement probably also required a mechanism identified by
another sociologist: Emile Durkheim. Not anarchy or *anomie* but
normative regulation was provided at first primarily by
Christendom. Political and class struggles, economic life and even
wars were, to a degree, regulated by an unseen hand, not Adam
Smith's but Jesus Christ's. . . . The community depended on the
general recognition of norms regarding property rights and free
exchange. These were guaranteed by a mixture of local customs
and privileges, some judicial regulation by weak states, but
above all by the common social identity provided by
Christendom. . . .

The main conclusion is unmistakable. The most powerful and
extensive sense of social identity was Christian, though this was
both a unifying transcendent identity and an identity divided by
the overlapping barriers of class and literacy. Cross-cutting all
these were commitments to England, but these were variable and,
in any case, included less extensive dynastic connections and
obligations. Thus, Christian identity provided both a common
humanity and a framework for common divisions among
Europeans. . . .

The Christian achievement was the creation of a minimal
normative society across state, ethnic, class and gender
boundaries. It did not in any significant sense include the Eastern
Byzantine Church. It did, however, integrate the two major
geographical areas of "Europe", the Mediterranean lands with
their cultural heritage, their historic and predominantly *extensive*
power techniques – literacy, coinage, agricultural estates and
trading networks – and north-western Europe with its more
*intensive* power techniques – deep ploughing, village and kin
solidarities and locally organized warfare. If the two could be kept
in a single community, then European development was a
possible consequence of their creative interchange.
(Mann, 1988, pp. 10–15)

In contrast to Mann, John Roberts brings cultural and ideological aspects to the fore:

> Europeans . . . now [took] a new view of themselves and their relation to the other peoples of the globe. Maps are the best clue to this change . . . They are always more than mere factual statements. They are translations of reality into forms we can master; they are fictions and acts of imagination communicating more than scientific data. So they reflect changes in our pictures of reality. The world is not only what exists "out there"; it is also the picture we have of it in our minds which enables us to take a grip on material actuality. In taking that grip, our apprehension of that actuality changes – and so does a wide range of our assumptions and beliefs.
>
> One crucial mental change was the final emergence of the notion of Europe from the idea of Christendom. Maps show the difference between the two. After the age of discovery, Jerusalem, where the founder of Christianity had taught and died, could no longer be treated as the centre of the world – where it appeared on many medieval maps. Soon it was Europe which stood at the centre of Europeans' maps. The final key to a new mental picture was provided by the discovery of the Americas. Somewhere about 1500 European map-makers had established the broad layout of the world map with which we are familiar. In the fifteenth century, Europe had usually been placed in the top left-hand corner of attempts to lay out the known world, with the large masses of Asia and Africa sprawled across the rest of the surface. The natural centre of such maps might be in any of several places. Then the American discoveries slowly began to effect a shift in the conventional arrangement; more and more space had to be given to the land masses of North and South America as their true extent became better known. . . .
>
> By the middle of the century the new geographical view of the world had come to be taken for granted. It was given its canonical expression in the work of Mercator . . . Mercator's new "projection", first used in a map in 1568, . . . drove home the idea that the land surface of the globe was naturally grouped about a European centre. So Europe came to stand in some men's minds at the centre of the world. No doubt this led Europeans for centuries to absorb unconsciously from their atlases the idea that this was somehow the natural order of things. It did not often occur to them that you could have centred Mercator's projection in, say, China, or even Hawaii, and that Europeans might then have felt very different. The idea still hangs about, even today. Most people like to think of themselves at the centre of things. . . . Mercator helped his own civilisation to take what is now called a "Eurocentric" view of the world.
> (Roberts, 1985, pp. 194–202)

Roberts argues that maps are "fictions" which "reflect changes in our pictures of reality." His larger claims, however, focus on the centrality of Christianity to the idea of "Europe." For centuries, the concepts "Europe" and "Christendom" were virtually identical. Europe's cultural identity – what made its civilization distinct and unique – was, in the first instance, essentially religious and Christian. Eventually, the idea of "Europe" acquired a sharper geographical, political, and economic definition. This brought it closer to the modern, secular concept of "the West." However, the West has never entirely lost touch with its Christian roots. The encounter with the new worlds – with *difference* – actually reinforced this new identity. It promoted that "growing sense of superiority," which Roberts calls a "Eurocentric" view of the world.

# 3   Discourse and Power

We have looked at the historical process by which an idea of "the West" emerged from Europe's growing internal cohesion and its changing relations to non-Western societies. We turn, next, to the formation of the languages or "discourses" in which Europe began to describe and represent the *difference* between itself and these "others" it encountered in the course of its expansion. We are now beginning to sketch the formation of the "discourse" of "the West and the Rest." However, we need first to understand what we mean by the term "discourse."

## 3.1   What is a "discourse"?

In common-sense language, a **discourse** is simply "a coherent or rational body of speech or writing; a speech, or a sermon." But here the term is being used in a more specialized way. By "discourse," we mean a particular way of *representing* "the West," "the Rest," and the relations between them. A discourse is a group of statements which provide a language for talking about – i.e. a way of representing – a particular kind of knowledge about a topic. When statements about a topic are made within a particular discourse, the discourse makes it possible to construct the topic in a certain way. It also limits the other ways in which the topic can be constructed.

A discourse does not consist of one statement, but of several statements working together to form what the French social theorist, Michel Foucault (1926–84) calls a **"discursive formation."** The statements fit together because any one statement implies a relation to all the others: "They refer to the same object, share the same style and support 'a strategy . . . a common institutional . . . or political drift or pattern'" (Cousins and Hussain, 1984, pp. 84–5).

One important point about this notion of discourse is that it is not based on the conventional distinction between thought and action, language and practice. Discourse is about the production of knowledge through language. But it is itself produced by a practice: "discursive practice" – the practice of producing meaning. Since all social practices entail *meaning*, all practices have a discursive aspect. So discourse enters into and influences all social practices. Foucault would argue that the discourse of the West about the Rest was deeply implicated in practice – i.e. in how the West behaved towards the Rest.

To get a fuller sense of Foucault's theory of discourse, we must bear the following points in mind.

1   A discourse can be produced by many individuals in different institutional settings (like families, prisons, hospitals, and asylums). Its integrity or "coherence" does not depend on whether or not it issues from one place or from a single speaker or "subject." Nevertheless, every discourse constructs positions from which alone it makes sense. Anyone deploying a discourse must position themselves *as if* they were the subject of the discourse. For example, we may not ourselves believe in the natural superiority of the West. But if we use the discourse of "the West and the Rest" we will necessarily find ourselves speaking from a position that holds that the West is a superior civilization. As Foucault puts it, "To describe a . . . statement does not consist in analysing the relations between the author and what he [*sic*] says . . . ; but in determining what position can and must be occupied by any individual if he is to be the subject of it [the statement]" (Foucault, 1972, pp. 95–6).

2   Discourses are not closed systems. A discourse draws on elements in other discourses, binding them into its own network of meanings. Thus, as we saw in the preceding section, the discourse of "Europe" drew on the earlier discourse of "Christendom," altering or translating its meaning. Traces of past discourses remain embedded in more recent discourses of "the West."

3   The statements within a discursive formation need not all be the same. But the relationships and differences between them must be regular and systematic, not random. Foucault calls this a "system of dispersion": "Whenever one can describe, between a number of statements, such a system of dispersion, whenever . . . one can define a regularity . . . [then] we will say . . . that we are dealing with a *discursive formation*" (Foucault, 1972, p. 38).

These points will become clearer when we apply them to particular examples, as we do later in this chapter.

## 3.2   Discourse and ideology

A discourse is similar to what sociologists call an "ideology": a set of statements or beliefs which produce knowledge that serves the interests of a particular group or class. Why, then, use "discourse" rather than "ideology"?

One reason which Foucault gives is that ideology is based on a distinction between *true* statements about the world (science) and *false* statements (ideology), and the belief that the facts about the world help us to decide between true and false statements. But Foucault argues that statements about the social, political, or moral world are rarely ever simply true or false; and "the facts" do not enable us to decide definitively about their truth or falsehood, partly because "facts" can be construed in different ways. The very language we use to describe the so-called facts interferes in this process of finally deciding what is true and what is false.

For example, Palestinians fighting to regain land on the West Bank from Israel may be described either as "freedom fighters" or as "terrorists." It is a fact that they are fighting; but what does the fighting *mean*? The facts alone cannot decide. And the very language we use – "freedom fighters/terrorists" – is part of the difficulty. Moreover, certain descriptions, even if they appear false to us, can be *made* "true" because people act on them believing that they are true, and so their actions have real consequences. Whether the Palestinians are terrorists or not, if we think they are, and act on that "knowledge," they in effect become terrorists because we treat them as such. The language (discourse) has real effects in practice: the description becomes "true."

Foucault's use of "discourse," then, is an attempt to side-step what seems an unresolvable dilemma – deciding which social discourses are true or scientific, and which false or ideological. Most social scientists now accept that our values enter into all our descriptions of the social world, and therefore most of our statements, however factual, have an ideological dimension. What Foucault would say is that knowledge of the Palestinian problem is produced by competing discourses – those of "freedom-fighter" and "terrorist" – and that each is linked to a contestation over power. It is the outcome of *this* struggle which will decide the "truth" of the situation.

You can see, then, that although the concept of "discourse" side-steps the problem of truth/falsehood in ideology, it does *not* evade the issue of power. Indeed, it gives considerable weight to questions of power since it is power, rather than the facts about reality, which makes things "true": "We should admit that power produces knowledge . . . That power and knowledge directly imply one another; that there is no power relation without the correlative constitution of a field of knowledge, nor any knowledge that does not presuppose and constitute . . . power relations" (Foucault, 1980, p. 27).

## 3.3   Can a discourse be "innocent"?

Could the discourse which developed in the West for talking about the Rest operate outside power? Could it be, in that sense, purely scientific – i.e. ideologically innocent? Or was it influenced by particular class interests?

Foucault is very reluctant to *reduce* discourse to statements that simply mirror the interests of a particular class. The same discourse can be used by groups with different, even contradictory, class interests. But this does *not* mean that discourse is ideologically neutral or "innocent." Take, for example, the encounter between the West and the New World. There are several reasons why this encounter could not be innocent, and therefore why the discourse which emerged in the Old World about the Rest could not be innocent either.

First, Europe brought its own cultural categories, languages, images, and ideas to the New World in order to describe and represent it. It tried to fit the New World into existing conceptual frameworks, classifying it according to its own norms, and absorbing it into western traditions of representation. This is hardly surprising: we often draw on what we already know about the world in order to explain and describe something novel. It was never a simple matter of the West just looking, seeing, and describing the New World/the Rest without preconceptions.

Secondly, Europe had certain definite purposes, aims, objectives, motives, interests, and strategies in setting out to discover what lay across the "Green Sea of Darkness." These motives and interests were mixed. The Spanish, for example, wanted to:

1   get their hands on gold and silver;

2   claim the land for Their Catholic Majesties; and

3   convert the heathen to Christianity.

These interests often contradicted one another. But we must not suppose that what Europeans said about the New World was simply a cynical mask for their own self-interest. When King Manuel of Portugal wrote to Ferdinand and Isabella of Spain that "the principal motive of this enterprise [da Gama's voyage to India] has been . . . the service of God our Lord, and our own advantage" (quoted in Hale, 1966, p. 38) – thereby neatly and conveniently bringing God and Mammon together into the same sentence – he probably saw no obvious contradiction between them. These fervently religious Catholic rulers fully believed what they were saying. To them, serving God and pursuing "our advantage" were not necessarily at odds. They lived and fully believed their own ideology.

So, while it would be wrong to attempt to reduce their statements to naked self-interest, it is clear that their discourse was molded and influenced by the play of motives and interests across their language. Of course, motives and interests are almost never wholly conscious or rational. The desires which drove the Europeans were powerful; but their power was not always subject to rational calculation. Marco Polo's "treasures of the East" were tangible enough. But the seductive power which they exerted over generations of Europeans transformed them more and more into a myth. Similarly, the gold that Columbus kept asking the natives for very soon acquired a mystical, quasi-religious significance.

Finally, the discourse of "the West and the Rest" could not be innocent because it did not represent an encounter between equals. The Europeans had outsailed, outshot, and outwitted peoples who had no wish to be "explored," no need to be "discovered," and no desire to be "exploited." The Europeans stood, vis-à-vis the Others, in positions of dominant power. This influenced what they saw and how they saw it, as well as what they did not see.

Foucault sums up these arguments as follows. Not only is discourse always implicated in *power*; discourse is one of the "systems" through which power circulates. The knowledge which a discourse produces

constitutes a kind of power, exercised over those who are "known."
When that knowledge is exercised in practice, those who are "known"
in a particular way will be subject (i.e. subjected) to it. This is always a
power-relation. (See Foucault, 1980, p. 201.) Those who produce the
discourse also have the power to *make it true* – i.e. to enforce its
validity, its scientific status.

This leaves Foucault in a highly relativistic position with respect to
questions of truth because his notion of discourse undermines the
distinction between true and false statements – between science and
ideology – to which many sociologists have subscribed. These
epistemological issues (about the status of knowledge, truth, and
relativism) are too complex to take further here. (Some of them are
addressed further in part III.) However, the important idea to grasp now
is the deep and intimate relationship which Foucault establishes
between discourse, knowledge, and power. According to Foucault,
when power operates so as to enforce the "truth" of any set of
statements, then such a discursive formation produces a "regime of
truth."

Let us summarize the main points of this argument. Discourses are
ways of talking, thinking, or representing a particular subject or topic.
They produce meaningful knowledge about that subject. This
knowledge influences social practices, and so has real consequences
and effects. Discourses are not reducible to class-interests, but always
operate in relation to power – they are part of the way power circulates
and is contested. The question of whether a discourse is true or false is
less important than whether it is effective in practice. When it is
effective – organizing and regulating relations of power (say, between
the West and the Rest) – it is called a "regime of truth."

# 4   Representing "the Other"

So far, the discussion of discourse has been rather abstract and
conceptual. The concept may be easier to understand in relation to an
example. One of the best examples of what Foucault means by a
"regime of truth" is provided by Edward Said's study of **Orientalism**. In
this section, I want to look briefly at this example and then see how far
we can use the theory of discourse and the example of Orientalism to
analyze the discourse of "the West and the Rest."

## 4.1   Orientalism

In his book *Orientalism*, Edward Said analyzes the various discourses
and institutions which constructed and produced, as an object of
knowledge, that entity called "the Orient." Said calls this discourse
"Orientalism." Note that, though we tend to include the Far East
(including China) in our use of the word "Orient," Said refers mainly to
the Middle East – the territory occupied principally by Islamic peoples.

Also, his main focus is French writing about the Middle East. Here is Said's own summary of the project of his book:

> My contention is that, without examining Orientalism as a discourse, one cannot possibly understand the enormously systematic discipline by which European culture was able to manage – and even produce – the Orient politically, sociologically, militarily, ideologically, scientifically and imaginatively during the post-Enlightenment period. Moreover, so authoritative a position did Orientalism have that I believe no one writing, thinking, or acting on the Orient could do so without taking account of the limitations on thought and action imposed by Orientalism. In brief, because of Orientalism, the Orient was not (and is not) a free subject of thought and action. This is not to say that Orientalism unilaterally determines what can be said about the Orient, but that it is the whole network of interests inevitably brought to bear on (and therefore always involved in) any occasion when that peculiar entity "the Orient" is in question. . . . This book also tries to show that European culture gained in strength and identity by setting itself off against the Orient as a sort of surrogate and even underground self.
> (Said, 1985, p. 3)

We will now analyze the discourse of "the West and the Rest," as it emerged between the end of the fifteenth and eighteenth centuries, using Foucault's ideas about "discourse" and Said's example of "Orientalism." How was this discourse formed? What were its main themes – its "strategies" of representation?

## 4.2   The "archive"

Said argues that, "In a sense Orientalism was a library or archive of information commonly . . . held. What bound the archive together was a family of ideas and a unifying set of values proven in various ways to be effective. These ideas explained the behaviour of Orientals; they supplied Orientals with a mentality, a genealogy, an atmosphere; most important, they allowed Europeans to deal with and even to see Orientals as a phenomenon possessing regular characteristics" (Said, 1985, pp. 41–2). What sources of common knowledge, what "archive" of other discourses, did the discourse of "the West and the Rest" draw on? We can identify four main sources:

1   **Classical knowledge**: This was a major source of information and images about "other worlds." Plato (c. 427–347 B.C.) described a string of legendary islands, among them Atlantis which many early explorers set out to find. Aristotle (384–322 B.C.) and Eratosthenes (c. 276–194 B.C.) both made remarkably accurate estimates of the circumference of the globe which were consulted by Columbus. Ptolemy's *Geographia* (2nd century A.D.) provided a model for map-makers more than a thousand years after it had been produced. Sixteenth-century explorers believed that in the outer world lay, not only Paradise, but that

"Golden Age," place of perfect happiness and "springtime of the human race," of which the classical poets, including Horace (65–8 B.C.) and Ovid (43 B.C.–A.D. 17), had written.

The eighteenth century was still debating whether what they had discovered in the South Pacific was Paradise. In 1768 the French Pacific explorer Bougainville renamed Tahiti "The New Cythera" after the island where, according to classical myth, Venus first appeared from the sea. At the opposite extreme, the descriptions by Herodotus (484–425 B.C.) and Pliny (A.D. 23–79) of the barbarous peoples who bordered Greece left many grotesque images of "other" races which served as self-fulfilling prophecies for later explorers who found what legend said they would find. Paradoxically, much of this classical knowledge was lost in the Dark Ages and only later became available to the West via Islamic scholars, themselves part of that "other" world.

2 **Religious and biblical sources**: These were another source of knowledge. The Middle Ages reinterpreted geography in terms of the Bible. Jerusalem was the center of the earth because it was the Holy City. Asia was the home of the Three Wise Kings; Africa that of King Solomon. Columbus believed the Orinoco (in Venezuela) to be a sacred river flowing out of the Garden of Eden.

3 **Mythology**: It was difficult to tell where religious and classical discourses ended and those of myth and legend began. Mythology transformed the outer world into an enchanted garden, alive with misshapen peoples and monstrous oddities. In the sixteenth century Sir Walter Raleigh still believed he would find, in the Amazon rain-forests, the king "El Dorado" ("The Gilded One") whose people were alleged to roll him in gold which they would then wash off in a sacred lake.

4 **Travellers' tales**: Perhaps the most fertile source of information was travellers' tales – a discourse where description faded imperceptibly into legend. The following fifteenth century German text summarizes more than a thousand years of travellers' tales, which themselves often drew on religious and classical authority:

> In the land of Indian there are men with dogs' heads who talk by barking [and] . . . feed by catching birds. . . . Others again have only one eye in the forehead. . . . In Libya many are born without heads and have a mouth and eyes. Many are of both sexes. . . . Close to Paradise on the River Ganges live men who eat nothing.
> For . . . they absorb liquid nourishment through a straw [and] . . . live on the juice of flowers. . . . Many have such large underlips that they can cover their whole faces with them. . . . In the land of Ethiopia many people walk bent down like cattle, and many live four hundred years. Many have horns, long noses and goats' feet. . . . In Ethiopia towards the west many have four eyes . . . [and] in Eripia there live beautiful people with the necks and bills of cranes.
> (quoted in Newby, 1975, p. 17)

A particularly rich repository was Sir John Mandeville's *Travels* – in fact, a compendium of fanciful stories by different hands. Marco Polo's

*Travels* was generally more sober and factual, but nevertheless achieved mythological status. His text (embellished by Rusticello, a romance writer) was the most widely read of the travellers' accounts and was instrumental in creating the myth of "Cathay" ("China" or the East generally), a dream that inspired Columbus and many others.

The point of recounting this astonishing mixture of fact and fantasy which constituted late medieval "knowledge" of other worlds is not to poke fun at the ignorance of the Middle Ages. The point is: (a) to bring home how these very different discourses, with variable statuses as "evidence," provided the cultural framework through which the peoples, places, and things of the New World were seen, described, and represented; and (b) to underline the conflation of fact and fantasy that constituted "knowledge." This can be seen especially in the use of analogy to describe first encounters with strange animals. Penguins and seals were described as being like geese and wolves respectively; the tapir as a bull with a trunk like an elephant, the opossum as half-fox, half-monkey.

## 4.3   A "regime of truth"

Gradually, observation and description vastly improved in accuracy. The medieval habit of thinking in terms of analogies gave way to a more sober type of description of the fauna and flora, ways of life, customs, physical characteristics, and social organization of native peoples. We can here begin to see the outlines of an early ethnography or anthropology.

But the shift into a more descriptive, factual discourse, with its claims to truth and scientific objectivity, provided no guarantees. A telling example of this is the case of the "Patagonians." Many myths and legends told of a race of giant people. And in the 1520s, Magellan's crew brought back stories of having encountered, in South America, such a race of giants whom they dubbed *patagones* (literally, "big feet"). The area of the supposed encounter became known as "Patagonia," and the notion became fixed in the popular imagination, even though two Englishmen who visited Patagonia in 1741 described its people as being of average size.

When Commodore John Byron landed in Patagonia in 1764, he encountered a formidable group of natives, broad-shouldered, stocky, and inches taller than the average European. They proved quite docile and friendly. However, the newspaper reports of his encounter wildly exaggerated the story, and Patagonians took on an even greater stature and more ferocious aspect. One engraving showed a sailor reaching only as high as the waist of a Patagonian giant, and The Royal Society elevated the topic to serious scientific status. "The engravings took the explorers' raw material and shaped them into images familiar to Europeans" (Withey, 1987, pp. 1175–6). Legend had taken a late revenge on science.

## 4.4 Idealization

"Orientalism," Said remarks, "is the discipline by which the Orient was (and is) approached systematically, as a topic of learning, discovery and practice." "In addition," he adds, Orientalism "designate[s] that collection of dreams, images and vocabularies available to anyone who has tried to talk about what lies east of the dividing line" (Said, 1985, p. 73). Like the Orient, the Rest quickly became the subject of the languages of dream and Utopia, the object of a powerful fantasy.

Between 1590 and 1634 the Flemish engraver Theodor de Bry published his *Historia Americae* in ten illustrated volumes. These were leading examples of a new popular literature about the New World and the discoveries there. De Bry's books contained elaborate engravings of life and customs of the New World. Here we see the New World reworked – re-presented – within European aesthetic conventions, Western "ways of seeing." Different images of America are superimposed on one another. De Bry, for example, transformed the simple, unpretentious sketches which John White had produced in 1587 of the Algonquin Indians he had observed in Virginia. Facial features were retouched, gestures adjusted, and postures reworked according to more classical European styles. The effect overall, Hugh Honour observes, was "to tame and civilize the people White had observed so freshly" (Honour, 1976, p. 75).

A major object of this process of idealization was Nature itself. The fertility of the Tropics was astonishing even to Mediterranean eyes. Few had ever seen landscapes like those of the Caribbean and Central America. However, the line between description and idealization is almost impossible to draw. In describing Cuba, for example, Columbus refers to "trees of a thousand kinds . . . so tall they seem to touch the sky," sierras and high mountains "most beautiful and of a thousand shapes," nightingales and other birds, marvellous pine groves, fertile plains and varieties of fruit (quoted in Honour, 1976, p. 5). Columbus's friend, Peter Martyr, later used his descriptions to express a set of rich themes which resound across the centuries:

> The inhabitants live in that Golden World of which old writers speak so much, wherein men lived simply and innocently, without enforcement of laws, without quarrelling, judges and libels, content only to satisfy Nature . . . [There are] naked girls so beautiful that one might think he [*sic*] beheld those splendid naiads and nymphs of the fountains so much celebrated by the ancients.
> (quoted in Honour, 1978, p. 6)

The key themes in this passage are worth identifying since they reappear in later variants of "the West and the Rest":

1   the Golden World; an Earthly Paradise;
2   the simple, innocent life;
3   the lack of developed social organization and civil society;
4   people living in a pure state of Nature;

5    the frank and open sexuality; the nakedness; the beauty of the
women.

In these images and metaphors of the New World as an Earthly
Paradise, a Golden Age, or Utopia, we can see a powerful European
fantasy being constructed.

## 4.5   Sexual fantasy

Sexuality was a powerful element in the fantasy which the West
constructed, and the ideas of sexual innocence and experience, sexual
domination and submissiveness, play out a complex dance in the
discourse of "the West and the Rest."

When Captain Cook arrived in Tahiti in 1769, the same idyll of a
sexual paradise was repeated all over again. The women were
extremely beautiful, the vegetation lush and tropical, the life simple,
innocent, and free; Nature nourished the people without the apparent
necessity to work or cultivate; the sexuality was open and unashamed –
untroubled by the burden of European guilt. The naturalist on
Bougainville's voyage to the Pacific said that the Tahitians were
"without vice, prejudice, needs or dissention and knew no other god
but Love" (Moorhead, 1968, p. 51). "In short," Joseph Banks, the
gentleman-scientist who accompanied Cook, observed, "the scene that
we saw was the truest picture of an Arcadia, of which we were going to
be kings, that the imagination can form" (quoted in Moorhead, 1987, p.
38). As Cook's biographer, J.C. Beaglehole, remarks, "they were
standing on the beach of the dream-world already, they walked straight
into the Golden Age and embraced their nymphs" (quoted in
Moorhead, 1968, p. 66). The West's contemporary image of tropical
paradise and exotic holidays still owes much to this fantasy.

Popular accounts by other explorers, such as Amerigo Vespucci
(1451–1512), were explicit – where Columbus had been more reticent –
about the sexual dimension. New World people, Vespucci said, "lived
according to Nature," and went naked and unashamed; "the
women . . . remained attractive after childbirth, were libidinous, and
enlarged the penises of their lovers with magic potions" (quoted in
Honour, 1976, p. 56).

The very language of exploration, conquest and domination was
strongly marked by gender distinctions and drew much of its
subconscious force from sexual imagery (see figure 6.3). In figure 6.3,
"Europe" (Amerigo Vespucci) stands bold and upright, a commanding
male figure, his feet firmly planted on *terra firma*. Around him are the
insignia of power: the standard of Their Catholic Majesties of Spain,
surmounted by a cross; in his left hand, the astrolabe that guided him,
the fruit of western knowledge; behind him, the galleons, sails
billowing. Vespucci presents an image of supreme mastery. Hulme
comments that, "In line with existing European conventions, the 'new'
continent was often allegorized as a woman" – here, naked, in a
hammock, surrounded by the emblems of an exotic landscape: strange
plants and animals and, above all, a cannibal feast (see Hulme, 1986, p.
xii).

Figure 6.3 Europe encounters America (van der Straet, c. 1600)

## 4.6  Mis-recognizing difference

Said says that "the essence of Orientalism is the ineradicable distinction between Western superiority and Oriental inferiority" (Said, 1985, p. 42). How was this strong marking of difference constructed?

Europeans were immediately struck by what they interpreted as the absence of government and civil society – the basis of all "civilization" – among peoples of the New World. In fact these peoples did have several, very different, highly elaborated social structures. The New World the Europeans discovered was already home to millions of people who had lived there for centuries, whose ancestors had migrated to America from Asia across the neck of land which once connected the two continents. It is estimated that sixteen million people were living in the western hemisphere when the Spanish "discovered" it. The highest concentration was in Mexico, while only about a million lived in North America. They had very different standards and styles of life. The Pueblo of Central America were village people. Others were hunter-gatherers on the plains and in the forests. The Arawaks of the Caribbean islands had a relatively simple type of society based on subsistence farming and fishing. Further North, the Iroquois of the Carolinas were fierce, nomadic hunters.

The high civilization of the Maya, with its dazzling white cities, was based on a developed agriculture; it was stable, literate, and composed of a federation of nations, with a complex hierarchy of government. The civilizations of the Aztecs (Mexico) and the Inca (Peru) were both large, complex affairs, based on maize cultivation and with a richly developed art, culture, and religion. Both had a complex social structure and a centralized administrative system, and both were capable of extraordinary engineering feats. Their temples outstripped in size anything in Europe, and the Royal Road of the Incas ran for nearly 2000 miles through mountainous terrain – further than the extent of the Roman empire from York to Jerusalem (see Newby, 1975, pp. 95–7).

These were functioning societies. What they were *not* was "European." What disturbed western expectations, what had to be negotiated and explained, was their *difference*. As the centuries passed, Europeans came to know more about the specific characteristics of different "native American" peoples. Yet, in everyday terms, they persisted in describing them *all* as "Indians," lumping all distinctions together and suppressing differences in one, inaccurate stereotype (see Berkhofer, 1978).

Another illustration of the inability to deal with difference is provided by Captain Cook's early experience of Tahiti (1769). The Englishmen knew that the Tahitians held property communally and that they were therefore unlikely to possess a European concept of "theft." In order to win over the natives, the crew showered them with gifts. Soon, however, the Tahitians began to help themselves. At first the pilfering amused the visitors. But when the natives snatched Banks's spyglass and snuff-box, he threatened them with his musket until they were returned. Cook's crew continued to be plagued by incidents like this. A similar misunderstanding was to lead to Cook's death at the hands of the Hawaiians, in 1779.

The first actual contact with local inhabitants was often through an exchange of gifts, quickly followed by a more regular system of trade. Eventually, of course, this trade was integrated into a whole commercial system organized by Europe. Many early illustrations represent the inauguration of these unequal exchanges (see figure 6.4). In Theodor de Bry's famous engraving of Columbus being greeted by the Indians, Columbus stands in exactly the same heroic pose as Vespucci ("Europe") in van der Straet's engraving. On the left, the Cross is being planted. The natives (looking rather European) come, bearing gifts and offering them in a gesture of welcome. As Columbus noted in his log-book, the natives were "marvellously friendly towards us." "In fact," he says, disarmingly, "they very willingly traded everything they had" (Columbus, 1969, p. 55). Subsequent illustrations showed the Indians laboring to produce gold and sugar (described by the caption as a "gift") *for* the Spaniards.

The behavior of the Europeans was governed by the complex understandings and norms which regulated their own systems of monetary exchange, trade, and commerce. Europeans assumed that, since the natives did not have such an economic system, they therefore had no system at all and offered gifts as a friendly and suppliant gesture to visitors whose natural superiority they instantly recognized. The Europeans therefore felt free to organize the continuous supply of such "gifts" for their own benefit. What the Europeans found difficult to comprehend was that the exchange of gifts was part of a highly complex, but different, set of social practices – the practices of reciprocity – which only had meaning within a certain cultural context. Caribbean practices were different from, though as intricate in their

Figure 6.4 Columbus being greeted by the Indians (de Bry, 1590)

social meaning and effects as, the norms and practices of European
exchange and commerce.

## 4.7 Rituals of degradation

The cannibal feast in the corner of the van der Straet engraving (figure
6.3) was an intrusive detail. It points to a set of themes, evident from
the first contact, which were, in fact, the reverse side – the exact
opposites – of the themes of innocence, idyllic simplicity, and
proximity to Nature discussed earlier. It was as if everything which
Europeans represented as attractive and enticing about the natives
could also be used to represent the exact opposite: their barbarous and
depraved character. One account of Vespucci's voyages brought these
two sides together in the same passage: "The people are thus
naked . . . well-formed in body, their heads, necks, arms, privy part, feet
of women and men slightly covered with feathers. No one owns
anything but all things are in common. . . . The men have as wives
those that please them, be they mothers, sisters or friends . . . They also
fight with each other. They also eat each other" (quoted in Honour,
1976, p. 8).

There were disturbing reversals being executed in the discourse here.
The innocent, friendly people in their hammocks could also be
exceedingly unfriendly and hostile. Living close to Nature meant that

they had no developed culture – and were therefore "uncivilized." Welcoming to visitors, they could also fiercely resist and had war-like rivalries with other tribes. (The New World was no freer of rivalry, competition, conflict, war, and violence than the Old.) Beautiful nymphs and naiads could also be "warlike and savage." At a moment's notice, Paradise could turn into "barbarism." Both versions of the discourse operated simultaneously. They may seem to negate each other, but it is more accurate to think of them as *mirror-images*. Both were exaggerations, founded on stereotypes, feeding off each other. Each required the other. They were in opposition, but systematically related: part of what Foucault calls a "system of dispersion."

From the beginning, *some* people described the natives of the New World as "lacking both the power of reason and the knowledge of God"; as "beasts in human form." It is hard, they said, to believe God had created a race so obstinate in its viciousness and bestiality. The sexuality which fed the fantasies of some, outraged many others. The natives were more addicted, it was said, to incest, sodomy, and licentiousness than any other race. They had no sense of justice, were bestial in their customs, inimical to religion. The characteristic which condensed all this into a single image was their (alleged) consumption of human flesh.

The question of cannibalism represents a puzzle which has never been resolved. Human sacrifice – which may have included cannibalism – was associated with some religious rituals. There may have been ritual sacrifice, involving some cannibalism, of captured enemies. But careful reviews of the relevant literature now suggest that the hard evidence is much sketchier and more ambiguous than has been assumed. The extent of any cannibalism was considerably exaggerated: it was frequently attributed by one tribe to "other people" – who were rivals or enemies; much of what is offered as having been witnessed first-hand turns out to be second- or third-hand reports; the practice had usually just ended months before the European visitors arrived. The evidence that, as a normal matter of course, outside ritual occasions, New World Indians regularly sat down to an evening meal composed of juicy limbs of their fellow humans is extremely thin (see, for example, the extensive analysis of the anthropological literature in Arens, 1978).

Peter Hulme (1986) offers a convincing account of how cannibalism became the prime symbol or signifier of "barbarism," thus helping to fix certain stereotypes. Columbus reported (January 13, 1493) that in Hispaniola he met a warlike group, whom he judged "must be one of the Caribs who eat men" (Columbus, 1969, p. 40). The Spanish divided the natives into two distinct groupings: the "peaceful" Arawaks and the "warlike" Caribs. The latter were said to invade Arawak territory, steal their wives, resist conquest, and be "cannibals." What started as a way of describing a social group turned out to be a way of "establishing which Amerindians were prepared to accept the Spaniards on the latter's terms, and which were hostile, that is to say prepared to defend their territory and way of life" (Hulme, 1986, p. 72).

In fact, so entrenched did the idea become that the "fierce" Caribs were eaters of human flesh, that their ethnic name (Carib) came to be used to refer to anyone thought guilty of this behavior. As a result, we today have the word "cannibal," which is actually derived from the name "Carib."

## 4.8 Summary: stereotypes, dualism, and "splitting"

We can now try to draw together our sketch of the formation and modes of operation of this discourse or "system of representation" we have called "the West and the Rest."

Hugh Honour, who studied European images of America from the period of discovery onwards, has remarked that "Europeans increasingly tended to see in America an idealized or distorted image of their own countries, on to which they could project their own aspirations and fears, their self-confidence and . . . guilty despair" (Honour, 1976, p. 3). We have identified some of these **discursive strategies** in this section. They are:

1  idealization;
2  the projection of fantasies of desire and degradation;
3  the failure to recognize and respect difference;
4  the tendency to impose European categories and norms, to see difference through the modes of perception and representation of the West.

These strategies were all underpinned by the process known as **stereotyping**. A stereotype is a one-sided description which results from the collapsing of complex differences into a simple "cardboard cut-out." Different characteristics are run together or condensed into one. This exaggerated simplification is then attached to a subject or place. Its characteristics become the signs, the "evidence," by which the subject is known. They define its being, its *essence*. Hulme noted that,

> As always, the stereotype operates principally through a judicious combination of adjectives, which establish [certain] characteristics as [if they were] eternal verities ["truths"], immune from the irrelevancies of the historical moment: [e.g.] "ferocious", "warlike", "hostile", "truculent and vindictive" – these are present as innate characteristics, irrespective of circumstances;
> . . . [consequently, the Caribs] were locked as "cannibals" into a realm of "beingness" that lies beyond question. This stereotypical dualism has proved stubbornly immune to all kinds of contradictory evidence.
> (Hulme, 1986, pp. 49–50)

By "**stereotypical dualism**" Hulme means that the stereotype is split into two opposing elements. These are two key features of the discourse of "the Other":

1  First, several characteristics are collapsed into one simplified figure which stands for or represents the *essence* of the people; this is stereotyping.

2  Second, the stereotype is split into two halves – its "good" and "bad" sides; this is "splitting" or *dualism*.

Far from the discourse of "the West and the Rest" being unified and monolithic, "splitting" is a regular feature of it. The world is first divided, symbolically, into good–bad, us–them, attractive–disgusting, civilized–uncivilized, the West–the Rest. All the other, many differences between and within these two halves are collapsed, simplified – i.e. stereotyped. By this strategy, the Rest becomes defined as everything that the West is not – its mirror image. It is represented as absolutely, essentially, different, *other*: the Other. This Other is then itself split into two "camps": friendly–hostile, Arawak–Carib, innocent–depraved, noble–ignoble.

# 5  "In the Beginning All the World was America"

Writing about the use of stereotypes in the discourse of "the Other," Sander Gilman argues that "these systems are inherently bi-polar (i.e. polarized into two parts), generating pairs of antithetical signifiers (i.e. words with apparently opposing meanings). This is how the deep structure of the stereotype reflects the social and political ideologies of the time" (Gilman, 1985, p. 27). He goes on to say:

> With the split of both the self and the world into "good" and "bad" objects, the "bad" self is distanced and identified with the mental representation of the "bad" object. This act of projection saves the self from any confrontation with the contradictions present in the necessary integration of "bad" and "good" aspects of the self. The deep structure of our own sense of self and the world is built upon the illusionary [sic] image of the world divided into two camps, "us" and "them". "They" are either "good" or "bad".
> (Gilman, 1985, p. 17)

The example Gilman gives is that of the "noble" versus the "ignoble savage." In this section, we examine the "career" of this stereotype. How did it function in the discourse of "the West and the Rest"? What was its influence on the birth of modern social science?

## 5.1  Are they "true men"?

The question of how the natives and nations of the New World should be treated in the evolving colonial system was directly linked to the question of what sort of people and societies they were – which in turn depended on the West's knowledge of them, on how they were represented. Where did the Indians stand in the order of the Creation? Where were their nations placed in the order of civilized societies? Were they "true men" (*sic*)? Were they made in God's image? The point was vital because if they were "true men" they could not be enslaved. The Greek philosophers argued that man (women rarely figured in these debates) was a special creation, endowed with the divine gift of reason; the Church taught that Man was receptive to divine grace. Did the Indians' way of life, their lack of "civilization," mean that they were so low on the scale of humanity as to be incapable of reason and faith?

The debate raged for most of the fifteenth century. Ferdinand and Isabella issued decrees saying that "a certain people called Cannibals" and "any, whether called cannibals or not, who were not docile" could be enslaved. One view was that "they probably descended from another Adam . . . born after the deluge and . . . perhaps have no souls" (see Honour, 1978, p. 58). However, Bartolomé de Las Casas (1474–1566), the priest who made himself the champion of the Indians, protested vigorously at the brutality of the Spaniards in putting Indians to work as forced labor. Indians, he insisted, *did* have their own laws, customs, civilization, religion, and were "true men" whose cannibalism was much exaggerated. "All men," Las Casas claimed, "however barbarous and bestial . . . necessarily possess the faculty of Reason . . ." (quoted by Honour, 1978, p. 59). The issue was formally debated before Emperor Charles X at Valladolid in 1550.

One paradoxical outcome of Las Casas' campaign was that he got Indian slavery outlawed, but was persuaded to accept the alternative of replacing Indians with African slaves, and so the door opened to the horrendous era of New World African slavery. A debate similar to that about the Indians was held about African slavery prior to Emancipation. The charter of the Royal Africa Company, which organized the English slave trade, defined slaves as "commodities." As slavery expanded, a series of codes was constructed for the Spanish, French, and English colonies governing the status and conduct of slaves. These codes defined the slave as a *chattel* – literally, "a thing," not a person. This was a problem for some churches. But in the British colonies the Church of England, which was identified with the planters, accommodated itself to this definition without too much difficulty, and made little effort to convert slaves until the eighteenth century. Later, however, the Dissenters in the anti-slavery movement advocated abolition precisely because every slave *was* "a man and brother" (see Hall, 1991).

## 5.2 "Noble" vs "ignoble savages"

Another variant of the same argument can be found in the debate about the "noble" versus the "ignoble savage." The English poet John Dryden provides one of the famous images of the "noble savage":

> I am as free as Nature first made man,
> E're the base Laws of Servitude began,
> When wild in woods the noble Savage ran.
> (*The Conquest of Granada*, I.I.i.207–9)

Earlier, the French philosopher Montaigne, in his essay *Des Cannibales* (1580), had placed his noble savage in America. The idea quickly took hold on the European imagination. The famous painting of "The Different Nations of America" by Le Brun in Louis XIV's (1638–1715) Versailles Palace was dominated by a "heroic" representation of an American Indian – grave, tall, proud, independent, statuesque, and naked (see Honour, 1978, p. 118). Paintings and engravings of American Indians dressed like ancient Greeks or Romans became popular. Many paintings of Cook's death portrayed both Cook and the natives who killed him in "heroic" mold. As Beaglehole explains, the Pacific voyages gave new life and impetus to the idealization of the "noble savage," who "entered the study and drawing room of Europe in naked majesty, to shake the preconceptions of morals and politics" (in Moorhead, 1987, p. 62). Idealized "savages" spoke on stage in ringing tones and exalted verse. The eponymous hero in Aphra Behn's novel *Oroonoko* (1688), was one of the few "noble" Africans (as opposed to American Indians) in seventeenth-century literature, and was fortunate enough to have "long hair, a Roman nose and shapely mouth."

"Heroic savages" have peopled adventure stories, Westerns, and other Hollywood and television films ever since, generating an unending series of images of "the Noble Other."

The "noble savage" also acquired sociological status. In 1749, the French philosopher Rousseau produced an account of his ideal form of society: simple, unsophisticated man living in a state of Nature, unfettered by laws, government, property, or social divisions. "The savages of North America," he later said in *The Social Contract*, "still retain today this method of government, and they are very well governed" (Rousseau, 1968, p. 114). Tahiti was the perfect fulfillment of this preconceived idea – "one of those unseen stars which eventually came to light after the astronomers have proved that it must exist" (Moorhead, 1987, p. 62).

The French Pacific explorer Bougainville (1729–1811) had been captivated by the way of life on Tahiti. Diderot, the philosopher and editor of the *Encyclopédie* (see chapter 1), wrote a famous *Supplement* about Bougainville's voyage, warning Tahitians against the West's intrusion into their innocent happiness. "One day," he prophesied correctly, "they [Europeans] will come, with crucifix in one hand and the dagger in the other to cut your throats or to force you to accept their customs and opinions" (quoted in Moorhead, 1987). Thus the "noble savage" became the vehicle for a wide-ranging critique of the over-refinement, religious hypocrisy, and divisions by social rank that existed in the West.

This was only one side of the story. For, at the same time, the opposite image – that of the "ignoble savage" – was becoming the vehicle for a profound reflection in European intellectual circles on the nature of social development. Eighteenth-century wits, like Horace Walpole, Edmund Burke, and Dr Johnson, poured scorn on the idea of the noble savage. Ronald Meek has remarked that contemporary notions of savagery influenced eighteenth-century social science by generating a critique of society through the idea of the *noble* savage; "It is not quite so well known ... that they also stimulated the emergence of a new theory of the development of society through the idea of the *ignoble savage*" (Meek, 1976, p. 2).

The questions which concerned the social philosophers were: What had led the West to its high point of refinement and civilization? Did the West evolve from the same simple beginnings as "savage society" or were there different paths to "civilization"?

Many of the precursors and leading figures of the Enlightenment participated in this debate. Thomas Hobbes, the political philosopher, argued in *Leviathan* (1651) that it was because of their lack of "industry ... and consequently no culture of the earth, no navigation, nor use of commodities" that "the savage people in many places of America ... live at this day in [their] brutish manner" (Hobbes, 1946, pp. 82–3). The English satirist Bernard Mandeville, in his *Fable of the Bees* (1723), identified a series of "steps" or stages in which economic factors like the division of labor, money, and the invention of tools played the major part in the progress from "savagery" to "civilization." The philosopher John Locke claimed that the New World provided a prism through which one could see "a pattern of the first ages in Asia and Europe" – the origins from which Europe had developed. "In the beginning," Locke said, "all the World was America" (Locke, 1976, p. 26). He meant by this that the world (i.e. the West) had evolved from a stage very much like that discovered in America – untilled, undeveloped, and uncivilized. America was the "childhood of mankind," Locke claimed, and Indians should be classed with "children, idiots and illiterates because of their inability to reason in abstract, speculative ... terms" (quoted in Marshall and Williams, 1982, p. 192).

## 5.3   The history of "rude" and "refined" nations

The "noble–ignoble" and the "rude–refined" oppositions belonged to the same discursive formation. This "West and the Rest" discourse greatly influenced Enlightenment thinking. It provided the framework of images in which Enlightenment social philosophy matured. Enlightenment thinkers believed that there was *one* path to civilization and social development, and that all societies could be ranked or placed early or late, lower or higher, on the same scale. The emerging "science of society" was the study of the forces which had propelled all societies, by stages, along this single path of development, leaving some, regrettably, at its "lowest" stage – represented by the American savage – while others advanced to the summit of civilized development – represented by the West.

This idea of a universal criterion of progress modelled on the West became a feature of the new "social science" to which the Enlightenment gave birth. For example, when Edmund Burke wrote to the Scottish Enlightenment historian William Robertson on the publication of his *History of America* (1777), he said that "the great map of Mankind is unrolled at once, and there is no state or gradation of barbarism, and no mode of refinement which we have not at the same moment under our view; the very different civility of Europe and China; the barbarism of Persia and of Abyssinia; the erratic manners of Tartary and of Arabia; the savage state of North America and of New Zealand" (quoted by Meek, 1976, p. 173). Enlightenment social science reproduced within its own conceptual framework many of the preconceptions and stereotypes of the discourse of "the West and the Rest."

The examples are too voluminous to refer to in detail. Meek argues that "No one who reads the work of the French and Scottish pioneers [of social science] of the 1750s can fail to notice that all of them, without exception, were very familiar with the contemporary studies of the Americans; that most of them had evidently pondered deeply about their significance and that some were almost obsessed by them. . . . The studies of Americans provided the new social scientists with a plausible working hypothesis about the basic characteristics of the "first" or "earliest" stage of socio-economic development" (Meek, 1976, p. 128). Many of the leading names of the French Enlightenment – Diderot, Montesquieu, Voltaire, Turgot, Rousseau – used the studies of early American Indians in this way.

This is also the case with the Scottish Enlightenment. In Adam Smith's *Theory of the Moral Sentiments* (1759), American Indians are used as the pivot for elaborate contrasts between "civilized nations" and "savages and barbarians." They are also pivotal in Henry Kames's *Sketches of the History of Man* (1774), John Millar's *Origin of the Distinction of Ranks* (1771), and Adam Ferguson's *Essay on the History of Civil Society* (1767).

The contribution which this debate about "rude–refined nations" made to social science was not simply descriptive. It formed part of a larger theoretical framework, about which the following should be noted:

1　It represented a decisive movement away from mythological, religious and other "causes" of social evolution to what are clearly recognizable as material causes – sociological, economic, environmental, etc.

2　It produced the idea that the history of "mankind" (*sic*) occurred along a single continuum, divided into a series of stages.

3　Writers differed over precisely *which* material or sociological factors they believed played the key role in propelling societies through these stages. But one factor assumed increasing importance – the "mode of subsistence":

> In its most specific form, the theory was that society had "naturally" or "normally" progressed over time through four more or less distinct and consecutive stages, each corresponding to a different mode of subsistence, these stages being defined as hunting, pasturage, agriculture and commerce. To each of these modes of subsistence . . . there corresponded different sets of ideas and institutions relating to law, property, and government and also different sets of customs, manners and morals.
> (Meek, 1976, p. 2)

Here, then, is a surprising twist. The Enlightenment aspired to being a "science of man." It was the matrix of modern social science. It provided the language in which "modernity" first came to be defined. In Enlightenment discourse, the West was the model, the prototype, and the measure of social progress. It was *western* progress, civilization, rationality, and development that were celebrated. And yet, all this depended on the discursive figures of the "noble vs ignoble savage," and of "rude and refined nations" which had been formulated in the discourse of "the West and the Rest." So the Rest was critical for the formation of western Enlightenment – and therefore for modern social science. Without the Rest (or its own internal "others"), the West would not have been able to recognize and represent itself as the summit of human history. The figure of "the Other," banished to the edge of the conceptual world and constructed as the absolute opposite, the negation, of everything which the West stood for, reappeared at the very center of the discourse of civilization, refinement, modernity, and development in the West. "The Other" was the "dark" side – forgotten, repressed, and denied; the reverse image of enlightenment and modernity.

# 6   From "the West and the Rest" to Modern Sociology

In response to this argument, you may find yourself saying – "Yes, perhaps the early stages of the 'science of man' *were* influenced by the discourse of 'the West and the Rest.' But all that was a long time ago. Since then, social science has become more empirical, more 'scientific.' Sociology today is, surely, free of such 'loaded images'?" But this is not necessarily the case. Discourses don't stop abruptly. They go on unfolding, changing shape, as they make sense of new circumstances. They often carry many of the same unconscious premises and unexamined assumptions in their blood-stream.

For example, some of you may have recognized in the Enlightenment concept of "modes of subsistence" the outline of an idea which Karl Marx (1818–83), a "founding father" of modern sociology, was subsequently to develop into one of the most powerful sociological tools: his theory that society is propelled forward by the class struggle; that it progresses through a series of stages marked by different modes of production, the critical one for capitalism being the transition from feudalism to capitalism. Of course, there is considerable divergence between the Enlightenment's "four stages of subsistence" and Marx's "modes of production." But there are also some surprising similarities. In his *Grundrisse*, Marx speaks in broad outlines of the Asiatic, ancient, feudal, and capitalist or bourgeois modes of production. He argues that each is dominated by a particular social class which expropriates the economic surplus through a specific set of social relations. The Asiatic mode (which is only sketchily developed), is that to which, in Marx's view, countries such as China, India, and those of Islam belong. It is characterized by: (a) stagnation, (b) an absence of dynamic class struggle, and (c) the dominance of a swollen state acting as a sort of universal landlord. The conditions for capitalist development are here absent. Marx hated the capitalist system; nevertheless, he saw it, in contrast with the Asiatic mode, as progressive and dynamic, sweeping old structures aside, driving social development forward.

There are some interesting parallels here with Max Weber (1864–1920), another of sociology's founding fathers. Weber used a very dualistic model which contrasted Islam with Western Europe in terms of modern social development. For Weber, the essential conditions for the transition to capitalism and modernity are: (a) ascetic forms of religion, (b) rational forms of law, (c) free labor, and (d) the growth of cities (see chapter 5 above). All these, in his view, were missing from Islam, which he represented as a "mosaic" of tribes and groups, never cohering into a proper social system, but existing under a despotic rule which absorbed social conflicts in an endlessly repeating cycle of factional struggles, with Islam as its monolithic religion. Power and privilege, Weber believed, had been kept within, and rotated between, the ruling Islamic families, who merely siphoned off the wealth through taxation. He called this a "patrimonial" or "prebendary" form of authority. Unlike feudalism, it did not provide the preconditions for capitalist accumulation and growth.

These are, of course, some of the most complex and sophisticated models in sociology. The question of the causes and preconditions for the development of capitalism in the West have preoccupied historians and social scientists for centuries.

However, it has been argued by some social scientists that *both* Marx's notion of the "Asiatic" mode of production and Weber's "patrimonial" form of domination contain traces of, or have been deeply penetrated by, "Orientalist" assumptions. Or, to put it in our terms, both models provide evidence that the discourse of "the West and the Rest" is still at work in some of the conceptual categories, the stark oppositions and the theoretical dualisms of modern sociology.

In his studies of *Weber and Islam* (1974) and *Marx and the End of Orientalism* (1978), Bryan Turner has argued that both sociology and Marxism have been unduly influenced by "Orientalist" categories, or, if you lift the argument out of its Middle Eastern and Asian context, by the discourse of "the West and the Rest":

> This can be seen . . . in Weber's arguments about the decline of Islam, its despotic political structure and the absence of autonomous cities. . . . Weber employs a basic dichotomy between the feudal economies of the West and the prebendal/patrimonial political economies of the East. . . . [He] overlays this discussion . . . with two additional components which have become the staples of the *internalist* version of development – the "Islamic ethic" and the absence of an entrepreneurial urban bourgeoisie.
> (Turner, 1978, pp. 7, 45–6)

Marx's explanation of the lack of capitalist development in the East is very different from Weber's. But his notion that this was due to the "Asiatic mode of production" takes a similar path. Turner summarizes Marx's argument thus:

> Societies dominated by the "Asiatic" mode of production have no internal class conflicts and are consequently trapped within a static social context. The social system lacks a basic ingredient of social change, namely class struggle between landlords and an exploited peasantry . . . [For example] "Indian society has no history at all."
>
> (Turner, 1978, pp. 26–7)

Despite their differences, both Weber and Marx organize their arguments in terms of broad, simple, contrasting oppositions which mirror quite closely the West–Rest, civilized–rude, developed–backward oppositions of "the West and the Rest" discourse. Weber's is an "internalist" type of explanation because "he treats the main problems of 'backward societies' as a question of certain characteristics *internal* to societies, considered in isolation from any international societal context" (Turner, 1978, p. 10). Marx's explanation also looks like an "internalist" one. But he adds certain "externalist" features. By "externalist" we mean "relating to a theory of development which identifies the main problems facing 'developing' societies as external to the society itself, which is treated as a unit located within a structured international context" (see Turner, 1978, p. 11). In this chapter, we have adopted an "externalist" or "global" rather than a purely "internalist" account of the rise of the idea of the West.

However, these additional features of Marx's argument lead his explanation in a very surprising direction. "Asiatic"-type societies, he argues, cannot develop into modern ones because they lack certain pre-conditions. Therefore, "only the introduction of dynamic elements of western capitalism" can trigger development. This makes "capitalist colonialism" a (regrettable) historical necessity for these societies, since it alone can "destroy the pre-capitalist modes which prevent them from entering a progressive historical path." Capitalism, Marx argues, must expand to survive, drawing the whole world progressively into its net; and it is this expansion which "revolutionizes and undermines pre-capitalist modes of production at the periphery of the capitalist world" (Turner, 1978, p. 11). Many classical Marxists have indeed argued that, however stunting and destructive it may have been, the expansion of western capitalism through conquest and colonization was historically inevitable and would have long-term progressive outcomes for "the Rest."

Earlier, we discussed some of the forces which pushed a developing Western Europe to expand outwards into "new worlds." But whether this was inevitable, whether its effects have been socially progressive, and whether this was the only possible path to "modernity" are subjects increasingly debated in the social sciences today (as is discussed in part III). In many parts of the world, the expansion of western colonization has *not* destroyed the pre-capitalist barriers to development. It has conserved and reinforced them. Colonization and imperialism have *not* promoted economic and social development in these societies, most of which remain profoundly under-developed. Where development has taken place, it has often been of the "dependent" variety.

The destruction of alternative ways of life has not ushered in a new social order in these societies. Many remain in the grip of feudal ruling families, religious elites, military cliques, and dictators who govern societies beset by endemic poverty. The destruction of indigenous cultural life by western culture is, for most of them, a very mixed blessing And as the human, cultural, and ecological consequences of this form of "western development" become more obvious, the question of whether there is only one path to modernity is being debated with increasing urgency. The historically inevitable and necessarily progressive character of the West's expansion into the Rest is no longer as obvious as perhaps it once seemed to western scholars.

We must leave these issues as open questions at this stage. However, this is a useful point to summarize the main thrust of the argument of this chapter.

# 7  Conclusion

In the early chapters of this book, we looked at how the distinctive form of society which we call "modern" emerged, and the major processes which led to its formation. We also looked at the emergence of the distinctive form of knowledge which accompanied that society's formation – at what the Enlightenment called the "sciences of man," which provided the framework within which modern social science and the idea of "modernity" were formulated. On the whole, the emphasis in those chapters was "internalist." Though the treatment was comparative – acknowledging differences between different societies, histories, and tempos of development – the story was largely framed from within Western Europe (the West) where these processes of formation first emerged.

This chapter reminds us that this formation was also a "global" process. It had crucial "externalist" features – aspects which could not be explained without taking into account the rest of the world, where these processes were not at work and where these kinds of society did not emerge. This is a huge topic in its own right and we could tell only a small part of the story here. We could have focused on the economic, political, and social consequences of the global expansion of the West; instead, we briefly sketched the outline history of that expansion, up to roughly the eighteenth century. We also wanted to show the *cultural* and *ideological* dimensions of the West's expansion. For if the Rest was necessary for the political, economic, and social formation of the West, it was also essential to the West's formation both of its own sense of itself – a "western identity" – and of western forms of knowledge.

This is where the notion of "discourse" came in. A discourse is a way of talking about or representing something. It produces knowledge that shapes perceptions and practice. It is part of the way in which power operates. Therefore, it has consequences for both those who employ it and those who are "subjected" to it. The West produced many different ways of talking about itself and "the Others." But what we have called the discourse of "the West and the Rest" became one of the most powerful and formative of these discourses. It became the dominant way in which, for many decades, the West represented itself and its relation to "the Other." In this chapter, we have traced how this discourse was formed and how it worked. We analyzed it as a "system of representation" – a "regime of truth." It was as formative for the West and "modern societies" as were the secular state, capitalist economies, the modern class, race, and gender systems, and modern, individualist, secular culture – the four main "processes" of our formation story.

Finally, we suggest that, in transformed and reworked forms, this discourse continues to inflect the language of the West, its image of itself and "others," its sense of "us" and "them," its practices and relations of power towards the Rest. It is especially important for the languages of racial inferiority and ethnic superiority which still operate so powerfully across the globe today. So, far from being a "formation" of the past, and of only historical interest, the discourse of "the West and the Rest" is alive and well in the modern world. And one of the surprising places where its effects can still be seen is in the language, theoretical models, and hidden assumptions of modern sociology itself.

# References

Arens, W. (1977) *The Man-Eating Myth: Anthropology and Anthropophagy*, New York, Oxford University Press.

Asad, T. (1973) *Anthropology and the Colonial Encounter*, London, Ithaca Press.

Barker, A.J. (1978) *The African Link: British Attitudes to the Negro in the Era of the Atlantic Slave Trade, 1550–1807*, London, Frank Cass.

Baudet, H. (1963) *Paradise on Earth: European Images of Non-European Man*, New Haven, Yale University Press.

Beaglehole, J.C. (ed.) (1961) *The Journals of Captain Cook on his Voyages of Discovery*, vol. 2 of 3, Cambridge, England, Cambridge University Press.

Berkhofer, R. (1978) *The White Man's Indian: Images of the American Indian from Columbus to the Present*, New York, Knopf.

Chiappelli, F. (ed.) (1978) *First Images of America: The Impact of the New World*, 2 vols, Berkeley, University of California Press.

Columbus, C. (1969) *The Four Voyages of Christopher Columbus* (ed. J.M. Cohen), Harmondsworth, England, Penguin.

Cousins, M. and Hussain, A. (1984) *Michel Foucault*, London, Macmillan.

Dryden, J. (1978) *The Works of John Dryden*, vol. 11, Berkeley, University of California Press.

Fairchild, H. (1961) *The Noble Savage: A Study in Romantic Naturalism*, New York, Russell & Russell.

Foucault, M. (1972) *The Archeology of Knowledge*, London, Tavistock.

Foucault, M. (1980) *Power/Knowledge*, Brighton, England, Harvester.

Gilman, S. (1985) *Difference and Pathology: Stereotypes of Sexuality, Race, and Madness*, Ithaca, Cornell University Press.

Hakluyt, R. (1972) *Voyages and Discoveries*, Harmondsworth, England, Penguin.

Hale, J.R. et al. (1966) *Age of Exploration*, The Netherlands, Time-Life International.

Hall, C. (1991) "Missionary positions," in Grossberg, L. and Nelson, C. (eds) *Cultural Studies Now and in the Future*, London, Routledge.

Harris, M. (1977) *Cannibals and Kings: The Origins of Cultures*, New York, Random House.

Hay, D. (1957) *Europe: The Emergence of an Idea*, Edinburgh, Edinburgh University Press.

Hobbes, T. (1946) *Leviathan*, Oxford, Basil Blackwell.

Honour, H. (1976) *The New Golden Land: European Images of America*, London, Allen Lane.

Hulme, P. (1986) *Colonial Encounters: Europe and the Native Caribbean, 1492–1797*, London, Methuen.

Jennings, F. (1976) *The Invasion of America: Indians, Colonialism, and the Cant of Conquest*, New York, Norton.

Joppien, R. and Smith, B. (1985) *The Art of Captain Cook's Voyages*, 2 vols, New Haven, Yale University Press.

Latham, R. (ed.) (1958) *Marco Polo: The Travels*, Harmondsworth, England, Penguin.

Léon-Portilla, M. (1962) *The Broken Spears: the Aztec Account of the Conquest of Mexico*, London, Constable.

Locke, J. (1976) *The Second Treatise on Government*, Oxford, Basil Blackwell.

Mandeville, B. (1924) *The Fable of the Bees*, Oxford, Clarendon Press.

Mandeville, Sir J. (1964) *The Travels*, New York, Dover.

Mann, M. (1988) "European development: approaching a historical explanation," in Baechler, J. et al. (eds), *Europe and the Rise of Capitalism*, Oxford, Basil Blackwell.

Marshall, P. and Williams, G. (1982) *The Great Map of Mankind: British Perceptions of the World in the Age of the Enlightenment*, London, Dent.

Marx, K. (1964) *Precapitalist Economic Formations* (ed. E.J.

Hobsbawm), London, Lawrence and Wishart.

Marx, K. (1973) *Grundrisse*, Harmondsworth, England, Pelican.

McNeill, W. (1963) *The Rise of the West: A History of Human Community*, Chicago, Chicago University Press.

Meek, R. (1976) *Social Science and the Ignoble Savage*, Cambridge, England, Cambridge University Press.

Montaigne, M. (1964) *Selected Essays*, Boston, Houghton Mifflin.

Moorhead, A. (1987) *The Fatal Impact: An Account of the Invasion of the South Pacific, 1767–1840*, Harmondsworth, England, Penguin.

Newby, E. (1975) *The Mitchell Beazley World Atlas of Exploration*, London, Mitchell Beazley.

Parry J.H. (ed.) (1968) *The European Reconnaissance: Selected Documents*, New York, Harper & Row.

Parry, J.H. (1971) *Trade and Dominion: The European Oversea Empires in the Eighteenth Century*, London, Weidenfeld & Nicolson.

Roberts, J.M. (1985) *The Triumph of the West*, London, British Broadcasting Corporation.

Rousseau, J.-J. (1968) *The Social Contract*, Harmondsworth, England, Penguin.

Said, E.W. (1985) *Orientalism: Western Concepts of the Orient*, Harmondsworth, England, Penguin.

Sale, K. (1991) *The Conquest of Paradise: Christopher Columbus and the Columbian Legacy*, London, Hodder & Stoughton.

Schama, S. (1977) *The Embarrassment of Riches: An Interpretation of Dutch Culture*, New York, Knopf.

Smith, B. (1988) *European Vision and the South Pacific*, New Haven, Yale University Press.

Turner, B.S. (1974) *Weber and Islam*, London, Routledge.

Turner, B.S. (1978) *Marx and the End of Orientalism*, London, Allen & Unwin.

Wallace, W.M. (1959) *Sir Walter Raleigh*, Princeton, Princeton University Press.

Williams, E.E. (1970) *From Columbus to Castro: The History of the Caribbean, 1492–1969*, London, Andre Deutsch.

Withey, L. (1987) *Voyages of Discovery: Captain Cook and the Exploration of the Pacific*, London, Hutchinson.

# Part II

# Structures and Processes of Modernity

# Introduction

## Don Hubert and Kenneth Thompson

"Structures and Processes of Modernity" continues the story of the formation of modern societies begun in part I of this volume. It takes as its starting point the emerging structures already in place, though not yet fully formed, at the start of the nineteenth century. In keeping with part I, modernity is understood as a cluster of trends and institutions emerging from the Middle Ages, including the industrializing capitalist economy and the nation-state system.

As with the previous chapters, modernity is conceived, at least initially, as a European phenomenon. Part II will, therefore, focus primarily on the advanced industrialized countries of Western Europe and North America. Following Stuart Hall's discussion of the relationship between the "West and the Rest," these chapters will also explore the increasing penetration of Western "civilization" throughout the rest of the world. While the notion of globalization will not be examined in detail until part III, the processes which underpin this phenomenon are understood to be operating and expanding through the historical period under consideration here as well.

Although the chapters in part II cover a broad historical scope, from the consolidation of the structures of modernity to the present, the focus is on the twentieth century, and particularly on the period after 1945. Many historians would accept this period as the peak of modernity's development, since at least some of these institutions now appear to be in historic decline. The accounts which follow do not observe a strict chronological order, but instead focus on the decisive turning points, and quintessential examples of particular social and institutional forms of modernity. Given the limitations of space, the chapters focus on those moments that are crucial for understanding the development of modern societies. Furthermore, the authors are interested not merely in the description and analysis of the structures and processes themselves, but also in the way in which these have been interpreted, theorized, and debated. Thus, while no chapter is explicitly devoted to social science as an enterprise through these years, there is considerable emphasis throughout part II on the theoretical and academic conceptualization, or "framing," of the institutions of modernity. Central to the claims made throughout this volume is the notion that there is considerable interplay between the evolution of social forms and structures, and both popular and academic beliefs and interpretations.

The subject matter of part II may seem to be familiar territory for a sociology textbook, especially in contrast to the historical character of part I and the projective nature of part III. Yet there are several ways in which these chapters do provide a unique account of modern societies. First, they place considerable emphasis on comparative analysis. While the following chapters emphasize the continuity and coherence of modernity as a cluster of institutional forms and structures, they are also eager to explain the different trajectories followed byindividual countries in Europe and North America. Second, the authors are particularly concerned to analyze the consolidation of the emergent forms of social practice and institutions through the twentieth century, and therefore give detailed accounts of historical development. Coupled with an examination of the defining features of contemporary forms of modern structures and processes, these chapters contain a thorough appraisal of the period under review. Third, these chapters highlight new trends in social and cultural studies. By focusing on the representation of social relations, and the discourses surrounding them, in conjunction with analyses of specific structures or organizations, the authors highlight challenging questions often left unexposed. This approach involves an emphasis on subjectivity and attention to the types and forms of social representation and signification, particularly where these processes enter into the construction of collective and individual identities. Finally, the authors reject a simple notion of the separation of the public and private spheres. What is socially relevant exists as much in the intimate and private sphere of gender relations and sexual identities as it does in class structure or large-scale organizations.

Part II can be divided roughly into two substantive sections, following the four constitutive dynamics of modernity: the political, the economic, the social, and the cultural. The first section focuses on the advanced industrial state in terms of its political orientations, productive capacity, and the labor market. The relationship between the state as the agent of warfare and as the provider of welfare, the transformation of production and the shift to a more service-oriented economy, and the changes in the divisions of labor are of particular interest here. The second set of chapters focuses on the consolidation of social and cultural forms of modernity, specifically the social construction of individual identities and roles, and the discourses which surround them. Emphasis is given to the family and the domestic sphere, discourses surrounding sexual identity, and the relationship between ideology and religion.

The history of social theory is marked by theoretical positions that place more emphasis upon one of these four constitutive components. Classical Marxists advance the strong thesis that economic structure is the major determinant in what ultimately happens in each of the other spheres. Subsequent efforts by Marxists to account for the apparent inadequacies of this thesis gave greater prominence to the other components: the State in the political sphere, gender and race in the social realm, and ideology in the cultural domain. While these revisions weakened the strong thesis considerably, the original position was not wholly abandoned. Neo-Marxists granted varying degrees of relative autonomy to the political, economic, and cultural spheres, but they maintained nonetheless that in the last instance the economic was the determining factor. The economic structure then is viewed within the neo-Marxist perspective as setting the broad parameters on the political, cultural, and social possibilities of a given society.

Political factors such as coercive force and the form of legitimate authority, social divisions based on status, and cultural formations consisting of certain world-views or rationality, have been given a much larger role in the analysis of modern societies within other theoretical conceptions. Max Weber, the German sociologist, emphasized the control over the means of violence as a source of power in social formation, operating independently of economic class. The history of the Russian Revolution and the development of communist regimes in Eastern Europe following World War II are important examples of how the control over the means of violence in a given territory can be crucial in determining the economic, political, and social/cultural systems that emerge. Weber's position, however, cannot be considered mono-causal, for while exploring the implications of the control of the means of violence, he also argued that the ways in which coercive authority or domination were legitimated and organized were important factors. In this regard he placed considerable emphasis on the expansion of modern rational-legal bureaucracies as a prominent feature of the modern social order. Perhaps even more famously, his book *The Protestant Ethic and the Spirit of Capitalism* argued that culture, in the form of values and world-views, had a profound impact on the emergence and consolidation of modern Europe.

Of course, cultural ideas and values do not cause major changes on their own – they have to be expressed in the lives of key *social* groups to have influence. This limitation on cultural explanations leads to what might be called a purely sociological position, emphasizing the social rather than the cultural, economic, or political alone. This theoretical stance is occupied most prominently by Émile Durkheim. He defined sociology as the scientific, objective study of the genesis and functioning of institutions. By "institution" he meant a set of beliefs and practices that achieve normative status and that relate to recurrent or continuous areas of social concern. In part II we are interested in the functioning and adaptation of institutions under changing circumstances. According to Durkheim, as institutions develop they become more differentiated and elaborated, and at the same time self-sustaining and self-justifying. In other words, institutions acquire a relative autonomy from the original circumstances which brought them into existence. For Durkheim, then, while economic factors may have been major determinants, they do not have a privileged analytical position, as institutions quickly become separated from their origins. His attention to the operation of norms as the foundations of institutions also led him away from a focus on the coercive power of the state. Rather, he was concerned with the legitimating effect produced by the "collective representation" or symbols that give norms the appearance of some superior standing. Durkheim argued that by internalizing categories and norms they become our own, while simultaneously exerting authority over us.

Durkheim's emphasis on social representations and the process by which they crystallize into institutions with normative force, thus reproducing social structures, has been echoed in different ways by many twentieth-century social theorists. His analyses of symbolic and social classification were influential on later structuralist theories as well as on the analysis of discourses surrounding gender, sexuality, ethnicity, and nationalism. Perhaps the most important contribution that Durkheim made was to show how systems of classification develop a moral force, resting on binary opposition – sacred versus profane, normal versus abnormal or pathological.

The focus on the sources of societal cohesion in Durkheim's work has also had considerable influence in twentieth-century social thought. Although he was fully aware that modern societies were a long way from achieving social and cultural integration, some sociologists, particularly in the optimistic atmosphere of post-war America, believed that a functionally integrated modern social system was rapidly evolving. The functionalist conception of a social system, in which all parts or structures articulate smoothly with one another, now seems to belong to a different era; it is as if the United States in the 1950s came to represent the high point of modernity according to one version of enlightenment social science. Subsequent decades, however, have seen radical critiques of such ideas, and a greater sociological consciousness of disarticulation and uneven development.

As discussed in the introduction to part I, one of the distinctive features of this volume is its emphasis on a multi-causal approach to social theory. Accounts which depend exclusively on one principal causal force are treated with considerable suspicion. This emphasis does not reflect the naïve belief that the more factors taken into account, the better the theory. Rather, it stems from the conviction that reductionism to any single causal factor is incapable of providing a convincing account, and that the complex phenomenon of modernity is bound up in multiple and interacting structures and processes. We leave it as an open question as to exactly where the balance should be placed, although it should be clear that the authors have adopted their own particular positions.

The general theoretical position adopted in this volume also places a special emphasis on the linkages and connections between what are often depicted as autonomous or unrelated events. Such an emphasis problematizes the very notion of neat analytical categories. It is important to recognize that while the divisions between the political, economic, social, and cultural spheres retain a certain degree of utility, many interesting and unexpected conclusions become apparent when the divisions are challenged. As with any analytical tools, they must be held up to constant scrutiny to ensure that they do not obscure more than they illuminate.

"Structures and Processes of Modernity" is composed of six chapters. It opens, in chapter 7, with a discussion of the state in advanced industrial societies. Since the emergence of its modern form, and particularly in the past four decades, the state has grown enormously in both size and influence. It has expanded its role in the provision of welfare, while at the same time consolidating its position as the focus of military power. Anthony McGrew argues that through the themes of military power and expanding bureaucracies, it is possible to identify a model of the Advanced Capitalist State. In presenting this claim, the chapter is also sensitive to the individual character of the various manifestations of modern industrialized states, specifically with regard to the scale of welfare provisions. McGrew makes clear that while some level of welfare support is a common characteristic of the advanced capitalist state, the level of commitment varies considerably.

The expansion of the modern state raises important questions regarding its roles and actions. McGrew outlines two broad theoretical positions which attempt to account for the sources of state decisions. The first, termed society-centered, suggests that state action or inaction reflects the interests of the dominant groups within society. Alternatively, the state-centered approach claims that the institutions representing the state have considerable autonomy from societal forces. McGrew concludes with a brief discussion of the implications of globalization on the advanced capitalist state. While states have always encountered substantial external constraints, the advanced capitalist state is increasingly caught in the dilemma of balancing the demands of effectiveness and autonomy in coping with emerging transnational issues.

Chapter 8, "Fordism and Modern Industry," continues the discussion of the development and formalization of the modern economy. In this chapter John Allen explores the central characteristics of Fordism: mass production based on the specialization of tasks and the automation of production techniques, large factories producing standardized goods, the creation of the interchangeable worker, and the role of the state in the formation of sufficient markets. This particular vision of production is considered by many to represent the culmination of modern industrial development. Based on the scientific management of production introduced by Taylor and Ford in America, factories were dramatically transformed around the turn of the century. These early shifts were consolidated through the following decades and reached their peak following World War II.

In addition to outlining components and assumptions, the author raises a series of questions about Fordism as a theoretical concept. As with all discourses, Fordism is not neutral: it contains an implicit logic with respect to the engine or motor of economic growth. Does it capture the essence of production in the twentieth century, and particularly the pattern of post-war growth across advanced capitalist economies; is it a catch-all that obscures more fundamental processes; and finally, has the term lost its utility given the considerable changes over the recent decades? While the debates about the utility of Fordism are likely to continue, there is no doubt that many of the processes it represents have left a deep and indelible mark on the post-war economies of the advanced industrial state. Allen will return to many of these issues in his chapter "Post-Industrialism/Post-Fordism" in part III.

Chapter 9, "Divisions of Labor," shifts the focus from modern industry itself towards the pattern of post-war labor and occupations. Peter Braham highlights the importance of a highly complex division of labor to modern economies. Modern industry is based on the division of skills, tasks, qualifications, and experience, yet the divisions of labor inside modern economies extend far beyond the factory floor. Braham explores four divisions of the labor market in particular. The first division is tied to the decline of employment in manufacturing industries and the corresponding rise in the service sector. This transition is a dominant characteristic of the post-war advanced economies. Another major change, especially pronounced following World War II, was the integration of women into the labor market. The discussion is not limited to an increase in the proportions of women looking for work, but also includes their position vis-à-vis men in terms of stereotypical female employment, their greater flexibility with regard to part-time or casual work, and the persistent problem of lower pay for equivalent jobs. The third division is the ethnic segregation that dominates many industries particularly in the inner cities of western states, and is closely tied to both legal and illegal migrants. Finally, the chapter examines the new international division of labor and its impact on the relocation of industries out of advanced western states and into developing countries to take advantage of a seemingly inexhaustible supply of cheap labor.

One aspect of economic activity only recently given much attention is that which takes place within the household. Helen Crowley's arguments reveal the porous boundaries between the economic and social realms. Chapter 10, "Women and the Domestic Sphere," is concerned both with the growing diversity of families and households and with changes in the sexual division of labor. The combined effect of the recent changes in patterns of marriage, cohabitation, divorce, family size, women's economic activity, types of families, and demographics, suggests that the domestic sphere remains in a period of transition where diversity, rather than the "traditional" family, remains the norm. Yet in spite of these considerable shifts, Crowley argues that some traditional behavior patterns remain largely unchanged, particularly in the area of the sexual division of labor. Her discussion of the division of work within the household along gender lines gives strong support to the contention that not only are women still presumed to be responsible for a majority of the work in the domestic sphere, but they also remain trapped inside pre-existing stereotypes of women as primary care-givers and nurturers. In assessing these circumstances, Crowley highlights the way in which areas of social life previously thought to be *natural* are increasingly recognized as being *socially constructed*. The constructed nature of women's identity, however, does not change the fact that these stereotypes continue to play an important role in the opportunities and constraints that women face, both within the household and beyond.

The theme of social construction is directed towards sexual identity in chapter 11, "The Body and Sexuality." Through a discussion of recent theoretical works on sexuality, Jeffrey Weeks argues that sexual identity is not predetermined but is shaped by our beliefs, ideologies, and imaginations within particular social and historic contexts. He defends this claim with a discussion of the ways in which the dominant definitions of sexuality have emerged and shifted throughout the modern era. Through an examination of historical and contemporary evidence, particularly around the "invention" of homosexuality, Weeks argues that sexual identities are social and political definitions, subject to negotiation and change, but also to manipulation. He concludes the chapter with a discussion of the nature of regulation and control around sexuality, and its position in contemporary political debates.

While chapters 10 and 11, in considering the social and cultural construction of women's roles and of sexual identities, explore important cultural aspects of modernity, chapter 12 brings culture directly to the fore. In "Religion, Values, and Ideology," Kenneth Thompson begins with the question: How important is a shared culture in binding people together in modern society? As discussed in part I, the Enlightenment can be understood as the attempt to loosen religious ties, believed to be a constraint on progress, and to replace them with a secular, rational-scientific culture. This "secularization thesis" predicted that the triumph of reason over religion would proceed irreversibly as part of the social differentiation that characterized modernity. There is considerable debate, however, as to the validity of this claim, on both empirical and theoretical grounds. There is evidence that some cultural elements of religious origin are more enduring than had previously been predicted. Religious beliefs and values remain widely held, even in highly secularized western industrialized states. Furthermore, religious ideas and practice continue to have profound influence in contemporary culture. Michel Foucault's work on discourse and discursive practices surrounding sex and confession supports this general claim, as do the rituals and symbols relating to identity and the maintenance of imagined communities. The fact that these symbols and rituals have become the site of considerable political struggle over the past decades is powerful evidence of the importance of culture in the institutionalization and reproduction of the structures of modernity.

Considerations of "progress" are a central theme throughout these chapters. Already in this period the early optimism of the Enlightenment and prospects for control over human destiny were beginning to fade. The following chapters demonstrate that the contemporary manifestation of modern processes and structures is far from homogeneous, and is in some respects contradictory. Both Marx and Weber recognized the double-sided character of modernity, yet they differed over how the modern era would develop. Where Marx emphasized the possibility of the struggle between two classes – capital and labor – leading to the emergence of a new kind of society based on less degrading social relationships, Weber stressed the negative characteristics of rationalist bureaucracy, in particular the imposition of impersonal rules which limit prospects for individual self-fulfillment and spontaneity. Looking back we can see that if Marx erred on the optimistic side of what the "modern" project would finally deliver,

Weber's view is perhaps too pessimistic in its neglect of the capacity for creativity and autonomy within modern organizations.

Nor is it just the economic domain of modernity that is characterized by the two sides of progress. In the political sphere, while essential attributes like the powerful attachment to military force and centrality of physical security were well established in the early period, the form and scale of activities undertaken by the contemporary state are vastly different from those seen in the nation-states of the early modern period. State responsibility for the welfare and material security of its citizens has mushroomed in the twentieth century alongside the traditional objectives of security and order. The combination of the two functions within the state – welfare and warfare, especially since the emergence of "industrialized warfare" – provides yet further illustration of the contradictory character of the developed modern world.

In the social and cultural spheres there has been a proliferation of new forms of division and differentiation. The Marxist forecast of a capitalist society increasingly characterized by a clear split in two opposing classes has been confounded by the prominence and complexity of the other divisions and distinctions, based on gender, ethnicity, sexuality, lifestyle, and locality. In the cultural sphere, it is not just a question of consumer society producing a widening choice of lifestyles and taste groupings; there has also been a surge of fundamentalist world-views and "culture wars." If the 1950s were the high point of modernity and optimism, then subsequent decades have been marked by increasing anxieties and tensions about social and cultural fragmentation.

Given the tragic events of the twentieth century – from the carnage of World War I, to Hitler's gas chambers and Stalin's *gulags* – a simplistic belief in progress has lost credibility. This is not to suggest that the darker side of modernity is necessarily dominant, but rather that the belief in progress, deeply implicated in the Enlightenment project, must be critically reevaluated. Part III, "Modernity and its Futures," will pursue in considerable detail the character of modernity and attempt to evaluate its prospects. In addition, the authors will respond to important questions regarding the resilience of the structures and processes of modernity discussed in part II. While the debate remains open, a considerable range of participants now claim that the Enlightenment project is no longer defensible, that the dominant western institutions of recent centuries are fading, and that we are witness to the eclipse of the modern era.

# 7 The State in Advanced Capitalist Societies

Anthony McGrew

## Contents

1 Introduction                                                      240

2     The Advanced Capitalist State: Diversity and Uniformity       242
2.1   The ACS: a comparative perspective                            243

3     The Formation of the Advanced Capitalist State                249
3.1   The logics of militarism                                      250
3.2   The logics of capital                                         256
3.3   The welfare–warfare state: a review                           261

4     Putting the Advanced Capitalist State in Perspective          261
4.1   Society-centered approaches                                   263
4.2   State-centered approaches                                     266
4.3   State autonomy and state power                                271

5     Putting the Advanced Capitalist State in its Place            272
5.1   Globalization and the ACS                                     273

6     The ACS: A Review                                             275

References                                                         276

# 1   Introduction

In all advanced capitalist societies the state has come to acquire immense influence over its citizens. Its activities permeate almost every single aspect of daily existence, such that few of us may claim that our lives are entirely "untouched" by the state. As citizens, members of households, consumers, recipients of welfare, employees, or employers we cannot escape the direct interventions of the modern state through its powers to tax, pass laws, coerce, enforce, and to re-distribute resources and life-chances. As Mann has observed:

> The state can assess and tax our income and wealth at source, without our consent or that of our neighbours or kin; it can enforce its will within the day almost anywhere in its domains; its influence on the overall economy is enormous; it even directly provides the subsistence of most of us (in state employment, in pensions, in family allowance etc.). The state penetrates everyday life more than did any historical state.
> (Mann, 1988, p. 7)

Undoubtedly, social historians in the late nineteenth century made very similar comments on the expanding role of the state in the era of liberal capitalism. Yet simply in terms of the size and complexity of the state apparatus, let alone the proportion of national income controlled by government, the advanced capitalist state (ACS) bears little direct resemblance to its nineteenth-century progenitor. Mann is therefore surely correct to assert the historically unique character of the ACS, particularly in relation to its pervasive influence within modern society. So central has it become to modern existence that the role of the state has emerged as a dominant theme in political, as well as intellectual, debates concerning the future development of advanced capitalist countries. On the one hand the "New Right" advocates curtailing its power while the left, and social democratic forces, continue to promote a vital role for the state in reforming advanced capitalist society. Yet despite the actual attempts (throughout the 1980s) of conservative administrations in Britain and the US to reduce the level of government intervention in social life, the state in both societies has not contracted significantly, although its activities have been re-directed. "Big government," as Rose characterizes it, appears to be a permanent feature of advanced capitalist nations: "Big government is here to stay . . . Whatever political perspective is adopted, within the immediately foreseeable future the size of government can change only marginally. This is true whether the margin for change involves growth or cutting back" (Rose, 1984, p. 215).

Understanding the nature of modern societies demands an understanding of the modern state. Certainly there exists a symbiotic relationship between the two: the state is embedded in social life, while social processes influence the form and activities of the state itself. In many respects ". . . states are central to our understanding of what a society is" (Mann, 1988, p. 19). Understanding the ACS involves exploring both its more "benign" activities – welfare – as well as its "darker" side – warfare and coercion. Without an appreciation of both these dimensions, any discussion of the ACS would be deficient. This is because the ACS is at one and the same time both a "welfare state" and a "warfare state."

Moreover, in making sense of the ACS, it is essential from the outset to recognize the incredible diversity of state forms among those nations which make up the advanced capitalist world: the West as opposed to the "Rest." Within the OECD (Organization for Economic Co-operation and Development) – which is essentially a "club" for western capitalist states – state forms vary dramatically in terms of institutional structures and modes of welfare provision. To make one obvious comparison, the US has a federal and presidential system of government combined with minimal public provision of welfare and minimal state intervention in the economy, while Sweden has a unitary and parliamentary system of government combined with extensive welfare programs and intervention in the economy. Developing a sophisticated understanding of the modern capitalist state requires acknowledging this diversity. However, in concentrating upon the ACS it is important not to forget the existence of quite different state forms in other industrial societies, such as the former command economies of Eastern Europe, and the newly industrializing nations of Latin America and South-East Asia. This chapter deals only with the ACS.

The fundamental aim of this chapter is to discover whether, in the light of this incredible diversity, it is possible to construct any meaningful general observations about the nature, functions, and role of the state within advanced capitalist societies. Without prejudging subsequent discussion the answer would appear to be a qualified "yes," acknowledging that a robust understanding of the modern capitalist state cannot be constructed from the purely particular but must embrace a "universalizing comparison" (Tilly, 1984, ch. 6). Such comparison contextualizes the diversity of state forms by bringing into focus the common features, structures, and processes which define the advanced capitalist state. Relying upon a comparative approach, the discussion in this chapter centers upon three key questions:

First, given the diversity of state forms within the advanced capitalist world is it possible to identify common patterns with respect to the development, characteristics, activities, and functions of the state?

Second, how are we to make sense of the role and actions of the state in governing advanced societies, and in whose interests does it "rule"?

Third, in what ways do international or global forces condition the activities of the modern capitalist state?

These questions define the intellectual boundaries of our inquiry while the substantive focus is advanced capitalist states. By the concluding section you should be in a position to develop your own responses to these three questions and to critically analyze the responses of others, including those of the author.


# 2   The Advanced Capitalist State: Diversity and Uniformity

Within the diplomatic world the state is generally taken to be coterminous with society and the nation. When the UK Ambassador to the United Nations delivers a speech to the Security Council, this is as a representative of the British state, the "official" voice of the nation and British society. From the outside the state therefore appears to be indistinguishable from "society." Not surprisingly, it is fairly common to find the terms frequently used interchangeably. But, from the "domestic" perspective, the state is commonly understood as simply "the government," the institutions of political rule: an entity separate from or even above society. These popular but conflicting understandings of the term "the state" suggest the need for a more rigorous conceptualization.

An obvious starting point is to view the state in terms of the "idea" of rule; a set of *public institutions* – government, parliament, armed forces, judiciary, administration; and a set of *public functions* – law-making, maintaining order and security. As the earlier discussion in chapter 2 indicated, the state is the locus of supreme authority within a delimited territory; authority which is reinforced by a monopoly of physical coercion. Mann offers a (neo-Weberian) definition of the state as:

1   a differentiated set of institutions and personnel embodying

2   centrality in the sense that political relations radiate outwards from a centre to cover

3   a territorially demarcated area, over which it exercises

4   a monopoly of authoritatively binding rule-making, backed up by a monopoly of the means of physical violence.

(Mann, 1988, p. 4)

Three important points flow from this definition. First, it emphasizes that the generic notion of the state embraces much more than the popular notion of "government" – e.g. the Major government or the Clinton administration etc. – since it refers to the whole apparatus of rule within society, e.g. government, police, army, judiciary, etc. Second, and closely associated with the first point, is the idea that the state defines the realm of supreme authority within society. The essence of the state is therefore to be distinguished from the specific agencies or institutions (the police, courts, social security, etc.) which give effect to that supreme authority. In simple terms the state as the realm of *public power* is to be differentiated from the agencies of rule within society. Third, as the embodiment of supreme authority, the state is thereby the primary law-making body within a defined territory. Through its institutions of rule the state formulates, implements, and adjudicates the laws and legal framework which govern civil society. Mention of "civil society" in this context demands a further conceptual clarification.

"Civil society" refers to those agencies, institutions, movements, cultural forces, and social relationships which are both privately or voluntarily organized and which are not directly controlled by the state. This includes households, religious groups, trade unions, private companies, political parties, humanitarian organizations, environmental groups, the women's movement, Parent-Teacher Associations, and so on. In simple terms, "civil society" refers to the realm of *private power* and private organizations, whereas the state is the realm of public power and public organizations. Of course, this is by no means a fixed or finely calibrated distinction since the public and the private can never be so readily differentiated. Feminists, for instance, would argue that power relations in the household are significantly structured by the welfare and regulatory activities of the state and so are not constituted solely in the private sphere. Through its powers to make law as well as its spending, taxing, employment, education, health, and social security policies, the state is deeply enmeshed in the institutions and processes of civil society. In effect, through its actions or inactions, the state effectively establishes the contours and constructs the framework of civil society. It is therefore possible to argue that the state constitutes civil society because of its power to define and redefine the legal and political boundaries between the public and private spheres. As Mitchell observes, "The distinction must be taken not as the boundary between two discrete entities, but as a line drawn internally within the network of institutional mechanisms through which a social and political order is maintained" (Mitchell, 1991, p. 78).

## 2.1   The ACS: a comparative perspective

While it is possible to define the state in abstract terms, the actual institutional forms of the contemporary state vary enormously among the advanced capitalist nations of the West. Constitutional arrangements, political structures, social formations, national wealth, and productive power differ considerably. Although all claim the democratic mantle, they differ, as Lijphart has shown, between federal (US, Germany) and unitary (UK, France, Japan) state structures as well as between parliamentary (UK, Japan) and presidential (US, Finland) systems of government (Lijphart, 1984). Militarily and economically, too, there is enormous diversity. To give one startling comparison: the US defense budget in 1990 was equal to almost twice the gross domestic product (GDP) of Belgium and approaching half that of the UK. These states also differ significantly in terms of the nature of their welfare state provision. Some countries, like Sweden, have a comprehensive welfare regime while others like the US have limited state provision of welfare. This diversity, along with its implications for how we progress beyond the particular to a more general understanding of the ACS, is analyzed in the following excerpt:

> In Western Europe, we can distinguish between a *Scandinavian and Anglo-Saxon version* of the welfare state (Denmark, Finland, Norway, Sweden, United Kingdom, Ireland) and a *Continental version* (Belgium, Netherlands, France, Italy, Austria, West Germany, Switzerland). The former emphasizes social services rather than social transfers, the transfer schemes have universal coverage with a focus on the provision of minima, and financing is heavily based on general revenues. The latter emphasizes earnings-related and status-preserving social transfer payments, places more limits on coverage, and relies to a lesser degree on general revenue financing. A second – and empirically more problematic – typology distinguishes "institutional" and "residual" welfare state models in the Western world. In the residual model, welfare state schemes are selectively targeted on the poorer strata with guaranteed minima and only a mildly progressive tax system, whereas in the institutional model the schemes have a more universal coverage and rather generous benefits financed with the help of a highly progressive system of taxation. . . .
>
> In a historical perspective, we can distinguish five general phases of welfare state development in Western Europe that to some extent cut across the national divergences (see table).

Phases of Welfare State Development in Western Europe

| Phases | Time | Core welfare state concept |
|---|---|---|
| Prehistory | 1600–1880 | Policing the poor |
| Takeoff | 1880–1914 | Social insurance to integrate workers |
| Expansion | 1918–1960 | Social services as an element of citizenship |
| Acceleration | 1960–1975 | Promotion of quality of life |
| Slowdown | 1975– | New mix of state, associational, and private responsibilities? |

First, in the *prehistory* of the modern welfare state, national poor laws were developed. The policy choices in this period structured subsequent welfare state developments. This period extended roughly to the late nineteenth century. Poverty was perceived as an individual shortcoming, and support was given only in combination with tight controls. Public policy centered on the maintenance of collective order rather than on individual well-being.

Towards the end of the nineteenth century, the policy conception changed radically. As social insurance programs were adopted, the collective causes of misery were highlighted and individual well-being became a recognized policy goal, firmly established in individual legal entitlements. However, the scope of welfare schemes was still targeted selectively on the working class. The concern with public order was still central, the major objective being to integrate the workers into the capitalist economy and the national state. Public efforts centered on income maintenance for workers, and the range of state services in health, housing, and education remained limited. Prior to World War I, the ratio of welfare spending to GDP remained below 5 percent throughout all Western European countries. However, as contemporary research on the impact of program age on current spending levels has shown, an important institutional basis for welfare provisions had been laid. This phase may therefore be considered the *takeoff* period of the modern welfare state.

After World War I, a long period of *expansion* began in which the scope and the range of welfare state activities was successively widened. The coverage of social insurance schemes was extended to white-collar strata and independent categories, health and education facilities were expanded, and public housing programs were adopted. Welfare services came to be perceived as a fundamental element of citizenship rights. National variations remained great, but in all countries the welfare expenditure ratio grew. The expansionary trend was spurred after World War II, which had strengthened national unity. In the leading country (Germany), the ratio of welfare spending to GDP had exceeded 20 percent during the interwar period. The Western European average climbed to 15 percent by 1960.

During the 1960s, welfare state expansion accelerated considerably. From 1960 to 1975, the average welfare expenditure ratio in Western Europe jumped from 15 to 27 percent. Income maintenance schemes now attained universal or nearly universal coverage, and benefit levels were repeatedly improved. Sizable resources were channeled into the health and housing sectors, and participation ratios in institutions of higher learning multiplied. The traditional idea of state provision of minima gave way to the new notion of state responsibility for optima. In several countries flat-rate minimum benefits were combined with earnings-related supplements. In institutional terms, the Western European welfare states came to resemble one another, as even the few remaining associational provisions were superseded by public schemes. In order to evaluate the effectiveness of public policy, several countries developed social indicator systems designed to measure the quality of life, for which the state now assumed a public responsibility. This was also part of a larger effort to move from a merely reactive social and economic policy to a more active engineering of societal development based on scientific analysis and forecasts. Thus, several countries set up national economic advisory councils to mobilize professional expertise (for example, the United Kingdom in 1961, West Germany in 1963).

With the recession of the mid-1970s these high-flying projects came to a sudden end. If we use the welfare expenditure ratio as the chief indicator, the speed of welfare state expansion was considerably curbed. Some countries even witnessed a *standstill* or slight decrease in welfare spending relative to GDP. However,

the wide variety of policy responses to the economic crisis seems to have led to an increase in national divergences.
(Alber, 1988, pp. 451–68)

Alber's approach to his subject matter is extremely instructive. Having alerted the reader to the substantial diversity of welfare regimes among advanced capitalist states, he nonetheless identifies common features and common patterns of development. Furthermore, he utilizes these common features in constructing broad typologies of states – Scandinavian and Continental versions of the welfare state; the austerity countries and the expansion countries – as an initial step in comparing different welfare state regimes. Building on this approach he suggests the feasibility of constructing general theoretical explanations which can account for the nature of different types of welfare state regimes or different types of national policy response to the crisis of the 1970s and 1980s. Thus it is both the *substantive content* as well as the *method* used by Alber in his study which is valuable here, since it confirms the value of comparison as a technique in sociological inquiry. Moreover, it indicates the feasibility of constructing general accounts of the state despite the obvious diversity of state forms within capitalist societies. While remaining sensitive to the differences between the OECD states which constitute the advanced capitalist world, we can now draw upon this comparative approach in the search for common features and general patterns with respect to the size, growth, and role of the state in advanced capitalist societies.

Since the turn of the century, one of the most striking features of all advanced societies has been the enormous expansion of the apparatus of government. Rose (in table 7.1) details the massive growth in central government departments in all western nations indicating the extensive bureaucratization of the state.

Table 7.1   The growth in central government departments 1849–1982

|  | 1849 | 1982 (number of ministries) |
| --- | --- | --- |
| France | 10 | 42 |
| Canada | 8 | 36 |
| Italy | 11 | 28 |
| United Kingdom | 12 | 22 |
| Denmark | 8 | 20 |
| New Zealand | 19 | 19 |
| Sweden | 7 | 18 |
| Germany | 12 | 17 |
| Norway | 7 | 17 |
| Belgium | 6 | 15 |
| Finland | 11 | 15 |
| Ireland | 11 | 15 |
| Australia | 7 | 14 |
| Austria | 9 | 14 |
| Netherlands | 9 | 14 |
| USA | 6 | 13 |
| Switzerland | 7 | 7 |
| Average | 9.4 | 19.2 |

Source: Rose, 1984, p. 157

Table 7.2  Public expenditure in fifteen OECD countries as % of GDP

| Year | Belgium | Denmark | W. Germany | Finland | France | UK | Ireland | Italy | Canada | Netherlands | Norway | Austria | Sweden | Switzerland | US |
|---|---|---|---|---|---|---|---|---|---|---|---|---|---|---|---|
| 1850 |  | 8.4 |  |  |  | 11.1 |  |  |  |  |  |  |  |  |  |
| 1855 |  | 9.4 |  |  |  |  |  |  |  |  |  |  |  |  |  |
| 1860 |  |  |  |  |  | 10.7 |  |  |  |  |  |  |  |  |  |
| 1865 |  | 11.2 |  |  |  |  |  |  |  |  |  |  |  |  |  |
| 1870 |  | 9.2 | 13.3 |  | 11.0 | 8.7 |  |  |  |  | 5.8 |  |  |  |  |
| 1875 |  | 8.3 |  |  |  |  |  |  |  |  | 5.9 |  |  |  |  |
| 1880 |  | 8.9 | 9.9 |  | 15.4 | 9.1 |  |  |  |  | 6.8 |  |  | 16.5 |  |
| 1885 |  | 10.0 |  |  |  |  |  |  |  |  |  |  |  |  |  |
| 1890 |  | 10.6 | 12.9 |  | 15.0 | 9.2 |  |  |  |  | 7.4 |  |  | 15.0 | 7.1 |
| 1895 |  | 10.3 |  |  |  | 10.4 |  |  |  |  |  |  |  |  |  |
| 1900 |  | 10.8 | 14.2 |  | 15.2 | 14.9 |  |  |  | 8.9 | 9.9 |  |  | 11.1 | 7.9 |
| 1905 |  | 10.0 | 15.1 |  | 14.6 | 12.4 |  |  |  | 8.8 |  |  |  |  |  |
| 1910 |  | 12.3 |  |  | 14.4 | 12.7 |  |  |  | 8.8 | 9.3 |  |  |  |  |
| 1915 |  | 11.5 | 17.0 |  |  | 12.7 |  |  |  | 9.1 |  |  | 11.2 | 14.0 | 8.5 |
| 1920 |  | 15.3 |  |  | 34.2 | 27.4 |  |  |  | 18.5 | 12.8 |  | 10.9 |  | 12.6 |
| 1925 |  | 13.4 | 22.4 |  | 21.9 | 23.6 | 21.5 |  |  | 14.9 |  |  | 14.1 | 17.0 | 11.7 |
| 1930 |  | 13.5 | 29.4 |  | 22.1 | 24.7 | 20.8 |  |  | 15.2 | 17.4 |  | 14.0 | 17.4 | 21.3 |
| 1935 |  | 17.5 | 29.8 |  | 35.4 | 23.7 | 27.8 |  |  | 18.0 | 18.1 |  | 17.1 | 23.7 |  |
| 1940 |  | 19.2 | 36.9 |  | 29.2 | 33.4 | 26.8 |  |  | 18.3 | 19.1 |  | 17.7 | 23.9 | 22.2 |
| 1945 |  | 20.0 |  |  | 37.2 | 45.5 | 22.6 |  |  |  | 29.3 |  | 19.3 | 29.3 |  |
| 1950 | 22.6 | 19.4 | 30.8 |  | 28.4 | 30.4 | 27.4 |  |  | 27.0 | 25.5 | 25.0 | 23.5 | 19.8 | 23.0 |
| 1955 | 24.7 | 23.6 | 30.0 | 26.7 | 32.2 | 30.2 | 27.5 | 27.8 | 27.1 | 28.5 | 26.8 | 27.5 | 26.4 | 17.4 | 24.9 |
| 1960 | 30.3 | 24.8 | 32.0 | 31.3 | 34.6 | 32.6 | 28.0 | 30.1 | 28.9 | 33.7 | 29.9 | 32.1 | 31.1 | 17.2 | 27.8 |
| 1965 | 32.3 | 29.9 | 36.3 | 31.3 | 38.4 | 36.4 | 33.1 | 34.3 | 29.1 | 38.7 | 34.2 | 37.9 | 36.0 | 19.7 | 28.0 |
| 1970 | 36.5 | 40.2 | 37.6 | 31.3 | 38.9 | 39.3 | 39.6 | 34.2 | 35.7 | 45.5 | 41.0 | 39.2 | 43.7 | 21.3 | 32.2 |
| 1975 | 44.5 | 48.2 | 47.1 | 37.1 | 43.5 | 46.9 | 47.5 | 43.2 | 40.8 | 55.9 | 46.6 | 46.1 | 49.0 | 28.7 | 35.4 |
| 1980 | 51.7 | 56.0 | 46.9 | 38.2 | 46.2 | 44.6 | 48.9 | 45.6 | 40.7 | 62.5 | 49.4 | 48.5 | 65.7 | 29.7 | 33.2 |

Source: Berger, 1990, p. 117

Similarly, the growth of public expenditure in western nations over the last one hundred years represents further evidence of the enormous expansion of state activity (see table 7.2). Commenting on similar public expenditure figures, Pierson observes that a state which controls 11 percent of GDP (near the average for the turn of the century) is a fundamentally different entity than one which controls three times that figure (the average for the contemporary western state) (Pierson, 1991, ch. 2).

Besides disbursing significant resources, the state in most advanced societies is also a major, if not the largest, single employer. Clearly the scale and changing patterns of public employment have important ramifications for national labor markets and the nature of work as well as social divisions and domestic political alignments. For example, the biggest growth in public employment has been in those sectors, such as health, education, and personal social services, which have tended increasingly to recruit women. In 1981, ". . . 65–75 percent of college educated women in Germany, Sweden and the US were employed in the social welfare industries" (Pierson, 1991, p. 135).

But it is not simply the scale of public expenditure and employment which distinguishes the ACS from earlier historical states; it is also the nature of its activities. In comparison with traditional state forms, the balance between the welfare and warfare activities of the state has shifted decidedly in favor of the former. The historical evidence appears to confirm that the transformation from a warfare-dominated to a welfare-dominated state has been particularly marked across all advanced capitalist nations in the post-World War II era. In terms of the post-war changes in the composition of state budgets (table 7.3), the changing pattern of major state activities and the expansion of non-military expenditure (table 7.4), the ACS has become increasingly welfare-oriented.

Table 7.3   Military expenditure as a percentage of state budgets 1850–1975

| Year[a] | Austria | France | UK | Netherlands | Denmark | Germany |
|---|---|---|---|---|---|---|
| 1850 | | 27.4 | | | | |
| 1875 | | 23.2 | | | 37.8 | 34.0 |
| 1900 | | 37.7 | 74.2 | 26.4 | 28.9 | 22.9 |
| 1925 | 7.7 | 27.8 | 19.1 | 15.1 | 14.2 | 4.0 |
| 1950 | | 20.7 | 24.0 | 18.3 | 15.6 | 13.5 |
| 1975 | 4.9 | 17.9 | 14.7 | 11.3 | 7.4 | 6.4 |

[a] Dates are very approximate
Source: Tilly, 1990, p. 124

Both Tilly and Therborn refer to this remarkable transformation as a process of "civilianization" of the modern state (Tilly, 1990; Therborn, 1989). But it would be more accurate to conceive of the state in the majority of advanced nations as both a welfare and a warfare state, a characterization which will be justified in a subsequent section.

It would appear reasonable, on the basis of this broad overview, to offer four general observations about the state in advanced capitalist countries. First, in terms of both the nature and scale of its activities, the contemporary state bears only mild resemblance to its historical

Table 7.4  State (Non-military) expenditures as a
percentage of GNP

| Year | Britain | France | United States | Japan |
|------|---------|--------|---------------|-------|
| 1890 | 3.8 | 9.6 | 1.9 | 6.3 |
| 1900 | 3.5 | 8.5 | 1.8 | 7.4 |
| 1913 | 4.0 | 6.1 | 1.0 | 8.3 |
| 1920 | 14.5 | 15.0 | 4.5 | 5.4 |
| 1930 | 14.7 | 11.2 | 2.7 | 8.1 |
| 1938 | | | 6.5 | 17.3 |
| 1950 | 19.2 | 21.9 | 10.4 | 16.0 |
| 1960 | 17.5 | 18.1 | 9.6 | 10.8 |
| 1970 | 22.7 | 23.5 | 11.9 | 10.3 |
| 1980 | 28.5 | 27.2 | 17.2 | 17.6 |

Source: adapted from Rasler and Thompson, 1989,
p. 152

counterparts depicted in earlier chapters. While there are obvious
continuities, such as the powerful attachment to military force and
military security, the nature and functions of the state have been
transformed over the last century. Second, its functional responsibilities
have expanded considerably to embrace the welfare and material
security of its citizens alongside the traditional goals of maintaining
security and order. Third, given its sheer size and complexity, it would
appear over-simplistic to treat the ACS as some kind of monolithic
entity which operates in a unified manner. Rather, the state is a highly
fragmented and in some respects de-centered apparatus of rule. Fourth,
despite the tremendous variation among ACSs in terms of political
structures, state forms, and welfare provision, they also exhibit many
common features and similar evolutionary patterns. In view of this fact,
it does not seem entirely fanciful to engage in generalizations about, or
to construct general theoretical accounts of, such a heterogeneous set of
states. On the contrary, an intriguing question arises: How do we
account for these common features and broad similarities among such a
diverse collection of states?

# 3  The Formation of the Advanced Capitalist State

In his overview of the formation of the modern nation-state in chapter
2, David Held focused on the role of war and the role of capitalism.
The modern state, it was argued, was forged by the intersection of
external and internal forces. Although much of the traditional literature
on the evolution of the state tends to give primacy to the latter, more
recent scholarship has combined this with an emphasis on the
profound significance of war and modern warfare in accounting for the
nature of the advanced capitalist state (Mann, 1986). Such an emphasis
is to be welcomed since "... who, living in the twentieth century,
could for a moment deny the massive impact which military power,
preparation for war, and war itself, have had upon the social world?"
(Giddens, 1985, p. 22). Accordingly, the approach adopted here will

extend the analytical framework deployed in chapter 2 to examine the underlying forces which have determined both the nature and the development of the state in advanced capitalist societies.

## 3.1   The logics of militarism

Tilly (as noted earlier) identifies one of the distinctive features of contemporary western states as the "civilianization" of government (Tilly, 1990, p. 122). In comparison with early modern states, the ACS is entirely in civilian hands. Paradoxically, this civilianization of government has been accompanied by the "militarization" of society in the wake of the industrialization of warfare. National security in the modern age is no longer a matter of ensuring that the barracks are constantly manned. Rather, it demands state intervention to organize society and industry so as to ensure that, should war occur, military requirements can be rapidly met. Modern warfare has become incredibly capital-intensive such that a sophisticated and well-resourced industrial and technological infrastructure, organized by the state, is essential to national defense. As a consequence: "Preparation for war . . . is a continuous activity, reaching into all aspects of society and eroding, even nullifying, conventional distinctions about the 'civil' and the 'military' spheres of life" (Pearton, 1982, p. 11).

One of the distinctive features of all advanced industrial societies is the interlocking nature of the civil and military domains. At one level, it finds expression in the technologies and infrastructure which are very much part of everyday existence. Advanced telecommunications, the miniaturized electronics found in many household appliances, satellite TV, jet aircraft, and nuclear power, not to mention modern management techniques, such as operational research, government statistics, and sophisticated satellite cartography, all have their origins or stimulus in the military sector or military requirements. Equally, many civil technologies or facilities have direct military uses. During the 1991 Gulf War, American military commanders were able to use portable telephones linked through private sector satellites, such as those of AT&T, to communicate directly with their home bases. But this erosion of the civil–military distinction is not solely expressed in the dual use which can be made of most modern technologies or facilities. Rather more significant is the fact that the traditional distinction between war-time and peace-time has been steadily eroded by the industrialization of warfare. While there are obvious political and international legal distinctions between the two conditions, in practice defense in the modern era totally depends on the constant preparation for war. This was demonstrated unambiguously in 1990 by the incredible swiftness with which the allied nations were able to deploy unprecedented military force to the Middle East in order to liberate Kuwait from Iraqi occupation.

Even with the passing of the Cold War, continuous preparation for war remains a perfectly "normal" feature of advanced societies. To ensure national security in an age of technological warfare the state must organize the industrial, technological, and economic resources of society in order to produce the sophisticated weapons systems required and to sustain a highly professional military machine. Militarism is therefore deeply embedded in all modern industrial societies.

While "embedded militarism" may be a normal feature of advanced societies, it is not accompanied, as in previous historical epochs, by military rule or a strong propensity for military aggression. On the contrary, modern militarism articulates ". . . an attitude or a set of institutions which regard war and the preparation for war as a normal and desirable social activity" rather than the military domination of society *per se* (Mann, 1988, p. 127). A cursory examination of most western societies would confirm that, despite the demise of the Cold War, defense remains a central preoccupation of all ACSs. In the US, Britain, France, Germany, and Japan, military or security-related functions may no longer account for the largest slice of state expenditure, yet national security and military requirements permeate the whole of society. This is simply because, in order to produce advanced weapons systems and to maintain a military-technological edge, the state is implicated in a "military-industrial-bureaucratic-techno-complex" (MIBT) (Thee, 1987).

According to Thee, the MIBT is a self-sustaining structure, representing a fusion of the state and agencies within civil society, whose sole purpose is to prepare for war. It embraces the common interests and symbiotic relationships between the military, the defense-related segments of the state bureaucracy, politicians whose constituencies receive military contracts, industries which rely on defense work, unions which seek to protect their members' jobs, and producers of knowledge (universities, research establishments, etc.), all of which depend upon the maintenance or expansion of defense spending. Moreover, it is a structure which has become internationalized, through the operation of alliance organizations like NATO (the North Atlantic Treaty Organization) and the increasing globalization of defense production.

With the decline of the Cold War, the deeply rooted nature of militarism within advanced capitalist societies has become more "visible." Successive attempts to reap a significant "peace dividend," through the contraction of the military machine, have met with powerful resistance from those sectors and communities likely to lose out. In the US and the UK (where the military are the largest single consumers of goods and services in their respective national economies), the defense effort so permeates society that attempts to reduce it threaten to undermine the technological competitiveness of the most advanced sectors of industry and the prosperity of those regions, such as the Sun-belt states or the South-East respectively, which have benefited from high levels of defense spending (Lovering, 1990; Gummett and Reppy, 1991).

Accounts of the MIBT vary in their interpretations of its causal dynamic. Many neo-Marxists locate its dynamic in the nature of capitalism, either in terms of the drive for profit on the part of capital or the state's use of military spending to regulate the capitalist economy. Power-elite theorists, such as C. Wright Mills, account for it in terms of the confluence of interests between military, political, and economic elites within capitalist societies (Mills, 1956). Others explain it as a product of coalition building among bureaucratic, political, military and industrial agents and groups who have essentially common interests in sustaining military innovation and capabilities (MacKenzie, 1990). A rather different approach is advocated by Mann and Giddens. They consider militarism within advanced societies, as expressed most visibly in the MIBT, to be a consequence of the industrialization of war in the context of a global states system in which "might is right" (Mann, 1988; Giddens, 1985). This particular argument, which combines insights from historical sociology and international relations, locates modern militarism in a comparative and global context. It explores why militarism has become "embedded" in the very fabric of advanced societies as well as how, together with the actual experience of two world wars, it has contributed to the transformation of the state within western nations since the turn of the century. Put simply, the argument is that in a global system of sovereign nation-states each state is the only guarantor of its own security. But, because each state arms to defend itself, this immediately generates insecurity in surrounding states. Insecurity is therefore a permanent structural feature of the global states system. Accordingly states must constantly prepare for the eventuality of war if they are to feel secure. Combine this with the industrialization of war, which requires the state to organize society in such a way that facilitates this permanent preparation for war, and the consequence is an "embedded militarism," to varying degrees, within all advanced societies.

In a magisterial study of the impact of modern warfare on society, Pearton argues that, since the close of the last century, the industrialization of war has played a primary role in transforming the relationship between state, society, and the economy in western countries (Pearton, 1982).

Industrialization required the state to forge direct links with private industry in order to secure the supply of modern military hardware. New technologies which had significant military implications, like the railway and the telegraph, were nurtured or supervised by the state. In Germany, for instance, railway construction was directed and controlled by the military, as was the development of the chemical industry (McNeill, 1983). State intervention in industry to strengthen the nation's military capability was driven by the fear that to lag behind a potential rival would be to court defeat should war occur. Competition between states, generated by the endemic insecurity of the inter-state system, combined with the industrialization of warfare rapidly eroded the traditional *laissez-faire* approach to the economy. By 1913, for instance, one-sixth of the entire British workforce was dependent solely on navy contracts. As Pearton comments "The state, in all countries, began to undermine the liberal economy in regard to its military requirements, even before the [First World] War broke out" (Pearton, 1982, p. 49).

When it came, industrial war brought with it destruction and human suffering on a scale never before witnessed in western civilization.

Unlike war in the seventeenth or eighteenth centuries, World War I was a total war. It involved the mobilization of entire national populations and economies.

In Britain, France, Germany, Russia, and the United States the state was forced to engage in direct regulation of the economy, controlling those sectors considered vital to the war effort. The concept of the "home front" entered common parlance as the "real" battleground – the Western front – and placed increasing demands upon society and the economy (see table 7.5).

Table 7.5   War expenditure and total mobilized forces, 1914–19

|  | War expenditure at 1913 prices (billions of dollars) | Total mobilized forces (millions) |
|---|---|---|
| British Empire | 23.0 | 9.5 |
| France | 9.3 | 8.2 |
| Russia | 5.4 | 13.0 |
| Italy | 3.2 | 5.6 |
| United States | 17.1 | 3.8 |
| Other Allies* | −0.3 | 2.6 |
| *Total Allies* | *57.7* | *42.7* |
| Germany | 19.9 | 13.25 |
| Austria-Hungary | 4.7 | 9.00 |
| Bulgaria, Turkey | 0.1 | 2.85 |
| *Total Central Powers* | *24.7* | *25.10* |

*Belgium, Romania, Portugal, Greece, Serbia
Source: Kennedy, 1987, p. 274

Industrialists and trade unionists were co-opted into the state machine to manage the "home front." Scientific knowledge and technological innovation were also harnessed to military requirements. During this period the state discovered a capacity to "manage" society and the economy; a realization which was to have important consequences for post-war reconstruction. As Beveridge, the "founder" of the British welfare state, remarked in 1920, "We have ... under the stress of war, made practical discoveries in the art of government almost comparable to the immense discoveries made at the same time in the art of flying" (quoted in Smith, 1986, p. 61).

Beyond the destruction – the human toll was appalling with over 7.7 million combatants killed – the unintended and unforeseen consequences of the war were far reaching. Pearton notes that "... industrialized war enabled the state to tighten its grip on society and make industry responsible to its demands" (Pearton, 1982, p. 174). In the political domain the need to mobilize entire populations accelerated processes of democratization.

It also, according to Pierson, helped lay the ideological foundations of both the "welfare state" and expanded notions of citizenship (Pierson, 1991). In the economic domain new industries, such as aircraft manufacture, grew rapidly while the traditional industries were modernized. The world of work changed too. Widespread diffusion of "Fordist" techniques of mass production were encouraged by wartime demands and state initiatives. In addition, the war also triggered a massive surge in trade unionism. Nor did the household escape change, with the temporary expansion of the female labor market and the decline of domestic service. According to McNeill, the extent of these changes added up to a "social metamorphosis" (McNeill, 1983, p. 317).

If the "Great War" marked a "... discontinuity in our culture" (Pearton, 1982, p. 49) World War II underwrote a further phase in the re-structuring of state–society relations in all western societies. By comparison with 1914 the war effort demanded state intervention in the economy and society on an unprecedented scale. For example, Allied armaments production in 1943 alone equalled that for the entire period 1914–18 (see table 7.6).

Table 7.6   Armaments production of the powers, 1940–3 (billions of 1944 dollars)

|  | 1940 | 1941 | 1943 |
| --- | --- | --- | --- |
| Britain | 3.5 | 6.5 | 11.1 |
| USSR | (5.0) | 8.5 | 13.9 |
| United States | (1.5) | 4.5 | 37.5 |
| *Total of Allied combatants* | *3.5* | *19.5* | *62.5* |
| Germany | 6.0 | 6.0 | 13.8 |
| Japan | (1.0) | 2.0 | 4.5 |
| Italy | 0.75 | 1.0 | – |
| *Total of Axis combatants* | *6.75* | *9.0* | *18.3* |

Source: Kennedy, 1987, p. 355

Along with the mobilization of industry and science, the mobilization of entire civil populations transformed the relationship between the state and its citizens.

In addition, some 13 million battle deaths and at least as many civilian deaths, combined with the unimaginable scale of the destruction and dislocation wreaked across Europe and the East, reinforced demands for extensive state intervention in the process of post-war reconstruction. In Britain, reconstruction witnessed the birth of the "welfare state," while in Germany and Japan reconstruction brought a complete social and political transformation as the "victors" imposed their own vision of liberal-capitalist democracy. Within all western countries the unforeseen legacy of war involved an expanded role for the state as well as a deepening of citizenship rights and democracy.

According to Milward, the war experience contributed to a decisive change in the role of the state within western capitalist nations:

> The hope that the economy could be managed, and the political will that it should be managed, were greatly reinforced by the knowledge of the more detailed workings of business and industry which central governments were forced to acquire between 1939 and 1945. That is perhaps the most immediately obvious historical consequence of the changes in the direction of the economy in the second world war. Capitalist economies had been made to function in a very different way and it is easy to see in the plans

> for reconstruction that their economic shibboleths had been much
> altered by the war experience. Governments were persuaded that
> their economic powers were much more extensive and their
> economic duties more compelling.
> (Milward, 1987, p. 128)

The war crystallized social and political forces around "managed
capitalism" – state intervention in and management of the economy to
ensure full employment combined with the provision of welfare
services. Titmus, a leading sociologist of the period, attributed this in
Britain to the fact that the war ". . . spread and quickened a trend
towards social altruism and crystallized within the nation demands for
social justice" (quoted in Fox, 1986, p. 36). Yet, in many other respects
the war, but particularly the Holocaust, stood as a clear indictment of
the central ideals of European civilization – the attachment to
inevitable social progress, instrumental rationality, and western cultural
supremacy – which had been fixed in the western imagination since the
age of the Enlightenment *philosophes*. In this sense, the war had a
dramatic impact upon the West, marking a new discontinuity in
western culture and its collective consciousness.

A further discontinuity between the pre-war and the post-war worlds
arose with the bombing of Hiroshima and Nagasaki in August, 1945.
The advent of nuclear weapons, which epitomized the harnessing of
science and technology for military purposes, transformed modern
warfare. With the development of the Cold War, two nuclear armed
camps confronted each other for over forty years in the knowledge that
"hot" war would extinguish humanity. In this context defense became
synonymous with deterrence. But for deterrence to be credible required
permanent preparation for war on a scale which demanded extensive
state activity in organizing society's economic, industrial, technological,
and human resources to ensure production of the most advanced
military hardware and to the highest possible technical standards. The
result was a post-war remilitarization of societies in both the East and
the West anchored into position by global alliance structures. President
Eisenhower, in his famous speech warning of the dangers posed by the
"military-industrial complex," feared this remilitarization would
undermine western societies through its corrosion of democratic
practices and its distortion of the capitalist economy. Paradoxically, the
military burden was more severely felt in the Eastern bloc, where it
helped along the decline of state socialism.

"Embedded militarism," despite the demise of a bipolar world,
remains a distinctive feature of all advanced societies. Of course within
the West there exists significant diversity with respect to both the scale
of national military efforts and the particular dynamics of militarism.
Yet, for all the major western states, embedded militarism retains its
common roots in the industrialization of warfare and the workings of a
global states system in which security is measured solely in units of
military-industrial capabilities. Thus, as Giddens and others have
argued, the logics of militarism together with the actual experience of

war in the twentieth century have been key processes in the formation of the ACS (Giddens, 1985). However, the story so far remains essentially one-dimensional.

## 3.2   The logics of capital

> The welfare state . . . is a major aspect of politics, policy, and states of our time. Alongside liberal democracy, it may be said to be the most pervasive feature of the everyday politics of western countries. Health and social care, education, and income maintenance constitute today the predominant everyday activities and pecuniary efforts of the states of advanced capitalism.
> (Therborn, 1989, p. 62)

The universal nature of the modern welfare state, to which Therborn refers, has been attributed to the dynamics of industrial capitalism. But the primacy now attached to welfare provision in all advanced capitalist societies is a recent and somewhat surprising development. No account of this development can ignore the complex interplay between endogenous factors, such as class conflict, and exogenous factors, such as war or international economic crises (Gourevitch, 1986).

In the post-war period, "managed capitalism" – through which, to varying degrees, the state in western societies accepted some responsibility for ensuring full employment, providing welfare services and a modicum of social justice – emerged as the dominant "framework" for organizing the continued reproduction of advanced capitalism. "Managed capitalism," it has been argued, was based on a historic class compromise between capital and labor in which the state played a critical mediating role. Through a combination of Keynesian and interventionist economic policies, the state sought to sustain economic growth and full employment while simultaneously, through its welfare programs, it attempted to redress some of the inequalities inherent in capitalism. Corporate capital and organized labor accepted in return the need to look beyond their own sectional interests to the furtherance of the collective interests of the nation. In Britain, "managed capitalism" was associated with the institutionalization of the welfare state – i.e. the establishment of the National Health Service, the extension of educational provision, the implementation of national social insurance – and an attachment to consensus politics. But in some respects the UK was atypical, insofar as the post-war commitment to managed capitalism in other countries, for example Sweden and the US, largely reflected the consolidation of a "historic compromise" between corporate capital, organized labor, and the state which had been arrived at in response to the trauma of the Great Depression.

Although the US and Sweden are viewed as polar opposites with respect to welfare state provision – with the US considered a "welfare laggard" in comparison to Sweden with its comprehensive welfare provision – both nonetheless have much in common insofar as they experimented with a kind of "welfare state project" as part of a social democratic/reformist response to the economic crisis of the 1930s. Underlying this reformist response was a coalition of agricultural, labor, and corporate interests which in partnership with the state forged a successful accommodation of interests around progressive policies of "managed capitalism." In the case of the US this was articulated in Roosevelt's New Deal, while in Sweden it took the form of the Saltsjobaden Accord and the entrenchment of social democratic rule (Gourevitch, 1986, ch. 4). However, in the UK, social reformism took hold in the process of post-war reconstruction, rather than in the context of international economic crisis. Despite the diverse trajectories of national developments, there can be no disputing the fact that the post-war period witnessed a universal expansion of the welfare state (coupled with an explicit attachment to Keynesian strategies of economic management) within the western capitalist world.

Within the last decade the social democratic account of the welfare state has drawn substantial criticism in relation both to its historical accuracy and its intellectual coherence. Historically, the social democratic "story" tends to play down the continued significance of deep social and class divisions within capitalist societies, with its stress on the social and political consensus surrounding the welfare state. Yet it is clear that in the majority of advanced capitalist nations the post-war consensus on bounded or "managed capitalism" has not survived the global economic crisis of the 1970s and the subsequent national economic re-structuring. In the UK, for instance, the emergence of "Thatcherism" in the 1980s is often taken to define the end of "consensus politics." Similar, though not as dramatic, political changes in Germany, the US, Sweden, and other western states in the 1980s underline the fragile and historically contingent character of "managed capitalism." Furthermore, this account fails to acknowledge that many of the original and more radical welfare state measures were introduced, not by social democratic or socialist regimes, but by liberal or conservative governments (Pierson, 1991).

Recent scholarship on the origins of the welfare state tends to place greater stress on the role of organized working-class interests as well as on the fragile nature of the coalitions which nurtured its formation (Esping-Andersen, 1985; 1990). Moreover, it seems simplistic, as do so many social democratic accounts, to assume that governments promoting social reform merely responded to societal pressures. Quite clearly, as much of the historical evidence confirms, the development of welfare programs was sometimes driven by the state's own requirements ". . . not least in the securing of a citizenry fit and able to staff its armies" (Pierson, 1991, p. 35). As Giddens observes, state managers had a political interest in developing welfare programs since they afforded an expanded scope for official "surveillance" and created new mechanisms of social control (Giddens, 1985). Nor should it be forgotten that, while much of the visible activity of the welfare state involves responding to the failings of the market, welfare programs and state intervention also function to support and sustain, rather than supplant, the market system (Therborn, 1987).

In comparison to the "social democratic paradigm," the Marxist tradition stresses the functional role of the welfare state in sustaining capitalism. Of course, within this broad tradition there is considerable theoretical diversity. Despite this diversity, two distinctive approaches can be discerned: the first locates the origins of the welfare state and "managed capitalism" in the class struggles of capitalist society; the second considers it a mechanism for "regulating" (but in no sense resolving) the contradictions within capitalist society. In both cases the emphasis is on the welfare state as a *capitalist* state.

The class struggle approach considers managed capitalism primarily as a regime for ensuring the continued reproduction and maintenance of an essentially exploitative capitalist socio-economic order. Unlike the social democratic paradigm, which considers the welfare state as a "real" class compromise, this approach conceives of it as an apparatus of social control:

> From the capitalist point of view state welfare has contributed to the continual struggle to accumulate capital by materially assisting in bringing labour and capital together profitably and containing the inevitable resistance and revolutionary potential of the working class . . .
> . . . the social security system is concerned with reproducing a reserve army of labour, the patriarchal family and the disciplining of the labour force. Only secondarily and contingently does it function as a means of mitigating poverty . . .
> (Ginsburg, 1979, p. 2)

Gough echoes this critique in suggesting that "managed capitalism" has never been based on a real accommodation of class interests but rather reflected the ". . . ability of the capitalist state to formulate and implement policies to secure the long-term reproduction of capitalist social relations" (Gough, 1979, p. 64). The development of the welfare state in the UK, Germany, Sweden, and the US is often cited to validate this argument. Piven and Cloward, for instance, argue that in the case of the US the New Deal reforms were essentially a response to ". . . the rising surge of political unrest that accompanied this [Great Depression] economic catastrophe" (Piven and Cloward, 1971, p. 45). However, this "social control" perspective is not entirely convincing. On the one hand, according to Pierson ". . . it is difficult to sustain the argument that the growth of the welfare state was exclusively or even preponderantly in the interests of the capitalist class" (Pierson, 1991, p. 54). On the other hand it adopts an uncomplicated view of the state as an extension of the ruling class with limited autonomy and no independent sources of power.

A second approach locates the origins of the welfare state in the contradictions of capitalist society, and more specifically in the dynamic tension between democracy and capitalism. A major exponent of this "neo-Marxist" position is Claus Offe. His analysis concentrates on the welfare state as a form of "crisis management" whose primary purpose is to regulate the contradictions between liberal democracy and market capitalism (Offe, 1984). Offe's argument is that the welfare state emerged as an apparatus to "reconcile" the demands of citizens, expressed through the democratic process, for a more secure standard of living with the requirements of a crisis-prone capitalist economy in which accumulation – continuous acquisition of capital – "rules." Because democracy and private accumulation can never be successfully reconciled, the welfare state functions as a form of "crisis manager," constantly attempting to secure both "continued accumulation" and "continued legitimation" (Pierson, 1991, p. 58).

Offe's approach provides a complex appreciation of the origins of the welfare state without denying the significance of the political struggles and class compromises – "managed capitalism." As he notes, underlying the development of the welfare state

> . . . is a politically constituted class compromise or accord . . . It is easy to see why and how the existence of this accord has contributed to the compatibility of capitalism and democracy . . . each class has to take the interests of the other class into consideration: the workers must acknowledge the importance of profitability, because only a sufficient level of profits and investment will secure future employment and income increases; and the capitalists must accept the need for wages and welfare state expenditures, because these will secure effective demand and a healthy, well-trained, well-housed and happy working class. (Offe, 1984, pp. 193–4)

This analysis emphasizes the "autonomous" character of the welfare state – i.e. actively reconciling contradictions – in comparison to other theories which stress its essentially class based or social democratic character. Moreover, unlike the social democratic/reformist account, it considers that this reconciliation is neither stable nor permanent but rather is subject to continuous negotiation and adaptation. In effect, the state is trapped in a cycle of crisis management. In Offe's view, the welfare state and "managed capitalism" are thus historically contingent; they have no fixed institutional or political form; and neither is necessarily a permanent feature of the political terrain of advanced capitalism. However, critics have pointed to the strong functionalist logic which underpins Offe's analysis: that is, the needs of capitalism seem to predetermine the action and responses of the state. As a consequence, the state is projected as a kind of "black box" rather than an arena within which socio-political struggles are played out.

If the logic of capitalism has shaped the formation of all modern welfare states, it has nonetheless been mediated by distinctive national social and political formations which have culminated in very different types of welfare regimes. Therborn attempts to impose some order on this diversity by creating a typology of welfare state regimes (Therborn, 1987). Welfare states are classified along two dimensions: whether the commitment to full employment is relatively strong or relatively weak; and whether entitlements to social benefits are extensive or restrictive. This, as table 7.7 shows, produces a four-fold categorization of welfare states from the strong-interventionist type, the Scandinavian model, to the market-oriented type, such as the US and the UK. You may notice,

Table 7.7   A typology of welfare states

|  |  | Social entitlements | |
|---|---|---|---|
|  |  | High | Low |
| Commitment to full employment | High | Strong interventionist welfare states | Full employment-oriented small welfare states |
|  | Low | Soft, compensatory welfare states | Market-oriented welfare states |

too, that the two highest defense spenders in the West (the US and the UK) also have in common minimal welfare state provision.

Thus, as Pierson notes, we can identify the following four categories:

**Strong interventionist welfare states** (extensive social policy, strong commitment to full employment)

Sweden, Norway, Austria, (Finland)

**Soft compensatory welfare states** (generous social entitlements, low commitment to full employment)

Belgium, Denmark, Netherlands, (France, Germany, Ireland, Italy)

**Full employment-oriented, small welfare states** (low social entitlements, but institutional commitment to full employment)

Switzerland, Japan

**Market-oriented welfare states** (limited social rights, low commitment to full employment)

Australia, Canada, USA, UK, New Zealand.

(Pierson, 1991, p. 186)

Capitalism has been a central force in the formation of the contemporary state. As this section has argued, both social democracy and neo-Marxism have much to say about the relationship between capitalism and the nature of the ACS. While these traditions have particular strengths and limitations both share one common failing: a tendency to underplay the significance of international or exogenous forces of socio-political change. As Gourevitch's study of the impact of international economic crisis on western capitalist states demonstrates, the emergence of "managed capitalism" and the welfare state had a powerful external stimulus in the global depression of the 1930s:

> Out of the traumas of the depression of the 1930s and of World War II the countries of Western Europe and North America had forged a "historic compromise". Bitter enemies had worked out a truce built around a mixed economy, a kind of bounded capitalism, where private enterprise remained the dynamo but operated within a system of rules that provided stability, both economic and political.
> (Gourevitch, 1986, p. 18)

International economic crises are in many respects the equivalent of war in the sense that they may disrupt established frameworks of national economic management as well as the political and social coalitions which sustain them. No account of the ACS can therefore afford to ignore the ways in which global economic forces intrude upon the processes of state formation. Alber has argued that the global economic recession of the 1980s disturbed the social and political basis of "managed capitalism" and promoted a restructuring, if not a retrenchment, of welfare provision in all western states. Whether this spells the end of organized or "managed capitalism," as some would argue, or whether it merely represents a temporary deviation from established practice, remains a vigorously debated topic. What is incontestable, however, is the increasing significance of global conditions in defining the types of welfare regimes which can realistically survive in a more economically interconnected world system. As Gourevitch observes in the contemporary era, ". . . pressure has built up to curtail state spending and interventions. Whatever the differences in partisan outcomes, all governments have been pressed in the same direction" (Gourevitch, 1986, p. 33). The implication is that exogenous forces of change have a strategic role in accounting for the form of the ACS.

### 3.3  The welfare–warfare state: a review

Mann argues that ". . . capitalism and militarism are both core features of our society but they are only contingently connected" (Mann, 1988, p. 127). The discussion in the preceding pages would appear to confirm his position. Taking the question of the welfare state, for instance, there can be little dispute that it is a product of both the dynamics of capitalism and the unintended consequences of war. Yet there is little common agreement on precisely how the intersection of these causal forces culminated in the institutionalization of the modern welfare state. Given such uncertainty, a reasoned conclusion might be that, while the ACS has been, and continues to be, fashioned by both militarism and capitalism, the intellectual temptation to give causal primacy to one over the other has to be resisted in favor of a more eclectic approach which recognizes the complex intersection of these forces. Such eclecticism reflects the reality that the ACS has always faced both inwards and outwards; inwards towards society and outwards towards a system of states. Accordingly the ACS continues to be defined by the complex interplay between endogenous and exogenous processes of change: the domestic realm of socio-economic conflict and the external realm of inter-state rivalry respectively.

# 4  Putting the Advanced Capitalist State in Perspective

The discussion so far has concentrated on the dynamic processes of formation: an overview of the development of the ACS but in "fast-forward" mode. In this section we shift from "fast-forward" mode, continuing the video metaphor, to a "freeze frame" or synoptic mode in an attempt to understand the functions and the power of the state in advanced capitalist nations. As the previous discussion has demonstrated, the post-war period witnessed a massive expansion of the state apparatus and state activity in all western societies. This raises a series of intriguing questions: Does this expansion represent an accretion of power by the state in capitalist societies? Or is it a sign of a weak state unable to resist societal demands? In whose interests does the ACS "rule"? Is the state best conceived as a "capitalist" state or an "autonomous" state? These are somewhat intimidating questions. Perhaps by engaging with some of the existing literature which has analyzed these issues we can begin to sketch in the outlines of some "answers." This will involve not only confronting different theoretical approaches to the state but also focusing on ". . . the state's authoritative actions and inactions, the public policies that are and are not adopted" (Nordlinger, 1981, p. 2): what the state does or fails to do.

As Alber has highlighted, the global economic crisis which began in the 1970s and continued into the early 1980s corroded the domestic social and political foundations of "managed capitalism," with the consequence that the role of the state has come under increasing scrutiny in all ACSs (Alber, 1988, pp. 451–68). Even in Sweden, social democratic governments have been forced to rethink the state's role in response to domestic political crises and international economic conditions. And in France a socialist government was forced to embrace aspects of the "New Right" agenda. By the 1990s, given the collapse of "state socialism" in Eastern Europe, the proper extent of state intervention in civil society and the legitimate boundaries of state power remain issues which continue to occupy a strategic position (if at times somewhat camouflaged) on the domestic political agenda within the majority of ACSs.

Political controversy within society over the proper role of the ACS has had the effect of rejuvenating the study of the state within sociology and associated disciplines. A "state debate" has emerged, delivering some new insights into the ACS. Within this debate, two distinct approaches can be identified to the key questions of state power and the relationship between state and civil society. "Society-centered" approaches, which embrace a variety of theoretical traditions, view the ACS as tightly constrained by the structure of power within society and heavily reliant, for the most part, on the political support and economic resources generated by powerful private actors. In effect, the tendency is for state action or inaction to reflect the interests of the dominant groups within society, whether dominant classes or elites. Thus Nordlinger writes that the ACS in such approaches ". . . is commonly seen as a permeable, vulnerable, and malleable entity, not necessarily in the hands of most individuals and groups, but in those of the most powerful" (Nordlinger, 1981, p. 3). In comparison "state-centered approaches" stress the power of the ACS in relation to societal forces and its ability to act ". . . contrary to the demands of the politically best endowed private actors, whether these are voters, well organized "special interest" groups, the managers of huge corporations, or any other set of societal actor" (Nordlinger, 1981, p. 2). Within each of these two general approaches can be located a heterogeneous grouping of theoretical accounts of the ACS. These are given more exposure in the two subsequent sections.

## 4.1  Society-centered approaches

The emergence of liberal democracy has often been identified with both the extension of the franchise and the consolidation of social and political pluralism. Representative government in all ACSs is supplemented by the existence of a universe of diverse social and political groupings within civil society. In addition to the "vote," citizens thus have the ability to channel their demands on the state through those social groups, organizations, or movements with which they are associated. Accordingly, liberal democracy, as the previous chapter implied, is commonly equated with polyarchy: a system in which power and political resources are largely fragmented. Within this classical pluralist tradition, the state's role is primarily conceived of as processing political issues and securing a societal consensus by delivering policy outcomes that do not diverge substantially from the status quo and which reflect the demands of the public. Such a conception implies an essentially neutral or broker model of the state, and a correspondingly wide dispersion of power throughout society such that no one group or set of interests systematically dominates the political process.

Few political scientists or sociologists would accept that classical pluralism offers even a remotely accurate account of the state or policy-making in ACSs. Even its original proponents, Robert Dahl and Charles Lindblom, no longer argue that it provides a fair representation of American liberal democracy at work, let alone democracy in other ACSs (Dahl, 1985; Lindblom, 1977). Coming to terms with the structural changes in capitalist societies in the 1960s and 1970s, particularly the growth of state bureaucracy and state interventionism within the economy, has forced advocates of classical pluralism to review their assumptions and adapt their account accordingly. In virtually all capitalist societies, the growth of corporate power and state bureaucracy has "distorted" the political process. Nordlinger even refers to the ACS as the "distorted liberal state" (Nordlinger, 1981, p. 157). Moreover, the increasing specialization, technical nature, and overwhelming volume of policy issues has encouraged the formation of functionally differentiated "policy communities," e.g., health, social security, energy, defense, education, etc. Within these "policy communities" officials and experts from the responsible state agencies concerned, together with representatives of the most influential or knowledgeable private organized interests, formulate public policy often with only very limited participation by elected politicians.

Health policy in most ACSs is formulated in this manner. In the UK, for instance, Department of Health officials, representatives of the professional medical associations and other major interests (i.e. pharmaceutical companies) jointly determine much health policy. Moreover, in most key policy sectors such consultative machinery or policy networks are institutionalized through formal or informal committee structures. Japan is a principal example of such institutionalization, since in almost every policy sector government departments have spawned considerable numbers of consultative committees through which the major organized interests and experts are co-opted into the policy formulation process (Eccleston, 1989). This "privileging" of the most powerful organized interests within the policy process limits effective democratic participation, since it excludes the less influential and specifically those critical of the status quo who become relegated to "outsiders." It also reinforces executive domination of the policy process since parliaments or legislatures are substantially bypassed. Accordingly, neo-pluralists paint a picture of the democratic process in most ACSs as one of unequal and restricted group competition in which there exists a "privileging" within the policy process of the more powerful organized interests within civil society. In the case of business and corporate interests, neo-pluralists argue that such "privileging" is a structural necessity rather than a consciously articulated choice made by state managers or politicians. For, as Lindblom acknowledges: "Because public functions in the market system rest in the hands of business, it follows that jobs, prices, production, growth, the standard of living, and the economic security of everyone all rest in their hands. Consequently government officials cannot be indifferent to how well business performs its functions" (Lindblom, 1977, p. 122). The consequence of this is that:

> It becomes a major task of government to design and maintain an inducement system for businessmen, to be solicitous of business interests, and to grant them, for its value as an incentive, intimacy of participation in government itself. In all these respects the relation between government and business is unlike the relation between government and any other interest group in society. (Dahl and Lindblom, 1976, p. xxxvii)

Neo-pluralism delivers an account of the ACS that is significantly removed from that of classical pluralism. Power in capitalist societies is argued to be highly concentrated while corporate interests and economic issues dominate the political agenda. The existence of such inequalities in the distribution of power resources and in access to government decision-makers undermines the classical pluralist notion of a highly competitive political process which no single set of interests can systematically dominate. Furthermore, since the state in a capitalist society has to be constantly attentive to the needs of corporate capital, the pluralist fiction of a neutral arbiter between competing interests is replaced with the notion of a "distorted liberal state."

Evidence of a further kind of "distortion" of the liberal democratic state is to be found in the numerous studies of social and political "elites" which some argue exercise extensive power within capitalist society (Mills, 1956). Elite theories stress the natural tendency for power within all social institutions and organizations to become centralized within the hands of a dominant group or *elite*. This is particularly the case in capitalist societies where mass politics, the centrality of huge organizations in social life, the growth of bureaucracy, reliance upon expertise, etc., encourage the formation of elites. Several recent studies of British and American society point to the domination of key social institutions, such as the military, civil service, church, business, finance, the press, the judiciary, and so on, by elites whose members share similar social backgrounds and often similar political outlooks (Scott, 1991; Domhoff, 1978). In Britain the key elites are remarkable in the degree to which they share common social origins. Corresponding studies of Japanese society suggest equivalent conclusions (Eccleston, 1989). Some elite theorists therefore argue that, because elites tend to be recruited from the same social strata, they function as a socially cohesive political group. Many decades ago, C. Wright Mills argued that American society was ruled by a power elite and this remains a "popularized" explanation of the American political process (Mills, 1956). As Lukes acknowledges, political influence rarely has to be exerted openly but rather operates more "informally" within elite networks. Accordingly, it is their ability to shape the political agenda, so avoiding open confrontation where their interests may be under threat, linked with a societal attachment to consensus decision-making, that enables elites to "control" the political process. But the existence of elites, however defined, does not convincingly demonstrate that the political process is directed or even considerably influenced by their activities. Elitist accounts share in common a view of the ACS as permeated at key levels by dominant social elites such that the state apparatus is perceived as functioning substantially in the interests of a (powerful) minority of its citizens.

If elite theorists point to the existence of a "ruling elite" within ACSs, Marxism, at least its classical brands, points to a "ruling class" (Scott, 1991). This distinction is critical, for within traditional Marxist accounts it is the class nature of capitalist society and the consequent class nature of the state itself that is fundamental to an understanding of power and the state in western societies. A classical Marxist account of the state is to be found in Ralph Miliband's *The State in Capitalist Society* (Miliband, 1969). Miliband argued that power within capitalist society resides within a fairly cohesive capitalist class. In effect, the state substantially expresses and acts to secure "bourgeois" dominance within capitalist society. This is achieved because, within Britain, the US, France, and other capitalist societies, state managers, those in senior positions in business, the military, the judiciary, and so on are largely recruited from the ranks of the dominant capitalist class. In addition, the "ruling class" can exploit its social networks to gain access to the key decision-making sites within state and civil society. The state is also constrained by the need to ensure continued capital accumulation. Taken together Miliband therefore constructed what is broadly regarded as an "instrumentalist" account – in the sense that the state is conceived of as an instrument of capital – of the ACS (Held, 1987, pp. 207–8).

This account attracted considerable criticism, mostly from within Marxist or *marxisant* circles. Poulantzas argued that an "instrumentalist" account was insensitive to the structural factors which conditioned state action, namely its need to secure the conditions for the continued reproduction of capitalist society even when the necessary action conflicted with the short-term interests of the capitalist class. For Poulantzas, the ACS often acted "relatively autonomously" of the capitalist class where such action was functional to the long-term stability of the capitalist order. Evidence for this, Poulantzas argued, was to be found in the institutionalization of the welfare state which appeared to conflict with the core interests of the capitalist class. These two polarized positions of "instrumentalism" and "structuralism" have shaped an on going debate within neo-Marxism on the role of the state in advanced capitalist societies.

Despite their origins in rather different theoretical traditions, the various accounts of the ACS which have been elaborated in the last few pages all share a common preoccupation with the societal constraints on and the social basis of state power. They represent the central core of "society-based approaches" to the ACS. For they consider that the autonomous power of the ACS is severely compromised by its dependence on dominant socio-economic groups for the political and economic resources essential to its continued survival. Whether exaggerated or not, this claim requires critical scrutiny.

## 4.2   State-centered approaches

When President Truman initiated the Marshall Aid Plan to provide direct financial assistance for the post-war reconstruction of Europe, he did so in the knowledge that powerful corporate, labor, and political elites at home openly opposed the policy.

Despite overwhelming opposition from industrialists, labor unions, and a significant section of its own party, the first Thatcher government in Britain pursued a severely deflationary economic strategy at the peak of an economic recession in which unemployment had reached well over 3 million. Japanese rice farmers faced the 1990s with the gloomy prospect of mass bankruptcies following their government's decision to liberalize the rice trade – so allowing imports of cheaper US rice to flood the domestic market – even though farmers remain a powerful force within the governing LDP party. What each of these vignettes appears to illustrate is the autonomous power of the state; its ability to articulate and pursue actions and policies which can run counter to the interests of the most dominant or powerful groups (classes) in society.

Nordlinger, in his extensive study of the autonomy of the liberal democratic state, delivers a powerful critique of "society-centered approaches" to the ACS precisely because they ". . . strenuously [deny] the possibility of the state translating its preferences into authoritative actions when opposed by societal actors who control the weightiest political resources" (Nordlinger, 1981, p. 3). Attempts to understand the autonomous power of the state have generated a range of "state-centered approaches" to the study of the ACS.

A very influential strand of theorizing has been that of the "New Right" which, as noted earlier, launched a sustained attack on the welfare state in the 1980s. Underlying "New Right" accounts of the ACS is an unusual juxtaposition of neo-conservative and neo-liberal political philosophies. The result is an interesting diversity of theoretical interpretations. Yet within this broad "school" there is a shared set of assumptions that the state is not subordinate to societal forces but can and does act quite autonomously. Focusing on the massive post-war expansion of the welfare state in capitalist societies, "New Right" accounts lay stress on the internal political and bureaucratic imperatives of the state rather than on a massive upsurge in societal demand for welfare provision. Governments and politicians are conceived of as having a rational, institutionally based interest in expanding state welfare programs and expenditure since this helps win votes and consolidates their own power-bases. Moreover, competition between parties for political office encourages politicians to ". . . create unrealizable citizen expectations of what the government can deliver . . ." (Dunleavy and O'Leary, 1987, p. 102), and so to increase citizen demands upon the state. State bureaucracy also has a rational incentive to expand since this enhances the budgets, career prospects, and bureaucratic power of state managers. Since welfare programs are labor-intensive, there are additional pressures from public-sector unions to sustain or increase spending levels. This suggests the conclusion that: "Under liberal democratic and adversarial political arrangements, and without some sort of constitutional constraint upon the action (and spending) of governments, politicians, bureaucrats and voters acting rationally will tend to generate welfare state policies which are . . . in the long run unsustainable" (Pierson, 1991, p. 47). As Alber highlights, during the late 1970s and throughout the 1980s, this analysis of the state captured the political imagination of many conservative politicians throughout the industrialized world since it appeared to offer a convincing account of the "crisis of the welfare state." Both in Britain and the US it strongly informed the political agenda of radical conservative administrations which sought to "roll back the state."

Central to "New Right" thinking is a conception of the ACS as a powerful and "despotic" bureaucratic apparatus which has its own institutional momentum. Rather than the highly responsive and responsible state envisaged in pluralism, many "New Right" accounts proffer an image of the ACS as a quasi-autonomous set of governing institutions with enormous resources and administrative power at its disposal.

This portrait of an extremely powerful state apparatus would not be rejected totally by all state theorists. Indeed, throughout the 1970s and 1980s there was a general awareness that, within all capitalist societies, the state had acquired a more directive role with respect to the economy and civil society. This was predicated on studies of the policy-making process which demonstrated a growing tendency towards the "institutionalization" of powerful organized interests – e.g. trade unions, professional associations, employers' organizations, corporate capital – within the state decision-making apparatus (Schmitter, 1974). Since trade unions and business interests could potentially disrupt or undermine state policy, the obvious solution was to "incorporate" them into the policy-making arena. In the environment of economic crisis which pervaded the 1970s, this appeared a highly effective political strategy for governments to adopt since it provided a formal framework within which the state could attempt to hold together the post-war consensus on "managed capitalism": a consensus increasingly threatened by rising unemployment and surging inflation. Accordingly, the 1970s witnessed an intensification of this process of incorporation as well as its regularization through formal institutional mechanisms. In Britain, the CBI (Confederation of British Industry – an employer organization) and TUC (Trades Union Congress) participated in many "tripartite" structures while in Sweden and other Scandinavian democracies such forums played a critical role in the formulation of national economic strategy. But in return for institutionalized access to government, so providing these groups with a privileged position in the policy process, the state acquired expanded control over these "private" associations. As a result, rather than limiting its scope for autonomous action such "corporatist" strategies enhanced the autonomous power of the state (Nordlinger, 1981, p. 171). Thus, in the mid-1970s the TUC and CBI found themselves locked into a "social contract" arrangement with the state in which, for few immediate tangible benefits, both agreed to contain national wage demands and price rises respectively. Despite the "social contract" operating against the direct material interests of their own members, each of these associations "policed" its operation on behalf of the state.

"Corporatism" (which describes this process of incorporation) is much more than a state strategy for dealing with the inherent crisis tendencies within advanced capitalist societies. Several writers have suggested that it is a novel institutional form of the ACS – a particular kind of state structure – which is evident to varying degrees in Sweden, Norway, Austria, Finland, and the Netherlands (Schmitter, 1974). Panitch, for instance, considers corporatism as ". . . a political structure within advanced capitalism which integrates organized socio-economic producer groups through a system of representation and co-operative mutual interaction at the leadership level and mobilization and social control at the mass level" (Panitch, 1980, p. 173). Others have pointed to a more limited conception of corporatism as a mode of public policy making, restricted to a delimited set of policy sectors in almost all ACSs. This is often referred to as *sectoral corporatism*. In this regard Japan is particularly interesting since the incorporation of the major organized interests into government is distinguished by its sectoral nature and by the exclusion of labor interests (Eccleston, 1989). While it is no longer as evident in the UK, Schmitter argues that corporatism nonetheless remains a visible feature of the political economy of most European nations (Schmitter, 1989) (see table 7.8).

Corporatist theoreticians accept that although corporatism may no longer reflect the political reality in all capitalist societies, nevertheless where they do exist, corporatist modes or forms of policy making articulate the autonomous power of the state. This is so because:

State officials have the greatest agenda setting capacity . . . since
they decide who is to participate in consultations and invariably
they chair the relevant committees. Hence their policy influence
seems bound to be considerable. Administrative elites in the
Scandinavian countries are disproportionately represented on all
the commissions and boards and committees engaged in
corporatist policy making. If the policy making area is technical
and complex, public officials have a decided advantage. . . . Finally
if the relevant interests in the corporatist process are conflicting
and balanced, then the opportunities for state elites to act
autonomously are immensely enhanced.
(Dunleavy and O'Leary, 1987, pp. 195–6)

Table 7.8   A cumulative scale of corporatism

| |
| --- |
| 1   Pluralism |
|     United States, Canada, Australia, New Zealand |
| 2   Weak corporatism |
|     United Kingdom, Italy |
| 3   Medium corporatism |
|     Ireland, Belgium, West Germany, Denmark; |
|     Finland, Switzerland (borderline case) |
| 4   Strong corporatism |
|     Austria, Sweden, Norway, the Netherlands |
| Not covered by the scale are cases of |
| 5   "Concertation without labour" |
|     Japan, France |

Source: Lehmbruch, 1984, p. 66

Contemporary neo-Marxist accounts of the ACS share some of the
same conceptual terrain with corporatist and "New Right" theorizing.
One significant area of overlap is in the primacy given to politics and
the corresponding emphasis upon the state as ". . . an actor in its own
right pursuing particular interests . . . different from those of societal
agents" (Bertramsen et al., 1991, p. 98). There is also a shared
recognition that there can be no effective differentiation between the
state and civil society. However, what distinguishes recent neo-Marxist
accounts is a concentration upon the "capitalist" nature of the
contemporary western state. According to such accounts, the state in
advanced societies is essentially "capitalist" not because it acts in the
interests of a dominant capitalist class, nor because it is constrained to
do so by structural forces which prevent the prosecution of alternative
anti-capitalist policies. Rather it is a "capitalist state" because, in the
process of sustaining and reproducing its own programs, state managers
must sustain and create the conditions for private capital accumulation.
Since the state itself is heavily dependent on the revenues derived from
the taxation of profits and wages to maintain its programs, failure to
facilitate capital accumulation is likely to have politically destabilizing
consequences (Carnoy, 1984, pp. 133–4). How state managers formulate
strategies for encouraging private accumulation, and precisely what
policies are followed, remain complex and indeterminate processes

suffused by politics since ". . . there can be no single, unambiguous reference point for state managers how the state should serve the needs and interests of capital" (Jessop, 1990, p. 357). In this respect the state in advanced capitalist societies is accorded extensive autonomy from capital, yet still remains essentially a "capitalist state." This is underwritten too by the state's need to secure the legitimacy of its actions within the context of a liberal-democratic polity.

Offe points to the apparent contradiction between the state's need to sustain its legitimacy and the need to sustain the conditions for private accumulation. By contradiction Offe is referring to the fact that both are essential to the survival of the state but each can pull it in opposing directions. Since the state's power derives in part from the legitimacy accorded it through the political process, it cannot afford to be perceived as acting with partiality, by systematically privileging corporate capital, without endangering its political support. Yet, to sustain mass support, it requires substantial revenues to finance welfare and other programs. However, revenues derive largely from the taxes on profits and wages so that the state is obliged to assist the process of capital accumulation and thus act partially. As a consequence, the state in advanced capitalist society is caught between the contradictory imperatives of accumulation and legitimation, i.e. between "capitalism" and "democracy." Reconciling this contradiction prises open a political space for the state to formulate and pursue strategies and policies which reflect ". . . the institutional self-interest of the actors in the state apparatus" (Offe, 1976, p. 6). This "autonomy" is enhanced further by the fact that there are diverse and conflicting interests between different sectors of capital, e.g. industrial, financial, national as against international, etc., and within civil society more generally. Accordingly, the precise strategies and policies adopted by the state to reconcile the conflicting demands of capitalist accumulation and legitimation are a product of political negotiation and the outcome of a rather indeterminate political process within which ". . . the personnel of the state try to ensure their own jobs and hence ensure the continued existence of the State apparatuses" (Carnoy, 1984, p. 136).

Alber has emphasized the diverse responses among advanced states to the economic crises of the late 1970s and 1980s (Alber, 1988, pp. 451–68). In the UK and the US, this was the era of "Thatcherism" and "Reaganomics" respectively. Both articulated strategies for rejuvenating and restructuring the domestic economy to make it more competitive with new centers of economic power such as Japan and Germany. "Thatcherism," in particular, articulated a break with post-war orthodoxy by pursuing an economic strategy, involving "rolling back the state," encouraging competition, privatization, and reforming the welfare state. This was accompanied by a distinctively "populist" political strategy designed to sustain essential support for and legitimation of these radical policy initiatives. Even so, many "unpopular" policy measures were adopted and implemented against the backdrop of considerable resistance. In other advanced countries, rather different, although equally unpopular and resisted, economic and political strategies were adopted to deal with the crisis. In France, a socialist government abandoned nationalization and in Sweden the social democratic government jettisoned the long-standing commitment to full employment (Gourevitch, 1986).

Recent scholarship has focused on the critical role of the state in organizing the appropriate political and economic conditions for the successful accumulation of capital. Jessop, in his analysis of the "Thatcher era" in the UK, suggests that the state adopted a highly proactive role throughout the 1980s (Jessop et al., 1988). Rather than simply reacting to the economic crisis, it sought to pursue a determined transformation of the British economy and society through a radical agenda of reform, marketization, industrial restructuring, and economic rationalization. Through the active assertion of an ideological program – "Thatcherism" – the state sought ". . . the mobilization and reproduction of active consent through the exercise of political, intellectual and moral leadership" (Jessop quoted in Bertramsen et al., 1991, p. 110). This was achieved by the state consciously building, manipulating, and consolidating its own "power-base": a dynamic coalition of quite different social groups and political actors, e.g. the skilled working class, the London financial establishment, "New Right" groups, moral crusaders etc., as well as appealing to more "populist" sentiments within British society (Jessop et al., 1988). In this regard the state is conceived more as a kind of "power broker" constructing and sustaining the political coalitions vital to the success of its strategy for enhancing corporate profitability while simultaneously marginalizing societal resistance to its policies. There exists here a trace of, what some would identify as "Marxist–pluralism."

## 4.3   State autonomy and state power

This short excursion into theories of the ACS has offered a variety of accounts concerning the functions of the state in advanced capitalist societies (see table 7.9) and the issue of in whose interests the state "rules." But equally it appears it has left us with a nagging question: Which of these two sets of approaches to the ACS – the society-centered or the state-centered – is the more convincing?

Table 7.9   Theoretical accounts of the ACS

|  | neo-Marxist | Weberian/pluralist |
| --- | --- | --- |
| Society-centered | structural and instrumental accounts (Miliband, Poulantzas) | elitist (Mills); neo-pluralism (Lindblom, Dahl) |
| State-centered | post-Marxist (Offe, Jessop) | (neo-)corporatism (Lehmbruch); New Right (neo-institutionalism) |

One way in which these two distinctive approaches can be reconciled is by acknowledging the significant differences between ACSs in terms of the resources (administrative, political, coercive, financial, ideological, knowledge), capacities, and instruments of state power. Mann refers to these resources and capacities as embodying the

"infrastructural power" of the state, by which he means the ability
". . . to penetrate civil society and implement decisions throughout the
realm" (Mann, 1988, p. 4). Some ACSs have considerable
"infrastructural power" and others relatively less. The greater the
infrastructural power of the state, the greater is its influence over civil
society. Accordingly, it is possible to differentiate, as do both Krasner
and Skocpol, between "strong" states and "weak" states (Krasner, 1978;
Skocpol, 1985). A "strong state" is one which is able to implement its
decisions against societal resistance and/or can resist societal demands
from even the most powerful private groups (Nordlinger, 1981, p. 22).
By comparison a "weak state" can do neither of these things ". . . owing
to societal resistance and lack of resources" (Bertramsen et al., 1991, p.
99). Studies which have exploited this typology tend to classify ACSs
such as Japan and France as "strong states" while the US and Canada
are classified as "weak states" (Atkinson and Coleman, 1990).

One logical implication of this typology is the conclusion that state-
centered approaches might best explain the power and policies of
"strong states," while society-centered approaches are better at
accounting for the actions and policies of "weak states" (Bertramsen et
al., 1991, p. 100). Furthermore, the distinction can be utilized to
account for the very different styles of policy making which occur in
different policy sectors within the same state. Thus, in some policy
sectors the state may be considered strong while in other policy sectors
it is considered weak (Atkinson and Coleman, 1990). In this case, both
society-centered and state-centered approaches provide equally helpful
insights into state action (see Goldthorpe, 1984). In addition, the
infrastructural power of any state varies over time with the result that
states historically can be conceived as becoming stronger or weaker.
Recognizing this underlines the relevance of both state-centered and
society-centered approaches to the ACS.

It would appear that the notion of choosing between state-centered
and society-centered approaches is somewhat spurious. As McLennan
observes, "statism," or state-centered accounts, may be ". . . designed to
complement rather than replace society-centredness" (McLennan, 1989,
p. 233). The upshot of this is that in attempting to explain the power
and actions of the ACS a "modest theoretical eclecticism" has to be
embraced even if it is intellectually uncomfortable.


# 5   Putting the Advanced Capitalist State in its Place

No contemporary analysis of the ACS can afford to ignore the stresses
to which it is subject because of its strategic location at the intersection
of international and domestic processes. As the earlier discussion has
made clear, both the formation and the nature of the ACS can only be
properly understood by reference to both endogenous and exogenous
forces of social change. Moreover, as patterns of global
interconnectedness appear to be intensifying, the distinctions between

the internal and the external, the foreign and the domestic, seem increasingly anachronistic. A moment's reflection on some of the critical social issues which confront the ACS, such as drug abuse or the environment, would confirm that each has a global or transnational dimension. Few issues can now be defined as purely "domestic" or specifically "international." On the contrary, it is more accurate to view states as confronted by "intermestic" problems. However we choose to recognize the erosion of this traditional distinction, the central point is that all ACSs are increasingly subject to globalizing forces which impose powerful constraints on state sovereignty and press heavily upon the everyday lives of their citizens.

## 5.1   Globalization and the ACS

Globalization ". . . should be understood as the re-ordering of time and distance in our lives. Our lives, in other words, are increasingly influenced by activities and events happening well away from the social context in which we carry on our day-to-day activities" (Giddens, 1989, p. 520). To talk of globalization is to recognize that there are dynamic processes at work constructing and weaving networks of interaction and interconnectedness across the states and societies which make up the modern world system. Globalization has two distinct dimensions: scope (or stretching) and intensity (or deepening). On the one hand it defines a process or set of processes which embrace most of the globe or which operate worldwide: the concept therefore has a spatial connotation. Politics and other social activities are becoming "stretched" across the globe. On the other hand it also implies an intensification in the levels of interaction, interconnectedness, or interdependence between the states and societies which constitute the world community. Accordingly, alongside the "stretching" goes a "deepening" of the impact of global processes on national and local communities.

   Far from being an abstract concept, globalization articulates one of the more familiar features of modern existence. A single moment's reflection on the contents of our own kitchen cabinets or fridges would underline the fact that, simply as passive consumers, we are very much part of a global network of production and exchange.

   In his analysis of the welfare state, Alber stresses the significance of global forces – the economic crisis of the 1970s and early 1980s – in stimulating a restructuring of welfare provision within all capitalist societies. A combination of factors made it increasingly difficult for governments, of whatever political persuasion, to sustain the growth in welfare programs which had occurred in the 1960s or to protect workers from the consequences of growing international competition. The kind of "managed capitalism" which had emerged in the post-war period no longer meshed with an increasingly globally integrated economic and financial system. Full employment or extensive welfare provision which require high levels of taxation are difficult to sustain when capital is so readily mobile and foreign competition so intense. Underlying this erosion of "managed capitalism" in the 1980s has been an acceleration in processes of economic globalization and the consequent break-up of the post-war global order.

As Keohane observed, "the European welfare state was built on foundations provided by American hegemony" (Keohane, 1984, p. 22). "Managed capitalism" did not simply reflect a domestic political settlement but rather was constructed upon the post-war global settlement of a liberal (free trade) world economic order underwritten by US military and economic power. Within this world order, structures of global economic management, such as the International Monetary Fund (IMF) and General Agreement on Tariffs and Trade (GATT), nurtured the economic conditions which helped sustain the rapid post-war growth of western economies and enabled the massive expansion of welfare provision. Both "managed capitalism" and a regulated world economy were mutually reinforcing. However, by the mid-1980s the combined effects of economic recession, the resultant global economic restructuring, the intensification of the financial and economic integration of western economies, and the emergence of new centers of economic power such as Japan and Germany, had seriously undermined the post-war global capitalist order. As the 1990s dawned, the conditions essential to the survival of the welfare state in its conventional form had been transformed:

> ... the reconstruction of the international political economy has definitively altered the circumstances in which welfare states have to operate. Exposing national economies and national corporatist arrangements to the unregulated world economy has transformed the circumstances under which any government might seek, for example, to pursue a policy of full employment ...
>
> The deregulation of international markets and of financial institutions, in particular, have tended to weaken the capacities of the interventionist state, to render all economies more open and to make national capital and more especially national labour movements much more subject to the terms and conditions of international competition.
> (Pierson, 1991, pp. 177, 188)

For some, this process of "reconstruction" signals an even more profound shift in the nature of global capitalism. Lash and Urry, for instance, argue that organized or "managed capitalism" is giving way to a form of "disorganized capitalism" in which national economies are becoming increasingly beyond the control of national governments, partly as a consequence of the accelerating globalization of production and exchange (Lash and Urry, 1987, p. 308; Offe, 1984). But it is not simply the capacity of the capitalist state to control its own economy that is at issue.

Writing in the early 1970s, Morse pointed to the ways in which the global movement of goods, money, ideas, images, knowledge, technology, etc., challenged the ability of the ACS to govern effectively within its own territory (Morse, 1976). Morse argued that growing international interdependence diminished the effectiveness of national governments and thereby encouraged a corresponding attachment to international forms of regulation or cooperation. Over the last three decades there has been a startling expansion in levels of international cooperation. Through a myriad of international institutions, such as the IMF, GATT, International Civil Aviation Organization, International Telecommunications Union, Organization of Economic Cooperation and Development etc., informal arrangements such as the G7 group of leading capitalist states, and international networks of key policy makers, advanced capitalist states have created a vast array of *international regimes*: sets of international rules, norms, procedures, modes of decision making and organizations. These embrace those issue-areas in which states have become increasingly interdependent or where transnational activities create common problems. Such regimes seek to regulate high policy domains, such as defense and global finance, as well as welfare policy domains such as the trade in narcotics, environmental issues, and AIDS.

International regimes, in effect, express the growing international-ization of the advanced capitalist state and the internationalization of state elites. Within Europe, this internationalization has culminated in the evolution of the European Community from a common market into a quasi-supranational political structure which can take decisions binding upon member governments. Advanced capitalist states are enmeshed in an extensive array of formal and informal international regimes which make them simultaneously both the determinants and the objects of an expanding field of international regulatory practices. In some domains, the sovereignty of the ACS is severely compromised by its participation in these regimes while in others it is sometimes enhanced. Clearly, ACSs have always operated under external constraints of all kinds. However, it is frequently argued that international cooperation restricts the exercise of state autonomy – the capacity to act independently, within circumscribed parameters, in the articulation and pursuit of domestic and international policy objectives – across a range of policy domains. Yet, in a more interconnected world, international cooperation has become increasingly vital to the achievement of a host of domestic policy objectives. For instance, dealing with drug addiction requires international cooperation to combat the global trade in narcotics, while domestic economic management demands cooperation on interest rates and currency fluctuations. The ACS thus confronts a major dilemma as it attempts to balance effectiveness against a potential loss of autonomy.

For some, such a choice merely reinforces growing evidence of the decline of the nation-state and calls into question its continued viability. However, for now that particular argument is left in abeyance to be explored in part III.

# 6   The ACS: A Review

This chapter set out to examine three questions:

First, given the diversity of state forms within the advanced capitalist world is it possible to identify common patterns with respect to the development, characteristics, activities, and functions of the state?

Second, how are we to make sense of the role and actions of the state in governing advanced societies and in whose interests does it "rule"? and

Third, in what ways do international or global forces condition the activities of the modern capitalist state?

In section 2 we adopted a broad comparative approach in order to isolate the common features and diverse forms of the ACS. This analysis was extended further in section 3 through a comparative historical examination of how the twin processes of militarism and capitalism have contributed to the formation of the ACS. In section 4 a rather more synoptic approach was adopted in exploring both society-centered and state-centered accounts of the role and functions of the state in advanced capitalist societies. Finally in section 5 we dealt with the consequences of globalization for the nature of the contemporary ACS and its capacity to ensure the welfare of its citizens.

Throughout this chapter great stress has been placed on the diverse forms as well as the common features of the state in advanced capitalist societies. Tremendous diversity is apparent with respect to institutional structures and welfare regimes. Yet commonalities do exist in so far as these states share broadly similar patterns of development, have acquired comparable roles and functions, and share a common experience in attempting to reconcile the often competing demands of private accumulation with liberal democracy. Moreover, as the chapter has argued, the traditional distinctions and boundaries between the public (the state) and the private (civil society), the civil and the military, and the foreign and the domestic have become increasingly blurred by the forces of modernity. As a result the state in all advanced capitalist societies may be entering a new "era" in which the very architecture of politics itself is experiencing a profound transformation (Cerny, 1990). Making sense of the ACS therefore demands a refreshing theoretical eclecticism in which the dynamic interplay between capitalism and militarism, as well as between national and international processes and conditions, is explicitly acknowledged (Giddens, 1985; 1990).

# References

Alber, J. (1988) "Continuities and changes in the idea of the welfare state," *Politics and Society*, vol. 16, no. 4, pp. 451–68.

Atkinson, M.M. and Coleman, W.D. (1990) "Strong states and weak states; sectoral policy networks in advanced capitalist economies," *British Journal of Political Science*, vol. 19, pp. 47–67.

Berger, J. (1990) "Market and state in advanced capitalist societies," in Martinelli, A. and Smelser, N. (eds) *Economy and Society*, London, Sage.

Bertramsen, R.B., Thomsen, J.P.F., and Torfing, J. (1991) *State, Economy and Society*, London, Unwin Hyman.

Carnoy, M. (1984) *The State and Political Theory*, Princeton, Princeton University Press.

Cerny, P. (1990) *The Changing Architecture of Politics*, London, Sage.

Dahl, R.A. (1985) *A Preface to Economic Democracy*, Cambridge, England, Polity Press.

Dahl, R.A. and Lindblom, C. (1976) *Politics, Economics and Welfare*, 2nd edn, Chicago, Chicago University Press.

Domhoff, G. (1978) *Who Really Rules?*, Santa Monica, CA, Goodyear Publishing.

Dunleavy, P. and O'Leary, B. (1987) *Theories of the State: the Politics of Liberal Democracy*, London, Macmillan.

Eccleston, B. (1989) *State and Society in Post-War Japan*, Cambridge, England, Polity Press.

Esping-Andersen, G. (1985) *Politics against Markets*, Princeton, Princeton University Press.

Esping-Andersen, G. (1990) *The Three Worlds of Welfare Capitalism*, Cambridge, England, Polity Press.

Fox, D.M. (1986) "The NHS and the Second World War," in Smith, H.L. (ed.) *War and Social Change*, Manchester, England, Manchester University Press.

Giddens, A. (1985) *The Nation-State and Violence*, Cambridge, England, Polity Press.

Giddens, A. (1989) *Sociology*, Cambridge, England, Polity Press.

Giddens, A. (1990) *The Consequences of Modernity*, Cambridge, England, Polity Press.

Ginsburg, N. (1979) *Class, Capital and Social Policy*, London, Macmillan.

Goldthorpe, J. (ed.) (1984) *Order and Conflict in Contemporary Capitalism*, Oxford, Clarendon Press.

Gough, I. (1979) *The Political Economy of the Welfare State*, London, Macmillan.

Gourevitch, P. (1986) *Politics in Hard Times*, Ithaca, Cornell University Press.

Gummett, P. and Reppy, J. (1991) "Military industrial networks and technical change in the new strategic environment," *Government and Opposition*, vol. 25, no. 3, pp. 287–304.

Held, D. (1987) *Models of Democracy*, Cambridge, England, Polity Press.

Jessop, B. (1990) *State Theory*, Cambridge, England, Polity Press.

Jessop, B., Bonnett, K., Bromley, S., and Ling, T. (1988) *Thatcherism*, Cambridge, England, Polity Press.

Kennedy, P. (1987) *The Rise and Fall of the Great Powers*, London, Unwin Hyman.

Keohane, R.O. (1984) "The world political economy and the crisis of embedded liberalism," in Goldthorpe, J. (ed.) *Order and Conflict in Contemporary Capitalism*, Oxford, Clarendon Press.

Kingdom, P. (1991) *Government and Politics in the UK*, Cambridge, England, Polity Press.

Krasner, S. (1078) *Defending the National Interest*, Princeton, Princeton University Press.

Lash, S. and Urry, J. (1987) *The End of Organized Capitalism*, Cambridge, England, Polity Press.

Lehmbruch, G. (1984) "Consertation and the structure of corporatist networks," in Goldthorpe, J. (ed.) (1984).

Lijphart, A. (1984) *Democracies*, New Haven, Yale University Press.

Lindblom, C. (1977) *Politics and Markets*, New York, Basic Books.

Lovering, J. (1990) "Military expenditure and the restructuring of capitalism," *Cambridge Journal of Economics*, vol. 14, pp. 453–67.

MacKenzie, G. (1990) *Inventing Accuracy: A Historical Sociology of Missile Guidance*, Boston, MIT Press.

Mann, M. (1986) *The Sources of Social Power*, vol. 1, Cambridge, England, Cambridge University Press.

Mann, M. (1988) *States, War and Capitalism*, Oxford, Basil Blackwell.

McLennan, G. (1989) *Marxism, Pluralism and Beyond*, Cambridge, England, Polity Press.

McNeill, W. (1983) *The Pursuit of Power*, Oxford, Basil Blackwell.

Miliband, R. (1969) *The State in Capitalist Society*, London, Quartet.

Mills, C. Wright (1956) *The Power Elite*, Oxford, Oxford University Press.

Milward, A. (1987) *War, Economy and Society 1939–1945*, London, Pelican.

Mitchell, T. (1991) "The Limits of the State," *American Political Science Review*, vol. 85, no. 1, March, pp. 77–96.

Morse, E. (1976) *Modernization and the Transformation of International Relations*, New York, Free Press.

Nordlinger, E. (1981) *On the Autonomy of the Democratic State*, Cambridge, MA, Harvard University Press.

Offe, C. (1976) "Laws of motion of reformist state policies," mimeo.

Offe, C. (1984) *Contradictions of the Welfare State*, London, Hutchinson.

Panitch, L. (1980) "Recent theorizations on corporatism," *British Journal of Sociology*, vol. 31, no. 2, pp. 159–87.

Pearton, M. (1982) *The Knowledgeable State*, London, Burnett.

Pierson, C. (1991) *Beyond the Welfare State?*, Cambridge, England, Polity Press.

Piven, F. and Cloward, R. (1971) *Regulating the Poor*, New York, Pantheon.

Rasler, K. and Thompson, W.R. (1989) *War and State Making*, Boston, Unwin Hyman.

Rose, R. (1984) *Big Government*, London, Sage.

Schmitter, P. (1974) "Still the century of corporatism?," *Review of Politics*, vol. 36, pt 1, pp. 85–131.

Schmitter, P. (1989) "Corporatism is dead! Long live corporatism," *Government and Opposition*, vol. 24, no. 1, pp. 54–73.

Scott, J. (1991) *Who Rules Britain?*, Cambridge, England, Polity Press.

Skocpol, T. (1985) "Bringing the state back in," in Evans, P.R., Rueschemeyer, D., and Skocpol, T. (eds) *Bringing the State Back In*, Cambridge, England, Cambridge University Press.

Smith, H.L. (ed.) (1986) *War and Social Change*, Manchester, England, Manchester University Press.

Thee, M. (1987) *Military Technology, Military Strategy and the Arms Race*, London, Croom Helm.

Therborn, G. (1987) "Welfare state and capitalist markets," *Acta Sociologica*, vol. 30, no. 3, pp. 237–54.

Therborn, G. (1989) "States, populations and productivity: towards a political theory of welfare states," in Lassman, P. (ed.) *Politics and Social Theory*, London, Routledge.

Tilly, C. (1984) *Big Structures, Large Processes, Huge Comparisons*, London, Sage.

Tilly, C. (1990) *Coercion, Capital and European States*, Oxford, Basil Blackwell.

# 8    Fordism and Modern Industry

John Allen

## Contents

| 1 | Introduction | 281 |

2    Ford, Fordism, and Modern Industry    282

2.1   Ford and mass production    283
2.2   Fordism as an industrial era    285
2.3   Was Fordism ever dominant?    292

3    Progress and Modern Industry    297

3.1   Manufacturing growth?    298
3.2   Industry and the rest    299
3.3   A discourse of industry    301

4   Conclusion: Globalization and Industry    304

References    305

# 1   Introduction

If the emergence of a modern industrial economy can be epitomized by the rise of factory production and a factory workforce, its characteristic image must surely be that of the giant industrial workplace in which car after car, or other consumer durable, is turned out on a seemingly endless assembly production line. A sea of men in blue overalls pouring through factory gates at the end of the working day, or mass, open-air union meetings attended by men with raised hands are all part of this dominant imagery. The period in question is post-1945 rather than the nineteenth century, and the typical form of industry can be summed up under the heading of *large-scale, mass production.*

As a process, mass production can be traced back to the volume production of goods such as (Singer) sewing machines and bicycles at the end of the nineteenth century, but the real development of mass production began with the combination of moving assembly lines, specialized machinery, high wages, and low-cost products at the Ford Motor Company between 1913 and 1914. Henry Ford's heyday was the "Model T" era in which car production at the Ford Motor plant soared from 300 000 in 1914 to more than two million in 1923, but the industrial era which he initiated and which subsequently became known as "Fordism" is best described as a post-war affair. If large-scale, mass production is one specific form of modern industry, its zenith was reached after World War II across a range of industrial economies. After a brief look at Henry Ford's development of mass production methods, the rest of the chapter takes this post-war moment of "Fordism" as its central focus.

As you work your way through this chapter, you should bear in mind that the use of the term "Fordism" to depict an industrial era is a highly contentious issue. The very idea that the term "Fordism" helps us to understand the dynamics of the long post-war boom is deeply contested. For some, the concept of "Fordism" captures all things modern about an economy: it is associated with scale, progress, science, control, technology, rationality, including the sea of disciplined workers that poured through the factory gates each working day. More than this, the concept of Fordism has been held up as a symbol of a new kind of society, indeed as a modernizing discourse: one that involves a new type of worker, a different kind of lifestyle, and a specific form of state and civil society.

For others, it is precisely the sweeping nature of such claims that irritates. The use of the term "Fordism" to make sense of the rather complex set of events and circumstances that lie behind the long post-war economic boom is regarded as at best misleading, at worst a gross caricature. Mass production has performed an important role in post-war economic history, but the conceptual leap from mass production to "Fordism," taking in mass consumption and the mass worker along the way, is said to offer a reductive image. It obscures more than it reveals. It obscures the varied organization of manufacture across different modern economies, the diversity of markets, the different types of labor and work, as well as simplifying post-war political developments in the advanced economies. In short, Fordism is rhetoric: it is part of a discourse of industry that sets out a powerful but misleading image of what a modern economy looks like in the second half of the twentieth century.

In this chapter, we are going to explore these claims, and in particular some of the *economic* implications that are entailed by the concept of Fordism. One of the initial aims of the chapter is to spell out what it is about Ford and Fordism that has generated such disagreement and caught the imagination of many. Section 2 looks at this issue and explores the relative importance of the mass production industries in the post-war period. A major concern of this section is to examine the claim that Fordist industries performed some kind of "lead" role or established an economic "dominance" in the post-war industrial economies. What does it mean to say that an economy is Fordist? Is there some kind of checklist of features involved which, if present, add up to an economy organized along Fordist lines? Or does the concept of Fordism draw its explanatory power from its ability to highlight the structural connections that shape an economy?

Section 3 extends this assessment of Fordism by widening the topic of inquiry to include an evaluation of the role of services in a modern economy. Fordism as usually understood is taken to represent a modern *manufacturing* economy. Growth and modern industry are invariably taken to be synonymous with a thriving manufacturing sector. What interests us in section 3 is why a modern economy should be regarded as manufacturing-based. What kind of economic discourse is in play which suggests that only certain kinds of economic activity generate growth and represent real wealth? Why are services usually represented in modern economies as unproductive or frequently seen as a poor form of economic progress?

Finally, in section 4, the chapter concludes with a summary of the arguments explored and also a brief consideration of the implications that an era of increased global interdependence may have for the pattern of growth in modern, national economies. But first let's consider Henry's part in all this.

## 2   Ford, Fordism, and Modern Industry

The name of Henry Ford is synonymous with the advent of the moving assembly line and mass production. The name conveys a sense of technological progress as well as a model of how manufacturing production is or should be organized. In contrast with the early stages of industrialization, Ford*ism* is conceived as an era of mass, standardized goods produced for mass markets, created by an interventionist state which gave people the spending power to make mass consumption possible. The two, however, are linked by a particular history.

## 2.1   Ford and mass production

In the introduction to this chapter, it was noted in passing that mass
production began with the combination of:

1   moving assembly lines;
2   specialized machinery;
3   high wages; and
4   low-cost products.

The stress here should be placed upon the term *combination*, for it was
the manner in which these elements were brought together at Ford's
Highland Park factory in Detroit between 1913 and 1914 which gave
rise to the *system of mass production*. It was this combination of
elements that lay behind the shift from craft to mass production. We
shall take a closer look at these elements before considering the system
as a whole.

First, let's consider the development of the moving assembly line
and specialized machinery. Before the opening of the Highland Park
factory in 1910, Henry Ford had already put into place one of the
keystones of assembly-line production at the company's Piquette and
Bellevue plants: the interchangeability of parts. Although much of the
production at Ford's early plants was craft-based, Ford and a handful of
skilled mechanics had already designed and developed fixtures, jigs,
and gauges with which unskilled workers could turn out uniform parts.
Special- or single-purpose machine tools followed, as did the practice
of arranging the flow of materials to follow the sequence of operations.
Hounshell (1984) has shown how these innovations drew upon and
extended earlier attempts to attain a high volume of production of
interchangeable parts, first in the American firearms industry and then
in the manufacture of sewing machines, agricultural machinery, and
bicycles. By 1913, Ford's refinements to the American process of
repetition manufacturing had laid the foundation on which the
technique of continuous-flow or assembly-line production rests: the
standardization and simplification of the product, the use of special-
purpose equipment together with the interchangeability of parts, and
the reduction of skilled labor. All that remained was to connect these
elements together through the introduction of the moving assembly
line.

Scientific management of the workplace significantly transformed the
nature of industrial production in the late nineteenth century. The
central figure in the initial transition was Frederick W. Taylor. His
contribution to the reconceptualization of the workplace was based on
two main principles: first, that production could be broken down into
specialized and discrete tasks, and second, that the relationship
between these various tasks could be logically structured through the
formal study of time and motion within the factory. One of the clearest
differences between the approaches of Taylor and Ford was that
whereas Taylor sought to organize labor around machinery, Ford
sought to eliminate labor by machinery. Where Taylor took for granted

the existing level of technology and sought greater efficiency from workers through the reorganization of work, Ford and his mechanics used technology to mechanize the work process. A second difference concerns the pace of work, which, for Taylor, was set by the workers themselves or the supervisors, whereas for Ford it was set by the machinery, the speed of the assembly line. Despite these radical differences, however, this new technology led to similar consequences for the modern workforce: fragmentation of tasks and a more detailed division of labor. With the introduction of fixed-speed, moving assembly lines, tasks were broken down and simplified further, removing previous skill requirements for the job. Such benefits achieved by the company from gaining greater control over the production process were not without their drawbacks, however. The most serious were the rapid increase in the turnover rate of labor, growing absenteeism, and broad dissatisfaction with work at the Ford plant. Yet, paradoxically, it was the growth in labor unrest on the shop floor that led to the introduction of the third element which was to give rise to the system of mass production, namely the payment of high wages, or the "Five-Dollar Day" policy.

The high-wage system which became known as the "Five-Dollar Day" effectively doubled the earnings of Ford workers (or rather those workers who qualified for the profit-sharing scheme if their private lives met the standards laid down by Ford's new Sociological Department). The impact on absenteeism, labor turnover, and labor productivity was dramatic: profits soared as absenteeism and turnover stabilized and productivity leapt. Ford's Five-Dollar Day had in effect laid the basis for a new contractual system whereby workers stayed "on the line" in return for high wages paid for by the dramatic increases in labor productivity. A new "mass worker" had been created – highly paid and unskilled – to accompany the introduction of the new mass technology.

The fourth and final element in the system of mass production, a low-price strategy, is perhaps the most understated feature of Ford's system of manufacture. Unlike most of his contemporaries, Ford recognized that there was an enormous demand in the US at that time for cheap, basic, reliable cars. Where companies like Singer had dominated the US sewing-machine market in the 1870s and 1880s by producing quality products at a high price, Ford sought to manufacture *low*-priced cars and to use a strategy of successive price reductions to boost demand further. Ford's Model T, a robust car, easy to repair and available in "any colour as long as it was black," sold in unprecedented numbers at a price well below that of its industrial competitors. Thus, alongside mass technology and the mass worker, the growth of mass markets represented the sum of Ford's *system* of mass production or modern manufacture.

Prior to Ford's technical innovations, the factory system of manufacture was based largely upon the division of the production process into a number of tasks which varied in terms of the degree of skill required. Thus, each worker would perform a specialized task within the factory, drawing upon their own craft skills to manufacture the required part of the overall product. (See chapter 4 for discussion of this type of low-technology production.) What broadly distinguished modern manufacture from the factory system was:

- the introduction of machinery to eliminate labor and skills;

- the introduction of machinery to wrest control from labor over the nature and pace of work.

In many ways it is the moving assembly line, accompanied by a high degree of specialization among workers and standardization of products, that symbolizes this shift to modern industry. But modern industry is not only characterized by technical innovations; the social innovations introduced by Ford – the high pay, the enforced labor discipline, and the attempt to cater for a mass market by continually dropping prices – are all part of what we take to be the fabric of modern industry.

By the early 1920s, the Model T had captured 55 percent of the US car market, brought about in part by the economies of scale reaped through large-scale mass production at Ford's new River Rouge plant. A massive complex with its own deep water port and railway, the plant was designed as a fully integrated manufacturing operation from steelmaking through to final assembly, employing tens of thousands of workers. With high fixed costs in plant and machinery, Ford's efficiency was achieved by high-volume production which reduced the cost per car as output rose. As a giant industrial workplace it looked capable of satisfying the demands of an expanding mass market and, in terms of economic efficiency, it had all the hallmarks of competitive advantage. The operation was widely admired and the diffusion of Fordism as an industrial model looked set to occur.

## 2.2 Fordism as an industrial era

In the years that followed Ford's successful market performance in the 1920s, the methods of mass production were borrowed liberally by US companies in housing, furniture, and other consumer goods industries. As Hounshell points out, Ford was neither slow nor reticent to bring his economic innovations to the attention of US manufacturing industry. In particular, the mass production technology was quickly seized on as a recipe for economic growth. However, the economic Depression of the 1930s across the industrial economies was soon to remove the gloss from Ford's ideas and methods. Alongside mass production, a different kind of mass phenomenon was about to arise: mass unemployment. Cyclical crises and recurrent disruptions in economic production as a result of the time-lags between effective demand and productive investment were a known feature of industrial economies. But the coupling of mass production and mass unemployment was a new experience – especially for those workers laid off by Ford and other car manufacturers in the Detroit area. The limited consumption levels of the mass of the population on the one hand and the sharp increase in the productivity growth of industry on the other had brought about what many considered to be a crisis in the very functioning of capitalism itself. President Roosevelt's New Deal staved off the US crisis, but it was not until after World War II that this mismatch between the amount of goods produced and the effective ability of the population to consume them was to be resolved in any general way. What became known as a crisis of "underconsumption" was about to give way to what others have termed "Fordist" growth.

Fordist growth – that is, a mode of economic growth based upon a system of mass production and sustained by mass markets – is widely regarded as a feature of the US, UK, and other European economies in the 1950s and 1960s. Such growth, it is argued, was fostered by what chapter 7 referred to as "managed capitalism," an institutional arrangement which owed much to the experience of state wartime mobilization and large-scale planning. It was this experience which enabled governments confidently to take an ever-increasing role in the regulation and direction of their national economies. In the UK, for example, Keynesian demand management policies (over levels of taxation, interest rates, and public expenditure) and the introduction of welfare payment systems helped to raise the spending power of the mass of the population to within a level capable of sustaining mass markets. In other modern industrial economies, the actual political forms of intervention by national governments in the regulation of their economies varied widely, although the outcome – in terms of the promotion of mass markets – is said to have varied less. The *bulk* of the additional spending power, however, was considered to be a direct result of real wages rising at an unprecedented rate in the industrial economies, broadly in line with the sustained growth in productivity. With the formation of mass markets across much of the industrialized world, a stable link between mass consumption and mass production was considered to be firmly in place. And it was this connection, this match between mass production and mass consumption, that was taken to be one of the hallmarks of the modern industrial era. However, of equal importance was the Depression of the inter-war period and the severe onslaught by employers and governments on labor movements in the late 1940s which, many now argue, cleared the way for the introduction of the new type of work discipline and economic trade-offs between high wages and high productivity that an economy organized along Fordist lines entailed.

We shall examine some of the general features of this Fordist era, especially the notion of a Fordist mode of growth. Before we do so, however, it is worth spelling out precisely what those general features are, primarily to avoid any potential misunderstandings over the sense in which I intend to use the term "Fordism."

Sayer (1989) has helpfully provided four different meanings attached to the term.

1   Fordism as a *labor process* involving moving assembly line mass production.

This refers to the tasks and technologies that should be familiar to you from the above account of the labor process developed by Ford at the

Highland Park plant. A Fordist labor process involves the use of semi-skilled labor performing few tasks at a pace determined by "the line." Control over all aspects of production is exercised by management through a hierarchical chain of authority.

2   Fordist sectors as the *lead growth sectors* capable of transmitting growth to other sectors of an economy.

This refers to the *dominant* role performed by the mass production industries in the post-war period. Such industries, it is argued, take a lead role in an economy because of their ability to *generate* growth. Thus, the car industry may literally be seen as the "motor" of an economy, setting both the pace and the direction of growth through rising productivity and ascending output levels (achieved through economies of scale). The lead sectors may also *transmit* growth to other sectors through their network of supply relationships. Taking the example of the car industry again, a range of industries from steel, rubber, and glass through to upholstery and electronics, as well as a host of services, are seen to depend on it, wholly or in part, for their own growth.

The sum total of this growth may be referred to as "Fordist" growth.

3   Fordist organization as *hegemonic*.

The term "hegemonic" refers to the pervasive influence of Fordist ways of organizing production, work, and labor. It can be considered as another aspect of a sector's *dominance*, although in this instance the criterion by which the influence of the mass production sector is measured concerns the *extent* of that influence. If, for example, a range of industries outside of the mass production sector are seen to adopt, say, collective bargaining procedures, contracts on a rate-for-the-job basis, management hierarchies which leave little discretion to the workforce, or the technical innovations of mass production, then the Fordist influence may be regarded as widespread throughout the economy.

4   Fordism as a *mode of regulation*.

In this sense of Fordism, the term "regulation" refers to more than the labor process or the lead sectors of growth in an economy, and moves beyond the strictly economic to include both political and cultural considerations. We have already noted some of the more central political considerations, in particular the kind of policy interventions made by national governments in their attempts to balance mass production and mass consumption and thus underpin long-term growth. Indeed, it could be said that *all* modes of regulation, of which there are a considerable variety, are geared towards the regulation of a particular pattern of growth, in this case Fordist growth. Thus, the continuation of Fordism as a pattern of growth can be considered to be as dependent on self-regulation by organized labor and leading industrial enterprises as it is dependent upon the state to secure a balance between profit and wage levels so that mass purchasing power is maintained.

Our concerns in the rest of section 2 are more narrowly economic, and will address in particular the meanings of Fordism outlined in (2) and (3) above, through an assessment of the relative importance of the mass production industries in modern industrial economies. The coverage will nonetheless include a consideration of Fordist forms of regulation, as these are regarded as indispensable to an understanding of the character of economic growth in the long post-war boom.

So far, we have loosely referred to a Fordist mode of growth as a feature of the advanced industrial economies in the 1950s and 1960s. However, in terms of actual growth rates, a more precise periodization is usually given, starting in the early 1950s and tailing off in the early 1970s around the time of the "oil crisis" of 1973 and the economic downturn of 1974. If we look back at that period, it is difficult not to be impressed by the sheer scale and pace of growth across the economies of Europe and the US, as well as that of Japan. Industrial output across the advanced economies virtually trebled between 1950 and 1973, with more produced in this period than in the whole of the previous seventy-five years – itself a period of not inconsiderable growth, especially in the late nineteenth century (Armstrong et al., 1991, p. 117). Also, in terms of the quality of life, the development and availability of a whole string of consumer goods – from washing machines, vacuum cleaners, fridges, cars, to color TVs – represented a real leap in living standards for a large part of the working population. Judged in either quantitative or qualitative terms, the pattern of post-war growth in the 1950s and 1960s can only be described as phenomenal. While it would be wrong to suggest that everybody in the industrial nations benefited from this development or indeed benefited equally, or to suggest that everyone was content with the direction of change towards standardized, mass consumer durables, nonetheless in aggregate output terms this pattern of growth was taken to be a clear sign of modernist progress. The question we need to ask now is, what makes this pattern of growth distinctively Fordist?

Armstrong et al. (1991) provide a framework within which we can pursue this question. Figure 8.1 lays out the context.

A wealth of information is presented in figure 8.1, but the main point of interest to note is the contrast between output growth and employment growth over the period. As you can see, the increase in output is far higher than the growth in employment, which suggests that output per person, the productivity rate within industry, grew rapidly in the 1950s and 1960s (as figure 8.1 also indicates). This growth in productivity could conceivably have stemmed from people working longer hours, but as the length of the "normal" working week declined during this period, the most likely factor behind the shift in productivity was the sharp rise in the amount of machinery and plant (as measured by capital stock) at the workplace. If you look again at figure 8.1, you will note that the amount of capital stock at the workplace more than doubled in the 1950s and 1960s, giving the impression that "each worker was confronted by two machines where one had stood before" (Armstrong et al., 1991, p. 119). However, the change in the *type* of machinery that confronted workers was just as

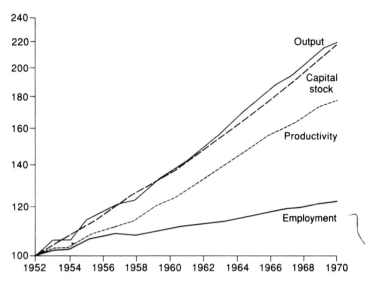

Figure 8.1 Output, capital stock, productivity, and employment in the advanced industrial economies, 1952–70 (index numbers, 1952 = 100, log scale)

Source: Armstrong et al., 1991, p. 118

important as (or even more important than) the multiplication of machinery. Increased mechanization of industrial production, in particular the forced pace of production, is singled out by Armstrong and his co-authors as one of the main causes of the rapid growth in productivity, along with changes in both work practices and the design of jobs. So, in both quantitative and qualitative terms, the new production technologies and their embodiment in new machinery lay behind the post-war boom in production. But, to restate the main question, how far was this pattern of rapid growth actually tied to Fordist production?

Certainly the car industry, that icon of Fordist production, was at the hub of post-war growth. Motor vehicle production rose dramatically in the 1950s across all the advanced industrial economies. In the UK, France, and Germany, annual average production went way above the million mark for the first time, while in the US it topped seven million. By the second half of the 1960s, annual average car production in Japan had risen to above four million from a low base in the 1950s; vehicle output in France, Germany, and Italy had more than doubled; and in the UK car industry, production reached its highest post-war figure of just over two million per year (Lee, 1986). Other industries geared directly to consumer durables, especially those concerned with the mass production of electrical goods, were at the forefront of post-war growth trends. Indeed, those industries involved in the production of complex standardized goods excelled as a result of the introduction of mass production techniques. But they were not alone.

Clearly, those industries geared to the mass consumption of consumer durables were among the high growth sectors in the post-war period, but the performance of other industries – notably those in the capital and intermediate goods sector which supply and feed into the manufacture of washing machines, ovens, cars, and the like, or those, such as chemicals, which do not – also exhibited strong growth rates. Technological advances and the introduction of new machinery were not restricted to the assembly of complex consumer goods, nor was the pattern of post-war growth simply the result of a boom in consumer durables. Nonetheless – and this is an important observation – technological innovation and economic growth were unduly concentrated on the manufacture and consumption of such consumer durables. And those who place Fordist production at the heart of the post-war boom would see much of the rest of the economy as *dependent* on the growth of mass produced consumer goods.

The car industry is also seen to hold a central position in the creation of mass markets and mass production. If real wages had not risen broadly in line with the rate of productivity growth in the 1950s, then (apart from a greater share of profits accruing to industry) production would have outstripped consumption and the industrial economies would have faced another "underconsumption" crisis similar to that of the 1930s. If we follow Murray (1989), the development of a national system of collective wage bargaining which effectively tied wage rises to rising productivity levels throughout industry in the 1950s and 1960s owed much to the *dominant* role of the car industry within the US and the UK. Although conditions varied between the two countries, the annual pay settlement negotiated by the mass unions within the vehicle industry, the "going rate" for the year as it were, was regarded as a kind of benchmark for wage settlements in the rest of the economy. As a "lead" industry, in this case one which had substantial connections with a range of other industries and their workforces through its supplier network, it was in a position to influence the wage pattern for much of the rest of the economy, especially in manufacturing. In wage negotiations with their own managerial bureaucracies, the unionized workers in dependent and other sectors would be guided by the pay settlement agreed in the vehicles sector. And so, it is argued, a predictable pattern of wage increases and a stable pattern of differentials between sectors occurred which, when linked to rising productivity, created the initial conditions for consumer spending to rise in line with increased goods production.

To this we can add a further condition which was also a characteristic of the post-war car industry as well as many other consumer durable industries, namely the domination of national markets by a few large companies. The significance of large companies in this period, apart from their ability to enjoy economies of scale, is usually taken to be their power to regulate the price of their products in domestic markets. The ability to operate oligopolistic markets – that is, markets which are run by a few large-scale enterprises which tend to use marketing ploys such as easy credit facilities or minor design changes (remember the chromework, "tail-fins," and "portholes" on the larger American cars in the 1950s?) to distinguish and sell their product

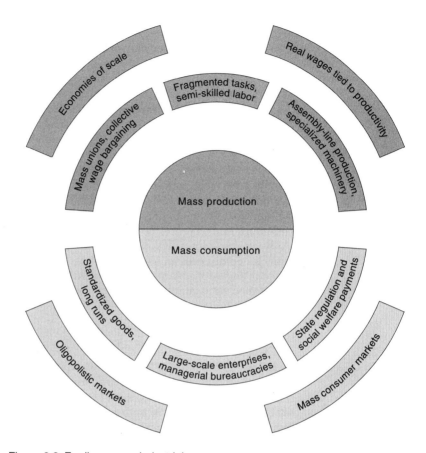

Figure 8.2 Fordism as an industrial era

rather than compete directly on price terms – can create long periods of price stability. Thus, the regulation of national markets by a few large companies can and arguably did provide another part of the post-war economic framework which enabled prices, wages, productivity, and investment to sustain one another. Under these conditions Fordist growth would certainly predominate.

We have covered a lot of ground in this sketch, perhaps more economic than historical, in order to bring to the fore the conditions that gave rise to Fordism as an industrial era. As with any historical generalization, we have sacrificed some of the rich detail that brings a period to life and we have been selective in our focus, concentrating on Fordist growth within national economies at the expense of the global economic and political regulatory structures that also enabled Fordist growth to continue. Chapter 7 touched upon some of the structures that lay behind the rapid growth in international trade in the early post-war period, such as the dominance of the US in the field of international finance and the range of institutions and networks that made up the Bretton Woods system, namely the International Monetary Fund, The World Bank, and The General Agreement on Tariffs and Trade (GATT).

On a broad scale, these arrangements were responsible for the long periods of stability in world trade and investment in the 1950s and 1960s and thus mirrored the stable pattern of growth within national domestic markets.

We shall return to the international dimension in section 4, but for now it is worth standing back to take stock of the general features of Fordist growth that we have highlighted. Figure 8.2 provides a diagrammatic representation of Fordism as an industrial era.

One of the things that always strikes me about this kind of general representation and, in this case, quite forcibly, is the number of different processes – economic, political, and cultural – that overlap and interact over a relatively short period to give rise to something that we now call Fordism. We have moved a fair way beyond the four elements in Henry Ford's system of mass production – moving assembly lines, specialized machinery, high wages, and low prices. And yet those four elements are clearly part of the preconditions for the emergence of Fordism as an industrial era. Whether or not Fordism as the contingent outcome of many elements and processes was ever as developed or as dominant a post-war model as many now take it to be remains, however, an open question.

## 2.3  Was Fordism ever dominant?

It is possible to approach this question by considering "Fordism" as a mode of growth (in Sayer's second and third meanings of the term, outlined in section 2.2), or, in a broader way, through a consideration of Fordism as a mode of national regulation. In practice, it is not particularly easy to separate the two senses. Having said that, the intention here is initially to separate the two senses of Fordism for analytical purposes and then to bring them together through the work of Jessop (1989).

The first thing that we need to do is to clear some ground. Earlier it was noted that the dominance of Fordist industries could be gauged by their ability to generate and transmit growth in the national economy, as well as influence ways of organizing work and labor. Let us take the issue of growth generation and transmission first.

A judgment that Fordist industries are dominant in an economy does not entail the simple view that mass production has spread throughout industry, or that assembly line production and dedicated machinery are now typical of factory work. On the contrary, mass production industries may represent a small part of the manufacturing sector, in both output and employment terms, yet remain dominant in terms of their ability to stimulate growth in small and medium batch production, especially in those industries that supply inputs to the mass production sector. In this case, "dominance" is a question of the structural *reach* of large-scale, mass industry; that is, how far it can transmit growth as a *propulsive industry*. Much depends upon the extent to which the mass production sector is integrated with other sectors of an economy. If it is well integrated, other firms – whatever their size – may prosper as suppliers of component parts or raw materials. If the ties are loose then, at the level of the national economy, imports will be sucked in to meet the needs of the Fordist industries and little growth transmission will take place. Indeed, it may be the case that batch production in the capital goods sector (for example, in the mechanical engineering industry) retains a critical national importance and assembly industries remain just that, plants which assemble complex products.

Turning to the second aspect of an industry's dominance, its ability to influence ways of organizing work or labor in its own and other sectors, then the issue *is* one of how widespread those changes are. For example, Tolliday (1986) has drawn attention to the fact that, among British car manufacturers in the inter-war period and beyond, there was extensive adaptation, rather than imitation, of Ford's production methods and labor strategies. Both Austin and Morris combined various aspects of Ford's moving assembly line production with a continued use of labor-intensive methods, and operated piece-work incentive systems rather than a payment system based on fixed daily rates. More generally, within Europe, even after 1945, few of the major car manufacturers ran plants which closely resembled the highly integrated River Rouge model. Most in fact relied upon operations outside of their plants to sustain their internal production processes (Williams et al., 1987). Indeed, it was the Ford Motor Company itself, through its multinational transplants (at Dagenham and Cologne), which brought about the direct diffusion of Fordist ways of organizing production.

At this *fine* level of detail it is of course possible to show that no other company or industry provides a perfect imitation of the Fordist model (other than Ford's own multinational transplants). But this type of exercise tends to under-estimate just how far Fordist ways of doing things, rather than the whole package, influenced the modern car industry and spread across other industries, such as electrical engineering. And although it is accurate to point out that mass production techniques are best suited to a narrow range of industries concerned with the manufacture of *complex* consumer durables, such as cars and electrical goods (Williams et al., 1987), this observation does not negate the pervasive influence or appeal of the *idea* of large-scale, mass produced, standardized products throughout the post-war period, in areas as diverse as clothing, construction, furniture, food processing, and, in some countries, schools and hospitals (Murray, 1989 and 1991).

You should bear in mind these two aspects of an industry's dominance as we consider the development of Fordism in its broadest sense in two European economies during the post-war period:

> Neither Britain nor Germany reveal a clear-cut case of Fordism if this is defined simply in terms of mass production and mass consumption. Britain failed to secure the productivity growth which Fordist methods could have brought to mass production and was hard-hit by de-industrialisation as a result. West German growth owes as much to the capital goods sector as to mass production of consumer goods and has also relied as much on its

highly qualified *Facharbeiter* as on semi-skilled, Fordist mass
workers. In its minimal sense, therefore, "Fordism" serves mainly
as an "ideal type" against which to assess the specificity of the
British and German regimes of accumulation. The broader concept
of Fordism is, however, both directly relevant and powerful. For
the Fordist wage relation based on institutionalised collective
bargaining around a wage tied to rising productivity and inflation
characterised both Britain and West Germany. Likewise private
credit and monopolistic competition played key roles in capital
accumulation; and state credit and tax expenditures were central
elements in economic management. If we adopt the broader
concept of Fordism as a regime of accumulation, therefore, we
can treat both Britain and West Germany as having Fordist
regimes.

The related concepts of "mode of regulation" and "mode of
growth" have proved even more relevant for our analysis. They
are clearly more concrete concepts and can generate significant
insights into the differential dynamic of the British and West
German regimes. The institutions of collective bargaining, the
relations between banks and industry, and the state play key roles
in a mode of regulation; and their contrasting natures in the two
cases investigated emerges very clearly. Likewise the modes of
growth in Britain and Germany are also significantly different –
reflecting their different industrial profiles and modes of insertion
into the international economy. By examining the contrasting
modes of regulation and growth in these two economies we can
better grasp the specificity of their post-war development and of
the forms assumed by the crisis of Fordism.
(Jessop, 1989, pp. 288–9)

Clearly Jessop is sympathetic to the heuristic value of the term Fordism
as a way of describing the post-war industrial era in Britain and (West)
Germany, but what is of particular interest is his willingness to accept
considerable national variation in how that Fordist era held together.
Take, for example, the issue of mass production.

So far we have referred to the mass production sector primarily in
terms of "lead" consumer industries, high productivity growth,
domestic markets, and semi-skilled workers. In the UK, there is some
degree of "fit" between this characterization and the profile of
manufacturing industry in the 1950s and 1960s. The consumer goods
industries were among the lead growth sectors and the mass worker did
indeed have a presence at the workplace. Yet, if we follow Jessop's
account, it is apparent that a thoroughgoing Fordist transformation of
industry did not occur in Britain. Industry failed to obtain the
productivity levels from mass production techniques that had been
secured elsewhere (recall the above reference to British car
manufacturers *adapting* rather than imitating Ford's innovations), and
one of the consequences of this failure was an increase in the level of
imports of mass consumer durables. Thus, in terms of growth
generation and indeed growth transmission through linkages to other

parts of the economy, it is debatable how far the mass production sector in Britain occupied a dominant role.

In (West) Germany the situation appears to be more clear-cut. The post-war growth of the German economy owed as much if not more to the export-oriented capital goods sector than to the consumer goods sector. Moreover, the dynamism and growth of the capital goods sector was largely attributable to the technologies employed and the use of highly skilled labor rather than to the operation of economies of scale in large companies and the use of a semi-skilled workforce. While it is important not to slip into the simple error of equating all mass production with the manufacture of consumer durables (think for example of the mass production of standard chips in the electronics industry), it is nonetheless unusual to talk about an export-oriented economy (like the German one), based on the lead role of the capital goods sector, in strictly Fordist terms. Industries such as iron and steel or mechanical engineering may well perform a propulsive role in an economy, but they are more likely to be characterized by small and medium batch production than by mass production.

If we turn our attention from the issue of growth generation and transmission towards the question of economic influence, then it is possible to see Fordist industries as in some measure hegemonic. In both Britain and (West) Germany, Jessop notes the practice of oligopolistic pricing by large companies (described in section 2.2), and he points to the formation of institutionalized collective bargaining arrangements which more or less tied real wages to rising productivity levels. What is more, he is prepared to argue that a Fordist wage relation was evident in the UK, despite the relative absence of mass industrial trade unions. Indeed, this is part of Jessop's portrayal of the British post-war economy as one of "flawed" Fordism.

So perhaps the broadest indication that we have from Jessop of the Fordist character of post-war Britain and Germany has less to do with the nature of modern industry and more to do with the manner in which it is regulated. This focus is certainly consistent with Jessop's concern to show how institutions such as the state attempted to secure and maintain the conditions for stable, Fordist patterns of growth. Although he is very careful to show the varied ways in which the two national governments actually intervened to engineer and sustain rising living standards and a growth profile, it is evident that the common threads of economic management represent a Fordist form of regulation for Jessop. Indeed, other commentators equally sympathetic to the characterization of post-war growth in industrial economies as Fordist go to considerable lengths to show how the forms of state regulation were nationally specific. For example, post-war France is usually characterized as a strong interventionist state concerned with the regulation of wages and prices; Italy is generally regarded as a state which was rather late in adopting a strategy of direct intervention; Germany, as we have seen, is said to have operated a decentralized, federal system which made it difficult to pursue a strategy of demand management; the Japanese state is depicted as one which coupled a

high level of public investment in industrial infrastructure with a low
level of social welfare provision, and so on.

If we place this political diversity alongside the industrial diversity
that we have just witnessed in the cases of Britain and (West) Germany,
and consider too Jessop's point about the different ways in which those
two countries are inserted into the global economic order, then we are
faced with a considerable *plurality* of Fordist economies. If the forms
assumed by Fordism across a range of industrial economies in the post-
war period are indeed the contingent outcome of many elements and
processes which come together in specific ways in different countries,
can we legitimately talk about Fordism as an industrial era or refer to
Fordist industries as in any way dominant? Is the general notion of
Fordism too broad, too encompassing, to convey such diversity?

We can start to answer this question by considering what strengths
and weaknesses are attached to Fordism as a broad historical
abstraction. On the plus side, it does point to a remarkable string of
general characteristics that, in different forms, were part of the long
post-war boom across the industrial economies. Those general
characteristics were set out in figure 8.2 and indeed act as a *vision* of a
particular industrial era. The articulation of those features through the
concept of Fordism provides a fixed image of an industrial landscape –
with its large manufacturing plants and big industrial cities – which
despite its reductiveness clearly strikes a chord with many. But perhaps
a more important strength of the concept of Fordism, in economic
terms at least, is that it represents *more* than a simple checklist of
features on which to check off the extent of Fordist-type development.
Implicit within the concept of Fordism is an evident prioritization of
features, with, for example, collective wage bargaining, oligopolistic
markets, economies of scale, and mass standardized consumer durables
each receiving a high weighting. If few of these features were
widespread in a national economy, then it is unlikely that we would
refer to it or describe it as Fordist. The point however is not simply
that a range of prioritized features should appear for the first time in
one place; rather, it concerns the presence of *actual* connections
between these features. For without such interconnections the concept
of Fordism is sapped of its explanatory power. This takes us closer to
the critical question of whether Fordist industries have performed a
*dominant* role in post-war national economies. As we have seen, this
can only be judged in terms of the extent of their integration or
interconnectedness in a national economy or their degree of influence
over issues of work and labor organization – issues which, it has to be
said, can only be settled by empirical evidence on a country-by
country-basis.

On the debit side, a central weakness of the concept of Fordism is
not so much its inability to adequately convey a pattern of national
diversity as its failure to see beyond large-scale mass production. There
is a tendency in the Fordist literature to overstate the key importance of
the mass production industries within an economy at the expense of
other kinds of manufacturing production. Equally, there is a tendency
to foreshorten the history of mass production by dating its demise

across the industrial economies from the early 1970s. As Sayer (1989) has pointed out, "western Fordist" mass production may have its problems today, but no such problems are apparent in South-East Asian mass production. We thus need to be alert to the twin dangers of overstating the significance of mass production in a national economy and mass production in the West. (In one sense this is just another example of how the discourse of "the West and the Rest" is played out; see chapter 6.)

A further major weakness of the concept of Fordism is that its reference does not include some of the most important developments in the post-war economies. When we fix the reference of a concept, we offer a description of its general features, as in figure 8.2. However, this industrial vision leaves out two prominent characteristics of the 1950s and 1960s: the activities of multinational corporations and their impact on national economies, and the role of the service industries. In the US economy for example, at the height of the long post-war boom, multinationals were increasingly locating plants offshore, in Europe and other parts of the globe. The relative neglect of this phenomenon in Fordist accounts can, in part, be traced to the emphasis they place upon the regulation of *national* economies. As for the limited attention paid to the service industries within the Fordist literature, this may be traced directly to the broad assumption that it is *manufacturing* which acts as the "engine" of growth within an economy. Service industries, for example those concerned with finance and commerce, are regarded as dependent on the Fordist manufacturing sectors for their economic well-being. In the next section, we explore this representation of services further, and examine the kind of "history" that tells us that modern manufacture equals progress. In the final section, the position of multinational and transnational corporations within a system of national markets is briefly considered.

# 3   Progress and Modern Industry

In discussing Ford's economic innovations and the relative importance of Fordist industries in the post-war period we have generally taken it for granted that the kind of modern economy which we have before us is a modern *manufacturing* economy. In fact, it is quite difficult to think otherwise. Modern progress is after all associated with the making of things, not in a craft sense, but rather, as noted in the introduction to this chapter, with the mass manufacture of objects: the ability to act on raw materials and to transform them into tangible goods in unprecedented quantity and volume. As the twentieth century progressed, the rise of assembly line manufacture represented for many the very apex of modern industrialism. In one sense it can be regarded as the culmination of a long line of economic development that reaches back to the rise of industry in the eighteenth century (see chapter 3). What interests us here is why the modern economy should be seen in this particular way. Why, for instance, is our image of industrialism linked so closely with that of heavy machinery, large workforces, physical outputs, and the overall process of manufacture? Why is manufacturing regarded as so important to a modern economy?

## 3.1   Manufacturing growth?

At one level the answer to the above question may appear quite straightforward: yes, industrialism and the process of manufacture are closely linked because the latter is the most dynamic, productive sector of an economy. Other sectors such as services are less able to generate high productivity gains, and act as adjuncts to the manufacturing process, keeping the factory going and ensuring that the goods reach the marketplace. So the line of argument that was used to justify the lead role of Fordist mass production industries earlier can also be extended to the *whole* of the manufacturing sector. Manufacturing represents the engine of growth within an economy insofar as it is capable of achieving increasing returns to scale. Put simply, this means that if the scale of production were to double in size, the increase in output would more than double. Unlike services, so the argument runs, the manufacturing industries can achieve successive productivity gains through the introduction of new machinery and the operation of larger plants.

Certainly there is strong empirical support for this line of argument in the post-war period. Across the advanced industrial economies there was a significant association between manufacturing growth and overall growth rates. And in the UK, Lee (1986) has shown how much of the growth in Gross Domestic Product was attributable to a strong manufacturing performance. Lee's work on the UK economy is, however, interesting for a number of other reasons.

Even though manufacturing exhibited a certain dynamism throughout the 1950s and 1960s in the UK, the service sector was not far behind in its overall contribution to growth. While the service sector may not have experienced the increasing returns to scale that manufacturing clearly did in this period, it did contribute just under half the rate of national growth. Indeed, Lee's study of growth rates in the UK economy over the past century and a quarter showed that the service sector consistently generated around half of GDP growth, with finance and commerce among the main contributors. It is this contribution of the service sector to GDP, especially commerce, that catches Lee's attention and leads him to ask why so little attention has been paid to services in accounts of the development of UK industry. Or, to put it another way, why is so much attention paid to manufacturing in accounts of the rise of modern industry?

The answer that he offers is reminiscent of the "increasing returns to scale" argument, insofar as he notes the pervasive assumption that services are dependent upon the dynamism of industry. The close interconnection of services and manufacturing in an industrial economy is regarded as a one-way relationship, with services growing, as we have seen, in response to manufacturing growth. Thus, the relative size of the service sector in output terms is *not* an issue in this context; it could exceed the contribution of manufacture (as it often did in industrial economies) yet still remain firmly dependent upon manufacturing as the "engine" of growth to drive the national economy. In some cases, this line of thought has been extended to refer to manufacturing as the part of an economy which produces wealth, and services as the part which is paid for and sustained by that wealth. The crucial issue for Lee, however, is not the productive capacity of services, but whether or not services only generate growth *through* manufacturing. His findings for the British economy are especially interesting.

Throughout much of the nineteenth century he found little evidence to show that services had grown in response to demands from manufacturing industry. On the contrary, he found strong links between services but few between manufacturing industries and services. Among banking, insurance, commerce, and several other sectors he found little dependence on manufacturing, and he argued that many such services may have actually paved the way for industrial development in the UK. A similar stress upon the diversity of sources which gave rise to service sector growth is also evident throughout the twentieth century, although perhaps less marked. Manufacturing was certainly an important stimulus for service sector growth in this period, but again no strong pattern of dependence was evident across the UK economy.

It is important to recognize that Lee is not suggesting here that there was a virtual absence of links between the manufacturing and service sectors in a modern economy. Clearly, most manufacturers require the services of banks, insurers, communications and transportation companies as well as retail distribution networks. His point is that such relationships are not simply one-way or dependent relationships. Banks and commercial practices require a variety of manufacturers too, as well as a range of services. In modern economies, services generate growth for one another, and those such as finance and banking may look beyond the national boundaries for global business – including that of international service corporations.

Having outlined Lee's concerns, we can now draw together the threads of the argument in this subsection. The significance of services may well have been under-estimated in our understanding of what it is that holds together and drives a modern economy. The exclusive focus upon manufacturing as a dynamic sector has perhaps presupposed more than we had been aware of; in particular, it tends to regard as irrelevant the volume of output generated by services. No one is suggesting that services and not manufacturing have held central ground throughout the industrial age; only that services have lost out to manufacturing as the dominant discourse of industry and industrialism.

## 3.2   Industry and the rest

So far, the discussion of the relationship between manufacturing and services has centered on growth statistics and growth dynamics. In this section, I want to alter that focus slightly by looking at how the relationship between manufacturing and services has been *represented* in the discourses about the modern economy. A *discourse* provides a language for talking about a topic which makes it difficult to think about that topic in any other way. *Representations* are part of a process of binding and work as a system; that is, they generate meaning as a cluster or set of images and ideas rather than standing alone. (For a discussion of the concept of "discourse", see chapter 6.)

When we talk about *industry*, many of the things that we have discussed in this chapter naturally come to mind: manufacturing, tools, machines, skilled labor, unions, factories, set perhaps against an urban backdrop. To this picture we can add one thing that we have yet to talk about: men, invariably in full-time work. When we talk about the *service industries*, however, a somewhat different picture tends to emerge. It is not quite the mirror image, but it is centered on the office or the store and involves people, often women, working with people and information rather than with machines or tools. Both accounts are exaggerations, one-sided in their coverage, but that is of less importance here. What interests me is that when we refer, quite legitimately, to services *as* industries we obtain one view of work and production, yet when we refer to industry on its own we obtain quite another view. Once the term "services" is disconnected from the term "industry," the latter seems to refer exclusively to manufacturing. One part of industry – manufacturing – has been substituted for the whole.

The meanings we attach to *production* appear to bind us to manufacturing in much the same way. Production is about making things; it calls up images associated with power sources, raw materials, physical labor, technology, and a productivity rate that can be measured down to the last nut and bolt. Yet when we connect services to production, a different, rather blurred image is evoked. There is a product, but it is more difficult to pin down exactly what it is, how it is produced, and what measure of productivity and output is best. In some cases, for example in health care, education, entertainment, and a range of personal services, the output is essentially intangible, produced at the same time as it is consumed, and judged by a measure of quality rather than quantity. But not all services fit this snug picture and many in fact possess characteristics which are not that dissimilar to the industries which make things. The production of audits, consultancy reports, legal briefs, insurance policies, advertisements, transportation systems, communications systems, restaurant meals, and even haircuts all take tangible forms. Electricity is just as much a power source as coal or steam in modern production; technologies have been a feature of much service production long before computers arrived; and although we need to be cautious about interpreting productivity and output statistics in the service industries, a range of quantitative measures operate across the sector.

In lots of ways, therefore, the distinction between making things and providing services is a *constructed* distinction. This is not to deny that there are differences between manufacturing and service production; rather it points to the fact that the differences between the two are less than are commonly thought. Yet the moment that we return to talking about production in a general way, the opposition between manufacturing and services reasserts itself and production connects with making things. Once again, we find ourselves back in the language of manufacturing. If you can touch it, it can only be something that has been manufactured, or so it would seem.

That some things are tactile, suggestive of touch, and other things are not is of particular interest here. Some things are easily grasped in our minds as tangible, whereas others, such as a haircut or a legal service, *seem* intangible. Arguably this is because the notion that services may actually be produced or the idea that services may possess a "hard" form lacks legitimacy. Such views contradict the language of industry and manufacturing. The image of services as industrial production remains unconvincing primarily because we appear to know what services are *not*. After all, services are not industry; it would seem that they are not machine-based, skill-based, exportable, or measurable, and above all they do not make things. Accordingly, they are not manufacturing. And it is this representation of services in terms of their *difference* from manufacturing which gives it its strength. It fixes the image, even though only certain services fall in the frame (for example, telecommunications and computing services fall outside), and thus limits the number of ways in which we can talk about services.

It is important to be aware that we are not only talking about a stereotype of services here. We have also seen how the *relationship* between manufacturing and services is represented through the language of industry. That language is not of recent origin, nor is it a seamless web of meaning which has remained intact since the Industrial Revolution. As a *discourse* of industry it contains statements that differ in form, statements that on occasions appear to contradict one another, and conceptions of economic life that do not sit easily alongside one another. Yet within this pattern of dispersion it may be possible to discern a certain regularity in the relation between statements which provides a constant way of talking about such differences. This unity of a discourse was described by Foucault (1972) as a "system of dispersion" (see chapter 6). We can think of this as a group of statements which systematically govern the different ways in which it is possible to talk about a particular topic. It is as if there are certain ground rules which allow us to make all sorts of comments and observations about the nature of industry, manufacturing, services, and yet the very same rules restrict the number of things that it is possible to say about these aspects of an economy.

Let me spell this out further.

## 3.3   A discourse of industry

What makes it possible to talk about a discourse of industry is the system according to which the different sectors of the economy can be specified and related. In talking about services, it is difficult to think of their role outside of their relation to manufacturing, the form of the connection, and the direction in which it flows. The discourse of industry thus only makes sense from this position and it is from this position that the sectors can be specified in terms of their contribution to society's wealth – or rather a nation's wealth, because the discourse itself makes its appearance first within a system of national economies: "engines of growth," "motors of the economy" refer to *national* modes of growth. In this way, a national economy can be systematically split into two: the productive, wealth-creating part and the other part – seen either as supportive of growth at the core, an obstacle to growth at the core, or a drain on wealth created at the core.

In consequence, there are theoretical choices to be made within this discourse. As we have stressed, not all the statements within a discourse point to the same set of conclusions or co-exist without contradiction. In the first place, given that the rules of industrial discourse presuppose that there is a productive core within a national economy, there are choices to be made over where that core is located – in which sector, or in what part of a sector, or in what combination of sectors.

For example, both the physiocrats, a group of eighteenth-century French economists, and Adam Smith specified economic sectors according to their capacity to generate wealth, yet each chose to locate that productive core in different parts of the economy. The physiocrats held that agriculture was the only source of wealth, whereas Smith ranked agriculture, manufacturing, and commerce in descending order. In both cases, their choices were linked not simply to the development of "industry" at that time but also to wider views of how an economy works and how it *should* work (for Smith, questions of the economy were linked with questions of morality, government, law, and jurisprudence). Since the eighteenth century, the productive core of an economy has been located in various positions, sometimes quite narrowly, as with its identification with the mass production industries of the post-war period, or, more recently, with the high-technology industries of advanced economies, and sometimes quite broadly to include the whole of manufacturing. The choices, however, are guided by questions of what is considered a *valid* form of wealth and how this is best understood through an analysis of the relationships that hold within and between sectors of the economy.

Thus, there are also choices to be made about how the sectors connect and relate. At various times in the past, the relationship between sectors, especially manufacturing and services, has been regarded as mutually beneficial at one extreme or mutually antagonistic at the other, with services representing a "drain" on the "surplus" created in the rest of the economy. It is of less importance here to spell out the various gradations in between the two extremes and of greater interest to note how statements about the sectors (even the concept of "sector" itself) presuppose a national economy as a complete interdependent system with interlocking parts. So the very act of formulating a theoretical opinion about how services relate to manufacturing requires a regular practice of seeing an economy as first, *national*, and second, a *system of internally related sectors – with links out to the wider international economy*. It is only within such a conception of the economy that statements about "engines of growth," "motors of the economy," "lead sectors," and "productive cores" are possible. In choosing to locate these phenomena, we find ourselves speaking from *within* this economic discourse.

And when we speak the discourse of industry today, we locate that core in a sector called manufacturing. However, such a location is neither innocent nor without its consequences. We can note two in passing. One consequence of the discourse of industry is that the qualities of manufacturing and service jobs tend to be regarded as quite different. Where manufacturing jobs tend to be associated with full-time employment and a full range of work skills, many service sector jobs are often seen as part-time and low-skilled. Where jobs in engineering and the car industry are accepted without thought as "real jobs," jobs in for example catering and cleaning have to battle for the accreditation. The origins of these ideas are to be found in nineteenth-century notions of which jobs are the most suitable for men and women (see chapter 4). In the following chapter, the discussion of modern divisions of labor will show how such notions remain linked to conceptions of technology which, in turn, are related to the "worth" of a job. If services are not regarded as a valid source of wealth, especially labor-intensive services, then this estimation is likely to be reflected in the payment of low wages for such work.

Another consequence of the discourse of industry is that it differentiates between a positive and negative direction of economic change. In its weakest version, we are told that an economy (which is to say, "national economy") cannot survive on services, by "taking in laundry" or "selling its heritage." This is probably true, although "niche economies" can specialize in tourism, off-shore data processing, specific financial practices, and the like. In its stronger and more plausible version, the importance of industry (by which is meant "manufacturing") is that it generates more exports (for the national economy). Invisibles (an interesting representation) – services such as banking, insurance, shipping, travel, and other activities that earn income abroad – account for a relatively small proportion of international trade. It is hard to see, therefore, how any (national) economy can rely on services to maintain a broad balance between imports and exports. Hence the importance accorded to mass production export industries in the post-war modern economies.

The logic is fine, but it is perhaps too much of an industrial logic. Visible trade is about the export of things that are made; goods produced in one country and then sold in another. But what does it mean to export a service? As the dominant representation of services is one of intangibility (which has helped to strengthen the view of service exports as "invisible"), statements about the measurement of service trade consistently refer to those aspects of the trade which are tangible – that is, which approximate to trade in goods. This "hard" service-trade element is however increasingly difficult to isolate in a modern global economy, characterized by large international flows of money in the financial sector and an increased transnationalization of services ranging from cleaning and security to property and advertising (UNCTC, 1988).

# 4   Conclusion: Globalization and Industry

Much of the previous section illustrated the importance of the national economy as the discursive framework within which discussions of the role and significance of modern industry have taken place. A modern economy is conceived of as an "economy-in-one-country," which has a "core" or an "engine of growth" and it is this part of the economy which is assumed to shape the pattern and trajectory of a national mode of growth. The state's management of the national economy, which took on such importance in the post-war period across the advanced industrial economies, sustained this view of an economy as a system of interdependent sectors – mining and agriculture, manufacturing, and services – whose borders coincided with those of the nation-state.

The concept of Fordism fitted neatly within this discursive framework. The explanatory power of the term "Fordism" could be demonstrated by tracing the connection between industries and sectors within a national economy. The dominance of Fordist industries could be assessed by the extent of their integration within a national economy. This led us to note the relative neglect of the activities of multinational and transnational corporations within Fordist discourse, especially in terms of their impact upon the regulation of national economies. We now need to consider briefly the relationship between national economies and the processes of internationalization that move across them. For if the modern economy takes its shape from a national mold, does that imply that the globalizing of modernity will break that mold?

The intention here is merely to clear some ground for the examination of this question and to raise some of the issues that flow from the topics discussed in this chapter (the question is dealt with in greater depth in part III). The first point to bear in mind is that internationalization is not a recent phenomenon. There have been international trade flows of some significance for much of the past two centuries, as well as considerable flows of portfolio (financial) investment between countries, and in both cases, in the early period, the UK economy was at the hub of these flows. Direct foreign investment, the establishment of production facilities in different countries, is a different form of internationalization and is connected with the rise of multinational corporations. Multinationals are simply large corporations which have spread their operations beyond their country of origin, and they are an important feature of the post-war period.

Given this history, it is quite possible therefore that none of these international movements, of trade, of finance, of production, will lead to the fragmentation of the modern national economy. On the contrary, it is often argued that multinational (manufacturing) industry is usually headquartered in one country and operates between countries. Similarly, the flows of finance, money, and jobs which take place occur between national economies. The stress here, then, is on relations *between* national economies of the kind that we have been concerned with in this chapter (i.e. the fully interlocking economy). There is, however, an alternative interpretation of global relations. With the contemporary growth in the volume of financial transactions across the globe, more specifically between a relatively small number of "world cities," and the expansion of *trans*national service firms alongside the many multinational concerns, it could be argued that national economies are increasingly becoming "sites" *across* which international forces flow. Note here that the emphasis has switched from processes which operate *between* countries to processes which operate *across* national economies.

The significance of this change in emphasis is profound as the latter approach points to the formation of dislocated "national" economies; economies that are characterized by co-existing modes of growth rather than one model of growth. On this interpretation, as the global processes themselves take an uneven pathway across countries, taking in some regions while passing around others, the "national" economy will exhibit lines of dislocation. In the UK, for example, it could be argued that the contemporary role of the City of London in the global financial system has shaped much of the southern economy while leaving the north relatively untouched. The notion of a "national" economy as a system of interdependent sectors thus falls away somewhat. Similarly, in the US, the rising industrial energies of the Southwest and California, resting on a high technology base, are very loosely connected to the decline of the mass production industries in the Midwest, around Chicago and Henry Ford's Detroit. Are we therefore witnessing the break-up of modern industrial economies in an era of greater global economic interdependence? If so, then this also calls into question the validity of the national growth models based upon "lead" sectors that we have considered in this chapter. As noted at the end of section 2.3, if mass production was the high point of modern industry, it is not so much disappearing as moving across the globe. The next chapter explores this issue further in the context of recent shifts in the international division of labor.

The full picture, however, will only become clear when we pick up the implications of globalization in part III. We shall also explore the nature of a modern economy *after* Fordism – or rather, *possibly* after Fordism, since the concept of "post-Fordism," signifying the end of the industrial era, is just as contested within the social sciences as we have discovered Fordism to be in this chapter.

# References

Armstrong, P., Glyn, A., and Harrison, J. (1991) *Capitalism Since 1945*, Oxford, Basil Blackwell.

Foucault, M. (1972) *The Archeology of Knowledge*, London, Tavistock.

Hounshell, A. (1984) *From the American System to Mass Production 1800–1932*, Baltimore, Johns Hopkins University Press.

Jessop, B. (1989) "Conservative regimes and the transition to post-Fordism: the cases of Great Britain and West Germany," in Gottdiener, M. and Komninos, N. (eds) *Capitalist Development and Crisis Theory: Accumulation, Regulation and Spatial Restructuring*, London and Basingstoke, Macmillan.

Lee, C.H. (1986) *The British Economy Since 1700: A Macroeconomic Perspective*, Cambridge, England, Cambridge University Press.

Murray, R. (1989) "Fordism and post-Fordism," in Hall, S. and Jacques, M. (eds) *New Times*, London, Lawrence and Wishart.

Murray, R. (1991) "The State after Henry," *Marxism Today*, May.

Sayer, A. (1989) "Post-Fordism in question," *The International Journal of Urban and Regional Research*, vol. 13, no. 4, pp. 666–95.

Tolliday, S. (1986) "Management and labour in Britain 1896–1939," in Tolliday, S. and Zeitlin, J. (eds) *The Automobile Industry and its Workers: Between Fordism and Flexibility*, Cambridge, England, Polity Press.

United Nations Center on Transnational Corporations (1988) *Transnational Corporations in World Development: Trends and Prospects*, New York, United Nations.

Williams, K., Cutler, T., Williams, J., and Haslam, C. (1987) "The end of mass production?" (review of Piore, M.J. and Sabel, C.F., *The Second Industrial Divide: Possibilities for Prosperity*, New York, Basic Books, 1984), *Economy and Society*, vol. 16, no. 3, pp. 405–38.

# 9 Divisions of Labor

Peter Braham

## Contents

| | | |
|---|---|---|
| 1 | Introduction | 308 |
| 2 | From a Manufacturing to a Service Economy? | 309 |
| 3 | Labor Market Segmentation | 312 |
| 4 | Gender and Labor Market Segmentation | 317 |
| 5 | Migrant Workers and Divisions of Labor | 321 |
| 6 | A New International Division of Labor? | 327 |
| 7 | The Division of Labor and Flexible Specialization | 332 |
| 8 | Conclusion | 337 |
| | References | 339 |

# 1   Introduction

This chapter will examine issues surrounding divisions of labor and
sectoral changes in the labor market. This will be done not only in
relation to the UK but, where appropriate, in a way that is both
international and comparative, and that reflects the growing
globalization of the economic system.

The notion of a modern economy takes certain things for granted.
Prominent among these is a specialized and educated workforce
organized to produce a highly differentiated range of goods for a world-
wide market. However, the extent to which an economy has become
modernized is also assessed according to the relative importance of
different sectors in terms of output and employment. Usually a modern
economy is seen as one where manufacturing industry is much more
important than agriculture, but the history of the twentieth century has
demonstrated that this sectoral composition is neither final nor
predetermined. Perhaps the most obvious development in most
industrially advanced countries (IACs) has been the decline of the
manufacturing sector and the rise of the service sector.

The term "division of labor" originally referred to these sectoral
divisions, as well as to occupational structures and to the organization
of tasks. More recently, the term has been applied to gender and racial
divisions of labor, and to the spatial division of production and the
movement of some elements outside the factory (Cohen, 1987, p. 228).
For example, the boundaries between male and female labor have
altered markedly; and the location of production may change too: a
typical case may involve a multinational corporation withdrawing from
established industrial areas to set up factories in low-wage, newly
industrialized countries (NICs), while its headquarters are relocated to
London or New York.

The most obvious labor market developments in all western IACs
since World War II concern the decline of manual and industrial
occupations and the rise of white-collar and service occupations. Once-
familiar jobs have disappeared and new jobs have appeared – often
involving new skills or demanding new categories of worker. These
developments – together with the erosion of the norm of full
employment – have raised a number of important questions. For
example, can "work" still be seen as a full-time, regular, job-for-life
performed by men? Or is full-time employment now too limited an area
for study, and does part-time employment – and specifically the role of
women within it – demand our attention?

The difference between part-time and full-time employment provides
a good starting point for introducing the contrast between "core" and
"periphery" in the labor market, which provides an underlying
connecting theme of this chapter. My use of the terms "core" and
"periphery" is both wider and less specific than that of others. I shall
treat the contrast between "core" and "periphery" as providing valuable
insights into the labor market position of women and of migrant
workers, as well as helping our exploration of labor market

segmentation, the new international division of labor, and the concept of flexible specialization, each of which will be explored in a separate section of this chapter.

Thus, a woman or a migrant worker is more likely to be directed to "peripheral" employment, while a man or an indigenous worker is more likely to be found in "core" employment. This process reflects long-standing beliefs about what *type* of work is appropriate for particular *types* of worker. And, by extension, if a worker can be adversely or positively categorized in more than one way, the disadvantage or advantage is likely to be commensurately greater. We can use the terms "core" and "periphery" not only to refer to workers and to jobs, but also to refer to contrasts between industries in a society and to refer to contrasts between developed and less developed societies. Through the use of these twin concepts, then, we can bring out connections between ostensibly disparate groups of workers in different locations.

Before proceeding it is worth saying that to use the terms "periphery" or "peripheral" is not to suggest that the entity or group so described is not of central importance to economic life or to production. Thus, if we categorize part-time workers – most of whom are women – as "peripheral," this is not intended to diminish the importance of female waged labor. Nevertheless, it does reflect the fact that part-time workers *are* seen by many employers and trade unionists as marginal, whether their work is of marginal or central importance to the production process. As Hakim points out, this prevailing view of part-timers has had substantive consequences for jobs which are low-graded, low-paid, lacking in promotion prospects, and denied the range of benefits generally given to full-time employees (Hakim, 1990, p. 163).

# 2   From a Manufacturing to a Service Economy?

Perhaps the most conventional way to describe the industrial structure of an IAC is to divide it into three sectors, namely:

1   the primary sector (extractive industries and agriculture);
2   the manufacturing sector (the production of commodities);
3   the service sector (where commodities are circulated or a service is provided).

The changing balance between these sectors may then be evaluated in accordance with, for example, the proportion of GDP accounted for by each sector or by the proportion of workers employed in each sector at various times.

As figure 9.1 shows, in the UK over the last two centuries there has been a significant change in the percentage of people employed in each of these three sectors. As the proportion of workers entering the

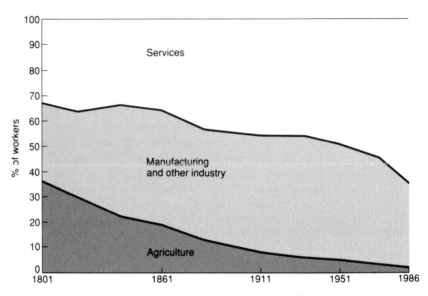

Figure 9.1　UK – approximate proportions of workers in different economic sectors, 1801–1986

Source: based on Abercrombie, Warde et al., 1988, p. 84

primary sector fell steadily, so more people entered manufacturing. It also shows that the growth in the proportion of the workforce entering the service sector is of long standing and that by the 1980s about two-thirds of all workers were in service industries.

The decline in employment in manufacturing in the UK has been very swift: for instance, between 1966 and 1985 it fell from 8.6 million to 5.4 million workers (Abercrombie et al., 1988, p. 82). Such a decline, and the corresponding rise of services, is a feature of all the IACs and is taken as signifying a new type of economy, a *post-industrial* economy (see part III). This is not simply a statistical extraction of the sort that can be derived from figure 9.1 (for instance, far fewer people now work in textile manufacture, shipbuilding, or car production, whereas many more people work in stores, hotels, the provision of financial services, and in health care and education). It also involves a view of historical change whereby the most developed service-based economies are held to chart the course that other aspiring economies will eventually replicate (see chapter 8 for discussion of this point).

The current emphasis on manufacturing decline may cause us to neglect the point that, as a source of employment, manufacturing in Britain has contracted quite consistently since the mid-1950s, and that at no time since World War II has manufacturing employed as many people as services. A number of reasons may be suggested for this decline, prominent among which are factors such as the loss of employment that often accompanies mechanization and automation, and the declining competitiveness of British manufacturing in the face of competition not only from low-wage, Third World countries but also from other IACs with higher rates of capital investment. It is not suggested that this decline is universal, but viewed solely in terms of aggregate employment even the expansion of the so-called "sunrise" industries, such as electronics, is more than matched by the contraction and/or demise of the so-called "sunset" industries, such as steel and shipbuilding.

The UK economy can be described as a service economy not only because the majority of *employment* is service employment and has been so since World War II but also because the majority of *output* is service output and has been so since the 1960s. However, it would be a mistake to consider the employment implications of "de-industrialization" and the emergence of a service economy as if they are quite separate and as if what "services" are is self-evident. As Gershuny and Miles (1983) point out, services comprise:

1   industries where the final output is non-productive – thus, "services" encompasses both manual and non-manual occupations;

2   occupations, whether in agriculture, manufacturing, or services, where there is no *direct* involvement in the production of material products;

3   service products, such as maintenance contracts, which may be delivered by manufacturing firms as well as by service enterprises; and

4   service functions – a more specialized usage, which reminds us that all products, whether material or otherwise, incorporate a service function.

What is important to note here is that services such as marketing, technical expertise, and finance are often integral components of modern manufacturing activities. Gershuny and Miles also argue that service jobs have grown in number in response to an increased demand for manufactured goods which is, in reality, a consequence of what they describe as a "self-service" economy. They therefore emphasize not the separateness of manufacturing and services, but the links between them. The view that there is, indeed, a linkage between the service and the manufacturing sector is also central to Porter's analysis of national competitive advantage (1990, pp. 252–3). In Porter's view, this link has become an important part of the argument that a nation cannot afford to neglect its international competitive position in manufacturing, assuming that services will fill the gap. This is not only because many service industries have been created through the de-integration of service activities by manufacturing concerns, but also because services are often tied to the sale of manufactured goods *and* manufactured goods are often tied to the sale of services.

The emergence of a post-industrial society, as evidenced by the decline of manufacturing and the rise of services, should not be seen only in domestic terms, and our attention should not be confined solely to sectoral movement within the IACs. In addition to taking into account the nature of the linkage between services and manufacturing, we should also emphasize the importance of the effect of the global relocation of manufacturing industry to NICs on the balance between services and manufacturing in the IACs.

# 3   Labor Market Segmentation

The scale of the long-term changes in the proportion of the population employed in each of the sectors and the degree of occupational change discussed in the previous section might almost convey a picture of free and unhindered movement, such that the labor market seems to be undifferentiated and unitary. However, this would be misleading: the labor market is not a single entity, but a whole series of labor markets marked by divisions not only between industries, but also between employing organizations, skills, hierarchies of authority, geographical locations, and so on. For example, geographical divisions are apparent in the UK economy of the 1930s and 1940s, notably the decline of large-scale industries located mainly in Scotland and north-east England and the rise of new industries in the Midlands and south-east England. Similarly, the "sunset" and "sunrise" industries of the 1970s and 1980s display a very unequal geography. And more generally there is a clear *inverse* relationship between de-industrialization and the rise of services: those regions that have experienced the largest falls in manufacturing employment have gained the least from the expansion of the private service sector (Massey, 1988, p. 60).

If we see the labor market in terms of these various divisions we can appreciate that movement within it is not free, but is constrained by one or more of a number of impediments, as well as by means of controls on entry operated by different "gatekeepers." Yet there are a number of powerful concepts relating to the labor market which, though they acknowledge divisions – particularly divisions based on skill, qualifications, and experience – seem to suggest that less relevant divisive factors (those unrelated to job performance) are of little or diminishing importance. For example, for the classical economists who examined the division of labor, relations of cooperation involving specialization of complementary tasks were of crucial importance. Their approach was set firmly within a framework of *laissez-faire* capitalism, where the relationship between worker and employer is treated purely in market terms: the worker selling labor and the employer hiring him or her. In this exchange it is irrelevant whether an individual worker is male or female, young or old, or white or black, provided the efficiency of production is maintained or enhanced. The status achieved by the worker is thus solely dependent on his or her individual efforts, skill, ability, and so on (Worsley et al., 1977, pp. 279–81).

It requires no significant conceptual leap to relate this perspective to contemporary characterizations of *meritocracy*:

> ... more and more it becomes possible for talent and hard work to reap their reward through an upward progress in what is

> sometimes called a meritocracy – a new aristocracy based on
> individual ability and effort instead of on birth and social rank.
> (Fox, 1974, p. 7)

A belief in an emerging meritocracy was particularly pronounced in the
IACs in the 1960s and was strengthened by a number of developments,
prominent among which were educational reforms and changes in
industrial structure. These in turn promised not only greater
opportunities, but also more objective and achievement-related methods
of selection and promotion.

   Nowadays the word "meritocracy" seems to have been supplanted by
the idea of "equal opportunity," which Seear defines as meaning "that
no one is denied training or a job for reasons that have nothing to do
with their competence or capacity" (Seear, 1981, p. 295). In one sense
these concepts seem mutually beneficial to employee and employer:
thus, if it is to the advantage of a suitably qualified job applicant to be
chosen on merit, it is equally to the advantage of the employer to have
the widest and best choice for selecting personnel. That this is so seems
borne out by Offe's *achievement principle*, which suggests that there
are qualitative differences between employees which can be objectively
identified and rewarded by selection, promotion, and so on (Offe,
1976). However, there are a number of problems in applying the
"achievement principle," particularly with respect to non-skilled jobs.
The low skill content of many jobs is indicated in Blackburn and
Mann's survey of manual jobs, carried out in the late 1970s. They
found that the *absolute* level of skill in all but the very highest jobs was
minimal: their research showed that 87 percent of workers exercised
less skill at work than they would have done by driving to work
(Blackburn and Mann, 1979, p. 280). In such circumstances it is
comparatively easy for employers to establish apparently objective
entry and promotion requirements which, though generally irrelevant
to the job in question, serve to exclude, deliberately or otherwise,
certain categories of worker. More widely, the definition of skill may
turn out to be somewhat elastic, as in the way in which it has been
manipulated to exclude or restrict the employment of women
(Cockburn, 1983). Thus, Offe prefers to see the "achievement principle"
not as a process of objective evaluation, but as an ideology within the
context of employer authority and control which, because of its very
imprecision, helps to support *partiality* in deciding whom to select or
promote. Functional or relevant criteria are likely to be overlaid "by a
second level of ascriptive qualifications . . . [which] then become
important as an additional criterion for occupational status and
mobility chances" (Offe, 1976, p. 90).

   It is sometimes argued that, with the steady upgrading of
employment as western IACs switch from having a preponderance of
manual and manufacturing occupations to being white-collar and
service based, so the functioning of labor markets becomes increasingly
homogenized. On this view, the labor market is conceived of as perfect
insofar as it is atomistic: that is, irrelevant criteria do not intrude in
determining wages and conditions of employment, and the existence of

segmentation, whereby workers of equal efficiency are differently rewarded, is regarded as of only marginal significance. Thus, the elimination of undesirable, dirty, and routine factory jobs and the proliferation of what are assumed to be more desirable, cleaner, and varied jobs in the service sector seem to promise both more attractive and less segmented employment.

The problem with this analysis is that there is absolutely no evidence that the atomistic or non-segmented labor market has ever existed. On the contrary, labor markets have always been, and continue to be, structured such that the higher the skill and status of workers, the better organized is their position, whereas where workers are continuously obliged to compete with their fellows, pay and conditions are much worse (Wilkinson, 1981, p. x). This phenomenon is not confined to manufacturing: many jobs in services have never offered more attractive pay and conditions than routine factory jobs, and many service occupations – notably those in clerical work – are being deskilled and rationalized (Abercrombie et al., 1988, p. 85).

The concept of the dual labor market (DLM) is perhaps the most influential theoretical perspective to challenge the assumption that the trend in IACs is towards economic homogeneity. It is premised on the belief that social and economic difference in these labor markets continues and may even become deeper. In essence the DLM hypothesis treats the labor market as separated into a primary sector, where jobs are categorized as skilled and where pay and conditions are good, and a secondary sector where jobs are categorized as unskilled and semi-skilled and where pay and conditions are markedly inferior (Roberts et al., 1985, p. 5).

The DLM thesis was developed in the 1960s to analyze labor market segmentation in the US, but subsequently applied to other western economies. Later variants of this thesis suggested that not only employers but also trade unions had an interest in maintaining these divisions. What was common to early and late versions alike, however, was the idea that firms had to devise a satisfactory means to adjust their labor force to fluctuations in demand, while contriving to retain more skilled workers in whom their investment was commensurably greater. What was expected of such "core" workers might be seen in terms of *functional flexibility* whereby they might have to perform different tasks or utilize different skills as the demand for the firm's output varied in type and quantity. By contrast "peripheral" workers – whether directly employed or employed by subcontractors – were required to provide necessary *numerical* flexibility: that is, they could more readily be hired and fired or move in and out of the labor market. This is a contrast to which we shall return in section 7. Typically, primary sector or "core" workers are to be found in large-scale enterprises whose strong market position permits them to offer reasonably good pay and conditions. By contrast, secondary workers are likely to be employed in smaller-scale enterprises whose market position is more precarious. In the secondary sector, the ease with which work tasks may be learned by newly appointed employees, and the constant pressure to reduce labor costs, means that there is little incentive to retain staff by matching the pay and conditions on offer in the primary sector.

Labor market segmentation theory in general (and the DLM thesis in particular) represents a substantial sociological contribution to a field which is otherwise the province of labor market economists (Hakim, 1990, pp. 159–60). Its key elements are presented in figure 9.2, which shows the fourfold classification developed by Loveridge.

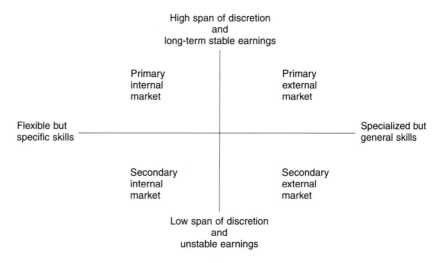

Figure 9.2   Organizational and firm-specific labor markets
Source: based on Loveridge, 1983, figure 7.1, p. 159

This classification is derived by cross-cutting internal and external labor markets with primary and secondary sectors. Thus, most jobs in the primary internal sector are permanent and full-time and offer a high degree of discretion and reasonable earnings; the primary external sector includes professional or skilled craft work supplied on a self-employed or subcontracted basis; the secondary internal sector refers most notably to part-time employment; and the secondary external sector involves, for example, seasonal, casual, and homeworking and unskilled labor.

Though DLM theory has been criticized on a number of grounds (for example, for neglecting the influence of worker organization on labor market structure and on the protection of vulnerable groups in the labor market), the basic distinction that is made between full-time employees in regular, stable, and permanent jobs and other forms of peripheral work remains a valuable one. Some writers prefer to use the term "flexible," not only because it avoids the pejorative connotations of "peripheral" and "unstable," but also because it points to the advantages accruing to employees, as well as to employers, in the availability of flexible work (Hakim, 1987, p. 550). The three most important groups within this flexible workforce are part-time workers, the self-employed, and those in temporary work. In the mid-1980s, the relative proportions of the "traditional" and "flexible" workforces in the

EEC as a whole were very similar to those in the US: in each roughly
two-thirds worked in the "core" workforce and one-third worked in the
flexible workforce (Hakim, 1987, pp. 553–4).

Technological changes have helped to deskill and routinize many
primary sector jobs, some of which have been relocated to low-wage-
labor countries. The advantages and bargaining power of primary sector
workers have also been diminished by the tendency of many large-scale
western enterprises to detach part of their production by means of
subcontract to smaller concerns. This trend, while designed to protect
large enterprises against fluctuations in demand and labor market
rigidities, often results in the creation of peripheral jobs as
subcontractors try to minimize costs. According to Goldthorpe, this
practice is particularly pronounced in France and Italy (1985, p. 142).
Hudson notes that the common practice of subcontracting services once
performed within these companies has led to increasing competition
between subcontracting companies, with predictable adverse effects on
the latter's wages and working conditions. Similarly, many previously
"core" workers have been re-hired by big companies on a casual or
part-time basis to meet temporary surges in demand, and on terms
which involve forgoing holiday entitlement, waiving redundancy rights,
and agreeing to work any pattern of shifts or days that management
might specify (Hudson, 1988, pp. 154–6). In other words, not only may
flexible or peripheral work grow in relation to or at the expense of
primary work, but primary workers may become transformed into
peripheral workers.

Though Goldthorpe sees this "dualistic" strategy being based in no
small measure on phenomena like subcontracting, he also places
particular emphasis on the recruitment of exceptionally vulnerable
migrant labor, which was of great value to employers in many western
IACs, especially in terms of its elasticity of supply and its tractability
(Goldthorpe, 1985, p. 439). This type of dualism also forms an
important element of Phizacklea's analysis of the British garment
industry and of the role of ethnic minority labor within it. She
contrasts the development before World War II of factory-based
production outside London with the traditional sweatshop based in the
inner cities. According to Phizacklea, the two sectors – one stable,
employing capital-intensive techniques, the other precarious and
undercapitalized – are sometimes linked by a complex web of
subcontracting: the dualism in this relationship is reflected not only in
technology and markets, but also in working conditions and in an
ethnic division of labor (Phizacklea, 1990, pp. 30 and 53).

In the next section the role of women in the labor force will be
explored, while the general significance of a reliance on migrant labor
will be discussed in section 5. However, before we end our
consideration of labor market segmentation, we should note the
relationship between location in either the primary or secondary sectors
on the one hand, and the risk of unemployment on the other. In IACs,
the least likely to become unemployed are those who would normally
fill the primary sector of the labor market: namely, men between the
ages of 24 and 54. Conversely, those who normally fill the secondary

labor market – the young and old, women and minorities – are more likely to be unemployed. The position in IACs in the early 1980s can thus be summarized as follows:

> ... ten persons out of 100 are unemployed. Of these ten persons, five are young and three of these are women. [A]mong the unemployed queuing up for unskilled jobs, the successful applicants will be the first adult males (between 24 and 54 years of age), then women of the same age, followed by young persons; the last will be minorities and older workers.
> (ILO, 1984, p. 46)

# 4   Gender and Labor Market Segmentation

In nineteenth-century Britain the majority of women did not enter regular waged employment – though many of them were engaged as homeworkers and domestic servants. Nevertheless, speaking of women who *were* in regular employment in the East End of London in 1888, Fishman says that "the crime of being born female meant that women were at the bottom of the pecking order." He cites a contemporaneous six-month research project carried out by Harkness, which revealed a picture of unmitigated exploitation: women were working in some 200 separate trades and, despite their low rates of pay and poor conditions of employment, Harkness found that "many a family is at present kept by the labor of one or two such girls" (Fishman, 1988, pp. 115–16).

Since 1945 the number of women in regular employment in Britain has grown sharply. For example, between 1951 and 1986 their number increased from almost 7.5 million to 9.4 million, at which point they accounted for more than 40 percent of the economically active workforce; and of the nearly 3 million growth in the civilian labor force between 1971 and 1989, some 90 percent has been among women. Of the projected increase between 1989 and 2001, again more than 90 percent is expected to be among women (*Employment Gazette*, April 1990, pp. 186 and 188).

Similar trends are visible in other IACs. In the US, for example, women made up only 28 percent of the labor force in 1948, but by 1990 they accounted for 45 percent of the total (Economic Report of the President, 1992, pp. 334 and 337). This increasing female participation may be explained by a number of factors: first, demand for labor has risen in sectors where women are concentrated, notably in services – where in 1960 46 percent of workers were women and in which 73 percent of all employed women worked (Dex, 1985, p. 77) – and in clerical occupations; second, there has been a decline in demand for labor in sectors in which men are particularly concentrated, notably in manufacturing; and third, the growth in real wages for women has been an important variable, though the effects of falling real male incomes and rising divorce rates should also be taken into account (Jacobsen, 1994, p. 225).

Although in broad terms the participation of women in the US labor force resembles the pattern in the UK and in Western Europe more generally, there are some important differences. For example, whereas women in the United States are much more likely to work part-time than are men, the differential is nothing like so marked as it is in the UK: in the early 1990s more than 25 percent of American women worked part-time as against 10 percent of men, whereas in the UK in 1989 the equivalent figures were 45 percent and 7 percent (US Department of Labor, 1992, p. 170; Employment Gazette (UK), April, 1990, p. 202). Another significant difference concerns the employment of married women with young children. For women in the US it is in this category that the most striking rise in labor force participation rates occurred between 1960 and 1990. They are much more likely to be in employment – and full-time employment at that – than their British counterparts, a difference that can be explained partly in terms of the availability of childcare in each country (Dex and Shaw, 1984).

Since 1950 it is evident that in the United States as in other IACs, women have increased their representation in virtually all occupations and industries, though their representation varies from one sector to another and there remains a high degree of segregation by sex. In the US, perhaps as a consequence of sex discrimination litigation against major employers, women are better represented among professionals and intermediate non-manual categories than is the case in Britain. Nevertheless, in both countries women remain concentrated in occupations like clerical work that are disproportionately and stereotypically "female" (Dex, 1985, p. 7; Jacobsen, 1994, p. 225). What we find is a mixture of change and continuity: growing "feminization" of the labor force is balanced by the uneven distribution of women within it such that they occupy a secondary position within employment. This unevenness can be ascribed to various factors ranging from the views that employers hold about the capabilities of women workers to the tensions that confront women, but which are less likely to confront men, between paid work and the demands of the domestic sphere.

As in the US, continuing "feminization" of the UK labor force reflects not only the expansion of services but also the decline in the number of jobs for men in manufacturing. For example, while in 1986 female employment levels were slightly below their peak of 1979, male employment fell in the same period by 1.5 million to 11.5 million, a decline of 11 percent (McDowell, 1988, p. 165). Thus, the 1989 Labour Force Survey shows that 81 percent of working women were employed in service industries as against just over 50 percent of men. By contrast, manufacturing industries employed only 16 percent of women as against 28 percent of men. Moreover, there was an even greater concentration in the service industries of women who worked part-time (88 percent) (UK *Employment Gazette*, December, 1990, p. 640). The expansion of part-time work and the dominant role of women within it is a continuing feature of the UK labor market and is a reflection of sectoral restructuring: while manufacturing and extractive industries employing full-time workers have declined as sources of employment, service industries have expanded. It is in these industries – often characterized by extended opening hours to meet consumer demand, as in the case of retailing – that part-time work and women's employment are concentrated.

The concentration of women in the service sector of the economy seems not only to indicate the feminization of the labor force, but also to lend credence to Bell's claim "that a service economy is very largely a female-centred economy" (1974, p. 146). It might be more accurate, however, to describe certain activities within the service sector and certain occupations as having become "feminized," rather than simply referring to the labor force as a whole having become so. Thus, as Werneke observes:

> Today, throughout the industrialized countries, one of the fundamental characteristics of the labour markets is the marked segregation by sex. Women are concentrated in a limited range of occupations and are most likely to be found working in relatively less skilled and lower paying jobs than their male counterparts. (Werneke, 1985, p. 400)

In the labor market, two kinds of segregation by gender can be distinguished:

1  *Horizontal segregation*, which refers to the extent to which men and women are concentrated in different jobs.
2  *Vertical segregation*, which refers to the differences within occupations with respect to pay, skill, status, promotion prospects, and the like. In broad terms we usually find women at the bottom of such hierarchies and men occupying more of the supervisory and managerial positions.

The degree to which women are concentrated in a narrow range of occupations, and are situated more often than not in the lower grades within occupational groups, owes much to the importance that part-time work has assumed for the growing number of women in employment. It was widely held in the period from the 1950s to the early 1970s that, against a background of shortages of labor, married women constituted the only major untapped source of labor. If this was so, then it seemed to follow that the most effective means to remedy the shortages was to expand part-time employment. The rise of part-time work, however, represents both a breakthrough and a trap for women seeking employment. This is because part-time workers often work under much less favorable conditions than do full-time workers. For example, part-time workers who work only a few hours per week are not covered by many of the items of employment protection legislation.

Women in employment – despite the extent of their participation – tend to be regarded differently from men. At one level they are seen as a *labor reserve*; that is, as a body of workers who may be tempted to move into work when and where labor is in short supply, yet who equally ought to be prepared to move out of the workforce once more if unemployment levels rise significantly. This expectation was perhaps demonstrated most graphically when, in the period after World War II, talk of the vital contribution of women's work was replaced by an emphasis on the "secondary" nature of women's earnings and on the virtues of domesticity. If women continue to be seen as a labor reserve or, equally, if they are regarded first and foremost as part-time workers, this gives credence to the idea that paid work is:

> ... of central importance in men's lives, but not as important in women's lives. This reflects the widespread view in our society that women have a choice about employment, at least at certain stages of their lives, in a way that men do not, as they will be primarily concerned with rearing children during their lives and so will either withdraw from the labour market or combine domestic responsibilities with part-time work.
> (Roberts, 1983, p. 236)

The significance of such attitudes and their implications for the organization of work are indicated in Beechey and Perkins' investigation of part-time work. They found, for instance, that it was invariably women's jobs that were arranged on a part-time basis; that part-time work was closely bound up with occupational segregation; and that employers and trade unionists alike made assumptions about the sort of work that was suitable for women and about why women did part-time work (Beechey and Perkins, 1985, p. 261). The attitudes of employers and trade unionists which they report demonstrate that the consequences of the domestic division of labor strongly influence the circumstances under which women – and especially married women – present themselves to the labor market: women are frequently characterized as having limited availability and limited ambition. Equally, the demands of women workers for shorter working hours to match the school day, the provision of day care facilities, or for paid leave in case of family illness and so on – whether or not seen as legitimate – can be said to reinforce the stereotype of women as primarily responsible for care in the family. Although one of the most important factors affecting women's participation in the labor market *is* the need to care for their children, we may nevertheless presume that *beliefs* about responsibilities for childcare are extended to justify the secondary status of women in the workforce more generally, even where their activity rates virtually match those of men.

How should we understand these different processes? At a general level, we can say that gender is central to the way work is organized. This is so not merely because of the implications that the domestic division of labor has for the employment of women, often in part-time jobs. The concentration of women in work that is labelled "unskilled" or "semi-skilled," and which is largely segregated from male employment, also reflects the way in which skill is attributed to a task (or to a number of tasks) depending on who is doing it:

> ... conventional notions of skill and deskilling cannot be applied to a predominantly female labour process because the very fact of

a job being labelled as "women's work" brings in enormous
ideological determinations which enable its skill content
"somehow" to be devalued.
(Barker and Downing, quoted in Harvey, 1987, p. 72)

We can also apply the concept of the dual labor market to the
employment profile of women by suggesting that, if it is in the interests
of employers to maintain and expand the primary sector, it may be
equally in their interests to maintain instability and low earnings in the
predominantly female secondary sector. However, "this strategy is
necessarily related to the availability of a supply of workers willing to
accept the poor pay, insecurity, low status and poor working conditions
of secondary jobs" (Barron and Norris, 1976, p. 52).


# 5   Migrant Workers and Divisions of Labor

At first sight, the differences between the position of women in the
labor market and that of migrant workers outweigh the similarities: for
example, many women are part-time workers, but most migrants work
full-time. Nevertheless, they are believed to share two important
characteristics. First, their participation in the labor market is seen by
employers and others to offer a (much-needed) degree of *numerical*
flexibility. Second, both groups are seen as entering the labor market
with lower expectations about pay, conditions, and prospects than
other workers have.

   The study of immigrant labor in the US has been mainly devoted to
the experiences of European migrants and to their contribution to US
economic development. By contrast, much less attention has been paid
to the movement of workers from Mexico and to their role in filling
gaps in low-wage sectors of the American economy. This neglect is
surprising for several reasons. It has been estimated that between 1900
and 1930 1.5 million people – 10 percent of Mexico's population at the
time – migrated from Mexico to the US. Subsequently, under the
*Bracero* program, which was initiated by the Federal Government in
1942 and afterwards extended by Congress until 1964, almost five
million Mexican contract workers were recruited. The *Bracero* program
represented what seemed to be an ideal solution to the long-standing
conflict between those who wanted cheap labor and those who wished
to restrict immigration for whatever reason. The details of this conflict
do not concern us here, but what is of interest is that the admission of
hundreds of thousands of such workers was permitted only on the
stipulation that they returned to Mexico each season. This resulted in
their confinement to, and identification with, a narrow range of back-
breaking tasks – tasks generally shunned by indigenous workers – and
in turn helped to prevent *permanent* Mexican immigrants from
achieving significant economic gains or acquiring skills (Reisler, 1976,
pp. 260–1). Since the late 1960s, Mexicans have accounted for a large
proportion of what Piore called "new" immigration to the US (1979,

pp. 141–66). For example, in fiscal years 1961–85, of the 10.68 million immigrant aliens admitted to the US for permanent residence, 1.42 million were Mexican. Furthermore, of the 5.42 million immigrant aliens admitted in fiscal years 1989–92, more than half were of Mexican origin (Statistical Abstract of the United States, 1994, p. 1404).

Though we can be sure about the *importance* of Mexican migration to the US, because of the extremely high rate of undocumented or illegal immigration it is very difficult to obtain reliable figures on *numbers* of migrant workers. For example, in the 1970s the US Immigration and Naturalization Service (INS) estimated that there were between 4 and 12 million illegal residents, finally opting for a figure of 6 million (Keely, 1977) and it was estimated that in the late 1970s between 500,000 and 1 million illegal migrants entered the country each year (Wachter, 1978). We might assume that the scale of illegal immigration is indicated by the number of undocumented persons identified by the INS. Much of this is, by common consent, Mexican. For example, of the 1.2 million "deportable aliens" identified by the INS in fiscal year 1991, 1.14 million were Mexican (Statistical Abstract of the United States, 1992, table 285). But this is to see the issue in narrow terms. We need to begin not with efforts to locate and deport "illegals," but with the claim that about one-third of full-time, low-skilled jobs in the US are filled by illegal workers (Wachter, 1978, p. 80) and to consider how far action against illegal workers by government agencies might be deflected or weakened by those who have an interest in obtaining cheap labor in abundance.

It is tempting to conclude that the employment of illegal workers takes place in what amounts to a separate labor market, characterized by low skill, poor conditions, and inadequate pay. However, this is a partial truth at best, for it conceals the way in which the continuing presence of illegal workers has depressed wage levels in particular industries and the probability that in the absence of such labor, employers would have been obliged to improve wages and conditions in order to attract sufficient numbers of indigenous Americans.

The specific consequence of this state of affairs is that there exists in the US a substantial number of workers who, even though they have avoided poverty and unemployment in their country of origin, not only work for little reward, but also are compelled to conceal their existence, for example by declining medical attention or by keeping their children out of school – anything to avoid the attention of the authorities. The wider consequence is that other "peripheral" workers, notably Blacks, Puerto Ricans, legal immigrants, and others, find themselves competing for jobs with illegal workers and, what is more, competing for jobs where wages and conditions have been adversely affected by the ready availability of illegal labor (North, 1977, pp. 8–9).

To draw attention to the high proportion of illegals among migrants to the US should not, however, dissuade us from appreciating what it is these migrants shared with migrants to the UK and Western Europe in the post-war period. Specifically, they are widely seen as being suitable people to perform undesirable jobs which, under prevailing economic conditions, attract insufficient numbers of indigenous workers.

Shortages of labor afflicted IACs to a greater or lesser degree between 1945 and 1970. One solution to this problem was to import foreign workers, though the extent to which these migrants satisfied the requirements to be available as demand for labor rose and to depart when demand for labor subsided varied from case to case. Their importance is to be understood not merely in terms of their overall numbers, but also in terms of their marginal contribution in particular sectors or in certain types of employment. For example, in the car industry, Cohen reports that 60 percent of the workforce at Ford's largest British plant (Dagenham) was black; that the proportion of Turkish workers in Ford's plants in Germany was higher still; and that migrant labor-power predominated in car factories generally in France and Germany (Cohen, 1987, p. 128).

Some observers believed that the importing of foreign workers had the effect of prolonging the life of relatively labor-intensive forms of production in the IACs, and thus, in the long run, economic growth was constrained. Others (for example, Kindleberger, 1967) argue that migrant labor was integral to economic growth as well as to developments in the production process. In the case of West Germany, for instance, foreign workers provided much-needed additional labor, particularly in growth industries such as engineering, chemicals, and plastics, at times when the number of indigenous German workers was stagnant or in decline (Castles, 1984, p. 127).

Migrant workers in West Germany offered a number of advantages both to employers and to the receiving economy more widely: for example, given their origins in less developed countries (LDCs), they had lower economic and social expectations than other workers and thus could be paid less; and they were easier to recruit *and* to dismiss. But possibly their greatest value lay in what it was that most obviously distinguished these migrants from their counterparts who left Europe to settle in North America in the nineteenth and early twentieth centuries. This concerns the range of *political* restrictions that most post-1945 international migrants have faced and, in particular, their exclusion from, or their limited opportunities to obtain, full citizenship in receiving countries. They can thus be seen as belonging to the category *unfree laborers* which Cohen describes as being "destined to be deployed either at the core or at the edge of the regional political economy" (Cohen, 1987, p. 26).

In these circumstances, migrant workers offered the additional advantage that, if and when they were discarded by employers, it could be expected that they would return to their families who, because of restrictions at the point of entry, had remained in the country of origin. The receiving economy would then be responsible only for the wage at the point of production, and the "social wage" (that is, the cost to society of providing for the worker's family and especially the costs associated with birth, education, and health) would be eliminated or sharply reduced. As far as employers and governments alike in the

labor-importing countries were concerned, there were good reasons for
seeing migrant workers not only as a source of labor that would
perform jobs others were unwilling to perform but also as a *flexible*
source of labor. In part, this could be ascribed to migrants themselves
who were believed to act as "target" workers, intending only to earn
enough to improve their position in their country of origin. Once this
was achieved, they would depart. In addition, there were strong
grounds for preferring temporary labor migration to permanent
settlement of immigrants together with their families. In the words of
the Chairman of the Committee on Foreign Workers of the German
Employers Association, "the great value of the employment of
foreigners lies in the fact that we have here at our disposal a *mobile
labour potential*. It would be dangerous to limit this mobility through a
large-scale assimilation policy" (quoted in Ward, 1975, p. 24, emphasis
added).

This "mobile labor potential" was referred to by the West German
government as the *Konjuncturpuffer* (meaning "boom-buffer"): that is,
the import of migrant labor during an economic boom served to protect
the indigenous labor force from some of the adverse consequences of
labor shortages – such as lay-offs or short-time working caused by
production bottlenecks – and, equally, the export of migrant labor in
time of economic recession cushioned the indigenous labor force
against unemployment. It was believed that such an objective would be
obtained by having a partially rotating workforce: new migrants on
short-term contracts would replace existing migrants whose contracts
had ended; the number of migrants could then be adjusted by the
government according to prevailing economic conditions, either by
increasing recruitment or (aided by the migrants' normally high rate of
return because they acted as "target" workers) by restricting it or
suspending it altogether.

But even in West Germany, where the system of controlling the
inflow and outflow of foreign workers was particularly elaborate, only a
proportion of the workforce remained "flexible" in the manner just
described. A larger element became an integral component of the labor
force, and as such were hardly more mobile than indigenous labor
either individually or collectively. One persuasive explanation of this
phenomenon is provided by Böhning's hypothesis (1981, pp. 28–9)
that, in what he termed a post-industrial society (which he defined as
comprising a relatively small agricultural sector, a large semi-automated
manufacturing sector which is in relative decline, and an equally large
but expanding service sector), committed to high economic growth and
to full employment:

1   because such a society is unable to change its traditional job
    structure, endemic labor shortages will arise in socially undesirable
    and low-wage jobs;
2   an attempt will be made to ameliorate these labor shortages by
    engaging foreign workers from LDCs; and consequently
3   the social-job structure will become rigidified, so forestalling an
    effective remedy to the initial problem of labor shortages and setting

in motion a process of migration which, under current trends of technological developments, is unending and self-feeding.

The transition from a "mobile labor potential" to a "self-feeding" process hints at the transformation of migrant workers into settled immigrant communities. Though it is true that migrants could be more easily hired and fired according to the dictates of the economy, it is also true that they were engaged as *replacement labor* to perform the dirty and socially undesirable jobs vacated by indigenous workers, who had taken advantage of expanding employment opportunities to secure more desirable jobs.

We can see this pattern clearly in the UK textile industry. In the post-war period, it faced severe labor shortages because indigenous workers had been generally unwilling to work in what was perceived as a declining industry in which pay and conditions were poor. The employers' response was to recruit large numbers of New Commonwealth immigrant workers (the majority from Pakistan), particularly for permanent night-shifts where the level of wages they judged to be low enough for them to remain competitive had failed to attract indigenous workers in any numbers. In performing this role, New Commonwealth immigrants followed in the footsteps of previous immigrants to Britain, for industries like textiles, iron foundries, clothing, and brickmaking have traditionally depended on immigrant labor.

The use of immigrant labor in the post-war period was not, however, simply the result of overall economic growth; it also reflected the form that this growth took – or, in the case of industries like textiles, the form of its retrenchment. The replacement of relatively labor-intensive methods of production by more capital-intensive methods involving the spread of automation and semi-automation did not eliminate poorly-paid, boring, or otherwise undesirable jobs. Indeed in some respects, as in the need to work some capital equipment on a continuous-shift basis in order to justify the cost of investment, it multiplied such jobs by necessitating the creation of permanent night-shifts. Much of the machinery that the expensive new capital equipment replaced had previously been worked by female labor. But there were both legal and social impediments to the employment of women on night-shifts. Given the reluctance of white males to accept the proffered rates of pay for this work, the introduction of the new machinery therefore resulted in black male immigrant labor being substituted for white female indigenous labor (Cohen and Jenner, 1981, pp. 109 and 126).

An examination of the role of immigrant workers in both the textile and garment industries provides strong evidence that their employment was associated with unpleasant working conditions and intensification of work. They consented to do such work where indigenous labor was not forthcoming because, as Cohen and Jenner concluded in their analysis of the textile industry:

> Firstly, the undoubted discrimination in employment against the immigrant restricts his choice of jobs severely. Secondly, his lack of suitable qualifications and language problems further restrict

opportunities. Thirdly, one can hypothesize that the immigrant newly established in this country is much nearer the economist's ideal of economic man. The majority of immigrants are simply adult males less constrained than the English worker by non-economic factors such as socially awkward hours of work, and are willing to work as long hours as possible to earn as much as possible.
(Cohen and Jenner, 1981, p. 122)

In this process, immigrant labor became a permanent part of the workforce, in the UK, France, West Germany, and Switzerland (Castles and Kosack, 1973). Immigrant workers performed jobs that indigenous workers were reluctant to undertake, even in time of recession: "Who else, after all, would shift the muck in Munich or do the dirty work in Stuttgart or Frankfurt? Certainly not the German unemployed" (*The Economist*, January 25, 1974). This is not to say they were made welcome: the attitude of many employers towards immigrant workers is, perhaps, encapsulated in the comment, "We haven't got to the point where we have to take them on. I suppose if things got bad enough we would" (Daniel, 1968).

Nevertheless, and notwithstanding this replacement role of immigrant labor, there is no doubt that the attraction of the "migrant solution" as a means of solving the sort of problems addressed in Böhning's self-feeding hypothesis had virtually disappeared by the mid-1970s. To some extent this was because the cost of maintaining what had gradually evolved into immigrant communities (the social wage) had become much higher. But of equal, if not greater, importance was the realization by many employers, for example in the garment and electrical industries, that their labor requirements could be better met by relocating all or a part of their production outside the national economy. A key question became, is it not more rational to move the machines to the workers than to bring the workers to the machines?

The use of cheap, immigrant labor in the American economy has also changed, completing what Burman perceptively calls a "three dimensional pattern." At first legal and illegal immigrant labor is employed within the US in agriculture, some services, and certain manufacturing sectors; subsequently, the assembly of cheap manufactured goods comes to be located near the US–Mexican border; and finally, the passage of the North American Free Trade Agreement (NAFTA) promises to give US employers unprecedented access to low-cost Mexican labor by allowing them to move without penalty to where the labor is, so avoiding the social costs and social problems associated with an influx of immigrants (Burman, 1994, p. 283).

Though, of course, this relocation of industry could not be applied in certain inherently immobile (immobile, that is, in international terms) spheres such as public transportation and the health service, the consequence of this migration of manufacturing was that, in summary, "an internal racial division of labour could be replaced by an international division of labour, and the sites of production could be switched to take account of market, transportation and labour conditions" (Cohen, 1987, p. 141). In broader terms, however, this involves more than the internal racial division of labor: it concerns the way employment opportunities in one part of the world are related to those in another. Thus when, in pursuit of lower labor costs, capital migrates in search of its own comparative advantage, this relocation will come at the expense of both indigenous and imported workers in the metropolis, whose job prospects are thereby reduced. It may be anticipated that this process will be particularly marked in labor-intensive and easily-relocatable industries such as textiles and clothing. Lipietz sees this as a process whereby poorly paid workers at the center are replaced with women workers at the periphery who receive minimal wages: in his view this is a "zero-sum game" involving no increase in world demand, in which it is employment at the center which is the loser, thus explaining protectionist reactions aimed at curbing NIC exports (Lipietz, 1987, p. 77).

In the face of this relocation the remaining immigrant workers will, however, experience higher levels of unemployment than indigenous workers. This is not only because of discrimination and because it is less skilled workers who tend to lose their jobs first, but also because immigrant workers are disproportionately represented in declining and vulnerable industries such as textiles. But this differential rate of unemployment should not cause us to overlook an important change in labor market dynamics that Wilkinson (1981) noted with reference to West Germany. In the period from 1960 to the early 1970s, when labor shortages were at their most pronounced and West German employers relied heavily on immigrant workers to fill secondary occupations, it would hardly be an exaggeration to say that the West German labor force was segmented along international lines. However, the subsequent economic slowdown permitted a much more selective provision of primary employment conditions by employers: while unemployment was concentrated among workers with "secondary characteristics," nevertheless "the margin between the primary and secondary segments of the West German labour force has shifted from that country's border to include a significant proportion of the domestic labour force" (Wilkinson, 1981, p. ix).

# 6  A New International Division of Labor?

As a rule, the discussion of employment prospects for migrant labor in the metropolis has been conducted in domestic terms. Most attention has been paid to questions of racial discrimination on the one hand, and labor market segmentation on the other. Conversely, little attention has been devoted to the connections between international migration of labor and international movements of capital. Yet, as suggested in the previous section, changing attitudes towards the recruitment of foreign workers are strongly related to mobility of capital in general and to the operations of multinational corporations (MNCs) in particular.

As their name suggests, MNCs can operate "geocentrically," planning the location of their production and the pattern of their investment according to the balance of advantage across the whole capitalist world economy. In the short-term these geocentric MNCs have the ability to increase the level of production in one country at the expense of another and in the longer term they could even shift the entire balance of their production between countries. The importance of MNCs can be illustrated by the fact that something like two-fifths of international trade occurs *within* firms, a proportion that becomes even higher if we take into account the flows between companies and their partners in subcontracting agreements. This and other considerations causes some observers to visualize national economies as mere organic elements within an all-embracing world system (e.g. Fröbel et al., 1980, p. 8).

In this section our interest is not, however, in the pursuit of comparative advantage in general, but in the way in which production is located to take advantage of differential wage rates (and by implication of the social and economic conditions which influence these wage rates). We shall explore this further by examining the idea of a "new international division of labour" (NIDL) developed by Fröbel et al. (1980). NIDL draws attention to the impact of MNCs, but its specific purpose is to point to the development of a world market in which manufacturing production (services are not addressed in its thesis) can be divided up into fragments and located in any industrialized or *less developed* part of the world, depending on where the most profitable combination of labor and capital can be obtained. Though this analysis is strong on contemporary empirical detail, it also presents a historical contrast between (a) a "classical" international division of labor, in which a minority of industrialized countries produced manufactured goods and less developed countries were integrated into the world economy solely as producers of food and raw materials, and (b) NIDL, in which the traditional "bisection" of the world economy is undermined (Fröbel et al., 1980, pp. 44–5).

In brief, what NIDL entails is the shutting down of certain types of manufacturing operations in IACs, and the subsequent opening up of these same operations in the foreign subsidiaries of the same company. In the view of Fröbel et al., the Federal German garment and textile industries represent one of the best examples of this process (though these industries in other IACs too have, in most cases, drastically cut production at traditional sites of manufacture as output became less competitive in world markets). An archetypal instance of this is that "Trousers for the Federal German market are no longer produced for example in Mönchengladbach, but in the Tunisian subsidiary of the same Federal German company" (Fröbel et al., 1980, p. 9).

The extent to which the most profitable combination of labor and capital for manufacturing is no longer to be found in the IACs is frequently explained with reference to a supposed crisis of Fordist production at the "center" (see chapter 8). However, we should not under-estimate the extent to which the optimum location for production shifts away from the center in response to the erosion of the *initial* advantages derived by IACs from the employment of imported labor. For instance, as action by trade unions on behalf of immigrant workers, action by immigrant workers on their own behalf, or the beneficial effects of health and safety legislation combine to improve the pay and conditions of immigrant labor, so the advantages of decamping to areas of low-cost labor – particularly for firms in labor-intensive spheres – become ever more appealing. It is therefore not surprising to discover that the industries that once expanded by using immigrant workers, or those industries which forestalled decline by the same means, were in the forefront of the drive to relocate production, often to the same countries from which their imported workers originated.

> [T]he old or "classical" international division of labour is now open for replacement. The decisive evidence for this hypothesis is the fact that developing countries have increasingly become sites for manufacturing – producing manufactured goods which are competitive on the world market. . . .
>
> This world market oriented industrialisation which is emerging today in many developing countries is not the result of positive decisions made by individual governments or companies. Industry only locates itself at those sites where production will yield a certain profit, sites which have been determined by five centuries of development of the world economy. In the "classical" international division of labour which developed over this period, industrial sites for manufacturing basically only existed in Western Europe, and later in the USA and Japan. Since it is evident that the developing countries are now providing sites for the profitable manufacture of industrial products destined for the world market to an ever-increasing extent, we quickly come up against the question: What changes are responsible for this development?
>
> Three preconditions taken together seem to be decisive for this development.
>
> Firstly, a practically inexhaustible reservoir of disposable labour has come into existence in the developing countries over the last few centuries. . . .
>
> Secondly, the division and subdivision of the production process is now so advanced that most of these fragmented operations can be carried out with minimal levels of skill easily learnt within a very short time.
>
> Thirdly, the development of techniques of transport and communication has created the possibility, in many cases, of the complete or partial production of goods at any site in the world – a possibility no longer ruled out by technical, organisational and cost factors. . . .
>
> The term which we shall use to designate this qualitatively new development in the world economy is the *new international division of labour.*
> (Fröbel et al., 1980, pp. 12–15)

In this extract Fröbel et al. refer to the creation of a virtually inexhaustible and easily exploitable supply of labor in developing countries, and elsewhere in their book they specify the characteristics of this labor force and the conditions under which these workers are employed. According to Lipietz, most of the jobs that are created in the developing countries involve "Taylorism" rather than "Fordism." (Taylorism and Fordism will be discussed in section 7 of this chapter; for further discussion, see chapter 8.) What he means by this is that the sort of jobs that are relocated – mostly in textiles and electronics – are not linked by any automatic machine system, yet they are fragmented and repetitive and thus labor-intensive in the strictest sense of the term (Lipietz, 1987, p. 74).

It is no wonder, then, that the preferred labor force in this environment is invariably female: this is not simply because in developing countries, as in the IACs, the price of female labor-power is lower, and often very much lower, than that of male labor-power; it also reflects beliefs about the intensity with which women may work when sitting at a sewing machine in textile production or in an electronics factory. The ideological character of these beliefs can be gauged from a variety of sources. For example, an article in the *Far Eastern Economic Review* stated that:

> Most manufacturers prefer female workers because they have a longer attention span than males and can adjust more easily to long hours on the assembly line. In addition they are willing to accept lower pay and are said to have more agile hands, which is especially important in electronics.
> (July 2, 1976; quoted in Fröbel et al., 1980, p. 348)

And in a feature on Mauritius in the *Financial Times* it was stated that:

> There has been some criticism of the fact that most zone industries, especially in the textile and electronic factories, employ mainly women. Some 85 percent are women, and efforts are being made to switch the trend . . . [It] is not necessarily due to the fact that women in Mauritius receive lower wages than men, but rather because industrialists have found that women are more adaptable than men to most of the skills required.
> (June 18, 1976; quoted in Fröbel et al., 1980, p. 348)

The role of female labor in what Fröbel et al. call "world market factories," and in particular the way in which the domestic division of labor is seen to prepare them for this role (women are referred to in another Malaysian investment brochure as being qualified "by both nature and tradition" for work on the assembly line requiring great manual dexterity) is further clarified by this impression gained on a visit to a British-owned Malaysian factory which assembled integrated circuit boards, of

> . . . well qualified young women who, whilst awaiting their parent-chosen bridegroom, work on flow lines doing minutely routinized assembly tasks under the supervision of generally less or equally qualified males. The latter have what they regard as a career in a "high tech" industry: the former seem well aware of their

> subjugation to market, domestic and religiously sanctified
> hierarchy.
> (Loveridge, 1987, p. 185)

Though Fröbel et al. emphasize the contrast between the old
international division of labor and the new, they see the latter as
deepening rather than reversing the historical underdevelopment of
LDCs: what applied to their agriculture and to mining is now replicated
in the industrial sector. In their view there is no discernible transfer of
technology involved in the new international division of labor (NIDL).
In part, this is because the technology being employed is generally
simple (and in any case is dependent on the expertise of foreigners),
but it is also because the skills acquired by the workforce in world
market factories are seen as minimal because training rarely lasts for
more than a few weeks. For these and other reasons, no significant
improvement is envisaged in either the material conditions of the
population or in its level of skill: only a fraction of the population is
employed – at very low wage levels – while the remainder forms a
permanent reserve army. In addition to this, Fröbel et al. see world
market factories remaining as industrial enclaves, unconnected to the
local economy except insofar as the latter provides new labor to be
freshly trained when the existing labor force is discarded (Fröbel et al.,
1980, p. 6).

There are, nevertheless, a number of criticisms to be made of this
general thesis. First, Phizacklea contends that the German pattern of
relocating the production of garments in the way described by Fröbel et
al. was not replicated on the same scale in the UK: in Britain, similar
ends were often achieved by subcontracting production to inner-city,
secondary sector firms (Phizacklea, 1990). If we examine the conduct of
British MNCs such as Coats Patons we see that, just like their German
counterparts, their response to being undercut by imports from
developing countries was to move much of their own production to
such countries in order to take advantage of lower labor costs.
(According to a report in the *Financial Times*, in 1981 comparative
labor costs for Coats Patons were as low as 10 percent of British levels
in the Philippines and 6 percent in Indonesia (*Financial Times*, June
29, 1981).)

A second criticism is that NIDL theorists have exaggerated the
scale of the relocation of production, for expressed as a proportion
of world-wide industrial output, that of the Third World remains
small. There is some truth in this, but what may be of more
significance for NIDL theorists is that in the 1970s and 1980s
the workforces of MNCs in their home countries fell quite
markedly as world-wide economic activity slackened, whereas
employment levels fell much less or even expanded in LDCs (Thrift,
1988, p. 34).

Thirdly, some commentators (e.g. Jenkins, 1984, and Lipietz, 1987)
have argued that where MNCs do relocate production they are as likely,
if not more likely, to do so to establish a market position in the
economy in question as to be in pursuit of cheap labor.

Though these are powerful criticisms, advocates of NIDL were generally well aware that the amount of direct foreign investment in LDCs was limited. What they sought to draw attention to was the likelihood that future flows of such investment would increase, attracted in particular by the prospect of cheap labor. Thus, the path established by the relocation of garment and textile production would be followed by other industries, notably the car component industry. The logic of this argument is that MNCs have in their operations transcended national boundaries. But what this logic overlooks is that reducing direct labor costs – whether by relocation or otherwise – is only one route to competitive advantage, and perhaps one of diminishing importance. An alternative approach is to increase labor productivity by means of technical innovation. In achieving this objective the role of the national environment is profoundly important: "It shapes the way opportunities are perceived, how specialized skills and resources are developed, and the pressures on firms to mobilize resources in rapid and efficient ways . . . Globalization makes nations more, not less, important" (Porter, 1990, p. 736). It is to aspects of this argument, and particularly to those which concern the concepts of "core" and "periphery" in the labor process, that we turn in the next section.

# 7   The Division of Labor and Flexible Specialization

In drawing attention to the relocation of manufacturing consequent upon the division and subdivision of production processes into fragments, often requiring only minimal skill, Fröbel et al. also assert that this has overtaken the traditional means of rationalizing production in IACs. This rationalization is perceived quite differently by other commentators, however. For example, according to Piore and Sabel (1984), contemporary capitalism is undergoing a period of restructuring which can be seen in terms of a divide between the eras of *mass production* and *flexible specialization*, the latter being linked to the new type of flexible electronics-based automation technologies.

In the era of mass production, particular models (whether cars or washing machines) were manufactured in large batches on assembly lines that required great investment in inflexible plant. In the era of flexible specialization, on the other hand, small batch production is possible. In this era, *flexibility* is at a premium not only in terms of the organization of production but also in terms of the *workforce*.

The transition to mass production associated with Taylorism and Fordism should be seen in terms of an evolving labor process which has both earlier and later manifestations (Kaplinsky, 1988, pp. 453–4; Hoffman and Kaplinsky, 1988, p. 330; see also the discussion in chapter 8).These developments have their roots in:

1   the division of labor discerned by Adam Smith, in which jobs are broken down into ever more specialized tasks, each of which can be done by a dedicated worker (however, it was the economies of scale associated with machine production of goods that vastly increased output, when complemented with the requisite pattern of work and production organization, rather than the division of labor in itself);

2   the so-called *Babbage principle*, which involved the identification and separation of unskilled tasks, thus simultaneously deskilling some work, permitting the employment of cheaper labor, and increasing managerial control by firing recalcitrant workers (or threatening so to do);

3   the attempt to compensate for the unreliability of skilled labor by mechanizing hitherto skilled sub-processes;

4   the introduction of Taylorism in an effort to maintain control of workers in larger factories;

5   the incorporation of Taylorism into a mass production system of moving production lines and standardized products (Fordism) in which one of the key elements was the keeping of high levels of inventory as an insurance against interruptions in the system; and finally

6   as we saw in the previous section, the three preconditions mentioned by Fröbel et al., which allow the process of task fragmentation, deskilling and large-scale production to be conducted on a world-wide basis in a "new international division of labor."

These developments need not and should not be seen as flowing inevitably from technological advances. Thus, the transition to mass production reflects *beliefs* about the gains to be derived from standardizing products, or about the economies of large-scale production. The choices between one form of technology and another are often shaped by a variety of non-technological, non-economic, and ideological considerations (Piore and Sabel, 1984, p. 57). We can see this type of influence, for example, in the success which Taylorism has had in establishing deskilling, task fragmentation, and decreased worker discretion as key elements of managerial control, to the extent that they are widely taken for granted as the way to approach the organization of work. Yet as Rosenbrock observes, if the urge is to seek subsequently to automate "unsatisfactory" (i.e. fragmented, deskilled) jobs out of existence, we must not overlook the extent to which, in order to apply the cure, to abolish the trivialized job, one first has to create the disease, the supply of trivialized jobs (Rosenbrock, 1987, pp. 281–2). Nevertheless, it is precisely this creation of trivialized jobs that is presented by Braverman (1974) as the dominant and inevitable form of the way work is organized in capitalist industrial production. For Braverman, a continuous process of fragmentation and deskilling was visible in IACs from the 1890s onwards. Eventually, work for virtually the whole labor force would have become routine, fragmented, and lacking in skill, and the distinctions between skilled and unskilled workers or between manual and non-manual workers would therefore be devalued. In Braverman's opinion Taylorism represented, capitalism in its purest form, embodying the maximum division of labor and, insofar as labor is regarded as a factor disruptive of production, the minimal amount of worker discretion (Lane, 1988, p. 141).

There are, however, a number of reasons for questioning the continued viability of Taylorism and Fordism at the center over and above the competition emanating from peripheral NICs taking advantage of lower labor costs. For example, markets have become less stable and predictable, and the inflexibility of the established mass production model with its reliance on dedicated machinery operated by semi-skilled workers has therefore become more evident (Lane, 1988, p. 142). In addition, the diminishing returns associated with the Fordist labor process can be attributed to the denial of human creativity in the workplace: if worker discretion is minimized, it is unlikely that the enterprise will benefit from incremental improvements which workers may suggest on the basis of their detailed observations of production – improvements which in other, more enlightened, circumstances would be a vital element of technical innovation (Kaplinsky, 1988, p. 455). It was in the light of these and other problems associated with Fordism that Piore and Sabel (1984) proposed a solution based on the concept of "flexible specialization."

Flexible specialization emphasizes flexibility in a number of areas: in terms of a response to the market, in terms of an ability to produce economically in small batches, and in terms of the flexibility demanded of the workforce. Piore and Sabel accept that the enhancement of workers' skills associated with more flexible forms of work organization may be balanced against, or even constrained by, the extension of management control which the introduction of new technology – particularly information technology – facilitates. Thus worker discretion may still be sharply circumscribed under flexible specialization. Nevertheless, they see the changes that flow from fragmented product markets as offering benefits to capital, labor, and consumers alike: instead of workers with narrowly defined jobs using dedicated machines to produce a standard product, broadly skilled workers use capital equipment capable of making different models to produce specialized goods.

It is apparent that this represents a significant break with two of the key elements of Fordism: an increased division of labor and the deskilling of work. For example, whereas in Fordist car production the line is halted while specialist die-changers key in their work, in flexible specialization production workers are "multi-tasked": not only are they responsible for changing the dies, but they have undergone training in routine maintenance and in a range of allied tasks. In addition to this, the new labor process is multi-skilling insofar as, in order to perform a range of tasks, workers must command a range of skills (Kaplinsky, 1988, pp. 457–8; Hoffman and Kaplinsky, 1988, p. 52).

What then is the evidence that a shift to flexible specialization has occurred or is occurring in IACs? Meegan concludes that although there are important changes going on of the type described by Piore and Sabel, they are happening more slowly and on a smaller scale than is sometimes claimed – claims that are often based on exaggerated accounts of the spread of flexible technologies like computer-integrated automation. In addition, Meegan argues that significant difficulties have been encountered in trying to automate "flexibly" many of the assembly line operations that epitomize Fordism (Meegan, 1988, p. 171).

Lane gives a rather different estimation of the development of flexible specialization in Germany. She makes particular reference to the importance widely given there to organizational and technological innovation and to the links between them, which seem to signify "an important change in capital's attitude to labour deployment which has more positive consequences for labour than the old Taylorist concept" (1988, p. 159). Drawing on Friedman's distinction between a labor process in which workers are given a measure of control over their working arrangements (*responsible autonomy*) and one where little or no discretion is granted (*direct control*) (Friedman, 1977), she explains the predisposition of German employers to adopt the former rather than the latter strategy both in terms of the availability of a large pool of skilled labor and in terms of how skill is produced. Lane describes how in Germany since 1945 there has been a predominance of skilled workers possessing a high degree of qualifications. She calls such workers "polyvalent"; that is, they have knowledge or capabilities in at least two areas gained in a systematic type of training.

On the basis of a review of several studies of industrial transformation in Germany in the 1970s and 1980s, Lane emphasizes the importance of developing forms of work organization which facilitate worker autonomy, job enrichment, and upskilling. Though she is uncertain whether this denotes a new industrial strategy or merely indicates islands of change, Lane emphasizes that in Germany a successful competitive strategy is widely seen to depend on a range of factors: not *only* on the availability of worker skills, as Piore and Sabel suggest, but also on high levels of investment and managerial competence.

One of the main criticisms of Braverman's deskilling thesis is that it portrays a relationship between technology and the labor process which is ineluctable. It therefore ignores the extent to which the same sets of machinery located in similar modes of production can, nevertheless, be linked to quite different forms of workforce organization. These differences are evident, for example, in the "extreme malleability of CNC [computer numerical control] technology" described by Hartman et al. They found that CNC could be operated either within a system where unskilled operators were neatly differentiated from skilled setters and technician planners, or near conventional machinery involving a skilled homogeneous workforce (1985, p. 359). More generally, it can be argued that, contrary to Braverman, it has *not* been equally true in all IACs that the labor process in the twentieth century has been one of deskilling. Thus, although the conditions described in *Working for Ford* (Beynon, 1973) seem to symbolize the deskilling thesis, according to which work is boring, repetitive, and fragmented, other ways of manufacturing cars have been developed.

The deskilling thesis seems also to neglect the extent to which new technology is conducive to the creation of new or extended skills, as well as to the disappearance of existing skills. In other words, management may pursue a variety of strategies, some of which may have a deskilling effect, others not. For example, we can see this in the way that management in the Japanese car industry seems to be able to give a substantial degree of control back to the workforce without having to worry that such control will be employed against company interests. Though some accounts of this phenomenon describe it as a matter of worker self-discipline rather than an indication that the workers control the production process, it seems more useful to see it in terms of the distinction drawn by Hoffman and Kaplinsky between "interior determination" and "exterior control." While the latter is a product of Taylorism, the former entails providing the workforce not just with quality circles, but also with the means to bring production to a halt, something that cannot be easily envisaged under Taylorism (Hoffman and Kaplinsky, 1988, p. 338). The most arresting example of this – and the word is used advisedly – is the installation of Andon lights and switches by Toyota on many of their production lines. Not only do these allow each line worker to bring the line to a standstill if a fault is noted, but it is *expected* that this power will be exercised. (Hoffman and Kaplinsky, 1988, p. 337).

In contrast to the German approach to technological innovation, Lane reports evidence of hesitancy (and worse) in the approach of British firms. But even where British management pursues a "new market strategy" and makes extensive use of technical innovations, she argues that labor force problems impede the realization of flexible specialization. In particular, this is attributed to an insufficient supply of skilled polyvalent labor. Similarly, Hartmann et al. conclude their Anglo-German comparison by predicting that British companies will train and utilize fewer skilled workers than their German counterparts, which are able to draw on a greater supply of trained labor at all levels (1985, pp. 352–3).

As we have seen, central to the flexible specialization thesis is the view that changes in the markets for products have had or will have extensive implications for the sort of labor force that is needed to satisfy the market. Broadly speaking, one designated path for IACs can be summarized in terms of an increasing reliance on the production of highly sophisticated goods and services for fast-changing needs. This will require highly qualified workers capable of selecting data and handling strategic information. But if this is so, it may be asked whether the "mixed strategy" that some commentators discern in the UK, which demands "functional flexibility" from a core workforce and "numerical flexibility" from a peripheral workforce (Hakim, 1990, p. 164), or a "polarized qualification pattern" (Hartmann et al., 1985, p. 358), is best suited to the posited product market.

We need to express some hesitation here, otherwise we may suggest, misleadingly, that a uniformly appropriate labor strategy is being pursued in one country whereas in another the strategy is largely inappropriate to changes in the product market. In reality the difference is not so extreme. Thus, if we consider Kaplinsky's analysis of the reasons for the success of Japanese manufacturers in fostering the creation of a multi-skilled, multi-tasked workforce and entrusting this workforce with a measure of control over the production process, we ought to note that the working conditions prevailing in Toyota stand in sharp contrast to those which exist in its subcontractors. In both the 200 highly specialized enterprises to which Toyota subcontracts directly and in the further 38 400 enterprises to which they, in turn, subcontract, wages are much lower than in Toyota, and there is no job security. In Kaplinsky's view, this constitutes a dual labor market so pronounced that it permits a structure of production costs that has traditionally been beyond the capacity of the older IACs to obtain (1988, p. 466). Thus, in assessing trends towards "enskilling," "upskilling," and the like, which may be associated with "interior determination" and the "manufacture of consent," we should note that these concepts may apply only in certain parts of the production process and to certain types of worker. Those who work part-time or are employed by subcontractors may be excluded from these improvements; flexible specialization does not therefore entail the obsolescence of the concepts of "core" and "peripheral" worker.

# 8  Conclusion

In this chapter I began my consideration of the division of labor in a conventional way by looking at sectoral divisions in the economy. But in emphasizing not only different aspects of the divisions of labor (with respect to gender, migrant workers, NIDL, and flexible specialization), but also the concepts of "core" and "periphery" as providing a theme which connects these disparate aspects, my approach has been somewhat less conventional.

Perhaps the key point, and one which can be applied to each of the groups and types of worker that I have dealt with, was set out in my reference in section 3 to the idea of a "dual labor market." In the general context of a labor market being separated into primary and *secondary* sectors – or more accurately where workers can be categorized as being "primary" or "secondary" workers – reference was made to the need for employers to find a suitable means of adjusting their labor forces to fluctuations in demand. Broadly speaking, they will contrive to retain more skilled workers, in whom training and investment is relatively high, while shedding less-skilled workers, in whom investment is relatively low and who are easy to replace. If this is so, we can go on to specify that the former group of workers is seen to be adaptable or "functionally flexible," while the latter group need only be disposable or "numerically flexible." But we must not exaggerate the permanence of this posited boundary. It does not follow that "once a primary worker, always a primary worker."

Nor is it wise to exaggerate what different groups of workers share. For example, if we compare the situation of women workers and migrant workers, we see immediately that part-time work is considered appropriate for women because work is not regarded as centrally important to women's lives, whereas the term "economic migrant" indicates that the desire to *work* is understood to explain the very act of migration itself. Nevertheless, women and migrants entering the labor market *do* have much in common. They are both perceived as being more easily disposable than are other groups of workers (though for different reasons): each is seen as providing a *labor reserve*, moving in and out of employment according to the demand for labor. And each is seen as suited to less-skilled work and to jobs with few prospects. The case of migrant workers in West Germany is particularly instructive. As was indicated in section 5, although they were employed to provide a "mobile labor potential," if anything, they turned out to be permanent, not temporary, replacements for indigenous labor. Nonetheless, the differences between the high-water mark of dependence on migrant labor and the subsequent recession, which also saw the growth of relocation of production to less developed countries described by Fröbel et al., reveals a significant movement in the boundary between "primary" and "secondary" employment in West Germany. When migrant workers were at their most numerous, it was, according to Wilkinson, not much of a distortion to say that the German economy was segmented along international lines: that is, to be an indigenous worker was to be a primary worker. Thereafter, however, the boundary between primary and secondary employment shifted to include a significant percentage of indigenous workers among the secondary workforce. In essence this means that *who* was disposable changed: at one point the use of migrant workers guaranteed the employment of indigenous workers *and* protected them from unemployment; at the next point both the guarantee and the protection disappeared.

We saw the element of *disposability* most clearly, however, when we examined NIDL in section 6. According to Fröbel and his colleagues, NIDL depends on a virtually inexhaustible and easily exploitable (thus disposable) supply of labor which, far from incidentally, is invariably female. Here there is no debate about work being of marginal importance to women's lives; instead, female workers are preferred because the price of their labor is lower, because of beliefs about the intensity with which they work (or can be made to work), and because of their perceived "dexterity" (an attribute which diminishes by about the age of thirty, when they can be replaced by younger workers).

At first sight, the discussion of *flexible specialization* as an emergent trend seems to fit less easily into this framework of "core" and "periphery" – with its attendant emphasis on "disposability." However, a careful reading of section 7 will show evidence to the contrary. We can see this most obviously in relation to the points about functional and numerical flexibility made at the beginning of this conclusion. As you will note, central to the flexible specialization thesis is the view that changes in the markets for products have far-reaching implications for the sort of workforce needed to satisfy those markets. These implications concern the degrees of skill that workers are required to possess and the degrees of control and autonomy that they are expected to exercise. However, you will also note that this emergent trend towards flexible specialization – if that is what we are witnessing – does not preclude a reliance on or a coexistence with forms of production where wages and conditions are much less attractive and where job security is much lower, and this often involves subcontracting relationships. In essence, therefore, a scenario in which workers are multi-skilled, relatively autonomous and, perhaps, indispensable, does not mean that other workers do not remain readily disposable.

# References

Abercrombie, N., Warde, A., Soothill, K., Urry, J., and Walby, S. (1988) *Contemporary British Society*, Cambridge, England, Polity Press.

Allen, J. and Massey, D. (eds) (1988) *The Economy in Question*, London, Sage.

Barron, R. and Norris, E. (1976) "Sexual divisions and the dual labour market," in Barker, D. and Allen, S. (eds) *Dependence and Exploitation in Work and Marriage*, London, Longman.

Beechey, V. and Perkins, T. (1985) "Conceptualizing part-time work," in Roberts, B. et al. (1985).

Bell, D. (1974) *The Coming of Post-Industrial Society: a Venture in Social Forecasting*, London, Heinemann.

Beynon, H. (1973) *Working for Ford*, London, Allen Lane.

Blackburn, R. and Mann, N. (1979) *The Working Class and the Labour Market*, London, Macmillan.

Böhning, W. (1981) "The self-feeding process of economic migration from low-wage to post-industrial countries with a liberal capitalist structure," in Braham, P. et al. (eds) (1981).

Braham, P., Rhodes, E., and Pearn, M. (eds) (1981) *Discrimination and Disadvantage in Employment*, London, Harper & Row.

Braverman, H. (1974) *Labour and Monopoly Capital: the Degradation of Work in the Twentieth Century*, New York, Monthly Review Press.

Burman, S. (1994) "America in transition: domestic weakness and international competitiveness," in Thompson, G. (ed.) *Markets – The United States in the Twentieth Century*, Sevenoaks, England, Hodder & Stoughton.

Castles, S. (1984) *Here for Good: Western Europe's New Ethnic Minorities*, London, Pluto.

Castles, S. and Kosack, G. (1973) *Immigrant Workers and the Class Structure in Western Europe*, Oxford, Oxford University Press.

Cockburn, C. (1983) *Brothers: Male Dominance and Technical Change*, London, Pluto.

Cohen, R. (1987) *The New Helots: Migrants in the International Division of Labour*, Aldershot, England, Avebury.

Cohen, B. and Jenner, P. (1981) "The employment of immigrants: a case study within the wool industry," in Braham, P. et al. (eds) (1981).

Daniel, W. (1968) *Racial discrimination in England*, Harmondsworth, England, Penguin.

Dex, S. (1985) *The Sexual Division of Work*, Brighton, England, Wheatsheaf.

Dex, S. and Shaw, L. (1984) *A comparison of British and US Women's Work Histories* (Report submitted to the Equal Opportunities Commission).

Economic Report of the President (1992) Washington, DC, US Government Printing Office.

*Employment Gazette* (monthly) London, Department of Employment.

Fishman, W. (1988) *East End 1888*, London, Duckworth.

Fox, A. (1974) *Man Mismanagement*, London, Hutchinson.

Friedman, A. (1977) *Industry and Labour: Class Struggle at Work and Monopoly Capitalism*, London, Macmillan.

Fröbel, F., Heinrichs, J., and Drey, O. (1980) *The New International Division of Labour*, New York, Cambridge University Press.

Gershuny, J. and Miles, I. (1983) *The New Service Economy: The Transformation of Employment in Industrial Societies*, London, Frances Pinter.

Goldthorpe, J. (1985) "The end of convergence: corporalist and dualist tendencies in modern western societies," in Roberts, B. et al. (1985).

Hakim, C. (1987) "Trends in the flexible workforce," *Employment Gazette*, November, pp. 549–60.

Hakim, C. (1990) "Core and periphery in employers' workforce strategies: evidence from the 1987 ELUS survey," *Work, Employment and Society*, vol. 4, no. 2, pp. 157–88.

Harris, L. (1988) "The UK economy at a cross-roads," in Allen, J. and Massey, D. (eds) (1988).

Hartmann, G., Nicholas, I., Sorge, A., and Warner, M. (1985) "Computerised machine tools, manpower consequences and skill utilisation: a study of British and West German manufacturing firms," in Rhodes, E. and Wield, D. (eds) *Implementing New Technologies*, Oxford, Basil Blackwell.

Harvey, J. (1987) "New technology and the gender divisions of labor," in Lee, G. and Loveridge, R. (eds) *The Manufacture of Disadvantage*, Milton Keynes, England, Open University Press.

Hoffman, K. and Kaplinsky, R. (1988) *Driving Force: The Global Restructuring of Technology, Labour and Investment in the Automobile and Components Industry*, San Francisco, Westview Press.

Hudson, R. (1988) "Labour market changes and new forms of work in 'old' industrial regions," in Massey, D. and Allen, J. (eds) (1988).

ILO (1984) *World Labour Report 1. Employment, Incomes, Social Protection, New Information Technology*, Geneva, International Labour Organization.

Jacobsen, J. (1994) "Gender aspects of the American economy," in Thompson, G. (ed.) *Markets – US in the Twentieth Century*, Sevenoaks, England, Hodder & Stoughton in association with the Open University.

Jenkins, R. (1984) "Divisions over the international division of labour," *Capital and Class*, no. 22, pp. 28–57.

Kaplinsky, R. (1988) "Restructuring the capitalist labour process: some lessons from the car industry," *Cambridge Journal of Economics*, vol. 12, pp. 451–70.

Keely, C. (1977) "Counting the uncountable," in *Population and Development Review*, vol. 3, no. 4, December.

Kindleberger, C. (1967) *Europe's Post-war Growth: The Role of Labor Supply*, Cambridge, MA, Harvard University Press.

Lane, C. (1988) "Industrial change in Europe: the pursuit of flexible specialisation in Britain and West Germany," *Work, Employment and Society*, vol. 2, no. 2, pp. 141–68.

Lipietz, A. (1987) *Mirages and Miracles: The Crisis of Global Capitalism*, London, Verso.

Loveridge, R. (1983) "Labour market segmentation and the firm," in Edwards, J. et al. (eds) *Manpower Planning: Strategy and Techniques in an Organisational Context*, Chichester, England, John Wiley.

Loveridge, R. (1987) "Social accommodations and technological transformations: the case of gender," in Lee, G. and Loveridge, R. (eds) *The Manufacture of Disadvantage*, Milton Keynes, England, Open University Press.

Massey, D. (1988) "What's happening to UK manufacturing?," in Allen, J. and Massey, D. (eds) (1988).

Massey, D. and Allen, J. (eds) (1988) *Uneven Redevelopment*, London, Hodder & Stoughton.

McDowell, L. (1988) "Gender divisions," in Hamnett, C. et al. (eds) *The Changing Social Structure*, London, Sage.

Meegan, R. (1988) "A crisis of mass production?," in Allen, J. and Massey, D. (eds) (1988).

North, D. (1977) *Illegal immigration to the USA: a quintet of myths*, APSA, Annual Meeting, Washington, DC, September.

Offe, C. (1976) *Industry and Inequality*, London, Edward Arnold.

Phizacklea, A. (1990) *Unpacking the Fashion Industry: Gender, Racism and Class in Production*, London, Routledge.

Piore, M. (1979) *Birds of Passage – Migrant Labour and Industrial Societies*, Cambridge, England, Cambridge University Press.

Piore, M. and Sabel, C. (1984) *The Second Industrial Divide*, New York, Basic Books.

Porter, M. (1990) *The Competitive Advantage of Nations*, London, Macmillan.

Reisler, M. (1976) *By the Sweat of Their Brow: Mexican Immigrant Labour in the United States 1900–1940*, Westport, CT, Greenwood Press.

Roberts, B. et al. (1985) *New Approaches to Economic Life: Economic Restructuring: Unemployment and the Social Division of Labour*, Manchester, England, Manchester University Press.

Roberts, C. (1983) "Research on women in the labour market: the context and scope of the women and employment survey," in Roberts, B. et al. (1985).

Rosenbrock, H. (1982) "Can human skill survive microelectronics?," in Rhodes, E. and Wield, D. (eds) *Implementing New Technologies*, Oxford, Basil Blackwell.

Rosenbrock, H. (1987) "Engineers and the work people do," in Finnegan, R., Salaman, G., and Thompson, K. (eds) *Information Technology*, Sevenoaks, England, Hodder & Stoughton in association with the Open University.

Seear, N. (1981) "The management of equal opportunity," in Braham, P. et al. (eds) (1981).

Smith, D. (1974) *Racial Disadvantage in Employment*, London, PEP.

The Statesman's Year Book (1994) Statistical and Historical Annual of the States of the World, 1994–1995, 131st edn (ed. Brian Hunter), London, Macmillan.

Statistical Abstract of the United States (1988 and 1992) National Data Books and Guide to Sources, 112th edn, Bureau of the Census, Washington, DC, US Department of Commerce.

Thrift, N. (1988) "The geography of international economic disorder," in Massey, D. and Allen, J. (eds) (1988).

US Department of Labor (1992) *Employment and Earnings*, Bureau of Labor Statistics, vol. 39, no. 1.

Wachter, C. (1978) "Second thoughts about illegal immigration," in *Fortune*, May 22, pp. 78–86, cited in Cohen, R. (1987).

Ward, A. (1975) "European capitalism's reserve army," *Monthly Review Press*, vol. 27, p. 6.

Werneke, D. (1985) "Women, the vulnerable group," in Forester, T. (ed.) *The Information Technology Revolution*, Oxford, Basil Blackwell.

Wilkinson, F. (ed.) (1981) *The Dynamics of Labour Market Segmentation*, London, Academic Press.

Worsley, P. et al. (1977) *Introducing Sociology*, Harmondsworth, England, Penguin.

# 10   Women and the Domestic Sphere

Helen Crowley

## Contents

| | | |
|---|---|---:|
| 1 | Introduction | 344 |
| 1.1 | The sexual division of labor | 344 |
| 2 | Women and the Family: Some Theoretical Issues | 348 |
| 2.1 | The changing state/family relation | 349 |
| 2.2 | Conceptualizing reproductive labor | 351 |
| 2.3 | The logic of the private sphere | 353 |
| 2.4 | Women's mothering | 354 |
| 2.5 | The social construction of femininity | 359 |
| 3 | Conclusion | 360 |
| | References | 361 |

# 1   Introduction

In terms of gender, recent social changes have been dramatic in many respects. Women now make up half the workforce and the span of their working lives contrasts with the greatly reduced time spent in caring for children in the home. Women with dependants are less reliant on the male wage and more directly supported by their own wages and state benefits. Marriage and the family have been transformed by changes in the law, by women's increased participation in the labor force, and by the extension of state welfare provision. Relations between women and men have been recast by these changes, particularly insofar as the balance of women's dependency on men has shifted. They have also been influenced by the emergence of the women's movement which challenged women's socially subordinate position within the domestic sphere, and demanded women's rights to independence and sexual equality.

Paradoxically, however, in spite of these changes, the position of women within the domestic sphere remains, in many respects, unaltered. Women continue to be responsible for the primary care of children and the private care of vulnerable adults such as the sick, the elderly, and the mentally and physically disabled. Women also continue to undertake the domestic servicing of able-bodied men, as well as the majority of tasks associated with the domestic maintenance of families and family life.

The aim of this chapter is to consider these continuities and discontinuities in the position of women, focusing in particular on the social and psychological processes that constitute women as primary carers. Within sociology, the place of women as primary carers is conventionally understood as an offshoot of the sexual division of labor, which is seen as naturally allocating nurturance and childcare to women. The merits of this position, along with some closely aligned feminist conceptualizations of the sexual division of labor, will be considered in the latter part of this introductory section. The second section will consider some of the theoretical issues raised by conceptualizing the sexual division of labor as a social, and not biological, natural, or even patriarchal division.

## 1.1   The sexual division of labor

In the process of slow but profound social change traced by the emergence of the modern social formation out of the pre-industrial, agrarian society it replaced, the lines of demarcation between the work undertaken by women and the work undertaken by men were drawn and redrawn, and gradually emerged in a division of the social world into public and private spheres, with women's work being firmly positioned in the latter. One of the dominant explanations for the positioning of women in the private sphere of the family and men in the public sphere of work and polity was, and remains, that women are naturally suited to mothering and caring.

This idea of a natural sexual division of labor is a very powerful one, not least because we take the categories of women and men as self-evident. They are seen as biological categories, and biological difference is accepted as the guarantee of the naturalness of women and men. However, the idea that biology underwrites the unambiguous authenticity of womanliness and manliness is itself a historical one (and will be considered in more detail in chapter 11). Far from being an absolute, biological difference is represented differently in different cultures, and in different historical periods within a culture.

The idea that women's reproductive biology casts them naturally and exclusively as mothers whose "true sphere" is in a separate social domain is also historically specific. It might seem difficult to reconcile this idea of a natural sphere for women with "modernity," since the idea of raising children as a purely natural activity sits uneasily with the grander Enlightenment claims of reason, progress, and the scientific domination of nature. However, historically, this dissonance was muted by the division of social life into "public" and "private," with all things intuitive and natural falling to women in the private sphere. Once these divisions were culturally consolidated, the link between gender (femininity) and sex (female) came to appear as both indissoluble and natural, thereby ultimately guaranteeing the social order as itself natural. Consequently, accepting sexual difference as natural and self-evident has led to acceptance of the social forms that sexual divisions take as themselves having a certain kind of inevitability.

Although mainstream sociology has directed attention to the historical and social circumstances of the divisions between men's tasks and spheres and those of women, it is presumed, rather than argued, that there is a natural association between women and mothering and caring. Sociology has analyzed a wide range of institutional aspects of the family, including the organization of the household economy, the consumption, work, and leisure activities of women and men, intersexual relations and intrafamily dynamics. However, woman's place in the family – a factor which links these different facets of the family together – has been assumed to be "given" and not to require a sociological explanation. Thus Durkheim, for example, noted that while "man is almost entirely the product of society," woman is "to a far greater extent the product of nature" (Durkheim, 1952, p. 385). Such an ideology not only makes women's labor in the private sphere appear to be natural, it also strips it of its status as *labor*, because women's work in the family is separated from the public domain of waged work. Consequently, a polarized view of the division between women and men has emerged as a division between non-work and work, and between the natural and the social.

Against such naturalistic conceptions of the sexual division of labor, some feminists have argued that the division between the public and private domains is a gendered structure in which women and men come to be identified with different social places, different values, and different activities and characteristics. This occurs through political and economic practices, as well as through those cultural and ideological systems which represent the social as naturally divided. These divisions between the public and private domains, and the work of women and men, are specific to modernity and mark the boundaries between historically specific forms of masculinity and femininity, and between different kinds of individuality. The public and the private have come to represent different values – rationalization, contract, and egalitarianism as counterposed to emotionality, bonding, and difference; and different kinds of activities – productive work and rational calculation in the public sphere, and reproductive caring and intuitive empathy in the private sphere (Pateman, 1989).

However, this polarization of women's work in the home and men's in the workforce has obscured the more complex parameters of the modern socio-sexual or gendered division of labor, in which women combine *two* kinds of labor which broadly can be defined as productive and reproductive labor. Both women and men undertake wage-earning activities, in addition to which women perform unwaged reproductive labor in the care of the young and dependent adults. In other words, the division between the work of women and men is asymmetrical, not symmetrical, and involves women combining productive and reproductive labor across the public/private divide.

The engendered separation of home and work, and the asymmetrical nature of the sexual division of labor, have constituted the position of women as economically subordinate and culturally inferior to that of men. While traditional sociology was content to analyze this situation under the rubrics of the family, marriage, and the *sexual* division of labor, feminist sociology has problematized it in the conceptual language of power, the *gendered* division of labor and patriarchy.

However, many feminist analyses which use patriarchy to explain the position of women tend not to question the fact that women *are* mothers and carers, and concentrate instead on the circumstances in which women perform these activities. Caroline Ramazanoglu, for example, argues that:

> Motherhood and childcare remain contradictory experiences for the majority of the world's women – an unparalleled experience of creativity, an area of limited control over their bodies for most, and a direct connection to economic and political subordination. Pregnancy and breastfeeding provide some restrictions on economic activity, but these natural functions cannot account for the social mechanisms by which women are very generally restricted to their roles as mothers, or potential mothers, or as motherly people, in relation to dominant males.
> (Ramazanoglu, 1989)

Here a distinction is made between women's natural functions and the social mechanisms of male power. However, what is foregrounded in this account are the natural functions of mothering ("pregnancy and breastfeeding"); what is eclipsed are the social determinants of the labor of mothering, what is entailed in this activity, and how it is that women come to mother. In this version of patriarchy, women's social position is explained as the outcome of male power, so that, once again, social and historical processes are reduced to the effects of biological (i.e. natural) differences (female/male).

Sylvia Walby gives perhaps the most detailed social account of patriarchy as an integrated system which socially subordinates women. Walby identifies women's position within the family as a subjugated one involving the exploitation of women by men. She argues, however, that the family no longer represents the primary site of patriarchal domination, which has shifted to the public domains of the state and the economy. The patriarchal closure of the labor market to women's equal participation as wage laborers is identified by Walby as the most significant determinant of women's continuing oppression within the family, and one which entraps women within both public and private patriarchy. For Walby, patriarchy operates in different sites – the family, economy, state, sexuality, male violence, and cultural institutions which make up "the system of social structures and practices, in which men dominate, oppress and exploit women" (Walby, 1990, p. 20).

However, while Walby gives a detailed analysis of the social mechanisms which restrict women, ultimately she understands these mechanisms as the product of male power. There are two difficulties with this. The notion of male power is an essentialist one; that is, it is one which assumes that there is something in maleness as such which determines this position of power. What this essence is, is unexplained; nevertheless, patriarchy is characterized as a social system which is controlled by men. However, not all men identify with this power, nor are all men committed to ensuring that women's social subordination be maintained. The other difficulty is that "men" cannot be abstracted as a homogeneous social group because of the intersections of gender, race, class, and sexuality which shape their identities differently. Social systems *constitute* women and men as social subjects, as feminine and masculine; these systems are not the *product* of individuals or a particular group of individuals, i.e. men.

So the problem with the patriarchal explanation of women's position is that it forecloses the question of how relations between women and men are socially constituted. It does not fully address the issue of how human reproduction is socially organized and controlled; for example, how it affects and is affected by such factors as economic production. Women's fertility is constituted in part by forms of economic organization, as is the allocation of reproductive labor, and relations between women and men, women and women, and men and men. In other words human reproduction, intersexual relations, and reproductive labor as well as productive labor are all social activities determined by historically specific forms of social organization. If women's reproductive labor is thus constituted, then the parameters of the issue go far beyond that of intersexual relations and male power (patriarchy). Most obviously it means that the position of women within the family casts women in a relationship to those *social* mechanisms and processes which give rise to particular forms of the family and gendered labor divisions. This is not first and foremost a relationship between women and men, but between women and "society" or between women and the social, political, and cultural institutions and processes which produce gendered labor divisions and construct intersexual relations.

Walby's account of patriarchy clearly shows how in modern societies these institutions are dominated by men and how women have politically engaged with that institutional power. But I am suggesting that the sociological parameters of engendered relations of reproduction are more important than those given by theories of patriarchy. They provide a wider framework in which to think about both the complex processes involved and the question of social change.

In this chapter we will consider the argument that gendered divisions of labor are neither natural, nor patriarchal, but *social*. They are a necessary and inevitable feature of all societies in much the same way as are production, politics, and culture. By this I mean that all societies have to incorporate ways of caring for successive generations, and providing for vulnerable adults and children. Although these activities are qualitatively different from those involving material survival, they are no less necessary. Gendered labor divisions represent the way in which mothering and caring are allocated (historically but not inevitably) to women, and the way in which women combine this with economic activity. Relations of reproduction are very wide-ranging. They encompass relations between women and men, between wealth production and distribution, between cultural values and sexual identities, between the regulation of sexuality and generational renewal, between political power and individual rights, between parents and children, home and work, and even between life and death – things which make up much of the substance of social existence. These relations are not separate, as the ideology of the public/private division would have it. Rather, they are relations to which production and politics are integral. Nor are they subordinate; for how could it be that "caring" is less important than "work"? From this viewpoint, then, the social becomes integrated and continuous, and women belong as fully and centrally to it as men. In considering the modes of organization and changes that have occurred in gendered divisions of labor, it will become even clearer just how *socially determined* and *integrated* these relations are, and therefore how much more encompassing our concept of "society" must be.

# 2   Women and the Family: Some Theoretical Issues

This section will consider several related theoretical issues which throw light on and help to explain both the changing patterns and the persistence of the link between women, femininity, and the family. First, we will attempt to explain the changes in state/family relations and in the shifting balance between reproductive labor and waged productive activity. Secondly, we will examine the different ways in which the link between women, the construction of femininity, and the domestic sphere has been conceptualized. In discussing the theoretical problems raised by these issues the central claim of this chapter – that gendered labor divisions are produced through the social organization of reproduction – will be developed further.

## 2.1 The changing state/family relation

Uniquely of all the modern state forms, the welfare state concerns itself with the private realm of domesticity. Social policy controls the level and type of the redistribution of resources to families through the provision of support services in health care, child welfare services, social security benefits, and public housing. Taxation allows for the reallocation of resources across the competing sectors of welfare, industry, and defense, and provides a mechanism for differentially subsidizing women's and men's labor. Labor legislation as well as equal opportunities and community programs mediate the relationship between women's waged and unwaged labor. State educational provision influences the balance between women's reproductive and productive labor. Family law defines and enforces legal obligations within the family, and the rights of individual family members. In all these areas gender divisions of labor are both assumed by the state and transformed according to the particular conception of the family sustained by the policies of the respective state agencies.

Yet notwithstanding these interventions of the state (which lies at the heart of the *public* sphere) the domestic domain retains its status as the *private* sphere of social existence. What are the consequences of the family's ambiguous position in this public/private division? How, theoretically, can we explain it?

In her critical overview of the different theoretical positions on the family/state relationship, Faith Robertson Elliot rejects the idea that the family is private and separate from the state. On the other hand, she rejects the suggestion that it is politically determined by either capitalist or patriarchal interests exercised through state power. Advocates of the family as a discrete and naturally distinctive institution (the first position) completely under-estimate the role and significance of political intervention in shaping familial relations. Conversely, those theorists who emphasize the importance of state policies in structuring the family in the interests of either capitalism or patriarchy (the second position) fail to account for the shifting legal and political balances between women and men within families, and between families and state regulation and support of those families. Even though state intervention into the family has increased, ultimately such intervention is limited in the degree to which it can influence people's behavior. Institutions other than the state have a role to play in shaping desires and aspirations. State policies are mediated by other factors, such as class, ethnicity, and religion. Women are not helpless victims but respond to, struggle against, and deflect the strategies of the state.

Against the idea that the private family is determined by a natural sexual division of labor, or produced by the public power of capitalism or patriarchy which construct an ideological divide between the public and private realms, Elliot considers less deterministic accounts of the family/state relationship. She concludes that a less monolithic conception of the state is preferable. The state is a complex and diverse institution, not a single instrument. It is composed of different agencies with their own histories and internal power relations. So the state influences which shape the domestic sphere are complex. Its multi-dimensional political processes are formed through the attempts of various competing interest groups, all seeking to influence the public contours of domestic life. Thus, state policies on the family cannot be seen as monolithic precisely because they are mediated by the concerns and responses of different groups, including feminist groups.

This pluralist-feminist approach to the family/state relationship acknowledges that the differing interest groups competing to influence state policy are not equally powerful, and that the state is in no way a "neutral arbiter" between them. The state arbitrates according to strategic interests. But this is not a form of state power which can be exercised unilaterally, either by a single group or without consideration of the balance of forces that make up the political process. The question of the family and the state is not, therefore, a question of centralized control but of negotiated and shifting relations of power; and within this process feminism has a long history of intervention in the political construction of women's position within the family, as well as, of course, within the public domain.

The questions this leaves unanswered are: What has necessitated the relationship between the welfare state and the family in the first place? What is the nature of the state's "domestic" policies? Why should the state have strategic interests in family life? Clearly all states are concerned with the relationship between the population and the economic resource base, both in terms of whether the resource base is large enough to support the population, and in terms of whether demographic trends meet the requirements of the economy. However, far from being simple and monolithic, these politically mediated interests of the state are complex and contradictory. In China, for example, where it is feared that population growth will exceed, in the very immediate future, the economic capacity of the country to sustain it, the state has attempted to implement – largely unsuccessfully – a policy of one child per family. This population policy reflects the impact on family life of strategic political decisions about the pace of China's economic expansion. It is these decisions which affect the resource base and in turn lead to birth control policies (Hillier, 1988). In the Soviet Union, by contrast, where the concern was with a contracting (Russian) population, Russian women were awarded the Order of Lenin if they had six children (Molyneux, 1985). Here, population was privileged over production. In the Eastern Bloc countries during the post-war period of rapid industrialization, women's labor, both as full-time workers and as mothers, was required; a situation which produced a level of public childcare provision necessary to "free" women as workers equal to men. However, when these demands on women's labor produced a radical drop in the birth rate, some socialist states withdrew women's legal right to abortion (Scott, 1974). In each of these instances political decisions attempted to affect the balance between women's productive and reproductive labor but the motivations for these interventions were different. Moreover, as Elliot points out, these strategic interventions have had limited success, not least because countervailing forces sometimes deflect or reverse them.

There is, however, another reason for the state's strategic interest in the private sphere. This arises out of the separation of reproductive labor from production and the attendant economic vulnerability of those caring for the young and the old. For example, the liberalization of divorce law has created additional pressure on governments in all advanced industrial societies to provide benefits adequate to support single parents. Other kinds of interventions have been made in this area. For example, in a recent ruling in the UK, the court decided that genetic fingerprinting can be used to establish paternity for the purposes of the mother gaining some financial support for the upbringing of the child. Clearly, then, the state has very different ways, in different periods, of ensuring the economic viability of families and the caring role of women in the family.

State policies can also have contradictory effects for women. The political economy of the gendered division of labor necessitates that women be supported in some way if they are to sustain the social requirements of mothering and caring. The family paycheck was one solution. Its failure is measured by women's growing economic activity. Public provision in the form of welfare is another means of support which is also inadequate – a fact confirmed by the historically consistent, and currently increasing, levels of poverty sustained by women. This "feminization of poverty" reflects the contradictory relation between women as carers and workers, and the welfare state. The state wants both to support women as carers and to keep public expenditure low. Social policy would be a far greater proportion of public expenditure if women's unpaid labor were to be adequately recompensed from the public purse. In this sense the position of women as reproductive laborers lies at the heart of the structurally and politically contested domain of the distribution of social wealth.

## 2.2  Conceptualizing reproductive labor

How then should we conceptualize the unpaid labor of women caring for the young as well as vulnerable adults in the private domestic sphere? The term "reproductive labor" which I have used in this chapter was chosen because it indicates a continuum between women's paid and unpaid work. This continuum is disrupted by the structural and ideological division between the public and the private but, notwithstanding this, reproductive labor represents socially necessary labor which constitutes an *integral* part of the social division of labor, and gives rise to a form of redistribution outside the wage form.

The private domestic sphere tends to be thought of as the domain of personal relations, those affective ties that bind us to particular people in a unique way. It is this area of emotionality and love, of caring and nurturance, which is seen as both quintessential to family life and beyond the imperatives of rational social organization. Emotional and sexual relations within private life are experienced as not dictated by public policy or economic necessity, as embracing personal desires and needs which are neither public nor necessarily rational. It is the private satisfaction of these needs and desires which shapes our domestic relations.

Affective relations, however, are not free-floating. Even when confined to the private sphere, they are grounded in the social conventions and practices of caring for people and being cared for which prevail in a particular culture. As Barrett and McIntosh (1982) have noted in their critique of the claim that the domestic sphere is a "haven in a heartless world," the haven, for women, is actually a place of *work*. This is not to deny its significance in the emotional lives of women as well as children and men. The family is privileged over all other institutions, by both men and women, as the place where emotional and sexual needs can be expressed and met. However, to conceptualize the family as an area of women's work raises questions about its "private" character and the extent to which it is a separate, discrete domain, since women's work spans the family and the workplace. If we conceptualize women's caring role as *labor*, then its relationship to other kinds of work quickly becomes apparent. But certain aspects of reproductive labor have resisted incorporation into the arena of public work and the processes of economic rationalization. Reproductive labor has never been fully drawn into the process of refinement and the specialization of tasks that has transformed the sphere of public production. What is it about the primary labor process of "people production" (Murgatroyd, 1985) that leads inevitably to locating it in the domestic sphere? What prevents us from defining reproductive labor as a non-gendered labor process like any other?

There are two aspects of domestic life that largely continue to resist incorporation into the rationalistic world of calculation and contract. These are (a) childcare and (b) emotionally intimate personal and sexual relations between adults. Of course, these relationships are not exclusive to the domestic sphere. Childcare is sometimes organized as a public service. Equally, the sex industry is an economic complex which trades internationally in emotions and desires as well as people, bodies, and services. What is distinctive about domestic relations is that they privilege the individual, emotionally and psychologically, in terms of the uniqueness of her/his emotional needs. In terms of the care of children, what is distinctive is the process of socially integrating the developing person through affective care, which actually brings a unique self into being. In terms of personal adult relationships, it is the sexual, emotional, and psychic needs of the individual which are satisfied in intimate interpersonal relationships. Thus, what we call reproductive labor – the "work" of producing and caring for these subjective personal needs – is socially necessary labor, in the sense that it is necessary and inevitable and has to be done in every society irrespective of who takes responsibility for it. However, because it is necessarily interpersonal it is therefore outside the scope of collective labor practices, and tends to be separated off into a distinct sphere of social activity – the private. The private sphere, then, is the sphere of the individual subject, grounded in and defined by her/his own personal subjective needs, desires, and history. What remains to be explained is how and why this domain of the private or domestic world came to be exclusively associated with the labor of women.

## 2.3 The logic of the private sphere

The linkage between women and the private sphere has been explored by Anna Yeatman. She suggests that the way sociological theory has analyzed the individual as socially constructed from within society is limited by the conventional view of socialization advanced by the leading American sociological theorist of the 1940s and 1950s, Talcott Parsons.

Yeatman begins by making two sets of propositions in her argument. The first is that the project within sociology to understand the individual as *socially* constituted is potentially one which contains the promise of an adequate sociological account of the domestic sphere. The second, however, is that in order to extend and develop this theoretical ground and deliver this promise, sociological explanation has largely proceeded as if gender divisions play no part in this process. What she is suggesting is that, unless we analytically separate the elements involved in the constitution of the individual subject – that is, the process of the personality development of the individual subject through the taking on of cultural values – from the way this process is currently divided between men and women, then we risk reducing these elements to a mere description of what women and men do within the family and interpersonal relations. Such a description fits with the prevailing relations in the domestic sphere. But it does not, Yeatman argues, allow the analysis to go beyond this division to consider *the necessity of the domestic sphere irrespective of the particular gender relations which currently sustain it.* The assumption that the domestic sphere and gender divisions are one and the same thing displaces the question of whether domestic tasks can be shared in ways which are not gender-defined as they are now. Ignoring this possibility is, in effect, to make the current gender division of labor in the family a natural and inevitable one.

Yeatman has several criticisms of the Parsonian account of socialization within the family. First, Parsons gives a behaviorist account of the mother's role in primary childcare. He does not analyze that role either socially or in terms of its unconscious motivations (see section 2.4 below). Secondly, Parsons argues that women as wives and mothers provide the necessary emotional work to satisfy the needs of men and children. This undermines the more general argument that, since the individuated personality must be able to gain satisfaction of its emotional needs, there is no necessity, as Parsons would have it, for one type of person (women) always to provide for the needs of other types of person (children and men). Finally, Parsons' account of domestic relations fails to develop the idea that the private sphere is necessary to the structure of *all* modern societies because private interpersonal relations are an inevitable part of the formation of the socialized individual subject whatever her/his gender. Parsons collapses this independent necessity of the private sphere into a theory of the *normative* family which in turn rests on the assumption that it is only women who can naturally mother.

If we accept Yeatman's argument that the domestic sphere is a necessary dimension of modern social life but that the nuclear family is only one of the many historic family forms in which its tasks have been performed, it follows that different kinds of relationships could potentially exist within the domestic sphere. The nuclear heterosexual family is currently the preferred form in the domestic sphere but it is not the only one and is certainly not *intrinsic* to it. What is intrinsic, or necessary, to the private sphere is simply that it provides support for these particularistic needs and relationships. How this is organized within different family and domestic arrangements varies widely from one culture to another and from one historical period to another. Indeed, the domestic sphere is increasingly diversified by different types of relationships. Yeatman's argument therefore tallies with Barrett and McIntosh's analysis of what they call "the anti-social family," in which they argue that the normative nuclear family seriously limits the kinds of intimate interpersonal relationship which are now potentially possible (Barrett and McIntosh, 1982).

## 2.4 Women's mothering

If the exclusive feminization of the role of women in mothering is central to the current dominant form of the nuclear family, but is neither necessary nor intrinsic to the process of individuation and socialization as such, then it still remains a problem to try to explain the position of women as mothers within the domestic sphere. Why does the domestic remain so fixedly "gendered"? One possible answer to this question is that there is, in addition to the social division of labor which organizes this sphere, an *unconscious logic* to women's identification with motherhood. In other words the identification of women with the domestic and familial may have both social and psychological foundations.

This is an argument put forward by Juliet Mitchell, the feminist theorist and psychoanalyst, who mobilizes psychoanalytic theory to explain the tenacity of gender identity and women's desire to mother. Mitchell's account of psychoanalytic theory is influenced by the work of the French psychoanalyst Jacques Lacan (1901–81), who emphasized the significance of language and the symbolic realm in bringing the individuated subject into being. According to Lacan, the child only gradually learns to live in a world that is differentiated. For Lacan, as for Freud, this takes place at the psychic level. It is related to those primary unconscious processes through which the infant comes to recognize and accept its separateness from others, enters the realm of language, and resolves its intense early relationships to its parental figures. Lacan argues that the entry of the subject into language (which is a system of differences) is closely related to, occurs at the same time in early childhood as, and follows the same pathways as, the entry of the individual subject into the system of *sexual* difference (masculine/feminine). For our purposes, what is interesting about Mitchell's account of the subject is the way in which she proposes that one of the consequences of the way that girls enter into the language and sexual systems of difference is an unconscious imperative which delivers women as mothers into, so to speak, the bosom of the family.

Before discussing Mitchell's argument further, it might be helpful to take you briefly through the main relevant points of psychoanalysis on which her exposition depends. Freud argued that infantile sexuality was made up of several sources of pleasure and was both active and passive. In the beginning, the child occupies a sexually undifferentiated world. It is only after a long, complex, and incomplete process that it learns to identify itself as "male" or "female." Children of both sexes take the mother as their primary love object because it is she who provides most satisfaction, and their pleasure in the early stages of life is dependent on her presence. In the beginning the child does not differentiate itself from the mother, and only comes to do so through recognizing her absences (in the same way as, in language, we know what "dark" is by what it isn't – it is the absence of "light"). Having acknowledged both its dependence on the mother and her independence, the child wants to possess the mother, to retain her presence, and, therefore, its own pleasure. But this is a contradictory desire since the child also desires its own independence, and resents the power that the mother represents.

In the process of psychophysical development the child comes to recognize that one way of gaining the presence of the mother is to acquiesce to her desires. If only it can become what the mother wants, the child will be guaranteed her continued affections. Freud argued that this dovetails with the child's own narcissistic curiosity about where babies come from since this is one of the "secrets" which the mother clearly possesses. Establishing that babies come from people, the child then wants to give the mother a baby, or to have the mother's baby. In the sexually undifferentiated world of the child, this is assumed to be a possibility by *both* little boys and little girls. The child takes this to be the ultimate gift it can give to or receive from the mother; that it will satisfy the mother's own desire and, therefore, sustain the child's wish for a possessive and exclusive relationship to the mother. Freud called this fantasy the "Oedipus complex," after the Greek myth of Oedipus, the hero who, by mistake, killed his father and married his mother. As Freud saw it, the child cannot take up a sexual identity until this complex relationship to the parental figures – the Oedipus complex – has been resolved.

Two things interrupt this unconscious infantile project. The child learns that only boys can give the mother a baby and that the father has greater powers to do this. He, therefore, has more privileged claims to the mother than the child. This recognition of the significance of sexual difference and the power of the father forces children to repress an aspect of their infantile sexuality. However, this repression is itself sexually differentiated. Boys have to surrender both their desire to have a baby and their expectation of claiming exclusive rights to the mother. Unable to dislodge the father, boys must renounce their Oedipal fantasy and instead become like their fathers. (In fact, the boy's renunciation of the Oedipal fantasy is often only a temporary surrendering which can be negated at a later stage in men's adult relationships with women, who symbolically represent the possibility of repossessing the mother of their unconscious desire.) For the little girl, on the other hand, the recognition that sexual relationships with women cannot produce that which women most desire, that is a baby, means that her only choice is to become like the mother. In this she transfers her affections to the father as the person who can give her a baby. These, according to Freud, are the unconscious origins of sexual difference.

The fact that the little girl has to surrender the mother as her primary love object means that her sense of self as powerful (or as Freud calls it, "phallic") is massively undermined. The little girl is unable to do that which she originally most desires. So she becomes contemptuous of her own desires, and instead tries to satisfy the desires of her father. In this way, her sense of autonomy is radically diminished, in that her desires become predicated on *meeting the expectations of someone other than herself.* Juliet Mitchell sees this predicament as generating what she calls "the inferiorized psychology of women."

In acquiescing to the patriarchal law of the power of the father, women have to deny the universal unconscious desire for the primary love of the mother. This means that women are forever trapped within the family, for it is only there that their qualified unconscious desire, that is the desire for a child, can find expression. In short, Mitchell is suggesting that powerful unconscious motivations mean that both women and men will continue to hold women in disregard and that women will always be drawn to the family and motherhood. At the same time, however, women as mothers are also immensely powerful figures.

It also follows from Mitchell's argument that sexuality is necessarily structured heterosexually, through the logic of reproductive sexual difference. At the level of the unconscious this logic works itself out in symbolic terms. This "desire for the mother" and the "recognition" of the symbolic power of the father are psychic processes which mean that both the boy and the girl have in different ways to give up the mother as primary love object. Unless they do so, they cannot leave the imaginary world of fantasy and accept their place in the social world of women and men, that is of *sexually differentiated people.* The pre-Oedipal child thinks it can be and do everything. It is omnipotent. But it learns that we only become someone by not being everyone. Femininity entails that women have to surrender this fantasy of infantile omnipotence. However, masculinity allows men to proceed as if that fantasy is still a possibility. When they grow up they will, symbolically, be able to assume the position of the powerful patriarchal "father." Hence, on one side of the equation we have the inferiorized psychology of women, and on the other, the over-valorized psychology of men. Or, as Mitchell puts it, we have women defined by nature and nurturance, and men by class and history. This is what Mitchell means by the "logic of sexual difference."

Since writing *Psychoanalysis and Feminism* (1974), Mitchell has qualified some of its arguments and rejected others. However, her account of the development of masculinity and femininity as outlined above remains largely intact. Mitchell is proposing a theory of psychosexual development to account for the way in which we come to accept our identities as heterosexual masculine and feminine subjects. In accepting this sexually differentiated structure the child is implicated in *both* a set of cultural, social meanings and in a set of unconscious motivations. Thereafter, gender differences are determined at both the cultural and psychic levels. You will recall, however, that these sexually differentiated unconscious structures emerge out of what Mitchell, following Freud, posited as a non-differentiated infantile sexuality. For both sexes therefore the possibility exists for resolving the Oedipus complex homosexually rather than heterosexually. Women could retain the mother as a love object and refuse to play the role accorded to them in the logic of reproductive sexuality. By implication then they would not become mothers, although, of course, their heterosexual desire would still remain part of their unconscious. This would be a "homosexual" rather than a "heterosexual" resolution to the Oedipus complex.

Mitchell gives no satisfactory account of why the heterosexual resolution of the Oedipus complex is the more commonplace one in our culture. She refers to motherhood as the most socially acceptable way for women to give expression to unconscious desire. But this is a sociological argument, not a psychoanalytic one. In Freud's account, heterosexuality is privileged over homosexuality because it encompasses more of the structure of desire. For women, to have a child satisfies the desire to be powerful (phallic) and whole, as well as to be like the mother. However, it could also be argued that women's homosexuality expresses a more "pure" form of phallic desire – not just to be like but actually to possess the mother/woman. This does not satisfy the desire for a child; on the other hand, heterosexuality does not fully satisfy this homosexual desire to possess "the mother." For Freud there is another factor which comes into play. This is that sexuality is necessarily structured and subsumed by the logic of biological reproduction. In other words, in the end, Freud's argument resolves itself heterosexually because of the facts of biological reproduction and the anatomical differences between men and women with which even unconscious fantasies must come to terms. This is not an argument that sits well in Mitchell's account, however, not least because, once we accept that women's position is defined by the logic of reproduction, there is little else to be said about it. However, what Mitchell is concerned with is how we enter the realm of the social as masculine and feminine subjects, the significance of the realms of the symbolic and cultural in this process of sexual differentiation, and the unconscious processes involved in these, rather than with purely anatomical or biological differences.

Another difficulty with Freud's account of normative heterosexuality is that his psychoanalytic theory lays out the paths of psychosexual development but cannot say in advance which of these paths any particular individual will take. As Mitchell points out, Freud establishes the complex history of the unconscious by reading the history of the individual backwards. He starts with the adult patient and reconstructs the "story" of how the patient's Oedipus complex was resolved. It was only by retracing the stories of his patients that Freud was able to understand retrospectively how their neuroses developed, and how and why they made the choices they did. However, if we can only "know" how the Oedipal drama is resolved retrospectively, then psychoanalytic theory cannot be used as a theory of *normative* femininity and masculinity (i.e. it cannot predict in advance what will be the normal paths). If there is no one, necessary, predetermined, and prescribed resolution, then more than one way of resolving the Oedipal dilemma must be "normal." We cannot account for this in advance. Clearly other factors must come into play to mobilize an individual's choice of normative heterosexuality and its resolution in the family.

Psychoanalysis tells the story of the differentiated personality as, within the limits of certain possibilities, a unique story. It is the story of how the individual subject enters culture and "becomes" social, and, for modern industrial societies, this marks out as distinctive the context of the domestic sphere of private relations in which this "becoming social" occurs. I have argued, however, that the gender division of labor cannot be exclusively derived from the psychoanalytic account of the process of social individuation. Although psychoanalytic theory can provide a *particularistic* explanation which is true for individual cases as to why some women want to mother, it cannot account for the *general* social fact of women's mothering. Clearly, the social construction of the gender division of labor is determined by social processes over and above those of the unconscious.

Masculinity and femininity exist not only as unconscious structures but also as cultural conventions which provide the socio-historical content and meanings of sexual identity. Moreover, unconscious desire is anarchic and diverse. It is not inevitably tied to the logic of reproduction and cannot easily be made to fit with, or give rise to, a system of gender relations organized around reproductive sexuality. The sexuality which Freud discovered in the unconscious is not necessarily geared to producing the neat package of gender differences that societies might require. How then do we explain the dominant resolution of sexuality in the normative familial relations typical of modern societies? We shall consider this question in the next part of this chapter.

## 2.5 The social construction of femininity

One school of thought which has critically measured itself against the version of psychoanalytic theory outlined above is the post-structuralist tradition (so called because it was influenced by structuralism but abandoned some of its rigidities as a methodology). This approach has stressed that meanings are *always* socially produced and cannot be understood outside this process, and neither can they be fixed or frozen, even by the language of the unconscious. In contrast with the psychoanalytic story, this post-structuralist position suggests that a symbol, or referent, cannot structure or organize the unconscious because meaning is not intrinsic to the sign. The meaning of any sign is given by its relationship to other signs and the systems of difference which articulate it. In themselves, "things" have no meaning because meaning is only produced *through* language. (You may remember the discussion of this theory of language and meaning from chapters 5 and 6.) This standpoint therefore rejects the idea of sexual identity and desire being fixed and determined by the unconscious. Instead it stresses how cultural meanings change, shaping psychic life through the patterning and prescribing of particular structures of desire at different times and in different cultures. (This approach is discussed more fully with respect to sexuality in chapter 11.)

One benefit of this perspective is that it emphasizes cultural values, how these may change, and their psychological significance in the formation of the individual subject. Its stress on social processes, rather than psychic determinants, alerts us to changes in the definitions and meanings of femininity and masculinity, arguing that it is these, rather than unconscious identifications and their "resolution," which structure sexual identities and relations.

The position taken by Rosalind Coward is radically divergent from that of Mitchell. Mitchell argued that femininity and masculinity arise out of the resolution of the child's infantile relation to its parents. For her, there is a basic unconscious structure to femininity which is the desire for a child/phallus and this "logic" determines women's dependent position in the family. However, Mitchell's framework tells us little of the changing patterns of gender relations and the shifts in meaning that occur in different periods and societies in definitions of masculinity and femininity and indeed of motherhood. These indices of historical change become negated, in Mitchell's account, by the overarching, predetermined power of the unconscious. In other words the domain of the social becomes subsumed by the ahistorical workings of the unconscious.

Coward, by contrast, is concerned to chart the way in which discourses and representations orchestrate desire not as a unitary structure but as a spectrum of pleasures. She rejects the idea that desire is psychically determined in the sense that it is possible to read off social relations directly from unconscious structures. Her argument is that desire is organized by cultural meanings which have the power to shape our deepest and innermost sense of selfhood. What it means to be a woman or man, a father or mother is, for her, socially produced and these changing cultural meanings alter the structures of desire. Coward also maintains that the discourses of femininity do not simply invoke motherhood as the exclusive source of identity and pleasure for women. Rather, a range of activities centering on, for example, the body, the home, or food, are held up as offering women feminine gratification. Social relations are organized around specifying what kinds of activities can give us pleasure and those relations involve us at the deepest level of our subjectivity.

This approach allows us to see how the cultural meanings which structure desire can anchor particular forms of social relationship. For example, our desire to find solace, love, and recognition within the confines of the family, structures an emotional commitment to ideas of the private, and to a narrow set of familial relations which in turn promise to meet some of the most fundamental needs surrounding our individuality. However, although this social constructionist perspective allows us to recognize the importance of sexuality in the organization of familial (and other) relations, it does have some weaknesses. It tends to assume that the structuring of desire is *exclusively* a social process. In this respect, the obverse of Mitchell's position prevails in Coward's version. Sexuality now comes to be seen, in Coward's account, as outside any form of psychic determination. But desire is not just a mechanism of social control. It is more complex than this. Our desires are invested with considerable power for which we cannot always rationally account. People also have a habit of resisting dominant cultural values, of parodying them, refusing them, or simply carrying on in spite of them; cultural meanings do not have any guaranteed effect on our identities. In short, Coward's constructionist framework begs the question of why it is *sexual difference*, and not some other factor, which is the main vehicle of cultural patterns of desire.

The cultural construction of gender relations, outlined by Coward, invokes and consolidates a particular structuring of female desire. But it fails to account for the psychic mechanisms which predispose women to *identify* with the cultural representations of maternal desire. It seems, therefore, that *both* the unconscious formations of sexuality, and the social structuring of desire, are necessary for an analysis of women's mothering. In short, we need both Mitchell and Coward. The affective and physical labor of mothering is socially organized; but the effectiveness of women as mothers relies on the unconscious resonance of maternal desire.

## 3 Conclusion

At the heart of the construction of familial relations, and our private existence as social individuals, are ideas about women's *natural* identity as mothers. However, from our study of the changing ways in which families and the domestic sphere are organized, we can see that the domestic sphere, and the gender division of labor, are increasingly becoming spheres of political and social contestation in which ideas about "the natural" and "the family" are increasingly being questioned.

With the changing status of marriage, the state has come to accept the need to support lone mothers with children and this, in conjunction with the increasing economic demand for women's labor, has meant that women are now less economically dependent on the family and on men, but more dependent on the state. However, this shift in the mode of economic support of reproductive labor has made the question of resource allocation a *public* issue, no longer simply a private one, requiring collective social recognition of changing relations in the domestic sphere. Women's growing ability to control their own fertility also means that motherhood can now be a choice exercised by women, and therefore that women have marginally greater control over the way in which they combine their labor as mothers and workers, and define their identity as women.

Increasingly, then, women's identities are formed outside the confines of marriage and motherhood. Neither marriage nor cohabitation are any longer cultural, or economic, prerequisites for women to have children. Women have acquired a political voice which challenges, among other things, the politics of redistribution and resource allocation. Indeed, the family and the sexual division of labor can no longer easily be explained as purely natural institutions. In many respects sociological analysis of these processes lags behind these changes because of the way in which the position of women in the domestic sphere has been conceptualized as a fact of nature and thus marginalized within much of sociology.

In spite of these changes women continue to mother. In this chapter, I have argued that to understand this process fully, it is necessary to include an analysis of *both* the unconscious structure of femininity and the relation of this to the social definitions and cultural representations of motherhood and domesticity.

The central argument of this chapter has been that modernity has located relations of human reproduction at the heart of the *social*, but continues to describe them in the *language* of the *natural*. The complex interplay of political, economic, and cultural forces which actually sustain gendered divisions of labor is, however, increasingly entering sociological discussion as a result of feminist theorizing. Once ideas about "the natural" are surrendered in analyzing the position of women within the family, the concepts of social structure and social process are expanded. Questions are then raised – both politically and theoretically – about sexuality, intersexual relations, mothering, childhood, old age, wealth redistribution, individual freedom, and social control. These *social* questions are becoming a real testing ground of modernity and of its original promise of liberty and equality for all – women as well as men.

# References

Barrett, M. and McIntosh, M. (1982) *The Anti-Social Family*, London, Verso.

Coward, R. (1985) "Female desire and sexual identity," in Diaz-Diocaretz, M. and Zavala, I. (eds) *Women, Feminist Identity and Society in the 1980s*, Amsterdam and Philadelphia, J. Benjamins.

Durkheim, E. (1952) *Suicide*, London, Routledge and Kegan Paul.

Elliot, F.R. (1989) "The family: private arena or adjunct of the state?," *Journal of Law and Society*, vol. 16, no. 4, pp. 443–63.

Finch, J. (1989) *Family Obligation and Social Change*, Cambridge, England, Polity Press.

Henwood, M., Rimmer, L., and Wicks, M. (1987) *Inside the Family: Changing Roles of Women and Men*, London, Family Policy Study Centre.

Hillier, J. (1988) "Women and population control in China: issues of sexuality power and control," *Feminist Review*, no. 29.

Kiernan, K. and Wicks, M. (1990) *Family Change and Future Policy*, London, Family Policy Study Centre.

Lister, R. (1984) "There is an alternative," in Walker, A. and Walker, C. (eds) *The Growing Divide*, London, CPAG.

Mitchell, J. (1974) *Psychoanalysis and Feminism*, Harmondsworth, England, Penguin.

Molyneux, M. (1985) "Family reform in socialist states: the hidden agenda," *Feminist Review*, no. 21.

Mount, F. (1982) *The Subversive Family: An Alternative History of Love and Marriage*, London, Jonathan Cape.

Murgatroyd, L. (1985) "The production of people and domestic labour revisited" in Close, P. and Collins, R. (eds) *Family and Economy in Modern Society*, London, Macmillan.

Pateman, C. (1989) *The Disorder of Women*, Cambridge, England, Polity Press.

Ramazanoglu, C. (1989) *Feminism and the Contradictions of Oppression*, London, Routledge.

Riley, D. (1983) *War in the Nursery: Theories of the Child and Mother*, London, Virago.

Scott, H. (1974) *Does Socialism Liberate Women?*, Boston, Beacon Press.

Titmuss, R. (1963) *Essays on the Welfare State*, London, Allen & Unwin.

Walby, S. (1990) *Theorizing Patriarchy*, Oxford, Basil Blackwell.

Wilson, E. (1977) *Women and the Welfare State*, London, Tavistock Women's Studies.

Yeatman, A. (1986) "Women, domestic life and sociology," in Gross, E. and Pateman, C. (eds) *Feminist Challenges: Social and Political Theory*, Sydney, Allen & Unwin.

# 11 The Body and Sexuality

Jeffrey Weeks

## Contents

| | | |
|---|---|---|
| 1 | What do we Mean when we Talk about the Body and Sexuality? | 364 |
| 1.1 | Introduction | 364 |
| 1.2 | The subject of sex | 365 |
| 1.3 | Historicizing the body | 368 |
| 2 | Sexuality and Sexual Norms | 372 |
| 2.1 | Establishing "the normal" and "the abnormal" | 372 |
| 2.2 | The social dimensions of sexuality | 374 |
| 3 | Sexuality and Power | 375 |
| 3.1 | Class and sexuality | 375 |
| 3.2 | Gender and sexuality | 376 |
| 3.3 | Race and sexuality | 378 |
| 4 | Sexual Identities | 380 |
| 4.1 | The institutionalization of heterosexuality | 380 |
| 4.2 | Inventing homosexuality | 382 |
| 4.3 | Rethinking sexual identities | 385 |
| 5 | Sexuality and Politics | 388 |
| 5.1 | Current debates | 388 |
| 5.2 | The future of sexuality | 390 |
| | References | 392 |

# 1   What do we Mean when we Talk about the Body and Sexuality?

## 1.1   Introduction

Let's start with an image that has haunted our imaginations in the past decade: the sunken eyes, the emaciated bodies, the apparently doomed courage of people with AIDS.

In a period which as never before saw the celebration of healthy, perfectly-tuned bodies (thousands of people running the Boston Marathon provides an apt memorial of this new fetish for fitness), a new syndrome emerged which ravaged the body. It was intimately connected with sex – with acts through which the HIV virus could be transmitted. Many people, not least in the tabloid press, presented AIDS as a necessary effect of sexual excess, as if the limits of the body have been tested, and found wanting by "sexual perversity." This, according to the more brazen propagandists, was nature's revenge on those who transgressed its boundaries.

The assumption seemed to be that the body expresses a fundamental truth about sexuality. But what can this truth be? We now know that the HIV virus, which causes the breakdown of the body's immunities and so in turn gives rise to AIDS, is not selective in its impact. It affects heterosexuals and homosexuals, women and men, young and old. Yet at the same time it does not affect everyone in these categories, or even necessarily the partners of people infected with HIV. Who gets HIV is partly a matter of chance, even for those who engage in what we now call "high-risk activities."

Of course, any life-threatening illness should arouse anxiety, and I am not seeking in any way to minimize the terrible effects of the syndrome. But AIDS has become more than a set of diseases: it has become a potent metaphor for our sexual culture. The response to it has been seen as a sign of our growing confusion and anxieties about our bodies and their sexual activities (Sontag, 1989). It has been presented as a dire warning concerning the effects of sexual change. In the process the experiences of people living with HIV and AIDS, stories of courage and resilience in the face of illness, have often been ignored.

What is the relationship between the body as a collection of organs, feelings, needs, impulses, biological possibilities, and limits, on the one hand, and our sexual desires, behaviors, and identities, on the other? What is it about these topics that make them so culturally significant and morally and politically fraught? These, and others like them, have become key questions in recent sociological and historical debates. In attempting to respond to them I will argue that though the biological body is the site for, and sets the limits on, what is sexually possible, sexuality is more than simply about the body. In fact, with Carole Vance (1984) I am going to suggest that the most important organ in humans is that between the ears. Sexuality is as much about our beliefs, ideologies, and imaginations as it is about the physical body.

This chapter is concerned, then, with the ways in which bodies and sexuality have been endowed with importance and rich meanings in modern societies. The remainder of this section, starting with a closer look at the literature on sexuality, will explore the significance of seeing sexuality as a social and historical phenomenon. It will argue that bodies have no intrinsic meaning, and that the best way of understanding sexuality is as a "historical construct."

Section 2 will then go on to discuss the ways in which the dominant definitions of sexuality have emerged in modernity. Section 3 will be concerned with how power relations, particularly with regard to gender, class, and race (that is, socially differentiated bodies), become meaningful in defining sexual behavior. Section 4 will be primarily concerned with the problem of defining sexualized identities, especially as they have been made and remade over the past 100 years or so, in an effort to understand the forces at work in shaping sexuality. It will explore the institutionalization of heterosexuality and the "invention" of homosexuality, and then look at ways of rethinking sexual identity.

Finally, section 5 will look in more detail at the social regulation of bodies and sexuality, concentrating on the implications of the public/private division – a division we take for granted as natural, but which also has a history; in fact, many histories. The chapter will conclude by posing the question: What is the future of sexuality and the body? – a vital issue in the wake of the crisis generated by HIV and AIDS.

## 1.2   The subject of sex

Although there is a strong case for arguing that issues relating to bodies and sexual behavior have been at the heart of western preoccupations for a very long time, until the nineteenth century they were largely the concern of religion and moral philosophy. Since then they have largely been the concern of specialists, whether in medicine, the professions, or among moral reformers. Since the late nineteenth century the subject has even produced its own discipline, sexology, drawing on psychology, biology, and anthropology as well as history and sociology. This has been enormously influential in establishing the terms of the debate about sexual behavior. Yet sexuality is clearly a critical social and political issue as well as an individual concern, and it therefore deserves a sustained historical and sociological investigation and analysis.

Sexology has been an important factor in codifying the way we think of the body and sexuality. In his famous study *Psychopathia Sexualis* (first translated into English in 1892), Richard von Krafft-Ebing, the pioneering sexologist of the late nineteenth century, described sex as a "natural instinct" which "with all conquering force and might demands fulfilment" (1931, p. 1). What can we deduce from this? First, there is the emphasis on sex as an "instinct," expressing the fundamental needs of the body. This reflects a post-Darwinian preoccupation in the late nineteenth century to explain all human phenomena in terms of identifiable, inbuilt, biological forces. Today we are more likely to talk about the importance of hormones and genes in shaping our behavior, but the assumption that biology is at the root of all things persists, and nowhere more strongly than in relation to sexuality. We talk all the time about the "sex instinct" or "impulse," and see it as the most natural thing about us. But is it? There is now a great deal of writing which suggests, on the contrary, that sexuality is in fact a "social construction," a historical invention, which of course draws on the possibilities of the body, but whose meanings and the weight we attribute to them are shaped in concrete social situations. This has profound implications for our understanding of the body, sex, and sexuality, which we will need to explore.

Take the second part of the Krafft-Ebing quote: sex is an "all-conquering force," demanding fulfillment. Here we can see at work the central metaphor which guides our thoughts about sexuality. Sex is seen as a volcanic energy, engulfing the body, as urgent and incessant in pressing on our conscious selves. Few people, Krafft-Ebing wrote, "are conscious of the deep influence exerted by sexual life upon the sentiment, thought and action of man in his social relations to others." I don't think we could make such a confident statement of ignorance today. We now take it for granted, in part because of the sexologists, that sexuality is indeed at the center of our existence.

The following quotation from the English sexologist Havelock Ellis, who was very influential in the first third of this century, illustrates the ways in which sexuality has been seen as offering a special insight into the nature of the self: "Sex penetrates the whole person; a man's sexual constitution is a part of his general constitution. There is considerable truth in the dictum: 'a man is what his sex is'" (Ellis, 1946, p. 3).

Not only is sex seen here as an all-conquering force, but it is also apparently an essential element in a person's bodily make-up ("constitution"), the determinant of our personalities and identities – at least, if we take the language at its surface value, if we are men. This poses the question of *why* we see sexuality in this way. What is it about sexuality that makes us so convinced that it is at the heart of our being? Is it equally true for men and women?

This leads us to the third point that we can draw from the original Krafft-Ebing quotation. The language of sexuality appears to be overwhelmingly male. The metaphors used to describe sexuality as a relentless force seem to be derived from assumptions about male sexual experience. Havelock Ellis appears to be going beyond the conventional use of the male pronoun to denote universal experience. Even his use of metaphors ("penetrates") suggest a sublimely unconscious devotion to male models of sexuality. On one level this may seem an unfair criticism, given that the sexologists did attempt to recognize the legitimacy of female sexual experience. In fact, sexologists often followed a long tradition which saw women as "*the sex*," as if their bodies were so suffused with sexuality that there was no need even to conceptualize it. But it is difficult to avoid the sense that the dominant model of sexuality in their writings, and perhaps also in our social consciousness, is the male one. Men were the active sexual agents; women, despite or because of their highly sexualized bodies, were seen as merely responsive, "kissed into life," in Havelock Ellis's significant phrase, by the man.

I am not attempting to suggest that definitions such as Krafft-Ebing's are the only ones, or even the dominant ones today. I have chosen this starting point to illustrate the major theme of this chapter – that our concept of sexuality has a history. The development of the language we use is one valuable index of that: it is in constant evolution. The term "sex," for example, originally meant "the results of the division of humanity into male or female *sections*." It referred, of course, to the differences between men and women, but also to how they were related. As we shall see below, this relationship was significantly different from the one our culture now understands as given – that men and women are fundamentally different. In the past two centuries or so, "sex" has taken on a more precise meaning: it refers to the anatomical differences between men and women, to sharply differentiated bodies, and to what divides us rather than unites us.

Such changes are not accidental. They indicate a complicated history in which sexual difference (whether we are male or female, heterosexual or homosexual) and sexual activity have come to be seen as of prime social importance. Can we therefore, with justice, describe sexual behavior as either "natural" or "un-natural" in any unproblematic sense? I believe not.

The second major theme of this chapter is closely related to this. Our sexual definitions, conventions, beliefs, identities, and behaviors have not simply evolved, as if propelled by an incoming tide. They have been shaped within defined power relationships. The most obvious one has already been signalled in the quotation from Krafft-Ebing: the relations between men and women, in which female sexuality has been historically defined in relationship to the male. But sexuality has been a peculiarly sensitive marker of other power relations. Church and state have shown a continuous interest in how we behave or think. We can see the intervention over the past two centuries or so of medicine, psychology, social work, schools and the like, all seeking to spell out the appropriate ways for us to regulate our bodily activities. Racial and class differences have further complicated the picture. But alongside these have appeared other forces, above all feminism and the sex reform movements of various types, which have resisted the prescriptions and definitions. The sexual codes and identities we take for granted as inevitable, and indeed "natural," have often been forged in this complex process of definition and self-definition that have made modern sexuality central to the way power operates in modern society.

In the discussion which follows we shall be very concerned with the use and meanings of terms, so to close this part of the argument I want to clarify the basic term we are going to use. "Sex" will be used in the sense mentioned above: as a descriptive term for the basic anatomical differences, internal and external to the body, that we see as differentiating men and women. Although these anatomical distinctions are generally given at birth, the meanings attached to them are highly historical and social. To describe the *social* differentiation between men and women, I shall use the term "gender." I shall use the term "sexuality" as a general description for the series of historically shaped and socially constructed beliefs, behaviors, relationships, and identities that relate to what Michel Foucault has called "the body and its pleasures" (Foucault, 1979).

The phrase "social constructionism" will be used as a shorthand term to describe the historically oriented approach towards bodies and sexuality that we shall be adopting. The phrase has perhaps a harsh and mechanistic ring to it, but all it basically sets out to do is argue that we can understand attitudes to the body and sexuality only in their specific historical context, by exploring the historically variable conditions that give rise to the importance assigned to sexuality at any particular time, and by grasping the various power relations that shape what comes to be seen as normal and abnormal, acceptable and unacceptable behavior. Social constructionism is counterposed to sexual "essentialism," the position expressed in the Krafft-Ebing definition, and dominant in most discussions of sexuality until recently. Essentialism is a viewpoint that attempts to explain the properties of a complex whole by reference to a supposed inner truth or essence. Such an approach reduces the complexity of the world to the imagined simplicities of its constituent parts, and seeks to explain individuals as automatic products of inner propulsions.

Against such assumptions I shall argue that the meanings we give to sexuality and the body are socially organized and sustained by a variety of languages which seek to tell us what sex is, what it ought to be, and what it could be.

## 1.3   Historicizing the body

The study by Michel Foucault (1926–84) of the "history of sexuality" has been central to recent discussions about the body and sexuality among historians and social scientists. Consider this quotation: "Sexuality must not be thought of as a kind of natural given which power tries to hold in check, or as an obscure domain which knowledge gradually tries to uncover. It is the name that can be given to a historical construct" (Foucault, 1979, p. 152). Who and what is he challenging here?

Most clearly it is a challenge to the essentialist views we have already surveyed. He is quite firmly stating that sexuality is not a "dark continent" (in Freud's famous phrase relating to female sexuality) that needs its specialist explorers. Sexologists, the would-be scientists of sex and the body, are the targets here, with a strong hint that they have, in part, helped to "construct" sexuality as a privileged domain of knowledge. By establishing a special sphere of knowledge, by seeking the "laws of nature" which supposedly govern the sexual world, by arguing that sexuality has a particular influence on all aspects of life and that the body speaks an ultimate truth, sexologists have, in a sense, helped to "invent" the importance we assign to sexual behavior.

There is also another target, however, and that is that particular tradition of sexual theorizing which has seen sexuality as itself a force which provides a form of resistance to power. Writers like Wilhelm Reich in the 1930s and 1940s argued that capitalist society survived and reproduced itself by repressing our natural and healthy sexuality (Weeks, 1985): if the body could be freed from the constraints of enforced labor, if its basically healthy instincts could have free play, then the ills of society would fade away. "Sexual liberation," therefore, offered the possibility of challenging the oppressive social order, and was a key element in the struggle for social change.

Foucault, on the other hand, rejected what he termed the "repressive hypothesis": the belief that society is all the time attempting to control an unruly natural energy emanating from the body. This was not because he did not want a more liberal sexual order; on the contrary. But he believed essentialist arguments ignored the central fact about modern society: that sexuality was a "historical apparatus" which had developed as part of a complex web of social regulation which organized and shaped ("policed") individual bodies and behavior. Sexuality could not act as a resistance to power because it was so bound up in the ways in which power operated in modern society.

Foucault has been the most influential of the theorists of the "social constructionist" approach to the history and sociology of sexuality. Foucault's own work can best be understood, however, if we appreciate that he was building on a sustained critique of sexual essentialism that had a number of discrete sources. I want to look briefly at some of the streams that have fed the historical approach. (For a fuller discussion, see Weeks, 1985.)

1   From social anthropology, sociology, and the work of sex researchers has come a growing awareness of the vast range of sexual patterns that exist both in other cultures *and* within our own culture. An awareness that the way we do things is not the only way of doing things can provide a salutary jolt to our own ethnocentricity. It should force us to ask searching questions about why things are as they are today. Other cultures and subcultures are a mirror to our own transitoriness.

What does this imply for our thinking about modern sexuality? The American sociologists John Gagnon and William Simon, in their book *Sexual Conduct* (1973), have argued that sexuality is subject to socio-cultural molding to a degree surpassed by few other forms of human behavior. This is quite contrary to our normal belief that sexuality tells us the ultimate truth about ourselves and our bodies; rather, it might tell us something more of the truth of our culture.

2   The legacy of Sigmund Freud and his theory of the dynamic unconscious provides another source for the new approach to sexuality. What psychoanalysis, at least in its original form, sought to establish was that what goes on in the unconscious mind often contradicts the apparent certainties of conscious life. It has been argued that we can detect, in neurotic symptoms, or through the analysis of dreams and the accidents of daily life, traces of repressed wishes or desires – repressed because the desires are of a "perverse" kind. Such arguments unsettle the apparent solidities of gender, of sexual need, and of identity

because they suggest that these are precarious achievements, shaped in the process of the "human animal" acquiring the rules of culture through a complex psycho-social development.

3   Alongside these theoretical developments, the "new social history" of the past two decades has explored areas hitherto ignored by historians, of which the history of gender and the body (e.g. Turner, 1984, Laqueur, 1990) as well as sexuality are of central interest to our concerns. Various studies have questioned the fixity of the prevailing ideas of what constitutes masculinity and femininity, have explored the changing nature of domesticity and work (see chapter 10), and have thrown new light on the development of social categorizations (for example, those of childhood, of prostitution, and homosexuality) and on the development of individual sexual identities (Weeks, 1989).

4   Finally, the emergence of a new politics around sexuality – such as feminism, lesbian and gay politics, and other radical sexual movements – have challenged many of the certainties of our sexual traditions, and have offered new insights into the intricate forms of power and domination that shape our sexual lives. Why is male dominance so endemic in culture? Why is female sexuality so often seen as subsidiary to that of men? Why does our culture celebrate heterosexuality and discriminate against homosexuality?

All these streams force us to confront questions which are fundamentally social and historical; to ask: What are the cultural forces that shape our sexual meanings? As Carole Vance has argued:

> The widespread use of social construction as a term and as a paradigm obscures the fact that constructionist writers have used this term in diverse ways. It is true that all reject transhistorical and transcultural definitions of sexuality and suggest instead that sexuality is mediated by historical and cultural factors. But a close reading of constructionist texts shows that social construction spans a theoretical field of what might be constructed, ranging from sexual acts, sexual identities, sexual communities, the direction of sexual desire (object choice) to sexual impulse or sexuality itself.
>     At minimum, all social construction approaches adopt the view that physically identical sexual acts may have varying social significance and subjective meaning depending on how they are defined and understood in different cultures and historical periods. Because a sexual act does not carry with it a universal social meaning, it follows that the relationship between sexual acts and sexual identities is not a fixed one, and it is projected from the observer's time and place to others at great peril. Cultures provide widely different categories, schemata, and labels for framing sexual and affective experiences. The relationship of sexual act and identity to sexual community is equally variable and complex. These distinctions, then, between sexual acts, identities, and communities are widely employed by constructionist writers.

A further step in social construction theory posits that even the direction [of] sexual desire itself, for example, object choice or hetero/homosexuality, is not intrinsic or inherent in the individual but is constructed. Not all constructionists take this step; for some, the direction of desire and erotic interest are fixed, although the behavioural *form* this interest takes will be constructed by prevailing cultural frames, as will the subjective experience of the individual and the social significance attached to it by others.

The most radical form of constructionist theory is willing to entertain the idea that there is no essential, undifferentiated sexual impulse, "sex drive" or "lust," which resides in the body due to physiological functioning and sensation. Sexual impulse itself is constructed by culture and history. In this case, an important constructionist question concerns the origins of these impulses, since they are no longer assumed to be intrinsic or, perhaps, even necessary. This position, of course, contrasts sharply with more middle-ground constructionist theory which implicitly accepts an inherent sexual impulse which is then constructed in terms of acts, identity, community, and object choice. The contrast between middle-ground and radical positions makes it evident that constructionists may well have arguments with each other, as well as with essentialists. Each degree of social construction points to different questions and assumptions, possibly to different methods, and perhaps to different answers. (Vance, 1989, pp. 18–19)

Carole Vance quite rightly asks us to recognize that we cannot forget the body. It is through the body that we experience both pleasure and pain. Moreover, there are male bodies and female bodies, and these give rise to quite different experiences, for example childbirth. Another powerful point is that we do not experience our sexual needs and desires as accidental, or as the product of society. They are deeply ingrained in us as individuals.

This does not mean that they cannot be explained socially: one of the attractions of psychoanalysis, for example, is that it does challenge us to ask about the relationship between psychic processes, social dynamics, and historical change. The meanings which we give to our bodies and their sexual possibilities do become a vital part of our individual make-up, whatever the social explanations.

This does not, nevertheless, invalidate the main lesson of social constructionist arguments, whose main purpose is not to offer dogmatic explanations about how *individual* sexual meanings are acquired. Constructionism is, in a sense, agnostic about this question. We are not concerned with the question of what causes heterosexuality or homosexuality in individuals, but rather with the problem of why and how our culture privileges the one and marginalizes – where it does not discriminate against – the other. Social constructionism also poses another central question: Why does our culture assign such an importance to sexuality, and how has this come about?

All these are legitimately questions for social investigation, and in the next section we shall begin to look at them in more detail.

# 2    Sexuality and Sexual Norms

## 2.1    Establishing "the normal" and "the abnormal"

One of the more intriguing of Michel Foucault's works is his "dossier" on the memoirs of a nineteenth-century French hermaphrodite, Herculine Barbin. He sums up the tragic story in the following terms:

> Brought up as a poor and deserving girl in a milieu that was almost exclusively feminine and strongly religious, Herculine Barbin, who was called Alexina by her familiars, was finally recognized as being "truly" a young man. Obliged to make a legal change of sex after judicial proceedings and a modification of his civil status, he was incapable of adapting himself to a new identity and ultimately committed suicide. I would be tempted to call the story banal were it not for two or three things that give it a particular intensity.
> (Foucault, 1980, p. xi)

Alexina/Herculine was born of indeterminate sex – that is, with bodily characteristics which made it difficult to determine clearly whether the child was a boy or a girl. This was an anomaly not particularly common then or now, but certainly not unknown. In this case the body was ambiguous; it did not reveal an unproblematical truth. Foucault's point is that, while awkward and graceless as a "normal" girl, nevertheless during her early life she was able to be accepted within a particular milieu without special stigmatization. She lived the "happy limbo of a non-identity" (Foucault, 1980, p. xiii).

Eventually, however, those "two or three things" mentioned by Foucault forced a choice about identity. It became necessary to insist on a "true sex," whatever the consequences. Chief among these factors, Foucault suggests, during the 1860s when the tragedy occurred, was the new concern among doctors, lawyers, and the like with classifying and fixing the different sexual types and characteristics. Because Alexina had certain evidence of a masculine body, that is a small penis, "she" had to become "he."

We can leave aside for present purposes the question of whether the dossier gives a full picture of the processes at work, or how representative Herculine Barbin's experience was of a new classifying zeal. Rather, this case should be seen as symbolic of a wider process: a complexly intertwined process by which the sharpening definition of "true" male and female characteristics is allied to a new zeal in defining what is "normal" or "abnormal" in judicial, medical, and political discourses. Indeed, by defining what is abnormal (a girl with bodily evidence of masculinity in this case), it became fully possible to attempt to define what is truly normal (a full correspondence between the body and socially acceptable gender identity).

As we have already seen, one characteristic way of perceiving this is as a process of discovery of the true facts about human sexuality by a new objective science. Foucault, like others who have been exploring the sexuality of modernity, is saying something much more: that this process is the result of a new configuration of power which requires us to place a person by defining his or her true identity, an identity that fully expresses the real truth of the body.

The history of sexuality is, for Foucault, a history of our discourses about sexuality: discourses through which sexuality is constructed as a body of knowledge which shapes the ways we think and know the body. The western experience of sexuality, he suggests, is not the inhibition of discourse. It cannot be characterized as a "regime of silence," but is, on the contrary, a constant and historically changing incitement to discourse about sex. This ever-expanding discursive explosion is part of a complex growth of control over individuals, control not through denial or prohibition, but through production: by the imposition of a grid of definition on the possibilities of the body through the apparatus of sexuality.

> The deployment of sexuality has its reasons for being, not in reproducing itself, but in proliferating, innovating, annexing, creating and penetrating bodies in an increasingly detailed way, and in controlling populations in an increasingly comprehensive way.
> (Foucault, 1979, p. 107)

Foucault's study of the sexual apparatus is closely related to his analysis of the development of what he sees as the "disciplinary society" characteristic of modern forms of social regulation – a society of surveillance and control that he sketches in his book *Discipline and Punish* (1977). He argues here that in the modern period we should see power, not as a negative force operating on the basis of prohibition ("thou shalt not"), but as a positive force concerned with administering and fostering life ("you must do this or that"). This is what he terms "bio-power," and here sexuality has a crucial role. For sex is the pivot along which the whole technology of life developed: sex was a means of access both to the life of the body and the life of the species; that is, it offered a way of regulating both individual bodies and the behavior of the population (the "body politic") as a whole (Foucault, 1979).

Foucault pinpoints four strategic unities which link together a variety of social practices and techniques of power since the eighteenth century. Together they form specific mechanics of knowledge and power centering on sex. These are concerned with the sexuality of women; the sexuality of children; the control of procreative behavior; and the pinpointing of sexual perversions as problems of individual pathology. In the course of the nineteenth century these strategies produced four figures for social observation and control, invented within the regulative discourses: the hysterical woman, the masturbating child, the married couple using artificial birth control, and "the pervert," especially the homosexual.

The significance of this argument is that it fundamentally challenges the idea that social regulation sets out to control pre-existing types of being. What is actually happening is that a generalized social concern with controlling the population gives rise to a specification of particular types of people, who are simultaneously evoked and controlled within the complex of power–knowledge. This does not mean that female sexuality, masturbation, birth control or homosexuality did not exist before. What it does mean is that the specification of people by these characteristics, the creation of "subject positions" around these activities, was a historical phenomenon.

## 2.2   The social dimensions of sexuality

Sexuality, we are suggesting, is shaped at the juncture of two major concerns: with our subjectivity (who and what we are); and with society (with the health, prosperity, growth, and well-being of the population as a whole). The two are intimately connected because at the heart of both is the body and its potentialities. As society has become more and more concerned with the lives of its members – for the sake of moral uniformity, economic prosperity, national security, or hygiene and health – so it has become increasingly preoccupied with disciplining bodies and with the sex lives of its individuals. This has given rise to intricate methods of administration and management, to a flowering of moral anxieties, medical, hygienic, legal, and welfarist interventions, or scientific delving, all designed to understand the self by understanding, and regulating, sexual behavior.

The Victorian period is a key one in understanding the process in all its complexity. Traditionally, historians have commented on the repressiveness of the period, and in many ways this is an accurate picture. There was indeed a great deal of moral hypocrisy, as individuals (especially men) and society avowed respectability but did something else. Women's sexuality was severely regulated to ensure 'purity' at the same time as prostitution was rife. Venereal disease posed a major health threat, but was met by attempts to control and regulate female sexuality rather than male. By the mid-nineteenth century, fuelled by the spread of epidemics such as cholera and typhoid in the overcrowded towns and cities, attempts to reform society concentrated on questions of health and personal morality. From the 1860s to the 1890s, prostitution, venereal disease, public immorality, and private vice were at the heart of debate, many choosing to see in moral decay a symbol of social decay.

Such preoccupations were not unique to the nineteenth century. If anything, sexuality became more and more a public obsession. In the years before World War I, there was a vogue for eugenics, the planned breeding of the best. Though never dominant, it had a significant influence in some countries in shaping welfare policies and the attempt to reorder national priorities in the face of international competition. It also fed into a burgeoning racism in the inter-war years as politicians feared a declining population which would give dominance to "inferior races." In the 1940s, the key period for the establishment of the welfare state in many western societies, there was an urgent concern with the merits of birth control ("family planning") in ensuring that the right sort of people built families, and with the appropriate roles of men and women (especially women) in the family in the brave new world of social democracy.

Linked with this, by the 1950s, in the depth of the Cold War, there was a new searching out of sexual "degenerates," especially homosexuals, who not only lived outside families but were also, apparently, peculiarly susceptible to treason. By the 1960s, a new liberalism ("permissiveness") seemed torn between relaxing the old authoritarian social codes and finding new modes of social regulation, based on the latest in social psychology, and a redefinition of the public/private divide. During the 1970s and 1980s there was, in effect, the beginning of a backlash against what were seen as the excesses of the earlier decade, and perhaps for the first time sexuality became a real front-line political issue as the emergence of the New Right identified the "decline of the family," feminism and the new homosexual militancy as potent symbols of national decline.

What is at stake in these recurrent debates about morality and sexual behavior? Clearly a number of different but related concerns are present: the relations between men and women, the problem of sexual deviance, the question of family and other relationships, the relations between adults and children, and the issue of difference, whether of class, gender, or race. Each of these has a long history, but in the past couple of hundred years they have become central concerns, often centering around sexual issues. They illustrate the power of the belief that debates about sexuality are debates about the nature of society: as sex goes, so goes society.

So far we have concentrated on the symbolic importance attributed to sexuality, and some of the reasons for this. But it is important to recognize that sexuality is not a unified domain. In the next section we shall look at some of the forces that shape sexual beliefs and behavior, complicating sexual identities.

The assumption here is that power does not operate through single mechanisms of control. In fact, it operates through complex and overlapping – and often contradictory – mechanisms which produce domination and oppositions, subordination and resistances. There are many structures of domination and subordination in the world of sexuality, but three interdependent elements or axes have been seen as particularly important today: those of class, gender, and race. We shall look at each of these in turn.

# 3   Sexuality and Power

## 3.1   Class and sexuality

Class differences in sexual regulation are not unique to the modern world, but they have become more sharply apparent over the past 200 years. Foucault has argued that the very idea of "sexuality" as a unified domain is essentially a bourgeois one, developed as part of the self-assertion of a class anxious to differentiate itself from the immorality of the aristocracy and the supposedly rampant promiscuity of the lower classes. It was basically a colonizing endeavor, seeking to remold both the polity and sexual behavior in its own image. The respectable standards of family life developed in the nineteenth century ("Victorian values"), with the increased demarcation between male and female roles, a new emphasis on the need to bring public behavior up to the best standards of private life, and a sharpened interest in the public policing of non-marital, non-heterosexual sexuality, became increasingly the norm by which all behavior was judged.

This does not mean, of course, that all or even most behavior conformed to the norm. Historians have provided plentiful evidence that the working class remained extremely resistant to middle-class manners. Patterns of behavior inherited from their rural predecessors continued to structure the sexual culture of working-class people well into the twentieth century. The fact that such patterns were different from those of the bourgeoisie does not mean that they were in themselves worse. Nevertheless, it is true that the patterns of sexual life of the present century are the results of a social struggle in which class and sexuality were inextricably linked. This is even reflected at the level of fantasy, particularly in the belief, evident in both heterosexual and homosexual upper-class male culture, that the working-class woman or man was somehow more spontaneous, closer to nature, than other people.

The result has been the existence of quite distinct class patterns of sexuality at various times. For example, attitudes to birth control varied considerably, with the professional classes leading the way in the adoption of artificial contraception from the 1860s, and working-class families on the whole having larger families until after World War II (McLaren, 1978; Weeks, 1989). But it is also unwise to generalize about class patterns. Textile workers from early in the nineteenth century tended to have smaller families. In the inter-war years there were marked differences between the contraceptive activities of female factory workers, who had access to cultures of knowledge about birth control, and domestic workers, who often did not. As in the Third World today, to have large families was often economically rational in many social situations, and inappropriate in others. Geographical, religious, employment, and other factors inevitably came into play.

The same is true in relation to many other aspects of sexual behavior, for example in attitudes to masturbation, acceptance of casual prostitution, attitudes to homosexuality, and the like (Kinsey et al., 1948, and 1953). Class, in other words, was a key factor, but not always a decisive one in shaping choices about sexual activity.

## 3.2   Gender and sexuality

This leads us to the question of gender itself. Classes consist of men and women, and class and status differences may not have the same significance for women as for men. Gender is a crucial divide.

Gender is not a simple analytical category; it is, as feminist scholarship has increasingly documented, a relationship of power. So, patterns of female sexuality are inescapably a product of the historically rooted power of men to define what is necessary and desirable.

The nineteenth century was a key point in the definition of female sexuality in terms which have greatly influenced our own concepts, and not least our assumptions about the importance of bodily differences. We have already looked at one example of the processes at work – that of Herculine Barbin, discussed in section 2.1. Let us now look at the issue again, in a wider historical framework. Thomas Laqueur (1990) has argued that the political, economic, and cultural transformations of the eighteenth century created the context in which the articulation of radical differences between the sexes became culturally imperative.

In a long and subtle examination of the evolution of concepts of the body and gender from the Greeks to the twentieth century, Laqueur suggests that there have been fundamental shifts in the ways we see the relationship between male and female bodies. He argues that, until the eighteenth century, the dominant discourse "construed the male and female bodies as hierarchically, vertically, ordered versions of one sex" (Laqueur, 1990, p. 10). The hierarchical but single-sex model certainly interpreted the female body as an inferior and inverted version of the male, but stressed nevertheless the important role of female sexual pleasure, especially in the process of reproduction. Female orgasm and pleasure were seen as necessary to successful impregnation. The breakdown of this model, in political as well as medical debates, led to its replacement in the nineteenth century by a reproductive model which emphasized the existence of two, sharply different bodies, the radical opposition of male and female sexualities, the woman's automatic reproductive cycle, and her lack of sexual feeling. This was a critical moment in the reshaping of gender relations, because it suggested the absolute difference of men and women: no longer a single, partially differentiated body, but two singular bodies, the male and the female.

Laqueur argues that the shift he traces did not arise straightforwardly from scientific advance, nor was it the simple product of a singular effort at social control of women by men. The emergent discourse about sexual difference allowed a range of different, and often contradictory, social and political responses to emerge. But at the heart of the emerging definitions were new cultural and political relations, the product of shifts in the balance of power between men and women. The new perception of female sexuality and reproductive biology has been absolutely central to modern social and political discourse because it stressed difference and division rather than similarity and complementarity.

While male dominance remains a central feature of modern society, it is important to remember that women have been active participants in shaping their own definition of need. Not only feminism, but the practices of everyday life have offered spaces for women to plot out their own lives. Since the nineteenth century, the acceptable spaces have expanded to include not only pleasure in marriage, but also relatively respectable forms of non-procreative behavior. The patterns of male sexual privilege have not been broken, but there is now plentiful evidence that such privilege is neither inevitable nor immutable.

## 3.3    Race and sexuality

Class and gender are not the only differences that shape sexuality. Categorizations by class or gender intersect with those of ethnicity and race. This aspect of sexuality has generally been ignored by historians and social scientists until recently, but it is a vital element of the history of sexuality nonetheless.

The sexual ideologies of the latter part of the nineteenth century presented the black person – "the wild savage" – as lower down the evolutionary scale than the white: closer to the origins of the human race; closer, that is, to nature. Such views survived even among the culturally relativist anthropologists who displaced many of the evolutionary theorists after the turn of the century (Coward, 1983). One of the attractions of portrayals of non-industrial cultures was precisely the subliminal feeling that the people there were indefinably freer of the constraints of civilization. Whether non-European peoples represented the childhood of the race, or the promise of a spontaneity free of the effects of a corrupting civilization, the common thread was the symbolic difference represented by the non-white body.

The awareness of other cultures, and of other sexual mores, therefore offered a challenge and a threat. For sexologists like Havelock Ellis the evidence from non-industrial societies provided a justification for their reformist critiques of western sexual norms. At the same time, Ellis, like many others of his generation, supported eugenicist policies, which were based on the belief that it was possible to improve the "racial stock" by the planned breeding of the best in society. The assumption that the racial stock could (and should) be improved was based on two related assumptions: first, that the laboring poor, whose bodies were enfeebled by ill-health and the effects of industrial society, were disqualified from the hope of social progress; and, second, that the world's "inferior races" posed a threat (particularly because of their fertility) to the future of the imperial races of Europe. The aim of people like Ellis was ostensibly to improve the human race rather than any particular race, but inevitably assumptions of what was socially desirable were filtered through beliefs of the time.

It can be argued that the very definitions of masculinity and femininity, and of the appropriate sexual behavior for either sex, during the past two centuries have to a high degree been shaped in response to the "Other" represented by alien cultures. Think, for example, of the myths of black men's hyper-sexuality and of the threat to female purity represented by them, common in many colonial situations as well as in the Deep South of the US. Consider the importance in South African apartheid of the banning of sexual relations between members of different racial groups. Or of the fascination with the exotic sexuality of women in other cultures as represented in art and literature. Western sexuality, with its norms of sexual differentiation, monogamy, heterosexuality, and (in some periods at least) respectability, has been both challenged and undermined, as well as triumphantly reasserted, by knowledge of other cultures, other bodies, and other sexualities. The following extract by Valerie Amos and Pratibha Parmar, two contemporary black feminists, suggests that we have not yet escaped this history:

> White feminists have fallen into the trap of measuring the Black female experience against their own, labelling it as in some way lacking, then looking for ways in which it might be possible to harness the Black women's experience to their own. Comparisons are made with our countries of origin which are said to fundamentally exploit Black women. The hysteria in the western women's movement surrounding issues like arranged marriages, purdah, female-headed households, is often beyond the Black woman's comprehension – being tied to so-called feminist notions of what constitutes good or bad practice in our communities in Britain or the Third World.
>
> In rejecting such analyses we would hope to locate the Black family more firmly in the historical experiences of Black people – not in the romantic idealized forms popular with some social anthropologists, and not merely as a tool of analysis. There are serious questions about who has written that history and in what form, questions which have to be addressed before we as Black people use that history as an additional element of our analysis. Black women cannot just throw away their experiences of living in certain types of household organization; they want to use that experience to transform familial relationships. Stereotypes about the Black family have been used by the state to justify particular forms of oppression. The issue of fostering and adoption of Black kids is current: Black families are seen as being "unfit" for fostering and adoption. Racist immigration legislation has had the effect of separating family members, particularly of the Asian community, but no longer is that legislation made legitimate just by appeals to racist ideologies contained in notions of "swamping." Attempts have actually been made by some feminists to justify such legislative practices on the basis of protecting Asian girls from the "horrors" of the arranged marriage system. White feminists beware – your unquestioning and racist assumptions about the Black family, your critical but uninformed approach to 'Black culture' has found root and in fact informs state practice. (Amos and Parmar, 1984, p. 11)

The examination of the relations of power concerning class, gender, and race demonstrates the complexity of the forces that shape sexual attitudes and behavior. These forces in turn open the way to the development of differentiated sexual identities. In the next section, we are going to look at the whole question of identity in more detail, to show the main factors that have shaped the divisions that we assume to be natural, but that are actually historically constructed.

# 4   Sexual Identities

## 4.1   The institutionalization of heterosexuality

Let's look again at words – at the language used to describe sexuality. In particular I want to look at the history of two principal terms we now take for granted to such an extent that we assume they have a universal application: "heterosexuality" and "homosexuality." In fact, these terms are of relatively recent origin, and I am going to suggest that their invention – for that is what it was – is an important marker of wider changes. To be more precise, the emergence of the two terms marks a crucial stage in the modern delimitation and definition of sexuality. No doubt it will surprise many that it was the attempt to define "homosexuality," the "abnormal" form of sexuality, which forced a sharper definition of "heterosexuality" as the norm, but the evidence now available suggests that this was the case.

The two terms were, it seems, coined by the same person, Karl Kertbeny, an Austro-Hungarian writer, and were first used publicly by him in 1869. The context in which these neologisms emerged is critical: they were deployed in relation to an early attempt to put on the political agenda in the soon-to-be unified Germany the question of sex reform, in particular the repeal of the anti-sodomy laws. They were part of an embryonic campaign, subsequently taken up by the developing discipline of sexology, to define *homosexuality* as a distinctive form of sexuality: a benign variant in the eyes of reformers of the potent but unspoken and ill-defined notion of "normal sexuality" (apparently another concept first used by Kertbeny). Hitherto, sexual activity between people of the same biological sex had been dealt with under the catch-all category of sodomy, which was generally seen, not as the activity of a particular type of person, but as a potential in all sinful nature. Early campaigners who aimed to change attitudes to same-sex relations were anxious to suggest that homosexuality was a mark of a distinctive sort of person. As Michel Foucault has noted, the sodomite was seen as a temporary aberrant, whereas the homosexual belonged to a species (Foucault, 1979).

The deployment of these terms must be seen, therefore, as part of a major effort at the end of the nineteenth and beginning of the twentieth centuries to define more closely the types and forms of sexual behavior and identity; and it is in this effort that homosexuality and heterosexuality became key oppositional terms. In the process, however, the implications of the words subtly changed. Homosexuality, instead of describing a benign variant of normality, as Kertbeny originally intended, became a medico-moral description in the hands of pioneering sexologists such as Krafft-Ebing. Heterosexuality, on the other hand, as a term to describe the hitherto untheorized norm, slowly came into use in the course of the twentieth century – more slowly, it should be noted, than its partner word. A norm, perhaps, does not need an explicit descriptor; it becomes the taken-for-granted framework for the way we think, part of the air we breathe.

What are the implications of this new language, and the new realities they signal? Our present-day common sense takes for granted that these terms demarcate a real division between people: there are "heterosexuals" and there are "homosexuals," with another term for those who do not quite fit into this neat divide, "bisexuals." But the real world is never as tidy as this, and recent historical work has demonstrated that not only do other cultures not have this way of seeing human sexuality, neither did western cultures until relatively recently.

We are not arguing of course that what we know today as heterosexual or homosexual activity did not take place before the nineteenth century. The real point is more subtle: that the way sexual activity is conceptualized, and consequently divided, has a history, and a history that matters. The argument over terms at the end of the nineteenth century signals a new effort at redefining the norm. A central part of this was the definition of abnormalities. The two efforts are inextricably linked.

The attempt to more rigorously define the characteristics of "the pervert" (descriptive terms such as "sado-masochism" and "transvestism" for sex-related activities emerged at the end of the nineteenth century alongside "homosexuality" and "heterosexuality") was an important element in what I am calling the institutionalization of heterosexuality in the course of the nineteenth and twentieth centuries. In part this was a sexological endeavor. Sexology took upon itself two distinct tasks at the end of the nineteenth century. First, it attempted to define the basic characteristics of what constitutes normal masculinity and femininity, seen as distinct characteristics of biological men and women. Second, by cataloguing the infinite variety of sexual practices, it produced a hierarchy in which the abnormal and the normal could be distinguished. For most of the pioneers, the two endeavors were closely linked: heterosexual object-choice was closely linked to genital intercourse. Other sexual activities were either accepted as fore-pleasures, or condemned as aberrations.

Sexology, however, only set the terms of the debate. The social history of heterosexuality in the twentieth century is much more complex than a simple sexological reflex. It is tempting to see this social history as the sum total of all the developments in relation to sexuality in the century, because even the changing ideas about sexual diversity make sense only in relation to an apparently nature-given norm. We can, however, point to some key elements which suggest that heterosexuality as an institution is itself a historically changing phenomenon. For example, consider:

• Changes in family life, and the recognition of diversity in patterns of domestic life, which suggest that the family itself is a historically changing form.

- The changing patterns of employment, and women's fuller integration into the paid workforce, which have inevitably shifted the balance between men and women, even if major inequalities survive and remain deeply entrenched.
- Changes in the patterns of fertility, the widespread use of birth control techniques, abortion, etc., that have opened new potentials in the sexual relations of men and women.
- A new emphasis in the twentieth century on sex as pleasure, reflected in the explosion of literature on how to attain sexual pleasure, how to avoid frigidity, premature ejaculation, etc., which has served to put an overwhelming emphasis on sexual relations in binding couples together.

Some feminist writers have suggested that what has happened is that heterosexuality has been institutionalized as "compulsory," in a way which binds women ever more tightly to men (Rich, 1984; Jackson, 1987). The interesting point to note here is that very little attention has been paid by historians and social scientists to this process of institutionalization.

## 4.2  Inventing homosexuality

Let us now turn to the history of homosexuality, about which a great deal has been written in the past twenty years. It may seem strange to look in detail at what will seem to many to be a minority activity. But I believe that in understanding the history of homosexuality we can gain new insights into the social construction of heterosexuality and of sexuality as a whole.

I shall begin with a bald assertion: before the nineteenth century "homosexuality" existed, but "the homosexual" did not.

Put simply, this suggests that while homosexuality has existed in all types of societies, at all times, and has been variously accepted or rejected as part of the customs and social mores of these societies, only since the nineteenth century, and in the industrializing societies of the West, has a distinctive homosexual category and associated identity developed. The emergence in Germany, and other Central and West European countries such as Britain, in the 1870s and 1880s of writings about, and crucially by, homosexuals was a critical stage in this shift. By defining the "contrary sexual feeling," or the existence of a "third" or "intermediate" gender, Richard von Krafft-Ebing, Magnus Hirschfeld, Havelock Ellis and others were attempting to signal the discovery or recognition of a distinct type of person, whose sexual essence was significantly different from that of the "heterosexual" – another category invented, as we have seen, at about the same time.

Now, I am not arguing that these newly defined homosexuals were figments of the imaginations of these distinguished writers. On the contrary, these writers were attempting to describe, and explain, individuals they were encountering through the law courts, their medical practices, their friends, or in their personal lives (Ulrichs and Hirschfeld, for example, were themselves homosexual; Havelock Ellis was married to a self-defined lesbian). What I do assert, however, is that this new categorizing and defining zeal towards the end of the nineteenth century was as significant a shift in the public and private definition of homosexuality as the emergence of an open and defiant lesbian and gay politics in American cities in the late 1960s and early 1970s. Both represented a critical transformation of what it meant to be sexual. They symbolized crucial breakthroughs in the meanings given to sexual difference.

So what existed before the nineteenth century? The American historian Randolph Trumbach (1989) has detected two major patterns of homosexual interaction in the West since the twelfth century, which in turn echo the two great patterns of the organization of homosexuality on a world scale, as revealed by the evidence of anthropologists. Around the year 1100, he argues, a distinctive western cultural pattern begins to emerge. Marriage was late and monogamous. Sexual relations outside marriage were forbidden, but licensed in the form of regulated prostitution. However, all forms of sexual activity which were not procreative were regarded as sinful, whether they were solitary, between men and women, men and men, men and beasts (relations between women, though sometimes noted, did not achieve the same ignominy).

Nevertheless, homosexual activities between men did occur. When they did, they were usually between an active adult and a passive adolescent. Usually, the adult male also had sexual relations with women. The boy, provided he adopted an active role in adulthood, did not suffer a loss of status or of manhood. On the contrary, as long as the role was active, homosexual activity could be seen as a sign of manhood. But the same was not true of those who retained a passive role in adulthood: they were stigmatized, and often abused.

This pattern is very common in various parts of the world. It is essentially the ancient Greek model, but has survived well into the twentieth century, particularly in Mediterranean countries, and also in some subcultures of western societies. Nevertheless, from the early eighteenth century it was gradually superseded by a second model, which increasingly associated any male homosexual behavior, whether active or passive, with effeminacy, with breaching the accepted or expected gender behavior. The emergence in the early eighteenth century of male transvestite subcultures in London and other major western cities marks the shift. Here "mollies," as they were called in England, could meet others like themselves, and begin to define some sort of sense of difference and identity. By the mid-nineteenth century, this sort of subculture was well-developed in cities such as London, Paris, and Berlin.

Basically, what seems to have happened is that the transformation in family life from the eighteenth century, and the sharpening distinctions of male and female social and sexual roles associated with it, had the effect of increasing the stigmatization of men who did not readily conform to their expected sexual and social roles. Those who breached the social expectations of what it was to be a man were categorized as being not real men, what Marcel Proust in the early twentieth century

called the *homme-femme* ("man-woman"). Attitudes to women were
significantly different, reflecting the social and sexual subordination of
women, and the expectation that they could not be autonomously
sexual (something I'll come back to in a moment).

If this overview is accurate, it suggests that what was taking place in
the late nineteenth century in countries such as Germany and Britain
grew out of subcultural developments which were already a couple of
hundred years advanced. In Britain, the flurry of scandals and court
cases, culminating in the most famous of all, Oscar Wilde's trials in
1895, revealed to an amazed public the existence of an already-complex
sexual underground alongside the now hegemonic sexual respectability.
The theorizing about "the urning" or "third sex" by writers such as
Ulrichs, Hirschfeld, or Edward Carpenter can then be seen as a
description of a type of person who had already differentiated himself
from the norm. Simultaneously, the construction of the sexological and
psychological category of "the homosexual" by the new sexual
scientists of the late nineteenth century was an attempt to define the
natural laws which explained what was usually seen as a pathology.
Similarly, the legal changes, for example in Germany and Britain,
which sharpened the penalties against male homosexuality, marked an
attempt to regulate and control sexual perversity.

But while in one sense these developments represented a
rationalization of long-term developments, and would not have been
possible without them, this is not the whole story. Just as the explosive
appearance of gay liberation in the US in 1969 grew out of well-
established community networks, but then began something distinctly
new, so the changes of the late nineteenth century put the discourse of
homosexuality on a new footing. Homosexuality became a scientific
and sociological category, classifying sexual perversity in a new way,
and this inevitably had its effects in legal and medical practice from
then on. It constructed the idea of a distinctive, and perhaps
exclusively homosexual, nature. And, possibly even more importantly,
it initiated a new phase of homosexual self-definition in the face of the
defining work of the new medical and psychological norms.

From the nineteenth century a new model of "the homosexual"
emerged from the scientific literature, though there were all sorts of
disputes about the explanations for this strange phenomenon:
biological, hormonal, environmental, psychological (Plummer, 1981a).
This model provided, in a sense, the norm around which the people so
defined were constrained to live their lives until very recently. But
their lives were of course differentiated by many other factors. Class
differences in gay lifestyles have been apparent since at least the
nineteenth century, since before Oscar Wilde "feasted with panthers,"
as he described his dalliances with working-class boys. More recently,
we have been forcefully reminded in the West that there are also sharp
racial and ethnic differences in attitudes towards, and responses to,
homosexuality (see below). But the best-documented differences are
between men and women.

The model of the homosexual that emerged in the nineteenth century
attempted to explain homosexual women and men in the same terms,

as if they had a common cause and common characteristics. In fact, the model was overwhelmingly based on male homosexuality, and was never straightforwardly applicable to women. Lesbian scholars have documented the ways in which intimate relations between women formed part of a continuum of close relationships, with no distinctive lesbian identity clearly developing until this century (Faderman, 1980). Men and women might be classified by the same psychological labelling, but their histories are different (Vicinus, 1989).

It should be apparent from what I have said that the new history of homosexuality is a history of identities: their emergence, complexities, and transformations. This does not, of course, exhaust the subject of homosexuality. Much same-sex activity goes on that is never defined as "homosexual," and does not radically affect someone's sense of self: in closed institutions such as prisons, in casual encounters, and in one-to-one relations which are seen as special, but not defining. For distinctive identities to emerge, and set themselves against the heterosexual norms of our culture, something more than sexual activity, or even homosexual desire, is needed: the possibility of some sort of social space, and social support or network which gives meaning to individual needs.

The growth from the eighteenth century onwards of urban spaces, making possible both social interaction and anonymity, was a crucial factor in the development of a homosexual subculture. The increasing complexity and social differentiation of a modern industrialized society in Europe and North America from the end of the last century provided the critical opportunity for the evolution of the male homosexual and lesbian identities of this century. More recently, gay historians have shown the essential role played by the development of highly organized gay communities in cities such as San Francisco, New York, and Sydney in providing the numbers necessary for the mass organization of gay politics.

As civil society in western countries becomes more complex, more differentiated, more self-reliant, so the lesbian and gay community has become an important part of that society. Increasingly, homosexuality becomes an option, or choice, which individuals can follow in a way which was impossible in a more hierarchical and monolithic society. The existence of a gay way of life provides the opportunity for people to explore their needs and desires in ways which were sometimes literally unimaginable at an earlier period. This is, of course, why homosexuality is still often seen as a threat to those wedded to the moral status quo, whether from the left or right of the political spectrum. The existence of positive lesbian and gay identities symbolizes the ever-increasing pluralization of social life, and the expansion of individual choice that this offers.

## 4.3   Rethinking sexual identities

Let us now look at the issue of sexual identities in a wider context. The idea of a *sexual* identity is an ambiguous one. For many in the modern

world it is an absolutely fundamental concept, offering a sense of
personal unity, social location, and even a political commitment. Not
many people may say "I am a heterosexual," because it is the great
taken-for-granted. But to say "I am gay" or "I am lesbian" is to make a
statement about belonging, and to take a specific stance in relation to
the dominant sexual codes.

Yet at the same time the evidence looked at above suggests that such
identities are historically and culturally specific, that they are selected
from a host of possible social identities, that they are not necessary
attributes of particular sexual drives or desires, and that they are not
*essential* parts of our personality. We are increasingly aware that
sexuality is as much a product of language and culture as of nature. Yet
we constantly strive to fix it, stabilize it, and say who we are by telling
of our sex.

How important, then, is sexual identity, and what does it tell us
about the question of identity in the modern and post-modern world?
Several different emphases on identity can be traced.

1  **Identity as destiny.** This is the assumption behind the essentialist
tradition as we have traced it. It underpins such phrases as "biology is
destiny." It assumes that the body expresses some fundamental truth.
But, as we have seen, such assumptions themselves have a history.
Everything we now know about sexuality undermines the idea that
there is a predetermined sexual destiny based on the morphology of the
body. We must find the justification for identity elsewhere.

2  **Identity as resistance.** For the social theorists of the 1950s and
1960s, who first brought the question of identity explicitly onto the
agenda by speaking of "identity crises" – psychologists and sociologists
such as Erik Erikson (1968) and Erving Goffman (see especially
Goffman's *Stigma*, 1968) – personal identity roughly equalled
individuality, a strong sense of the self, which was attained by
struggling against the weight of social conventionality. For the "sexual
minorities" coming to a new sense of their separateness and
individuality during the same period – especially male homosexuals
and lesbians – the finding of identity was like discovering a map to
explore a new country. As Plummer put it, the processes of
categorization and self-categorization (that is, the process of identity
formation) may control, restrict, and inhibit, but simultaneously they
offer comfort, security, and assuredness (Plummer, 1981a).

So, the preoccupation with identity among the sexually marginal
cannot be explained as an effect of a peculiar personal obsession with
sex. It can be seen, more accurately, as a powerful resistance to the
organizing principle of traditional sexual attitudes. It has been sexual
radicals who have most insistently politicized the question of sexual
identity. But the agenda has largely been shaped by the importance
assigned by our culture to "correct" sexual behavior.

3  **Identity as choice.** This leads us to the question of the degree to
which sexual identities, especially those stigmatized by the wider
society, are in the end freely made choices. Many people, it has been
argued, "drift" into identity, battered by contingency rather than guided

by will. Four characteristic stages in the construction of a "stigmatized personal identity" have been identified:

(i)  *sensitization:* the individual becomes aware through a series of encounters of his or her difference from the norm, e.g. through being labelled by peers as a "sissy" or "tomboy";

(ii)  *signification:* the individual begins to assign meaning to these differences, as she or he becomes aware of the range of possibilities in the social world;

(iii)  *subculturization:* the stage of recognizing oneself through involvement with others, e.g. through first sexual contacts;

(iv) *stabilization:* the stage of full acceptance of one's feelings and way of life, such as through involvement in a supportive subculture of similarly inclined people.

There is no automatic progression through these stages. Each transition is as dependent on chance as on decision. There is no necessary acceptance of a final destiny, an explicit socio-sexual identity, for example, as gay or lesbian. Some individuals have choices forced on them, through stigmatization and public obloquy – for example, through arrest and trial for sexual offenses. Others adopt open identities for political reasons.

It can be argued that sexual feelings and desires are one thing, while acceptance of a particular social position and organizing sense of self – that is, an identity – is another. There is no necessary connection between sexual behavior and sexual identity.

Take, for example, Alfred Kinsey's best known statistic: some 37 percent of his male sample had had homosexual experiences leading to orgasm. But less than 4 percent were exclusively homosexual, and even they did not necessarily express a homosexual identity (Kinsey et al., 1948). So the apparent paradox is that there are some people who identify themselves as gay and participate in the gay community, but may not have any homosexual sexual activity. And others may be homosexually active (for example, in prison) but refuse the label of "homosexual."

The conclusion is inescapable. Feelings and desires may be deeply embedded, and may structure individual possibilities. *Identities,* however, can be chosen, and in the modern world, with its preoccupation with "true" sexuality, the choice is often highly political.

Take an example of this. During the 1980s, questions of race and ethnicity assumed a new prominence, and often these challenged many of the assumptions about the unitary nature of the newly openly-expressed lesbian and gay identities. The result was to highlight the different implications of homosexuality in different communities, and therefore the different meanings it might have. Here, for example, are the comments of an Asian gay man:

> Our community [i.e. the Asian community] provides a nurturing space. . . . [Families] are often bulwarks against the institutional and individual racism that we encounter daily. . . . And then we discover our sexuality. This sets us apart from family and

> community, even more so than for a white person. . . . More often
> than not, we live two lives, hiding our sexuality from family and
> friends in order to maintain our relationships within our
> community, whilst expressing our sexuality away from the
> community.
> (quoted in Weeks, 1990, p. 236)

The conflicting loyalties posed by "identity" are real. But again, they
suggest the importance of choice in adopting an identity that can help
an individual negotiate the hazards of everyday life.


# 5  Sexuality and Politics

## 5.1  Current debates

Concern with sexuality has been at the heart of western preoccupations
since before the rise of Christianity. And it has been a key element of
political debate for most of the past two centuries. More recently, it has
become a major factor in the redefinition of political battle lines
associated with the rise of the New Right in the US and Britain. It
seems that for many people the struggle for the future of society must
be fought on the terrain of contemporary sexuality.

It has been argued that this intense preoccupation with the erotic
grows out of, and simultaneously contributes to, a growing sense of
crisis about sexuality. At its center is a crisis in the relations between
the sexes, relations which have been profoundly unsettled by rapid
social change and by the impact of feminism, with its wide-ranging
critiques of the patterns of male domination and female subordination.
This in turn feeds into a crisis over the meaning of sexuality in our
culture, about the place we give sex in our lives and relationships,
about identity and pleasure, obligation and responsibility, and about
the freedom to choose. Many of the fixed points by which our sexual
lives were organized have been radically challenged during the past
century. But we do not seem quite certain what to put in their place. A
growing willingness to recognize the huge diversity of sexual beliefs
and behaviors has only sharpened the debate about how to cope with
these in social policy and personal practice.

A crisis about the meaning(s) of sexuality has, then, accentuated the
problem of how we are to regulate and control it. What we believe sex
is, or ought to be, structures our response to it. It is difficult to separate
the particular meanings we give to sexuality from the forms of control
we advocate. If we regard sex as dangerous, disruptive, and
fundamentally anti-social, then we are more likely to adopt moral
positions which propose tight, authoritarian regulation. This I shall call
the *absolutist* approach. If, on the other hand, we believe that sexual
desire is fundamentally benign, life-enhancing and liberating, we are
likely to adopt a relaxed, and perhaps radical set of values, to support a
*libertarian* position. Somewhere between these two approaches we can
find a third, which may be less certain as to whether sex is good or

bad. It is convinced, however, of the disadvantages both of moral authoritarianism and of excess. This is the *liberal* position. These three strategies of regulation have been present in our culture a long time. They still provide, I suggest, the framework for most current debates about sexual morality.

Historically, we are heirs of the absolutist tradition. This has assumed that the disruptive powers of sex can only be controlled by a clear-cut morality that is embedded in social institutions: marriage, heterosexuality, family life, and monogamy. Though it has its roots in the Judaeo-Christian religious tradition, absolutism is now grounded much more widely. It is basically the case that an essentially authoritarian moral code dominated the regulation of sexuality until the 1960s.

The libertarian position can best be seen as an oppositional tendency, whose task has been to expose the hypocrisies of the dominant order in the name of a greater sexual freedom. Its politics have been an important part of various radical political movements over the past 150 years. From the point of view of the analysis we have been following, however, perhaps the most interesting feature of libertarianism is its structural affinity with the absolutist approach: both assume the power of sexuality, and take for granted its disruptive effect. They draw, however, fundamentally divergent conclusions from this.

In practice, the regulation of sexuality for the past generation has been dominated by various forms of the liberal tradition. The duty of the law was to regulate the public sphere and, in particular, to maintain public decency. There were limits, however, to the law's obligation to control the private sphere, the traditional arena of personal morality. Churches might strive to tell people what to do in private; it was not the task of the state to attempt to do the same. The state, therefore, had little place in the enforcement of private standards, except (a major qualification) when harm was threatened to others. By such an approach there was an implicit assumption that society was no longer governed – if indeed it ever had been – by a moral consensus. The law should therefore limit itself to maintaining common standards of public decency.

It is important to note, however, that the argument that the law should be cautious about intervening in private life, to impose a single moral standard, did not lead to the belief that no control of sexuality was necessary. The liberal reforms of the 1960s did not involve a positive endorsement of either homosexuality, abortion, divorce, or explicit sexual representations in literature, film, or theater. Just as the liberal approach was uncertain about the merits of legal enforcement in a complex society, so it was undecided about the merits of the activities to which it directed its attention. The main purpose of the reforms was to relieve the burden of increasingly unworkable laws, while maintaining the possibility of a more acceptable form of social regulation: what Stuart Hall (1980) has called the "double taxonomy" of freedom *and* control.

I am arguing that the liberal reforms of the 1960s were attempts to come to terms with social change, and to establish a more effective form of social regulation. That is not, however, how they have been seen. Here, for example, are the views of a conservative commentator, Ronald Butt, concerning what became known as "permissiveness." Its essence, he suggested, was:

> ... permissiveness in one strictly limited social area (i.e. sex) coupled with the exaction of strict obedience to new norms prescribed by the liberal orthodoxy in another. In some matters, a charter of individual licence was granted which unleashed an unprecedented attack on old commonly held standards of personal behaviour and responsibility. . . .
> (Butt, 1985)

The attack on permissiveness as an attempt to establish a new norm has been central to conservative mobilization around sexual issues in the 1970s and 1980s. It has focused in particular on what it sees as several significant changes:

- the threat to the family;
- the challenge to sexual roles, particularly that posed by feminism;
- the undermining of heterosexual normality particularly through the attempts of the lesbian and gay movement to advance the full equality of homosexuality;
- the threat to values posed by a more liberal sex education, which was seen as inducting children into the acceptance of hitherto unacceptable sexual behavior;
- all these fears were compounded by, and thought to be symbolized in, the emergence of a major health crisis associated with HIV and AIDS.

It can be seen that all these concerns are related to a number of central questions that have existed throughout the modern history of sexuality: questions concerning family, the relative positions of men and women, sexual diversity, children. These remain the issues on which the history of sexuality still revolves.

There is, in fact, growing evidence that the distinctions between public and private life are perhaps not subtle enough to deal with some of the sexual issues which are now to the fore. If we take an issue like child sex abuse, it becomes clear that intervention to stop abuse may be regarded as transcending any respect for the inviolability of private life. What we think should be legitimately allowed in private is always controlled by wider values about the sort of society we want to see. These values, I would argue, are at the moment in a period of great flux and change. This is why issues such as pornography, which turn on the public impact of private taste and fantasy, become so controversial.

## 5.2   The future of sexuality

Despite the counterattack against "permissiveness" there are clear signs that less authoritarian attitudes towards sexuality continue to grow. The framework for this is a profound change in family relationships, which has two main aspects. The first is a critical shift in attitudes towards marriage and the family. Most people still get married, and this key feature of institutionalized heterosexuality does not appear to be threatened. But, to an important extent, the idea that marriage is for life does seem to have been undermined. A third of marriages now end in divorce, as do a high percentage of second marriages. The fact that people remarry so enthusiastically underlines the importance given to formal legal bonds. But even more importantly, there seems to be a will to try to get it right, by trying again.

This can be related to the belief that domestic intimacy is of fundamental importance as the basis for social life. "Modern society is to be distinguished from older social formations," Niklas Luhmann has argued, "by the fact that it has become more elaborate in two ways: it affords more opportunities both for impersonal and for more intensive personal relationships" (1986, p. 12). Marriage remains the dominant focus for the latter, as is suggested both by the continuing public disapproval of extra-marital relations, and the acceptance of pre-marital sexual relations if they are seen to be stable, marriage-like relations. But this is accompanied by a strong sense that modern marriage has to be worked at, and if it goes wrong it should be tried again.

The second feature about attitudes to the family that deserves attention is the growing perception that there are many different types of families. Families change over the life-cycles of their members. More importantly, however, for historical and cultural reasons different forms of family life have evolved, and the term "family" is now often used to describe domestic arrangements that are quite different from what was once "the norm." The best examples of this are provided by the phrase "one-parent families," and the gradual disappearance of the stigma of illegitimacy.

Alongside these changes there exists the widespread acceptance of birth control and support for liberal abortion laws, both of which underline a general belief that sexual activity should involve a degree of choice, especially for women.

There has been, however, one major exception to this gradual liberalization, and that is in attitudes towards homosexuality. There now seems to be a general acceptance that homosexual relations should not be subject to punitive laws, but their legality is still subject to tight limits. There is no general acceptance of homosexual relations as being on a par with heterosexual ones (Weeks, 1989). The British government even passed legislation in 1988 to ban the promotion of homosexuality as a "pretended family relationship." The phrase was new, and like all innovations in the language of sexuality was an attempt to deal with an emergent reality: this time, the claims of lesbians and gay men that their sexual choices were on a par with those of heterosexuals.

Clearly, the background to this, as well as to the public's hesitant attitudes towards homosexuality generally, was the crisis caused by the emergence of HIV and AIDS as a major health threat. The fact that the first people in the West identified as having AIDS were gay men has profoundly shaped responses to the health crisis, leading to a general stigmatization of people with the syndrome. AIDS served to crystallize a range of anxieties about shifts in sexual behavior that focused on the growth of a self-assertive gay consciousness since the 1960s. These anxieties seem, in turn, to have been part of the social anxiety generated by wider shifts in the culture of western societies caused by a growing social diversity. Alongside gay men, especially in the US, black people were seen as a potent source of "pollution" – they too were strongly linked to the new virus. Both sexual and racial diversity were seen as portending a threat to the hegemonic values of modernized societies.

What we are seeing is a growing recognition of the *facts* of social and sexual diversity, but only to a limited degree so far has this recognition been turned into a positive acceptance of diversity and moral pluralism. On the contrary, as we have seen, diversity, and the ever-growing social complexity which gives rise to it, arouses acute anxieties, which provide the basis of a constituency for the revival of more absolutist values. A more pluralist position, however, would seem to be more in line with the complexity and variety that can be observed in the history of sexuality as we have traced it. It seems likely that in the years ahead the challenge of sexual diversity will grow rather than diminish.

But will the question of sexuality remain central to social and moral debates? Rosalind Coward (1989) has suggested that, as we approach the end of the twentieth century, "the body," its fitness, health, and well-being, particularly in the wake of the AIDS crisis, is displacing a concern with "sex" in the traditional sense as focus for social concern. A final question we might ask ourselves is whether we are beginning to see the end of what Foucault called the "regime of sexuality." Is the throne of "King Sex" beginning to totter? And if so what would this mean?

Everything we have learned about the history of sexuality tells us that the social organization of sexuality is never fixed or stable. It is shaped in complex historical circumstances. As we enter the period known as "post-modernity" we are likely to see a new and radical shift in the ways we relate to our bodies and their sexual needs. The challenge will be to understand the processes at work in a more effective way than was apparent in the period of modernity.

# References

Amos, V. and Parmar, P. (1984) "Challenging imperial feminism,' in *Feminist Review*, no. 17, pp. 3–19.

Butt, R. (1985) "Lloyd George knew his followers," *The Times*, September 19.

Coward, R. (1983) *Patriarchal Precedents: Sexuality and Social Relations*, London, Routledge and Kegan Paul.

Coward, R. (1989) *The Whole Truth: The Myth of Alternative Medicine.* London, Faber.

Davidoff, L. (1983) "Class and gender in Victorian England," in Newton, J.L. et al. (eds) *Sex and Class in Women's History*, London, Routledge.

Ellis, H. (1946) *The Psychology of Sex*, London, William Heinemann.

Erikson, E. (1968) *Identity: Youth and Crisis*, London, Faber and Faber.

Faderman, L. (1980) *Surpassing the Love of Men*, London, Junction Books.

Foucault, M. (1977) *Discipline and Punish: The Birth of the Prison*, London, Allen Lane.

Foucault, M. (1979) *The History of Sexuality. Vol. 1: An Introduction*, London, Allen Lane.

Foucault, M. (1980) *Herculine Barbin, Being the Recently Discovered Memoirs of a Nineteenth Century French Hermaphrodite*, Brighton, England, Harvester.

Gagnon, J. and Simon, W. (1973) *Sexual Conduct*, London, Hutchinson.

Goffman, E. (1968) *Stigma. Notes on the Management of Spoiled Identity*, Harmondsworth, England, Penguin.

Hall, S. (1980) "Reformism and the legislation of consent," in Clarke, J. et al. (eds) *Permissiveness and Control: The Fate of the Sixties Legislation*, London, Macmillan.

Home Office (1957) *Report of the Committee on Homosexual Offences and Prostitution*, Command 247, London, HMSO.

Jackson, M. (1987), "'Facts of life' or the eroticisation of women's oppression? Sexology and the social construction of heterosexuality," in Caplan, P. (ed.) *The Cultural Construction of Sexuality*, London, Tavistock.

Kinsey, A. et al. (1948) *Sexual Behaviour in the Human Male*, Philadelphia and London, W.B. Saunders.

Kinsey, A. et al. (1953) *Sexual Behaviour in the Human Female*, Philadelphia and London, W.B. Saunders.

Krafft-Ebing, Richard von (1931) *Psychopathia Sexualis*, New York, Physicians and Surgeons Book Company.

Laqueur, T. (1990) *Making Sex: Body and Gender from the Greeks to Freud*, London, Harvard University Press.

Luhmann, N. (1986) *Love as Passion*, Cambridge, England, Polity Press.

McLaren, A. (1978) *Birth Control in Nineteenth Century England*, London, Croom Helm.

Plummer, K. (ed.) (1981a) *The Making of the Modern Homosexual*, London, Hutchinson.

Plummer, K. (1981b) "Going gay: identities, life cycles, and lifestyles in the male gay world," in Hart, J. and Richardson, D. (eds) *The Theory and Practice of Homosexuality*, London, Routledge.

Rich, A. (1984) "Compulsory heterosexuality and lesbian existence," in Snitow, A. et al. (eds) *Desire: The Politics of Sexuality*, London, Virago.

Sontag, S. (1989) *AIDS and its Metaphors*, London, Allen Lane.

Trumbach, R. (1989) "Gender and homosexual roles in modern western culture: the 18th and 19th centuries compared," in van Kooten Niekerk, A. and van der Meer, T. (eds) *Homosexuality, which Homosexuality?*, London, GMP Publishers.

Turner, B.S. (1984) *The Body and Society*, Oxford, Basil Blackwell.

Vance, C. (1984) "Pleasure and danger: towards a politics of sexuality," in Vance, C. (ed.), *Pleasure and Danger: Exploring Female Sexuality*, London, Routledge and Kegan Paul.

Vance, C. S. (1989) "Social construction theory: problems in the history of sexuality," in van Kooten Niekerk, A. and van der Meer, T. (eds) *Homosexuality, which Homosexuality?*, London, GMP Publishers.

Vicinus, M. (1989) "They wonder to which sex I belong: The historical roots of the modern lesbian identity," in van Kooten Niekerk, A. and van der Meer, T. (eds) *Homosexuality, which Homosexuality?*, London, GMP Publishers.

Walkowitz, J.R. (1980) *Prostitution and Victorian Society: Women, Class and the State*, Cambridge, England, Cambridge University Press.

Weeks, J. (1985) *Sexuality and its Discontents: Meanings, Myths and Modern Sexualities*, London, Routledge and Kegan Paul.

Weeks, J. (1989) *Sex, Politics and Society: The Regulation of Sexuality since 1800*, 2nd edn, Harlow, England, Longman.

Weeks, J. (1990) *Coming Out: Homosexual Politics in Britain from the Nineteenth Century to the Present*, 2nd edn, London, Quartet.

# 12 Religion, Values, and Ideology

Kenneth Thompson

## Contents

| | | |
|---|---|---|
| 1 | Introduction | 396 |
| 2 | Enlightenment: The Dilemmas of Modernity | 398 |
| 3 | Secularization and Community | 403 |
| 4 | Foucault: Integration through Discourses | 407 |
| 5 | Gramsci: The Struggle for Ideological Hegemony | 410 |
| 6 | Ideological Community | 412 |
| 7 | Conclusion | 420 |
| | References | 420 |

# 1 Introduction

How important is a shared culture in binding people together in a modern society? Is it necessary for a society's existence that people should share certain values and beliefs in order for them to engage in social cooperation, or is it enough that they seek to maximize their individual interests or that they submit to the dull compulsion of routine and necessity? Finally, does culture affect how people perceive their interests and, even, their sense of themselves as individuals with an identity derived from membership of some larger community or grouping? (See chapter 5, which deals with cultural formations in the emergence of modern society, and chapter 6, which discusses the links between discourses and power in the construction of a new sense of cultural identity in Western Europe.)

These questions about the part played by culture in modern society have been central to sociology since its emergence in the nineteenth century, and religion has figured prominently in the debates. This is not surprising in view of the derivations of the two terms "religion" and "sociology":

> The term "religion" is derived from *religio*, the bond of social relations between individuals; the term "sociology" is derived from *socius*, the bond of companionship that constitutes societies. Following Durkheim (1961), we may define religion as a set of beliefs and practices, relating to the sacred, which create social bonds between individuals. We may define sociology, naively, as the "science of community" (MacIver, 1917, p. 45). Sociology in general and the sociology of religion in particular, are thus concerned with the processes which unite and disunite, bind and unbind social relationships in space and time.
> (Turner, 1983, p. 8)

However, modern industrial societies are often referred to as "secular societies," meaning that religious or other absolute moral values no longer play a central role as cultural bonds uniting and disuniting social relationships (as Robert Bocock explained in chapter 5). Is this the case? Or might there be another side to the story in which there could still be some such cultural bonds operating as a kind of cultural "cement" to varying degrees in modern society? This is the main issue we will be addressing in this chapter. It seems to be a topical question if we are to judge from some of the most heated public controversies of recent years. The political movements of the New Right that came to prominence during the 1980s in Britain, America, and some other western countries, were also moral reform movements, supported by the so-called "Moral Majority" and various pressure groups campaigning over moral issues concerning the family, sex, abortion, education, broadcasting, etc. Above all, however, these were struggles to define or redefine national culture and identity. On some issues, such as government social policies, some of the most prominent critics of the New Right were to be found among bishops of the Church of

England and the American Catholic Bishops Conference (both churches produced official reports that criticized government social and economic policies on moral grounds). Whatever the merits of the arguments coming from different sides of these controversies, the amount of attention devoted to them by the mass media suggested that questions concerning the cultural and moral bases of society were still regarded as vitally important.

The discussion of the issues in this chapter will be structured as follows:

1   We will begin by considering what social thinkers in the wake of the Enlightenment had to say about the dilemma which the development of modernity had produced: namely, how to reconcile the critique, even the overthrow, of traditional social bonds with the need for some new basis of moral community. Some of the heirs of the Enlightenment, whether in the social sciences or in liberal, reformist, and socialist political movements, believed that science, and the reorganization of society along more rational lines, would supply adequate foundations for the new social order. At the same time, there were occasional suggestions that some elements of the sacred basis of social order might still persist, even though the process of secularization in the *public* sphere would mean that religion and other "pre-modern" or "irrational" philosophies would be increasingly confined to the *private* sphere.

2   We will examine some of the theories and evidence about the process of secularization in order to determine to what extent these predictions have been borne out. Some attention will be given to the suggestion by a recent social philosopher, Alasdair MacIntyre, that bonds of community based on shared moral values of an absolute sort have declined, leaving only appeals to people's feelings as the ground for moral judgment. However, we will see that surveys of beliefs and values show that some values are quite widely shared in modern societies.

3   These considerations lead on to a critique of that aspect of the secularization thesis which maintains that there is a separation between the public and private spheres, and that religion is increasingly confined to the private sphere. Foucault's account of the ways in which social integration is ensured on the basis of power mediated through dominant discourses will be used to raise questions about the separation of the public and private spheres. It also raises questions about the authority of such discourses and whether they are purely secular, or whether they still have traces of a religious, or sacred/ absolute element, which produce feelings of moral obligation and guilt.

4   Finally, we will combine insights drawn from a number of theorists, including Gramsci, Althusser, and Durkheim, who have analyzed those cultural processes that have the effect of creating ideological communities and identities. Here the emphasis is on the symbolic and ritual aspects of discourses. Our aim is to examine the claim that, although there may not be a single dominant ideology based on shared values in a modern society, there are cultural processes that reproduce

some social integration. For example, there is a certain degree of cultural integration to the extent that people are won over by the symbolic appeal of a combination of discourses, as in the appeal of the "imagined community" of the nation.

To summarize: It will be argued that the transition to modernity has not been marked by total eradication of the sacred and the triumph of the secular-profane. As Durkheim predicted, there will always be some sacred cultural elements in even the most modern, secularized society. On a day-to-day basis, these are likely to be less prominent than the rationalities and routines of mundane activities. However, there are traces of such sacred elements on three levels of culture that we will examine: belief in God and certain traditional moral values; discourses and discursive practices that regulate behavior; and ideological or "imagined" communities such as the nation. In this chapter, therefore, we will look for the traces which may reveal elements of culture that have a sacred character, or can take on such a character when activated by emotional appeals or threats. Gramsci described this search for traces as making an inventory of the "stratified deposits" of all the previous ways of thinking that make up a culture. This can be a way of knowing oneself "as a product of the historical process to date which has deposited in you an infinity of traces, without leaving an inventory" (Gramsci, 1971, p. 324). You might like to think of the sections of this chapter as suggesting ways in which you could draw up your own inventory of such traces in yourself.

## 2   Enlightenment: The Dilemmas of Modernity

The critical thought of the Enlightenment challenged the dominance of religion in the realm of ideas, including social and political thought, and the French Revolution seemed to deal a fatal blow to traditional institutions that embodied those ideas. Both in the realm of thought and the institutional sphere, modern societies were loosening their religious ties: they were described as undergoing a process of "secularization." The question for an emerging sociology was: What, if anything, will take the place of these ties? Could there be, or need there be, new ties that would serve the same social functions as religion?

Sociology was born in the nineteenth century in the aftermath of the French Revolution and in the midst of the socially disruptive developments of industrialization and urbanization. Old community ties were being broken and the new social relations were largely contractual, as between individual buyers and sellers, including individuals who sold their labor and those who bought it. According to Karl Marx, this kind of relationship was bound to produce alienation and conflict. In the short term, the conflict might be kept down if the real nature of the exploitative relations could be masked by "ideology" – ways of thinking that distract or distort perception – and so produce a "false consciousness." He explained the persistence and apparent revivals of religion by arguing that these served the interests of the dominant class, while recognizing that it answered some real needs for believers, even if the causes of those needs were socially derived. Marx's radical diagnosis was that religion, or ideologies serving similar functions, would not finally disappear, despite the intellectual critiques of the Enlightenment, until there was a revolutionary change in social relations. The political revolutions in France had not gone far enough because they had not produced a revolutionary change in economic relations. For this reason, Marx and Engels did not expect to see an automatic process of secularization in which religion would wither away, particularly in its adaptable modern form. Marx explained that, as far as western capitalist society was concerned, Christianity, especially Protestantism, was an ideally suitable belief system:

> The religious world is but the reflex of the real world. And for a society based upon the production of commodities, in which the producers in general enter into social relations with one another by treating their products as commodities and values, whereby they reduce their individual private labour to the standard of homogeneous human labour – for such a society, Christianity with its *cultus* of abstract man, more especially in its bourgeois developments, protestantism, Deism, etc., is the most fitting form of religion.
> (Marx, 1974, vol. 1, p. 83, and in Marx and Engels, 1955, p. 135)

Engels maintained that such modern forms of monotheistic religion would prove extremely durable: "In this convenient, handy, and universally adaptable form, religion can continue to exist as the immediate, that is, the sentimental form of men's relation to the alien natural and social forces which dominate them, so long as men remain under the control of these forces" (Engels in Marx and Engels, 1955, p. 148).

Less radical social theorists feared that society would indeed disintegrate if there was not religion, or an equivalent belief system to bind it together. In France, Alexis de Tocqueville (1805–59) warned of the socially disintegrative effects of the decline in shared "public virtues" and the increasing individualism, which involved the apathetic withdrawal of individuals from public life into a private sphere, absorbed in pure egoism, with a dangerous weakening of social bonds. He pinned his hopes on the development of voluntary associations between the state and the individual. Later in the century, this theme was developed by Émile Durkheim, who made causal connections between high rates of suicide resulting from conditions of egoism (an exaggerated emphasis on the self) and "anomie" (that is the absence of shared values and norms of behavior). Durkheim found lower rates of suicide among Catholics and Jews than among Protestants. He thought that the excessive individualism of Protestantism was a major cause of this, compared to the stronger communal ties among Catholics and Jews. Similarly, there were lower rates in wartime, when even Protestants felt their social ties more strongly and had a sense of common national identity. He noted that the French Revolution had given rise to attempts to establish a religion of reason, in order to create a new sacred basis for society. He thought that such efforts to create such a basis for a nation-state would recur in one form or another.

According to Max Weber, with the disappearance of the ethical foundations of economic activity, such as those provided by the Protestant Ethic, cooperation would rest on the narrow basis of individuals' rational calculation of how far they could pursue their interests without breaking the law. The ideas of pursuing a vocation and of altruistic service, which provided a religious foundation for the ethic of the professions, would wither in this climate. With the decline in traditional bases of authority, the only alternatives were rational-legal authority (such as rule-following in a bureaucracy) or charismatic authority, based on irrational attraction to a leader, in a devotion and identification akin to that of love. While Durkheim believed that there would inevitably be periodic revivals of sacred social ties, Weber was more skeptical and simply expressed the hope that "entirely new prophets," or charismatic leaders, would emerge to give a new moral basis to modern societies.

The issue of whether modern societies are exhausting their "cultural capital" of shared values and are likely to face increasing social problems as a result was given a topical expression in the 1990 BBC Reith Lectures on "The Persistence of Faith." In his first lecture, the British Chief Rabbi-elect (as he then was), Jonathan Sachs, claimed that the crumbling of communism in Eastern Europe during 1989 had been as significant a turning point in history as 1789, the year of the French Revolution and the birth of the secular state. In the middle of it all, the American historian Francis Fukuyama wrote an article, "The end of history?" stating that the struggle between competing ideologies, or sets of social values and ideals, was virtually dead. (This article (Fukuyama, 1989) is discussed more fully by David Held in chapter 13.) Instead, we would increasingly see societies based on nothing but "economic calculation, the endless solving of technical problems, environmental concerns, and the satisfaction of sophisticated consumer demands." Sachs responded by arguing that: "The human being as consumer neither is, nor can be, all we are, and a social system built on that premise will fail." He set out the dilemmas posed by the transition from traditional communities, where identities, beliefs, and life chances were narrowly circumscribed, to a modern situation in which careers, relationships, and lifestyles have become things to be chosen from a superstore of alternatives:

> Modernity is the transition from fate to choice. At the same time it dissolves the commitments and loyalties that once lay behind our choices. Technical reason has made us masters of matching means to ends. But it has left us inarticulate as to why we should choose one end rather than another. The values that once led us to regard one as intrinsically better than another – and which gave such weight to words like good and bad – have disintegrated, along with the communities and religious traditions in which we learned them. Now we choose because we choose. Because it is what we want; or it works for us; or it feels right to me. Once we

have dismantled a world in which larger virtues held sway, what is left are success and self-expression, the key values of an individualistic culture.

But can a society survive on so slender a moral base? It is a question that was already raised in the nineteenth century by figures like Alexis de Tocqueville and Max Weber, who saw most clearly the connection between modern liberal democracies and Judaeo-Christian tradition. It was de Tocqueville who saw that religion tempered individualism and gave those engaged in the competitive economy a capacity for benevolence and self-sacrifice. And it was he who saw that this was endangered by the very pursuit of affluence that was the key to economic growth.

Max Weber delivered the famous prophetic warning that the cloak of material prosperity might eventually become an iron cage. It was already becoming an end in itself, and other values were left, in his words, "like the ghost of dead religious beliefs." Once capitalism consumed its religious foundations, both men feared the consequences.

The stresses of a culture without shared meanings are already mounting, and we have yet to count the human costs. We see them in the move from a morality of self-imposed restraint to one in which we increasingly rely on law to protect us from ourselves. In the past, disadvantaged groups could find in religion what Karl Marx called "the feeling of a heartless world." A purely economic order offers no such consolations. A culture of success places little value on the unsuccessful.

The erosion of those bonds of loyalty and love which religion undergirded has left us increasingly alone in an impersonal economic and social system. Emile Durkheim was the first to give this condition a name. He called it anomie: the situation in which individuals have lost their moorings in a collective order. It is the heavy price we pay for our loss of communities of faith.
(Sachs, 1990, p. 6)

Although advanced from a religious point of view, this statement of the dilemmas faced by modern societies corresponds in many respects to those identified by social theorists in the post-Enlightenment period, as the references to figures such as Marx, de Tocqueville, Durkheim, and Weber make clear. According to these theorists, the long historical processes which formed modern industrial society included fundamental cultural developments. (Some examples of these are discussed by Robert Bocock in chapter 5.) They included such tendencies as increased differentiation of institutions, thereby increasing cultural variations between social spheres, progressive rationalization of more and more areas of life, demystification of the world, and the civilizing of patterns of behavior in everyday life. An underlying theme was that of "secularization": the reduction of the space occupied by religion in social life. This theme of secularization has remained central to sociological theories of modernity. However, as mentioned above, from the beginning of sociology there has been a debate about whether modern societies could exist without some balancing tendency to that of progressive secularization: that is, what might be termed "sacralization" tendencies. Even Max Weber, who emphasized the role of processes of demystification and progressive rationalization giving rise to secularization of the modern world, nevertheless talked about periodic explosions of "charisma" and charismatic leadership; he also emphasized the part played by religion in the formation of modern notions of the individual and in the development of capitalism. Similarly, his French contemporary Émile Durkheim, while emphasizing increasing specialization of the division of labor and the rights of the individual, also wrote about periodic revivals of sacred elements in society:

> Also, in the present day just as much as in the past, we see society constantly creating sacred things out of ordinary ones. If it happens to fall in love with a man and if it thinks it has found in him the principal aspirations that move it, as well as the means of satisfying them, this man will be raised above the others and, as it were, deified. . . . This aptitude of society for setting itself up as a god or for creating gods was never more apparent than during the first years of the French Revolution. At this time, in fact, under the influence of the general enthusiasm, things purely laical by nature were transformed by public opinion into sacred things: these were the Fatherland, Liberty, Reason.
> (Durkheim, 1961, pp. 243–5)

During World War I, Durkheim noted that the communal experience of warfare had created a moral consensus in France and an involvement in public ceremonies, which had served to accentuate the sense of being part of a sacred community.

It seems to be the case, therefore, that for the early sociologists, both tendencies co-exist in the cultures of modern societies – secularization *and* sacralization. Societies do become more differentiated into specialized institutional spheres of activity, with each institution enjoying a degree of relative autonomy, and so there is less scope for tight social integration by an overarching belief system, particularly one that prescribes standard norms for behavior in all public and private spheres. However, this does not rule out the possibility that some inherited values, symbols, and discourses may persist and be drawn on in recurring efforts to create cultural or ideological unity. These efforts may take various forms, such as moral crusades, revivals of nationalism, or religious revivals. We will concentrate on just two questions. The first is to ask whether there is an inevitable tendency in modern society for secularization to result in a loss of moral consensus and so of any shared cultural basis for social solidarity or community. The second question asks whether there are contrary tendencies, such as tendencies that make the "imagined community" of the nation into a sacred collectivity. The latter tendency occurs where there is an appeal to some collective identity derived from membership of an "imagined community" (Anderson, 1983), which can involve combinations of the discourses of nationalism, ethnicity, and religion. In the next section, we will examine some of the cultural processes involved in these trends.


# 3   Secularization and Community

Rabbi Sachs' concern about the loss of moral community in modern society bears a strong resemblance to the theme of "secularization" that has been a major strand in the theoretical legacy of Enlightenment social theory. At one level, secularization refers to a process of institutional differentiation, commencing in the Middle Ages and linked to the processes of industrialization, urbanization, and the rise of science. According to the secularization thesis, the bonds of community are subject to irreversible decline, and relationships between persons are reduced to the instrumental/technical level outside close family and friendship networks (Wilson, 1982; Dobbelaere, 1981). This historical process of secularization is said to be paralleled by a rejection of philosophical notions of an essential human nature and purpose, such as those of Aristotle which informed medieval thinking. According to the social theorist, Alasdair MacIntyre, the coherence of the medieval moral scheme was destroyed and the Enlightenment project of discovering rational secular foundations for morality collapsed in failure (MacIntyre, 1981). In his view, the result is a decline into "emotivism" in the twentieth century, where the only ground for making moral judgments is that which appeals to feelings. Although some claim that this represents an increase in individual choice and freedom from moral constraints, it runs the danger of leaving individuals open to manipulation. The commercial appeal is to individual rather than collective satisfaction, which makes it difficult to appeal for restraint (e.g. appeals for wage restraint to curb inflation) or to encourage community care on a moral basis. According to Wilson, the collapse of community means that "the large-scale social system . . . seeks not to rely on a moral order, but rather . . . on a technical order . . . Where morality must persist, then it can be politicized, and subject to the direct coercive power of the state": for example in the case of sexual or racial discrimination (Wilson, 1982, p. 161).

Is it the case that there is now no moral community in modern society? And are the main cultural processes that reproduce social order to be found in various institutional discourses, or in the manipulation of emotions, such as those evoked in nationalism? If there are still significant traces of religion in these different cultural processes then it could be that modern societies have not yet used up that part of their "cultural capital."

In contrast to the stark version of the secularization thesis, there are a number of alternative perspectives. One perspective, while accepting that aspect of the secularization thesis concerning institutional differentiation and loss of the overarching social significance of religion, argues that religion does not necessarily decline, but rather evolves and changes its form. It adapts in response to wider social and cultural forces. The adaptation will vary between societies, groups, and periods. One obvious contrast is between the high level of religious activity in America and the relatively low levels in Western Europe. (Eastern European countries have varied, with high involvement in Poland and lower levels in some other countries such as Hungary.) There are also variations in terms of strategies of resistance or accommodation to wider cultural trends, and in terms of what is "sacred." (Although we will focus on western societies, it is in non-western societies that one might find some of the most striking examples of varied strategies of resistance or accommodation to global trends such as modernization and secularization. It would be instructive to compare Islamic and Buddhist cultures in this respect.)

The main adaptations of religion in modern Western societies are divided into two sorts. The first sort concerns formal religious groups (churches, denominations, and sects) and the extent to which they accommodate themselves to mainstream social trends. American religious organizations appear to have been particularly successful in fitting in with the demands of the wider society and meeting the needs of their constituents. European churches have been less successful at adaptation, although the prominence of religion in the recent changes in some East European countries suggests that religion can still be a powerful force when combined with other discourses, such as nationalism. The second sort of adaptation is concerned with informal or "invisible" religion, which would seem to be infinitely variable as it leaves individuals free to construct their own meaning systems and versions of the sacred. However, there are problems in pinning down such beliefs and in discovering how much commitment people have to them.

Religious involvement is clearly not uniform throughout society, but is related to key socio-demographic indicators, such as age, sex, class, occupation, and education. Other important determining factors that have been suggested include experiences of deprivation of various kinds (e.g. loss of health, loss of close relatives or friends, loss of status, etc.), involvement in certain types of industry, and the decline or persistence of local community. Forecasts of future trends on the basis of the present religious involvements of different age groups have sometimes produced contradictory conclusions.

Strategies of religious adaptation in modern society range from accommodation – going along with cultural trends (sometimes referred to disparagingly as "internal secularization") – to various strategies of resistance. Weber, and his colleague Tönnies, drew a sharp contrast between the church type of religious organization, which represented the response of accommodation to society, and the sect type, which was oppositional. However, Bryan Wilson points out that the picture is more complicated and he has sub-divided sects into seven types of response to the world:

1   The *conversionist* sect: typical of evangelical, fundamentalist Christianity, which aims to change a corrupt world by changing

individuals, as in the case of the Salvation Army in its early days. This response may also take the form of a cult of those who follow a charismatic leader, as in the case of followers of certain "televangelists" in America.

2   The *revolutionary* sect: these groups look forward to the passing of the present social order, as in the case of Jehovah's Witnesses, and the Fifth Monarchy Men of seventeenth-century England.

3   The *introversionist* sect: here the response to the world is not to try to convert it or to overturn it, but to retire from it and seek the security of personal holiness, as with certain "holiness movements."

4   The *manipulationist* sect: examples of this type are Christian Scientists, Rosacrucians, and Scientologists, who claim some special knowledge and techniques for attaining goals generally accepted by society.

5   The *thaumaturgical* sect: this is composed of people who come together more as an audience than a fellowship, in order to make contact with the supernatural for personal purposes, as with Spiritualists who seek contact with dead relatives.

6   The *reformist* sect: this is often a later stage, rather than the original orientation, of a sect (such as the Quakers), and the sect remains separate and apart in order to provide a critique and an ethic for the society to which it is no longer hostile or indifferent.

7   The *utopian* sect: here the response to the world is mainly that of withdrawal into a perfectionist community life, as with the Tolstoyan communities and some "hippie" communes in the 1960s.

It is worth noting that at the time when Wilson developed this typology of sectarian responses (Wilson, 1963), its relevance seemed to be confined to relatively small groups in marginal organizations. Such groups were on the fringes of society and had little impact on mainstream political and cultural life. The subsequent "cultural revolutions" of the late 1960s and the conservative reactions of the late-1970s and 1980s have shown that such sectarian responses to the world can be much more widespread in their impact and have an effect on mainstream culture. The rise of the New Christian Right or Moral Majority in support of Reaganism in America, and the controversies over religion and Thatcherism in Britain in the 1980s, testify to the capacity for religious discourses to enter into potent combinations with others, such as political, economic, and nationalist discourses. It is clear that the contrast between accommodation and resistance does not necessarily equate with different types of religious organization, such as the church-sect typology. The political ideology of Thatcherism was supported by many fundamentalist sect members and opposed by a number of bishops of the Church of England. Meanwhile in Latin America and Eastern Europe the Roman Catholic Church provided some of the strongest resistance to the dominant political forces.

The extent to which religion continues to play an important role in the public life of modern societies depends on a combination of factors.

For example, Wallis and Bruce (1986) compared the relationship between a particular form of religion – conservative Protestantism – and politics in several societies, and found that there was a limited range of patterns. These were placed on a continuum between two types of society. The first type of society was that in which conservative Protestantism had a high degree of impact on politics (e.g. Northern Ireland and South Africa). At the other end were societies where conservative Protestantism had little continuous significant impact on politics, but in which it might be periodically mobilized for issue specific campaigns to amend some unacceptable feature of society (e.g. Canada, Australia, New Zealand, England, and Scotland). Occupying an intermediate position were societies in which conservative Protestants were able to exercise some continuing influence on the political process over a broad range of concerns and possessed established institutional machinery for articulating their political views, but did not dominate the social and cultural basis of politics, having to compete with other organized blocks of opinion (e.g. the US, the Netherlands, and Scandinavia). Wallis and Bruce suggested that these patterns can be explained in terms of certain specifiable factors:

1   the circumstances of formation of the socio-religious culture;
2   the changes which have occurred affecting the socio-religious culture, especially patterns of migration, secularization, and church accommodation;
3   the structure of politics and communications in the surrounding society (Wallis and Bruce, 1986, p. 231).

In summary, their argument is that a high level of political involvement on the part of conservative Protestants results from:

1   a socio-religious culture formed by sectarianism, rather than more tolerant denominations or a state church;
2   a situation where subsequent social changes continue to threaten the dominance of the ethnic group, but its own identity is not diluted by subsequent waves of immigrants of heterogeneous cultural character;
3   a structure of politics and communication which inhibits a cohesive two-party system along class lines.

Perhaps the most interesting examples are the intermediate cases, such as the United States and the Netherlands, because they illustrate how a minority religious group can maintain a strong base within an advanced industrial society and exert considerable influence at times. In the American case, conservative Protestantism has been able to benefit from the high degree of regionalism in American politics, the susceptibility of national politicians to pressure groups (e.g. "political action committees"), and from the fact that groups can buy time on radio or television or purchase their own station. Although there is some debate about how important "New Christian Right" organizations such as the Moral Majority were in American politics during the 1980s, there is no doubt that they had considerable influence, especially in local politics. In the Netherlands there is a different structure. The Calvinists created a series of institutions to oppose the influence of secular liberalism and Catholicism, including separate trade unions, schools, and a political party, the Anti-Revolutionary Party. These divisions were carried into almost every sphere of Dutch life, producing three integrated "pillars" (*zuilen*) containing all the institutions essential to modern life, within which individuals could conduct their activities and form their own *weltanschauung* (world-view). This situation is known as *verzuiling*: "columnization" or "pillarization" (Wallis and Bruce, 1986, p. 231).

Such examples of the public role of religion also call into question the assumption in the secularization thesis that religion retreats into the private sphere. However, there is some truth in Luckmann's contention that the secularization thesis ignores the extent to which "invisible" religion thrives in the private sphere, even if it appears to decline in the public sphere (Luckmann, 1967). Luckmann shares his colleague Peter Berger's phenomenological perspective in which individuals are seen as creating their own private meaning systems, which provide them with an interpretative framework and chosen identity. This view is contradicted by Foucault's work on discourses, which insists that prevailing notions of individuality tend to be molded to suit the interests of the dominant powers. As Beckford puts it,

> Indeed, the most provocative and disturbing aspect of Foucault's thought is the implication that the very idea of privatized religion, far from being marginal to the operation of modern society, might actually be a pre-condition for the latter's success. It would be thoroughly in keeping with his philosophical position for Foucault to have regarded the belief that private thoughts and feelings were marginal to the reproduction of societal domination as evidence that exactly the opposite was true, namely, that effective control and surveillance was conditional upon the belief that the individual could be considered as an autonomous monad. (Beckford, 1989, p. 127)

Foucault's ideas are explored further in the next section of this chapter.

# 4  Foucault: Integration through Discourses

Foucault calls into question the usefulness of examining cultural integration on the basis of a single dominant ideology. In particular, he questions the assumption that societies have ever been integrated on the basis of anything other than power, mediated through the dominant discourses of the period. The religious input to these discourses has always been considerable: discourses and discursive practices concerning the self, the body, sexuality, death, illness, health, and spiritual well-being, as well as discourses of human rights, justice, and peace. (Foucault's work on power and on sexuality was discussed in chapter 11.) As Beckford points out, one of the effects of Foucault's approach is to show that the very distinction between private and public spheres is itself a cultural product; similarly, the meaning attributed to the "individual" and to the individual's rights and beliefs derives from particular cultural-historical contexts. Foucault would have been reluctant to accept the idea that personal meanings, or values, have been cut adrift from systems of public regulation in modern societies.

> Since the Middle Ages at least, western societies have established the confession as one of the main rituals we rely on for the production of truth.
> ... For a long time, the individual was vouched for by the reference of others and the demonstration of his ties to the commonweal (family, allegiance, protection); then he was authenticated by the discourse of truth he was able or obliged to pronounce concerning himself. The truthful confession was inscribed at the heart of the procedures of individualization by power.
> In any case, next to the testing rituals, next to the testimony of witnesses, and the learned methods of observation and demonstration, the confession became one of the West's most highly valued techniques for producing truth. We have since become a singularly confessing society. The confession has spread its effects far and wide. It plays a part in justice, medicine, education, family relations, and love relations, in the most ordinary affairs of everyday life, and in the most solemn rites; one confesses one's crimes, one's sins, one's thoughts and desires, one's illnesses and troubles; one goes about telling, with the greatest precision, whatever is most difficult to tell. One confesses in public and in private, to one's parents, one's educators, one's doctor, to those one loves; one admits to oneself, in pleasure and in pain, things it would be impossible to tell to anyone else, the things people write books about. One confesses – or is forced to confess. When it is not spontaneous or dictated by some internal imperative, the confession is wrung from a person by violence or threat; it is driven from its hiding place in the soul, or extracted from the body. Since the Middle Ages, torture has accompanied it like a shadow, and supported it when it could go no further: the dark twins. The most defenseless tenderness and the bloodiest of powers have a similar need of confession. Western man has become a confessing animal.
> ... The confession is a ritual of discourse in which the speaking subject is also the subject of the statement; it is also a ritual that unfolds within a power relationship, for one does not confess without the presence (or virtual presence) of a partner who is not simply the interlocutor but the authority who requires the confession, prescribes and appreciates it, and intervenes in order to judge, punish, forgive, console, and reconcile; a ritual in which

the truth is corroborated by the obstacles and resistances it has
had to surmount in order to be formulated; and finally, a ritual in
which expression alone, independently of its external
consequences, produces intrinsic modifications in the person who
articulates it: it exonerates, redeems, and purifies him; it
unburdens him of his wrongs, liberates him, and promises him
salvation. For centuries, the truth of sex was, at least for the most
part, caught up in this discursive form.
    . . . The confession was, and still remains, the general standard
governing the production of the true discourse on sex. It has
undergone a considerable transformation, however. For a long
time, it remained firmly entrenched in the practice of penance.
But with the rise of Protestantism, the Counter Reformation,
eighteenth-century pedagogy, and nineteenth-century medicine, it
gradually lost its ritualistic and exclusive localization; it spread; it
has been employed in a whole series of relationships: children
and parents, students and educators, patients and psychiatrists,
delinquents and experts. The motivations and effects it is
expected to produce have varied, as have the forms it has taken:
interrogations, consultations, autobiographical narratives, letters;
they have been recorded, transcribed, assembled into dossiers,
published, and commented on. But more important, the
confession lends itself, if not to other domains, at least to new
ways of exploring the existing ones. It is no longer a question
simply of saying what was done – the sexual act – and how it was
done; but of reconstructing, in and around the act, the thoughts
that recapitulated it, the obsessions that accompanied it, the
images, desires, modulations, and quality of the pleasure that
animated it. For the first time no doubt, a society has taken upon
itself to solicit and hear the imparting of individual pleasures.
(Foucault, 1980, pp. 58–63)

Foucault's work on discourses and discursive practices, such as sex
and confession, helps us to understand some of the ways in which
modern societies cohere at the cultural level by constructing and
regulating individuals and their subjectivity. One of the social functions
of discourses is that they close off alternative ways of speaking and
thinking, often in ways that reflect the distribution of power in society.
In this respect discourses have an effect similar to that of ideology as
portrayed by Marx, for whom "the ideas of the ruling class are, in every
age, the ruling ideas: i.e. the class which is the dominant material force
in society is at the same time its dominant *intellectual* force" (Marx and
Engels, 1972, p. 172). However, although Foucault showed that
there may be similarities (or articulations) between discourses of
different topics at any one time, which strengthen their power, it is
important to stress that they may also conflict. At various moments in
the history of western societies, for example, different and
contradictory discourses of the individual have co-existed, some of
which stressed a freedom to act, while others emphasized the
individual's duty to society.

## 5   Gramsci: The Struggle for Ideological Hegemony

Marx's ideas on ideology have also been developed by Gramsci in directions that emphasize the fact that there may be conflict and struggle over ideologies in modern society. The *Selections from Prison Notebooks* (Gramsci, 1971), written between 1929 and 1935, have been important in this respect. Gramsci insisted on the relative independence of politics and ideology from economic determinants and emphasized the ways in which people can change their circumstances by struggle. The capitalist class could not secure domination by economic factors alone, and it might have to resort to political coercion through the state, but increasingly it sought to attain domination through the ideological apparatuses of civil society – the churches, the family, education, and even trade unions. (If he were alive today, he would probably give a prominent place in that list to the media of mass communication.) He suggested that this ideological domination (hegemony) was seldom complete because the working class had a dual consciousness, one part of which reflected the ideas of the capitalist class and its intellectuals, while the other part was a common-sense knowledge derived from the workers' everyday experience of the world.

Gramsci's ideas have been particularly influential in the study of ideologies in relation to the culture of everyday life and popular culture. Gramsci maintained that moral and philosophical intellectual leadership (hegemony) could only be achieved by connecting up with the common-sense, or popular culture, of the subordinate classes. There are many layers of different cultural elements within such cultures: residues of old philosophies and practices, folklore, superstitions, popular religion (as distinct from intellectually formulated, official religion), local and family customs. In modern society this popular culture is frequently penetrated by elements of mass media culture, which become lodged in the common consciousness: hence the popularity of "golden-oldies" programs, particularly at times of nostalgic remembrance, such as Christmas and New Year's Eve. A number of other ideological themes or discourses are articulated with, or grafted onto, a concern with the family, especially discourses of community and of the nation, through which real social divisions are transcended and an idealized past symbolically recaptured. Raymond Williams, in his *The Country and the City* (1975), provided a detailed historical study of this ideology, showing how the series of contrasts it draws – between the past and present, the country and the city, the simple and the complex, the individual and the mass, the naïve and the corrupted – have been strongly present in English literature since the sixteenth century, and especially since the development of industrial capitalism in the early nineteenth century. It is probably not fortuitous that a nostalgic idealization of the past has been a core element in the inherited repertoire of ideological themes handed down to us from the Victorian period. In his *Leisure in the Industrial Revolution* (1980), Hugh Cunningham argues that the development of the provision of

Christmas parties for members of the working class by philanthropic organizations in England such as the Mechanics Institutes during the 1830s and 1840s, a period of acute class conflict, was conceived very much as an enterprise in class amelioration. He suggests that the symbols of "Olde England," with which such parties were festooned, formed part of "a romantic attempt to re-create a socially-harmonious medieval past" (p. 101), to transport the members of different classes from the real antagonism of the present into an imaginary universe of class-concord founded on tradition. These symbols are still at work in Christmas card scenes of snow-covered villages and families of all classes flocking into the village church or singing carols with neighbors round the Christmas tree. Many of the customs and rituals that regulate our practice of Christmas – rituals of neighborliness and charity, family and local traditions – can be seen as binding us at the level of our behavior to an imaginatively reconstructed past, a golden age of warm community. Such Christmas themes, with their idealized solutions to social difficulties, cannot be separated, in western societies, from their Christian basis:

> It is by virtue of this sedimented substratum of Christian belief that, no matter how much Christmas may have been secularized, Christmas is the period of the year *par excellence* in which we are constituted as subjects of the "as if"; that is, induced to live our relations to the world *as if* certain conditions that we know do not obtain did exist, *as if* imaginary ways of posing and resolving real difficulties were practicable.
> (Open University, 1981, p. 63)

Of course, there is another side to Christmas, as we all know. The idealized picture of harmony in family, community, and nation is constantly in danger of being shattered. Christmas is often a time of tension and strain for families. Local communities, and the nation at large, may be shocked by the realities of homelessness, drunken behavior, and violence. Even the Church has had to struggle to safeguard this Christian festival against complete take-over by popular culture, whether carnivalesque revelry or commercialization.

Gramsci insisted that there was nothing automatic about the working of ideology – the different discourses and cultures were not articulated together without constant effort and even contestation. He frequently illustrated this problem by reference to religion and the efforts of the Catholic Church to cement different classes and their cultures into a single social bloc:

> The problem is that of preserving the ideological unity of the entire social bloc which that ideology serves to cement and unify. The strength of religions, and of the Catholic Church in particular, has lain, and still lies, in the fact that they feel very strongly the need for the doctrinal unity of the whole mass of the faithful and strive to ensure that the higher intellectual stratum does not get separated from the lower. The Roman church has always been the most vigorous in the struggle to prevent the "official" formation of

> two religions, one for the "intellectuals" and the other for the
> "simple souls."
> (Gramsci, 1971, p. 328)

Insofar as ideological unity is achieved in a culturally complex and
class-divided society, it is secured by an articulating principle which
ties together the various cultural elements or discourses. Ideological
struggle is concerned with efforts to put such an articulating principle
into effect, which can entail "disarticulation" and "rearticulation" of
cultural layers or discourses. Gramsci gave some indication as to what
would determine the victory of one hegemonic principle over another
when he declared that a hegemonic principle did not prevail by virtue
of its intrinsic logic but rather when it manages to become a "popular
religion." He explained what this means by stating that a class which
wishes to become hegemonic has to "nationalize itself," and that:

> the particular form in which the hegemonic ethico-political
> element presents itself in the life of the state and the country is
> "patriotism" and "nationalism," which is "popular religion," that
> is to say it is the link by means of which the unity of leaders and
> led is effected.
> (Gramsci, 1975, vol. 2, p. 1084, and in Mouffe, 1981, p. 232)

In the next section, on "Ideological Community," we will examine
some of the ways in which different discourses are articulated together
(combined in new ways) to construct particular versions of the nation
as an imagined community. The analysis will draw on Durkheim's
sociology of religion and Althusser's theory of ideology in addition to
the ideas that we have already covered. Althusser's contribution is
significant because it marked another step forward in the reformulation
of Marx's theory of ideology, moving away from economic determinism
and the idea that ideology is merely an illusion, and also developing
Gramsci's ideas on hegemony through the concept of ideological state
apparatuses.

# 6   Ideological Community

Durkheim's theory of religion was based on the study of totemism in
the aboriginal, classless, societies of Australia and North America, but
it was intended to have a wider applicability to modern societies.
Although he did not use the word "ideology" in this connection, it can
be argued that his theory has some similarities to theories of ideology
as developed by Marxists such as Althusser. Both Durkheim and
Althusser described the socially binding functions of ideologies, and
emphasized the ways in which they gave individuals a sense of
identity. According to Durkheim, religious beliefs and practices are
collective representations that carry and bestow authority because they
seem to emanate from a transcendent source: they transcend the
individual, sectional interests, utilitarian or mundane considerations.

They have a "halo of disinterestedness," as Benedict Anderson says of the ties that bind us to the nation as an "imagined community" (Anderson, 1983). Durkheim also provides examples of the symbolic codes through which these systems of representation are constructed in the form of discursive chains that articulate differences and unity. (Durkheim's structuralist approach was discussed by Bocock in chapter 5.) For example, in the case of the totemic religion of the clan-based societies of the Australian aborigines, sometimes the collective representations are arranged in terms of differences that accord with a binary logic of opposition, such as sacred versus profane; others are unitary like the clan totem. These categories are socially constraining; they set rules of thought and behavior which have the power to elicit obedience. However, the social conditions or relations that gave rise to them are no longer evident; they seem to have taken on a life of their own. In other words, these symbolic codes, or discursive chains, have become relatively autonomous, although they may still bear the imprint of the conditions that gave rise to them.

Marx had suggested that there was an affinity or fit between religion and economic relations, which he described in terms of a fairly direct (although distorted) reflection. He gave the example of the fit between capitalist relations, where labor was reduced to standard units whose value depended on commodity prices, and a corresponding Christian doctrine, especially in Protestantism, which talked in terms of abstract individuals (Marx, 1974, vol. 1, p. 83). Althusser attempted to move away from this economic determinism in which superstructural elements like religion are seen as simply "reflections" of the economic base. He developed the concept of Ideological State Apparatuses – institutions such as religion, the media, and education – which helped to reproduce the conditions which made it possible for the relations of production to continue.

Althusser says that Ideological State Apparatuses (ISAs), which appear as "private" institutions, such as the Church, law, media, trade unions, schools, political parties, are really part of the public state because they function for the state in reproducing ruling-class power, and they are called ideological because they function primarily through ideology (Althusser, 1971). They function by incorporating all classes in society within a dominant ideology, securing the hegemony of the dominant classes. Through the process of what Althusser called "interpellation," people are made into agents, or carriers, of social structure. Interpellation is analogous to hailing a person in the street: ideologies "address" people and give them a particular identity or subjectivity and a position in society.

A number of criticisms have been made of Althusser's theory. One criticism is that it is still too deterministic and ignores the fact that, throughout history, subordinate groups have developed their own interpretations of beliefs and symbols and frequently opposed those of dominant classes (Abercrombie et al., 1990). It also ties ideology too closely to serving the function of reproduction of the relations of production. One consequence of this is that he downgrades the contemporary importance of religion and says that the crucial ideological institution is now education. Clearly, there is some reason for this downgrading if the comparison is being made between the role of the Church in reproducing the relations of production in feudalism and the situation in contemporary capitalism. However, it offers no insights for comparing different capitalist societies, or different ideological tendencies between groups within the same society. For this purpose it is more fruitful to adopt a sociological approach that is sensitive to cultural differences, concentrating on the actual articulation of various discourses or institutions in concrete social formations (e.g. Britain compared with America, in particular periods). Furthermore, although education may be found to contribute more directly to the reproduction of relations of production in all capitalist societies, religion may still be a potent factor in combination with other discourses in the construction of ideological communities, such as the imagined community of the nation.

Benedict Anderson defines the nation as "an imagined political community – imagined as both inherently limited and sovereign" (outside it are "alien Others," inside there is a demand for total allegiance). He adds that "It is *imagined* because the members of even the smallest nation will never know most of their fellow members, meet them, or even hear of them, yet in the minds of each lives the image of their communion" (Anderson, 1983, p. 15). The fraternity of nationalism is so deeply established that people are prepared to kill or die for it. With the pluralization of religions and the break-up of dynastic empires, which had preceded nation-states, the nation emerged as the ultimate ideological community for most people, and the one with the strongest imagined sense of timelessness, disinterestedness, and naturalness. These are the same characteristics that Durkheim said gave a society its god-like power and its binding sacredness.

Despite the assumption of theories of secularization stemming from the Enlightenment that religion would steadily decline in significance, it continues to play a prominent role in the ideological construction of national communities. Islamic Iran and Catholic Poland are obvious examples. In Britain, a variety of discourses, and sets of differences, have been rearticulated to construct the imagined community of the British nation at different times. Some of the most interesting are those in which religious and political discourses were combined in attempts to produce an ideologically unifying nationalism. In the period of internal upheaval and class conflict that accompanied the Industrial Revolution, such a combination occurred in response to the perceived threat posed by revolutionary France. New politically conservative theories of the nation were developed by Burke, Coleridge, and others, drawing on religious as well as political discourses. Public opinion was mobilized against the alien threat and British national characteristics were rediscovered or invented. Religious discourse was one of the key sites where there was a struggle to produce the required ideological effect of cementing national unity and rooting out any divisive tendencies. Nowhere was this more evident than in the remarkable change that took place in Methodism, which at one stage was regarded as something akin to a revolutionary fifth column, but which after the French Revolution became a pillar of support for King and country, and during the French wars passed resolutions to that effect at its annual conferences (Andrews, 1970; Thompson, 1986).

The great theorist of English conservatism, Edmund Burke, in his *Reflections on the Revolution in France* (1790), emphasized cultural practices which instilled social and moral discipline, and an essential part of that discipline derived from the established Church, which consecrated the state and provided powerful incentives to obedience and order. Similarly, Samuel Taylor Coleridge argued against religious individualism, such as that featured in the ideas leading to American independence. He said that the French wars had made the nation more serious, moral, and unified, and in 1834 he suggested that another threat of invasion might be good for morale (Stafford, 1982). This yearning for a return to wartime unity has sometimes been heard again in the post-World War II period and appears to be a recurring feature in the construction of the imagined community of the British nation: a closing of ranks against the external threat of an alien Other, variously represented by Revolutionary France, Napoleonic France, Fascist Germany, Communist Russia in the Cold War, Galtieri's Argentina in the Falklands War of 1982, and the Iraq of Saddam Hussein in 1991. Although there were economic and political conflicts involving national interests in each case, they were also efforts at ideological self-definition of the national community, contrasting Britain's virtuous characteristics with the dangerous and even insane vices of the alien Other.

It is not difficult to understand why periods of social tension or crisis should give rise to more pronounced efforts to articulate a dominant discourse defining the sacred character of the imagined community by contrasting it with an alien opponent. Most people would agree that in such periods of social tension public discourse becomes more like that of an intense social drama and that there is a shift away from the mundane concerns with means and ends that characterize the discourses of everyday life. What is more controversial is whether modern societies *need* to incorporate members into a dominant ideology with shared values. The authors of *The Dominant Ideology Thesis* (Abercrombie et al., 1980) are critical of Althusserian and Durkheimian theories for suggesting that ideology, or shared values, have to fulfill such a need in order for capitalist societies to go on reproducing themselves. They are particularly critical of the neo-Durkheimian argument put forward after the Coronation of Queen Elizabeth II by Edward Shils and Michael Young in their famous article "The meaning of the coronation" (1953). The critics interpret this neo-Durkheimian argument as being to the effect that modern capitalist societies require a powerful set of rituals in order to sustain a core of common values, into which the British working class had supposedly been incorporated at that time. This interpretation appeared to be borne out by Shils's subsequent statement that "the coronation of Elizabeth II was the ceremonial occasion for the affirmation of the moral values by which the society lives. It was an act of national communion" (Shils,

1975, p. 139). This was certainly a common view shared by many sociologists, such as Talcott Parsons in America, who had developed Durkheim's ideas in a functionalist direction. It was attacked at the time by the Marxist sociologist Norman Birnbaum, who criticized Shils and Young for providing no evidence for the supposed value consensus in Britain and for under-estimating the extent to which there existed conflicting values and even outright political opposition on the part of the working class (Birnbaum, 1955). The critique was extended by Abercrombie and his colleagues to cover studies such as that by Blumler of the investiture of the Prince of Wales, where the ceremony was said to serve the social function of reaffirming values associated with family solidarity and national pride (Blumler et al., 1971).

However, there is a difference between a functionalist Durkheimian theory which assumes that modern capitalist societies need rituals in order to incorporate the working class into a core of common values, and a more structuralist Durkheimian theory of ideology. The latter does not assume that a capitalist society is held together by incorporating the working class into a common culture including a set of core values held by all members. Durkheim himself did not believe that existing modern societies were very successful in integrating their members through shared values, even though he hoped that some day they might develop such a moral unity. He charted their failure by reference to their high suicide rates and other indicators of lack of social integration. Although he left unspecified the degree to which civic rituals and ceremonies might continue to have some solidifying effects, he believed that certain national symbols, such as the flag, and ceremonies like those of Bastille Day in France, clearly had some effect. They re-presented significant events as portrayed in discourses concerning the nation's history and they generated in people a sense of common identity.

The lesson to be drawn from this debate is not that civic symbols and ceremonies testify to an existing unity, or that these are essential to the very existence and functioning of a capitalist society. The implication of Durkheim's sociology is that modern society contains a variety of "collective representations" – discourses and practices that are economic, political, religious, etc. – and that sociological analysis is concerned with showing how they "articulate" with each other to promote or hinder different sorts and levels of social solidarity. Some social pressures towards cooperation will be based on routine and custom, including customary working practices; or on "disciplinary regimes" mediated by institutions such as education and the law. Other sources of cooperation rest on complementarity of functions and exchange of services, as in many market transactions. At the most general cultural level of moral values the secularization thesis suggests that there is a weakening of consensual ties in modern society, although the European Value Systems Study and other research reveals a surprisingly high level of general agreement. Finally, Durkheim seems to have been proved right in coming to the conclusion that there would continue to be some solidarity ties that resulted from the awe and reverence inspired by symbols and ceremonies expressive of the experience of the transcendence and power of the collectivity itself. Viewed from this perspective, it does seem plausible to suggest that, in Britain for example, discourses concerning royalty and religion can articulate together to produce a sense of awe and reverence for the imagined political community of the nation. International sporting contests may both heighten the sense of national bonding and emphasize national differences. None of these can be taken as representing a core set of values that are essential for the reproduction of capitalist relations of production. But they are nonetheless important in constructing ideological communities and interpellating individuals as subjects within such communities. However, individuals and groups are not passive receivers of such discourses; they are actively involved, in varying degrees, in interpreting and sometimes even contesting them, as illustrated by the different sectarian subcultural responses described by Bryan Wilson. The question of exactly how, and to what extent, people are integrated into ideological communities, can only be answered by following up the theoretical analysis with empirical investigations of the creation of ideologies, their transmission, and responses to them.

In the case of civic symbolic events and rituals, such as those which involve heads of state or royalty, analysis shows that they have some success in combining several discourses to produce dramatizations of the nation as a symbolic or imagined community. In the United States "civil religion" includes events and ceremonies such as Memorial Day, the birthdays of Washington and Lincoln, the Fourth of July, and Veterans' Day. These phenomena have taken on a significance that purely religious festivals had in societies with an established or state religion. In the US, the secular saints are figures such as Washington and Lincoln, and the sacred shrines can be visited at Arlington and Gettysburg. The civil religion is also prominent in its ceremonial form at Presidential Inaugurations, when the authority of the state receives its sacred legitimation.

In Britain, the Queen is spoken of as the head of the great family of the nation (and head of a family of nations – the Commonwealth); she is also Head of State and Head of the Church. Familial discourse features prominently in combination with political and religious discourses. Many civic rituals celebrate points in the life-cycle of members of the royal family, such as the marriage of Prince Charles and Lady Diana in 1981 and the annual celebrations of the Queen's birthday. They frequently involve and cement a link with other institutions, as when the Queen as Head of State takes part in the State Opening of Parliament, or engages in the military ritual of the Trooping of the Colour on the monarch's official birthday. Not the least important function is the link forged with the nation's past by ceremonies such as that on Remembrance Day, when members of the royal family lay wreaths honoring the war dead, and veterans of past wars join in the parade. All of these events contain "manufactured" or "invented" traditions, many of them of quite recent origin, which are broadcast to the nation, and members of the vast audience are drawn to identify with the imagined community and its past: in this way they are constituted and addressed ("interpellated") as subjects. The development of the 1953 coronation ceremony in Britain as a televised event is a good illustration of the invention of tradition, and of the manufactured nature of the process of creating a sense of community. The ceremony was adapted to the needs of television, while the BBC took upon itself the responsibility for deciding what kind of tone and impression should be created and transmitted, even down to the specification of what sorts of scenes and objects should be given prominence. The decision to go for a "reverential" approach, with one-third of the total footage taken up with symbolic shots (focused on inanimate features of Westminster Abbey – the altar cross, Coronation Plate, stonework, etc.), was aimed at eliciting a sense of respectful awe and reverence, which was further communicated by the invention of an appropriate style of hushed-voice commentary by Richard Dimbleby (Chaney, 1983). These are all aspects of the process of communalization and interpellation of subjects through which discourses can have ideological effects. To the extent that millions of viewers and listeners are won over by the discourse, with all its attractive pageantry, nostalgia, and familiar symbols, they recognize themselves as the subjects addressed, and willingly consent to their "subjection" to the sovereign power that it represents: that of the transcendent or "sacred" collectivity, the imagined community.

What is being suggested here is not a defense of the "dominant ideology thesis," which was effectively criticized by Abercrombie et al. (1980; 1990). There is no question of there being any functional necessity for, or economistic determination of, these ideological discourses. It cannot be established that they are essential to the reproduction of capitalist relations of production or that they are determined in the last instance by the economy. What is being argued is that various forms of culture – Durkheim's "collective representations," Foucault's "discourses," or what are more generally referred to as symbols, beliefs, values, rituals, and socially meaningful practices – can all have ideological effects. That is to say, they are ideologically effective if they persuade people that their society is a particular kind of unitary entity in which they have a particular kind of identity.

Modern societies are complex entities and it is not surprising that they are often described as "multicultural." In Britain and the US there are minority groups whose religions are not Christian – e.g. Jews, Muslims, Hindus, Buddhists, and others. However, even if there is seldom a single dominant ideology that unites all social classes and subcultural groups together, there is evidence of ideological processes at work in binding many of them together to varying degrees. We have mentioned some of these, including civic rituals, various inherited religious beliefs and values, ceremonies, and popular culture. Individuals, groups, and institutions that wish to influence people or exercise power will struggle to control this cultural "capital." Politicians, preachers, advertisers, managers, and other professional "cultural persuaders" are adept at manipulating symbols and constructing discourses that have an emotional appeal. The more deeply sedimented the layers of culture that they appeal to, the greater will be their persuasiveness. Much of the debate about the relative success or failure of the New Right movement for ideological renewal in the 1980s, particularly the British version labelled "Thatcherism," has been concerned with identifying the key elements in its cultural appeal and assessing their impact on different groups. It is worth taking note of these assessments, but the main purpose in considering them here is to illustrate the ways in which cultural processes do have ideological effects without there being a unitary dominant ideology.

As Gill Seidel pointed out, in an article comparing the British and French New Right, their ideology combined a neo-liberal emphasis on individual enterprise and free markets with more conservative ideas of national culture and identity (Seidel, 1986). In Gramsci's terms, their proponents were engaged in a cultural struggle to create a counter-hegemonic ideology to replace what they saw as the dominant ideology of the post-war era – the liberal and social democratic consensus. The French New Right group GRECE (*Groupement de Recherche d'Étude pour une Civilisation Européenne*) referred to this strategy quite explicitly as "right-wing Gramscism" (Seidel, 1986, p. 108). The British conservative philosopher, Roger Scruton, editor of *The Salisbury Review* and author of a weekly column in *The Times*, expressed this in terms of rhetoric:

> The main tasks for conservative rhetoric are to establish in the public mind the inseparability of market freedom and economic leadership, and to integrate the philosophy of the market into the underlying principle of order which both motivates conservative politics, and attracts the votes of a conservative electorate . . . Such a rhetoric . . . must . . . be taken from the broader realms of political ideology . . . Conservative rhetoric is, or ought to be . . . a rhetoric of order.
>
> (Scruton, 1982, p. 38)

This rhetoric constitutes what Foucault called a "discursive ensemble" – a network of interlinked words and meanings with its own internal coherence. Scruton argued that the most important social forces are "language, religion, custom, associations and traditions of political order – in short, all those forces that generate nations" (Scruton, 1982, p. 14).

Whether a political ideology such as Thatcherism, Reaganism, or the New Right represents a good example of the ways in which different discourses have ideological effects is open to debate. It might be more realistic to regard such political ideologies as merely the most overt and explicit examples of cultural processes that have ideological effects: changing or sustaining relations of domination in a society. Such relatively short-lived movements for ideological change or renewal as the New Right are interesting mainly for what they reveal about these underlying and continuing cultural processes. Thus, in this chapter we have chosen to focus not so much on the many sources of social and cultural division within an advanced industrial society, but on cultural processes which may have the ideological effect of sustaining the existing social order.

## 7 Conclusion

It is not difficult to see why the study of culture should occupy an important place in sociological analysis. If it has such ideological effects – persuading people to see their society as a particular kind of unitary entity in which they themselves have a certain identity and so sustaining or changing relations of domination – then it is indeed powerful. The very legitimacy of the state's claim to exercise power over individuals rests on its success in convincing people that it acts in their interests. In circumstances of international economic competition and periodic crises, the state depends on its success in harnessing the solidarity feelings of national community in support of its power. It is in such circumstances that we are likely to witness the sorts of upsurges of nationalist symbolism, including civil religion involving royalty and civic rituals, that we have discussed.

However, there is nothing mechanical or inevitably determined in the working of such ideologies. Whether culture has particular ideological effects depends on processes of social construction and transmission of meanings and their reception. The sense of being part of a unitary entity such as a national community may well be rooted in real elements of shared characteristics and common history, but these are frequently matters of dispute and contestation, linked to different interests and power struggles. Territory, language, religion, race, etc., are all sources of dispute and have to be ideologically constructed, or interpreted, in order to produce a sense of belonging to a national community.

The imagined community of the nation is the site of ideological contestation and power struggles, as is evident in the resurgence of ethnic-religious nationalisms throughout the world. In this chapter we have tried to show how ideological community is produced, or imagined, and individual identity constructed. We have also shown that older symbols and values, such as those deriving from religious sources, do not necessarily disappear from modern society as the inevitable result of a unilinear process of secularization. There are strong traces of them in various layers of culture and they are capable of being adapted, or articulated with non-religious elements in new combinations. The extent to which these have an ideological impact depends on a range of factors, as we have seen.

## References

Abercrombie, N., Hill, S., and Turner, B.S. (eds) (1980) *The Dominant Ideology Thesis*, London, Unwin Hyman.

Abercrombie, N., Hill, S., and Turner, B.S. (eds) (1990) *Dominant Ideologies*, London, Unwin Hyman.

Abrams, M., Gerard, D., and Timms, N. (eds) (1985) *Values and Social Change in Britain*, London, Macmillan.

Althusser, L. (1971) *Lenin and Other Essays*, London, New Left Books.

Anderson, B. (1983) *Imagined Communities*, London, Verso.

Andrews, S. (1970) *Methodism and Society*, London, Longman.

Beckford, J.A. (1989) *Religion and Advanced Industrial Society*, London, Unwin Hyman.

Birnbaum, N. (1955) "Monarchs and sociologists: a reply to Professor Shils and Mr Young," *Sociological Review*, vol. 3, no. 1, pp. 5–23.

Blumler, J.G. et al. (1971) "Attitudes to the monarchy: their structure and development during a ceremonial occasion," *Political Studies*, vol. 19, pp. 149–71.

Chaney, D. (1983) "A symbolic mirror of ourselves: civic ritual in mass society," *Media Culture and Society*, vol. 5, no. 2, pp. 119–35.

Cunningham, H. (1980) *Leisure in the Industrial Revolution*, London, Croom Helm.

Dobbelaere, K. (1981) "Secularization: a multi-dimensional concept," *Current Sociology*, vol. 29, London, Sage.

Durkheim, É. (1961) *The Elementary Forms of the Religious Life*, New York, Free Press. Original published in French, 1912.

Foucault, M. (1980) *The History of Sexuality*, vol. 1, New York, Vintage Books. Original published in French, 1976.

Fukuyama, F. (1989) "The end of history?," *The National Interest*, no. 16 (Summer), pp. 3–18.

Gerard, D. (1985) "Religious attitudes and values," in Abrams, M. et al. (eds) (1985).

Gramsci, A. (1971) *Selections from Prison Notebooks*, London, Lawrence and Wishart.

Gramsci, A. (1975) *Quaderni dal Carcere*, vol. 2 (ed. V. Gerratana), Turin, Italy, Einaudi.

Luckmann, T. (1967) *The Invisible Religion*, London, Macmillan.

MacIntyre, A. (1981) *After Virtue*, London, Duckworth.

MacIver, R.M. (1917) *Community, a Sociological Study*, London, Heinemann.

Marx, K. (1974) *Capital*, London, Penguin.

Marx, K. and Engels, F. (1955) *On Religion*, Moscow, Foreign Languages Publishing House.

Marx, K. and Engels, F. (1972) "The German ideology," in Tucker, R.C. (ed.) *The Marx-Engels Reader*, New York, W.W. Norton. First published in 1845–6.

Mouffe, C. (1981), "Hegemony and ideology in Gramsci," in Bennett, T. et al. (eds) *Culture, Ideology and Social Process*, London, Batsford.

Open University (1981) U203 *Popular Culture*, Units 1–2, Milton Keynes, England, The Open University.

Sachs, J. (1990) "The persistence of faith," the Reith Lectures, Lecture 1 "The environment of faith," *The Listener*, November 15, pp. 4–6.

Scruton, R. (1982) *The Salisbury Review*, vol. 1 (Autumn).

Seidel, G. (1986) "Culture, nation and 'race' in the British and French new right," in Levitas, R. (ed.) *The Ideology of the New Right*, Cambridge, England, Polity Press.

Shils, E. (1975) *Centre and Periphery: Essays in Macrosociology*, Chicago, University of Chicago Press.

Shils, E. and Young, M. (1953) "The meaning of the coronation," *Sociological Review*, vol. 1, pp. 63–82.

Stafford, W. (1982) "Religion and the doctrine of nationalism in England at the time of the French Revolution and Napoleonic Wars," in Mews, S. (ed.) *Religion and National Identity*, Oxford, Basil Blackwell.

Thompson, K. (1986) *Beliefs and Ideology*, London, Tavistock.

Turner, B.S. (1983) *Religion and Social Theory*, London, Sage.

Wallis, R. and Bruce, S. (1986) *Sociological Theory, Religion and Collective Action*, Belfast, The Queen's University.

Williams, R. (1975) *The Country and the City*, London, Paladin.

Wilson, B.R. (1963) "A typology of sects in a dynamic and comparative perspective," *Archives des Sciences Sociales des Religions*, vol. 16, pp. 49–53.

Wilson, B.R. (1982) *Religion in Sociological Perspective*, Oxford, Oxford University Press.

# Part III
# Modernity and its Futures

# Introduction

Stuart Hall, David Held, and Gregor McLennan

"Modernity and its Futures" is the third and final part in
*Understanding Modern Societies*, which has sought to examine the
emergence and characteristic institutional forms of modernity. Through
interpretative analysis the book as a whole has adopted a dual focus
which aims, on the one hand, to explore the central, substantive
features of social reproduction and transformation in the modern epoch
and, on the other, to highlight the nature of the theories and categories
that social scientists draw upon in order to make sense of those
processes. The volume has been concerned to examine both the
concept of "modernity" and modernity as an institutional nexus.

In many respects, the following chapters continue the storyline
begun by the previous two parts. Substantively, part III follows the
fourfold analytical division of modern society into its political,
economic, social, and cultural dimensions. Whereas the first part,
"Formations of Modernity," investigated how modern political and
economic forms first emerged, and the second part, "Structures and
Processes of Modernity," explored their consolidation in some detail,
this final part asks about their durability and prospects. As we
approach the twenty-first century, the volume tries to assess, among
other things, the meaning and implications of the collapse of
communism in Russia and Eastern Europe; shifts in the dynamics and
organization of the global capitalist economic order; the changing forms
of contemporary culture and identity formation; the growing
interconnectedness between states and societies; and challenges to that
quintessentially modern political institution, the nation-state. At the
same time, "Modernity and its Futures" is concerned with the changing
role of social science and the nature of modern "knowledge," which we
have depended on in the past to make sense of these changes and
which, if these shifts are taken far enough, could undercut some of the
underlying intellectual assumptions of leading forms of human inquiry.
These latter issues will be elaborated later in this introduction.

For the moment, it should be emphasized that in none of the
chapters which follow is it simply asserted that we have left modernity
behind and are moving rapidly into a new "post-modern" world. A
great deal of careful conceptual work, argument, and evidence is
needed before this scenario can be affirmed or denied with any
confidence. The signs of contemporary change point in different, often
contradictory, directions and it is difficult to make sense of them while
we are still living with them. Also, much depends on the specific
features of the particular institutional dimension being examined.
Accordingly, each chapter in this volume attempts to lay some common
basis for discussion about the direction and extent of recent social and
intellectual change before addressing the question of modernity's
future. For this reason, one of the main tasks of the chapters is to

introduce *debates*: debates about the likely directions, central dimensions, and proper naming of these changes; debates about whether the future of modernity will sustain the Enlightenment promise of greater understanding and mastery of nature, the progress of reason in human affairs, and a steady, sustainable development in the standard and quality of life for the world's populations; debates about whether there is any meaningful future for specific classical social theories (such as liberalism or Marxism); and debates about the very role and possibility of social science today.

## A Résumé of Some Earlier Reflections

In the previous chapters, a number of elements of modernity have been explored and questioned. These have formed a set of orientation points or recurrent themes to which our examination of modern societies has frequently returned. It may be useful briefly to summarize the main elements here, before addressing the issue of how far the shape and character of "modernity" remain intact as we approach the end of the twentieth century. We have examined the following propositions:

1   "Modernity" is that distinct and unique form of social life which characterizes modern societies. Modern societies began to emerge in Europe from about the fifteenth century, but modernity in the sense used here could hardly be said to exist in any developed form until the idea of "the modern" was given a decisive formulation in the discourses of the Enlightenment in the eighteenth century. In the nineteenth century, modernity became identified with industrialism and the sweeping social, economic, and cultural changes associated with it. In the twentieth century, several non-European societies – for example, Australasia and Japan – joined the company of advanced industrial societies. Modernity became a progressively global phenomenon.

2   Modernity has had a long and complex historical evolution. It was constituted by the articulation of a number of different historical processes, working together in unique historical circumstances. These processes were the political (the rise of the secular state and polity), the economic (the global capitalist economy), the social (formation of classes and an advanced sexual and social division of labor), and the cultural (the transition from a religious to a secular culture). Modernity, one might say, is the sum of these different forces and processes; no single "master process" was sufficient to produce it.

3   Modernity developed at the intersection of national and international conditions and processes. It was shaped by both "internal" and "external" forces. The West forged its identity and interests in relation to endogenous developments in Europe and America, and through relations of unequal exchange (material and cultural) with "the Rest" – the frequently excluded, conquered, colonized, and exploited "other."

4   Modernity can be characterized by a cluster of institutions, each with its own pattern of change and development. Among these we would include: the nation-state and an international system of states; a dynamic and expansionist capitalist economic order based on private property; industrialism; the growth of large-scale administrative and bureaucratic systems of social organization and regulation; the dominance of secular, materialist, rationalist, and individualist cultural values; and the formal separation of the "private" from the "public."

5   Although modern capitalism was from the beginning an international affair, capitalist market relations have been organized on an increasingly global scale. Capitalist relations continue to provide modernity with its economic dynamic for growth and expansion, though forms of mass production and consumption are changing. Industrial capitalism has characteristically involved striking patterns of social inequality: in particular, distinctive class relations, based on those who own and control the means of production and those who only have their laboring power to sell. These social divisions have persisted over time, while becoming more complicated as a result of the emergence of new social strata and occupational groupings. Modernity also produced distinctive social patterns of gender and racial division, as well as other social divisions which intersect with, but are not reducible to, class. This has given rise to complex patterns of asymmetrical life chances, both within nation-states and between them.

6   Modern societies are increasingly characterized by their complexity: by the proliferation of consumer products and by a variety of lifestyles. The hold of tradition has weakened in favor of individual choice and creating one's own life project; the individual is increasingly aware of the possibility of constructing new identities. Emphasis on personal life and on the spheres of intimacy has weakened the boundaries between the public and private. Nevertheless, this greater cultural pluralism and individuation has been accompanied by a growth of organizations (from hospitals to schools) seeking greater regulation and surveillance of social life.

7   Power is a constitutive dimension of all modern social relations; and social struggles – between classes, social movements, and other groups – are "inscribed" into the organization of society as well as the structures and policies of the state. Modern states are large, interventionist, administratively bureaucratic and complex systems of power *sui generis*, which intervene to organize large areas of social life. Liberal democracy in its contemporary form is the prevailing type of political regime in the industrial societies. It is partly the result of the struggles between different social groupings and interests, and partly the result of opportunities and constraints created by "power politics" and economic competition in national and international arenas. Socialism, an alternative to the predominantly capitalist path to modernity, developed historically into a number of different forms. State socialism, the comprehensive attempt to substitute central planning for the market and the state for the autonomous associations of civil society, is nearly everywhere on the retreat. Social democracy,

the attempt to regulate the market and social organizations in the name of greater social justice and welfare, continues to enjoy widespread support, especially in parts of Europe. Yet, it is also an intensively contested project which has had both its aims and strategies questioned.

8   Globalization, a process reaching back to the earliest stages of modernity, continues to shape and reshape politics, economics, and culture, at an accelerated pace and scale. The extension of globalizing processes, operating through a variety of institutional dimensions (technological, organizational, administrative, cultural, and legal), and their increased intensification within these spheres, creates new forms and limits within "modernity" as a distinctive form of life.

Part III seeks to explore these propositions further while also asking whether developments are leading towards an intensification and acceleration of the pace and scope of modernity, broadly along the lines sketched above, or whether they are producing an altogether altered or new constellation of political, economic, social, and cultural life. In pursuing these issues, we are primarily concerned, it should be stressed, to pose *questions* about modernity and its possible futures, rather than to deliver (or encourage) snap judgments, as some versions of each pole in the debates tend to do. At the same time, we are convinced that the very idea of what lies at the edge of, and beyond, modernity changes the experience of living in the modern world and sets an exciting and powerful agenda for social theory and research. We also feel that, complicated as the exchanges about the shape of the future often become, they should not be the exclusive property of established academics. Part of the great attraction of the issues confronted here is that they are not only of cerebral interest: they touch fundamentally on the changing identities of a great many people today, and affect in key ways their everyday experience of "being-in-the-world."

It is, therefore, important that the question of post-modernity be accessibly presented and engaged at a number of different levels of familiarity and scholarship. The topics we handle certainly have the sharp tang of the contemporary about them, but they are not going to be definitively resolved for some time to come, and this is another reason for ensuring that the driving concepts and evidential support for generalizations about modernity's future are addressed in an open and critical manner. Let us now begin to address these issues by putting aside for the moment the business of the precise label that we may wish to stick on the "new times" that we confront, and asking the question: What is going on in the social world of the 1990s?

## The Structure of Part III

In the political sphere, a number of earthquakes have shaken both social reality and social thinking in recent years. Most obviously, the collapse of communism in the USSR and Eastern Europe from the late 1980s has constituted a remarkable set of changes which few, if any, fully anticipated. These changes have set in motion not only wide-ranging transformations in Europe and the global order, but also intensive discussion about the significance of these world historical events. Do these events herald the victory of liberal democracy as an ideological tradition and as an institutional form? Do they herald the end of socialism and the final consolidation of capitalism on a world scale? Or, are the terms of these questions too simple and the underlying reality more complex?

David Held, in chapter 13, explores these issues and explains why the revolutions of 1989–90 constitute a profound shaking up of our very ideas of democracy and the state. Contrary to many recent claims, he explains why the future of democracy "as we know it" is not at all secure, partly because of the high levels of uncertainty and risk that accompany many of the sweeping changes across the globe today, partly because of contradictions and tensions among different dimensions of change, and partly because an adequate blend of the positive elements in both liberal and socialist democracy has not yet been achieved either in theory or in practice. The debate about 1989–90 turns out to be a debate about, as Held puts it, "the character and form of modernity itself: the constitutive processes and structures of the contemporary world."

This debate is carried through into chapter 14 by Anthony McGrew, who focuses on the prospects for the nation-state faced with the extension and deepening of regional and global interconnectedness. The consolidation of the modern states system was the result of the expansion of Europe across the globe. Key features of the European states system – the centralization of political power, the expansion of administrative rule, the legitimation of power through claims to representation, the emergence of massed armies – became prevalent features of the entire global system. Today, in the context of globalization, as McGrew explains, the viability of a sovereign, territorially-bounded, culturally and ethnically delineated state appears to be in question.

Economic processes (multinational companies, international debt, world trade, global financial institutions), ecological imperatives, and global or transnational political movements are putting sustained pressure on national economies and the nation-state. The "national" form of organization for political, economic, and cultural life, once a central feature of modernity, appears to have been weakened or badly damaged, although the difficulty of establishing a stable political form "beyond" the nation-state leads to an intricate spectrum of possible directions.

Globalization has resulted in a very *contradictory* social experience for many. On one hand, the universal spread of electronic media has rendered communications between different cultures astonishingly rapid. Along with economic pressures, the political and cultural reference points for the peoples of the world are more uniform than ever before. Our very experience of *space and time*, indeed, has been condensed and made uniform in an unprecedented fashion. Distances have been drastically compressed and people almost everywhere are more "aware" of the existence of others than ever before.

And yet — possibly as a direct result of increasing globalization — another very significant cultural phenomenon of recent times has been a growing sense of how particular people and their social interests *differ* radically from one another; or at least a sense of the *variety* of values and customs which abound. In addition, in a globalizing world system, people become more aware of, and more attached to, their *locality* as the appropriate forum for self-assertion and democratic expression. This desire to preserve something meaningful and tangible in the existing local culture in the context of profound universalizing tendencies is arguably what lies behind many of today's most intense political phenomena, from ethnic revivalism, to political separatism, to movements for local democracy.

The impact of globalization and the tension between the "global" and the "local" runs through a number of chapters in the volume. It lies at the heart of the environmental movement and the astonishing growth of "green" consciousness around the world, which have linked an awareness of the fragile character of human ecology with a concern for local environments and forms of life. In his contribution to this volume, Steven Yearley in chapter 15 addresses a number of immensely important issues concerning the sustainability of any society today, whether it be traditional or high-tech. The problems of coping with social waste and the need to rapidly prevent further erosion of the world's forests and ozone layer are so urgent that any remotely similar ecological agenda would have been simply unimaginable only thirty years ago. Here, as elsewhere, the modernist ideas of progress and infinite growth are questioned.

Yearley carefully analyzes the ecological threats to contemporary society, and some of the strengths and weaknesses of the burgeoning green ideology. No matter how potentially severe ecological problems are, he reminds us, the momentum of economic growth continues and the basic values and institutions of western society have not yet been fundamentally eroded by green thought. Moreover, he soberly concludes, "the lack of international accord over global warming and non-renewable resources indicates that a prosperous green future is not currently on offer to everyone on this planet."

It would be wrong to conclude from the above that the entrenched institutions oriented towards economic growth, and the economic structures geared to ever-increasing production, have not themselves undergone significant transformation in recent times. In the economic sphere, a number of central changes are apparent. For example, there appears to be a significant move "beyond" the typical industrial structure of the modern economy. In chapter 16, John Allen sets out these changes in detail, focusing on a move from mass production to "flexible specialization," and from mass consumption patterns to lifestyle niches in the marketplace. In terms of the techniques of production and economic calculation, the role of computerized information and designer modelling is critical in a way it never could have been before. Some would even say that we should now speak of "modes of information" rather than, in the old Marxist usage, "modes of production." And along with the change of emphasis from material production to the knowledge-based economy, we need to note the universal growth of "knowledge" workers (programmers, financiers, marketeers, designers, administrators) within an increasingly *service-*oriented labor force (where "servicing" includes a great variety of casual and menial work tasks as well as well-paid ones – the former often being undertaken by women). John Allen stages a debate about these issues between protagonists who, though differing in emphasis among themselves, tend to fall into the position of arguing, either that the fundamental dynamic which shaped the modern growth-oriented industrial economy is still operating, or that the changes taking place add up to the emergence of some new, post-industrial form of capitalist economic organization.

The economic dimension, of course, has significant implications for modern social structures – for social class and other social divisions, as well as for cultural and personal identities. In the era of mass production and manufacturing industry, social classes were tangibly related to basic patterns of *ownership* of wealth and resources, and rested upon common cultural experiences centered around the workplace and the community. Class was always hard to define precisely in sociological theory, but it was seldom disputed that the predominant forms of work, ownership, and local lifestyle were all important and related. It thus provided a major category of social and political analysis. Nowadays, the touchstone of "class" in both social *analysis* and social *experience* seems much less solid. Patterns of economic ownership have continued to move away from the image of individual persons or families being the *owning class*, while the dramatic decline of manufacture and extraction, and the changing nature of work, have turned the imposing image of the mass working class into that of a dwindling minority grouping – in the so-called "advanced" countries at any rate. The extensive fragmentation of the broad working class into a series of highly differentiated income groups and labor market "segments" has further prompted the thought that the end of class (in its customary image, anyway) is nigh. The extent to which the recomposition of the laboring class in western societies affects our understanding of the class structure of society as a whole is thus a major area for investigation. At the same time, other social processes, like the spread of mass consumption, and other social divisions, like those associated with gender, race, and ethnicity, have assumed greater salience, producing a greater complexity of social life, and a plurality of social groupings and communities of identification.

A final point to make on the economic–social interface is that the perceived significance of work itself has shifted. There has been a marked decline in the work "ethic," and a sharp rise in popular awareness of the possible uses of *non-work* time in people's lives. Moreover, the association of work with the physical transformation of natural materials for basic human needs is far less powerful in modern societies than it once was. We live in an epoch where the manipulation

of financial symbols on a screen is arguably truer to the spirit, and
perhaps more crucial to the overall well-being, of a global capitalist
economy than the wrenching of coal from the earth or trading goods for
banknotes. Or so it seems. And the social composition of those who
work, as well as the nature of the work itself, is now highly
differentiated, by class, race, and gender, and by position in the
international division of labor. How significant these developments
actually are is itself intensely debated. Assessments vary, from those
who think the broad march of modernity has only been marginally
knocked off its stride, to those who believe that multifaceted processes
of change have transformed the modern social landscape beyond recall
or regret.

"Modernity" has always served to identify a distinctive form of
experience and culture, as well as patterns of social, economic, and
political organization, and the shifts which characterize late twentieth-
century life are as dramatic in the cultural as in other spheres. The
growing social pluralism and cultural complexity of modern societies,
the global impact of the electronic media of communication spreading
the images and messages of "modernity" world-wide, the permeation of
daily life by the mediation of symbolic forms, the aesthetic revolution
in the design of physical environments as well as in contemporary art
forms – these have accelerated the pace of cultural innovation, the
production of new languages, and the pursuit of novelty and
experiment as cultural values. The early aesthetic movements of the
twentieth century, known as modernism, ushered in a new,
experimental period in aesthetic form and expression, breaking with
earlier, more realist forms of representation. Now, as this cultural
revolution transforms everyday life, popular culture, and the social
environment (and not only in "the West"), people are questioning
whether, just as a new post-industrial economy may be replacing the
old industrial economy, modernism is being displaced by a new post-
modern epoch.

It comes as little surprise, therefore, that some social scientists claim
that our political and social values, our cultural identities, and even
our very sense of *self* are in considerable flux and disarray. What is
sometimes called "late-modernity" "unfreezes" traditional values,
political alignments, and emotional allegiances, which in turn renders
the whole picture of social existence in the late modern world still
more fluid.

In the advanced heartlands of the West, we might imagine – just for
the sake of argument – how individuals may have lost a strong sense of
class-determined identity, and how their political reference points are
now criss-crossed with a variety of conflicting points of identification,
thus transforming notions about who they are and what they should be
thinking and doing. Ethnic, gender, local, party, family, consumer-
produced, media-inspired, self-contrived passions and aspirations now
blend and clash in this unstable amalgam of the self. In the "marginal"
countries, identities evolved from once-stable rural or traditional
cultures compete with those borrowed from or disseminated by "the
West"; and religious allegiances for their part either get modified and

modernized in order to adjust to, or mobilized in order to belatedly challenge, western-led globalization. At the "micro-level," in the fine mesh of interpersonal relations, the fresh instability and pluralism of social and political identities bring a different range of subjective expectations, and more complex notions of intimacy, trust, and dependency (see Giddens, 1991).

In chapter 17, Kenneth Thompson explores the debate about the characteristics of this new "post-modern" culture and whether it can be said to constitute a new cultural and social epoch. He describes its aesthetic features and introduces some major protagonists in the debate about how far these "new times" are characterized by a new level of social pluralism and fragmentation. In chapter 18, Stuart Hall outlines and appraises the implications of "new times" for our sense of self, our identities and cultural "belongingness." Hall presents the argument that a more unified conception of the modern self is being "de-centered" and that some of the social identities which stabilized the modern world and gave individuals firm locations in the cultural landscape of modernity are being dislocated. He explores the unsettling impact of globalization on national identities, but also discusses its contradictory outcome – the tendency towards both a "global post-modern" culture *and* simultaneously the resurgence of nationalism, ethnicity, and fundamentalism.

In this apparently shifting, novel context, what relevance can traditional social science have? Can the modern world undergo such rapid and extensive transformation while our analytic and explanatory models remain untouched? If our cultural understandings form as "real" a part of social change as do economic and technological processes, then the same might be said about our cognitive models and intellectual allegiances. Social scientists have frequently assumed that their theories and categories offer a "window on the world," and indeed that their concepts actually "pick out" bits of society and reveal their inner workings. Thus, even to conceive of society as divided into four distinct dimensions or sectors, having labels such as "the economic," "the political," etc., is to exemplify that classical social science assumption whereby theories and categories somehow "represent" social reality.

But let us pause for a moment to see what this aspiration to "represent" reality involves. For one thing, in this volume we have been keen to portray society, not as one unified thing "out there," but rather as a process of overlapping institutional dimensions, each with its own patterns of change and development. The capitalist economic order, the nation-state system, military and industrial organization, administrative and bureaucratic power: none of these institutional "clusters" is wholly separate from the others, yet each retains its special emphasis. And within any given social formation, these processes have resulted historically in very different social configurations. There are always likely to be a number of relevant causal influences to account for the evolution of distinctive patterns of inequality and structuration: class, gender, ethnicity, age, and so on. Now it could reasonably be argued that much social theory, up to the late 1970s, aspired at least in principle to an overarching or meta-theoretical perspective, which could somehow finally bring together and *rank* all these dimensions, in order to give a coherent overall picture of society. Social theory, in other words, aspired in principle to a "total theory" which would map society as a whole.

Today, this aspiration has been severely questioned, and the Enlightenment project from which it ultimately stems seems to some commentators to lie in tatters, as Gregor McLennan shows in chapter 19. What is interesting for our purposes here is to see how much the transformations of late-modernity challenge, even if they do not wholly undermine, the explanatory models of modern social sciences – showing as they do, for example, how hard it is to "hold the line" at a small number of "priority" societal factors in the explanation of social phenomena. In effect, there are always a great number of social factors to consider in any "total picture," and the outcomes are likely to be variable, and to show the effects of contingency in historical development rather than leading to one predictable historical result.

Against this background, the role of social theory as a "picturing" enterprise, that is, as a representational form, is put under strain. Rather than somehow representing reality, theories can instead be seen to produce variable *insights* into the complex and multiple existence that we happen to call "society." Similarly, it could be maintained that phrases such as "the economic dimension" do not in effect "pick out" bits of reality called "the economy." Rather, they are analytical devices which we use to say, not "this is how things really are," but rather, "look at it this way for a moment." Social theory thus becomes a much more suggestive business than anticipated by the positivist strands of the Enlightenment vision of an all-encompassing science of society. And social theorists, for their part, become more aware of the ways in which they produce different social descriptions, and consequently are more hesitant and provisional in their assertions than their more ambitious predecessors.

It follows that even the attempt in this book to highlight certain processes, developments, and dimensions in analyzing modernity could be regarded as a more or less useful way of *organizing inquiry*, rather than an attempt to *partition and wrap up* reality in any definitive sense. This is part of what was referred to in the introduction to "Formations of Modernity" as the remarkable growth of "reflexivity," both in common experience and in social science thinking. To regard social inquiry as a hesitant process of self-understanding in a rapidly changing world is a far cry from the view that social scientists must strive to reflect reality as it is in itself, formulating the inner essence of society in abstract scientific terms.

In conclusion, it is important to note that this dialogue and occasional antagonism between two powerful images of social understanding is not new; it may even be a kind of "eternal" oscillation in western thinking. Basically – and leaving aside for a moment our specific theoretical allegiances – there are those who habitually feel the "pull" of strong overarching concepts and applaud the ambition of "grand theory." Here the primary impulse is to perceive and articulate a sense of coherence and shape in the social world and thus to pinpoint our own place within that world. Ironically, the very concept of post-modernity as a general condition of society which follows the rise and fall of another stage called modernity itself embodies the idea that social theory can provide large-scale models of order and sequence.

On the other side are those who are suspicious of enforced order and grandiose ambition, whether in society at large or in social scientific reflection. Here the main impulse is to debunk big concepts and easy generalizations. The emphasis is not on progress, totality, and necessity, but on the very opposite of these intellectual emphases, namely discontinuity, plurality, and contingency (see Rorty, 1989). Post-modernism in this vein is more a "deconstructive" style of reasoning and inquiry, offering itself as a stimulant to dialogue and to conversation among human beings without the universalizing pretensions of Enlightenment philosophies. People, it is hoped, will be able to talk to one another and, in the process of playing vocabularies and cultures off against each other, produce new and better ways of acting on problems in the world.

The authors of the following chapters have their own views on the nature of modernity and its future. They also have views on the very possibility of "rational" social science. In one sense, we all believe that social scientific inquiry can proceed quite a long way and "deliver" a substantial amount before profound philosophical decisions have to be made about whether social science is a necessarily "totalizing" operation, or whether it can perfectly well survive instead by conducting "local" forms of investigation and by promulgating a probing, critical style. However, we are also sure that at some point we do face the overall issues of whether social science can provide an adequate ordering framework, or whether it would be more enlightening and liberating to throw to the winds our overweening intellectual ambitions. It should immediately be said that among the contributors there is a typical range of responses to that question, as the reader will discover in the pages which follow.

# References

Giddens, A. (1991) *Modernity and Self-Identity*, Cambridge, England, Polity Press.

Rorty, R. (1989) *Contingency, Irony, Solidarity*, Cambridge, England, Cambridge University Press.

# 13 The 1989 Revolutions and the Triumph of Liberalism

David Held

## Contents

| 1 | Introduction | 437 |
|---|---|---|
| 1.1 | The structure of the chapter | 438 |
| 1.2 | The historical backdrop | 439 |
| 2 | The Triumph of Liberalism? | 442 |
| 2.1 | Critical response | 445 |
| 3 | The Necessity of Marxism? | 447 |
| 3.1 | Critical response | 449 |
| 4 | From Modernity to Post-Modernity? | 452 |
| 4.1 | Critical response | 455 |
| 5 | The Story So Far, and the Question of the Political Good | 457 |
| 6 | Democracy: Between State and Civil Society? | 459 |
| 7 | Conclusion | 463 |
| | References | 464 |

# 1 Introduction

At the end of World War II Europe lay devastated and divided. The emergence of Nazism and fascism had shattered any complacent views of Europe as the cradle of progress in the world. The Holocaust appeared to negate Europe's claim – a claim made with particular force since the Enlightenment – to represent the pinnacle of civilization. Some philosophers even began to think of the Enlightenment as the origin of domination and totalitarianism in the West (see Horkheimer and Adorno, 1972). The war itself, moreover, had destroyed millions of lives, wrecked Europe's infrastructure, and left the world increasingly polarized between the democratic, capitalist West and the communist East.

Yet, scarcely more than forty years later, some were proclaiming (by means of a phrase borrowed most notably from Hegel) the "end of history" – the triumph of the West over all political and economic alternatives. The revolutions which swept across Central and Eastern Europe at the end of 1989 and the beginning of 1990 stimulated an atmosphere of celebration. Liberal democracy was proclaimed as the agent of progress, and capitalism as the only viable economic system; ideological conflict, it was said, was being steadily displaced by universal democratic reason and market-oriented thinking (Fukuyama, 1989).

The subtitle of this chapter could be "1989 and all that," for its objective is to explore and tentatively assess the debate about the meaning of the changes and transformations which swept through Europe during 1989 and 1990, and which were accelerated further by the popular counter-movement to the coup attempt in the Soviet Union during August 18–21, 1991. Has the West won? Has liberal democracy finally displaced the legitimacy of all other forms of government? Is ideological conflict at an end? These and related questions will be explored below.

It will become apparent in the course of the chapter that the debate about 1989 is much more than a debate about the events of that year and subsequent occurrences, important as these are. For it is also a debate about the character and form of modernity itself: the constitutive processes and structures of the contemporary world. The chapter presents, in microcosm some of the key issues, problems, and discussions about modernity, its past, present, and possible futures. In other words, "1989 and all that" is a stimulus to a variety of fundamental questions about the world unfolding before us. Is the distinctively modern world a world shaped and reshaped according to liberal political and economic principles? Was 1989 important because it represented a crucial formative movement in the development and consolidation of the liberal polity and the free market economy in the global order? Or, is it significant because it was the moment at which capitalism scored a decisive victory over socialism and communism and, accordingly, finally captured modernity for itself? Is socialism dead in the face of the apparent collapse of Marxism? Or will socialism be reborn when capitalism finally establishes itself on a world scale? In short, did 1989 represent a moment at which modernity was decisively shaped by one particular set of forces and relations? Or does it represent something more complex and uncertain?

The debate about 1989, and about the form and character of modernity, is a debate about the world as it is and might be. That the debate spans *analytical* and *normative* considerations should come as no surprise. While this distinction may be useful as an initial point of orientation, it is hard to use as a precise classificatory device for political and social theories. Events, processes, and political dramas do not simply "speak for themselves"; they are, and they have to be, interpreted; and the framework we bring to the process of interpretation determines what we "see": what we notice and register as important. All theoretical and analytical endeavor, whether it be that of lay people or professional social scientists, involves interpretation – interpretation which embodies a particular framework of concepts, beliefs, and standards. Such a framework should not be thought of as a barrier to understanding; for it is, rather, integral to understanding (Gadamer, 1975). It shapes our attempts to understand and assess political action, events, and processes, and provides points of orientation. However, such a framework does mean that particular positions in political and social theory – relating, for example, to modernity and its consequences – ought not to be treated as offering the correct or final understanding of a phenomenon; for the meaning of a phenomenon is always open to future interpretations from new perspectives, each with its own practical stance or interest in political life. (For further discussion of these themes, see the introduction to part III and chapter 19.)

This chapter, accordingly, considers a range of analytical and normative questions which thread through the debate about 1989, and it highlights, especially towards the end, some of the competing conceptions of the "political good" (the virtuous, desirable, and preferred form of human association) – particularly those offered by liberalism, Marxism, and, for want of a better label, a "multi-dimensional" approach to modernity. These positions proffer quite different conceptions of the political good and some of their strengths and limitations will be explored in subsequent discussion. Consideration of the political good readily becomes, it will be seen, an analysis of, and debate about, the nature and meaning of democracy, an issue so forcefully put on the agenda by the events of and since 1989. And a sustained reflection on democracy, it will be suggested, offers clues to a more coherent and cogent account of the political good than can be found in the other positions considered here.

## 1.1   The structure of the chapter

This chapter has a number of sections. After a brief examination of the historical background to 1989 (section 1.2), sections 2–4 will examine the debate about 1989 through accounts which offer sharply contrasting views.

Section 2 focuses on an essay by Francis Fukuyama which became *a* if not *the* reference point for discussions – particularly in the Anglo-American world – of the political transformations sweeping the East. Fukuyama's main thesis amounts to the claim that socialism is dead and that liberalism is the sole remaining legitimate political philosophy.

Section 3 addresses writings by Alex Callinicos, who takes an entirely different view. He interprets the East European revolutions as a victory for capitalism – but a victory which makes Marxism more relevant today, not less.

Section 4 then presents an argument by Anthony Giddens about modernity and its consequences. Taking modernity to represent four institutional dimensions – capitalism, industrialism, administrative power, and military might – Giddens argues that the future of modernity, like its past, is more complicated than either liberalism or Marxism can grasp.

The claims of Fukuyama, Callinicos, and Giddens have been selected, in particular, because they exemplify central voices or perspectives (albeit while making original contributions) in the attempt to think through and assess the revolutions and their impact. If Fukuyama is primarily concerned with examining the significance of liberalism in the contemporary era, Callinicos is preoccupied with showing how Marxism retains its integrity and critical edge despite the weakening appeal of communism throughout the world. Giddens, by contrast, rejects the premises of both these types of position and argues that a theory of the transformations of modernity must go beyond them. Together, these three perspectives set up a striking debate.

Section 5 offers a brief summary of the text to that point, drawing together the threads of how the different positions conceive of the political good and the role and nature of democracy. The debate among these conceptions is further explored in section 6 through an analysis of democracy itself. It is argued here that it is possible to develop a conception of the political good *as the democratic good*, and that this offers a more promising approach to questions about the proper form of "government" and "politics" than is offered by the positions set out earlier.

Section 7 briefly concludes the chapter and raises questions about the proper form and limits of political community today. In this way it provides a link with the following chapter (chapter 14) by Anthony McGrew.

## 1.2   The historical backdrop

The changes of political regime which swept through Central and Eastern Europe in 1989–90 – in Poland, Hungary, East Germany, Bulgaria, Czechoslovakia, and Romania – were world-shaking events by any standard. An extraordinary sense of exhilaration was created within and beyond Europe. As Callinicos aptly put it:

> Far beyond the countries directly affected, people shared a sense
> of suddenly widened possibilities. Parts of the furniture of the
> postwar world that had seemed irremovable suddenly disappeared
> – literally in the case of the Berlin wall. Previously unalterable
> assumptions – for example, that Europe would be permanently
> divided between the superpowers – abruptly collapsed.
> (Callinicos, 1991, p. 8)

The sharp division between the democratic capitalist and state socialist
worlds, created in the aftermath of World War II, began to disappear.
The pattern of intense rivalry between the superpowers, perhaps the
single most significant feature of world politics in the second half of
the twentieth century, was transformed almost at a stroke (see Lewis,
1990a). If this were not considered a revolution (or series of
revolutions) within the affairs of the communist bloc, and within the
international order more generally, it is hard to see what would qualify
as revolutionary change.

But things are rarely as straightforward as they seem. While the term
"revolution" may seem to accurately describe the sweeping, dramatic
and unexpected transformations of the state socialist system, and the
extraordinary movements of people who ushered in these changes on
the streets of Warsaw, Budapest, Prague, Berlin, and other cities, it
draws attention away from the momentum of changes and processes
already underway by November, 1989. Although I shall continue to
refer to the "revolutions" of 1989–90, it is as well to bear in mind that
these had roots stretching back in time.

To begin with, significant political changes had begun to get
underway in Poland in the early 1980s, and in Hungary a little later:
the Communists had been defeated in elections in Poland and the
principle of one-party rule had been renounced in Hungary before the
"dramatic" events of 1989–90 took place. There was also the massive
student uprising in Tiananmen Square, Beijing, so brutally put down
on June 3–4, 1989, which provided the reminder, if one was at all
needed, that change in state socialist regimes might, at the very best, be
tolerated only at a slow and managed pace.

Underpinning the slow but significant changes in Central and
Eastern Europe in the late 1980s was, of course, the reform process
initiated in the USSR by Mikhail Gorbachev – the so-called process of
perestroika ("restructuring"). Shifts in strategic thinking in the Kremlin
were probably the proximate cause of the East European revolutions,
alongside the gradual erosion of communist power in the civil societies
and economies of the Soviet bloc (see Lewis, 1990a and 1990b). In
particular, the Soviet decision to replace the "Brezhnev Doctrine" (i.e.
the policy of protecting the "achievements of socialism" in Eastern
Europe, by force if necessary) with the "Sinatra Doctrine" (i.e. the
policy of tolerating nationally chosen paths to progress and prosperity:
"do it your way") had decisive consequences, intended and otherwise,
for the capacity of state socialist regimes to survive. By removing the
threat of Red Army or Warsaw Pact intervention, and by refusing to
sanction the use of force to crush mass demonstrations, the Sinatra

Doctrine effectively pulled the carpet from under East European communism. The developments in East Germany were a notable case in point. When Hungary opened its border with Austria, and triggered the massive emigration of East Germans to the West, pressures within East Germany rapidly intensified and demonstrations, held in Leipzig and nearby cities, escalated. Without the routine recourse to force, the East German authorities sought to placate their rebellious citizenry by sanctioning access to the West *via* new openings in the Berlin Wall. The result is well known: the authorities lost control of an already demanding situation, and within a short time both their legitimacy and effectiveness were wholly undermined.

The roots of the events of 1989–90 can be traced back further. Three particular sets of pressures can usefully be mentioned, for they shed some light not only on why a shift in strategic thinking occurred in the Kremlin, but also on why the changes took the direction they did. First, the Soviet economy's lack of integration into the world economic system protected it in the short-term from the pressures and instabilities attendant on achieving the levels of competitive productivity necessary for a sustained role in the international division of labor; in the *long-run*, however, the same lack of integration left it weak and uncompetitive, particularly in relation to technology and innovation. Ever more dependent on imported technology and foreign sources of funding and investment, the centrally administered economy, rigid and relatively inflexible at the best of times, found few avenues through which to deliver better economic performance.

In the second place, this situation was compounded by renewed geopolitical pressures which followed from the intensification of the Cold War in the late 1970s and 1980s. A new arms race, in which "smart" weapons and ever more sophisticated weapon-systems played an increasing role, put a greater and greater burden on the financial, technical, and managerial resources of the Soviet Union. The costs of the Cold War became profoundly difficult to contain on both sides, but were particularly draining on the crumbling organizations and infrastructure of the Soviet economy.

Thirdly, significant conflicts and schisms had emerged in the Soviet bloc during the previous few decades, leading to massive acts of repression to contain dissent in Hungary (1956), Czechoslovakia (1968), and Poland (1981). While these acts may have effectively contained protest in the short term, they were not a permanent obstacle to the spawning of dissent, social movements, and autonomous organizations in civil society. The developments in Poland in the 1980s, particularly the formation of the trade union Solidarity, were by no means typical of what was happening in Eastern Europe as a whole. For the events in Poland were shaped by a remarkable ethnic and national unity, the power of the Catholic Church, and a strong sense of a foreign enemy on Polish soil corrupting its growth and identity. Nevertheless, they were indicative of a certain growing democratic pressure to "roll back the state" and to create an independent civil society in which citizens could pursue their chosen activities free from immediate political pressure. Solidarity sought to foster such a society throughout the 1980s by creating independent networks of information, cultural interchange, and social relations. In so doing, it recast and expanded the meaning of what it was to be a democratic social movement, while drastically weakening the appeal of state-dominated political change.

The above account is by no means intended to be a thorough analysis of the remarkable events and developments of 1989 and subsequent years. Rather, it is intended as a historical sketch which provides a context for the main focus of the chapter – namely, the consideration of what the revolutions mean, how they should be interpreted, and what light they shed on the development of modernity and its futures.

# 2   The Triumph of Liberalism?

Following the American defeat in the Vietnam War and the rise of the Japanese economic challenge to American economic interests, a detectable gloom settled over Washington policy-makers in the late 1970s. This gloom was reinforced by a spate of major academic publications in the 1980s, including Robert Keohane's *After Hegemony* (1984) and Paul Kennedy's *The Rise and Fall of the Great Powers* (1988), which charted the (relative) decline of US power and considered the implications of this for world politics and the world political economy. Focusing on the growing costs of maintaining the US's military strength, and the erosion of its productive and revenue-raising capacities by economic rivals, these authors raised alarms about the US's future and about the consequences of decline for the defense and stability of the West. Few foresaw, however, how thoroughly these considerations, important as they were, would have to be reassessed in the light of the dramatic decline of the West's main adversary at the end of the 1980s: the Soviet Union.

A major effort of reassessment was made by Francis Fukuyama in his 1989 essay "The end of history?"; this not only provided a reassuring counterpoint to the earlier preoccupation with the US's loss of hegemony, but, in its confident and assertive tone, went some way towards restoring faith in the supremacy of western values. Fukuyama, formerly deputy director of, and currently consultant to, the US State Department Policy Planning Staff, celebrated not only the "triumph of the West" but also, as he put it, "the end of history as such; that is, the end point of mankind's ideological evolution and the universalization of Western liberal democracy as the final form of human government" (1989, p. 3). Fukuyama's message became widely reported in the press and the electronic media more generally. While subjecting him to considerable criticism, most of Fukuyama's detractors seemed to concede that his "main point – the current lack of competitors against political and economic liberalism in the world ideological market place – is surely hard to refute" (Mortimer, 1989, p. 29).

Fukuyama's message recalls earlier debates in the 1950s and 1960s on "the end of ideology" (see Held, 1989, ch. 4). But whereas these debates focused on the significance in the West of a decline in support for Marxism by intellectuals, trade unions, and left-wing political parties, and on a reduction in the differences among political parties towards government intervention and welfare expenditure, Fukuyama's thesis goes much further, philosophically and politically. His thesis comprises four main components. First, there is a broad emphasis on conflict among *ideologies* as the motor of history. Drawing some inspiration from Hegel, Fukuyama argues that history can be understood as a sequence of stages of consciousness or ideology; that is, as a sequence of systems of political belief which embody distinctive views about the basic principles underlying social order (Fukuyama, 1989/90, pp. 22–3). The sequence represents a progressive and purposive path in human development from partial and particularistic ideologies to those with more universal appeal. In the modern period we have reached, in Fukuyama's judgment, the final stage of this development.

Secondly, the end of history has been reached because ideological conflict is virtually at an end. Liberalism is the last victorious ideology. At the heart of this argument, Fukuyama notes, "lies the observation that a remarkable consensus has developed in the world concerning the legitimacy and viability of liberal democracy" (1989/90, p. 22). The chief rivals to liberalism in the twentieth century, fascism and communism, have either failed or are failing. And contemporary challengers – religious movements such as Islam, or nationalist movements such as those found in Eastern Europe today – articulate only partial or incomplete ideologies; that is to say, they champion beliefs which cannot be sustained without the support of other ideologies. Neither religious nor nationalist belief systems provide coherent alternatives to liberalism in the long term and, therefore, have no "universal significance." Only liberal democracy, and market principles of economic organization, constitute developments of "truly world historical significance" (Fukuyama, 1989/90, p. 23).

The third distinctive element of Fukuyama's thesis is that the end of history should not be taken to mean the end of all conflict. Conflict can arise – indeed, is likely to arise – from diverse sources, including advocates of various (dated) ideologies, nationalist and religious groups, and peoples or collectivities locked into history or pre-history: i.e. those who remain "outside" the liberal world (certain Third World countries) or who remain "outsiders inside" (individuals and groups within the liberal world who have not yet fully absorbed its inescapability). Moreover, there is a danger of a progressive "bifurcation" or splitting of the world into those who belong to the "post-historical" liberal societies and the rest – the traditional unmodernized world. Bifurcation could certainly generate intense and violent struggles, but none of these will lead, Fukuyama maintains, to new systematic ideas of political and social justice which could displace or supersede liberalism.

The end of an era? The removal of the statue of Felix Edmundovitch Dzerzhinsky, founder of the KGB, from Moscow on August 22, 1991. G. Pinkhassov, Magnum.

Finally, Fukuyama is not wholly unambivalent about the "end of history." It will, he suggests, be "a very sad time" (1989, p. 18). There will no longer be daring leaps of human imagination and valiant struggles of great principle; politics will become an extension of the regulative processes of markets. Idealism will be replaced by economic management and the solving of technical problems in the pursuit of consumer satisfaction. In short, recalling one of the central themes of post-modernism, Fukuyama proclaims the exhaustion of the bold, even heroic, "grand narratives" of human emancipation which once struggled with one another for dominance in the world. (See the introduction to part III and chapter 19 for a discussion of the key ideas of post-modernism.) But while there is a detectable note of regret in his tone, it barely qualifies his generally optimistic affirmation of liberalism. Ideological consensus today may be neither "fully universal nor automatic," but it exists to a "higher degree than at any time in the past century" (1989/90, p. 22). The "liberal democratic revolution" and the "capitalist revolution" form the final stage of a clear-cut pattern of historical evolution.

## 2.1   Critical response

Fukuyama's essay was widely acclaimed as one of the "key texts for our age" (*The Guardian*, Sept. 7, 1990). In a sense, it provided a sophisticated justification for many of the commonplace pronouncements made by the leading governments of the West in the 1980s, especially those of Margaret Thatcher and Ronald Reagan (Hirst, 1989, p. 14). It reinforced the message of the neo-liberal New Right, which throughout the 1980s had proclaimed the imminent death of socialism, and praised the market and minimal state as the only legitimate and viable forms for the future (see, for example, Friedman, 1989). But it would be wrong to suggest that Fukuyama's arguments were supported only by the Right. A broad spectrum of political opinion found the general political message of Fukuyama's article hard to brush aside, even if there was intense disagreement about most of its details.

There are, however, also serious questions to be raised about Fukuyama's essential argument. In the first instance, liberalism cannot be treated simply as a unity. There are distinctive liberal traditions set down by such figures as Adam Smith, John Locke, and John Stuart Mill which embody quite different conceptions concerning the individual agent, autonomy, the rights and duties of subjects, and the proper nature and form of community (see, for example, Dunn, 1979). Fukuyama does not analyze the different forms of liberalism, nor does he provide any arguments about how one might choose among them. This is a striking omission, since liberalism itself is an ideologically contested terrain.

In addition, Fukuyama does not explore whether there are any tensions, or even perhaps contradictions, between the "liberal" and "democratic" components of liberal democracy; that is, between the liberal preoccupation with individual rights or "frontiers of freedom" which "nobody should be permitted to cross" (Berlin, 1969, pp. 164ff.), and the democratic concern with the regulation of individual and collective action, i.e. with public accountability. Those who have written at length on this question have frequently resolved it in quite different ways (see Held, 1987). Where Fukuyama stands on the balance between "liberalism" and "democracy" is unclear. Furthermore, there is not simply one institutional form of liberal democracy. Contemporary democracies have crystallized into a number of different types – the Westminster, federal, and consensual models, for example – which make any appeal to a liberal position vague at best (see Lijphart, 1984; Dahl, 1989). Fukuyama essentially leaves unanalyzed the whole issue of the meaning of democracy and its possible variants.

Fukuyama's affirmation of the principles of economic liberalism and the mechanisms of the market also raises questions. Following a central assumption of *laissez-faire* liberalism – that markets are basically self-equilibriating and "clear" if various "imperfections" are eliminated (wage and price "stickiness," for instance) – Fukuyama interprets markets as essentially "powerless" mechanisms of coordination. He thus neglects to inquire into the extent to which market relations are themselves power relations which can constrain and limit the democratic process. He fails to consider whether persistent asymmetries in income, wealth, and opportunity may not be the outcome of the existing form of market relations: capitalist market relations. For, one particular liberty – the liberty to accumulate wealth and to organize productive activity into hierarchically ordered enterprises – poses a challenge to the extent to which political liberty can be enjoyed by all citizens: i.e. the extent to which citizens can act as equals in the political process (see Dahl, 1985). Not to examine this challenge is to risk ignoring one of the main threats to liberty in the contemporary world: a threat deriving not, as thinkers like de Tocqueville and J.S. Mill thought, from demands for equality, but from inequality – inequality so great as to create violations of political liberty and democratic politics (Dahl, 1985, p. 60).

Moreover, despite his remarks on the dangers of a bifurcated world, Fukuyama barely considers the degree to which inequalities of ownership and control, and determinate asymmetries of life chances, can create differences of interest which may spark clashes of value, principle, belief – i.e. ideology – within the West, and between the West and "Third World" countries. He under-estimates the potential for struggles between different ideological accounts of the nature of the economic order, and of desirable alternative forms of economic organization at national and international levels. It is by no means self-evident, for example, that the existing economic system can generate the minimum life conditions for the millions of people – 27 million at the current estimate – who currently face death by starvation in Africa and elsewhere; or, for that matter, the minimum life conditions for all the planet's population faced with possible global warming, ozone depletion, and the continued destruction of life-sustaining natural resources. It is far from self-evident that the existing economic system is compatible with the central liberal concern to treat all persons as "free and equal" (see Miller, 1989). In the absence of such compatibility, one can surmise that liberalism is likely to face renewed criticism as the search for a "fairer" and "safer" economic order continues.

Fukuyama's own account of the potential sources of ideological conflict is, in addition, weak. Leaving aside his characterization of ideology, which is itself problematic (see the discussion in chapter 12; and Thompson, 1990), Fukuyama's attempt to explain away the persistence of nationalism and religious movements, especially religious fundamentalism, is unconvincing. For example, he dismisses Islam as a political ideology on the grounds that it is highly unlikely to generate a universal appeal: its appeal is restricted to the Muslim world. But this is a poor argument. For the same reasoning must surely lead one to conclude that liberalism itself should be dismissed as a political ideology because it, too, cannot generate a universal appeal; it has, after all, had limited impact on the Muslim world, on China, and so on. Furthermore, Fukuyama fails to examine some of the most vigorous sources of political debate to have emanated in the West recently, for example, from social movements like feminism and the Greens.

Finally, Fukuyama's claims about "the end of history" are implausible, in my view. For he ignores the continued contestability of liberalism and of the liberal conception of the political good both within and beyond the borders of the western nation-state. His claims also ignore the fact that we cannot fully know what all the major sources of conflict and ideological struggle will be in a world shaped as much by the contingent, the unanticipated, and the imponderable as by determinate causal forces and bounded patterns of institutional change (Himmelfarb, 1989). What we know is largely based on what has happened – on what was, and not on what will be. We cannot, therefore, rule out the possibility that new doctrinal orthodoxies with mass-mobilizing potential and capable of legitimating new kinds of regime, benevolent or authoritarian, will arise (see Beetham, 1991). After all, who could have predicted the fall of the Berlin Wall, the peaceful reunification of Germany, the collapse of communism in Eastern Europe, and the end of the Cold War?

# 3  The Necessity of Marxism?

Liberal theory in both its classical and contemporary guises generally assumes something that should, in fact, be carefully examined: namely, whether existing relationships between men and women, the working, middle, and upper classes, blacks and whites, and between various ethnic groups allow formally recognized liberties to be actually realized. The formal existence of certain liberties in liberal *theory* is, while not unimportant, of restricted value if these liberties cannot be exercised in practice. An assessment of freedom must be made on the basis of liberties that are tangible; liberty that is merely theoretical can scarcely be said to have profound consequences for everyday life. If liberals like Fukuyama were to take these issues seriously, they might have to come to terms more directly with the massive number of people who, for want of a complex mix of resources and opportunities, are systematically restricted from participating actively in political and civil affairs.

Pursuing ideas such as these, Alex Callinicos, one of the most vigorous defenders of classical Marxism today, argues that liberal democracy has broken its promises. Following the Italian political theorist Norberto Bobbio, Callinicos conceives these promises as: (a) participation, (b) control from below, and (c) freedom to protest and reform (Callinicos, 1991, pp. 108–9; cf. Bobbio, 1987, pp. 42–4). "Really existing liberal democracy" fails, he contends, on all three counts. For it is distinguished by: the existence of a largely passive citizenry (less than 50 percent of eligible citizens in the US vote in presidential elections, for example); the erosion and displacement of parliamentary institutions by unelected centers of power (typified by the expansion of the role of bureaucratic authority, of functional representatives, and of the security services); and substantial structural constraints on state action and, in particular, on the possibility of the piecemeal reform of capitalism (the flight of capital, for example, is a habitual threat to elected governments with strong programs of social reform) (Callinicos, 1991, p. 109).

Against this background Callinicos seeks to defend the classical Marxist tradition by arguing that democracy, and a feasible socialist program, can only come from "below," from the self-organizing activity of the working class. A democratic alternative to liberal democracy can be found, Callinicos claims, in the "rich twentieth century tradition of soviet democracy, of workers' councils ..." (1991, p. 110). From this point of view, Stalinism, which dominated the Soviet Union's history until recently, can be seen as the negation of socialism. Callinicos interprets Stalinism as a counter-revolutionary force which, at the close of the 1920s, created a state capitalist regime; that is, a regime in which the state bureaucracy collectively extracts surplus value and regulates capital accumulation, fulfilling the role once performed by the bourgeoisie. For Callinicos, Stalinism destroyed the possibility of a radical workers' democracy of the sort briefly installed in the Soviet Union in October 1917 under Lenin's leadership. The collapse of Stalinism in 1989, therefore, cannot be understood (in Fukuyama's terms) as the defeat of classical Marxism; for what was defeated, Callinicos insists, was an authoritarian distortion of Marxism. And what won in 1989 was not "democracy," but capitalism. Therefore, what the East European revolutions achieved was a political reorganization of the ruling classes – one that allowed the technical, bureaucratic elites of Eastern Europe to integrate their economies fully into the world market, and aided the transition from state to globally integrated capitalism (Callinicos, 1991, p. 58).

Callinicos attacks the equation Marxism = Leninism = Stalinism. A "qualitative break," he argues, separates Stalinism from Marx and Lenin (1991, p. 16). Neither Marx's theory nor Lenin's practice sanctioned a system characterized not simply by one person's rule, but by "the hierarchically organised control of all aspects of social life, political, economic, and cultural, by a narrow oligarchy seated at the apex of the party apparatuses" (p. 15). In addition, there are resources in the classical Marxist tradition, particularly in the Trotskyist tradition and the Leftist opposition to Stalinism, which provide a basis for making sense of the demise of the Stalinist regimes. Three themes are, according to Callinicos, of special relevance (pp. 16–20). First, Marx's work, subsequently enriched and refined by later Marxist scholars, provides an account of epochal transformations, resulting from the essential conflict that develops between the relations and forces of production, and from class struggle which both mediates and intensifies such conflict. This account offers an indispensable framework for understanding the progressive collapse of the Stalinist order.

Second, in the work of the Trotskyist tradition, particularly as elaborated by Tony Cliff, a basis exists for understanding the specific nature and evolution of Stalinism (see Cliff, 1948; cf. Cliff, 1974). Cliff's account of "state-capitalism" identifies, Callinicos maintains, the contradictions that exist in Stalinist regimes – between an exploiting dominant class which runs the bureaucracy and state factories, and the working classes, excluded from any effective control of the productive forces. It was this contradiction which brought the Stalinist regimes to an "immense crisis." While the crisis has been resolved temporarily by the integration of the East European economies into the world capitalist order, the contradictions of this latter order are likely to result in still greater economic and political instability in the future.

Finally, in defining a project of human emancipation, classical Marxists provide an alternative to existing class-ridden regimes in both West and East. In championing a conception of socialism as "the self-emancipation of the working class," classical Marxism upholds a vision of a "self-conscious independent movement of the immense majority, in the interest of the immense majority," as Marx once wrote (quoted in Callinicos, 1991, p. 18). This is a vision of "socialism from below," wholly at odds both with the form of governance which used to prevail in the USSR and the Eastern bloc and with the emasculated democracies of the West (Callinicos, 1991, p. 18).

The contemporary era is constituted by a single unified economic system (Callinicos, 1991, p. 134). However, it is a system marked by exploitation and inequality. "Really existing capitalism," unlike the myth of self-equilibriating markets, is characterized by: the concentration and centralization of economic power; the growth of multinational corporations beyond the control of individual nation-states; cyclical crises involving over-production, anarchy, and waste; poverty in the heartlands of the West and massive disparities in life chances between the West and the Rest; and the creation of life-threatening side-effects of uncontrolled capitalist accumulation, for example in the form of global warming (Callinicos, 1991, pp. 98–106). In Callinicos's judgment, "capitalism stands condemned"; it is time to resume the classical Marxist project (pp. 106, 134–6).

## 3.1 Critical response

In the liberal tradition of the nineteenth and twentieth centuries, the political has often been equated with the world of government and the citizen's relation to it. Where this equation is made, and where politics is regarded as a sphere apart from the economy or culture, a vast domain of what is central to politics in other traditions of thought tends to be excluded from view. Marxism has been at the forefront of the criticism of this position, maintaining that it proceeds as if classes did not exist, as if the relationship between classes were not exploitative, as if classes did not have fundamental differences of interest, and as if these differences of interest did not largely define economic and political life. The key source of contemporary power – private ownership of the means of production – is, Marxism holds, ostensibly depoliticized by liberalism; that is, it is arbitrarily treated as if it were not a proper subject of politics.

The Marxist critique of liberalism, as Callinicos rightly stresses, raises important questions – above all, about whether productive relations and market economies can be characterized as non-political and, thus, about whether the interconnections between economic power and the state can be anything but a central matter in politics. But it also raises difficulties by postulating (even in its subtler versions) a direct connection between the political and the economic spheres. By seeking to understand the political by reference to economic and class power, and by rejecting the notion of politics as a unique form of activity, Marxism itself tends to marginalize or exclude from politics certain types of issues: essentially, all those issues which cannot be reduced to class-related matters. Important examples are ecological questions, or issues raised by the domination of women by men or of certain racial and ethnic groups by others. Other central matters neglected include the power of public administrators or bureaucrats over their clients, the use and role of resources which build up in most social organizations to sustain authority, and the form and nature of electoral institutions.

One of the chief problems with a position such as Callinicos's, therefore, concerns the questions which arise when the capitalist order is presented as an all-embracing totality within which all aspects of social, political, and cultural life are, in principle, located. Some mechanisms of institutional ordering (the states-system, the military order, for instance) and some types of social relationship (gender inequality and ethnic discrimination, for example) pre-existed the advent of modern capitalism, and have retained a distinctive role in the formation and structuring of modernity (see the discussions in chapters 2 and 7). Among the implications of this are that the concepts of mode of production and class analysis are too limiting. The thesis of the primacy of production and class relations has to be discarded, though this should not be taken to mean that the analysis of class and class conflict becomes insignificant (see the introduction to part III).

There are additional questions to raise, especially about the relationship of classical Marxism to democracy. If not all differences of interest can be reduced to class, and if differences of opinion – for example, about the allocation of resources – can stem from a variety of positions, it is important to create the institutional space for the generation of, and debate about, alternative political strategies and programs, as many of the social movements in Central and Eastern Europe sought to do from 1989 onward. Indeed, without such a space it is hard to see how citizens could be active participants in the determination of the conditions of their own association. Politics involves discussion and negotiation about public policy – discussion and negotiation which cannot take place according to wholly impartial or objective criteria, for there are none. (Even the philosophy of science is well known for continuous controversy about what criteria are suitable for the resolution of disputes among competing theoretical positions (see chapter 19).) A series of institutional procedures and mechanisms for debating and taking decisions about public affairs is, accordingly, essential. Marx defended the role of elections to choose those who might represent local views and interests: delegates who would be mandated to articulate particular positions and who would be subject to recall if they failed in this respect. He was aware of the practical importance of being able to remove delegates from office. Callinicos shares this view. But such a position is, in my judgment, by no means sufficient (see Held, 1987, pp. 135–9).

The fundamental problem with Marx's view of politics, and "the end of politics" in a post-capitalist order (for politics will end when class is abolished, in this account), is that it cannot accept as legitimate in and of itself any description of political difference; that is, it does not accept the notion that an individual or group has a right to hold, and negotiate about, a politically different opinion as an equal member of a polity (Polan, 1984, p. 77). Marx's conception of politics in fact radically delegitimizes politics within the body of the citizenry. He saw systematic differences of political view as reflecting, above all, class interests in capitalist societies. Consequently, after the revolution, there is the strong likelihood that there can be only one genuine form of "politics"; for there will no longer be any justified grounds for fundamental disagreement. The end of class means the end of any legitimate basis for dispute: only classes have irreconcilable interests.

It is hard to resist the view that implicit in this position is a propensity to an authoritarian form of politics (Held, 1987, pp. 135–9). There appears to be no scope for systematically encouraging and tolerating disagreement and debate about public matters. Marx, it seems, under-estimated the significance of the liberal preoccupation with how to secure freedom of criticism and action – i.e. choice and diversity – in the face of political power (although this is by no means to say that the traditional liberal formulation of the problem is fully satisfactory; see section 6).

The upshot of this argument is that Stalinism is not simply an aberration of the Marxist project – a wholly separate and distinct political phenomenon. Rather, it is an outcome – though by no means the only possible one – of the "deep structure" of Marxist categories, with their emphasis on the centrality of class, the universal standpoint of the proletariat, and a conception of politics which roots it squarely in production. The contributions to politics of other forms of social structure, collectivity, agency, identity, interest, and knowledge are severely under-estimated. This argument does not imply that Stalinism was the inevitable result of the Revolution of 1917; there were many complex conditions which determined the fate of the revolution. But it does imply that Marxism has misunderstood the liberal and liberal-democratic preoccupation with the form and limits of state power, and that this misunderstanding is an inextricable part of classical Marxist political theory. Moreover, it is a misunderstanding rich in implications for how one conceives of politics, democracy, and the nature of political agency. (For an alternative view – one which, however, I find ultimately unconvincing – see Callinicos's reply to this criticism in chapter 4 of *The Revenge of History* (Callinicos, 1991).)

The argument that what failed in the Soviet Union is simply Stalinism, or the state-capitalist regime, is problematic. For it was not a form of capitalism which failed but, rather, a form of what I call "state-administered socialism." There are several different variants of state-administered socialism, from the state socialist societies of the former

Eastern bloc to the traditional social democratic regimes of the West.
While there are major differences between these types, which I by no
means wish to under-estimate, they also have certain elements in
common: all can be associated with centrally controlled bureaucratic
institutions. The program of state-administered socialism lost its radical
appeal precisely because it failed to recognize the desirable form and
limits of state action.

State-administered socialism assumed that state power could become
the caretaker of existence. Intervening in social life by securing capital
investment, managing employment, and expanding welfare
opportunities, the state tended to assume omniscience over questions of
needs and wants. In retrospect, it is hardly surprising that among its
unforeseen effects were the generation of a marked distrust of those in
charge of the apparatus of government, a deep skepticism about
expertise, and a general decline in the legitimacy of "socialism" (see
Held, 1989, chs 5–6). Many citizens came to assume that socialism
meant bureaucracy, surveillance, red tape, and state control – views
prevalent not only in the New Right (and in the mass media's images of
the Soviet Union), but also among those in daily contact with, for
example, certain branches of the western welfare state, e.g. social
security offices, social services, housing authorities, and city planners.

To summarize, the "crisis of socialism," in theory and in practice,
goes much further than the "crisis of Stalinism." The relationship
between socialism and democracy has to be re-thought, as does the
relationship between capitalism and modernity more broadly. There are
notable theoretical and practical reasons, I have suggested, for
skepticism about some of the dominant elements of the traditional
socialist project.

# 4   From Modernity to Post-Modernity?

For Fukuyama, modernity can be characterized as the victory of a
distinctive concept of the political – the liberal concept. Modernity is
the reshaping of the world according to liberal principles. For
Callinicos, modernity is *capitalist* modernity. It is the capitalist nature
of modern societies and states which gives them their distinctive
character. Anthony Giddens is among those who have resisted the
equations of modernity with liberalism, or modernity with capitalism.
While Giddens draws heavily on the thought of Marx, among others, he
does so in a critical way, emphasizing the multi-dimensional nature of
modernity, its complex causal patterns and institutional logics, and the
inherently contingent qualities of political and social change.

In Giddens's view, there are four main institutional aspects to
modernity: (a) capitalism (the system of production of commodities for
markets, in which wage labor is also a commodity); (b) industrialism
(the application of inanimate sources of power through productive
techniques for the transformation of nature); (c) coordinated
administrative power focused through surveillance (the control of

information and the monitoring of the activities of subject populations by states and other organizations); and (d) military power (the concentration of the means of violence in the hands of the state). These four institutional dimensions of modernity are irreducible to one another, for the form and logic of each one are quite different from those of the others. The development and dynamics of military power and warfare, for example, affected the shape and structure of capitalist development as well as particular patterns of class and class conflict, and helped generate an alternative power system to capital: the modern system of nation-states. The formation of the nation-state system and the dynamics of international security (and insecurity) cannot, therefore, simply be understood by reference to the logic and dynamics of capitalism (see Giddens, 1990b; and chapter 2). In Giddens's judgment, each of the four institutional dimensions consists of a distinctive set of causal processes and structures. Taken together, however, they provide a framework for understanding some of the central features, developments, and tensions in modern societies.

Giddens holds that Marx's analysis of the mechanisms of capitalist production and exchange, and his critical deciphering of the forms of class domination and exploitation, retain their relevance today. But he argues that, however important Marx's contributions may be, there are massive gaps in Marx's thought and in Marxism more generally, which mean that it cannot simply be updated or amended. These omissions relate to the different dimensions of modernity and include: the absence of a satisfactory account of power, particularly military power and the use of violence by individuals, collectivities, and states; an inadequate analysis of administrative power and its distinctive crystallization in nation-states; and a refusal to consider sources and forms of systematic conflict which cannot be related directly to class.

According to Giddens, each institutional complex of modernity should be understood as an area of contestation or conflict. The working-class or labor movement was always only one type of collective response to the process of change inaugurated by modern conditions. By equating capitalism with modernity, and working-class struggles with non-sectarian, progressive interests – i.e. by making the standpoint of the labor movement the general or universal standpoint – Marx failed to grasp two central matters: first, that there are forms of politics which cannot be understood from the perspective of class alone; and second, that a "critical" account of modernity must embrace a far wider perspective than labor interests if it is to claim to represent "a humane and just social order."

Giddens explores connections between the four central dimensions of modernity and four social movements which are both constituted by these dimensions and active agents in their re-formation. If the labor movement emerged as a product of, and critical response to, the capitalist labor contract, the environmental movement can be seen as the outcome of, and challenge to, ecological degradation which has followed in the wake of industrialism. The sites of the civil and human rights movements have been systems of unaccountable power, while the peace movement is the product of, and a key force against, the contemporary structure of military power. Linking the "alternative visions" of these movements to an analysis of the structural possibilities of transition offered by the institutions of modernity – a perspective Giddens calls "utopian realism" – yields a reconceptualization of what might be "beyond modernity." Figure 13.1 maps the institutional clusters and movements of modernity to the future projects and institutional elements of a "post-modern" order.

Rethinking socialism after the revolutions of 1989–90, Giddens contends, means exploring alternative institutional orders to each of the key dimensions of modernity. Only such an exploration can take us beyond modernity to envisage a post modern order. Such an order is both far more difficult to imagine and far more complex to realize than earlier socialists or utopians had thought. Nonetheless, future-oriented social movements and an understanding of the institutional dynamics of modernity provide clues to new possibilities. While a post-modern order will be institutionally complex, it will represent a movement beyond modernity along each of the four dimensions already distinguished.

The unregulated pursuit of capitalist expansion is as unviable an option in contemporary circumstances as the survival of state socialist societies. If socialism means rigorously planned production, organized primarily within the nation-state, we know that it cannot work any longer. But neither can ceaseless capitalist accumulation, for it is not self-sustaining in terms of resources, and the massive disparities it creates between the life chances of different groups and regions bear a cost in human terms that few can accept on reflection. (The number of people who die of malnutrition each year is equivalent to dropping a Hiroshima bomb every three days, yet this is not for want of adequate food production on a global scale (see Bennett and George, 1987).) In contrast, Giddens defends the possibility of a regulated market order

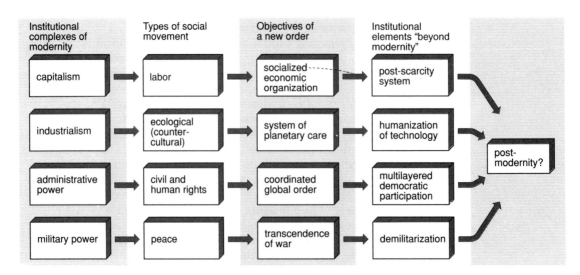

Figure 13.1   From modernity to post-modernity: Giddens's scheme

embedded in a post-scarcity economic system in which the developed societies make major adjustments in their economies and lifestyles in order to foster greater prosperity in the less-developed world.

Such a development depends, in turn, on a more coordinated global political order, and this, Giddens believes, could emerge. Trends towards increasing globalization are forcing states to collaborate ever more with one another (albeit in a variety of different forms), just as they are increasing spaces "below" the level of nation-states for enhanced democratic participation – by groups and movements, for example, that have gained greater autonomy as a result of the weakening of old state structures. These trends can only be effective, however, if they are linked to transformations in the sphere of military power, and these too Giddens thinks are possible. Few states today stand to gain anything durable from territorial aggrandizement, faced as they are with the destructive power of military technology and the interconnectedness of peoples and territories.

Finally, Giddens argues that while certain destructive trends in the earth's eco-systems may have proceeded too far to be reversed, it is also the case that there are significant counter-trends, which might be safeguarded by the institutional complexes of a post-modern order. Although one can make no assumption that world events will move in the direction outlined by these various "utopian considerations," "all discussions," Giddens holds, "which propose . . . possible futures, including this one, can by their very nature make some impact" (1990b, p. 171). A critical account of modernity remains an indispensable project.

## 4.1 Critical response

Giddens's emphasis on the multi-dimensional nature of modernity, with its distinctive and complex patterns of change and development, offers advantages over theories which ignore or play down the significance of certain crucial institutions (e.g. military power) because of their single-minded focus on one set of explanatory terms (e.g. class struggle); or which fail to recognize the role of certain phenomena (e.g. forms of economic power) in relation to their categories (e.g. market relations) and, hence, conveniently disregard important questions (e.g. the links between economic and political liberty). Likewise, Giddens's view of the interconnectedness of states and societies, and of the entwinement of the national and international in shaping the modern era, offers significant advances over most of the leading nineteenth- and twentieth-century perspectives on societal change which assumed all too often that the origins of social transformation are to be found in processes internal to society – in its power structures (liberalism) or productive relations (Marxism). Moreover, his consistent attempt to think about the "far side" of modernity – i.e. whatever lies beyond modernity – along a number of institutional axes offers important insights into both the autonomy and interrelatedness of different types of social change and, accordingly, into the weaknesses of most existing models of transformation (based, for instance, on politics or economics, on structural factors or social processes, on the local or the global).

Giddens's broad theoretical position is close to that found in a number of chapters in this volume. This is due partly to his influence on contemporary sociological debate and partly to a general rethinking of the classical sociological tradition undertaken in the last two decades; a process that has led to a convergence of viewpoints on some questions. Giddens's stress on the constitution of modernity by a cluster of institutions overlaps in particular with the standpoint of some of the authors in part 1; see, for example, chapter 2. Yet, it is also striking that certain institutional dimensions and spheres of activity play no part in his scheme; for instance, law, culture, and the separation of "the public" and "the private," the latter being perhaps one of the most distinctive features of modernity (see chapter 4). These absences raise questions about the comprehensiveness of Giddens's account and about its ability to illuminate some central shifts in social and political relations – for example, changing patterns and forms of public law, transformations in national and cultural identity, alterations in the relation between the domestic and familial spheres and those of waged work and politics; or, to put the point differently, between gender relations and citizenship, participation in politics and social welfare.

Likewise, many social movements – from religious groups to feminist activists – have no role in Giddens's scheme, suggesting again that his conceptual framework may not make adequate allowance for some of the key pressure points in contemporary culture and politics; indeed, that it mistakenly allows no place for those movements, or for the institutions to which they can be related, because they are not part of modernity and its dynamics, as he understands them. In addition, the type of connections Giddens draws between distinctive social movements and institutional clusters are themselves far from clear. Different movements, changing orientations over time (from civil concerns to perhaps wider political and social issues), and their different institutional locations at any given moment (economy, polity, local community, etc.), cannot easily be accommodated on a conceptual map which posits essentially fixed or static relations between particular institutional clusters and social groupings (see Held, 1989).

While Giddens rightly emphasizes the shifting significance and causal weight to be allocated to particular institutional dimensions over time, his account is ambiguous on certain significant questions: complexity of categories is no guarantee of either comprehensiveness or precision on key issues. For instance, Giddens does not adequately establish how and to what extent the modern state is enmeshed in industrial capitalism and, thus, the degree to which it can become an effective site of political transformation. Giddens's position wavers between seeing the state as a "capitalist state" and as a "power system" in and of itself. Or, to put the point another way, "the relative primacies of class vs. non-class conflicts and economic vs. political power in Giddens's analysis of capitalist nation-states remains uncertain" (Jessop, 1989, p. 122). The implications of this ambiguity are important, because if the non-capitalist features of the modern state are not adequately separated out, one cannot grasp many of the distinctive elements of modern politics – for instance, the centrality (in principle) of an "impersonal" structure of public power, of constitutional forms, and of a diversity of power centers within and outside of the state. Nor can one grasp many of the central factors involved in shaping the dynamics and forms of the existing state-system itself – factors which relate directly to the interrelations of states, to the structural features of the international political system, and to the "security dilemma" facing modern states, putting pressure on them to prepare for war in order to secure peace (see chapters 2 and 7). And if these factors are not adequately understood, it is doubtful whether the "far side" of modernity can be properly conceived.

Finally, the persuasiveness of Giddens's conception of a post-modern order is weakened by difficulties on three additional counts. First, it is not underpinned by a political theory which systematically recasts the meaning of the political good in relation to the interconnected institutions and issues we face today. Giddens's own conception of "a humane and just social order," "a common concern with the stewardship of the globe's resources," and a "post-scarcity" economic system is, at best, insufficiently clear. Secondly, the institutional prescriptions he sets forth are in need of further elaboration, because the relation of the institutional clusters to one another is barely theorized and, accordingly, it is hard to know how the institutional logics might mesh together. And, thirdly, the question of which institutions and which agencies might provide a path from modernity to its "far side" – the whole issue of transitional stages – remains largely unaddressed, though it should not be if "utopia" is to be "realistic."

In short, some fundamental issues are left aside. Of course, it is easy to put difficult questions to an author; and it is unreasonable to expect them all to be fully addressed. Nonetheless, it does not seem wholly unfair to put a wide range of issues to theorists like Giddens, precisely because they offer visions of life not only as it is, but also as it might and should be. Before we accept their accounts as guiding orientations, we need to be sure of their coherence and cogency.

# 5   The Story So Far, and the Question of the Political Good

The East European revolutions were, without doubt, a historical watershed. The collapse of the Soviet empire, and the retreat of communism across Europe, were not only major events of the twentieth century but probably of modern history as well. Ripples of change spread through political institutions and conventional beliefs across the globe.

The diverse interpretations of the revolutions, and of their impact on the contemporary world, reflect at least two things: history is not at an end and ideology is not dead. Liberalism and Marxism, prominent modernist ideologies with roots stretching back into the formative moments of modernity, remain alive and kicking. While liberalism is clearly in the ascendant, Marxism is not yet exhausted. Nonetheless, both positions, I have argued, are wanting, in fundamental respects. New accounts of the complexity of modernity have been elaborated which throw further into relief some of the limitations of earlier traditions of political and social thought. But these new accounts, exemplified here by Giddens's multi-dimensional view of the modern world, also generate new questions, not all of which are answered satisfactorily.

Among these questions is a concern about the meaning of the political good, or how one should define the "good life" in contemporary politics. This is a matter about which Fukuyama, Callinicos, and Giddens all have something to say (whether directly or indirectly) and it provides, accordingly, a useful point around which to draw together some of the strands of the previous sections.

For Fukuyama, the good life follows from the progressive recasting of the modern world on liberal principles. For him, political life, like economic life, is – or ought to be – a matter of individual freedom and initiative, and the more it approximates this state of affairs, the more justifiably one might claim that the political good has been achieved. The individual is, in essence, sacrosanct, and is free and equal only to the extent that he or she can pursue and attempt to realize self-chosen ends and personal interests. Equal justice can be sustained between individuals if, above all, individuals' entitlement to certain rights or liberties is respected, and all citizens are treated as equals before the law. The preoccupation here is with the creation and defense of a world in which "free and equal" individuals can flourish with minimum political impediment, West and East, North and South.

By contrast, Callinicos, and classical Marxists more generally, defend the desirability of certain social or collective goals and means. For them, to take equality and liberty seriously is to challenge the view that these values can be realized by individuals left, in practice, to their own devices in a "free market" economy and a restricted or minimal state. Equality, liberty, and justice – recognized by them as "great universal ideals" – cannot be achieved in a world dominated by private ownership of property and the capitalist economy; these ideals can be realized only through struggles to ensure that the means of production are socialized, i.e. subject to collective appropriation and to procedures which ensure social control. Only such procedures can ultimately guarantee that "the free development of each" is compatible with the "free development of all."

Although the revolutions of Central and Eastern Europe put democracy at the forefront of politics across the globe, the appeal and nature of democracy itself remains inadequately considered by both Fukuyama and Callinicos. In Fukuyama's writings, democracy is eclipsed by the affirmation of individualist political, economic, and ethical doctrines. The question and problem of democratic accountability takes second place, at best, to the imperative of individual liberty in the face of political regulation. In Callinicos's work, the categories of class, class conflict, and production displace the necessity of a thorough analysis of democracy. Giddens's conception of the political good shares some of these weaknesses. Not only is the political good under-theorized by him generally, but his position offers no account of the meaning of democracy in the contemporary era. For all its complexity, Giddens's theory of a post-modern order, with its emphasis on the necessity to create a post-scarcity economic system, humanized technology, demilitarized international relations, and increased participation, side-steps the question of how and in what particular ways it will actually be democratic.

Despite the near ubiquity of some form of democracy, its common use in political discourse, and its practically universal invocation by political regimes in the late twentieth century, the concept has not been at the center of theories of modernity or post-modernity. Democracy bestows an "aura of legitimacy" on modern political life: policies and strategies appear justified and appropriate where they are claimed to be democratic. Yet, under what conditions they may reasonably be considered democratic, and when one can legitimately claim the mantle of democracy, remains unclear. In the final section of this chapter, I should like to turn to this issue in a preliminary way, offering some thoughts on why democracy is so central in the current period, and on what it might mean today. Addressing these issues will, hopefully, throw further light on the meaning of the "good life" in contemporary politics.

# 6  Democracy: Between State and Civil Society?

Part of the appeal of democracy lies in its denial *in principle* of any conception of the political good other than that generated by "the people" themselves. From the pursuit of "no taxation without representation" in seventeenth-century England, to the diverse struggles to achieve a genuinely universal franchise in the nineteenth and twentieth centuries, advocates of greater accountability in government have sought to establish satisfactory means for choosing, authorizing and controlling political decisions. In the East European revolutions, the principle of self-determination and the principle of consent to government action have (once again) challenged the principle of "single person" or, in this particular case, "single party" rule (see chapter 7). Democracy is conceived of as a way of containing the powers of the state and of mediating among competing individual and collective projects. In political circumstances constituted by a plurality of identities, cultural forms, and interests, each perhaps articulating different prescriptive regimes, democracy is seen, moreover, as offering a basis for tolerating and negotiating over difference.

In this section I want to argue that democracy should be conceived of as the privileged conception of the political good because it offers –

in theory at least – a form of politics and life in which there are fair and just ways of negotiating values and value disputes. Democracy is, I think, the only "grand" or "meta-narrative" which can legitimately frame and delimit the competing "narratives" of the contemporary age. Or, to put the point somewhat differently, democratic reason (i.e. thinking democratically) ought to be regarded as the legitimate heir of the Enlightenment project: the project of self-reflection which finds its *raison d'être* in the determination of the conditions of human association (see the introduction to part III, and chapter 19). But why exactly should this be so? What is significant about democracy in an age in which some think it represents the end point of history, and others that it represents a sham in its existing form?

The *idea* of democracy is important because it does not just represent one value among many, such as liberty, equality, and justice, but is the value which can link and mediate between competing prescriptive concerns. It is a guiding orientation which can help generate a basis for the specification of the relation among different normative concerns. Democracy does not presuppose agreement on diverse values. Rather, it suggests a way of relating values to each other and of leaving the resolution of value conflicts open to participants in a political dialogue, subject only to certain provisions protecting the shape and form of the dialogue itself. In this lie further elements of its appeal.

What form or conception of democracy engenders or encourages political dialogue in practice? Answers to this question, it has already been suggested, cannot simply be found in liberalism or Marxism. Liberalism's desire to create a diversity of power centers and a world marked by openness, controversy, and plurality is compromised by the reality of the "free market," by the structure and imperatives of the system of private capital accumulation. If liberalism's central failure is to see markets as "powerless" mechanisms of coordination and, thus, to neglect the distorting nature of economic power in relation to democracy, Marxism's central failure is to reduce political power to economic power and, thus, to neglect – as liberal democrats, among others, point out – the dangers of centralized political power and the problems of political accountability. Marxism's claim to represent the forces of progressive politics is tarnished by socialism's relation in practice, both in the East and in the West, to bureaucracy, surveillance, hierarchy, and state control. Accordingly, liberalism's account of the nature of markets and economic power must be rejected, while Marxism's account of the nature of democracy must be severely questioned.

It follows that the liberal and Marxist conceptions of what it is for people to be "free and equal" in a social order are too limited. Liberals like Fukuyama neglect a wide range of questions concerning the spheres of productive and reproductive relations. Marxists like Callinicos neglect pressing issues about the proper form and limits of the state, and under-estimate the dangers of centralized political power and the problems of political accountability. While Giddens's position takes issue with the premises of both liberalism and Marxism, he also leaves out of account certain key political and cultural domains (for instance, those concerning human reproduction and the organization of the household) and, partly as a result, fails to specify some of the central conditions of involvement of women (and men) in public life. These positions generate an unnecessarily, and unacceptably, restricted view of politics and democracy – a view which obscures significant requirements for the realization of a democratic order.

The history of the clash of interpretations about democracy has given rise over time to three basic variants or models of democracy, which it is as well to keep in mind. First, there is *direct* or *participatory democracy*, a system of decision-making about public affairs in which citizens are directly involved. This was the "original" type of democracy found in Ancient Athens, among other places. Second, there is *liberal* or *representative democracy*, a system of rule embracing elected "officers" who undertake to "represent" the interests or views of citizens within the framework of the "rule of law." Representative democracy means that decisions affecting a community are not made by its members as a whole, but by a group of people whom "the people" have elected for this purpose. In the arena of national politics, representative democracy takes the form of elections to congresses, parliaments, or similar national bodies. Third, there is a variant of democracy based on a *one-party* model. Until recently, the former Soviet Union, many East European societies, and some Third World countries have been dominated by this conception. The principle underlying one-party democracy is that a single party can be the legitimate expression of the overall will of the community. Voters choose among different candidates ostensibly proposing divergent policies within an overall framework, not among different parties.

What should be made of these various models of democracy today? The participatory model cannot easily be adapted to stretch across space and time. Its emergence in the context of city-states and under conditions of "social exclusivity" was an integral part of its successful development. (In Athens, women, an extensive slave population, and many other marginal groups were excluded from participating in the polity.) In contemporary circumstances, marked by a high degree of social, economic, and political differentiation, it is very hard to envisage how a democracy of this kind could succeed on a large scale (see Held, 1987, ch. 9). The significance of these reflections is reinforced by examining the fate of the model of democracy advocated by Marx, Engels, and their followers. The suitability of their model as an institutional arrangement which allows for mediation, negotiation, and compromise among struggling factions, groups, or movements, is open to doubt, as I have already noted. A system of institutions to promote discussion, debate, and competition among divergent views – a system encompassing the formation of movements, pressure groups, and/or political parties with leaderships to help press their cases – appears both necessary and desirable. Further, the changes in Central and Eastern Europe since 1989 seem to provide remarkable confirmatory evidence of this, with their emphasis on the importance of political and civil rights, a competitive party system, and the "rolling back of the state," i.e. the freeing of civil society from state domination.

In my judgment, one cannot escape the necessity of recognizing the importance of a number of fundamental liberal tenets: concerning the centrality, in principle, of an "impersonal" structure of public power, of a constitution to help guarantee and protect rights, of a diversity of power centers within and outside the state, of mechanisms to promote competition and debate between alternative political platforms. What this amounts to, among other things, is confirmation of the fundamental liberal notion that the separation of state from civil society must be an essential feature of any democratic political order. Conceptions of democracy that assume that the state can replace civil society, or vice versa, must be treated with the utmost caution.

To make these points is not, however, to affirm any one liberal democratic model as it stands, although many advocates of democracy in Eastern Europe appear to take this view. It is one thing to accept the arguments concerning the necessary protective, conflict-mediating, and redistributive functions of the democratic state; quite another to accept these as prescribed in existing accounts of liberal democracy from J.S. Mill onward. Advocates of liberal democracy have tended to be concerned, above all else, with the proper principles and procedures of democratic government. But by focusing on "government," they have attracted attention away from a thorough examination of the relations between:

1 formal rights and actual rights;
2 commitments to treat citizens as free and equal, and practices which do neither sufficiently;
3 concepts of the state as, in principle, an independent authority, and involvements of the state in the reproduction of the inequalities of everyday life;
4 notions of political parties as appropriate structures for bridging the gap between state and society, and the array of power centers which such parties and their leaders cannot reach.

To ignore these questions is to risk placing "democracy" in the context of a sea of political, economic, and social inequality. And it is to risk the creation of, at best, a very partial form of democratic politics – one in which the participation of some bears a direct relation to the limited or non-participation of others.

The implications of these points are, I believe, profound: for democracy to flourish today it has to be reconceived as a *double-sided* phenomenon; concerned, on the one hand, with the reform of state power and, on the other hand, with the restructuring of civil society. This entails recognizing the indispensability of a process of "double democratization": the interdependent transformation of both state and civil society. Such a process must be premised on two principles: (a) that the division between state and civil society must be a central feature of democratic life; and (b) that the power to make decisions must be free of the inequalities and constraints which (as Marx foresaw) can be imposed by an unregulated system of private capital. Of course, to recognize the importance of both these points is to recognize the necessity of substantially recasting their traditional connotations. (For texts which seek to do this, see Held, 1987, 1991; and Keane, 1988.)

If democratic life involves no more than a periodic vote, the locus of people's activities will be the "private" realm of civil society and the scope of their actions will depend largely on the resources they can command. Few opportunities will exist for citizens to act as citizens: i.e. as participants in public life. But if democracy is understood as a double-sided process, this state of affairs might be redressed by creating opportunities for people to establish themselves "in their capacity of being citizens" (Arendt, 1963, p. 256). Of course, this model of democracy faces an array of possible objections which cannot be pursued here. Hopefully, however, the necessity to think beyond the positions of liberalism and Marxism, and beyond the gaps in Giddens's theory of modernity and post-modernity, has – at the very least – been established.

# 7 Conclusion

One of the abiding lessons of the twentieth century must surely be that history is not closed and that human progress remains an extraordinarily fragile achievement, however one defines and approaches it. Fascism, Nazism, and Stalinism came close to obliterating democracy in the West only fifty years ago. The outcomes of human action, intended and unintended, always generate surprises, some catastrophic, some offering grounds for hope. In this sense, history remains to be made; though, to adapt a saying from Marx, it cannot always be made in circumstances of one's own choosing, for it is often the result of circumstances directly given and transmitted from the past (Marx, 1963, p. 15). The struggle for democracy, for a democratic conception of the political good – the "good life" defined under "free and equal" conditions of participation – is without guarantees, but it is a struggle for which all can find equally good grounds for commitment, or so I have argued.

Of course, groups or agencies can *refuse* to participate in a democratic dialogue, and if they do there is nothing intrinsic to the idea of democracy that can compel them to participate. If democracy is rejected as a legitimate form of governance, the politics of other forms of governance will come into play. Against this, "1989 and all that" affirmed growing support for the idea of democracy. But it also highlighted the gulf that exists today between different models of democracy, between contemporary liberal democracy and models such as those outlined above in section 6. By ignoring such differences, Fukuyama could proclaim "the end of history"; however, I would rather say that we remain in the flux of history with many decisive choices about the character of the contemporary order still to be made.

One area of "decisive choices" connects the idea of democracy directly to the larger framework of international relations. If the history and practice of democracy has until now been centered on the idea of locality (the city-state, the community, the nation), it is likely that in the future it will be centered on the international or global domain. In a world of progressive global interconnectedness, mediated by modern communications systems and information technology, there are pressing questions about the very future and viability of national democracies. There are no immediate solutions to the problems posed by interconnectedness, with its complex and often profoundly uneven effects; but there is an inescapably important series of questions to be addressed, some of which are the topic of the next chapter. Certainly, one can find many good reasons for being optimistic about finding a path forward, and many good reasons for thinking that at this juncture democracy will face another critical test.

# References

Arendt, H. (1963) *On Revolutions*, New York, Viking Press.

Beetham, D. (1991) *The Legitimation of Power*, London, Macmillan.

Bennett, J. and George, S. (1987) *The Hunger Machine*, Cambridge, England, Polity Press.

Berlin, I. (1969) *Four Essays on Liberty*, Oxford, Oxford University Press.

Bobbio, N. (1987) W*hich Socialism*? Cambridge, England, Polity Press.

Bocock, R. and Thompson, K. (eds) (1992) *Social and Cultural Forms of Modernity*, Cambridge, England, Polity Press.

Callinicos, A. (1991) *The Revenge of History: Marxism and the East European Revolutions*, Cambridge, England, Polity Press.

Cliff, T. (1948) "The nature of Stalinist Russia," *Revolutionary Communist Party Internal Bulletin*, June.

Cliff, T. (1974) *State Capitalism in Russia*, London, Pluto.

Dahl, R.A. (1985) *A Preface to Economic Democracy*, Cambridge, England, Polity Press.

Dahl, R.A. (1989) *Democracy and its Critics*, New Haven, Yale University Press.

Dunn, J. (1979) *Western Political Theory in the Face of the Future*, Cambridge, England, Cambridge University Press.

Friedman, J. (1989) "The new consensus. Part 1: The Fukuyama thesis," *Critical Review*, vol. 3, nos. 3–4, pp. 373–410.

Fukuyama, F. (1989) "The end of history?" *The National Interest*, no. 16, pp. 3–18.

Fukuyama, F. (1989/90) "A reply to my critics," *The National Interest*, no. 18, pp. 21–8.

Gadamer, H.-G. (1975) *Truth and Method*, London, Sheed and Ward.

Giddens, A. (1990a) "Modernity and utopia," *New Statesman*, November 2, pp. 20–2.

Giddens, A. (1990b) *The Consequences of Modernity*, Cambridge, England, Polity Press.

Held, D. (1987) *Models of Democracy*, Cambridge, England, Polity Press.

Held, D. (1989) *Political Theory and the Modern State*, Cambridge, England, Polity Press.

Held, D. (1991) "Democracy, the nation-state and the global system," in Held, D. (ed.) *Political Theory Today*, Cambridge, England, Polity Press.

Himmelfarb, G. (1989) "Response to Fukuyama," *The National Interest*, no. 16, pp. 24–6.

Hirst, P.Q. (1989) "Endism," *London Review of Books*, November 23, p. 14.

Horkheimer, M. and Adorno, T. (1972) *Dialectic of Enlightenment*, New York, Herder and Herder.

Jessop, B. (1989) "Capitalism, nation-states and surveillance," in Held, D. and Thompson, J.B. (eds) *Social Theory of Modern Societies: Anthony Giddens and his Critics*, Cambridge, England, Cambridge University Press.

Keane, J. (1988) *Democracy and Civil Society*, London, Verso.

Kennedy, P. (1988) *The Rise and Fall of the Great Powers*, London, Unwin.

Keohane, R.O. (1984) *After Hegemony: Cooperation and Discord in the World Political Economy*, Princeton, Princeton University Press.

Lewis, P. (1990a) "The long goodbye: party rule and political change in Poland since martial law," *The Journal of Communist Studies*, 6.1, pp. 24–48.

Lewis, P. (1990b) "Democratization in Eastern Europe," *Coexistence*, 27, pp. 245–67.

Lijphart, A. (1984) *Democracies*, New Haven, Yale University Press.

Marx, K. (1963) *The Eighteenth Brumaire of Louis Bonaparte*, New York, International Publishers.

Miller, D. (1989) *Market, State and Community: Theoretical Foundations of Market Socialism*, Oxford, Clarendon Press.

Mortimer, E. (1989) "The end of history?," *Marxism Today*, November, p. 29.

Polan, A.J. (1984) *Lenin and the End of Politics*, London, Methuen.

Thompson, J.B. (1990) *Ideology and Modern Culture*, Cambridge, England, Polity Press.

# 14      A Global Society?

Anthony McGrew

## Contents

| | | |
|---|---|---|
| 1 | Introduction | 467 |
| 1.1 | Themes and structure | 468 |
| 2 | Modernity and Globalization | 469 |
| 2.1 | "Globe talk": the discourse of globalization | 470 |
| 3 | Mapping the Dimensions of Globalization | 473 |
| 3.1 | Logics | 473 |
| 3.2 | Dynamics | 478 |
| 4 | A Global Society? | 480 |
| 4.1 | A global civilization | 480 |
| 4.2 | A capitalist world society | 482 |
| 4.3 | A bifurcated world | 484 |
| 4.4 | A global society of states | 485 |
| 4.5 | Trajectories of change | 487 |
| 5 | Globalization and the Future Political Community | 488 |
| 5.1 | Dissolving the nation-state | 488 |
| 5.2 | Rejuvenating the nation-state | 493 |
| 5.3 | Rethinking sovereignty and political community | 495 |
| 6 | Globalization and a Universal Sociology | 497 |
| | References | 499 |

# 1 Introduction

One of the most significant legacies of the Enlightenment for modern social and political thought has been the belief that the universal community of humankind is in all respects ". . . the end or object of the highest moral endeavour" (Bull, 1977, p. 27). Underlying this vision is an assumption that at root the needs and interests of all human beings are universally similar. Such a vision has shaped the emancipatory aspirations of both liberalism and Marxism, which have been committed to the eradication of those structures – the state and capitalism respectively – deemed to suppress the realization of a cosmopolitan world order based on liberty, justice, and equality for all of humanity. As the end of the twentieth century approaches, the growing recognition, reinforced by satellite images from space, that planet earth is a single "place" has reawakened intellectual interest in Enlightenment notions of a universal community of humankind. Moreover, "surface" events, such as the end of the Cold War, the collapse of communism and the Soviet Union, the transition from industrialism to post-industrialism, the global diffusion of democratic institutions and practices, together with the intensification of patterns of world-wide economic, financial, technological, and ecological interdependence, have signalled to many observers the final clearing away of the old world order, with all its menacing features, and the inauguration of a new world order which contains the promise of an evolving world society, a single global "community of fate." Certainly, there can be little doubt that the world is being remade around us, that radical changes are underway which may be transforming the fundamental parameters of modern human, social, and political existence. Rosenau proclaims that the world has entered the era of post-international politics, a "historical breakpoint" in which ". . . present premises and understanding of history's dynamics must be treated as conceptual jails" (Rosenau, 1990, p. 5).

The notion of post-international politics suggests that, at the century's end, globalization – simply the intensification of global interconnectedness – is *transforming* the existing world order most conspicuously through its direct challenge to the primacy of the nation-state in its present form. One of the principal issues examined in this chapter is therefore the question of whether humanity is witnessing the unfolding of a new historical epoch (one which is distinguished by a progressive globalization of human relations and the emergence of the first truly "global historical civilization"), or alternatively whether the present "phase" of globalization simply conceals a renewed strengthening of the existing structures of western modernity – capitalism, industrialism, and the nation-state system. Within this discursive framework, the implications of the globalization of social life, both for the viability of the modern nation-state (in its present form) and for the "sociological imagination," will be systematically and critically explored.

## 1.1  Themes and structure

Most traditional sociology textbooks tend to open with the claim that the sociological enterprise is primarily concerned with the study of "modern society," understood as a cohesive, bounded totality, an integrated social system. Society, in effect, therefore becomes indistinguishable from the nation-state. This conflation of the two concepts is hardly surprising since, as a discipline, "modern" sociology reflects its nineteenth-century origins, during an age of virulent nationalism and nation-state formation. Despite the emphasis the founding "fathers" gave to comparative sociology, much contemporary theorizing still remains focused on the "national society." As Turner notes, although it sought to be a universal science of human affairs, ". . . in practice sociology has been developed to explain and understand local or national destinies" (Turner, 1990, p. 343). However, in a "shrinking" world, where transnational relations, networks, activities, and interconnections of all kinds transcend national boundaries, it is increasingly difficult to "understand local or national destinies," without reference to global forces. The dynamics of the global financial system; the tremendous expansion of transnational corporate activity; the existence of global communications and media networks; the global production and dissemination of knowledge, combined with (among other factors) the escalating significance of transnational religious and ethnic ties; the enormous flows of peoples across national boundaries; and the emerging authority of institutions and communities above the nation-state: all these factors provide a powerful case for reassessing the traditional conception of society (and by association the nation-state) as a bounded, ordered, and unified social space – a coherent totality. If, as many would argue, globalization is reconstituting the world as "one place," then a re-focusing of the sociological project – away from "society" and the "nation-state" towards the emerging "world society" – would seem a logical prerequisite for making sense of the contemporary human condition. Bauman puts the point clearly: "With the sovereignty of nation-states vividly displaying its limitations . . . the traditional model of society loses its credence as a reliable frame of reference . . ." (Bauman, 1992, p. 57).

Globalization strikes at many of the orthodoxies of social science, and more particularly the sociological project. At one level, the prospect of a "world society" resurrects the highly contentious issue, first posed and answered by the Enlightenment *philosophes*, as to the validity of universalist accounts of social phenomena. If globalization is characterized by universal socio-economic processes, does this not suggest the need for universal accounts of social affairs, and by definition the existence of some universal truths? Globalization also brings into question foundational concepts – "society" and the "nation-state" – which still retain a privileged position in the discourse of modern sociology and the social sciences more widely. Finally, globalization poses an interesting set of normative questions concerning the future of the nation-state and the nature of the modern political community. For, in an age in which global interconnectedness appears to be intensifying, the most pressing issue must be whether the nation-state and the national political community will remain viable and sustainable forms of political and social organization. In effect, globalization raises the prospect of the "end of the nation-state" as the primary container of modernity. It is somewhat ironic that, as the century draws to a close, the pace of "progress" is being indicted for dissolving one of the quintessential institutions of modernity: the nation-state. It seems equally ironic that, at the very moment sociology encounters the possibility of a "world society," it is gripped by the discourse of post-modernity which denies the plausibility of any universal truths or knowledge through which such an emerging "global social formation" might be comprehended (Archer, 1991).

While the conclusion of the chapter will confront these apparent ironies, the main narrative will be devoted to an exegesis of the contemporary debates about globalization, with specific emphasis on its consequences for the nation-state and the sociological imagination. The discussion will embrace:

1   an examination of the discourse of globalization;
2   a review of the dimensions of globalization;
3   the emerging debate on globalization and the formation of a global society;
4   the implications of a global society for the continued viability of the nation-state and the national political community; and
5   an assessment of why globalization invites the return of a more universal sociology, and the corresponding demise of "society" as the basic unit of sociological analysis.

## 2   Modernity and Globalization

In comparison with previous historical epochs, the modern era has supported a progressive globalization of human affairs. The primary institutions of western modernity – industrialism, capitalism, and the nation-state – have acquired, throughout the twentieth century, a truly global reach. But this has not been achieved without enormous human cost, since western globalization has been fuelled by a tremendous "arrogance and violence" (Modelski, 1972, p. 49). While early phases of globalization brought about the physical unification of the world, more recent phases have remade the world into a single global system in which previously distinct historical societies or civilizations have been thrust together. This should not be taken to imply that globalization involves global cultural homogenization or global political integration. Rather, it defines a far more complex condition, one in which patterns of human interaction, interconnectedness, and awareness are reconstituting the world as a single social space.

## 2.1    "Globe talk": the discourse of globalization

During the 1980s, the concept of globalization began to permeate a diverse body of literatures within the social sciences. This intellectual fascination with globalization and its consequences was stimulated in part by a concern to understand the nature of the socio-economic changes which appeared to be enveloping all advanced capitalist societies. In part the fascination was also associated with a perception that the fates of individual national communities were increasingly bound together, a perception underlined by the global economic recession of the early 1980s, the renewed threat of nuclear armageddon following the intensification of Soviet–American rivalry, and the impending eco-crisis. These, and other events, became significant reference points in a growing literature which sought to analyze the ways in which daily existence within most countries was becoming increasingly enmeshed in global processes and structures..This expanded awareness of global interconnectedness was reinforced by the electronic media, which were capable of bringing to their audience's immediate attention distant events, so creating a sense of a globally shared community. Today, "globalization" has become a widely used term within media, business, financial, and intellectual circles, reflecting a fairly widespread perception that modern communications technology has shrunk the globe. However, popular use of the term and its many definitions within the social sciences have imbued the concept with multiple meanings. How then should we understand the term?

Globalization refers to the multiplicity of linkages and interconnections that transcend the nation-states (and by implication the societies) which make up the modern world system. It defines a process through which events, decisions, and activities in one part of the world can come to have significant consequences for individuals and communities in quite distant parts of the globe. Nowadays, goods, capital, people, knowledge, images, communications, crime, culture, pollutants, drugs, fashions, and beliefs all readily flow across territorial boundaries. Transnational networks, social movements, and relationships are extensive in virtually all areas of human activity from the academic to the sexual. Moreover, the existence of global systems of trade, finance, and production binds together in very complicated ways the prosperity and fate of households, communities, and nations across the globe. Territorial boundaries are therefore arguably increasingly insignificant insofar as social activity and relations no longer stop – if they ever did – at the water's edge. It is thus largely irrelevant to continue to make distinctions between the internal and the external, the foreign and the domestic spheres of socio-economic activity, when globalization has resulted in a "stretching" of social relations across national territorial boundaries (Giddens, 1990, p. 14). But the concept of globalization articulates something much more profound about modern social existence than the simple fact of growing interconnectedness between nation-states.

Within the literature, two authors – Giddens and Harvey – have made a significant contribution to the theorization of globalization. Giddens considers globalization to be one of the most visible consequences of modernity. This is because globalization involves a profound reordering of time and space in social life – what Giddens refers to as "time–space distanciation" (1990, p. 14). He stresses how the development of global networks of communication and complex global systems of production and exchange diminishes the grip of local circumstances over people's lives. Thus, the jobs of Scottish miners may be more dependent on the pricing decisions of Australian and South African coal companies in the global market than on the immediate decisions of local management. In Giddens's view, this "disembedding" of social relations – lifting them out "from local contexts of interaction" and recombining them across time and space – is primarily associated with the forces of modernity. However, globalization expands the scope of such disembedding processes, with the consequence that ". . . larger and larger numbers of people live in circumstances in which disembedded institutions, linking local practices with globalized social relations, organize major aspects of day-to-day life" (Giddens, 1990, p. 79). This certainly does not mean that "place" or "locale" are no longer significant in structuring social life, but rather that ". . . the truth of experience no longer coincides with the place in which it takes place" (Jameson, quoted in Harvey, 1989, p. 261). The point is that, in today's world, social relations and interaction are not dependent on simultaneous physical "presence" within a specific location, since the structures and institutions of modern societies, facilitated by instantaneous communication, foster intense ". . . relations between 'absent' others, locationally distant from any given situation of face-to-face interaction" (Giddens, 1990, p. 18). Globalization articulates, in a most dramatic manner, this conflation of "presence" and "absence" through its systemic interlocking of the "local" and the "global." For Giddens, the concept of globalization therefore embraces much more than a notion of simple interconnectedness: ". . . the concept of globalization is best understood as expressing fundamental aspects of time–space distanciation. Globalization concerns the intersection of presence and absence, the interlacing of social events and social relations 'at a distance' with local contextualities" (Giddens, 1991, p. 21).

In his exploration of the "post-modern condition," Harvey, too, conceives of globalization as an expression of our changing experience of time and space – what he labels "time–space compression" (Harvey, 1989, p. 240). By using this term, he highlights dramatically the sense in which, under the pressures of technological and economic change, space and time have been continually collapsed such that ". . . today we have to learn how to cope with an overwhelming sense of compression of our spatial and temporal worlds" (Harvey, 1989, p. 240). What is distinctive about Harvey's analysis of globalization is the emphasis placed on the "speeding up" or intensity of time–space compression.

For Harvey, today's "global village" is not the product of some smooth linear or exponential process of time–space compression, but rather results from a more discontinuous historical process, a process punctuated by discrete phases or bursts of intense time–space compression. These phases, he argues, are associated with the periodic crises and restructuring of capitalism, which involve a "speeding up" of economic and social processes. We are all aware from our own experiences of the way in which, particularly in the current era, the quickening pace of change seems to have become a "normal" feature of social life. Virtually as they are launched, new fashions, new products, even major historical events, seem to become redundant "history." One of the consequences of this speeding up of socio-economic change is an intensification of time–space compression, and with this comes an acceleration in the pace of globalization.

According to Harvey, ". . . we have been experiencing, these last two decades, an intense phase of time–space compression that has had a disorienting and disruptive impact upon political-economic practices, the balance of class power, as well as upon cultural and social life" (Harvey, 1989, p. 284). This phase coincided with a deep crisis of capitalist accumulation, which was at its most intense in the late 1970s and early 1980s, and has been associated with a dramatic intensification of globalization. This intensification of globalization has been most pronounced in the spheres of manufacturing production and finance. In both these sectors, the speeding up of technological and organizational change has fostered an increased global mobility of capital, such that a new international division of labor appears to be emerging. Central to this has been the creation of the first truly global financial system, with twenty-four-hour-a-day trading: "The formation of a global stock market, of global commodity (even debt) futures markets, of currency and interest rate swaps, together with an accelerated geographical mobility of funds, meant, for the first time, the formation of a single world market for money and credit supply" (Harvey, 1989, p. 161). Globalization, in Harvey's analysis, is therefore intimately associated with the speeding up or intensification of time–space compression in social life.

These distinctive "meanings" attached to the concept of globalization share much in common, even though the theoretical approaches of Giddens and Harvey are very different. How can these "meanings" be distilled into a general conceptualization of the term? An acceptable solution is to conceive of globalization as having two interrelated dimensions: scope (or "stretching") and intensity (or "deepening"). On the one hand, the concept of globalization defines a universal process or set of processes which generate a multiplicity of linkages and interconnections between the states and societies which make up the modern world system: the concept therefore has a spatial connotation. Social, political, and economic activities are becoming "stretched" across the globe, such that events, decisions, and activities in one part of the world can come to have immediate significance for individuals and communities in quite distant parts of the global system. On the other hand, globalization also implies an intensification in the levels of interaction, interconnectedness, or interdependence between the states and societies which constitute the modern world community. Accordingly, alongside this "stretching" goes a "deepening," such that, even though ". . . everyone has a local life, phenomenal worlds for the most part are truly global" (Giddens, 1991, p. 187). Thus, globalization involves a growing interpenetration of the global human condition with the particularities of place and individuality (Giddens, 1990, 1991).

# 3 Mapping the Dimensions of Globalization

Clarifying the meaning of globalization invites further consideration of how it has been theorized within the literature. There is considerable debate concerning both the main driving force(s) behind globalization and how exactly it is reconstituting the world into a single social space. Section 3 will outline the theoretical debates with respect to the underlying causal logic(s) and dynamics of globalization. It will introduce the main protagonists in these debates and their respective theoretical positions on these issues.

## 3.1 Logics

A review of the literature on globalization highlights one fundamental axis of theoretical disagreement. As David Held noted in chapter 13, accounts of modernity divide into two camps: those which stress a single causal logic, and those which emphasize a complex multi-causal logic. Similarly, in discussions of globalization, it is possible to distinguish between those accounts which give primacy to a single causal dynamic, such as technology or the economy, and others which rely on a multi-causal logic. Obviously, this is a somewhat crude typology of theoretical approaches, and no single account fits snugly within either category. Nevertheless, despite the oversimplification, this typology has considerable utility in structuring this brief discussion of the primary theorizations of globalization.

Turning initially to those accounts which stress the primacy of one particular causal logic, the three key authors are Wallerstein, Rosenau, and Gilpin. Wallerstein has introduced the concept of the world system into the social sciences and has stressed the centrality of capitalism to the process of globalization (both past and present). Rosenau and Gilpin, in comparison, are located within the discipline of international relations and have exploited some of its orthodoxies in accounting for globalization. Thus, Rosenau associates globalization with technological "progress," while Gilpin considers it to be an expression of politico-military factors (power politics). Accordingly, each of these three authors locates the causal logic of globalization in a specific institutional domain: the economic, the technological, and the political, respectively.

In his pioneering studies of the emergence of "one world,"

Wallerstein focuses primarily on the dynamics of historical capitalism, ". . . that concrete, time-bounded, space-bounded integrated locale of productive activities within which the endless accumulation of capital has been the economic objective or 'law' that has governed or prevailed" (Wallerstein, 1983, p. 18). For Wallerstein, the logic of historical capitalism is necessarily global in reach. From its origins in sixteenth-century Europe, capitalism has acquired a truly global reach inasmuch as, nowadays, ". . . the entire globe is operating within the framework of this singular social division of labour we are calling the capitalist world-economy" (Wallerstein, 1984, p. 18). Wallerstein considers this capitalist world-economy to be historically unique, in that, while it has gradually created a universal economic space, humanity remains fragmented into discrete nation-states, each with its own center of sovereign political rule. Moreover, the world-economy is conceived of as having a distinctive, unequal structural arrangement with core, semi-peripheral, and peripheral areas – each of which has a specific functional role in sustaining the overall integrity of the system. The material fate of states, communities, and households flows from their location in this structure; a structure which maintains enormous inequalities in power and wealth. In addition, the periodic crises of capitalism mean that the world-economy is subject to discrete phases of global economic restructuring which reinforce these inequalities of power and wealth. But this restructuring also heightens the internal contradictions of the world-economy. Wallerstein argues that the universalization and deepening of capitalism provoke resistance on a global scale in the form of anti-systemic movements (e.g. environmental, socialist, and nationalist movements). The institutionalization of the world capitalist economy therefore embraces both processes of global integration and fragmentation, and this produces instabilities and contradictions which Wallerstein believes will eventually lead to its collapse (Wallerstein, 1991). Embedded in this analysis is an unambiguous thesis: namely, that the driving force of globalization is to be located in the logic of the capitalist world-economy.

If Wallerstein gives primacy to capitalism as a globalizing imperative, Rosenau privileges technology and its transformative capacities. An international relations scholar, Rosenau has written extensively on the growth and significance of global "interdependence" (Rosenau, 1980, 1989, 1990). In his attempt to make sense of the intensification of global interconnectedness he attaches enormous significance to technology:

> It is technology . . . that has so greatly diminished geographic and social distances through the jet-powered airliner, the computer, the orbiting satellite, and the many other innovations that now move people, ideas and goods more rapidly and surely across space and time than ever before. It is technology that has profoundly altered the scale on which human affairs take place . . . It is technology, in short, that has fostered the interdependence of local, national and international communities

that is far greater than any previously experienced.
(Rosenau, 1990, p. 17)

Rosenau considers that an underlying shift from an industrial to a post-industrial order is transforming the global human condition. Accordingly, he argues that humankind has escaped the age of international politics – an age in which nation-states dominated the global scene – and is today witnessing the arrival of the era of "post-international politics" – an era in which nation-states have to share the global stage with international organizations, transnational corporations, and transnational movements. The state is therefore no longer the primary unit of global affairs. Although a novel account of globalization, Rosenau's thesis derives from a fairly extensive literature, with its origins in nineteenth-century sociology, which views industrialism (and now "post-industrialism") as a powerful agent of global socio-economic and political transformation (Parkinson, 1977, ch. 6). (This particular strand of theorizing will be explored further in section 4.3.)

In comparison with Rosenau, Gilpin's account of globalization issues very much from within the orthodox approach to the study of international relations. Highly skeptical of any claim that globalization is transforming the world in which we live, Gilpin nonetheless acknowledges that nation-states are now profoundly interconnected in many different ways (Gilpin, 1987a). But, unlike Rosenau and Wallerstein, he argues that the process of globalization is a product of political factors, in particular the existence of a "permissive" global order – a political order which generates the stability and security necessary to sustain and foster expanding linkages between nation-states. In a global states system, where sovereign nations recognize no authority above their own, the creation of such a permissive political order can only arise from the exercise of power. For Gilpin, globalization is therefore a historically contingent process; contingent in the sense that it relies on the hegemonic (i.e. dominant, most powerful) state(s) in the international system to impose a form of world order which fosters interaction, openness, cooperation, and interdependence (Gilpin, 1981, 1987a). Thus, he asserts:

> My position is that a hegemon is necessary to the existence of a liberal international economy . . . historical experience suggests, that in the absence of a dominant liberal power, international economic cooperation has been extremely difficult to attain or sustain and conflict has been the norm . . . The expansion and success of the market in integrating modern [global] economic life could not have occurred without the favourable environment provided by the liberal hegemonic power.
> (Gilpin, 1987a, pp. 88 and 85)

Historically, globalization has been associated, particularly in the era of the European empires, largely with the expansionist drives of hegemonic powers. But, for Gilpin, the age of empires has now passed. Accordingly, more recent phases of globalization can be attributed instead to the permissive nature of the liberal world order, nurtured by the might of the hegemonic liberal state(s). Thus, in the age of Pax Britannica, high levels of international interdependence existed, while during the era of Pax Americana globalizing processes intensified, underwritten by a stable security order and US military might (Gilpin, 1986). The key point, for Gilpin and those who share his analysis, is that in the modern era global interconnectedness (and its intensification) is conditional on the existence of a stable and secure world order guaranteed by the power and military supremacy of a hegemonic (liberal) state. Globalization is shaped primarily by a political logic: the rise and decline of hegemonic powers in the inter-state system. So, in recent history, the most intense periods of globalization have been associated with the apogee of the hegemonic state's power in the global system (e.g. the US in the post-war era), while the decline of the hegemon (for instance, the United States today) can bring increased instability and an attenuation of global "interdependence" (Gilpin, 1987b).

Wallerstein, Rosenau, and Gilpin provide quite different accounts of globalization, although they share in common the fact that each privileges a single causal logic. However, a rather different "school" of theorizing exists within the literature, giving weight to a multi-causal logic in accounting for globalization. Giddens and Robertson are among the central figures within this particular "school."

As part of his systematic exploration of the contours of modernity, Giddens approaches the phenomenon of globalization by distinguishing between what he understands to be its constituent dimensions (Giddens, 1990, p. 70). Instead of a single causal logic, Giddens points to four discrete, but nonetheless intersecting, dimensions of globalization: capitalism; the inter-state system; militarism; and industrialism. Each of these dimensions embodies a distinctive globalizing imperative, nurtured by quite different institutional forces and constituencies. Thus, the logic and contradictions of the capitalist world-economy influence the pace and pattern of economic globalization while, within the inter-state system, it is the "universalism of the nation-state" form which is responsible for the creation of a single world (Giddens, 1987, p. 283). Similarly, "... the globalising of military power ..." (Giddens, 1990, p. 75) is tied to the logic of militarism, while the changing global division of labor is conditioned by the logic of industrialism. By theorizing these institutional dimensions of globalization, Giddens articulates an account of the global condition in which the "... connections between the emergence and spread of capitalism, industrialism and the nation-state system" are emphasized (Giddens, 1987, p. 288). Globalization is therefore understood as something "... more than a diffusion of Western institutions across the world, in which other cultures are crushed," but rather embraces a complex, discontinuous, and contingent process, which is driven by a number of distinct but intersecting logics; it is "... a process of uneven development that fragments as it coordinates" (Giddens, 1990, p. 175). Within Giddens's analytical framework, globalization and "... the world system should be seen as influenced by several sets of primary processes associated with the nation-state system, coordinated through global networks of information exchange, the world capitalist economy and the world military order" (Giddens, 1987, p. 288).

While Robertson disagrees with important aspects of Giddens's analysis, he too is highly critical of the fact that ". . . in the present climate of 'globality' there is a strong temptation for some to insist that the single world of our day can be accounted for in terms of one particular process or factor . . ." (Robertson, 1990, p. 22). Stressing that ". . . in the contemporary period a major task for sociological theory is to account for the trajectories of globalization in a multidimensional fashion" (Robertson and Lechner, 1985, p. 113), Robertson advocates a theoretical approach which goes ". . . beyond simple models of 'world polity' or a 'world economy' by [pointing] to the independent dynamics of global culture . . . to cultural aspects of globalization" (Robertson and Lechner, 1985, p. 103). This requires a theory of globalization which involves ". . . the analytical separation of the factors which have facilitated the shift towards a single world – e.g. the spread of capitalism, western imperialism and the development of a global media system – from the general and global agency-structure (and/or culture) theme" (Robertson, 1990, p. 22). Although he does not fully develop a systematic account of the interrelationships between the political, economic, and cultural dimensions of globalization, it is abundantly evident from Robertson's work that each is understood to have a distinctive logic (Robertson, 1990; 1991a; 1991b). However, his approach is fundamentally different from that of Giddens, since he is less concerned with mapping the intersections between these dimensions, or their independent logics, than in understanding how they foster the duality of universalization and particularization – themes which will be explored in chapter 18 in the context of culture and the formation of identity in "one world" (Robertson, 1991a).

This brief exegesis of the two most important "schools" of theorizing about globalization raises many difficult questions. Most obviously, it elicits a desire to establish the "truth" or at least the validity of these accounts: are they competing or contradictory views, can they be conflated, are there criteria by which we can judge their worth as "explanations"? As will become apparent in chapter 19, such questions are driven by a particular view of knowledge which has come under increasing attack from post-modernist challenges to the prevailing orthodoxies within the social sciences. Rather than engage with those issues here, it is sufficient to acknowledge that a healthy debate exists between two distinctive "traditions" of theorizing about globalization – between those theorists such as Wallerstein, Rosenau, and Gilpin who privilege one causal "logic" in their accounts of globalization, and those theorists such as Giddens and Robertson who emphasize intersecting causal "logics." However, my own sympathies lie with the work of Giddens and others who stress the multi-causal logic shaping the nature of contemporary globalization (McGrew, 1992). This attachment to a multi-causal account of globalization reflects the intellectual position adopted in many of the chapters of this volume. For the present, our gaze must turn away from the logics of globalization to its dynamics.

## 3.2  Dynamics

It should be apparent by this stage that the discourse of globalization – "global babble" or "globe talk" – is characterized by considerable complexity. This may well reflect the "real" nature of globalization, or it may simply issue from the nature of the discourse itself. In exploring the dynamics of globalization, a more intense sense of complexity, and even ambiguity, surfaces. This arises because, within the existing literature, globalization is understood as a process which is essentially *dialectical* in nature and *unevenly* experienced across time and space.

Sophisticated accounts of globalization are not teleological in the sense that they assume the existence of an inexorable historical process leading to a universal human community. Rather, globalization is generally understood to be a *contingent* and *dialectical* process; dialectical in the simple sense of embracing contradictory dynamics. As Giddens explicitly acknowledges, globalization "... is a dialectical process because ..." it does not bring about "... a generalized set of changes acting in a uniform direction, but consists in mutually opposed tendencies" (Giddens, 1990, p. 64). But what is the substantive form which these "opposed tendencies" take? Several "binary oppositions" or dualities are commonly identified within the discourse of globalization:

*Universalization versus particularization*    In the same way that globalization universalizes aspects of modern social life (e.g. the nation-state, assembly line production, consumer fashions, etc.), it simultaneously encourages particularization by relativizing both "locale" and "place" so that an intensification (or manufacturing) of uniqueness (or difference) is thereby fostered (e.g. the resurgence of nationalism and ethnic identities) (Robertson, 1990; Wallerstein, 1991; Harvey, 1989).

*Homogenization versus differentiation*    Inasmuch as globalization brings about an essential "sameness" to the surface appearance and institutions of modern social life across the globe (e.g. city life, religion, McDonalds, the existence of human rights, bureaucratization, etc.), it also involves the assimilation and re-articulation of the global in relation to local circumstances (e.g. human rights are interpreted in very different ways across the globe; the practice of Islam is quite different in different countries, etc.) (Hannerz, 1991).

*Integration versus fragmentation*    While globalization creates new forms of global, regional, and transnational communities or organizations which unite people across territorial boundaries (e.g. the transnational corporation, international trade unions, transnational class formations), equally, it also divides and fragments communities, both within and across traditional nation-state boundaries. For example, labor becomes increasingly divided along local, national, and sectoral lines; and ethnic and racial divisions become more acute as the "Others" become more proximate (Bull, 1977; Bozeman, 1984).

*Centralization versus decentralization* Although globalization facilitates an increasing concentration of power, knowledge, information, wealth, and decision-making authority (e.g. the European Community, transnational companies), it also generates a powerful decentralizing dynamic as nations, communities, and individuals attempt to take greater control over the forces which influence their "fate" (e.g. the activities of new social movements, such as the peace, women's, or environmental movements) (Rosenau, 1990; Wallerstein, 1991).

*Juxtaposition versus syncretization* By compressing time and space, globalization forces the juxtaposition of different civilizations, ways of life, and social practices. This both reinforces social and cultural prejudices and boundaries while simultaneously creating "shared" cultural and social spaces in which there is an evolving "hybridization" of ideas, values, knowledge, and institutions (e.g. the mixing of cuisines, New Age lifestyles, architecture, advertising images, etc.) (Perlmutter, 1991; Jameson, 1991).

These contradictory tendencies are inscribed in the very dynamics of globalization; a process which is by definition dialectical. For the participants in "globe talk," the contradictory nature of globalization serves to remind us of its essential contingency and complexity. This is further reinforced by the *unevenness* with which globalization has been experienced across time and space.

In *The Principles of World Politics*, Modelski (1972) provides what must be among the first – if not the first – serious use and systematic discussion of the concept of globalization within the social sciences. Central to his analysis is the notion of globalization as a historical process; a process which has distinctive (if not discrete) phases during which the pace of globalization appears to "speed up" or be attenuated. With respect to the present historical epoch, many writers, including Rosenau, Harvey, and Jameson, point to an intensification of globalization which marks a profound break with the past. Whether the current epoch is defined as "post-international politics" (Rosenau, 1990, p. 6), an emerging "postmodern global space" (Jameson, 1991, p. 363), or a new world capitalist order (Harvey, 1989, ch. 9), what is common to these authors is a sense of globalization as a discontinuous historical process.

This unevenness across time is also reflected in the differential reach of globalization. Not only is it considered to "speed up" at various historical conjunctures, but similarly its consequences are not uniformly experienced across the globe. Some regions of the globe are more deeply implicated in global processes than others, and some are more deeply integrated into the global order than others. Within nation-states, some communities (e.g. financial ones) are tightly enmeshed in global networks, while others (e.g. the urban homeless) are totally excluded (although not entirely unaffected) by them. And, even within the same street, some households are more deeply embedded in global processes than others. This unevenness characterizes a highly asymmetrical structure of power relations. For globalization tends on the whole to reinforce (if not to increase) inequalities of power and wealth, both between nation-states and across them, so reproducing global hierarchies of privilege, control and exclusion (Walker, 1988). Yet, as noted above, there are contradictory forces at work here, since globalization generates new centers of resistance. As Modelski comments, "... globalization has ... been profoundly divisive and the effects of this divisiveness are yet to be fully experienced" (Modelski, 1972, p. 55).

# 4  A Global Society?

Both liberalism and Marxism have their roots in an "enlightened" universalism which looked forward to the eventual emergence of a cosmopolitan world society; a global community in which transnational social bonds and universally held notions of peace, justice, equality, and freedom would define the conditions of human existence. To some extent much of our present-day thinking about globalization is imprisoned within these nineteenth-century traditions. Thus, as discussed in the previous chapter, Fukuyama considers the recent "triumph" of liberalism across the world as the beginning of a new era of "perpetual peace" (Fukuyama, 1989), while Wallerstein represents the contemporary era not as the triumph of capitalism but as an epoch of crisis which will bring in its wake emancipation on a global scale (Wallerstein, 1991). But liberalism and Marxism are increasingly inadequate guides to the complex global social architecture associated with recent phases of globalization. For globalization is transforming the basic parameters of modern social life. In doing so, it provokes the question as to how we as students (as well as subjects) of globalization should reflect on, represent and theorize the contemporary global condition. This in turn involves tracking the potential trajectories of social change brought about by globalization. In what follows, four discrete answers are provided to the question of where globalization might be leading humanity.

## 4.1  A global civilization

Howard Perlmutter delivers a powerful argument for viewing globalization as the harbinger of the first truly global civilization. His account of where globalization is leading is representative of a substantial and progressive body of literature which discerns in the growing intensification of global interconnectedness the emerging infrastructure of a "world society." Rather than conceiving of humanity as organized vertically into discrete nation-state units, this "world society" perspective considers humanity as a single, universal "community of fate." As Modelski observes, today's extensive patterns of global interaction and global awareness, combined with the deepening of universal values (e.g. environmentalism, human rights, survival, etc.), point to "the reality of world society" (1972, p. 227). The complex web of transnational ties, which connects communities, households, and individuals across national boundaries, undermines the image of humanity as imprisoned within bounded national societies, and instead supports a rather different image in which humanity is pictured as being organized horizontally into multiple, overlapping, and permeable communities or systems of social interaction. This image of a world society suggests that the ". . . boundaries of states would be hidden from view" (Burton, 1972, p. 43). Perlmutter writes:

> By the *first global civilization* we mean a world order, with shared values, processes, and structures: (1) whereby nations and cultures become more open to influence by each other, (2) whereby there is recognition of the identities and diversities of peoples in various groups, and ethnic and religious pluralism, (3) where peoples of different ideologies and values both cooperate and compete but no ideology prevails over all the others, (4) where the global civilization becomes unique in a holistic sense while still being pluralist, and heterogeneous in its character, and (5) where increasingly these values are perceived as shared despite varying interpretations, e.g. such as we currently see for the values of openness, human rights, freedom, and democracy. . . .
>
> For the first time in human history and with the help of major political and technological changes, we have the possibility of a real time, simultaneously-experienced global civilization with almost daily global events, where global cooperation is in a more horizontal than vertical mode. This is why we now see the possibility of the emergence of one single world civilization with great diversity in its constituent cultures and interdependence among poles. In fact, it would be a civilization whose distinctiveness comes from the attitudes toward and acceptance of diversity along with some shared values which act as a glue for the civilization. . . .
>
> So for us, the first global civilization is a vision seen at the dawn of universal history, as Raymond Aron (1961) has put it, not the end of history as Fukuyama (1989) has recently proclaimed. From this historical perspective, there is but one human civilization which is seamless and global in its character but with a magnificent variety of indigenous variations on the life experience. This is the meaning Teilhard de Chardin (1965) gave to the planetization of humankind.
> (Perlmutter, 1991, pp. 898, 902–6)

Interestingly, Perlmutter does not equate globalization with westernization. Rather, he considers globalization to be a complex process, for he points, later in the article, to the transformation within western societies (in medicine, cuisine, lifestyles, ethnic divisions, etc.)

brought about by the widespread appropriation and global diffusion of non-western values and social practices. Indeed, he believes globalization is responsible for creating a world civilization in which there is a dynamic form of global "syncretization." He defines syncretization as ". . . the attempted reconciliation or union of different or opposing principles, practices, or parties as in philosophy or religion" (Perlmutter, 1991, p. 911). For Perlmutter, world society is a much more pluralistic and de-centered construct than our traditional "models" of the hierarchical, ordered nature of domestic (i.e. national) society. But, for most post-modernists, even domestic (national) society can no longer be conceived of as a highly integrated, highly structured social space (Bauman, 1992, p. 350). Accordingly, Perlmutter implies that, in a post-modern world of cultural fragmentation and the de-centering of power, globalization is re-articulating on a global scale the pluralism, syncretism, and diversity of contemporary domestic society. Thus, the first "global civilization" may be a post-modern one.

## 4.2   A capitalist world society

Neo-Marxists would consider Perlmutter's account somewhat naïve, since it fails to recognize the global power structures created by processes of globalization. With the integration of the former command economies of Eastern Europe and the former Soviet Union into the world-economy, the global grip of capitalism now appears firmer than ever. Thus, rather than representing the present epoch as the dawning of a "global civilization," it might be more accurate to describe it as the final consolidation of a "capitalist world society." For one factor alone has a crucial bearing on the material well-being – and thus the fate – of the bulk of the world's population: namely, the dynamics of the capitalist world-economy.

To argue, as Wallerstein does, that there is a single, capitalist world-economy is to acknowledge that the prospects of the constituent parts of that economy (the states, peoples, communities, and households) are intimately bound up with the functioning of the whole. Despite the appearance of fragmentation, the nature of global markets and the global mobility of capital ensure that few states or peoples can opt out of the logic of this capitalist world political economy. According to Harvey and Jameson, in the last thirty years capital has extended its reach and, because of new technologies of communication and control, has become ever more mobile (Harvey, 1989; Jameson, 1991). Furthermore, they argue that this increasingly global form of capitalism is associated with a profound transformation in the nature of the existing world capitalist order. A new form of global capitalism ("late capitalism," "disorganized capitalism," or "transnational capitalism") has extended and deepened its reach across the globe. With this has come an increasing penetration and consolidation of capitalist social relations on a global scale. However, those excluded from or resisting this transformation have become ever more marginalized. Thus, within this world capitalist society there exist simultaneous processes of transnational integration and national disintegration, as some communities are incorporated into the system and others organized out. So, within the same state, community, and street, there will be those whose lives are deeply implicated in and tied to this new "transnational capitalism," and many others who are either its victims or exist on its margins.

Perhaps the most visible "agent" of this new form of global capitalist order is the transnational corporation (TNC). Production, trade, and finance are now increasingly organized on a transnational basis to reap maximum economic advantage in a highly competitive world. Leslie Sklair points to the transnational organization of production and exchange as producing distinctively capitalist global social arrangements and practices. This world capitalist society is one in which the primary capitalist dynamic is located at the transnational as opposed to the national level, and in which the social relations of production are no longer imprisoned within national territorial boundaries.

Thus, to think in terms of a territorially bounded "British" economy or an "American" economy is to overlook the complex transnational networks of production, ownership, finance, and economic activity which make national territorial boundaries almost meaningless; as King notes, "Germany's largest industrial city is Sao Paulo in Brazil" (King, 1990, p. 69). Alongside these networks is also an expanding array of elite interactions. Indeed, a number of writers have suggested that these ". . . are coming together to produce a transnational capitalist class or class fraction with its own particular form of "strategic class" consciousness" (Gill and Law, 1989, p. 484).

This shift to a more complex and spatially differentiated global capitalist order has also contributed to the internationalization of the state. The "territorial non-coincidence of capital," as Murray conceives of it, has forced states to cooperate more intensively at the global level (Murray, 1971). An enormous range of functional international regimes, global and regional institutions (e.g. the International Monetary Fund (IMF), the European Community (EC), etc.) is required, both to manage the problems associated with this capitalist order, and to ensure its continued reproduction. The Group of Seven leading capitalist states (the G7), for instance, operates as a powerful forum for global economic coordination (Lewis, 1991). Thus, world capitalist society is subject to extensive processes of "governance" or regulation, even though no formal world government exists. These global regulatory structures are far from democratic, but rather sustain a geometry of power relations which is conducive to the needs of global capital. Because labor is primarily organized at the national level, it is therefore incredibly weak in the face of transnational capital. This is also the case for other anti-systemic movements and for poorer states. As a result, there is an imperative for greater international collaboration and coalition-building among those marginalized by this new order. Yet these are the very groups whose political and economic resources are minimal.

## 4.3   A bifurcated world

Rosenau locates the logic of globalization in technology – specifically the shift to a post-industrial order – and arrives at correspondingly different conclusions as to the developing form of the contemporary global system. His position shares much in common with the intellectual tradition established by Auguste Comte, one of the founding figures of modern sociology, who envisaged a world society arising from the global diffusion of techno-industrial civilization (Parkinson, 1977, p. 68). Comte's faith in the universalizing imperatives of modern industrialism has been reflected since in the work of many other writers, including Rosenau, who identifies the arrival of "post-industrialism" with yet a further transformation in the global system.

Rosenau has produced a highly original account of the contemporary global condition. He rejects not only the notion of a "global civilization" but also that of a "capitalist world society." Instead, he identifies a complete fracturing of the global system, a structural bifurcation, as the full force of post-industrialism is experienced across the globe. His argument indicates that there is no longer a single global society (or system) but rather two: a society of states, in which diplomacy and national power remain the critical variables; and a world in which multifarious organizations, groups, and individuals, each pursuing its own interests, create an ever more intricate web of transnational relations, structures, and interactions which are outside the control of any single nation-state and which constitute a kind of hyper-pluralist "transnational society."

This "multi-centric world," as Rosenau labels it, is a world of:

- *transnational organizations*, such as Greenpeace, transnational banks, the Catholic Church, the International Sociological Association, the Red Cross, Oxfam, IBM, Ford, drug cartels, international trade unions, social movements, etc.;

- *transnational problems*, such as pollution, drugs, aid, ethnicity, currency crises;

- *transnational events* or happenings, such as live TV broadcasts from Baghdad and Riyadh during the Gulf War of 1991; or the publication of Salman Rushdie's novel in the UK leading to riots in Pakistan and the withdrawal of ambassadors from Iran; or US and British foundations and political parties advising politicians in Poland, Czechoslovakia, and other states on democratic process, etc.;

- *transnational communities*, based on religion (e.g. Islam, Catholicism), knowledge (e.g. academic networks), lifestyles (e.g. environmentalists), culture (e.g. the art world), or ideology (e.g. the New Right), etc.; and

- *transnational structures*, such as those of production, finance, and knowledge.

Of course, as Rosenau makes clear, these two worlds (the state-centric and the multi-centric) do interact. Thus, Greenpeace can be found lobbying the US government, the EC, the British government, and the World Bank to make lending policies to the Third World sensitive to environmental concerns. Conversely, governments and inter-governmental agencies legislate the global or regional rules (e.g. technical standards for pharmaceuticals, or for high-definition television), within which transnational corporations and other agencies operate. However, because each of these worlds has its own norms, structures, and principles, they co-exist in an unstable and indeterminate relationship. As a consequence, global order appears to be breaking down as the world, given the dynamics of post-industrialism, undergoes a profound de-centering of power and action. Turbulence, rather than stability, is the defining characteristic of the present epoch. Accordingly, Rosenau argues, this is now the era of the bifurcated world – the age of post-international politics.

## 4.4 A global society of states

One of the criticisms of Rosenau's "world-view" is that by concentrating on the visible turbulence and "disorder" in the global system he completely misreads the significance of the continuities in global life. To some observers, the continued existence (if not strengthening) of the nation-state, combined with the reassertion of nationalism across the globe, and (following the collapse of communism) the formation of a host of new states, suggests that globalization has far from transformed the global situation. In other words, there is no "post-international politics," or capitalist world society, or even an emerging global civilization. Rather, the primary trajectory of global development is to be tracked in the tightening hold of the nation-states system over human affairs. The nation-state and the inter-state system, it is argued, are and will continue to remain the dominant "reality" of modern social life.

A further criticism of Rosenau's thesis (and of the other three positions elaborated in this section) concerns its ethnocentricity. It extrapolates the experience of socio-economic transformation within late capitalist societies on to the global level. Yet, as John Allen indicates in chapter 16, there is enormous controversy concerning both the nature of that transformation (post-industrial, post-Fordist, post-capitalist) and how far it is appropriate even to think in terms of socio-economic transformations.

These criticisms provide a launching pad for the claims of Robert Gilpin. For it is Gilpin's contention (which, by the way, has a great deal of support within the transnational community of international relations scholars) that globalization has not fundamentally altered the structure of the global system, nor does it require a reorientation of our thinking or theorizing with respect to the future trajectory of global socio-political development.

Gilpin's argument is a very powerful restatement of "realism" in the context of accelerated globalization. While he does not dispute that the

world may be increasingly interconnected, he is adamant that this by
no means prefigures the arrival of a "world society." On the contrary,
his position is that, in a global system in which there is no authority
above the sovereign nation-state, there exists the constant danger
of conflict and even war. This danger is compounded by the absence
of any institution to enforce the peace. The result is a condition of
anarchy and insecurity which pushes the political leaders of all
states to maximize national power capabilities. Realists, such as
Gilpin, therefore view the global states system as a system of power
politics in which conflict and insecurity are the norm. In this context,
the state acquires a critical role in securing and defending the interests
and safety of its peoples in a dangerous world. Despite the enormous
expansion in transnational and global activity, for realists it is still the
case, as it was in Greek times, that only state power can secure the
peaceful milieu within which such activity is able to flourish. In
contrast with Rosenau's thesis of "two worlds," Gilpin argues
unambiguously for the primacy of the nation-state system.

Moreover, realists would take issue with their "idealist" colleagues
who conceive of globalization either as a permanent fixture of the
modern age or as necessarily leading to a more interdependent world.
Instead, Gilpin, as noted earlier (see section 3.1), argues vehemently
that the more historically recent phases of globalization have depended
on a specific configuration of global power. It is worth quoting him in
full:

> As I have argued, a liberal [interdependent] international
> economy rests on three political foundations (Gilpin, 1981, p.
> 129). The first is a dominant liberal hegemonic power, or, I
> would also stress, liberal powers able and willing to manage
> and enforce the rules of a liberal commercial [capitalist] order.
> The second is a set of common economic, political, and
> security interests that help bind liberal [capitalist] states
> together. And the third is a shared ideological commitment to
> liberal values . . . Thus, since the end of the Second World War,
> American global hegemony, the anti-Soviet alliance, and a
> Keynesian welfare state ideology . . . cemented together economic
> relations among the three principal centres of industrial power
> outside the Soviet block – the United States, Japan and Western
> Europe.
>
> It was on the basis of this conceptualization of the relationship
> between international economics and politics that I and a number
> of other "neo-realists" were highly sceptical of the argument of the
> more extreme exponents of interdependence theory. Their
> projections into the indefinite future of an increasingly
> interdependent world, in which nation-states and tribal loyalties
> (read nationalism) would cease to exist, seemed to us to be a
> misreading of history . . . Such theorizing assumed the
> preeminence and autonomy of economic and technological forces
> over all others in effecting political and social change. Thus, it
> neglected the political base on which this interdependent world

economy rests and, more importantly, the political forces that
were eroding these political foundations.
(Gilpin, 1986, pp. 311–12)

To summarize: for Gilpin, globalization has been contingent
historically upon strategic and political factors, the geometry of global
power relations and the ideological predispositions of the dominant
states. This is a very timely argument, since the relative decline of the
US, the absence of a global ideological threat to unite the most
powerful capitalist states, and the resurgence everywhere of nationalist
and protectionist political forces suggest the end of "the golden era" of
globalization. Accordingly, for "realists," globalization does not
prefigure the emergence of a "world society." On the contrary, the
world is still best described (and understood) as a "society of states."

## 4.5 Trajectories of change

Each of the authors discussed in section 4 identifies globalization with
quite different trajectories of change. Each tells a different story about
where globalization is leading and what form of global society appears
to be emerging. Indeed, there is little common ground between these
positions, in the sense that each delivers its own distinctive response to
the critical issue of the consequences of globalization for the social
architecture of modernity. By their very nature, none of these positions
can be judged to be either wholly right or wrong, true or false, since
each is essentially attempting little more than claiming to represent the
most judicious assessment of where contemporary trends are leading.
Moreover, the intellectual debate on these great matters remains
extremely fluid while, as Rosenau suggests, the world of experience
remains highly turbulent. As the "jury" is likely to remain out for some
time, the issue becomes one of which account(s) appears to be more or
less convincing.
    Although these four perspectives offer quite different visions
of the global predicament, they do share some common ground. In
particular, while each posits a quite different kind of global social
architecture arising from globalization, they all share a belief that
modern societies can only be understood within a global setting.
Additionally, each raises the question of whether the nation-state
is any longer the most appropriate political unit for organizing
human affairs in a more interconnected world system. Even Gilpin, a
staunch champion of realism, acknowledges that the intensification of
economic interdependence ". . . has decreased national economic
autonomy," and that it is unclear what the implications of ". . .
contemporary military and economic developments will be on
the scale of political organization" (Gilpin, 1981, p. 229). As the
end of the century draws near, globalization is forcing us to rethink
the nature of the "political community," the basic unit of human
affairs. Indeed, globalization appears to be challenging the modern
orthodoxy that the nation-state defines the "good community"
(Modelski, 1972, p. 56).

# 5  Globalization and the Future Political Community

Writing in 1957, John Hertz predicted the "demise" of the territorial state as the primary political unit in world affairs (Hertz, 1957). His prediction derived from the argument that nuclear weapons made it impossible for states to defend their citizens against attack. Once states could no longer fulfill this essential duty they became, Hertz suggested, obsolete. Slightly in excess of three decades later, Jameson, commenting on the ". . . prodigious expansion of capitalism in its third (or multinational) stage" (1991, p. 319), observed that ". . . not merely the older city but even the nation-state itself has ceased to play a central functional and formal role in a process that has in a new quantum leap of capital prodigiously expanded beyond them, leaving them behind as ruined and archaic remains of earlier stages in the development of this mode of production" (1991, p. 412). However, to talk the now-fashionable language of the "end of the nation-state" may be to invite the twin dangers of completely misreading its contemporary predicament while simultaneously neglecting the real underlying challenges to the nature of the "modern political community" inscribed within the processes of globalization.

## 5.1  Dissolving the nation-state

Globalization has been, and continues to be, associated with a "crisis of the territorial nation-state." Daniel Bell, writing about the US position in the future global order, captured this sentiment memorably in his comment that the nation-state was ". . . too small for the big problems of life, and too big for the small problems of life" (Bell, 1987, p. 14). While the unevenness of globalization and the diversity of modern state forms mean that any generalization on this issue demands careful qualification, nevertheless, with respect to the late (or advanced) capitalist states, there is a powerful argument which indicates that globalization is dissolving the essential structures of modern statehood. In effect, globalization is understood to be compromising four critical aspects of the modern nation-state: its competence; its form; its autonomy; and, ultimately, its authority or legitimacy.

In a global economic system in which productive capital, finance, and trade flow across national boundaries, the traditional distinction between the internal and external domains no longer holds. Such interconnectedness creates a situation in which decisions in one state can produce major consequences for the citizens of many other states. A recession in the United States, for instance, takes its toll in the factories of Europe, Japan, Latin America, and Asia. States therefore face extensive pressures from their citizens and domestic groups to regulate those transnational activities which directly impinge on their interests and livelihoods. Such pressures, as in the environmental or economic issue-areas, generate a significant political momentum for the expansion of international regimes and international regulatory frameworks at the regional or global levels. Accordingly, as Morse argues, in conditions of systemic "interdependence," the inability of governments to fulfill the demands of their citizens without international cooperation is evidence of the declining competence of states (Morse, 1976). While this may be particularly acute in the economic domain, a dwindling number of policy problems can now be resolved through purely domestic actions or decisions (e.g. drugs, environment, national security, immigration, etc.). Moreover, the corollary is also the case, since the resolution of international problems increasingly demands domestic action. Throughout the 1980s, for example, western governments, in response to the greater mobility of capital, were forced into extensive international coordination of ". . . monetary and fiscal policies – policies that had traditionally been considered 'internal'" (Webb, 1991, p. 311). Morse argues that "interdependence" has eroded the traditional boundaries between the internal and external domains, so encouraging an expansion in the functions and responsibilities of the state while simultaneously denying it effective national control over policy formulation and policy outcomes (Morse, 1976). This condition has been referred to as the "widening and weakening" of the state, or, as Rosenau prefers to label it, "the widening and withering" of the state's competence.

Strongly associated with this declining competence is an erosion of the capacity of the state to enforce its demands on others as the traditional instruments of policy are undermined by accelerating globalization. Whereas military force has been fundamental to state power, it is now of limited utility in achieving all but the most restricted of national goals (Jervis, 1991). Military force remains a last resort, and is largely irrelevant to the resolution of some of the key problems confronting modern states, such as economic welfare, environmental problems, trade matters, etc. According to Rosecrance, economic power and economic diplomacy are central to state security in the contemporary age because economic capabilities are extremely "fungible" (i.e. transferable into direct influence or power) (Rosecrance, 1986). In effect, the suggestion is that the currency of power in the global system has been transformed from military to economic capabilities (Nye, 1989). In the post-Cold War era of rapid demilitarization, this shift in the primary currency of power has doubly compounded the problems for states in trying to protect and secure their interests in a highly complex and dynamically interconnected world order (Shaw, 1991). The result is a significant shift towards multilateral diplomacy and collective action, which in the process further erodes the competence of states to control their own destiny.

It is not only the competence of states which is diminished by globalizing pressures; the form of the state is also subtly altered. With the increased emphasis upon international coordination and cooperation has come a staggering expansion in the numbers of inter-governmental organizations and international regimes. Thus, in whatever sector of state policy one cares to name, there exists a corresponding set of international regulatory institutions or agencies. For instance, there exists an international monetary regime which embraces inter-governmental organizations (e.g. the IMF) together with a set of international norms, rules, principles, regulations, and decision-making arenas, supplemented by informal policy coordination networks between the finance ministries of the major western states (the G7), as well as between central banks, and the major private transnational banks. In the post-war era, there has been an explosive growth in the number and significance of international regimes and organizations. Cox refers to this as the "internationalization" of the state (Cox, 1987). While not juridically above the state, most western governments are so deeply enmeshed in these regulatory and decision-making structures that national and international policy formulations have become inseparable. Moreover, some international organizations and regimes have acquired quasi-supranational powers. The European Community is a primary example, in that decisions (in some domains) taken by a majority can be legally imposed on other member governments, thus compromising their juridical sovereignty.

In effect, the "internationalization" of the state has created forms of international governance in which collective policy making and coordination of policy between governments have become vital to the achievement of national and international goals. Without knowing it, many aspects of people's daily existence are now shaped by the regulatory activities of a host of international regimes. This process of the "internationalization" of the state has fundamental implications for the coherence of the state apparatus and, ultimately, challenges democratic practices. Domestic bureaucracies become internationalized with the result that ministers and cabinets find it difficult to maintain direct control over policy formulation. Within international agencies, transgovernmental coalitions of bureaucrats develop with the result that policy outcomes are no longer decided by elected politicians or by the organs of central government (Keohane and Nye, 1977). This kind of multi-bureaucratic decision making, as Kaiser calls it, dissolves the notion of the state as a monolithic creature pursuing a coherent national interest (Kaiser, 1972). Instead, the state appears on the international stage as a fragmented coalition of bureaucratic agencies each pursuing its own agenda with minimal central direction or control.

If the institutional form of the state is recast by the processes of globalization, its effects are also experienced at a deeper structural level. Recent studies have begun to explore the relationship between globalization and the effectiveness of state strategies for managing the domestic socio-economic domain. What emerges from many of these studies is an awareness of how greater interconnectedness between states imposes intense pressures for a convergence in state socio-economic strategies. Gourevitch argues that the global economic and competitive pressures on states in the 1980s forced them ". . . to curtail state spending and interventions. Whatever the differences in partisan outcomes, all governments have been pressed in the same direction" (Gourevitch, 1986, p. 33). As a result, most governments have discarded strategies of full employment and interventionism because they might reduce their competitive edge in global markets. In a highly competitive but interconnected global economy, state strategies and the domestic socio-political coalitions which underpin them are increasingly sensitive to world economic conditions. According to Garrett and Lange, "The new international economic environment has undercut the effectiveness of the partisan strategies of the left and right based respectively on broadly 'Keynesian' and 'monetarist' fiscal and monetary policies" (Garrett and Lange, 1991, p. 541).

The discussion so far points to a third aspect of the consequences of globalization: the diminution of state autonomy. Clearly, states have always operated under constraints of all kinds; none has ever been free to act completely independently from external pressures. However, it is frequently argued that globalization has imposed tighter limits on the exercise of state autonomy across a range of policy domains (McGrew, 1992). State autonomy can be defined in terms of a state's capacity to act independently, within circumscribed parameters, in the articulation and pursuit of domestic and international policy objectives. State autonomy can be further differentiated with respect to both its "scope" and the "domains" within which it can be exercised. By "scope" is meant the level or intensity of constraints on state action, while "domains" refers to the policy spaces or issue-areas within which such constraints operate (McGrew, 1992). This conceptual definition allows an important distinction to be made between sovereignty – the *de jure* use of power through supreme legal authority or competence within a defined territory – and autonomy. It also suggests that the notion of a loss of state autonomy has to be specified and qualified quite carefully.

As implied already, one of the structural consequences of globalization is to deny the relevance or practicality of autarky – strategies of self-reliance. Thus, states operate within a set of prefigured strategic and policy options which immediately restrict the menu of policies from which state managers can choose. This is particularly evident in the economic and financial policy domains. The scale of financial transactions is such that no single state by itself can effectively control the system in which it is enmeshed. Frieden observes that, "In April 1989, foreign exchange trading in the world's financial centres averaged about $650 billion a day, equivalent to nearly $500 million a minute and to forty times the amount of world trade a day" (Frieden, 1991, p. 428). This, as Webb indicates, was twice the amount of the total foreign reserve holdings of the US, Japanese, and UK central banks combined for the entire month (Webb, 1991, p. 320). A very convincing argument can thus be made that the "... implications of interdependence ... are clear: governments no longer possess the autonomy to pursue independent macroeconomic strategies effectively, even if they were to seek to do so" (Garrett and Lange, 1991, p. 543). This is simply because it is exceedingly difficult to "buck" the global markets, for "... differences in the macroeconomic policies pursued by various countries immediately trigger large flows of capital" (Webb, 1991, p. 318). However, while shifts in state socio-economic strategies are severely constrained, this does not mean that governments are completely immobilized.

While state autonomy appears most compromised in the economic and financial domains, similar intense constraints operate in other areas too. Global warming compromises state autonomy, as does the parcelling out and regulation of the world airwaves, without which effective global communications would be impossible (Starke, 1990; Vogler, 1992). While acknowledging the constraints on state autonomy, it is nevertheless important to recognize that effective diminution of state autonomy varies considerably between different kinds of nation-state, as well as across time and in different policy sectors. Thus, advanced capitalist states may have greater autonomy in the global system than peripheral states, while the US has greater autonomy in some domains (e.g. military) than in others (e.g. financial). Propositions suggesting the general erosion of state autonomy in the face of increasing globalization therefore demand considerable qualification.

Finally, the combined consequences of eroding competence, converging forms, and diminishing autonomy have contributed to an erosion of state authority and legitimacy. Influenced by "crisis of governability" theories of the 1970s, a number of writers have argued that globalization is contributing to a crisis of compliance and authority within the nation-state (Rosenau, 1990; Burton, 1972). This view is driven by a conception of authority and legitimacy located in a discourse of performance and effectiveness. Very succinctly, the thesis is that, because globalization undermines the competence and autonomy of the nation-state, it reduces the effectiveness of government which, in turn, undermines the legitimacy and authority of the state (Rosenau, 1990). Moreover, in a world of global communications, where citizens can readily observe the global context of "domestic" problems and the parochial nature of domestic political debate, further strains are placed on compliance and authority relationships. Governments too contribute enormously to the sense of immobilization and despair which this situation generates by constantly stressing the international constraints on state action. In consequence, the dwindling efficacy of the state and its bases of authority is underlined.

In addition, the existence of global regimes and international organizations poses a further challenge to the actual authority of the state. Global and regional institutions, such as the IMF and the EC, may directly challenge the sovereignty and authority of member states when they impose decisions and policies upon them. National authorities, in some circumstances, may appear as little more than the "local" machinery for implementing regional or international policies. In a system in which international regimes and forms of international regulatory activity are expanding rapidly, the "threat from above" to the authority of the nation-state is arguably a real one.

But globalization also enhances the "threats from below." What Rosenau refers to as the proliferation of "sub-groupism," and others the fragmentation of civil society, is fuelled by globalizing imperatives (Rosenau, 1990, p. 40). As section 3.2 discussed, transnational integration and national disintegration of communities, the rise of ethnicity, the resurgence of nationalism, and the surfacing of new loyalties (e.g. environmentalism) are all associated with the dynamics of accelerating globalization. Globalization stimulates a search for new identities, so challenging the traditional "integrating" ideologies which have defined the boundaries of the "national" political community. As Rosenau observes, because of the diverse ethnic make-up of most states, the label ". . . nation-state fits only a quarter of the members of the global states system" (Rosenau, 1990, p. 406). This suggests that the divisive consequences of globalization operate on an enormously fertile terrain. Globalization is therefore considered by a number of writers to be undermining compliance and contributing to the erosion of state authority "from below."

A powerful argument can be made that globalization is compromising the authority, the autonomy, the nature, and the competence of the modern nation-state. While generalizing is fraught with dangers, there is a significant community of scholars within the social sciences who would agree with Freeman that ". . . the nation-state has become at best immobilized and at worst obsolete" (quoted in Frieden, 1991, p. 427). However, countervailing tendencies do exist.

## 5.2 Rejuvenating the nation-state

Convincing though the "declinist" argument appears, it is also crucial to acknowledge the significance of powerful countervailing forces which may be strengthening the nation-state. Here we will examine briefly the four main countervailing forces which are identified in the literature: the state's monopoly of military power; the potency of nationalism; the empowerment of states through international cooperation; and finally the "myth" of interdependence.

As Gilpin claimed, the primary focus in the global states system remains the prevention of war and the maintenance of peace. States, through their monopoly over the means of violence, and their attention to the balance of power, are therefore critical agents in maintaining global order. While military power may appear of less utility in the modern context, this, as Waltz argues, is a tribute to its vital role in sustaining the peace: "Possession of power should not be identified with the use of force, and the usefulness of force should not be confused with its usability . . . Power maintains an order; the use of force signals its breakdown" (Waltz, 1979, p. 185). Thus, the fact that military force is used infrequently to sustain the global order is not an indictment of the declining relevance of military power (and by implication the nation-state), but, on the contrary, can be seen as evidence of its centrality to the contemporary global order. Thus, for Bull, the state retains a "positive role" in the modern world primarily because its monopoly of military power provides its citizens with relative security in a highly dangerous world (Bull, 1979).

Alongside security, the state also provides a focus for personal and communal identity. As Modelski comments, the "nationalization" of the global system is a fairly recent phenomenon and it is, as daily events indicate, a largely unfinished project. Nationalism along with the newly resurgent forms of ethnic nationalism are extremely powerful evidence that, even if the state is functionally redundant, culturally and psychologically it remains of critical significance in structuring the

political and social organization of humankind. As Hanreider notes:
"Nationalism ... is alive and well. Far from being secondary or
obsolete, the nation-state, nationalism, and the idea of the national
interest are central elements in contemporary world politics"
(Hanreider, 1978, p. 1277).

While pursuing their national interest through cooperation and
collaboration, states also empower themselves. As Keohane and Gilpin
argue, the creation of international regimes and institutions of
cooperation does not in any sense weaken the nation-state (Keohane,
1984; Gilpin, 1987a). On the contrary, in many cases, international
cooperation, as opposed to unilateral action, allows states
simultaneously to pursue their national interests and to achieve more
effective control over their national destiny. Within the context of a
global economy, international coordination of exchange rates (for
instance, the European Exchange Rate Mechanism) can enhance state
autonomy rather than diminish it because it affords, through collective
action, greater security and benefits than any corresponding attempts at
unilateral action. To suggest that globalization necessarily undermines
state autonomy is therefore to ignore the ways in which states empower
themselves against the vagaries of global forces through collective
action. According to Gordon:

> ... the role of the state has grown substantially since the early
> 1970s; state policies have become increasingly decisive on the
> international front, not more futile ... And small consolation
> though it may be ... everyone including transnational
> corporations has become increasingly dependent upon
> coordinated state intervention for restructuring and resolution of
> the underlying dynamics of the [economic] crisis.
> (Gordon, 1988, p. 63)

Finally, a number of writers question whether globalization is really
creating a more "interdependent" world or convergence among state
policies. Care must be taken here to distinguish between the concepts
of interconnectedness and interdependence; interdependence should
not be elided with notions of interconnectedness (or globalization).
Interdependence implies a condition of *mutual* vulnerability to external
events, whereas dependence implies a condition of *asymmetrical*
vulnerability. While processes of globalization may generate
interdependencies between national communities, equally they can
generate relationships of dependence and reinforce existing inequalities
in the world system. Moreover, globalization often involves little more
than interconnectedness, which implies a *sensitivity*, as opposed to a
*vulnerability*, to external events or actions. Accordingly, globalization
embraces both interconnectedness and interdependence, but these are
radically different outcomes of the same process. Definitions aside,
what is significant is the emphasis given in the "declinist" argument to
the evidence of an increasingly *interdependent* world in which state
strategies and policies are converging. Yet both Krasner and Gordon,
coming from radically opposing analytical positions, conclude that,
although it may be more *interconnected*, the world is less

*interdependent* today than it was before World War I (Krasner, 1991; Gordon, 1988). Similarly, Scharpf argues convincingly that states do matter by demonstrating that, despite global constraints, state strategies of socio-economic management in the 1980s have not converged as much as the "declinist" view suggests (Scharpf, 1991).

It follows from these points that the "declinist" vision of the "end of the nation-state" seems somewhat premature. Yet there are contradictory processes at work, so that it would seem equally untenable to suggest either that the state has been left unscathed by globalization or that it has been strengthened. None of these conclusions seems entirely convincing, recognizing the dialectics of globalization and the adaptive capacities of the modern nation-state. Cerny discerns in this growing intersection of global and domestic forces the beginnings of the "changing architecture of the modern state" (Cerny, 1990). Globalization, in other words, requires us to accept the uncomfortable conclusion that the modern nation-state is ". . . both indispensable and inadequate" (Deutsch, 1988, p. 54). But it also invites us to rethink our understanding of the modern political community.

## 5.3   Rethinking sovereignty and political community

Sovereignty is concerned with the location of ultimate power within a territorially bounded political community. Indeed, sovereignty defines the "good community" by manufacturing the political space which separates the "community" from the "others." In the modern era the "good community" has come to be associated with the "national community," although this was not always the case. But today globalization may be tearing away the notion of sovereignty from its rootedness in the national community and the territorially bounded state (Beitz, 1991). As Held observes:

> The modern theory of the sovereign democratic state presupposes the idea of a "national community of fate" – a community which rightly governs itself and determines its own future. This idea is challenged fundamentally by the nature and pattern of global interconnections . . . National communities by no means exclusively "programme" the actions, decisions and policies of their governments and the latter by no means simply determine what is right or appropriate for their citizens alone.
> (Held, 1991, p. 202)

Rather than the decline or the transcendence of the modern nation-state, globalization may be bringing about a ". . . re-articulation of international political space" (Ruggie, 1991, p. 37), introducing a much more complex architecture of sovereign political power than presently exists. Sovereignty, along with the notion of political community, has become imbued, in Bauman's language, with incredible ambiguity (Bauman, 1992). In his explanation of the consequences of globalization for national sovereignty, Held concludes that globalization reveals:

... a set of forces which combine to restrict the freedom of action
of governments and states by blurring the boundaries of domestic
politics, transforming the conditions of political decision making,
changing the institutional and organizational context of national
polities, altering the legal framework and administrative practices
of governments and obscuring the lines of responsibility and
accountability of national states themselves. These processes alone
warrant the statement that the operation of states in an ever more
complex international system both limits their autonomy and
impinges increasingly upon their sovereignty. Any conception of
sovereignty which interprets it as an illimitable and indivisible
form of public power is undermined. Sovereignty itself has to be
conceived today as already divided among a number of agencies,
national, regional and international, and limited by the very
nature of this plurality.
(Held, 1991, p. 222)

This model of overlapping and pluralistic authority structures has
much in common with medieval political practice and organization
(Cook and Hertzman, 1983, ch. 8). Bull, for instance, refers to a "new
medievalism":

If modern states were to come to share their authority over their
citizens, and their ability to command their loyalties, on the one
hand with regional and world authorities, and on the other with
sub-state or sub-national authorities, to such an extent that the
concept of sovereignty ceased to be applicable, then a neo-

A global political forum: the United Nations takes on a vital role in the "new world
order" following the end of the Cold War. George P. Windham, AP.

mediaeval form of universal political order might be said to have
emerged.
(Bull, 1977, pp. 254–5)

This "new medievalism" suggests a reconstitution of political
community, such that it is no longer identified solely with the
territorial nation-state but is conceived in more pluralistic terms.
Thus, as in medieval times, we are forced to think in terms of
overlapping global, regional, transnational, national, and local
political communities. It is in this sense that globalization can be
said to be dissolving, rather than contributing to, the
transcendence of the sovereign nation-state and the bounded
national political community. Sovereignty, and with it the nature
of the "political community," is being reconstituted by the forces of
globalization.

# 6   Globalization and a Universal Sociology

If globalization invites us to rethink our notions of the sovereign
nation-state and political community, then it certainly demands a
reconsideration of the foundational concept in modern sociological
thought: the concept of "society." Bauman defines the problem in
transparent terms:

> It seems that most sociologists of the era of modern orthodoxy
> believed that – all being said – the nation state is close enough to
> its own postulate of sovereignty to validate the use of its
> theoretical expression – the "society" concept – as an adequate
> framework for sociological analysis . . . In the postmodern world,
> this belief carries less conviction than ever before.
> (Bauman, 1992, p. 57)

There is little need to rehearse again the arguments which make
Bauman's proposition so convincing, since they have been discussed in
previous sections. Instead, the objective here is to think through the
implications of the "globalist turn" for the contemporary sociological
enterprise. For it should be evident that, if the "society" – the ordered,
bounded totality – of modern sociology turns out to be a porous,
fragmented, and permeable social space, then a new "subject," or
primary unit of analysis, is required. In some respects the recent
writings of Mann, Giddens, Robertson, and Bauman can be seen as
attempts to refocus the discipline around a conception of the social
which acknowledges the significance of the "globalist turn" and thereby
distances itself from the orthodox approach in which "society" is the
central focus (Mann, 1986; Giddens, 1990, 1991; Robertson, 1990;
Robertson and Lechner, 1985; Bauman, 1992). Mann, for instance,
states: "I would abolish the concept of 'society' altogether" (Mann,
1986, p. 2). Instead, he conceives of societies not as unitary social
systems or bounded totalities but as constituted by ". . . multiple

overlapping and intersecting sociospatial networks of power" (p. 1). Giddens too stresses that "The undue reliance which sociologists have placed upon the idea of 'society', where this means a bounded system, should be replaced by a starting point that concentrates upon analysing how social life is ordered across time and space – the problem of time–space distanciation" (Giddens, 1990, p. 64). Globalization thus dislodges "society" from its focal position in the discourse of modern sociology. But what is to replace it?

Post-modernists might appear initially to have the answer, because of their attachment to diversity, difference, and the plurality of communities and identities which define the post-modern condition. Proponents of post-modernism on the whole argue that the notion of "society" is a totalizing concept which is completely redundant in the contemporary era. This is because post-modernism is associated with ". . . a view of the human world as irreducibly and irrevocably pluralistic, split into a multitude of sovereign units and sites of authority, with no horizontal or vertical order, either in actuality or potency" (Bauman, 1992, p. 35). Understanding this world, for many post-modernist theorists, requires accepting its essentially incoherent character and avoiding the temptation to impose order on it through totalizing and universal theoretical discourses. As Jameson notes, post-modernism prosecutes a "war on totality" (Jameson, 1991, p. 400). It denies the possibility of universal reasoning and accounts of the social life which claim universal validity. Paradoxically, for post-modernists, the existence of a "postmodern global space" (Jameson, 1991, p. 363) is not considered problematic, despite the implication that it assumes the operation of universal processes which are actively unifying humankind. Thus, Robertson refers to "the universalization of particularism" and the "particularization of universalism" (Robertson, 1991a). Yet this seems a logical contradiction. It might therefore be argued that post-modernism too, alongside the orthodox conception of society, is a victim of globalization. Indeed, in significant respects post-modernism, like much conventional sociological thinking, fails to confront the profound implications for its own conceptual categories and theoretical discourse which flow from globalization. Rather than looking to post-modernism to redress our uncertainty about the primary focus of the contemporary sociological enterprise, Archer suggests the solution is to be found elsewhere in a "sociology for one world" – a re-visioning of the Enlightenment project (Archer, 1991).

The Enlightenment project was based on a belief in the universality of reason and the universal character of scientific explanation. A science of society was thus by definition a universal enterprise. However, as chapter 19 will indicate, few social scientists today would accept that it is possible to construct wholly objective or universal accounts of social phenomena. Within modern sociology (whose intellectual foundations are rooted in the Enlightenment project's commitment to rational inquiry and human emancipation), post-modernism and the critique of a positive science of social affairs have prosecuted a "war on universalism." Yet the intensity of globalization in the current epoch produces a startling irony: just as the world is being compressed into one "place," sociology is becoming increasingly localized and relativized (Archer, 1991).

In a stinging critique of the "post-modernizing" and "relativizing" of sociology, Archer delivers a convincing case that globalization ". . . supplies us with good reasons for overhauling our theoretical assumptions and frameworks" (Archer, 1991, p. 133). This involves accepting that ". . . the globalization of society means that societies are no longer the prime units of sociology" (p. 133). What is to replace this focus on societies is a "sociology of One World" which recognizes that "global processes are now partly constitutive of social reality everywhere" (p. 134).

In cultivating this position, Archer is delivering a radical challenge to both orthodox and post-modernist sociological thinking. For, put simply, she is arguing that globalization demands a critical rethinking of the sociological enterprise to reflect the arrival of "One World." Such rethinking, she proposes, has to be fired by a commitment to both reason and humanity, and so requires a re-centering of reasoning and the human being within the sociological enterprise. In some respects she invites a reconstitution of the Enlightenment project, but shorn of its pretensions to be a positive science of social affairs and its de-humanizing of the human subject. For Archer, ". . . reasoning and humanity constitutes the bridge to international sociology" and so to delivering a "sociology for one world" (Archer, 1991, p. 144).

This chapter began with the claim that globalization invites a reconceptualization of the social architecture of modernity. In exploring this claim it has examined the dimensions of globalization, competing visions of today's global society, and the implications of globalization for the future of the nation-state and political community. What has emerged from this discussion is the urgent need for a re-visioning of the sociological project to confront the existence of a late twentieth-century "global social formation." As Archer concludes, this sociology for one world must aim ". . . at no less than the mobilization of Humanity itself as one self-conscious social agent. What ecologists have done for the protection of the natural world, only the sociologist can attempt for the most dangerous and endangered species . . . For commitment to Humanity is also an affirmation that it is ultimately one and indivisible" (Archer, 1991, p. 146).

# References

Archer, M.S. (1991) "Sociology for one world: unity and diversity," *International Sociology*, vol. 6, no. 2, pp. 131–47.

Bauman, Z. (1992) *Intimations of Postmodernity*, London, Routledge.

Beitz, C. (1991) "Sovereignty and morality in international affairs," in Held, D. (ed.) *Political Theory Today*, Cambridge, England, Polity Press.

Bell, D. (1987) "The world and the United States in 2013," *Daedalus*, vol. 116, no. 3, pp. 1–32.

Bozeman, A. (1984) "The international order in a multicultural world," in Bull, H. and Watson, A. (eds) *The Expansion of International Society*, Oxford, Oxford University Press.

Bull, H. (1977) *The Anarchical Society*, London, Macmillan.

Bull, H. (1979) "The state's positive role in world affairs," *Daedalus*, vol. 108, no. 3, pp. 111–24.

Burton, J. (1972) *World Society*, Cambridge, England, Cambridge University Press.

Cerny, P. (1990) *The Changing Architecture of the State*, London, Sage.

Cook, W. and Hertzman, R. (1983) *The Medieval World View*, Oxford, Oxford University Press.

Cox, R. (1987) *Power, Production and World Order*, New York, St Martin's Press.

Deutsch, K. (1988) "Learning-state and the self-transformation of politics," in Campanella, M. (ed.) *Between Rationality and Cognition*, Torio, Italy, Albert Meynier.

Featherstone, M. (ed.) (1990) *Global Culture*, London, Sage.

Frieden, J. (1991) "Invested interests: the politics of national economic policies in a world of global finance," *International Organization*, vol. 45, no. 4, pp. 425–53.

Fukuyama, F. (1989) "The end of history?," *The National Interest*, no. 16, pp. 3–18.

Garrett, G. and Lange, P. (1991) "Political responses to interdependence: what's 'left' for the left?," *International Organization*, vol. 45, no. 4, pp. 539–65.

Giddens, A. (1985) *The Nation-State and Violence*, Cambridge, England, Polity Press.

Giddens, A. (1990) *The Consequences of Modernity*, Cambridge, England, Polity Press.

Giddens, A. (1991) *Modernity and Self-Identity*, Cambridge, England, Polity Press.

Gill, P. and Law, D. (1989) "Global hegemony and the structural power of capital," *International Studies Quarterly*, vol. 33, no. 4, pp. 475–500.

Gilpin, R. (1981) *War and Change in World Politics*, Cambridge, England, Cambridge University Press.

Gilpin, R. (1986) "The richness of the tradition of political realism," in Keohane, R. (ed.) *Neo-Realism and its Critics*, New York, Columbia University Press.

Gilpin, R. (1987a) *The Political Economy of International Relations*, Princeton, Princeton University Press.

Gilpin, R. (1987b) "American policy in the post-Reagan era," *Daedalus*, vol. 116, no. 3, pp. 33–69.

Gordon, D. (1988) "The global economy: new edifice or crumbling foundations?," *New Left Review*, no. 168, pp. 24–65.

Gourevitch, P. (1986) *Politics in Hard Times*, New York, Cornell University Press.

Hannerz, U. (1991) "Scenarios for peripheral cultures," in King, A. (ed.) (1991).

Hanreider, W. (1978) "Dissolving international politics: reflections on the nation-state," *American Political Science Review*, vol. 72, no. 4, pp. 1276–87.

Harvey, D. (1989) *The Condition of Postmodernity*, Oxford, Basil Blackwell.

Held, D. (1991) "Democracy, the nation-state and the global system," in *Political Theory Today*, Cambridge, England, Polity Press.

Hertz, J. (1957) "The rise and demise of the territorial nation-state," *World Politics*, vol. 9, pp. 473ff.

Inkeles, A. (1975) "The emerging social structure of the world," *World Politics*, vol. 27, no. 4, pp. 467–95.

Jameson, F. (1991) *Postmodernism or the Cultural Logic of Late Capitalism*, London, Verso.

Jervis, R. (1991) "The future of world politics," *International Security*, vol. 16, no. 3, pp. 39–73.

Kaiser, K. (1972) "Transnational relations as a threat to the democratic process," in Keohane, R. and Nye, J. (eds) *Transnational Relations and World Politics*, Cambridge, MA, Harvard University Press.

Keohane, R. (1984) *After Hegemony*, Princeton, Princeton University Press.

Keohane, R. and Nye, J. (1977) *Power and Interdependence*, Boston, Little Brown.

King, A. (1990) *Urbanism, Colonialism and the World-Economy*, London, Routledge.

King, A. (ed.) (1991) *Culture, Globalization and the World System*, London, Macmillan.

Krasner, S. (1991) "Economic interdependence and independent statehood," mimeo.

Lewis, F. (1991) "The 'G-7½' Directorate," *Foreign Policy*, no. 85, pp. 25–40.

Maddox, C. (1990) *Salvador Dali*, Cologne, Benedikt Taschen.

Mann, M. (1986) *The Sources of Social Power*, Cambridge, England, Cambridge University Press.

McGrew, A. (1992) "Global politics in transition," in McGrew, A. and Lewis, P. (eds) (1992).

McGrew, A. and Lewis, P. (eds) (1992) *Global Politics*, Cambridge, England, Polity Press.

Modelski, G. (1972) *The Principles of World Politics*, New York, Free Press.

Morse, E. (1976) *Modernization and the Transformation of International Relations*, New York, Free Press.

Murray, R. (1971) "The internationalization of capital and the nation-state," *New Left Review*, no. 67, pp. 84–109.

Nye, J. (1989) *Bound to Lead*, New York, Basic Books.

Parkinson, F. (1977) *The Philosophy of International Relations*, London, Sage.

Perlmutter, H.V. (1991) "On the rocky road to the first global civilization," *Human Relations*, vol. 44, no. 9, pp. 897–1010.

Robertson, R. (1990) "Mapping the global condition," in Featherstone, M. (ed.) (1990).

Robertson, R. (1991a) "Social theory, cultural relativity and the problem of globality," in King, A. (ed.) (1991).

Robertson, R. (1991b) "The globalization paradigm," in Bromley, D.G. (ed.) *Religion and the Social Order*, London, JAI Press.

Robertson, R. and Lechner, F. (1985) "Modernization, globalization and the problem of culture in world systems theory," *Theory, Culture and Society*, vol. 2, no. 3, pp. 103–19.

Rosecrance, R. (1986) *The Rise of the Trading State*, New York, Basic Books.

Rosenau, J. (1980) *The Study of Global Interdependence*, London, Frances Pinter.

Rosenau, J. (1989) *Interdependence and Conflict in World Politics*, Brookfield, VT, Avebury.

Rosenau, J. (1990) *Turbulence in World Politics*, Brighton, England, Harvester Wheatsheaf.

Ruggie, J. (1991) "Finding our feet in territoriality: problematizing modernity in international relations," mimeo.

Scharpf, F. (1991) *Crisis and Choice in European Social Democracy*, Ithaca, NY, Cornell University Press.

Shaw, M. (1991) *Post-Military Society*, Cambridge, England, Polity Press.

Sklair, L. (1991) *Sociology of the Global System*, Brighton, England, Harvester Wheatsheaf.

Starke, L. (1990) *Signs of Hope*, Oxford, Oxford University Press.

Turner, B.S. (1990) "The two faces of sociology: global or national?," in Featherstone, M. (ed.) (1990).

Vogler, J. (1992) "Regimes and the global commons: space, atmosphere and the oceans," in McGrew, A. and Lewis, P. (eds) (1992).

Walker, R. (1988) *One World, Many Worlds*, New York, Lynne Rienner.

Wallerstein, I. (1983) *Historical Capitalism*, London, Verso.

Wallerstein, I. (1984) "Patterns and prospectives of the capitalist world-economy," in Wallerstein, I. *The Politics of the World-Economy*, Cambridge, England, Cambridge University Press.

Wallerstein, I. (1991) "The lessons of the 1980s," in Wallerstein, I. *Geopolitics and Geoculture*, Cambridge, England, Cambridge

University Press.

Waltz, K. (1979) *Theory of International Politics*, New York, Addison-Wesley.

Webb, M.C. (1991) "International economic structures, government interests and international co-ordination of macroeconomic adjustment policies," *International Organization*, vol. 45, no. 3, pp. 309–43.

# 15 Environmental Challenges

Steven Yearley

## Contents

| | | |
|---|---|---:|
| 1 | Introduction | 505 |
| 2 | Ecological Threats to Modern Society: An Overview | 507 |
| 2.1 | Waste and air pollution | 507 |
| 2.2 | Earth-bound wastes | 511 |
| 2.3 | Depletion of resources | 512 |
| 2.4 | Additional ecological issues | 513 |
| 3 | Developing a Green Political Ideology | 514 |
| 3.1 | Taking Green ideas to the polls | 518 |
| 3.2 | Public awareness and citizens' action | 521 |
| 4 | Growth, Capitalism, and Green Consumerism | 523 |
| 4.1 | Bringing greenery about | 526 |
| 4.2 | Beyond the greening of the West | 527 |
| 5 | Conclusion: Environmental Challenges and the Enlightenment | 529 |
| | References | 530 |

# 1    Introduction

At the start of the 1990s it appears that everyone is an environmentalist of some sort, be they politicians, supermarket chains, advertisers, the media, or big business. Even McDonalds, long associated with the modern American values of convenience and disposability, is now cultivating a "green" image. The firm is careful to boast that its cattle farming does no damage to the world's rainforests and that the company has withdrawn ozone-threatening CFCs from its burger packaging. A major aim of this chapter is to understand why such concern for the environment is now so prominent. But my analysis will go further than this and develop the theme in two directions. First, I shall assess the wider consequences of this "greening" for modern societies: for example, its impact on political parties and on people's attitudes to economic growth. Secondly, I shall examine how social scientists have themselves been affected by a growing awareness of environmental issues and how, in many cases, their interpretation of contemporary society has been influenced; in particular, how an appreciation of western societies' environmental problems has encouraged social scientists to question in a new way the Enlightenment "achievements" of economic growth, technological progress, and scientific advance.

In the course of this analysis I shall look at two major issues: (a) the environmental threats confronting modern societies, and (b) environmentalists' challenges to modern forms of social and political organization. By the former, I refer to our leading ecological problems, such as global warming or the build-up of toxic wastes – problems which may pose a physical threat to the viability of present-day society. By the latter, I mean the claims by environmentalists or "greens" that our current way of living is unsustainable and that the ambitions which predominate in contemporary society (particularly the wish for our society to become steadily more wealthy) are fundamentally mistaken.

While the ecological threat is a physical one, the environmentalists' challenge takes an ideological form. Naturally, these two issues are closely related. In the absence of ecological problems, environmentalists would find it hard to gain public support for their arguments. Equally, it has in many cases been members of the environmental movement who have brought ecological threats to public attention. But there is no automatic relationship between the two. Environmental consciousness does not arise just because there are ecological problems. As we shall see, social and political forces have played an important role in preparing the way for, and in shaping responses to, ecological issues.

I shall shortly present a brief account of the principal environmental problems with which our society is faced. However, before this it will be useful to set our problems in historical perspective.

One of the most significant, although often unnoticed, achievements of western society has been to radically diminish our subordination to natural forces and constraints. For example, in practical terms, we have vastly shortened distances between our cities through innovations in transportation technology. Nowadays, electronic communications permit virtually instantaneous interaction between one continent and another. Our ability to harness energy from coal, gas, and petroleum has lessened our dependence on the climate. In this way people can live essentially similar lives, using essentially the same products, eating more or less the same food, whether in Glasgow or Paris, in New York or Sydney. Through technology we have even tried to combat the tendency for food to perish: in many countries, food may now be irradiated to forestall natural deterioration. In other words, people (or at least *some* people) have more or less overcome the environmental constraints presented by distances, the climate, and even the limitations which stem from the nature of living organisms.

In all these and in many other ways, human dependence on the natural environment has been so reduced that an author such as McKibben (1990, pp. 43–60) has recently been able to speak of the "end of nature." In other words, no inhabitants of the West typically have to face nature without its effects being mediated by human technologies. And even in those parts of the world where nature's force is still felt in an apparently unaltered manner, nature itself has been affected by human activity. Traditional inhabitants of the Amazonian rain forests are having their "natural" environment altered by development policies; traditional fishing peoples of the Pacific are having their catches affected by the fish-processing ships of the developed world. Even the low-lying farm landscape of Bangladesh – which suffered the worst effects of the flooding of early 1991 – has been decisively shaped by western-led drainage policies and by development projects which have caused erosion in the uplands. Nature isn't what it was. In McKibben's words, "we have ended the thing that has, at least in modern times, defined nature for us – its separation from human society" (1990, p. 60).

This line of thinking may lead one to assume that past societies – in touch with nature as they had to be – were also in harmony with it. They may not have dominated nature in the way that we hope to, but, by being subordinate to it, they may perhaps have lived sustainably with it. Ironically, this view of the past has been encouraged by the lenses through which we usually look at history. As modern industrial society has developed, nature has been progressively marginalized. In parallel with this development, when historians have come to reflect on the factors which have exerted the greatest influence on human history they have tended, over the years, to grant nature a smaller and smaller role. Yet a plausible case can be put forward for the disruption of early civilizations by essentially ecological factors.

Seymour and Girardet (1990) argue, for example, that there are significant ecological elements underlying the decline of Rome. "Deforestation, loss of topsoil [and] the spread of swamps" led to diminishing agricultural productivity at home and spurred the pursuit of colonial territories, with first Sicily and then North Africa serving as sources for the staple food, wheat (Seymour and Girardet, 1990, p. 49). But years of intensive agricultural exploitation in these conquered regions led to erosion and a loss of soil fertility. Quite apart from external military threats, the empire was unsustainable:

> The Romans were the first to test the viability of large-scale commercial agriculture. They could only make it work by gaining access to ever larger areas of land. But, clearly, in the end they recognized the limits to growth. They left much exhausted land behind them, as well as a trail of human tragedy.
> (Seymour and Girardet, 1990, p. 54)

In putting their case, Seymour and Girardet seem too ready to dismiss non-ecological explanations for major social change. But they make a convincing – and, to many, surprising – argument that excessive exploitation of the Mediterranean forests, and remorseless extension of foodcrop agriculture, resulted in the collapse of an advanced civilization on Crete and in the declining viability of the Roman Empire. But these societies were not alone in precipitating environmental catastrophe. Ponting (1990) makes a related case for the downfall of the sophisticated Mayan society in the lowland rainforest of upper Central America (now parts of Mexico, Guatemala, Belize, and Honduras), and for the dwindling of the ancient Mesopotamian civilization in the Middle East (see also Thomas, 1984, p. 24).

These studies and their examples have two significant implications. First, they dispel any excessively romantic view of how well in touch with nature past cultures were: we are not alone in facing ecological problems. But if this realization is comforting, its corollary most certainly is not: this is that ecological problems can help bring about the downfall of whole societies. Therefore, according to these authors, we had better take ecological threats seriously.

# 2 Ecological Threats to Modern Society: An Overview

By 1990, some of the ecological threats to modern western societies had become very widely known. No comedy routine was complete without some joke about global warming, about pollution from cars, or about the ozone layer. Shelves in the newly created "green" departments of bookstores strained under the weight of rainforest picture books and environmental diaries. But there was still widespread confusion. Given this lack of clarity about environmental problems a short overview is probably useful (for a more comprehensive account, also from a social scientific perspective, see Yearley, 1991, pp. 11–46; see also FoE, 1990; and Elsworth, 1990). There is no single best way to classify these problems, though we can make a helpful initial division into problems of wastes and of declining resources. I shall deal with them in this order, picking up a few neglected themes at the end.

## 2.1 Waste and air pollution

Some waste is produced by nearly everything we do, at home, at work, driving in the car, and so on. Most often we think of waste in terms of the solid garbage that goes into our trash cans and the liquids which enter the sewers. But environmentalists also focus a great deal of attention on gaseous wastes. In particular, there are three kinds of gaseous effluent which give cause for the most concern: (a) the carbon dioxide which results from burning fossil fuels such as coal and petroleum in furnaces, power stations, and motor vehicles; (b) the acidic gases (notably sulphur dioxide) which arise mainly from the combustion of impurities in these fuels; and (c) the ozone-destroying gases which are released into the atmosphere from the use of aerosols, and from the manufacture and ultimate breakdown of insulating foams, refrigerators, and air-conditioning units.

In each case, the dangers which result from these gases have not been immediately apparent. For example, carbon dioxide is odorless and colorless; it is not poisonous and is produced naturally when animals breathe out and when organic matter decays. However, the burning of fossil fuels – predominantly in the industrialized world – has led to an increase in the proportion of this gas in the atmosphere. Although it still makes up only a tiny fraction of the atmosphere (just over a thirtieth of 1 percent by volume), it is steadily increasing and is believed to be far more plentiful now than at any other time since early prehistory (Leggett, 1990, pp. 26–7). Carbon dioxide (as well as other even rarer gases) tends to trap the sun's heat in the atmosphere. Acting rather like the panes of glass in a greenhouse, molecules of carbon dioxide permit the sun's rays to pass through (and thus to warm the earth), and then tend to prevent the resulting heat (in the form of infrared radiation) from passing back out through the atmosphere and being dissipated in space. Accordingly, the earth's average temperature is likely to rise, disrupting our climate, affecting vegetation and agriculture, and – most notoriously – prompting a rise in sea levels as the oceans warm and expand, and as land-based ice melts into the seas. This seemingly innocuous waste gas could have catastrophic consequences on a world-wide scale.

If fuelstuffs were chemically pure, waste gases would comprise virtually only water vapor and oxides of carbon. But they are not. The gases emitted from power stations, from cars, from domestic heating systems and from industry contain small amounts of acidic gases: sulphur dioxide and various oxides of nitrogen. As these gases spread through the atmosphere they mix with water vapor to form acidic compounds which, sooner or later, fall as "acid rain." Although acid emissions make up only a small part of waste gases, our overall output of such waste is so large that Britain alone generated over six million tonnes of acid gases in 1988 (FoE, 1990, p. 3).

Acid rain gives rise to many problems (see Elsworth, 1990, pp. 1–17). Rivers and lakes can become acidified, especially in areas of Scandinavia and Canada where the make-up of the soil means that it has only a limited ability to neutralize acidity. Acidity can kill fish, and some other animals, especially birds, are susceptible to acid poisoning too. In concentrated form – for example, from vehicle exhaust fumes in congested traffic – acidic gases can be harmful to human health. Acid rain is also believed to contribute to the death of trees by lowering their tolerance to disease and other biological hazards. Lastly, it erodes buildings and monuments.

Debate about the exact effects of acid rain and about different countries' respective responsibility for causing it persisted over the last two decades. This debate dragged on for several reasons: because the alleged results were often found very far away from the presumed causes; because the precise chemistry of acid rain production was open to dispute; and because acidification can be caused in other ways too: through algal activity, for example. The countries held chiefly responsible were able to claim that there was no definitive proof that it was their pollution which was to blame for other countries' acid rain. And since the evidence was not decisive, they could argue for a delay in taking practical action until even stronger proof was available.

The third major problem with effluent gases concerns the accidental destruction of ozone. Ozone is a gas very closely related to oxygen, but is relatively unstable and is very liable to enter into reactions and to be converted into oxygen in the process. At ground level, ozone is therefore short-lived. But high in the atmosphere (between about 12 and 30 miles up), ozone is more common, although still very rare. At these altitudes, some molecules of oxygen convert naturally into ozone which is then able to make up a shield, absorbing a great deal of the harmful ultraviolet radiation striking the atmosphere.

However, some gases synthesized for industrial uses this century – notably, but not exclusively, CFCs (chlorofluorocarbons) – have gradually drifted into the upper atmosphere, where they have broken down under the influence of solar radiation. The reactive components formed by their breakdown are very effective in encouraging the decomposition of ozone, and it is believed that it is these chemicals which have led to severe thinning of the ozone layer at both Poles. Damage to the ozone layer threatens to allow more high-energy radiation into the atmosphere, which is likely to cause an increase in the incidence of skin cancer and to lead to disruption of the marine food chain through its harmful effect on planktonic plants in polar waters – the most basic source of food in the oceans.

It is important to note in this case that the CFCs causing the damage are themselves not directly harmful. Indeed, they were developed precisely to be non-toxic and incombustible so that they could be safely used in aerosols, in insulating materials, and so on. But it is this very stability that has allowed them to get as far as the stratosphere without breaking down. Now that there is wide agreement on the dangers of "ozone-eaters," action can be taken to limit their production and release. Once their release is stopped the ozone layer will eventually heal itself. But there are still millions of tonnes of them on their way into the atmosphere, as well as vast amounts left in insulating foams and discarded refrigerators. It is also uncertain that we have identified all the potential ozone-eaters; Friends of the Earth has noted that solvents used in typing-correction fluids and for other industrial applications, as well as some of the proposed substitutes for CFCs, may also lead to ozone depletion.

I have described these problems in some detail for two reasons: first,

Table 15.1   Gaseous wastes and air pollution

| Effluent type | Source | Impact |
|---|---|---|
| Carbon dioxide: the leading "greenhouse" gas | Carbon dioxide is released when fossil fuels are burned. It is produced in roughly equal proportions by power stations, industry, and vehicle exhausts. | Carbon dioxide absorbs infrared energy and thus traps heat in the atmosphere. The more carbon dioxide we release, the hotter the atmosphere is likely to become. Such heating is expected to affect the climate, disrupt agriculture, and cause flooding. |
| Acidic gases | Sulphur dioxide comes mostly from the burning of impurities in coal and oil. Oxides of nitrogen come partly from impurities and partly from the nitrogen already in the air which is oxidized at very high temperatures. | Acidic gases react with rainwater and moisture in the air to produce "acid rain." The gases can travel large distances causing problems hundreds of miles from their source. Acid rain is harmful to trees, river life, soils, and even buildings. The acidic gases can also be directly harmful to human health. |
| Ozone-destroying gases | The most important of these are the CFCs which are produced commercially for use as solvents and cleaning fluids, and for use in refrigerators and air-conditioning equipment. They are also used to blow foams for insulating and packaging materials, and as propellants in aerosols. | CFCs are very long-lived chemicals. When they escape into the atmosphere (when solvents evaporate, for example) some eventually drift upwards and come into contact with the earth's protective ozone layer. They help break down that layer, which in turn permits harmful radiation from the sun to reach the earth's surface. That radiation is dangerous to many forms of life including human beings in whom it can promote cancer. Currently, the ozone layer is most affected at the Poles, so very northerly and very southerly peoples are at most risk. |

to show that exhaust gases, though less obvious than some other questions of waste disposal (such as the treatment of radioactive materials), do highlight the basic connection between waste and pollution. As Elsworth sharply points out, "Pouring industrial garbage into the air is a cheap form of waste disposal [especially if] it drifts into someone else's back yard" (1990, p. 15). Even waste which is apparently quite innocuous, such as carbon dioxide and CFCs, can pose a serious pollution hazard. Secondly, these gases pose major international, possibly global, threats. Even on its own, global warming might just result in the deaths of hundreds of thousands of people, and devastate the world economy. The atmosphere has been treated in a careless way; people have polluted our common environment presuming, if they thought about it at all, that the atmosphere was large enough to absorb anything we could dump into it. It looks as though the atmosphere is far more sensitive than we had assumed. These waste gases show us just how pervasively harmful modern forms of pollution can be.

## 2.2 Earth-bound wastes

Our other waste disposal problems can be viewed within the same general perspective. Seas and rivers have too often been seen as useful, free waste repositories, and refuse from firms, farms, and houses has been dumped in fresh and salt waters. This waste disposal has led to serious pollution. For example, human and animal wastes can, under the right conditions, break down in a natural and harmless way. In principle, they could be applied as fertilizers to farmland or just allowed to decay in watercourses and in the ocean. But they have often been discharged in such concentrations that they have upset the biological balance of rivers and estuaries. These wastes have poisoned fish and so contaminated shellfish (which feed by straining nutrients out of water) that these creatures have become inedible. Growing human and livestock populations threaten to make this problem worse.

Similarly, in industrialized areas, firms have released small (and sometimes large) amounts of chemicals – for example, the metals mercury and cadmium – into watercourses. Often these chemicals have subsequently become concentrated in the fatty parts of aquatic animals' bodies to such an extent that the chemicals can become hazardous at the top of the food chain; that is, for otters, large fish, or even humans. Elsewhere, small quantities of dangerous chemicals discharged into sewers mean that the sewage sludge becomes contaminated and cannot be applied as a fertilizer. It is not only big companies which are responsible for this pollution, but also ordinary citizens and small businesses who empty engine oil and other chemicals into the drains.

Additionally, there is solid waste from industry and from domestic sources. In principle, much of this could be recycled if the appropriate techniques could be devised and implemented and suitable markets developed. But at the moment, domestic waste (composed of vegetable wastes and cinders, paper, metals, glass, and plastics, roughly in that descending order) is not usually sorted. It is usually dumped in holes in the ground: in former quarries, or onto the beds of drained lakes. But these sites are rapidly filling up and the price of waste disposal is no longer negligible. Worse, these dumps themselves pose a threat. Rainwater seeping through them can leach out chemicals which can then enter water supplies. Natural decay in the dumps also leads to the production of methane gas which can spontaneously ignite. Although dumping on such sites is now regulated (in theory at least), it is difficult to prevent dangerous materials from finding their way on to these tips. Indeed, in the past, dangerous wastes were disposed of by "diluting" them with ordinary refuse; this procedure was dignified with the name "co-disposal." Accordingly, the threat of poisoning from long-established dumps could be much worse than we realize.

There are some wastes, both solid and liquid, which are known to be highly dangerous. Such toxic materials – typically coming from the chemical, pharmaceutical, and nuclear industries, and even from hospitals – generate acute disposal problems since nobody is keen to have them incinerated, dumped, or even stored close to their home or town. The difficulties posed by the management of these materials have increased recently, both because people are more aware of their potential dangers and because the old practice of incineration at sea has virtually ceased. The disposal costs of these wastes are now very high, a fact which has attracted the attention of unscrupulous, sometimes criminal operators. Some "entrepreneurs" have spotted the opportunity to take these materials to Third World countries (notably the poor nations of west Africa) where they can be dumped very cheaply. This dumping can be carried out either because these countries lack laws specifically prohibiting the dumping of these toxic materials – materials which, of course, they do not make themselves – or because the material has been misleadingly relabelled. Closer to home, the "processing" of these substances has proved attractive to illegal operators who may be willing to "lose" them at sea or to subcontract people to dump them illicitly (for an example, see Allen and Jones, 1990, pp. 230–1).

The final problem I wish to mention is not strictly one of waste, but of the pollution caused by chemicals applied on farms, in parks, and on railway and road shoulders. Fertilizers and herbicides are not completely absorbed by the plants on to which they are sprayed. The remainder is then carried away by rainwater into underground watercourses or rivers. Either way, chemicals which are designed to have a biological impact, to kill bugs or weeds for instance, may end up in our drinking water. Such pollution can be directly harmful to human health.

In all the ways highlighted here, our problems of waste disposal – understood in the widest sense – lead to dangers for our society. For a long time economists referred to such issues as "externalities," meaning costs which are borne neither by the consumer nor the producer but assumed by the environment. These can no longer be seen as just a side issue (see Pearce et al., 1989, pp. 5–7). Our wastes threaten our health and that of innocent citizens of Third World countries, they endanger wildlife and the natural environment, and may even jeopardize the global temperature-control system. Aside from these dangers, wastes and pollution pose a growing economic problem: the costs of pollution control are rising and the price of dumping can be expected to rise steeply. Waste endangers our health and our wealth.

## 2.3  Depletion of resources

If the way of life of our civilization is imperilled by the manner in which we have polluted the globe, it is also under threat because we are using up the world's resources. Economic growth since World War

II has been consistently large for all the First World and for parts of the Third World. To feed this economic growth we have consumed more and more energy, minerals, and agricultural products, which plainly cannot go on for ever. Stocks of minerals (whether metal ores, or nitrates for fertilizers, or whatever) are finite. Nor are agricultural crops an infinite, replenishable resource; first, because agricultural productivity is currently only maintained by the use of agrochemicals which themselves rely on other mineral resources, and second, because some agricultural exploitation is so intensive that it exhausts the land, in some cases turning it into infertile desert.

Of course, there are always likely to be more, as yet undiscovered, deposits of the natural resources, but they can be expected to be increasingly remote or difficult to work. Alternatively, new technologies may allow us to utilize existing resources more efficiently, or permit us to substitute a relatively common resource for an uncommon one. For instance, in the early years of the Industrial Revolution a projected catastrophic timber shortage was offset by the introduction of coal power. In the 1950s and 1960s it was hoped that nuclear power generated from uranium would replace that from fossil fuels; however, as it turned out, nuclear power was also very expensive once the costs of waste disposal and decommissioning were taken into account.

Thus, the argument about resource depletion is not cut and dried. The anticipated shortages have not yet occurred, at least if we judge by the continuing low prices of minerals. Certainly, successive gloomy forecasts – that minerals will *soon* begin to be in short supply – have left their authors embarrassed. Thus, the simple, logical point that resources obviously *must be* finite is complicated by the question of when their scarcity will become felt.

Still, it cannot be denied that with economic growth consumption not only increases but increases faster and faster. Every year the number of cars on the world's roads grows, on average, by more than the amount it grew the year before. We are thus using up our steel at a faster and faster rate. Furthermore, the low price of raw materials in the 1980s has been accompanied by huge Third World debts and falling real incomes in many under-developed countries. In terms of resources, therefore, our way of life may be sustainable for some time to come, but probably only at the cost of Third World poverty. Even people who are optimistic about the continued potential for growth are unclear about where the energy resources would come from if we were to try to provide everybody with the same standard of living as is currently enjoyed by an average West European or North American citizen.

## 2.4  Additional ecological issues

Pollution and resource depletion act together as a joint threat to modern society. But there are other important issues highlighted by environmentalists; in particular, threats to animals, to plants and trees, and to natural habitats. In fact, the largest and most established environmental organizations have tended to be devoted not to questions of resources and pollution, but to nature conservation.

However, it is important to note that while such groups have retained nature conservation as their central focus, they have lately broadened their objectives to include more wide-ranging environmental concerns. Many of these groups originally tended to concentrate on threats to particular creatures or to certain endangered species, but more recently they have switched most of their attention to threats to the habitats in which wild animals live. This has meant, for example, that rather than concentrate on hunting or shooting which endangers particular birds, they have worried more about changes to agricultural practices which threaten to obliterate the hedges and small woods in which the birds live and find their food. For this reason, nature conservation groups are increasingly involved in environmental campaigns, addressing issues such as the siting of roads, agricultural policy, pollution from factories, and the treatment of the rainforests (see Yearley, 1991, pp. 54–67).

There are other issues which have also been important to the growth of the green movement and have motivated people to become concerned about their environment: from the perceived threat from nuclear power and its closeness to the nuclear weapons industry, through anxieties about cruelty to animals and the use of animal testing in the developing of medical and cosmetic preparations, to worries about the loss of landscape and the destruction of our architectural heritage. In many cases, as I will show, these particular anxieties have been decisive in encouraging people's interest in the green movement. My review, therefore, cannot claim to be comprehensive, but it does serve to outline the issues which have most preoccupied the leading environmental groups. In particular, it helps us understand the twin threat, from pollution and resource depletion, which many greens would argue hangs over the contemporary world.

## 3   Developing a Green Political Ideology

There are a great number of pressure groups which together have put green arguments on the political agenda. Indeed they are rather more diverse than one would expect, ranging from small nature conservation groups through to the huge and wealthy organizations committed to heritage as well as wildlife conservation. There are also the well-known campaigning bodies such as Friends of the Earth (FoE) and Greenpeace. Given all this variation, the groups could probably be classified in any number of ways. But one particular divide has been accentuated by Jonathon Porritt, former director of FoE in England and Wales, who noted that, in a survey published in 1988:

> FoE is quoted as the only environmental organization "which argued that green growth is logically impossible."
>
> I can't say I'm surprised by that, but I continue to be fairly depressed by it. . . . The vast majority of UK environmental groups, consciously or subconsciously, have been co-opted by the growthist [sic] obsessions of our industrial culture.
> (Porritt, 1988, p. 22)

The argument about limits to growth, specifically about resource depletion, has already been mentioned and I will return to it later. The present point (indeed, Porritt's point too) is that those groups in the UK which have played the largest part in bringing green issues to public attention have not (publicly at least) espoused the need for a sharp break with current societal arrangements. They have challenged some specific things which we do (such as using leaded gasoline or buying "biological" detergents) but have stopped short of criticizing our basically capitalistic "industrial culture." This verdict matches that given by Lowe and Flynn (1989), who emphasized the "reformist strategies" of the UK green movement. In practice, even FoE has been reformist; it has tacitly supported the replacement of ozone-eating deodorants with non-ozone-depleting ones, rather than campaigning directly for the elimination of aerosols (an expensive, energy consuming, non-recyclable form of packaging).

Yet this reformist view is not the only available approach to current environmental threats: the last two decades have also witnessed the formulation of more radical green political ideologies. In his recent analysis of this line of political thought Dobson refers to reformist environmental concerns as "green" while the more radical, ecologist line he calls "Green." (This distinction can also be made using the terms "deep green" and "light green.") For presentation purposes, Dobson's distinction is a useful device and one which I shall adopt from now on.

How then does "green" differ from "Green"? In Dobson's view, Green political ideology, or "ecologism,"

> ... questions growth and technology, and suggests that the Good Life will involve more work and fewer material objects. Fundamentally, ecologism takes seriously the universal condition of the finitude of the planet and asks what kinds of political, economic and social practices are (a) possible and (b) desirable within that framework. Environmentalism [i.e. green thinking], typically, does no such thing.
> (Dobson, 1990, p. 205)

In his book *Green Political Thought*, Dobson sets out to give an objective description of ecologism and to establish that it is a coherent political ideology. This ideology contains a twofold critique of contemporary society, arguing both that it is, in fact, unsustainable (because of resource depletion and pollution) and that it is undesirable. It is undesirable because our "industrial culture" demands that we adopt an exploitative attitude to the natural world and that we alienate ourselves from our natural environment. In principle, therefore, Green beliefs could be persuasive even to people who did not yet feel themselves threatened by environmental disaster. But the present environmental crisis lends the Green argument an immediate credibility.

Greens take our current ecological problems very seriously, arguing that we must take immediate steps to decrease our consumption of energy and raw materials, and to reduce drastically our polluting behavior. In their view, we must lower our expectations of material goods and learn to enjoy simpler, sustainable lives. We must begin to decentralize our societies and learn to live predominantly with the resources of our local region. They argue, however, that this will not be a deprivation for us; both because our standard of living will be better than that which awaits us if we continue on our present course to its catastrophic end, and because the simpler life brings its own communal and spiritual dividends.

Part of the basis for these positive claims about the appeal of a Green lifestyle comes from a critical interpretation of the development of western thought, particularly scientific thought, which has been directed to taking nature apart (mentally and, often, physically) and considering its parts in isolation. By contrast, Greens value holistic thinking. The rational orientation, epitomized in the Enlightenment, is viewed by Greens as having played a large part in encouraging our exploitative attitude to the natural world. In their view, this way of thinking is partly responsible for precipitating the environmental crisis. Green political thought is thus opposed to the Enlightenment in many respects:

> The Green movement . . . is self-consciously seeking to call into question an entire world view rather than tinker with one that already exists. For the sake of convenience, but at the risk of blind blundering on territory where specialists themselves quite properly fear to tread, the world view that modern political ecologists challenge is the one that grew out of the (early) Enlightenment. Norman Hampson has suggested a number of characteristics salient to the Enlightenment world view: "a period when the culture of the educated man was thought to take in the whole of educated knowledge"; "that man was to a great extent the master of his own destiny"; that "God was a mathematician whose calculations, although infinite in their subtle complexity, were accessible to man's intelligence"; and that "universal reason" was held to be preferable to "local habit", principally because it helps to drive out superstition (Hampson, 1979, pp. 11, 35, 37–8, 152).
>
> The general tenor of these characteristics is the exaltation of human beings and their particular faculties (e.g. reason) – the placing of the human being in a pre-eminent position with respect to the rest of, not only terrestrial phenomena, but the universe at large . . . the Enlightenment attitude was that the world had been made for human beings and that, in principle, nothing in it could be kept secret from them.
>
> In a tortuous way this attitude has remained dominant ever since in the cultures and societies that have most obviously incubated the modern Green movement. They inform, too, [a dominant interpretation] of what post-industrial society both is and ought to be: Baconian science has helped produce its technology and its material affluence, and the Promethean project to which the Enlightenment gave birth in its modern form is

substantially intact. Now the historical significance of Green politics as I see it is that it constitutes a challenge to this project and to the norms and practices that sustain it. Green politics explicitly seeks to decentre the human being, to question mechanistic science and its technological consequences, to refuse to believe that the world was made for human beings – and it does this because it has been led to wonder whether dominant post-industrialism's project of material affluence is either desirable or sustainable. All this will be missed if we choose to restrict our understanding of Green politics to what is becoming its principal guise: an environmentalism that seeks a cleaner service economy, sustained by cleaner technology and producing cleaner affluence.

These thoughts on the Enlightenment help to identify ecologism's present historical significance, but there is danger here too. The analytic temptation is to see the ideology as a recreation of the romantic reaction that the Enlightenment and then early forms of industrialization themselves brought about. So we cast ecologism in terms of passion opposing reason, of the joys of a bucolic life and of mystery as against transparency. And of course it is true that most manifestations of the Green movement argue for a repopulation of the countryside and for the reawakening of a sense of awe in the face of natural phenomena.

At the same time, however, modern Green politics turns out to be based on a self-consciously hard-headed assessment of the unsustainability of present political and economic practices – it is remarkable, indeed, to see the extent to which the success of modern political ecology has been mediated and sustained by scientific research. This could hardly be said of the romantic reaction to the Enlightenment. Similarly, ecologism's political Utopia is (by and large) informed by interpretations of the principle of equality – a principle that was minted and put into circulation during the Enlightenment, and certainly not popular with romantics. Again, as far as romanticism is concerned, Green politics has little time for individualism or for geniuses, and one suspects (although this will be disputed by members of the movement) that the nonconformity so beloved of romantics would be a pretty scarce commodity in Green communities. Finally, if we hold the Green movement to believe that one can only recognize the value of the natural world through intuition (as we are likely to do if we see it merely as a resurgence of romanticism), then we are blind to the enormous range and influence of rationalist attempts to account for such value, and which are of great importance to the movement's intellectual archaeology.

So while (in terms of its present historical significance) Green politics ought to be characterized as a challenge to the contemporary consensus over norms and practices that has its most immediate sources in the early Enlightenment, it would be a mistake to think it pays no mind whatever to those norms and practices. And this would be an especially big mistake if we were to jump to the conclusion that modern Green politics is only a

form of reincarnated romanticism. To guard against this we should say that its challenge most generally takes the form of an attempt to shift the terms of the burden of persuasion from those who would question the dominant post-industrial embodiment (an affluent, technological, service society) of politics and society, onto those who would defend it. In doing so Greens may sometimes speak, even if often *sotto voce*, in the Enlightenment idiom.
(Dobson, 1990, pp. 7–10)

Dobson concludes by noting that ecologism, despite the occasional pronouncements of its advocates, is not anti-Enlightenment. By this he means that Greens are actually profoundly in debt to, and make active use of, aspects of Enlightenment thinking. Thus, Green thinking typically wishes to grant extensive rights to non-human (as well as human) forms of life, to recognize the inherent value of animal and vegetable life. And the fact that Greens talk about this process in terms of rights is indicative of ecologism's continuity with Enlightenment political thinking. Similarly, Greens tend to stress freedom of information and many kinds of equality. Yet these principles are not demanded by the need for ecological survival; they draw on other, pre-existing traditions of political analysis, particularly "socialistic" ones (Dobson, 1990, p. 183). Lastly, as Dobson mentions, Greens even depend on science to a large extent, for example in determining the threat from ozone depletion or the dangers of acid rain. The Green case is in many respects a scientific one (Yearley, 1991, pp. 113–48). At the risk of seeming sophistical, one might say that Greens put forward an enlightenment critique of the Enlightenment rather than a romantic one.

## 3.1 Taking Green ideas to the polls

The connection between Green thought and existing, especially Left-leaning, political philosophies is an important one and I shall return to it in section 4 when I consider the connection between growth, capitalism, and environmental problems. But there is a prior empirical question to be addressed – namely, what has happened to Green political ideas when people have attempted to convince the public on a large scale? For those convinced of the correctness of Green ideas there is clearly an urgent need for change. But it is far from clear how that change is to be brought about. For example, Greens may feel compelled to make radical alterations in their own lifestyles: they will try to consume much less, to live sustainably, to live non-exploitatively. They may even join together in communities to pursue this way of life. But they will also know that even if they give up their cars, travel by motor vehicles only when it is necessary, radically economize on power, and so on, this will not make a great deal of difference to the burdens of pollution and resource depletion. Greens may argue that their example will become infectious, that others will be attracted by what they see. There is little evidence so far to support this notion. Many Greens will believe that although they know the planet is heading for ecological disaster the rest of the world will not be won over in time just by the force of their example. Accordingly, the most obvious strategy is to seek to bring about change through intervention in the political process, in particular, by forming Green political parties.

Party formation offers at least two advantages. First, it provides a public platform from which to expound Green views. A party, particularly an innovative and reasonably successful one, is assured of publicity and is likely to gain media time at elections. Second, a party may become politically successful and thus win the opportunity to influence legislation. It can do this not only by entering government itself but also by becoming sufficiently popular at the polls that other parties are obliged to adopt some of its policies for fear of losing support to it. This was arguably the biggest impact of the UK Green Party after its unexpectedly successful showing in the 1989 European elections, when it won just short of 15 percent of the vote. Sensing the rise in the importance of the environmental vote, both the leading parties quickly set about greening their own images and – to some extent – their policies.

However attractive it may be to form a Green political party, it is by no means straightforward. No doubt it is difficult to launch any new party, but there are special, internal ideological obstacles to party formation within ecologism. For one thing, Greens are uneasy about appointing leaders or introducing hierarchies. They are attracted to the notion of direct democracy and have typically resisted the delegation of power to parliamentary representatives. There is also a tendency to view existing political structures (parliaments, councils, governmental committees, and so on) as part of the old "growthist" order. There is a corresponding fear that elected Green representatives would become seduced by the system. Worse still, since any early successes have resulted in Green parties acquiring only a few seats, there has been the problem of forming political alliances. If they hold firm to their principles, Green parties are unlikely to achieve any legislative changes, but if they compromise and form alliances with existing parties – especially larger parties – their radical Green identity is likely to be lost.

All party-based systems depend on electoral competition which in turn demands that voters be wooed. Greens face the problem that if their manifesto stresses the more austere aspects of Green beliefs, then support is likely to be reduced. If, however, the claims are moderated, support may rise but the intensity of commitment is likely to fall. This dilemma is felt very acutely in relation to economic growth, something routinely promised by all other parties.

While it is difficult to put forward an electorally attractive package which is also true to Green sentiments, Green parties have been successful in entering national parliaments in, for example, Germany, Austria, Italy, Sweden, and Belgium. Of these, the Green Party in pre-unification West Germany – die Grünen – has attracted the most attention since it was one of essentially only four parties in the parliament of Europe's strongest and most influential economy. The

West German electoral system was so arranged that parties had to cross
a threshold of support (effectively 5 percent) before they were eligible
for any representation. But once past this minimum, they gained a
reasonable number of seats (for *die Grünen*, 27 in 1983 and 44 in 1987
(Urwin, 1990, p. 155)). The two largest parties were close in size and a
coalition with the third, small, liberal party was vital for the exercise of
power. *Die Grünen* could thus be reasonably hopeful that it too might
come to wield real parliamentary power before too long. This prospect
obliged the West German Greens to confront difficult political choices:
if the chance presented itself, should they make an arrangement with
the social democrats (the SPD) in the hope of passing green (even
Green) legislation, or would they lose their integrity if they cooperated
with a much larger party which was committed to economic growth
and increased prosperity?

With German reunification and the triumph of the Right in the all-
German election of December, 1990, these questions lost much of their
immediacy. In what was formerly West Germany, *die Grünen* polled
less than the crucial 5 percent of the vote. But this setback for the party
is itself instructive since it shows the diversity of factors involved in
determining the success of Green groups. In part, success is affected by
the voting system. In the first-past-the-post systems of the UK and –
effectively – the US, it is difficult for small parties to achieve any
success. At the other extreme, in multi-party parliaments with
proportional representation, Greens may readily win seats but still not
be well placed to make a large impact on policy. Success is also
affected by the timing of the election and the kinds of issues which
have the highest political profile. In the case of Germany in 1990, the
dominant issue was reunification and the economic management of the
new Germany. This eclipsed matters on which Greens had distinctive
views. Voting is also affected by the conduct of the parties themselves
and by the composition of the Green movement within particular
countries. These factors have produced a variety of ecology parties, as
Urwin observes:

> The input into the green parties of the many disparate groups that
> made up the ecology movement varied from country to country. In
> general, the combinations produced two broad categories of party.
> On the one hand were those – the majority – where the dominant
> element was environmentalist [i.e. green] and the strategy broadly
> reformist within the prevailing neocapitalist system. Others, by
> contrast . . . rejected more explicitly the prevailing modes of
> participation and decision-making. No matter how vaguely, they
> expressed a broader and alternative world picture that, if
> implemented, would entail far-reaching reform of the social order,
> and rejected any form of political cooperation except on their own
> terms.
> (Urwin, 1990, pp. 155–6)

According to Urwin, therefore, the situation of ecology parties is very
diverse and complex. Nature conservationists and many environmental
groups may be green; though in Dobson's view only "political

ecologism" is Green. It now seems that ecology parties may be either Green or green. In other words, while Dobson is fundamentally correct that ecologism provides a distinctive Green political philosophy, it is very difficult to run a successful Green political party in modern western societies. Such parties face considerable pressures leading them to moderate their Greenness in much the same way that successful parliamentary socialist parties have tempered their socialism. In both cases the parties find themselves open to persistent ideological attack from those in the vanguard of their respective movements.

## 3.2 Public awareness and citizens' action

Up to this point I have emphasized the role of organizations – particularly pressure groups and political parties – in putting environmental issues on the public agenda. But their actions have been complemented by a public response. Membership of environmental pressure groups reached record levels at the start of the 1990s. Similarly, the persistent use of boasts about "environmental-friendliness" in advertising and in marketing slogans is clear testimony to sustained public sympathy for these issues.

As with virtually all voluntary associations, environmental groups have received most of their support from the middle classes. Cotgrove and Duff's research suggests that this support is strongest among those members of the middle classes who work in public services (1980, pp. 340–4). It is important to note that people's response to green issues is also affected by features of their own locality. As I have noted elsewhere:

> While individuals or families may be beset by a range of environmentally related problems, there appear to be certain types of development which frequently lead to collective responses. Some characteristics of these developments are rather obvious. All other things being equal, large projects are likely to catalyse action since they disturb many people at once. Yet while motorways will disturb large numbers of people, those people are socially and geographically dispersed. Airports, large factories and nuclear power plants on the other hand are concentrated. The last of these, as well as some factories, are additionally associated with insidious dangers, even occasional catastrophes. It is not surprising therefore that nuclear power plants have been rallying points for environmental action and "politicization" throughout almost the whole of the first world.
> (Yearley, 1991, p. 83)

As western governments proceeded with nuclear power programs after the sudden oil price rise of the early 1970s, opposition mounted, bringing together local residents or working people (though not necessarily the working class), members of the traditional nature conservation groups, more radical green groups, and representatives of the new Left (see Rüdig, 1986, pp. 378–80; and Lowe and Flynn, 1989,

p. 273). Such alliances fused the so-called NIMBY (not in my back yard) interests of locals, the green/Green concerns of environmentalists, and the anti-nuclear, often anti-militarist, attitude of the Left. These groupings – whose members initially seemed to have little in common – encouraged some of the participants to adopt a comprehensive green/Green political outlook and directly fed the growth of Green parties (Scott, 1990, pp. 82–5). The precise make-up of these parties, as we have seen, varies from one country to another, but in every case support has been driven up by a section of the population's experience of environmental protest.

Although these protests have often been directed against the construction of nuclear power stations – indeed such stations seem to be the "ideal" provocation for political action – they have not been the sole spur to protest. Facilities for the dumping of nuclear waste, the construction of large airports (notably in Germany and Japan) and incinerators for toxic materials (in Ireland; see Allen and Jones, 1990, pp. 237–42), and even plans to build over local beauty spots and wildlife sites have had similar effects.

Thus, an understanding of the reasons for particular individuals' participation in the green movement needs to encompass the dynamics of specific environmental protests as well as the effects of social-class position and the campaigning work of pressure groups. Seen from the environmentalists' perspective, however, this fact has an ironic consequence: it is typically harder to mount a strong public campaign about the allegedly global problems of atmospheric warming and ozone depletion than it is to get people to take political action about a local development.

The difficulties in getting the public involved in international issues are compounded in the cases of global warming, ozone depletion, and acid rain because, as I mentioned earlier, the evidence is remote from everyday experience and the scientific details are complex and contested. The scientific uncertainty over the mechanism of global warming can be used by industrialists and governments as a "reason" to wait-and-see before making policy changes. With authoritative sections of society keen to stress the uncertainty surrounding these issues, environmentalists have found it hard to make their case in an incontrovertible way. Their difficulties have been aggravated by the fact that some radical environmentalists are, in any case, skeptical of science and of our high-technology society. Accordingly, science has proved a rather slippery friend to environmental campaigners (see Yearley, 1991, pp. 113–48).

Despite these difficulties, environmental groups have recognized the importance of campaigning on international issues and have devised appropriate techniques. First, the groups have themselves cooperated and organized at an international level: notably Greenpeace and FoE International, but also more "establishment" groups such as, in Britain, the Royal Society for the Protection of Birds (RSPB), which has established relationships with conservationists in the countries to which (and over which) birds migrate.

Environmentalists have also used international comparisons to outflank national governments, arguing – for example – that if catalytic converters can be adopted in the US without endangering its motor industry, there can be no obstacle to their use in Britain. Lastly, these organizations have quickly learned to enlist the power of European Community legislation to circumvent national governments. In 1986, FoE began to threaten to take the British government to court over its failure to comply with European regulations on the quality of drinking water; in the end the government backed down (FoE, 1990, pp. 31–2). Equally, the World Wide Fund for Nature (WWF) has been quick to appreciate the power of European legislation to hasten environmental reform and to force the hand of reluctant governments. Thus, by organizing internationally, environmental groups can sometimes gain access to more information and authority than are available to national governments; this compensates to a large extent for the difficulties inherent in campaigning on non-local issues.

# 4   Growth, Capitalism, and Green Consumerism

Although large numbers of people throughout Europe are now members of green groups and many are prepared, at least sometimes, to vote Green, even larger numbers of people can participate in the movement through green consumerism. They can use their purchasing power to favor products which are less polluting than average or which contain recycled components. Some commentators take this phenomenon very seriously: Richard Adams of the consumers' magazine *New Consumer* was quoted in 1989 as proclaiming to the Green Party that "The shopping centre was the polling station and the cash till the ballot box" (*The Guardian*, September 22, 1989, p. 6). Others are more hostile, seeing dangers lurking behind the attractions of green consumerism.

Critics of green consumerism tend to adopt one or other of two sorts of response. On the one hand, it is possible to feel equivocal about green consumerism because of a fear that it may get highjacked. Knowing how much effort manufacturers are prepared to put into appearing to give customers what they want, one may legitimately fear that the greening of produce may be largely cosmetic. Already we are seeing bags and cans which bear the legend "recyclable." This does not mean that they have been recycled; it's a reminder that, in principle, they could be recycled in the future. There is no guarantee that the consumer will find a handy facility for recycling bags (in fact it's unlikely), nor any assurance that the manufacturer will prefer to buy materials from recycled sources. In short, the label may attract and comfort the greenish consumer while barely altering the environmental impact of our lifestyles.

The second line of criticism is more Green. It regards the idea of shopping your way to the salvation of the planet as a contradiction in terms. We need to consume less, not just carry on buying, though in a more discriminating way (Dobson, 1990, p. 17). This point of view leads us directly into a major debate within the environmental movement concerning the compatibility of economic growth and environmental protection. Advocates of green consumerism have to believe that we can reform our current economic system in such a way that it is sustainable *and* can still offer us new goods and growth. Others, such as Porritt, argue that we must forgo growth:

> Green growth *may* turn out to be less polluting, less wasteful and more efficient in terms of energy and resources (all of which are highly desirable goals, enthusiastically to be campaigned for), but its adherents still seem to subscribe to one all-powerful item of economic dogma: that it is only through a *permanent* process of expansion in production and consumption that it is possible to meet human needs, improve standards of living, and ensure that wealth trickles down to the unfortunate *billions* who haven't yet had "their share of the cake".
>
> It is indeed the lack of logic in all this which really irks me. Let us assume that all readers of this article subscribe to a vision of an equitable, just and sustainable future. That is easily said, but not so easily achieved. Though equity does not entail absolutely equal shares, it certainly implies far fairer shares for everyone. That either means that our existing material standard of living will gradually become available to all five billion souls with whom we currently share this planet (let alone the ten billion souls with whom we shall be sharing in the not so distant future), or it means that we must be prepared to reduce our own standard of living to a point where some approximation of equity may be achieved.
>
> If you subscribe to the former view, then you cannot, *by definition*, subscribe to the principles of sustainability. Five billion people abusing the planet as we in the developed world do now – bearing in mind that it is only such uncompromising abuse which affords us such a high material standard of living – would precipitate irreparable ecological damage before we even get halfway through the next century. If you subscribe to the latter view, then you must also accept that an equitable, just and sustainable future cannot possibly derive from *any* variation of today's industrial materialism – not even a marginally greener one. If you're into logic, green growth and green consumerism are therefore highly dubious notions. On balance, I still believe that more good will be done by them than harm, but only if they are seen as part of a transitional strategy to a genuinely green economy, the success of which is **not** exclusively measured by increases in GNP or further industrial expansion.
> (Porritt, 1988, pp. 22–3)

Porritt's attack is directed at what he calls "industrialism" rather than at a more narrowly defined socio-economic system: capitalism or state socialism. Many Left-leaning analysts who are otherwise sensitive to Green arguments would maintain that it is crucial to recognize the special connection between capitalism, growth, and environmental despoliation (see Yearley, 1991, pp. 104–7; and Dobson, 1990, pp. 186–90).

Essentially, their argument is as follows. The capitalist system is inherently competitive and firms have to compete by raising their productivity. As a capitalist, if you stay still you perish. Accordingly, growth is necessary to the system. Moreover, the system continually generates growth. Now, this "growth" may not all be desirable – indeed, it may in a certain sense be self-defeating. It may include more powerful cars *and* better in-car entertainment for passing the long hours spent in traffic jams. It may even include new forms of junk food. "Growth" will certainly include money spent on cleaning up environmental disasters such as oil spills. Furthermore, huge resources need to be spent on encouraging consumers to want the new products, such as DAT recorders or domestic ultra-violet lamps, for which they never knew they had a craving. Capitalist production leads to the proliferation of "gift shops" selling wholly useless executive toys and valueless presents. For these reasons, capitalist industrialism is seen by many as the special enemy of the environment. And among some neo-Marxists it is believed that capitalism will be undermined by the environmental problem to which it inevitably gives rise. Ecology here takes on the role of capital's implacable enemy, a role which the proletariat has been so slow to fill (for an early exposition of this view, see Bosquet, 1977).

Greens have not, by and large, been too impressed with this argument, pointing out that the environmental problems of state socialist countries (in terms of air pollution, the contamination of water, health and safety at work, and so on) have been, if anything, considerably greater than in capitalist countries. Certainly, more environmental problems have been caused under state socialism per dollar of wealth created. Less radical greens have been equally unimpressed; they are, as I mentioned, reformist in their attitudes and look to the market as part of the solution to our environmental problems – through green consumerism and related initiatives.

Just like the debate over resource depletion, the argument about the supposed incompatibility of capitalism and sustainable development is impossible to assess in abstract, logical terms. It is an empirical issue. Advocates of capitalism will argue that, even if capitalism does need growth, growth need not be polluting. For example, most recent economic growth has occurred in the service and information sectors. It is not certain, in principle, that growth has to entail greater depletion of scarce resources or the creation of ever more pollution. Of course, there will always be some pollution, but the planet can tolerate *some* and, anyway, capitalist societies have seen falls in certain forms of environmental contamination, for example, as a result of the phasing-out of smoky fuels.

Critics of capitalism will reply that, even if markets could respond to ecological problems (for example, by including the environmental impact of goods in their price; see Pearce et al., 1989, pp. 55–6), this will typically not come about soon enough. Capitalist economies develop through booms and slumps precisely because warnings feed back into the system too slowly. This will be true for ecological warnings too, as illustrated by the hunting of many species to extinction.

## 4.1   Bringing greenery about

Greens have good reason to be skeptical about existing forms of capitalist and socialist economies. They believe that profound social change is needed and they know some of the characteristics which they would like to see in the new order (for a sympathetic but critical overview, see Dobson, 1990, pp. 81–129). But, as both Scott and Dobson make clear, Greens often appear naïve about how this change may come about. On their behalf, Dobson asks how change might come about, and then suggests:

> The answer to this question might just turn on initially sidestepping it and asking instead: who is best placed to bring about social change? A central characteristic of Green political theory is that it has never consistently asked that question, principally because the answer is held to be obvious: everyone. (Dobson, 1990, p. 152)

In other words, if we are all threatened by global warming or by the contamination of drinking water, then it is in all our interests to bring about change. But of course the matter is not this simple. Many people may not believe the warnings about climate change; I have already described how the complexity of the scientific evidence allows plenty of room for the determined skeptic. And, even if our drinking water is badly polluted, the pollution is not the same everywhere, and the wealthy among us can buy bottled water or purification equipment. Many of us, business owners and workers alike, actually profit from polluting aspects of current society. There is therefore little prospect of us all combining to bring about profound social change.

Rudolf Bahro, formerly a leading socialist thinker, now espouses a radical Green (or fundamentalist) position. Alan Scott sums up Bahro's views as follows:

> The only viable means of averting ecological catastrophe is the importation of small-scale models of production into industrial societies. . . . [Furthermore] Bahro maintains that the working class cannot be agents of progressive change since they too have a stake in the growth model: "If I look at the problem from the point of view of the whole of humanity, not just that of Europe, then I must say that the metropolitan working class is the worst exploiting class in history".
> (Scott, 1990, pp. 90–1)

But Scott then goes on to criticize Bahro's vision, particularly on the grounds that Bahro does not spell out how the desired changes could be brought about. As Scott observes, Bahro does not "identify agents who could bring about" the social changes that he believes are desirable. The activists in environmental organizations, as we have seen, tend to be drawn from the middle classes. Although some of these people may adopt Green lifestyles out of personal conviction, in general the middle classes are the people who can best cocoon themselves from ecological problems (by living in the country, eating organic foods, and so on) and who would have most to lose from wholesale political and economic changes. Indeed, as Berger has made clear, the "knowledge class," from which environmentalists are mostly drawn, owes its very existence to the productive success of modern industrial society; without economic surplus this class would wither away. The middle classes can hardly be expected to sweep radical Greens to power; they are much more likely to adopt reformist positions.

In Marxist thought, the working class is expected (however erroneously) to usher in socialism precisely because workers are the victims of the capitalist system. It is in their political and material interests to alter the system. Marx anticipated that conditions would become sufficiently bad that workers would risk participating in radical social change. Greens find it hard to identify any group that is in an analogous position. As Bahro noted, the working class is barely a contender. Dobson views the long-term unemployed and others marginalized from western industrial society as the only group which might fulfill this role (1990, pp. 167–9). They have little to wed them to the system, share few of the benefits of growth, might not suffer materially from the introduction of a Green society, and might be attracted by the notion of a decentralized society with local economic initiatives. This idea has a certain plausibility but there is as yet little evidence of political consciousness developing in this group, nor of mass affiliation to Green organizations. Further, it is unclear how a group composed chiefly of the marginalized could hope to obtain political power. In other words, the majority of current sociological thinking suggests that, even if radical Greens are correct in their diagnosis, there is little prospect of collective action to bring about the changes they seek.

## 4.2 Beyond the greening of the West

It is clear that if environmentalists are at all justified in their arguments then green issues are not just pressing for the West but for all countries. Global warming is likely to be intensified as China and India begin to expand their power generation facilities and increase industrial development; and Bangladesh will be one of the nations most threatened by any associated rise in sea level. Acid rain over southern Asia from the burning oil-fields of Kuwait in 1991 is likely to be a precursor of industrial pollution in that region. Mining, mineral processing, logging, and agribusiness will all add to the likely environmental burden of development. Yet, for the Third World there is no choice about the need for development, as is expressed in the report of the World Commission on Environment and Development:

> While attainable growth rates [in the Third World] will vary, a certain minimum is needed to have any impact on *absolute*

*poverty*. It seems unlikely that, taking developing countries as a whole, these objectives can be accomplished with per capita income growth of under 3 percent. Given current population growth rates, this would require overall national income growth of around 5 percent a year in the developing economies of Asia, 5.5 percent in Latin America, and 6 percent in Africa and West Asia. (1987, p. 50; my emphasis)

Just to reduce absolute poverty, these economies have to grow at these rates for around twenty years, tripling (for instance) the size of the Latin American economies.

Consequently, although I have so far concentrated on the West, the Third World must not be omitted from any assessment of ecological threats to present-day society. Of course, there are good reasons for focusing on the West: the western countries are the major polluters and the major consumers of raw materials, our current scientific understanding of environmental threats was largely worked out there, western nations have witnessed the greatest growth in environmental politics and protest, and the Green challenge to Enlightenment attitudes was initiated there (Dobson, 1990, p. 10). But any proposals for addressing our (the West's) ecological problems must take into account the rest of the globe too. And I say "must" not just because many commentators believe that we should, but because the West cannot insulate its environment from that of the rest of the world. In the long run, it could be threatened by marine pollution, by atmospheric contamination, by threats to species, or by resource depletion. Already this interdependence has been graphically illustrated by the contamination in Western Europe from the Chernobyl explosion and by Europe's own experience of "trans-boundary" pollution through acid rain. The message that ecological threats do not respect national boundaries has been reinforced by environmental groups campaigning at a European and supranational level, as described above. Recognizing the importance of international environmental problems, and the general reluctance of national governments to engage in coordinated responses, these groups have begun to lobby governments, official aid agencies, and international bodies such as the World Bank and the International Monetary Fund, bodies which largely determine the West's attitude to Third-World countries' problems (see Hayter, 1989; and Searle, 1987).

Poor nations with an urgent need for economic growth naturally find it difficult to resist western development proposals or offers of trade even if the environmental implications are not likely to be benign. Typically, the West has not helped them to resolve this dilemma. Considerations of commercial and political self-interest still appear uppermost in the West's dealings with the Third World. But there are encouraging signs that, at least in the case of the threat posed by CFCs, the West may be willing to organize technical assistance to Third World countries to enable them to manufacture safer alternatives. Given the dangers associated with ozone depletion, this is only enlightened self-interest, but it is a start. The next major negotiations will concern greenhouse gases and these are likely to proceed much less smoothly. In this case there is no "technical fix," no ready substitute to allow emissions to be reduced. Just to limit pollution to present-day levels, the West will have to reduce its output of greenhouse gases while Third World industrialization proceeds. Already, the US and Japan – the largest polluters – have shown themselves willing to make very few concessions. It is unclear how this sharp conflict of interests can be resolved.

In this context of uncertainty, the only safe prediction is that environmental questions will figure ever more conspicuously in discussions of development, and that green groups will increasingly direct their campaigning work to international causes. Thus, in 1990, FoE ran a campaign aimed at encouraging banks to reduce Third World debt, hoping thereby to limit the short-term pressures which are leading to rainforest destruction and environmentally-damaging mining. Such internationalism can only grow.

# 5 Conclusion: Environmental Challenges and the Enlightenment

In this chapter we have seen that the ecological hazards of pollution and resource depletion pose a potentially catastrophic threat to industrial society, perhaps even to the planet. Since the earth's material resources must be finite, one might think it certain that economic growth cannot long continue on its present path. But successive predictions about resource depletion have appeared alarmist. The predicted shortages have so far failed to appear. It has turned out that, to date, pollution has had a much more pronounced impact on the West, with widespread experience of acid rain, of agricultural pollutants in our foodstuffs, and the loss of species from our countryside, rivers, and seas. Particularly within the last decade, environmental threats have come to be widely recognized in the West. We have explained this increased recognition partly in terms of individuals' experience of these ecological problems. But other factors have played a large role in this explanation too, notably shrewd environmental campaigning – aided by the media – and the growth of a "knowledge class" whose members' structural position makes them receptive to the environmental message.

No matter how potentially severe these ecological problems are, the majority response has been reformist and gradualist. Campaigners have lured us on to more "environmentally friendly" aerosols, and legislators have begun to tighten up the limits on acidic emissions from power stations. Still, economic growth is continuing and the basic values and institutions of western society have not been challenged.

However, some environmentalists have taken this opportunity to devise a new, comprehensive Green ideology which claims to offer new social and political goals, to transcend the old divisions of Right and

Left, and to displace humans from their central position in our moral philosophy. In this new view, all of nature is to command the same moral respect that used to be reserved for humans alone. We have seen that this Green ideology poses a challenge to many of the Enlightenment assumptions of our society: it questions our commitment to growth and material progress, it stresses restraint and thrift, it favors holism over individualism. But this ideology is not simply anti-Enlightenment. As Dobson showed, it retains elements of Enlightenment thought, such as a concern for rights (even animal rights) and a heavy dependence on scientific modes of thinking. Without science we could know little of the greenhouse effect or of the ozone layer.

Green thought thus offers an innovative and challenging political ideology, but, as we saw, it is not an easy ideology to introduce into contemporary western democracies. The tenets of the Green political philosophy make life difficult for Green parties since they breed a resistance to leadership, authority, and political compromise. Moreover, the audience for Green views is much smaller than that for environmentalist views. Accordingly, social support for this new ideology is growing only very slowly, a fact reflected in generally poor performances by Greens in European elections in the early 1990s.

By contrast, the reformist, green position appears firmly established throughout the West. Welcomed on the "soft" Left and in the liberal middle classes, it has even begun to find a home in conservative parties.

Yet there is no proof that the reformist path is sustainable. Nobody has shown that green reforms can penetrate deeply enough to overcome the global threats of pollution, species extinction, and habitat loss. In any case, companies or nations can at any time dig their heels in and resist reforms which are particularly unfavorable to them (as the British electricity supply industry did for so long over acid rain). Capitalist, market-based growth and sustainability may just not be compatible. Moreover, the lack of international accord over global warming and non-renewable resources indicates that a prosperous green future is not currently on offer to everyone on this planet.

In summary, therefore, radical Green thinking does challenge the Enlightenment project, but its challenge lacks a firm social basis; greens, on the other hand, try to accommodate to the Enlightenment, but there is no guarantee that they can pull this trick off.

# References

Allen, R. and Jones, T. (1990) *Guests of the Nation: People of Ireland versus the Multinationals*, London, Earthscan.

Berger, P.L. (1987) *The Capitalist Revolution*, Aldershot, England, Wildwood House.

Bosquet, M. (1977) *Capitalism in Crisis and Everyday Life*, Brighton, England, Harvester.

Cotgrove, S. and Duff, A. (1980) "Environmentalism, middle class radicalism and politics," *Sociological Review*, vol. 28, pp. 333–51.

Dobson, A. (1990) *Green Political Thought*, London, Unwin Hyman.

Elsworth, S. (1990) *A Dictionary of the Environment*, London, Paladin.

FoE, *see* Friends of the Earth.

Friends of the Earth (UK) (1989) "Your tap water, pure or poisoned?," *Observer Magazine*, August 6, pp. 16–24.

Friends of the Earth (UK) (1990) *How Green is Britain?*, London, Hutchinson.

Hampson, N. (1979) *The Enlightenment*, Harmondsworth, England, Penguin.

Hayter, T. (1989) *Exploited Earth: British Aid and the Environment*, London, Earthscan.

Leggett, J. (1990) "The nature of the greenhouse threat," in Leggett, J. (ed.) *Global Warming: The Greenpeace Report*, Oxford, Oxford University Press.

Lowe, P. (1983) "Values and institutions in the history of British nature conservation," in Warren, A. and Goldsmith, F.B. (eds) *Conservation in Perspective*, Chichester, England, John Wiley.

Lowe, P. and Flynn, A. (1989) "Environmental politics and policy in the 1980s," in Moran, J. (ed.) *The Political Geography of Contemporary Britain*, London, Macmillan.

McKibben, B. (1990) *The End of Nature*, Harmondsworth, England, Penguin.

Parkin, S. (1989) *Green Parties: An International Guide*, London, Heretic Books.

Pearce, D., Markandya, A., and Barbier, E.B. (1989) *Blueprint for a Green Economy*, London, Earthscan.

Pezzey, J. (1989) "Greens and growth – a reply," *UK Centre for Economic and Environmental Development Bulletin*, no. 22, pp. 22–3.

Ponting, C. (1990) "Historical perspectives on the environmental crisis," paper presented to the British Association for the Advancement of Science, Swansea.

Porritt, J. (1988) "Greens and growth," *UK Centre for Economic and Environmental Development Bulletin*, no. 19, pp. 22–3.

Rüdig, W. (1986) "Nuclear power: an international comparison of public protest in the USA, Great Britain, France and West Germany," in Williams, R. and Mills, S. (eds) *Public Acceptance of New Technologies: An International Review*, London, Croom Helm.

Scott, A. (1990) *Ideology and the New Social Movements*, London, Unwin Hyman.

Searle, G. (1987) *Major World Bank Projects*, Camelford, England, Wadebridge Ecological Centre.

Seymour, J. and Girardet, H. (1990) *Far From Paradise: The Story of Human Impact on the Environment*, London, Green Print.

Thomas, K. (1984) *Man and the Natural World*, Harmondsworth, England, Penguin.

Urwin, D. (1990) "Green politics in Western Europe," *Social Studies Review*, vol. 5, no. 4, pp. 152–7.

World Commission on Environment and Development (1987) *Our Common Future*, Oxford, Oxford University Press.

Yearley, S. (1991) *The Green Case*, London, HarperCollins.

# Post-industrialism/Post-Fordism

John Allen

## Contents

| | | |
|---|---|---|
| 1 | Introduction: The Economy in Transition | 534 |
| 1.1 | Directions of change | 535 |
| 2 | From Industrialism to Post-Industrialism and Beyond | 536 |
| 2.1 | Post-industrial possibilities | 537 |
| 2.2 | The post-industrial turn? An overview | 544 |
| 3 | From Fordism to Post-Fordism | 546 |
| 3.1 | The regulationist context | 546 |
| 3.2 | After Fordism? An overview | 553 |
| 4 | Assessing Economic Transitions | 555 |
| 4.1 | The scope of change | 556 |
| 4.2 | The pace and tempo of change | 558 |
| 5 | Conclusion: Beyond the Modern Economy? | 560 |
| | References | 562 |

# 1   Introduction: The Economy in Transition

It is perhaps one of the characteristics of modern life to claim that the changes which we witness around us represent the beginnings of something qualitatively new. That such a claim has a familiar ring and causes little surprise is due in no small way to the quickened pace and widespread scale of change in the latter half of the twentieth century. This state of affairs holds true for all aspects of modern life, especially those of work and the economy. This chapter considers the structure of the modern capitalist economy and examines the view that far-reaching changes are underway in the make-up of modern industry; changes which may signal the end of the old manufacturing economy and the emergence of a very different kind of economic order.

A sense of economic transformation within the western industrial economies has been present for quite some time, at least since the 1970s. It may not be surprising, therefore, to learn that there are a number of different views in circulation about what kind of economy we are moving away from and the type of economy that we are moving towards.

For some, it is a world of industrialism and its long-standing imagery that we are leaving behind – the modern factories in an urban setting, the heavy machinery and the ever-present noise, along with the massed ranks of workers in overalls. In its place, we are told that we have entered a *post-industrial* era; one that is characterized by information technologies and networked offices rather than by coal or steam power and sprawling workshops.

For others, it is not the whole of industry which is disappearing from view, but rather one specific form of industry – that of large-scale, mass production or, as it is otherwise known, Fordist manufacture. (For a discussion of the concept of "Fordism," see chapter 8.) Opening up before us, it is claimed, is an altogether different kind of economy; one which is organized around flexible forms of production, in both the technologies used and in the kinds of work expected. In contrast to mass production and mass markets, it is argued that flexible production techniques are becoming increasingly important as a means of responding to the greater diversity of consumer demand and fragmented market tastes. The name given to describe this shift from a mass to a more pluralistic kind of society is *neo-* or *post-Fordist*, depending on which characteristics of the route out of Fordism you wish to stress. The former emphasizes the continuities with Fordism, while the latter stresses a break with the Fordist era. However, both neo- and post-Fordist accounts regard flexibility as the hallmark of the new economic era, overcoming what many take to be the rigidities of an economy organized along Fordist lines.

There is also another sense of ending which is apparent in both the post-industrial and the post-Fordist discourses. It is the sense that the ideas of progress that we associate with a modern industrial economy, especially those based on the methods of mass production, are also losing their relevance. Among the foundations of a modern industrial economy is the notion that progress can be measured by the extent to which the natural world is transformed into tangible goods. The modern economy is, above all, a manufacturing economy; one that regards the making of things, the transformation of raw materials, as its core activity. But in their daily round of work, fewer and fewer people in the West experience work in this way.

Moreover, if the sheer volume and scale of modern mass manufacture can rightly be regarded as the height of industrial progress, then the passing of this moment must surely call into question the appropriateness of the term "modern" to describe the economic trends that have been labelled variously "post-industrial" or "post-Fordist." Thus, the perceptible shift away from bureaucratization and centralization towards more flexible, less hierarchical modes of economic organization may well signify a movement *beyond* economic modernity. Alternatively, such trends may simply represent a *continuation* of the dynamics of a modern economy: the emergence of a new form of industry, perhaps in much the same way that mass manufacture displaced the factory system in the earlier part of this century.

The transformation of the *modern* economy is one of the underlying issues discussed in this chapter. The question of economic modernity connects with the broader theme of the future shape of modern societies, but here it acts as a backdrop to the claims that we are in a *transitional* period – one that is taking us beyond industrialism, beyond Fordism. And in any period of transition, if we wish to make sense of the emergent trends, we need to identify the directions of change.

## 1.1 Directions of change

There are a number of sound reasons for stressing the importance of discerning the *direction* of economic change. In the first place, those who argue that modern industrial economies have undergone major changes in recent times are not necessarily suggesting that a total transformation of the economy has occurred. The emphasis placed on the transitional nature of events is intended to convey something of the *incomplete* and *uneven* character of the changes underway. At best, we can distinguish the lines of direction – the direction in which an economy faces and is moving towards.

The implication here is that some kind of qualitative shift in the organization of the economy is underway; one which is greater than the sum of a number of potentially disparate changes. Of course, it is possible to misread such shifts: to confuse short-term, ephemeral changes for those of a more long-term, substantial nature. But that is a risk one has to take when attempting to make sense of the present as opposed to the past. Economies are always in a state of change, but they are less often in the midst of a period of transformation that leads to a *radical shift* in the direction of the economy.

We can minimize such misreadings by spelling out what is entailed by a radical shift in the direction of an economy.

First, it should be possible to detect changes on a number of fronts which, together, are radically altering the general direction of an economy. The stress here is on the *interconnected* nature of such changes, so that what happens in one part of an economy will have some effect upon the rest of the economy. So, for instance, if we look at some recent trends – such as the growth of service jobs and the decline of manufacturing employment; the introduction of new technologies based upon the microchip; the shift in the structure and composition of labor markets, from a male, full-time workforce towards a female, part-time workforce; a change in consumption practices, with a greater emphasis placed on choice and specialization; and so on – which changes, if any, are interconnected? And if they aro interconnected, whal kind of economy is taking shape?

Secondly, a radical economic shift implies that a different set of *dynamics* is driving an economy. So identifying such a shift is not simply a question of tracing the connections between a variety of changes; it also involves an identification of which elements are key to the direction of change. For example, in the discussion of the contours of post-industrialization which follows, the movement beyond industrialism is not marked merely by a sectoral shift in an economy from manufacturing to services; rather, it is defined by the generation of knowledge and information which act as the dynamics of change. Indeed, as we shall see, the transformation of office work by information-processing technology is regarded by some, such as Manuel Castells, to be equivalent to the radical shift in industrial society from craft-based, factory production to a system of mass manufacture.

Bearing these two points in mind, we are now in a position to look at the claims that lie behind the first of our two possible directions, that of post-industrialism.

# 2   From Industrialism to Post-Industrialism and Beyond

Industrialism, as we have noted, has a long-standing imagery attached to it, one that conjures up heavy machinery, smokestacked factories, and large workforces. The dominant role of machinery in the manufacture of goods, driven first by coal and steam and then by oil and electricity, gives a more precise focus to this industrial imagery. With the rise of post-industrialism a new kind of dynamic is said to have displaced the centrality of manufacturing technologies and the making of things. We referred to this in passing as the generation of knowledge and the control of information, a less tangible form of economic power organized around the "clean" technologies of information and microelectronics. In common with such phenomena as rationalization and bureaucratization, post-industrialism is seen to cut across capitalist economies, radically reshaping the social structure and patterns of work. This section will explore the context in which such claims have been advanced, and the different emphases that such claims have been given by writers on post-industrialism.

## 2.1   Post-industrial possibilities

The idea that we may be moving towards a post-industrial society first took hold in the United States in the 1960s against a background of rising prosperity and increased automation at the workplace. The image of post-industrialism was given a certain currency by a popular belief that an age of economic plenty was just around the corner and a general expectation that technology would solve the problem of mind-numbing jobs. Commentators from across the political spectrum in the US spoke about the emergence of a new kind of society, although the clearest statement of what that society might look like is attributed to Daniel Bell. In *The Coming of Post-Industrial Society*, published in 1973, he outlined the nature of the transition that industrial societies had embarked upon.

Drawing upon the works of two economists writing in the 1930s, Fisher and Clark, Bell adopted a "stages" model of development which identified three successive phases of economic progress: a pre-industrial, an industrial, and a post-industrial phase. The first phase is dominated by agriculture; the second by manufacturing; and the third, the phase that he suggests we have now entered, is dominated by services. In this scenario, historical progress involves a march through these three sectors. The movement refers to historical shifts in the bulk of the workforce, with the majority moving first from agriculture to manufacturing, and then on to the service sector. Today, for example, the US, Japan, and all the major European economies have more than half of their workforce in the service sector. And behind all this, driving the movement, as it were, are rises in productivity levels; initially in agriculture and then in manufacturing. This movement of labor, in turn, is said to have been spurred by a shift in the pattern of demand as rising affluence among consumers leads them to purchase more services relative to manufactured goods and foodstuffs.

According to Bell, the general direction of economic change within the western economies is therefore clearly towards a *service economy*. However, his account of economic change amounts to more than a series of aggregate sectoral shifts in the economy. He wants to argue that each successive economic phase is organized around what he refers to as "axial principles." Loosely translated, Bell is referring to the mechanisms or dynamics that give shape to an economy. The "axial principles" are, so to speak, its driving force. In an industrial society, the driving forces are seen as those of production and profit, the rational pursuit of economic growth through the application of energy and machinery. In contrast, the dynamic forces of post-industrial society are, as we have seen, taken to be those of *knowledge and information*. On this view, it is the generation of knowledge and the processing of information that stimulate economic growth. They act as a source of innovation in the organization and management of the economy and take the form of a final product. Alongside the new technologies that are transforming and automating goods production we find a different product – reams of information. We shall look more closely at this dynamic of knowledge and information shortly, but for

the moment I want to draw your attention to the wide range of changes
in the social structure that Bell points to as a consequence of this new
economic dynamic. There are three aspects to consider.

The first is a shift in the *kinds of work* that people do. Work is
transformed, as knowledge (through its embodiment in the new
technologies) leads to a fall in the number of manual, manufacturing
jobs. At the same time, the growth of the service sector is represented
as a source of non-manual work which involves at least some degree of
creativity and sociability. Instead of working on things, people work
with other people to deliver a service, which for some provides a more
rewarding and interesting form of work. The second, related, aspect is
the change in the *occupational structure* as manual jobs give way to
white-collar and professional occupations. In this view, old skills
requiring strength and physical dexterity have given way to new forms
of "think" work. It is these two trends which lie behind the assertion
that we are witnessing the transformation of the working class,
although it is the rise of a professional middle class which draws Bell's
attention. Finally, Bell's emphasis on knowledge and information as the
key resources of a post-industrial society alert him to the significance of
those who actually control those resources, the *knowledge elites*, as he
refers to them. On his view, the entrepreneurs who held sway in
industrial society are giving way under a post-industrial ethos to the
new technical elites in the universities, government institutions, and
economic enterprises. Moreover, as intellectual work becomes more
specialized, he sees the emergence of new hierarchies of technical elites
alongside the increased professionalization of work and a shift towards
the bureaucratization of "think" work within the advanced western
economies.

The emergence of a post-industrial society, however, was not
something that was hailed only in the US. In France, in the 1960s,
against the backdrop of a radical student movement, Alain Touraine in
*The Post-Industrial Society* (1971) spoke about a move from one kind of
society to another. Although less explicit than Bell about the economic
characteristics of the new society, he also gave central place to the
disposal of knowledge and the control of information, and stressed the
importance of technology in what he termed the "programmed society."
Like Bell, he too identified the agents of change with the control of
knowledge and referred to them, among other terms, as a
"technocracy." At this point, however, these two accounts of post-
industrialism part ways.

At the base of their differences is their treatment of social conflict –
or, in Bell's case, its relative neglect. Pivotal to Touraine's analysis of
post-industrialism is the formation of a new social divide between, on
the one hand, technocrats and bureaucrats, and, on the other, a range of
social groupings, including workers as well as students and consumers.
On this account, the principal opposition between social classes does
not stem from the ownership and control of private property but from
access to information and its uses. To speak of a dominant class in this
context is thus to refer to those who have power over the livelihood
and lifestyle of social groups within and beyond the sphere of

economic production. This view represents a shift away from the more conventional Marxist views of social conflict held at that time, which located class tensions at the point of production, in the factory or workplace. The lines of protest may now take a variety of forms, which have little connection to industry or particular material needs, and thus generate *new social movements* that are quite distinct from the older forms of class conflict. In the 1960s, the student movement and the women's movement were among the best known examples and, today, it is probably the environmental movement which is taken to represent the move beyond class politics.

Despite the absence of popular resistance in Bell's account of social change, it would be wrong to caricature his position as one of consensual change. Writing from a conservative standpoint in *The Cultural Contradictions of Capitalism* (1976), he attempts to demonstrate how a (post-)modern culture based on an unrestrained individualism is increasingly at odds with the economic rationality of a post-industrial society in which the work ethic still holds firm. Economic progress in this instance, he argues, is rapidly being undermined by a cultural lifestyle that owes its very existence to that self-same economic progress. Whereas Touraine sees post-industrial society as a setting in which the lack of power among certain social groups provides the basis for new lines of social conflict and resistance, Bell identifies a structural dislocation between the economic and the cultural realms of post-industrialism in which the Protestant values of economic efficiency and restraint, on the one hand, are undercut by a material sufficiency, on the other. The self-same values which created the expansion of the post-war US economy and the rise of mass consumption are thus now threatened by the desire among many for a more individualistic and culturally expressive lifestyle. In short, there is a clash between the work ethic and the desire for a more hedonistic lifestyle in post-industrial society.

Aside from the differences of emphasis among post-industrial writers, however, there is considerable agreement over the *idea* of post-industrialism and the economic direction in which it faces. The general thesis attracted much criticism in the 1970s, partly from those who mistook Bell to be saying that post-industrialism heralded the demise of capitalism as a competitive economic system, but also because the advanced economies had begun to experience a more sustained downturn in the pattern of post-war economic growth. Nonetheless, the term "post-industrial" proved to be quite resilient and slipped into popular usage in a largely uncritical manner, until it resurfaced in the 1980s in the midst of a new, but related, set of debates.

*The information society* The first debate concerned the celebrated arrival of the *information society*. Drawing extensively on post-industrial arguments, information in all its various guises was projected as a major force in the shaping of advanced economies, affecting the nature of work as well as the occupational structure. Again, Daniel Bell was a key contributor to the debate, arguing that the information society is a recent expression of post-industrial society. In an article entitled "The social framework of the information society" (1980), he spelled out the parameters of an information society and how it rested on a *knowledge theory of value*. By this, he meant that knowledge has replaced (productive) labor as the source of value which yields future profits. One way to think about this is to see knowledge and its applications as *the* resource, one that has the potential to transform almost any kind of activity in an economy. If we take the example of information processing activities, then virtually every sector of the economy may be subject to its influence, from education to telecommunications through to the health services and the social benefits system. In this sense, information processing has the ability to radically alter familiar ways of doing things. Moreover, behind such a capacity lie the new information technologies, which it is argued have the potential to reshape the ways in which we produce and consume, as well as where we perform these activities.

Information in Bell's projection is regarded as more than a resource, however. It is also regarded as a commodity which can be bought and sold in the marketplace. For example, the commercialization of information has opened up a whole new sector of the modern economy, which includes anything from personalized "junk mail" and tradeable mailing lists to remote sensing systems capable of charting the planet's natural resources, or to satellite TV broadcasting. Little, it would seem, is left untouched by the new technologies, including the commodification of culture and the appearance of the "wired" home.

Overall, then, the image of the information society is one of a qualitative change in the nature of the western economies, with an ever-increasing proportion of the social structure consisting of professional and technical workers, many of whom are concerned with the production, processing, or distribution of information. Following Porat (1977), Bell argues that it is these *information occupations* which are now becoming increasingly important to the success of post-industrial economies and that the wider diffusion of information technologies will enhance this trend. Indeed, when you reach the final chapter of this volume, you will find that commentators such as Lyotard (1984) have argued that the transformation of knowledge and its effects in the current period represent the economic basis of an emergent post-modern age. The role of information, therefore, as both an economic resource and as a commodity, is central to arguments which may take us beyond the modern period. We shall return to this overarching question in section 2.2, but for the moment I want to remain with the discussion of the rise of the information society and to take it further by considering the more recent account offered by Manuel Castells.

There are principally two points to note. The first is that Castells – although keen to draw attention to the central importance of informational activities within western economies and the US in particular – is also anxious to distance himself from the concept of post-industrialism. The intention is not to reject or dismiss the analyses put forward by Bell and Touraine. On the contrary, it is to stress that an information-based society "is no more post-industrial than the industrial society was post-agrarian" (Castells, 1989, p. 367). It is important to Castells that the information society is not simply confused with a service society in which the manufacturing sector has all but disappeared from view. Like Bell and Touraine, he identifies the dynamic of the coming society as the role of knowledge and the use of information, not the predominance of any one particular sector of an economy.

The second point to note is that Castells is responding to earlier accounts of an emergent information society which tended to adopt a rather mechanistic stance towards the social impact of the new technologies. At worst, some of the more "futuristic" post-industrial writers spoke about changes in the nature of work and the occupational structure *as if* they were inscribed within the technologies themselves. Little sensitivity, if any, was displayed over the fact that societies mold their technologies and select their patterns of use, both within the workplace and beyond. For Castells, however, who draws his ideas from a Marxist tradition, technological change can only be understood in the context of the prevailing social relations of capitalism:

> [S]tructural trends, emerging and converging in a society largely dominated by the industrial mode of development, pave the way for the transformation of that mode, as information processing, with its core in knowledge generation, detracts from the importance of energy in material production, as well as from the importance of goods-producing in the overall social fabric. However, this transformation of the mode of development could not be accomplished without the surge of innovation in information technologies which, by creating the material basis from which information processing can expand its role, contributes to the change both in the structure of the production process and in the organization of society. It is in this sense that I hypothesize the formation of a new, informational mode of development: on the basis of the convergence through interaction of information technologies and information-processing activities into an articulated techno-organizational system.
> (Castells, 1989, pp. 28–32)

All economies, past and present, would in different ways acknowledge a role for technology and knowledge in shaping the way in which they organize their processes of production. What is novel about the information mode of development as outlined by Castells is that knowledge is used to generate new knowledge which itself acts as a catalyst for further economic development. Put another way, because information is both a raw material, a resource to be worked on, and the outcome of the process of production, a commodity in its own right, it is regarded as a central means of improving economic performance. It intensifies the process of economic innovation. Information, as noted at the beginning of this sub-section, can be used to transform a wide range of economic activities – as a technological process or as a product embodied in a variety of manufactured goods and services. Its centrality within the contemporary economy is regarded as crucial, especially as a considerable number of recent social and economic changes rest on this claim.

One of the more interesting changes identified by Castells is that the new technologies have enabled corporations, especially the large multinationals, to operate in new ways. First, the combined advances in communication technologies, systems of management, and technologies of production have provided corporations with the potential to operate in a more "footloose" fashion, while retaining their links with markets and production complexes. As you may recall from chapter 14, there is a sense here in which social distances and time are being "shrunk" or compressed. The second example is related and concerns the growth of multiple networks between corporations. These networks enable companies to develop products jointly or to serve specific markets, and thus represent a different economic strategy from the establishment of multinational "empires." And what both examples speak to is *power*, especially in relation to the kinds of labor employed by these large corporations. Among the changes that informationalism holds for today's workforce, Castells identifies the move towards a core–periphery model of the labor market, the concentration of "information power" among a knowledge elite in the corporations, and the automation of low-skilled jobs, especially among the unionized workforce in manufacturing. In other words, there is a marked trend towards the polarization and segmentation of the social structure.

Overall, then, many of the trends that Castells identifies do accord with earlier post-industrial themes. The focus on the activities of multinational corporations is different, but the priority accorded to knowledge and information as the driving forces of the coming society is there, as is the stress on technology. What is absent from the Castells's age of information, however, is the historical optimism present in some of the early post-industrial accounts.

*The divided society*   A related debate around the future shape of the post-industrial society is to be found in the work of André Gorz. In *Farewell to the Working Class* (1982), Gorz develops a set of arguments concerning the changing *role of work* in post-industrial economies. The strong claim advanced by Gorz is that the new technologies are altering the structure of employment within society, and that this has led to a social division between an "aristocracy" of secure, well-paid workers, on the one hand, and a growing mass of unemployed, on the other. In between, the majority of the population are said to belong to a post-industrial working class, for whom work no longer represents a source of identity or a meaningful activity. Automation at the workplace has created "jobless growth" and its rapid extension will, it is argued, progressively undermine the quality and status of the remaining working-class jobs. Work, in this scenario, thus becomes an instrumental activity for the majority, undertaken solely to earn a wage with little or no satisfaction or skill content attached.

Gorz's interpretation of the impact of the new technologies thus stresses a particular aspect of the post-industrial transition. It runs parallel to Castells's concerns about the growing segmentation of the workforce, but it is expressed in more social terms and without undue stress on the role of information as a dynamic which is shaping the social structure. A casualized and disorganized working class is in the foreground of his account, with a privileged minority akin to Bell's knowledge elite occupying the background locations. In a later text, *Critique of Economic Reason* (1989), Gorz intensifies this vision by referring to a society polarized between an emergent "servile" class and a securely employed, professional class:

> Certainly, the existence of a servile class is less obvious today than it was during the periods when the affluent classes employed a large number of domestic servants (according to British censuses – in which they were categorized as "domestic and personal servants" – the latter represented 14 per cent of the working population between 1851 and 1911). The difference is that nowadays these personal services are to a large extent socialized or industrialized: the majority of servants are employed by service enterprises which hire out labour (insecure, part-time employment; piece-work; and so on) which is then exploited by private individuals. But this does not alter the basic fact that these people are doing servants' work, that is, work which those who earn a decent living transfer, for their personal advantage and without gains in productivity, on to the people for whom there is no work in the economy.
> (Gorz, 1989, p. 7)

Gorz's reasoning is rather dense on this point, although it would appear that the advances in technology, far from enabling society as a whole to enjoy more free time, have resulted in an economic elite being able to purchase at low cost the services that they had previously been capable of doing for themselves. The commodification of domestic tasks, the incorporation of such tasks into the realm of economic rationality, has worked to the advantage of those who already have secure, well-paid employment. In the language of post-industrialism, work for the new "servile" class lacks any dignity that may have been associated with industrial tasks at the time of, say, mining and heavy manufacture. For Gorz, it would appear that the new service jobs not only lack economic rationality from the point of view of society as a whole, they are also not considered "real jobs' – whatever that may mean.

This line of argument thus stresses a growing social inequality as a marked feature of post-industrialism, and this places Gorz's account closer to that of Touraine's post-industrial vision and Castells's information age rather than to Bell's information society. In his later work, Gorz puts less theoretical weight upon the concept of post-industrialism, but it is apparent that the direction of economic and social change which he outlines represents an extension of his earlier speculations. It may also be useful to note that whereas both Touraine and Gorz wrote within a broad European context, Bell's account is US-centered, as is that of Castells. In many of the western economies, however, the arguments for post-industrialism still chime with the experience of many in work and out of work. And it is this resonance that gives the discourse of post-industrialism its coherence.

## 2.2   The post-industrial turn? An overview

Despite differences of emphasis and the range of aspects stressed among post-industrial writers, the arrival of post-industrialism can be signalled on a number of economic and social fronts. Above all, the writers seem to agree on one thing: that there has indeed been a shift away from industrialism. In broad terms, this movement can be identified with a shift in the balance of the western economies from a manufacturing to a service base, primarily in terms of employment, although it is often extended to include the output of an economy. However, not all of the writers that we have considered stress this aspect of the transition. Touraine and Gorz, for example, are less concerned than Bell to emphasize the changes that have taken place in the sectoral division of labor.

On the occupational and class fronts, it becomes harder to identify common post-industrial themes. At best, it could be said that Bell and Gorz focus on different aspects of the same transition. Where Bell sees the growth of white-collar occupations and the formation of knowledge elites, Gorz emphasizes the irrelevance of work to the majority and the fate of a deskilled working class forced to serve those elites. Where one offers the prospect of an end to harsh manual labor, the other holds out for a better world outside of, rather than within, work. Even so, it is evident that both Gorz and Castells see social and economic polarization as part of the general direction of change.

One of the main features of the post-industrial society, however, is not its simple lines of division, but rather the cross-cutting nature of the new social movements, as stressed by both Touraine and Castells. The impact of these movements is clearly meant to direct our attention beyond industrial forms of class politics, but it is an open question in the work of the three writers – Touraine, Castells, and Gorz – as to the nature of the relationship between the "old" and the "new" lines of conflict.

There *is*, nonetheless, complete agreement on one principal feature of the coming society among all the writers that we have discussed: namely, the central importance of knowledge and information in the transition, especially as a source of technological innovation. Information and its uses is regarded as a major resource, which has already begun to reshape activities in the manufacturing and state sectors as well as in private services such as finance and commerce. Strong claims have also been advanced for the importance of information technology as a "heartland technology'; that is, one capable of generating further innovations at the workplace and beyond. To convey the significance placed on this dynamic we need only to remind ourselves of the observation by Castells (noted in section 1.1) that information generation and processing is to office work what mass production was to craft-based manufacture – a radical shift in the

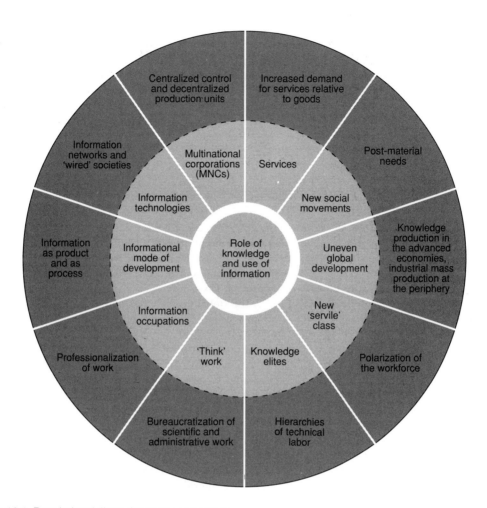

Figure 16.1 Post-industrialism: dynamics and trends

structure and organization of the economy. Figure 16.1 provides an impression of the post-industrial changes that could be involved in such a shift.

Of course, if valid, Castells's observation raises a further question as to what it is exactly that we are said to have gone beyond? We know that it is not capitalism, for instance. In the West, a competitive economic system based on the purchase and sale of commodities is still intact, as are the social relationships which underpin this system. But we also know that there *is* agreement over the passing of industrialism. If post-industrialism or informationalism is therefore a new phase of capitalism, have we then also moved beyond the *modern* economy and its associated ideas of progress? If mass manufacture and mass markets may be regarded as the height of modern industrial progress, how should we then regard the dynamic of information and the emergence of a more divided society? Should we consider these characteristics as a new *form* of economic modernity, or as something that takes us beyond the modern economic era, as Lyotard suggests in his post-modern argument outlined in chapter 19?

Section 5 will place this question in the context of the global economy and the uneven development of modern societies (and it will resurface in a discussion of Frederic Jameson's (1984) views on late capitalism and post-modernity in the following chapter). Before that, we turn our attention to an alternative account of the direction of economic change – post-Fordism.

# 3   From Fordism to Post-Fordism

Although it is claimed that the first signs of the decline of Fordism as an industrial era were apparent in the late 1960s and early 1970s, at about the time when a post-industrial society was also said to be emerging, the directions of change sketched within the two transitions and the debates surrounding them have taken rather different routes. At the risk of caricature, if the debate over what comes after industrialism focused on the rise of services and the role of information, the debate over the end of Fordism has largely concerned itself with what kind of manufacturing and product demand has replaced that of mass production and mass markets. With the shift to post-Fordism a new kind of economic era is said to have opened up: one based, as was noted in the chapter introduction, on flexible forms of economic organization and production, along with a more pluralistic set of lifestyles.

Earlier we referred to mass production as a twentieth-century *form* of industrialism. It is useful to bear this periodization in mind as a means of locating the two debates. Post-Fordist manufacture does not signal the end of industrialism, it is merely regarded as a more recent form of industry. For some writers, however, post-Fordism has taken on a wider set of meanings, as the economic basis for a post-modern culture. This section is primarily concerned with the economic implications of what is said to come after Fordism, although certain political and cultural considerations will be indispensable to the analysis.

## 3.1   The regulationist context

Before we explore the different pathways out of Fordism, we need to have a broad sense of what Fordism as an industrial era looks like. (As noted in the introduction to this chapter, you will find a full discussion of the concept of "Fordism" in chapter 8.)

A sketch of the structures specific to Fordism might include the following characteristics:

- The combination of standardized parts, special-purpose machinery, the fragmentation of labor skills, and the moving assembly line.

- Economies of scale reaped through large-scale mass production. (Although this entailed high fixed costs in plant and machinery, the sheer volume of production reduced the cost per car as output rose.)

- Long runs of standardized goods linked to a system of protected national markets.

- A concentration of highly paid, semi-skilled "mass workers" in large factories.

- A hierarchical, bureaucratic form of work organization, characterized by a centralized management.

- State management of the national economy through a range of "Keynesian" policies which regulated levels of income, demand, and welfare.

- And finally, and most importantly, the link between mass production and mass consumption that enabled the whole process to reproduce itself.

There is certainly more to this vision than the simple idea that the economy has, in some way, been transformed into something that resembles a giant car plant. In fact, it was Antonio Gramsci, an Italian Marxist writing in the early 1930s, who first used the term "Fordism," to refer to a new industrial lifestyle based on the "American way." As an industrial era, however, Fordism is primarily a post-war affair, and it was not until the 1970s that the first attempt to systematically construct a "history" around the concept of Fordism appeared. Michel Aglietta, a member of what is known as the French regulationist school, published his account of Fordism in 1976, and it appeared in English in 1979 under the title *A Theory of Capitalist Regulation: The US Experience.*

In this text, on the basis of evidence drawn from the US economy, Aglietta outlined the structure of Fordism and also pointed to its coming crisis. At that time, in the 1970s, a state of economic uncertainty was evident across the western economies as a slow-down in productivity and declining profitability, which had appeared first in the US in the late 1960s, spread across the other industrial economies, notably those of Europe. Compounded by the "oil shock" of 1973, which led to a dramatic increase in energy costs in the western nations, the long post-war boom which had lent credibility to the notion of Fordism as an industrial *era* appeared to be at an end. In a moment, we shall take a closer look at the nature of this economic crisis and the *limits* to Fordism. First, however, it would be helpful to say a little more about the regulationist approach.

Let me sketch the background. There is a variety of schools which talk about economic regulation, but the Parisian school, of which Aglietta is a central figure, is probably the best known. What is distinctive about the Parisian school, or for that matter all regulationist approaches, as their title suggests, is a concern with the regulation of the economy. This may sound a rather ordinary concern, yet in the context of much economic theory it is unusual in two respects. First, regulationists assume that the frequent disruptions and recurrent crises that an economy is subject to owe little to the "hidden hand" of the competitive market for their resolution. There is no short- or long-term tendency towards equilibrium in the market-place. Secondly, and relatedly, they recognize a role for political and cultural relations in attempts to regulate the instability of advanced economies. In particular, this approach stresses the role of *institutions*, such as the state, in attempting to balance the patterns of production and social demand. The pattern of accumulation and growth in the advanced economies is thus secured as much by *social* regulation as it is by economic regulation. What marks out the Parisian regulationist school, however, is its characterization of the processes of growth and accumulation.

Periods of growth and decline in the advanced economies are understood through two key concepts, *a regime of accumulation* and *a mode of regulation. Regimes of accumulation* are periods of growth characterized by whatever it is that ensures a compatibility between what is produced and what is consumed in an economy. Under a Fordist regime of accumulation, for example, production and consumption, as we have seen, are both characterized by mass standards. Production involves large batch, standardized runs (of cars, fridges, washing machines, and the like) that offer rapid productivity gains which, in turn, feed through to workers' incomes and the formation of mass markets. The *wage relation* is regarded as critical, as it influences levels of productivity and the share of profits accruing to industry, as well as shaping the overall level of employment. The wage relation connects the sphere of production with the sphere of consumption, and it is this connection which is said to give a regime of accumulation its distinctive shape. Moreover, it is this connection which enables the multitude of firms to make their investment and production decisions in the knowledge that the markets will not dramatically change in the foreseeable future. Equally significant, however, is the *labor process*: the tasks that workers perform and the technologies that they use. It is this aspect of production which provides the initial boost in productivity that gets a regime underway. So, for instance, under Fordism, it would have been the mass technologies and the highly specialized, semi-skilled, and unskilled workforce which exhibited the most dynamic forms of organization.

*A mode of regulation* is of a rather different order and, for want of a better way of expressing it, it functions as a support framework for growth regimes. It pulls together and directs the wide variety of actions taken by firms, banks, retailers, workers, state employees, and the like, into some kind of regulated network. In other words, it enables a particular regime of accumulation to develop in a particular direction in a more or less stable manner. How this process of regulation occurs is itself complex, although the support framework does include a whole host of cultural styles and political practices, ranging from popular aspirations and social expectations to the more formal interventions of the state, such as the politics of "Keynesianism." Under Fordism, for instance, an institutionalized expectation of stable growth, rising consumption levels, and increased social welfare, were said to have made up the "social cement" of the regime. Thus, even something as basic as the largely unquestioned acceptance of full-time factory work (among men) helped to ensure the stability of the regime. Indeed, it could be asserted that it is the mode of regulation that "holds together" a particular industrial era, albeit in different ways in different countries.

It is important to note, therefore, that any national economy, whether it is that of the US, France, Japan, Germany, or the UK, will find its own "route" through Fordism. A nation's past history, its cultural and political peculiarities, and the nature of its connections with the global economy, all combine to produce a *national mode of growth*. Thus, for example, it is generally assumed that the post-war productivity levels achieved in the UK were never comparable to those achieved under conditions of mass production in the US. In contrast, the welfare benefits system in the UK offered a more developed form of state regulation than in the US. This kind of uneven development is regarded as a common characteristic across national economies.

Having said that, the broad concept of Fordism *is* taken to encompass post-war developments across the advanced economies. In regulationist terms, these developments represent a distinctive period of economic growth in which a certain regime of accumulation *came together* with a supportive mode of regulation. By the early 1970s, however, as we have noted, the cohesion between the two was showing signs of fracture.

Crises are regarded by regulationists as an endemic feature of capitalist economies, although not all economic crises are of the same magnitude. Some offer an opportunity to bring an economy back into balance, while others are regarded as more fundamental; that is, as representing a threat to the basic structure of an economy. In such cases, the whole process of regulation starts to break down and with it the dynamic of capital accumulation.

It is possible to trace the structural crisis of Fordism to a number of factors, although disagreement exists over their relative significance. (See Boyer, 1990, for a comprehensive account of the structural crisis of Fordism.) However, two factors are widely regarded as key to the crisis. The first is rooted in the Fordist labor process and concerns the inability of mass production methods to realize further productivity gains within manufacturing, as well as their limited applicability to areas of the economy such as services. On this view, the *limits* of Fordism had been reached, both in a technical sense and in relation to a mass collective workforce whose resistance to the dull, repetitive rhythms of work had peaked. From a technical standpoint, increasing returns to scale from ever larger mass production complexes were said to have been frustrated by the difficulties experienced in balancing what is produced with what is in demand at any one point in time. Fluctuation in the pace of demand, shifting patterns of taste, delays in re-starting the line, and the time taken to re-tool machinery, all contributed towards a trend of declining productivity. And from the point of view of labor, the excessive bureaucratization of control, coupled with the tedium of work, had led to increased absenteeism and strife among the workforce. The very characteristics, therefore, which had once contributed to the success of the Fordist regime were now blocking the accumulation process.

The second factor is located at the international level. In essence, it concerns a shift in the post-war pattern of global demand. This, it is argued, occurred partly in response to the steady erosion of the US dollar as an international regulatory currency. As strong economies such as Japan and Germany challenged the hegemony of the US in the world economic order, the impact of increased competitiveness fuelled global instability and enhanced the prospect of international recession. Another related consequence of increased internationalization was the breakdown of oligopolistic pricing methods within national markets. The overall result was further disruption in the post-war economic momentum.

Thus, within the spheres of both production and consumption, the national and international dynamics that had sustained Fordist economic growth were, on this view, beginning to crack, and with them the forms of social regulation that supported the regime. If correct, therefore, the coming era may actually hold the prospect of a resolution to the crisis of Fordism. Broadly speaking, the nature of this resolution has been sketched in two ways – a neo-Fordist resolution and a post-Fordist resolution. We can distinguish them insofar as the first scenario represents an *extension* to the Fordist era, whereas the latter scenario represents a *break* with Fordism. We shall consider each resolution in turn.

*Neo-Fordism*    As there is nothing certain about the emergence of a new link between production and consumption, nor anything automatic about the rise of a mode of regulation compatible with it, the Parisian regulationists, and Aglietta in particular, are cautious about naming a successor to Fordism. In general, they have spoken about developments on two economic fronts which may possibly transcend the limits to Fordism. The first points to a transformation of the labor process, and the second draws attention to the global shifts in the organization of production.

Changes in the labor process which, in themselves, offer a partial resolution to the crisis of Fordism in the western economies include both increased automation at the workplace and the introduction of new working practices. Technological innovations such as computer-numerically controlled and computer-integrated manufacturing systems are held to signify the direction of economic change. Such systems, it is argued, lead to an overall reduction in the amount of labor required, a shift in control away from machine operators to skilled technicians, and, above all, a greater *flexibility* in production scale without incurring further substantial costs. The ability to switch from mass production to small-batch production is held to be one of the key features of this technology. Moreover, this kind of flexible technology finds its counterpart in the formation of flexible work groups and social innovations such as "quality circles." Taken together, the new technologies and the new work practices within manufacturing hold out the prospect of a new lease of life for Fordism – and not only within the western economies.

One of the implications of the new production technologies is that a greater decentralization of production is possible. The centralization of managerial control, combined with the Fordist break-up of the labor process into discrete elements, has enabled larger firms to move parts of their production processes to peripheral locations. At first, this movement of capital took place within the advanced economies, although by the 1970s it included less developed countries such as Hong Kong, Taiwan, Singapore, South Korea, and Brazil. This movement of production did not represent a break with Fordism, however. On the contrary, the search for new locations was based on a quest for new mass markets and attempts to maintain productivity levels by tapping available pools of unskilled, cheap labor. According to Lipietz (1987), the spread of Fordism across the globe, albeit in an uneven and partial manner, represents an attempt to overcome the crisis of Fordism at the "center" – that is, in the western economies.

In fact, the "center/periphery" distinction offers a useful way of summarizing the directions of change that neo-Fordism represents. In the central or core western economies, new technologies are said to be creating a polarization of the workforce that is not dissimilar to Gorz's projection. So while a highly skilled, technical elite amasses the advantages gained from increased automation, the majority are either deskilled or unemployed. Meanwhile, at the global periphery, routinized, labor-intensive methods of production predominate. The latter should not be read as an entirely negative scenario, however, as this type of production has created the possibility for economic advance among the newly industrializing countries (witness the Asian economies, for example).

The neo-Fordist scenario is nonetheless a cautious vision; one based on the centrality of the labor process in the movement from one regime of accumulation to another. As neo-Fordists move beyond the labor process to consider the cultural and political dimensions of the mode of regulation, their vision tends to become somewhat blurred.

*Post-Fordism* Post-Fordism, as noted above, represents a movement *beyond* Fordism. It signifies a qualitative shift in the organization of production and consumption, as well as a break in the mode of regulation. As a thesis, however, post-Fordism is not generally associated with the French regulationist school, although the framework of meaning that informs the thesis clearly binds it to the theoretical stance adopted by the French regulationists.

In the arena of production, it is possible to note a number of features which post-Fordism shares with neo-Fordism. The role of *flexible manufacturing systems* with their ability to switch from economies of scale (mass) to economies of scope (batch) is an important shared feature, and so too is the introduction of new ways of organizing work to improve product quality. In both cases, however, there is a further twist to the post-Fordist characterization. Where neo-Fordists tend to associate the new technologies with job deskilling and an increased centralization of managerial control, post-Fordists, while recognizing this prospect, point to a more positive side of the technologies. Alongside job deskilling, the new technologies are also seen as creating opportunities for enskilling and reskilling. Moreover, they are said to hold out the prospect of a multi-skilled labor force operating in a less hierarchical work environment.

Robin Murray highlights a series of production changes less often considered by neo-Fordists (Murray, 1989). Across the sectors there have been changes in product life and product innovation, with shorter, flexible runs and a wider range of products on offer; changes in stock control, with just-in-time methods removing the need to hold large amounts of costly stock; and changes in design and marketing in response to an increasingly diverse pattern of consumer demand. It is also interesting to note that services occupy an important "lead role" for Murray, especially retail services. It is doubtful, however, that the retail sector could match the propulsive role performed by the consumer goods industries in the Fordist era.

Turning to consumption, Murray sees a firm link to the changes in the way that goods and services are produced. With the emphasis on niche markets, segmented markets, and rapidly changing consumer tastes, he notes that cultural expectations and aspirations are in the process of shifting from standardized (Fordist) styles towards a greater acceptance of difference and plurality within the West. Naturally, it is difficult to gauge the extent of such a trend, but we should remind ourselves that we are concerned with *directions* of change, rather than any complete set of practices.

Similarly, at the national political level Murray points to the displacement of Keynesianism by a more strident neo-liberal economic strategy; that is, one based upon the economic rationality of the private market. Elsewhere, Jessop (with others, 1988 and 1990) has written about the significance of a neo-liberal strategy for the development of a post-Fordist route out of the economic uncertainty of the 1970s in the UK. In this strategy, we see the outline of an attempt to mobilize certain key social groups within the class structure around a direction of change secured by the competitiveness and morality of the market-place. However, Jessop and Murray are too aware of the contrasts in political strategies across Europe, the US, and Japan in the 1980s to be able to draw general conclusions about the regulatory structures which would support and direct a more flexible regime of accumulation.

Taken as a whole, then, Murray's approach has much in common with the regulationists, insofar as he is trying to think through the connections between the dynamics of accumulation and their social coordination, as well as how the relationships between classes enter into the formation of renewed stability between production and consumption. In terms of substance too, there are shared concerns with another writer who works loosely within a regulationist framework. David Harvey's ideas concerning the complex mix of forces which are said to have led to an altered rhythm and an acceleration in the pace of modern economic life were discussed in chapter 14. In *The Condition of Postmodernity* (1989), the argument that the pace of economic life has quickened dramatically since the 1960s is linked closely by Harvey to the dynamics of a more flexible regime of accumulation. Alongside the by-now-familiar developments in flexible workplace technologies, "flat" organizational structures, increased cooperation and coordination between companies, and diverse consumer markets, we also find knowledge and information playing an important part in the speed-up of market trading and in coordinating responses to the volatility of global demand. What is distinctive about Harvey's view of the new flexible regime, however, is that he traces many of these developments to what has been happening in the sphere of modern *finance*.

Where others locate the dynamic of the new regime within the flexible modes of production and consumption, Harvey locates it in the emergence of new financial systems. He argues that, since the 1970s, the banking and the financial system has achieved a degree of autonomy relative to industrial production which carries with it the ability to create havoc with the stability of material production as well as to overcome the rigidities of Fordist-type production and consumption. The formation of new financial markets, the introduction of new financial instruments, the opening up of new systems of global coordination between financial centers, have, according to Harvey, carried capitalism into a new era in which the rapidity and scale of capital flows make it more difficult for nation-states to secure stable accumulation strategies. At the same time, innovation within financial systems has enabled companies, governments, and consumers to adopt more flexible strategies towards the "blockages" of Fordism. It is in this sense that the emergence of a flexible regime of accumulation can be understood as *one* type of response to the transformation of the global financial system.

## 3.2 After Fordism? An overview

As with post-industrialism, it is possible to identify a number of economic and social fronts which take us beyond Fordist mass production and mass consumption. How far beyond is a rather moot question, although all commentators do agree that Fordism, however conceived, is in crisis. Moreover, attempts to overcome this crisis suggest a wider use of flexible production techniques and the promotion of flexible patterns of work organization. Both neo-Fordists, such as Aglietta, and post-Fordists, such as Murray, stress the significance of greater flexibility in the organization of production. Harvey would also agree on this aspect.

At a more detailed level, however, there is less agreement over the kinds of flexibility that are actually taking place within the sphere of production and, indeed, their extent. Aglietta offers a specific account of flexible automation related to changes in the labor process, whereas Murray, in addition, entertains a notion of flexibility around supply networks, product runs, job demarcation boundaries, labor market practices, stock control, and the like. Perhaps more importantly, there is an undercurrent in Murray's account that all the changes underway offer a potentially progressive mode of development, whereas the pitch

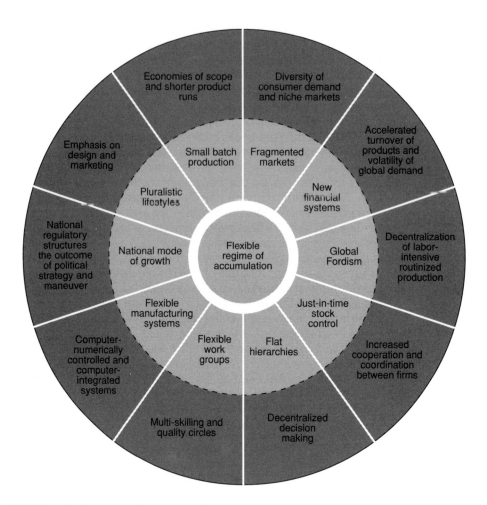

Figure 16.2 After Fordism: dynamics and trends

in Aglietta's account is generally regressive – for the majority of working people at least.

However, the sharpest expression of difference between neo-Fordist and post-Fordist accounts is found in their respective interpretations of the end of Fordism. Neo-Fordism represents an *adjustment* to the problems of Fordism, a way forward that extends the period of Fordism. In contrast, post-Fordism represents a qualitatively new economic direction, a *step beyond* Fordism. As such, post-Fordism signals a new *era*, in much the same way that Castells spoke about an information *age*. This can be gleaned from the breadth of the post-Fordist scenario which attempts to outline the kinds of social regulation that may support the rise of a new flexible regime. It would, however, be an exaggeration to claim that either Murray or Harvey had adequately sketched the lines of a new mode of regulation.

At the global level there is perhaps more rather than less that neo-Fordism and post-Fordism hold in common. Lipietz, above all, has drawn attention to the rise of "global Fordism"; that is, the spread of labor-intensive, routinized production across the globe in response to crisis conditions in the "core," western economies. Interestingly, this is said to be happening alongside the decline of "core" economies such as that of the UK, and the growth of post-Fordist-type regimes in Japan and Germany. And in Harvey too, there is the similar notion of different work regimes existing alongside one another, both within countries and between countries. What happens after Fordism therefore may involve a mix of regimes rather than the straightforward replacement of one mode of development by another.

There is, however, complete agreement over the passing of Fordism, conceived, that is, as a dynamic of mass manufacture and mass markets. Figure 16.2 provides an impression of what could replace it, if a number of trends were combined.

On the question of economic modernity, it is harder to discern the common ground. Certainly, all would agree that it is capitalism and its drive for profitability which gives modernity its restless, ceaseless quality. Today, however, it is this very same quality, speeded up, as it were, which according to Harvey represents the economic basis of post-modernism. By this, I take him to mean more than flexibility at the workplace. The economic basis also comprises the rapidity of capital flows, the accelerated turnover of products and consumer tastes, the speed up of communications, and, more generally, a sharp increase in the pace of economic life. Murray too refers to the quickening consumption of images in the "postmodern market place," although the lines of post-modernism do not *form* a central part of his analysis. (In the following chapter, Jameson's (1984) account of post-modernism as the cultural logic of late capitalism is explored at length.)

For Aglietta and the Parisian regulationist school, Fordism may well have represented one of the peaks of modernist progress in terms of its scale and pattern of growth, but it is not altogether certain that they would regard a movement beyond this era as involving anything other than a new *form* of economic modernity.

# 4   Assessing Economic Transitions

Assuming that you now have a broad sense of the kinds of economic transformation which are said to be underway in the major western economies, we need to turn our attention to the question of assessment. How do we decide just how far the industrial economies have changed? What are the right questions to ask? This section examines the strengths and weaknesses of the post-industrial and post-Fordist transitions through a consideration of the *scope* and the *pace* of the different developments. It will look at the role of empirical *evidence*, as well as providing an assessment of the *theoretical* strengths of the arguments. The section is thus not so much a debate between possible lines of development, as an assessment of what each argument has to offer. It will ask how successful the claims are in providing us with a sense of what is happening around us and the direction of economic change that we face.

## 4.1   The scope of change

The tentative nature of change in a period of transition, as noted in the chapter introduction, leaves us with little choice over the starting point of our assessment. We have to begin with the directions of change suggested by post-industrialism, post-Fordism, and neo-Fordism, for that is all that is available. This will involve more than an exercise in measuring the extent of empirical change, however. A wide assortment of potentially disparate changes, for example, do not add up to a shift in the overall direction of an economy. To assess, say, the direction in which neo-Fordism is pointing we need to identify the *kinds* of change involved, trace the *connections* between them, and then make a *judgment* about which of the changes, if any, are the more robust or decisive. Merely to list the empirical changes or to refer to their magnitude would not settle the issue, as the significance of such trends is essentially a theoretical question.

Consider the example of post-industrialism, which in Bell's hands *connects* the shift in the balance of employment from manufacturing to services, to the shift from blue-collar to white-collar professional work, to the shift in demand from goods to services, to the shift from an economy organized around raw materials and machinery to one organized around knowledge and information technology. Now, in my view, these substantive claims have a certain strength which stems from the actual sequence of connections drawn rather than from any one set of changes. Even though we should not anticipate complete agreement among post-industrial writers about the relative significance of these shifts, few are likely to dispute the sequence of connections drawn. Yet it would be premature to acknowledge the strength of the post-industrial claims.

Before doing so, we would need to satisfy ourselves on three counts.

1   In the first place, we would need to know whether the sequence of connections drawn by Bell and others is correct.

Consider, for example, the firm link drawn by Bell between the growth in service employment and an increase in the demand for services across the major western economies. This link has been challenged on the grounds that service workers are not only employed in the service sector; they are also directly employed in the manufacture and sale of goods (as clerks, accountants, designers, sales people, and the like). Thus, a boost in manufacturing growth is just as likely to lead to a rise in service employment as is an increase in the demand for service products (see Gershuny, 1978). We need to be alert therefore to a mis-specification of connections between changes that are taking place on a number of fronts. The causal chain of the argument may, on closer inspection, turn out to be illusory. The exact same kind of concern may be addressed to the connections drawn by post-Fordists between flexibility in manufacturing systems, product markets, and work organization, on the one hand, and the new institutional forms that comprise a mode of regulation on the other (see Rustin, 1989). Such links, if present, will naturally vary between nations, but in each mode of national growth it is important to trace the emergent patterns of regulation and their relation to processes of economic accumulation.

2   Secondly, we would need to know how widespread are the changes. Are the shifts as well-developed as some writers would have us believe?

Consider the types of flexibility we have spoken about above. How widespread, for instance, is the use of the new computer technologies within manufacturing? Are product markets fragmenting to the extent that Murray and others have indicated? And what of the new patterns of work organization – how pervasive is the influence of multi-skilling, flexible work groups, and of "quality circles"? Wood (1989), among others, remains skeptical, for instance, over the extensive adoption of each of these aspects. It is not evident, for example, why the advance of flexibility in one area should be followed by advances in other areas. Market diversification, for example, can be met by the assembly of different products from production runs organized along mass production lines (see Sayer, 1989). The real issue with these developments, however, as it is with the introduction of information technologies, is not the number of cases which can be cited across the industrial economies, but whether such innovations can sustain a new kind of economy. Even if we had extensive empirical data on these developments (which is unlikely as we are discussing *emergent* trends), such data would not amount to a *decisive* answer in favor of or against a movement towards a new kind of economy.

3   Our final concern is that we would need to know the geographical scope of the developments.

Take the example of Bell's post-industrial vision. It is strictly a vision of the First World which, interestingly, has its counterpart in a shift to industrialism in the Third World. In *The Coming of Post-Industrial Society*, Bell speaks of a geographical divide between knowledge-production and mass production, with the latter increasingly taking place outside of the advanced economies. However, a more explicit account of this global division of labor is to be found in the work of Lipietz. As we have seen, while neo-Fordism is said to have taken hold in the West, more "primitive" forms of Fordism, shed of their social welfare element, co-exist in less developed economies. Thus, in both Bell's post-industrialism and in Lipietz's neo-Fordism, it is apparent that what is happening in the West is certainly changing the lives of people elsewhere.

This view of global connections is also central to Castells' and Harvey's assessments of uneven global development. Castells argues that, in the coming information age, the internationalization of the economic order is being reconstructed through advances in information technology. Power and knowledge rest with an international, professional elite which controls the networks of information through which the global reorganization of production and markets is taking

place. For Harvey, it is nothing less than the accelerated speed-up of
capitalism which is making the world smaller, so to speak, as the "old
idea" of the "West and the Rest" breaks down under the impact of the
interpenetration of economies and cultures (see chapter 14).

Clearly there are many examples of such global connections.
Whether the dynamics which lie behind these connections are
sufficiently robust to support the scope of these claims begs a further
issue however – that of *economic dominance.*

*Structural reach*   By *economic dominance,* I mean that some changes
are considered more fundamental than others, more central to the
direction of an economy and events beyond. These are the dynamics
which drive change. We have encountered a variety of such dynamics:
the propulsive effects of the Fordist industries of mass production;
Bell's view of knowledge as the "principle" or driving force of a post-
industrial economy; similarly, the importance attached by Castells to
the catalytic role of information in an economy; the stress placed upon
the new flexible sectors of the economy by post-Fordists; and the
speed-up of capital circulation identified by Harvey, which gives causal
weight to the new financial systems.

In each of these cases a dominant influence is identified which may
manifest itself in one of two ways (see chapter 8 for a discussion of
economic dominance). Either the influence will be *extensive* (that is,
something like information technologies or flexible working
arrangements will spread widely across an economy), or the influence
will be *structural* (this implies that such dynamics have a *reach* across
an economy which is not matched by their widespread adoption within
an economy). So, for example, it could be argued that Fordist mass
production techniques were structurally dominant in the post-war
period because of their ability to generate and transmit growth to other
parts of the economy. This did not mean, however, that the whole
economy had been turned over to the mass production of consumer
durables.

## 4.2   The pace and tempo of change

This represents the second part of our assessment of economic
transitions. Even though we may feel confident about the direction and
scope of change, we may still overemphasize its long-term significance.
Leaving to one side the fact that there are always continuities present
in any period of transition, the pace and tempo of change is often left
unstated in assessments of economic change. The price paid for this
neglect is a loss of any notion of *historical time.*

Following Braudel (1972), we can distinguish between different sorts
of historical time. There are rapid, critical periods of time, of the kind
talked about by Castells, where sharp bursts of technological change are
followed by phases of consolidation as a variety of industries adapt to
the new information practices. A similar irregular and disruptive note
of change is present in Gorz's descriptions of how industries and

occupations contract, expand, or disappear. There are periods of medium duration, of up to half a century, which may also experience a disruptive tempo as the groundwork for a transition is laid down. Post-Fordism, for example, would fit into this medium time period, with the last twenty or so years representing the initial phase of development. There are also periods of long-term change, in which time unfolds in a more gradual manner. Post-industrialists, or rather, early post-industrial accounts, tend to emphasize this conception of historical time. On this view, economies are considered to evolve in a particular sequence, with the most developed economies, those that are knowledge-based, setting out the path of development that others are likely to follow. If this were so, then in the present period the US or Japan would be seen as the "lead" role model. In more recent versions of post-industrialism, however, this cumulative account of change is played down and the contingent character of transitions emphasized. Finally, there are other sorts of historical time, such as the "explosive event" that precipitates a war or political upheaval, but our concerns here are mainly with the long term and the medium term.

One of the advantages of thinking about time in these ways, as you may have already realized, is that it enables us to *periodize* the claims of the different versions of change. This is helpful in two ways.

1   The periodization of change provides a temporal yardstick by which we can gauge the length and form of any transition.

Commentators, for example, are often quick to point out that suggested developments have not in fact taken place. But if we know the pace and tempo of the projected changes, and their likely duration, then this may help us to weigh up such comments.

Consider, once again, the post-industrial views of Bell, which date back to 1973. Some of the developments he described concerning the potential impact of information-based activities on the social structure of a modern economy were strongly criticized at the time for their sweeping nature. It is quite possible, however, that we are only now in a position to see the consequences of the information society across a range of economies. Certainly, Castells is of this view. Alternatively, we may still have some time to wait before the significance of information as an economic dynamic is felt.

2   The periodization of change also offers a further check on the range of trends which suggest a potential economic direction.

Are some of the trends identified cyclical or short-term, perhaps in response to economic recession or recent political developments? Have we been misled by an awkward combination of the familiar and the new? The trend towards the fragmentation of consumer tastes and the significance of niche markets in the current period, for example, is one broad phenomenon that has received skeptical support as a permanent feature of a new economic order. For some, it may well be a short-term response to the economic crisis that started in the 1970s, or simply the temporary outcome of the current pattern of income distribution. It may even be the combined result of the two. Similarly, Harvey's stress on the accelerated pace of capitalism and the dominance of finance over industrial production may also represent a misreading of the global situation. Gordon (1988), for example, has argued that the recent volatility of financial markets and flows may also be understood as *part of* the contemporary economic crisis, and not as a sign of a new global order opening up before us.

In considering potentially far-reaching changes, therefore, the periodization of change also draws attention to some of the pitfalls that accompany the task of theorizing economic change.

# 5  Conclusion: Beyond the Modern Economy?

The long rise of the modern economy, dating back to its commercial and agrarian roots in the eighteenth century and culminating in the recent phase of mass industry, represents the historical backdrop to the arguments set out in this chapter (see chapters 3 and 8 for a discussion of these respective economic "moments"). That we are witnessing a transformation of the present structure of modern western economies is, I would have thought, not in doubt. As we have seen, however, there is considerable disagreement over the direction, scope, and pace of change. Equally, there is much dispute over whether the baggage of concepts associated with industrialism, and with Fordism and mass production, can serve to explain what is happening to economic life in the West and beyond.

We have considered some of the strongest claims concerning a coming economic era; namely, those of post-industrialism and post-Fordism (and relatedly neo-Fordism). We noted that the path of development in each of the two scenarios had a different starting point and a different trajectory, as well as being driven by a particular kind of dynamic. For the post-industrialists, it is the dynamic of information and knowledge which is taking us beyond the industrial era and into a world of services centered on information technologies and networked offices. For those who would move us beyond Fordism and mass production, it is the dynamic of flexibility which is taking us towards a more pluralistic, less bureaucratic, more decentralized mode of economic life. However, it is also of interest to note the points at which the lines of direction in the two scenarios intersect. There are at least three areas of common concern which are worth specifying.

The *first* shared concern is that of knowledge and the development of new technologies. Both post-industrial and post-Fordist accounts stress the role of knowledge and innovation in the organization of production, and the rise of "lead" industries based on breakthroughs in microelectronic and information technologies. The emphasis placed on these technologies differs somewhat, as do the consequences derived for society, but, nonetheless, knowledge as an asset appears to lie behind both post-industrial and flexible futures. Furthermore, it could be argued, following Giddens (1990), that such technological settings, rather than taking us beyond industrialism, represent a new *form* of industry; albeit one that is powered by electricity rather than by coal or steam, and where microcircuit-based machinery organizes the nature and the pace of work. On this view, Castells's observation that the new technologies represent some kind of shift in the economy on a par with the shift from craft to mass manufacture points to a *continuation* of the modern economic era rather than a move beyond it. What is perhaps more difficult to think through, however, is how all of this meshes with our notions of modern economic progress – ideas that are based on mass manufacturing and mass standards.

The *second* area of common concern is revealing in this context. In both post-industrial and post-Fordist accounts, there is a tendency towards greater, not less, economic and social inequality. It is a world of professional elites and multi-skilled workers, on the one hand, and a class of service workers, often employed on a casual or part-time basis, on the other. And far from being an accident of economic development, this segmentation or polarization of the social structure appears to be a *structural* tendency of the new economic order. Low-paid, insecure service work represents the down side of both post-industrial and post-Fordist forms of growth. And in both scenarios it is women who are disproportionately concentrated in this kind of "servile" work, to use Gorz's term. We can read this tendency towards greater inequality in one of two ways, however. We can regard it as a sign of the limits to modern progress, or we can interpret it as yet another illustration of the "double-sided" character of modernity – with women comprising most of the new "servicing" class.

Finally, the *third* area of common concern is one that perhaps raises the sharpest questions over the character of modern economic life, namely, its globalization. Despite, for example, a difference of emphasis and description in the accounts of Castells and Harvey, both point to aspects of the modern global order which are, in their view, undergoing fundamental change. As noted in chapter 14, and intimated earlier in this chapter, the accelerated pace of modern life, the "shrinking" of space, and the extent to which the fortunes of people in diverse places across the globe are increasingly interconnected and interwoven have all called into question our ability to think of modern progress in terms of *national* economic progress, and also in terms of developed and less developed *national* economies. There are two aspects to mull over here.

In the first place, there is the presence of "backward" enclaves *within* the economies of the First World cities. Alongside the financial and commercial practices of New York and London, for example, we find the sweat shops and outworking practices that are more often associated with Third World economies. Yet they are not opposing developments; nor are they unrelated. There is no simple equation of finance with post-industrialism and the informal economic practices often undertaken by a migrant workforce with pre-industrialism. On the contrary, they are part and parcel of the same global economic forces which are eroding the identity of the West, as the "Rest," as it were, move to the centers of the modern world. Chapter 18 explores this issue of cultural identity in greater depth.

The second aspect raises a question mark over the very idea that it is possible to discern a dominant direction of economic change within a modern economy. After all, if national economies are increasingly becoming "sites" across which international forces flow, with some parts of a country passed over by the new growth dynamics, then the new uneven global order will very likely be characterized by *more* than one line of economic direction within and between countries. The idea that a single dominant economic dynamic, such as information or flexible manufacturing, is capable of transforming much of the world economy may therefore represent the thinking of a *modern discourse* whose economic moment has now passed.

# References

Aglietta, M. (1979) *A Theory of Capitalist Regulation: The US Experience*, London, Verso.

Bell, D. (1973) *The Coming of Post-Industrial Society*, New York, Basic Books.

Bell, D. (1976) *The Cultural Contradictions of Capitalism*, New York, Basic Books.

Bell, D. (1980) "The social framework of the information society," in Forester, T. (ed.) *The Microelectronics Revolution*, Oxford, Basil Blackwell.

Boyer, R. (1990) *The Regulation School: A Critical Introduction*, New York, Columbia University Press.

Braudel, F. (1972) "History and the social sciences," in Burke, P. (ed.) *Economy and Society in Early Modern Europe*, London, Routledge and Kegan Paul.

Castells, M. (1989) *The Informational City*, Oxford, Basil Blackwell.

Gershuny, J.I. (1978) *After Industrial Society? Emerging Self-Service Economy*, London and Basingstoke, Macmillan.

Giddens, A. (1990) *The Consequences of Modernity*, Cambridge, England, Polity Press.

Gordon, D. (1988) "The global economy: new edifice or crumbling foundations?," *New Left Review*, no. 168, pp. 24–65.

Gorz, A. (1982) *Farewell to the Working Class: An Essay on Post-Industrial Socialism*, London, Pluto.

Gorz, A. (1989) *Critique of Economic Reason*, London, Verso.

Harvey, D. (1989) *The Condition of Postmodernity*, Oxford, Basil Blackwell.

Jameson, F. (1984) "Postmodernism, or the cultural logic of late capitalism," *New Left Review*, no. 146, pp. 53–92.

Jessop, B., Bonnett, K., Bromley, S., and Ling, T. (1988) *Thatcherism: A Tale of Two Nations*, Cambridge, England, Polity Press.

Jessop, B., Bonnett, K., and Bromley, S. (1990) "Farewell to Thatcherism? Neo-Liberalism vs New Times," *New Left Review*, no. 179, pp. 81–202.

Lipietz, A. (1987) *Mirages and Miracles: The Crises of Global Fordism*, London, Verso.

Lyotard, J.-F. (1984) *The Postmodern Condition*, Manchester, England, Manchester University Press.

Murray, R. (1989) "Fordism and post-Fordism," in Hall, S. and Jacques, M. (eds) *New Times*, London, Lawrence and Wishart.

Porat, M. (1977) *The Information Economy: Definition and Measurement*, Washington, DC, US Dept of Commerce.

Rustin, M. (1989) "The politics of post-Fordism: or, the trouble with 'New Times'," *New Left Review*, no. 175, pp. 54–77.

Sayer, A. (1989) "Post-Fordism in question," *The International Journal of Urban and Regional Research*, vol. 13, no. 4, pp. 667–95.

Thrift, N. (1989) "New times and spaces? The perils of transition models," *Environment and Planning D: Society and Space*, vol. 7, no. 2, pp. 127–8.

Touraine, A. (1971) *The Post-Industrial Society*, New York, Random House.

Wood, S. (1989) *The Transformation of Work? Skill, Flexibility and the Labour Process*, London, Unwin Hyman.

# 17 Social Pluralism and Post-Modernity

Kenneth Thompson

## Contents

| | | |
|---|---|---|
| 1 | Introduction | 565 |
| 2 | Post-Modernism | 569 |
| 3 | Post-Modernism as the Cultural Logic of Late Capitalism | 572 |
| 3.1 | Culture and economy | 572 |
| 3.2 | Culture and politics | 575 |
| 4 | Rejections of Post-Modernism | 578 |
| 5 | Reconstructions in Post-Modernity or New Times | 580 |
| 6 | Post-Modernity: Consumption and Appearances | 583 |
| 7 | New Connections of Constructive Post-Modernism | 586 |
| 8 | Conclusion | 591 |
| | References | 592 |

# 1 Introduction

> The first half of the twentieth century was dominated by
> Modernism – a movement that rejected the legacy of the past, that
> was caught up in the early enthusiasm for technological progress,
> and that sought to create the world anew. It accompanied and may
> even be seen as the cultural equivalent of the Russian Revolution.
> Rejecting tradition, it was the culture of innovation and
> change . . . Fifty years later, however, by the second half of the
> century, this dramatic, daring and innovative trend had become
> the cultural norm accepted by Western Establishments . . . The
> revolutionary impulses that had once galvanized politics and
> culture had clearly become sclerotic. The Brave New World was
> in retreat. In its place has emerged a new movement that seeks to
> recover tradition, a world that seems to prefer stability to change.
> Just as the whole socialist idea has gone into retreat, so too the
> great Modernist project has been largely abandoned. Into this
> vacuum steps Postmodernism, an eclectic movement of parody
> and pastiche that fits happily into a world where conservation has
> become the rage, where new pubs can be built with Victorian
> fittings, where Modernist tower blocks are replaced with
> "vernacular" retreats into the archaic . . . Postmodernism, of
> course, can also be portrayed in a progressive light. Some
> advocates of the Postmodern believe Modernism to have been a
> phallocentric, imperialist affair. In this light, Postmodernism
> appears as a form of liberation, a fragmented movement in
> which a hundred flowers may bloom. Such people might also
> argue that while Modernism was the product of a particular
> Western culture, Postmodernism heralds the recognition of a
> plurality of cultures.
> (Richard Gott, 1986)

The above quotation is from Richard Gott's article "The crisis of
contemporary culture," which introduced *The Guardian*'s three-day
major series *Modernism and Post-modernism* in December, 1986.
Clearly this newspaper thought the subject of an alleged cultural shift
from modernism to post-modernism sufficiently important for it to
devote many pages and several issues to the subject. The reason it was
considered important is indicated by the sub-heading: "Why did the
revolutionary movement that lit up the early decades of the century
fizzle out? In a major series, *Guardian* critics analyse late twentieth
century malaise" (Gott, 1986, p. 10). The subsequent articles made it
even clearer that the cultural "malaise" represented by the shift from
modernism to post-modernism was regarded as symptomatic of a
deeper social and political malaise.

If post-modernism had simply been about a change in cultural styles
in architecture, film, painting, and novels, it is unlikely that it would
have merited such attention. But, as Gott suggests, most of those who
write about the culture of post-modernism believe that, for good or ill,

it is related in some way to the emergence of a new social epoch of post-modernity. Some of the related social developments have already been discussed in previous chapters: the collapse of communism and the loss of confidence, not only in revolutionary Marxism, but also in social planning as epitomized by post-war housing estates and tower blocks; the alleged economic changes from mass production to flexible specialization, and from mass consumption patterns to lifestyle niches in the marketplace, with a consequent fragmentation of social classes; the perception that the modernist ideas of technological progress and economic growth may be the cause of problems of pollution, waste, and wars, rather than the solutions; the decline of the politics of party, legislature, and trade unions, and the growth of "micropolitics" marked by struggles over power at the institutional and local levels, or over single issues.

To these possibly epochal changes might be added one that is particularly relevant to the cultural sphere, although it is also involved in the economic, political, and social changes, and that is the astonishing growth and pervasiveness of the mass media of communication, particularly the visual (or figural) media of film, television, and graphic design. If we are entering a post-modern age, then one of its most distinctive characteristics is a loss of rational and social coherence in favor of cultural images and social forms and identities marked by fragmentation, multiplicity, plurality, and indeterminacy.

Do we need post-modern social theories to evaluate these changes, or is there nothing happening that could not be encompassed by theories developed to explain the formations of modernity? (The issue of whether post-modernism marks the end of the "Enlightenment project" is discussed further in chapter 19.) As we will see, the theorists to be discussed take different positions on this question. In the end, the neo-Marxists, Harvey and Jameson, believe that post-modernist developments can be incorporated into a renovated Marxist framework. In contrast, Foucault and Baudrillard eventually proclaimed that all-encompassing theories such as Marxism were incapable of explaining current developments, although both were uncomfortable with the label "post-modernist" to describe their positions (perhaps in keeping with the fragmentation and diversity of post-modern culture). This chapter will focus on four issues:

1   Is there a distinctive cultural trend towards post-modernism?

2   Is post-modernism related to *economic* developments? For example, can post-modernity be explained as the latest stage in the development of capitalism?

3   What are the *political* implications of post-modernism? Does it mark the end of class-based politics and the emergence of a new kind of politics?

4   Is post-modernism the cultural expression of an increasing *social* pluralism that warrants its description as "post-modernity" – a new social epoch?

The discussion of these issues is structured as follows. Section 2 considers David Harvey's description of the culture of post-modernism and his account of the ways in which various theorists have attempted to relate it to economic, political, and social processes. Harvey's own position is that of a neo-Marxist who accepts that certain cultural trends have gathered pace to such an extent that they merit the label "post-modernist," but believes these can ultimately be explained as the result of developments within the capitalist economic system.

Section 3 examines one of the most influential attempts to relate post-modernist culture to political, economic, and social developments, that of another neo-Marxist, Frederic Jameson, and looks at his thesis of "post-modernism as the cultural logic of late capitalism." Jameson maintains that there *is* a distinctive culture of post-modernism, but that it is nothing more than the cultural logic of the latest stage of capitalism. He admits that the cultural logic of post-modernism may be difficult to map on to the structural developments of capitalism, but he still believes it will be possible once Marxism has assimilated some of the theoretical insights generated by cultural analysts and the new social movements, such as feminism. For him, post-modern culture does not necessarily herald a new epoch:

> The post-modern may well in that sense be little more than a transitional period between two stages of capitalism, in which the earlier forms of the economic are in the process of being restructured on a global scale, including the older forms of labour and its traditional organizational institutions and concepts. That a new international proletariat (taking forms we cannot yet imagine) will re-emerge from this convulsive upheaval it needs no prophet to predict; we ourselves are still in the trough, however, and no one can say how long we will stay there.
> (Jameson, 1991, p. 417)

In the end, therefore, despite his acknowledgement that there is a culture of post-modernism and his appreciation of the perspectives brought by new political movements and a plurality of social groups, it appears that he still believes in the subordination of these to the Marxist categories of class analysis. Despite this, as discussed in section 4, he is criticized by a more orthodox Marxist such as Callinicos for conceding too much to those who maintain that we are entering a new cultural and social epoch, and who claim that overarching theories (or metanarratives) such as Marxism cannot do justice to the diversity and fragmentation of post-modernity.

Section 5 considers the case for a constructive view of post-modern politics as "New Times." It focuses on the argument of Hebdige, who, along with others, such as Laclau and Mouffe, claims that the new social movements point to the complexity of the contemporary social field and the range of identities on offer, which are irreducible to class positions and the logic of production.

Section 6 looks at Baudrillard's account of the distinctive culture of the present era, which seems to support the case for seeing post-modernity as a new epoch, even though he rejects the post-modernist culture. He emphasizes the impact of the mass media in producing a culture based on images or copies (simulations) in which it is no longer possible to distinguish the "real" from the copy that "improves on the real" (the "hyperreal"). Having begun by criticizing the consumer economy from a Marxist perspective, Baudrillard has rapidly lost faith in such attempts to penetrate beneath the cultural surface to find the causal explanation in an economic base. Indeed, he seems to have come to the conclusion that it is impossible to develop general theories or political strategies in the new epoch. This is a more extreme position than that of Foucault, another theorist who has also been singled out as a source of post-modernist theory. Foucault rejected totalizing theories such as Marxism and psychoanalysis as reductionist and coercive in their practical implications, preferring microanalyses of the many different discourses and institutional practices through which power was exercised. But, unlike Baudrillard, he continued to believe that such analyses could inform positive political strategies of resistance to power.

Section 7 turns to a selection of more positive or constructive views of post-modernism and post-modernity. As Richard Gott noted, advocates of the post-modern believe that modernism tended towards intellectual and political domination, often in the name of science and progress, whereas post-modernism can appear as a form of liberation, in which the fragmentation and plurality of cultures and social groups allow a hundred flowers to bloom. The perspectives of minority groups – for example, ethnic groups, feminists, gays, sects, and cults – are tolerated, and post-modernism may even give rise to unexpected combinations and pastiches of cultural codes and discourses that modernism would have dismissed as "irrational," "mindless eclecticism," or "politically unsound." (Modernist critics of post-modernism believe that those charges are still justified.) Some examples of these post-modern social forms and perspectives are examined: Judith Stacey's study of post-modern family regimes in California; "New Age" religions, and other efforts to forge new individual and group identities by combining seemingly disparate discourses.

These different figures are therefore taken as representing different facets of the debate on post-modernism and adopt different positions towards it. Both Harvey and Jameson, who provide vivid descriptive accounts of the phenomenon, in the end, wish to retain a neo-Marxist account of developments in "late capitalism" as providing the best explanatory key to what they acknowledge are the significant cultural trends which post-modernism has set in motion.

Callinicos offers a "root and branch" rebuttal of post-modernism's claims, and reaffirms the primacy of class politics from a classical Marxist position. Baudrillard believes post-modernism signals the "death of meaning" in modern culture but, though he is deeply pessimistic about it, he argues that there is no alternative and delights in offering an "extreme" account of post-modern culture. Hebdige, Laclau, Mouffe, and the New Times theorists take a more positive view of the social and cultural pluralism and political possibilities which post-modernism opens up. And the "New Age" movements examined at the end of the chapter inhabit the post-modern break-up of modern culture but are seeking new, "post-modern" forms of community and belief to put in the place of "the end of the grand narratives."

My own position in these debates is one which welcomes the opening created by the concept of post-modernity, because it allows us to focus on some of the diverse and contradictory trends which were glossed over by sociological theories of modernity and modernization and by orthodox Marxist theories that stressed economic determinism and class polarization. This position does not prejudge the issues to be considered here of whether post-modernity is a distinct period and cultural configuration, and exactly how it is related to economic and political developments.

# 2  Post-Modernism

There are many ways of trying to describe what is meant by post-modernism. Post-modernism is the very loose term used to describe the new aesthetic cultural and intellectual forms and practices which are emerging in the 1980s and 1990s. As the word suggests, "post-modernism" follows, and is rapidly replacing, modernism, the term used to describe the cultural styles and movements of the first half of the twentieth century. Modernism – including the practices of abstraction, non-representational art in painting, the high-tech functionalism of modern architecture, avant-garde experiments with form in literature, and so on – set out in the early years of the twentieth century to challenge nineteenth-century realism and to "shock" bourgeois tastes with its experimental and avant-garde techniques. But, post-modernists argue, eventually it was "tamed," becoming institutionalized as the International Style, dominating the skylines of every modern city, the "monuments" of corporate capitalism, the fashionable museums and art galleries and the international art market. Now a new, more populist culture is emerging, closer to everyday life, to the marketplace, to consumption, and to the new popular culture of the media – a culture which renounces purity, mastery of form, and elitism, and is more playful, ironic, and eclectic in style.

One of the clearest summaries of some of the issues is provided by David Harvey in his book *The Condition of Postmodernity* (1989).

The broad contours of his account can be outlined in twelve points:

1  In architecture, post-modernism prefers the popular and vernacular styles, symbolized by Las Vegas, rather than the modernist "soulless" buildings like the Manhattan skyscrapers or the residential tower blocks of post-war urban planning.

2  In philosophy, various schools of thought have intermingled in a wave of reaction against the Enlightenment legacy and its faith in the powers of technology, science, and reason. Harvey mentions American Pragmatism, post-Marxist, and post-structuralist thought in this connection. At the same time, in religious thought, there have been

attempts to develop a post-modern theology which reaffirms spiritual and moral bases of action neglected by secular modernism, while not abandoning the powers of reason. (Sometimes this takes the form of a pastiche of religious ideas and selected elements of science and secular reason as in New Age religion, which we will consider later.)

3   Post-modernism seems to revel in fragmentation, ephemerality, and discontinuity, preferring difference over uniformity.

4   Post-modernist thinkers, such as Foucault and Lyotard, attack any notion that there might be a metalanguage, metanarrative, or metatheory through which all things can be connected, represented, or explained.

5   There is an emphasis on looking for "local" factors or partial explanations, such as the micro-politics of power relations in different social contexts and in relation to specific discourses, language games, or interpretative communities.

6   Politically, post-modernism entails engaging in multiple, local autonomous struggles for liberation, rejecting the imperialism of an enlightened modernity that presumed to speak for others (colonized peoples, blacks and ethnic groups, religious minorities, women, and the working class) with a unified voice.

7   Post-modernists have a different view of language and communication from that held by modernists. Modernists presupposed a tight and identifiable relation between what was said (the signified or "message") and how it was being said (the signifier or "medium"), whereas post-structuralists see these as continually breaking apart and re-attaching in new combinations. "Deconstructionism" (associated with the work of the French philosopher Derrida) views cultural life as intersecting "texts"; deconstructive cultural analysis is concerned with "reading" texts by deconstructing them or breaking down the narrative to show how it is composed of different textual elements and fragments.

8   Post-modernism's preoccupation with the fragmentation and instability of language carries over into a conception of the post-modern personality as "schizophrenic" (not in the clinical sense, but in relation to a fragmented sense of identity). Words gain their meaning from being part of a sequential chain of linked "signifiers" in a sentence. If the links become unstable and the sequence disjointed, then there will be a fragmentation of meaning, manifested in an inability to think things through – including an inability to think through one's own biography and to unify the past, present, and future in one's psychic life. Experience is reduced to a "series of pure and unrelated presences in time" and the experiences of the present become overwhelmingly vivid as they are communicated by mass-media images and sensational spectacles (not just in entertainment, but also political, military, and scientific). The immediacy of events and the sensationalism of the spectacle become the stuff of which consciousness is forged.

9   The other side of loss of linear or sequential ideas of time and the search for instantaneous impact is a parallel loss of depth. Jameson

emphasizes the "depthlessness" and concern for surface appearance of contemporary culture.

10    High-brow authority over cultural taste collapses and is replaced by popular culture and consumerism.

11    Some social and cultural analysts of post-modernism take a positive and constructive view, insisting that various groups, such as youth and ethnic groups, develop their own sub-cultures by using consumer culture and fashion to construct a sense of their own public identities.

12    Finally, some Marxists, such as Jameson, maintain that post-modernism is simply the cultural logic of late capitalism.

Harvey's own view on the links between the economy and post-modernity is that there is a close relationship, although he admits it may be difficult to prove that it is a causal relationship. He sees links between Fordism (e.g. assembly-line mass production) and modernism as the dominant economic and cultural trends in the period up to 1970, and a similar association between post-Fordism (e.g. flexible accumulation in which international financial markets come to dominate the economic order and Japanese productive organization the industrial) and post-modernism in the subsequent period. (Debates about the extent of such trends in the economic sphere were discussed in chapter 16.) Speed-up of communication, transportation, fashion cycles, commodity life-spans, and the associated shrinking of distances and spaces – what he calls "time–space compression" – have radically affected the codes of transmission of social values and meanings. He gives a good example in the case of food: supermarkets and restaurants in cities such as London or Los Angeles now offer foods from all over the world. The cuisines of the world are now assembled in one place in the same way that the world's geographical complexity is reduced to a series of images on a television screen each evening. On television, as in Disneyland, it is now possible to experience the world's geography vicariously through images or "simulacra." In some cases these reproductions may fit the stereotype even better than the original (just as Indian curries in a supermarket may come closer to our ideal than those served in Bombay!): they are "hyperreal."

Harvey does not insist on a distinct break between modernity and post-modernity. He agrees that the conditions of post-modern time–space compression exaggerate tendencies that have been present in capitalist modernization in the past, generated by successive waves of compression arising from the pressures of capital accumulation, with its perpetual search to annihilate space through time and reduce turnover time. However, Harvey tends towards the view that there has been a change in the "mode of regulation" of capitalist economies as a result of the first major post-war slump in 1973. (This view was discussed in chapter 16.) That slump inaugurated a period of extremely rapid change, flux, and uncertainty. However, he is cautious about reaching a final judgment on whether or not the new systems of production and marketing, characterized by more flexible labor processes and markets, of geographical mobility and rapid shifts in consumption patterns, warrant the title of a new regime of accumulation, and whether the revival of entrepreneurialism and neo-conservatism, coupled with the cultural turn of post-modernism, warrant the title of a new mode of regulation. He notes many signs of continuity rather than rupture with the Fordist era (Harvey, 1989, p. 170) and even concedes that the cultural traits of modernism and post-modernism may simply represent opposing dynamic tendencies that have always existed within capitalism, which would explain why similar cultural forces were described in the previous *fin de siècle* in cities such as Vienna. As the sociologist Simmel remarked, it is in such places and at such times of fragmentation and economic insecurity that the desire for stable values leads to a heightened desire for charismatic authority and sacred attachments through family, religion, and state (Simmel, 1900). Harvey remarks that there is abundant evidence of a revival of support for such institutions and values throughout the western world since about 1970. The resulting cultural configuration or pastiche of novel and nostalgic elements is what gives post-modernity its paradoxical and intriguing character.

# 3   Post-Modernism as the Cultural Logic of Late Capitalism

## 3.1   Culture and economy

In his essay "Post-modernism or the cultural logic of late capitalism" (1984), Jameson presents the thesis that post-modern culture logically corresponds to a stage in the development of capitalism. He rejects the idea of the conservative sociologist Daniel Bell that we are living in a post-industrial society (Bell, 1973), or that class conflict has ended. Adapting the ideas of the Marxist economist Ernest Mandel, Jameson distinguishes three periods in the development of capitalism: market capitalism, characterized by the growth of industrial capital in largely national markets (from about 1700 to 1850); monopoly capitalism in the age of imperialism, when European nation-states developed international markets, exploiting the raw materials and cheap labor of their colonial territories; and, most recently (Mandel dates it from 1945, Jameson from the 1960s), the phase of late capitalism, of multinational corporations with global markets and mass consumption. Furthermore, in Jameson's account of late capitalism, increasingly it is culture itself that is "commodified" and consumed:

> Where an older Marxist social theory saw cultural forms as part of the ideological veil or distorting mirror preventing the real economic relations in a society from being seen, this theory sees the production, exchange, marketing and consumption of cultural forms – considered in their widest sense and therefore including advertising, TV and the mass media generally – as a central focus

and expression of economic activity. Here, images, styles and representations are not the promotional accessories to economic products, they are the products themselves. In a similar way, the explosion of information technology makes information not merely a lubricant of the cycles of exchange and profit, but itself the most important of commodities. If it is possible to imagine this nostalgically as a final greedy swallowing-up of culture by the forces of commodity capitalism then this is in itself to reproduce a notion of the autonomy or separateness of culture which, Jameson wants us to believe, is itself out of date.
(Connor, 1989, p. 46)

According to Jameson, a better way of modelling this situation is as "an explosion: a prodigious expansion of culture throughout the social realm, to the point at which everything in our social life – from economic value and state power to practices and the very structure of the psyche itself – can be said to have become 'cultural'"
(Jameson, 1984, p. 87). His key point about the post-modern economic phase is that culture has become integrated into commodity production and this makes it different from modernism in the earlier stages of capitalism.

What has happened is that aesthetic production today has become integrated into commodity production generally, the frantic economic urgency of producing fresh waves of ever more novel-seeming goods (from clothing to airplanes), at ever greater rates of turnover, now assigns an increasingly essential structural function and position to aesthetic innovation and experimentation.
(Jameson, 1984, p. 56)

Whereas modernist culture could be judged against certain dominant standards (hence the distinction between high culture and low or popular culture), and might even be oppositional or shocking, post-modernist culture is totally commodified and tends to be judged in terms of what gives immediate pleasure and makes money. Indeed, Jameson admits that his ideas about post-modernism emerged in response to architectural debates where, more decisively than in the other arts or media, post-modernist positions occupied the space left as a result of the criticisms of high modernism, which was credited with the destruction of the fabric of the traditional city and older neighborhoods. Hence, his references to Robert Venturi's influential manifesto *Learning from Las Vegas* (Venturi et al., 1977), which pointed out the popular success of buildings which purists would regard as "fake" and "tacky." He notes that post-modernists have been fascinated by the whole "degraded" landscape of schlock and kitsch, of TV series and Readers' Digest culture, of advertising and motels, of the television late show and the grade B Hollywood movies, of so-called "para-literature" with its airport paperback categories of the Gothic and the romance, the popular biography, the murder mystery, and the science fiction or fantasy novel (Jameson, pp. 54–5).

Excalibur Castle Hotel in Las Vegas, Nevada

The constitutive stylistic features of post-modernist culture for
Jameson are: a fondness for pastiche; the "flat" multiplication and
collage of styles, as opposed to the "deep" expressive aesthetics of
unique style characteristic of modernism; retreat from the idea of the
unified personality to the "schizoid" experience of the loss of self in
undifferentiated time. He gives a good example from mass culture:
nostalgia movies (what the French call *la mode retro* – retrospective
styling), such as *American Graffiti*, which in 1973 set out to recapture
the atmosphere and stylistic peculiarities of the 1950s America of the
Eisenhower era, as does Polanski's film *Chinatown* for the 1930s. They
are not the same as the older historical novel or movie, which sought to
represent historical events, but rather they approach the past through
stylistic connotation, conveying "pastness" by the glossy qualities of
the image and fashion. Pastiche does not set out to interpret the past or
to judge it against some standard, but simply plays images off against
each other to achieve its effects and with no clear reference to an
external or "deeper" reality. This superficial pastiche of images
("signifiers") with no referent except other signifiers, also has a kind of
"schizophrenic" character because the individual loses all sense of time
as the experiences of the present are overwhelmingly vivid.

Not only does post-modern culture disrupt our sense of time and
historical distancing, post-modern architecture also produces
"something like a mutation in built space itself," which leaves us
disoriented because "we do not yet possess the perceptual equipment
to match this new hyperspace" (Jameson, 1984, p. 80). Jameson's
famous example is that of the Bonaventure Hotel, built in the new Los
Angeles downtown area by the architect and developer John Portman.
Although some architectural experts describe it as "late-modernist,"
Jameson calls it post-modernist because it meets his criteria of being
populist and it produces a disorienting sense of "decentered

The Bonaventure Hotel

hyperspace": there is no single, focal point to give one a sense of direction, just as there is no sense of proportion in the spatial arrangements. Its reflector glass skin achieves a "peculiar and placeless dissociation of the Bonaventure from its neighbourhood," the elevators are like great Japanese lanterns or gondolas, passing inside and outside the building and splashing down into an internal moat, while the vast internal spaces are confusingly laid out, "transcending the capacities of the individual human body to locate itself" (Jameson, 1984, p. 83).

## 3.2 Culture and politics

We now move on to the second issue, the question of whether post-modernism is also related to the end of the primacy of class-based politics as the result of an increased social pluralism – a multiplicity of social groups and sources of identity, giving rise to different political interests. Jameson agrees that one of the most profoundly post-modern phenomena is the emergence of a whole range of small-group, non-class political practices – micropolitics. However, Jameson criticizes those whom he describes as "post-modernist ideologues" who claim that these new social movements (women, gays, blacks, ecologists, regional autonomists, etc.) "arise in the void left by the disappearance of social classes and in the rubble of the political movements organized around those" (Jameson, 1991, p. 319). According to Jameson, the conditions that give rise to these social movements or groups are real social changes, but they are nothing to do with the disappearance of classes and class conflicts.

> How classes could be expected to disappear, save in the unique special-case scenario of socialism, has never been clear to me; but

> the global restructuration of production and the introduction of
> radically new technologies – that have flung workers in archaic
> factories out of work, displaced new kinds of industry to
> unexpected parts of the world, and recruited work forces different
> from the traditional ones in a variety of features, from gender to
> skill and nationality – explain why so many people have been
> willing to think so, at least for a time. Thus the new social
> movements and the newly emergent global proletariat both result
> from the prodigious expansion of capitalism in its third (or
> "multinational") stage; both are in that sense "post-modern", at
> least in terms of the account of post-modernism offered here.
> (Jameson, 1991, p. 319)

Despite his criticisms of those he labels as "post-modern ideologues"
Jameson is careful to avoid the impression that he is advocating a
return to a base-superstructure deterministic type of explanation of the
new social movements:

> Two positions must be distinguished here, which are both wrong.
> On the one hand, for a properly post-modern "cynical reason" the
> new social movements are simply the result – the concomitants
> and the products – of capitalism itself in its final and most
> unfettered stage. On the other hand, for a radical-liberal populism
> such movements are always to be seen as the local victories and
> the painful achievements and conquests of small groups of people
> in struggle (who are themselves figures for class struggle in
> general, as that had determined all the institutions of history, very
> much including capitalism itself). In short, and no longer to put
> so fine a point on it, are the "new social movements"
> consequences and after effects of late capitalism? Are they new
> units generated by the system itself in its interminable inner self-
> differentiation and self-reproduction? Or are they very precisely
> new "agents of history" who spring into being in resistance to the
> system as forms of opposition to it, forcing it against the direction
> of its own internal logic into new reforms and internal
> modifications? But this is precisely a false opposition, about
> which it would be just as satisfactory to say that both positions
> are right; the crucial issue is the theoretical dilemma, replicated in
> both, of some seeming explanatory choice between the alternatives
> of agency and system. In reality, however, there is no such choice,
> and both explanations or models – absolutely inconsistent with
> each other – are also incommensurable with each other and must
> be rigorously separated at the same time that they are deployed
> simultaneously.
> (Jameson, 1991, p. 326)

The position taken by Jameson on this dilemma as it related to the
issue of the "new social movements" and their relationship to
capitalism leaves him open to the charge that he wants to "have his
cake and eat it too." He maintains that there is the simultaneous
possibility of active political commitment working through such partial

and limited movements and, at the same time, of continuing to develop a more totalizing and systematic social theory, "and not some sterile choice between those two things" (Jameson, 1991, p. 320). In other words, he believes it is right to take part in non-class-based social movements, but his Marxist systematic analysis would also insist that such alliances (or the "Rainbow Coalition") are generally not as durable as those organized around class and the development of class consciousness. It is for this reason that he prefers the example of Jesse Jackson's attempt to develop a Rainbow Coalition in American politics during the 1980s, because "he rarely makes a speech in which working-class experience is not 'constructed' as the mediation around which the equivalence of the coalition is to find its active cohesion" (Jameson, 1991, p. 331). Whereas the post-modern approach of Ernesto Laclau and Chantal Mouffe in *Hegemony and Socialist Strategy* (1985) is criticized because, although they provide a good description of the way in which alliance politics function – in the establishing of an axis of equivalence along which the parties line up – the equivalence could be in terms of non-class issues such as abortion or nuclear energy, and so lacks durability.

The political problem, as Jameson sees it, is that people can identify with *groups*, as represented through the media, but they cannot identify with large, amorphous classes. Consequently, in the era of post-modernism, it is virtually impossible for the metanarrative of class conflict and of the eventual triumph of the proletariat to succeed in encompassing all developments. Classes can no longer function or be represented as the "agents" or "subjects" of history. On the other hand, while the plurality of protest groups and social movements can attract allegiance and offer an identity, their "very lively social struggles of the current period are largely dispersed and anarchic" (Jameson, 1991, p. 349). It is difficult to unite them in some metanarrative of alliance and combined struggle because there is not a single enemy group against which they can struggle. Late capitalism has become such an impersonal system that it is difficult to develop convincing representations of a "ruling class" as an identifiable group. An actual group of influential businessmen, such as those who advised and backed President Ronald Reagan in the late 1970s and 1980s, is more likely to be regarded as a local network of cronies (in Southern California and the Sun Belt) engaged in conspiracy, rather than bringing discredit on business or being regarded as representatives of the ruling class (Jameson, 1991).

According to Jameson, the different groups should unite against a common enemy, which he calls corporate capitalism. But this entity is dispersed throughout the whole social system and culture: there are many levels and centers of power. Furthermore, post-modern culture itself would have to be identified as decadent and simply a ruling-class culture, which is difficult to do convincingly because of its seeming popularity and the pleasures that consumption offers. Opposition to it can seem puritanical or a form of out-of-date elitism. Despite these problems, Jameson maintains his faith in the Marxist metanarrative of history and a belief in the eventual emergence of a global class struggle

combining the many local groups at present engaged in dispersed
power struggles:

> I'm convinced that this new post-modern global form of capitalism
> will now have a new class logic about it, but it has not yet
> completely emerged because labour has not yet reconstituted itself
> on a global scale, and so there is a crisis in what classes and class
> consciousness are. It's very clear that agency on the Left is not
> there in those older forms but the Marxist narrative assures us that
> some form of agency will reconstitute itself and that is the sense
> in which I still find myself committed to the Marxist logic.
> (Jameson, 1991, p. 31)

As he himself admits, although this belief is supported by the logic of
the Marxist metanarrative, his faith is based on individual belief and
"could just be an aberrant personal religion of some sort" (1991, p. 31).
His own brilliant analysis of the fragmented post-modern culture makes
clear how difficult it is for such metanarratives to survive in
contemporary society.

# 4   Rejections of Post-Modernism

Outright rejections of the thesis that we are entering a post-modern
epoch take several forms. Perhaps the most outright rejection is that
voiced by orthodox Marxists who seek to reaffirm the revolutionary
socialist tradition and the primacy of class-based politics against those
they regard as "revisionists" or proponents of more pluralistic "New
Times." Such rejection is to be found in the work of Callinicos,
especially in his aptly titled book *Against Post-modernism: a Marxist
Critique* (1989). Callinicos describes his approach as

> continuing in a very minor key Marx's critique of religion, where
> he treats Christianity in particular not simply, as the
> Enlightenment had, as a set of false beliefs, but as the distorted
> expression of real needs denied by class society. Similarly I seek
> here not simply to demonstrate the intellectual inadequacy of
> post-modernism, understood as the claim, justified by appeal
> to post-modern art, post-structural philosophy, and the theory of
> post-industrial society, that we are entering a post-modern epoch,
> but to set it in historical context. Post-modernism, then, is best
> seen as a symptom.
> (Callinicos, 1989, p. 6)

It is interesting that Callinicos should treat post-modernism as Marx
treated religion, merely as a symptom of something more "real," by
which he means economic conditions associated with capitalism, and
as a set of political attitudes reflecting those conditions. Thus, "post-
modernist" ideas are said to be a reflection of opportunities for an
"over consumptionist lifestyle offered upper white-collar strata by
capitalism in the 1980s and political disillusionment in the
aftermath of 1968" (Callinicos, 1989, p. 7).

Jean-François Lyotard in France, and Ernesto Laclau and Chantal Mouffe in Britain, are cited as examples of leading "post-Marxists" who argue that socialists should abandon "classism" – the classical Marxist stress upon the class struggle as the driving force of history, and of the working class as the agency of socialist change. The resulting fusion of post-modernism and post-Marxism was exemplified in the 1980s by the magazine *Marxism Today*, which expressed the idea that we are living in "New Times," as follows:

> Unless the Left can come to terms with those New Times, it must live on the sidelines . . . At the heart of New Times is the shift from the old mass-production Fordist economy to a new, more flexible, post-Fordist order based on computers, information technology and robotics. But New Times are about more than economic change. Our world is being remade. Mass production, the mass consumer, the big city, the big-brother state, the sprawling housing estate, and the nation-state are in decline: flexibility, diversity, differentiation, mobility, communication, decentralization and internationalization are in the ascendant. In the process our own identities, our sense of self, our own subjectivities are being transformed. We are in transition to a new era.
> (*Marxism Today*, October, 1988)

Callinicos's criticisms of the thesis of New Times and the era of post-modernity include detailed arguments about the extent to which Fordist mass production has declined (an issue discussed in chapter 16), and whether post-modernist cultural trends are any different from modernism. He makes a strong case against the thesis that there has been a decisive shift from a modern to a post-modern era, although the case against the more moderate thesis of a gradual change is less conclusive. However, the crux of his argument is directed against any distraction from the predominant importance of class conflict.

The response of those who argue that we are in New Times or a post-modern era is that other social positions and identities have become more important or "real" for people, irrespective of whether or not that is a distraction from their supposed class interests and so a form of "false consciousness." Capitalism may be a major cause of some problems addressed by feminists, ecologists, New Age religionists, fundamentalists, and other groups, but they define their concerns differently. And, as one of the early American sociologists, William I. Thomas, pointed out: "If men (*sic*) define situations as real, they are real in their consequences." In other words, we have to take their reasoning seriously, not prejudge the question of the most significant factors in each situation. This is particularly important in a period when there is an apparent increase in social pluralism and new cultural formations. (It is still possible to follow Callinicos's example and to question the *degree* of social pluralism or cultural novelty, provided the evidence is considered in an open-minded way and takes account of the views of the people being studied, particularly their judgments as to where their interests and allegiances lie.)

# 5   Reconstructions in Post-Modernity or New Times

Most of the theorists who have written about post-modernity have viewed it as some kind of transition period in which older systems of production are giving way to newer ones, as in the change from Fordist to post-Fordist production; services are overtaking manufacturing occupations; supranational forms of organization are increasing at the expense of national forms; "civil society" is expanding and becoming more diversified, not only in terms of different consumer groups and lifestyles, but also with respect to a pluralization of social life in which ordinary people in industrialized societies have a greater range of positions and identities available in their everyday working, social, familial, and sexual lives. There are different opinions about the extent of these changes (particularly about whether they only apply to industrialized countries and to the better-off two-thirds of the people in those countries) and also about whether they are capable of being subsumed under the logic of a new stage of global capitalism. However, leaving aside the question of whether it is possible to predict a future stage of social development in the way that the Enlightenment project envisaged, there is no doubt that analyses of post-modernity or New Times are attempting to develop new concepts and categories that are adequate to the rich kaleidoscope of contemporary social life and that they have succeeded in opening up fresh and stimulating debates.

What distinguishes those I have called the "constructive post-modernists" from some other post-modernists and critics of post-modernism is their tendency to look for positive developments through their efforts to create new "emancipatory narratives," new identities, original syntheses, and rearticulations of otherwise divergent or fragmented elements. Dick Hebdige provides a good description of some of these developments in Britain during the 1980s, particularly those that sought to use popular culture and the media. His comments are made from the political point of view of a committed socialist who is concerned about the political implications of these developments, but they have a wider relevance irrespective of any political project. In reading the following quotation from Hebdige's article, *After the Masses*, you should form your own judgments about the social significance of such efforts to construct new identities and communities. Do they justify a more positive view of post-modernity or New Times than is allowed by the outright critics of the idea of post-modernism such as Callinicos?

In the following extract from Hebdige's article, he begins by showing how consumer identities and lifestyles constitute social types and categories that could be used in a more positive way by sociologists so as to develop a "sociology of aspiration" (what people desire to be). He does not envisage this as a substitute for class analysis, but he believes it is another important dimension of social stratification that has become more significant in these New Times.

One of the features of post-Fordist production is the leading role given to market research, packaging and presentation. While it doesn't literally *produce* the social, it's none the less the case that marketing has provided the dominant and most pervasive classifications of "social types" in the 1980s (the yuppie is the most obvious example). We use these categories as a kind of social shorthand even if we are reluctant to find ourselves reflected in them. We live in a world and in bodies which are deeply scored by the power relations of race and class, sexuality and gender but we also live – whether or not we know it consciously – in a world of style-setters, innovators, sloanes, preppies, empty nesters (working couples with grown up families), dinkies (dual-income-no-kids), casuals, sensibles, the constrained majority, and today's prime targets, the pre-teens and woofies (well-off-older folk).

These are the types outlined in commercial lifestyling and "psychographics" – forms of research which don't present descriptions of living, breathing individuals so much as hypothetical "analogues" of "aspirational clusters". In other words the new intensive but speculative forms of market research are designed to offer a social map of desire which can be used to determine where exactly which products should be "pitched" and "niched". All these types could no doubt be translated back into the old language (it would perhaps be relatively easy to return them to the axis of social class) but everything specific would be lost in the translation.

It is clear that such research methods and the marketing initiative associated with them have been developed precisely to cut across the old social–sexual polarities. The parameters are designed to be transcultural and transnational (the spread of "psychographics" in the UK is linked to the drive to go pan-European in preparation for 1992). We may find such forms of knowledge immoral, objectionable or sinister – a waste of time and resources which are unforgiveable in a world where people are starving and in a country where people are still sleeping in the streets – but the fact is that they do actively create and sustain one *version* of the social. They depend for their success on the accurate outlining and anticipation (through observation and interviews with "target" subjects) not just of what (some) people think they want but of *what they'd like to be*. A sociology of aspiration might begin by combining the considerable *critical* and *diagnostic* resources available within existing versions of sociology and cultural studies with the *descriptive* and *predictive* knowledge available within the new intensive market research to

get a more adequate picture of what *everybody* says they want and
what they want to be in all its radical plurality.
(Hebdige, 1989, pp. 89–90)

The key point that Hebdige is making in this discussion of lifestyles
and consumer groups is that these are social phenomena that are no
less real than previously privileged sociological categories such as
"class," and they are now more important and complex than in earlier
periods. Consequently, the Left has to take them more seriously and
accept "what certain forms of post-modernism recommend: a
scepticism towards imposed general, 'rational' solutions: a relaxation of
the old critical and judgemental postures, although without retreating
from its principles" (Hebdige, 1989, pp. 89–90).

The second set of new collectivities that requires positive appraisal,
according to Hebdige, are those that actively use the mass media to
construct an identity. Unlike more pessimistic post-modernist analysts,
and the critics of post-modernism, Hebdige emphasizes the capacity of
people to develop new communities and identities through popular
culture and the mass media, rather than being passive masses:

It may well be true that the two great collective identities through
which the masses came together to "make history" in the last two
hundred years – the first associated with nation, the second with
class – are breaking down today in the overdeveloped world. But
new "emancipation narratives" are being written round collectives
other than the imaginary community of nation or the international
brotherhood of socialist *man*. This is true even in popular culture
and the "depthless" field of the media upon which Baudrillard
operates.

Within the transfigured "public realm", established by
transnational communication networks, new forms, both of
alliance and contestation, are possible. One of the things ignored
in the more "fatal" versions of new times is the binding power of
the new transnational media systems: the power they have to
move people not just to buy the products of the culture industries
but to buy *into* networks that offer forms of community and
alliance which can transcend the confines of class, race, gender,
regional and national culture. Popular music offers many
examples of this kind of bonding. Some of these "communities of
affect" (rather than "communities of interest") are explicitly
utopian. The simultaneously most spectacular yet most
participatory examples to date of the kind of bonding made
possible across transnational communication systems have been
the televised events organized round Band Aid, Sport Aid, Live
Aid and the Free Mandela movement. This is where you see the
optimistic will in action. Televangelism is another less engaging
example of this kind of mobilization specific to the media age.

Rather than "psychic autism" (Baudrillard) or the waning of
affect (Jameson) such phenomena suggest the possibility of a new
kind of politics existing primarily in and through the airwaves
and organized around issues of universal moral concern. Such

> crusades are likely to be extended in the 1990s. Once again the
> desire to feel and to feel *connected* to a transitory mass of other
> people, to engage in transitory and *superficial* alliances of this
> kind is not intrinsically either good or bad. Instead it has to be
> *articulated*. Jimmy Swaggart managed to articulate the yearning for
> community and righteousness one way. Jerry Dammers, founder of
> the Two Tone movement and co-organizer of the Mandela concert,
> helped to direct the flow of similar desires in a radically different
> direction.
> (Hebdige, 1989, pp. 90–1)

This discussion of new forms of "communities of affect" or emotionally
based collectivities takes us beyond the consumer identities and their
related images as focused on by theorists such as Jameson and
Baudrillard. They cannot be "read-off" or understood simply as the
"cultural logic of late capitalism" (Jameson).

The remaining two alternatives draw different conclusions about the
implications of the increasing and diverse social pluralism that has
attracted the label "post-modernity." The first position, which we will
discuss next, is represented by Jean Baudrillard, who maintains that in
the post-modern era "appearances are everything." The second
position, to be discussed later, is that of the various constructive post-
modernists, who hold that it is possible to combine cultural codes that
were thought to be irreconcilable or contradictory according to
Enlightenment thought (including radical Enlightenment theory, such
as Marxism). An example of this in practice would be the varied "post-
modern" family regimes described by American sociologist Judity
Stacey in *Brave New Families* (1990), with their surprising linkings and
crossover codes involving fundamentalist religion, left-wing politics,
feminism, patriarchalism, and other seemingly incongruent elements.
Other examples include New Age religion and various charismatic
movements.

# 6 Post-Modernity: Consumption and Appearances

Baudrillard's account of the post-modern era is significant for the light
that it throws on two aspects that distinguish it from earlier eras: the
proliferation of communications through the mass media, particularly
television, and the full emergence of consumer society. The new mass
media use a montage of images (unlike print) and juxtapose or collapse
time–space distancing. The result is that culture is now dominated by
simulations – objects and discourses that have no firm origin, no
referent, no ground or foundation. Signs get their meanings from their
relations with each other, rather than by reference to some independent
reality or standard. There is a multiplicity of constantly shifting
cultural codes, with no fixed metacode to which they all relate and
against which they can be judged. Similarly, with respect to the

economy, activities and styles of consumption often play a larger role in defining people's identities and consciousness than position in the production system. Baudrillard rejects Marxism and other structuralist theories that deny the surface "appearance" of things in favor of a hidden underlying structure. Such interpretative strategies all privilege some form of rationality. Like the philosopher Nietzsche, Baudrillard criticizes such claims to "truth" and favors a model based on what he calls "seduction." Seduction plays on the surface; it is the surface appearance that is effective in determining action, not some latent or hidden structure as claimed by Marxism or Freudianism.

Baudrillard's position has become progressively more radically opposed to the Enlightenment tradition of rational thought and its project of promoting progress through scientific means. In his early works, *Le Système des Objets* (The System of Objects) (1968) and *La Société de Consommation* (Consumer Society) (1970), he simply sought to extend the Marxist critique of capitalism to areas beyond the scope of the theory of the mode of production, so as to take account of the meaning and communicational structure of commodities in post-war society. He explored the possibility that consumption had become the chief basis of the social order and of the classification system that encodes behavior and groups. Such classifications could not be explained by reference to some other structure, such as the mode of production and economic classes, or by reference to "real" needs or use value. Consumer objects constituted a system of signs that took their meaning from the play of differences between the signs, and these were inexhaustible in their ability to incite desire (or to seduce). Consequently, like many social and literary theorists who took a "linguistic turn" in the 1960s, he moved steadily in the direction of analyzing linguistic or symbolic codes purely in terms of their internal relationships and without reference to some external objects that they might be supposed to represent. In his later work, *Simulacres et Simulations* (1981), Baudrillard's theory of commodity culture removes any distinction between object and representation. In their place he pictures a social world constructed out of models or "simulacra" which have no foundation in any reality except their own.

> A simulation is different from a fiction or lie in that it not only presents an absence as a presence, the imaginary as the real, it also undermines any contrast to the real, absorbing the real within itself. Instead of a "real" economy of commodities that is somehow bypassed by an "unreal" myriad of advertising images, Baudrillard now discerns only a hyperreality, a world of self-referential signs. He has moved from the TV ad which, however, never completely erases the commodity it solicits, to the TV newscast which creates the news if only to be able to narrate it, or the soap opera whose daily events are both referent and reality for many viewers.
> (Baudrillard, 1988b, p. 6)

A good example of Baudrillard's use of the concepts of simulation and hyperreality is to be found in his statements about Disneyland in Los

Angeles. He describes it as a perfect model of the ways in which simulation works. At first glance it appears to be simply a play of illusions and phantasms, such as pirates, the frontier, future worlds, etc. "This imaginary world is supposed to be what makes the operation successful. But what draws the crowds is undoubtedly much more the social microcosm, the miniaturized and *religious* revelling in real America, in its delights and drawbacks" (Baudrillard, 1988b, p. 171). In Disneyland, all of America's values are exalted in miniature and comic-strip form. It is not just a question of Disneyland providing an idealized digest of American life and values, which works ideologically to conceal "real" contradictions in American society;

> Disneyland is presented as imaginary in order to make us believe that the rest is real, when in fact all of Los Angeles and the America surrounding it are no longer real, but of the order of the hyperreal and simulation. It is no longer a question of a false representation of reality (ideology), but of concealing the fact that the real is no longer real, and thus of saving the reality principle . . . It is meant to be an infantile world, in order to make us believe that the adults are elsewhere, in the "real" world, and to conceal the fact that real childishness is everywhere, particularly among those adults who go there to act the child in order to foster illusions of their real childishness.
> (Baudrillard, 1988b, p. 172)

Although this is a rather paradoxical statement – suggesting that there is no "real" Los Angeles or America – it does make sense if we accept it as an exaggerated version of the point that society itself is increasingly composed of constructed images (simulacra). Nowhere is this more clearly demonstrated than in Los Angeles, the site of Hollywood and Disneyland. However, critics of Baudrillard on the political left, while echoing some of his ideas about simulation and hyperreality, accuse him of lapsing into political apathy. One critic said that Baudrillard's version of California, in his short book *America* (1988), was "Reaganized and yuppified" and that in it "there are no migrant workers, no Chicano barrios, no Central American refugees, no Vietnamese refugees or Asians, not even any blacks . . ." (Kellner, 1989, pp. 171–2).

Baudrillard would probably respond that such groups are themselves co-opted into the world of simulacra and hyperreality, of which Disneyland and Hollywood are merely the most extreme examples. He notes sarcastically that, because America imagines itself as an "achieved utopia," minorities and the poor must disappear from view: it is only bad taste if they continue to show themselves (Baudrillard, 1988a, p. 111).

It is difficult to form a conclusive judgment about Baudrillard's contribution, partly because of the rather convoluted expressions he uses, but also because he seems to adopt an extreme position in order to shock his readers and perhaps jolt them out of what he would regard as their complacency or dogmatism. Nevertheless, he does focus on some important features of contemporary social life that distinguish the present period from earlier epochs and so might justify the label "post-modernity," although he rejects the label "post-modernist" for his own position.

The key contribution is to make us aware of how radically social life and our perceptions have been changed by the development of endlessly differentiated consumer lifestyles, the constant stream of television images, and the expanded capacity of the media to seduce us in a strange new world of "hyperreality": a world of simulations which is immune to rationalist critique, whether Marxist, liberal, or any other metatheory of reality. Baudrillard's radical, post-modernist message is that the media images do not merely represent reality; they *are* reality, because their meaning derives from their position within a system of signs, not from some referent in a "real" world outside that system. Whereas earlier sociologists, such as the founders of Symbolic Interactionism, George Herbert Mead (1863–1931) and Charles H. Cooley (1864–1929), emphasized the development of the individual's self concept through primary group interaction (family and other significant relationships) and seeing ourselves through the eyes of those "significant others," Baudrillard emphasizes the influence of the mechanically reproduced images of the media. For Baudrillard, the mass media are not a means of communication because there is no feedback or exchange of information. (He regards media surveys and opinion polls as just another media spectacle.) The only political strategy he can recommend to the masses (a term which encompasses everyone, not as in the older distinction between elite and masses) is to refuse to take the media seriously; that is, to refuse to play the game and so merely regard the media as nothing but spectacles.

Needless to say, Baudrillard's position is thought to be far too accepting of the status quo by those who believe the media do distort reality, or reflect a reality that must be changed. Critical theorists, such as Jürgen Habermas, believe that it is possible to establish rational criteria for judging the adequacy of representations of reality, and they are prepared to advocate social changes that would create the conditions for non-distorted communication and debate in civil society. (This is discussed further by Gregor McLennan in chapter 19.) Others such as Hebdige argue that groups and social movements can offer resistance by resignifying the meanings that are presented to them by the media and in consumer objects. We will turn to some examples of other strategies in the next section, which focuses on efforts to combine different cultural codes in everyday life.

# 7   New Connections of Constructive Post-Modernism

Hebdige's comment that some of the media-related movements were sometimes explicitly utopian, and usually sought to provide a bond of moral community, gives us a link to the ideas of other writers who have taken a constructive approach to post-modernism. These are the various scholars from different disciplines who have discerned post-modernist trends that constitute a challenge to the negative aspects of modernism, such as its materialism, secularism, individualism, patriarchy, scientism, anthropocentrism, and ecological vandalism. Constructive post-modern thought seeks new connections and syntheses that might offer alternatives to the negative aspects of modernism. The kinds of phenomena studied include some that modernist thought would have regarded as marginal or antithetical to modern life: the sacred, charisma, passion, spirituality, cosmic meaning and unity, enchantment, community, and so-called "feminine" qualities such as "love" and "romance." Some of these were emphasized in the nineteenth-century Romantic movement, which was a reaction against assumed negative aspects of Enlightenment thought and modernity. However, there is an important difference in that constructive post-modernism does not have a romanticized view of the pre-modern, but seeks to combine the benefits of modernity with values and qualities that it believes were devalued by modernism as an ideology (*materialistic* capitalism is viewed as a contributory factor, but not the sole cause).

Judith Stacey's book *Brave New Families* (1990), as mentioned above, describes the varied pattern of family regimes in an area of California, Silicon Valley, where there seem to be surprising linkings and crossovers involving fundamentalist religion, left-wing politics, feminism, patriarchalism, and various other seemingly incongruent elements. On the basis of her case studies of these extremely complicated family patterns, in which some of the women were finding that membership of a "born again" religious movement provided "a flexible resource for reconstituting gender and kinship relationships in post-modern and post-feminist directions" (p. 18), she came to the conclusion:

> We are living, I believe, through a transitional and contested period of family history, a period *after* the modern family order, but before what we cannot foretell. Precisely because it is not possible to characterize with a single term the competing sets of family cultures that co-exist at present, I identify this family regime as post-modern. The post-modern family is not a new model of family life, not the next stage in an orderly progression of family history, but the stage when the belief in a logical progression of stages breaks down. Rupturing evolutionary models of family history and incorporating both experimental and nostalgic elements, "the" post-modern family lurches forward and backward into an uncertain future.
> (Stacey, 1990, p. 18)

The various "post-modern" family forms that Stacey found in Silicon Valley were marked by differences rather than uniformities. At first glance they resembled the traditional, extended family household, but on closer examination they were found to be composed of various mixtures of friends and relatives, and the members of the household subscribed to sets of beliefs and rationalities that would traditionally have been regarded as incongruous. They do not conform to any single cultural code or form of social organization, and in that sense they are "disorganized." But for these Californians, who had experienced rapid and acute economic and cultural change, they represent pragmatic attempts to hold together their different subject positions (e.g. as partner, mother, feminist, worker, political liberal, and religious fundamentalist) and to provide a buffer against the effects of further disruptive changes.

It is just such reactions to modernity that we need to focus on in our discussion of post-modernity. These reactions are interesting not only because they represent new and often surprising combinations and crossovers of codes and discourses, but also because they offer a challenge to the grand theories and concepts derived from the Enlightenment tradition concerning the course of social development. On the whole, such tendencies or movements are not seeking to turn the clock back to a pre-modern "golden age," as did some conservative reactionaries in responding to the emergence of the modern age. They are efforts to articulate new identities, communities, and even utopias, in the face of increasing ephemerality and social life that lacks foundation – a society of spectacles and fashions, fragmentation of work and class identities, destruction of local communities and natural resources.

Another example of constructive post-modernism that combines elements of religion, psychology, and business is that of "New Age" religions. Heelas has traced these to the distinctive view of the self that began to take root in the 1960s and to what the sociologist Talcott Parsons (1975) called "the expressive revolution," which is concerned with discovering one's "true" nature, delving within in order to experience the riches of "life" itself, and which is all about authenticity, liberation, creativity, and natural wisdom (Heelas, 1991). Many people have been content with a more psychological version of expressivism, seeking self-development or self-actualization, in which importance is attached to getting in touch with feelings and being oneself. Others, however, have become involved with a more utopian version of the quest within. For these New Age or self-religionists, the key belief is that God lies within. "Rather than the self being quasi-sacralized" as in the more psychological wing of expressivism, it is now accorded an explicitly sacred status (Heelas, 1991, p. 1). In many respects the contemporary New Age religion is the direct descendant of the late 1960s and early 1970s hippie counter-culture, but New Age religionists do not think that it is necessary to "drop out" in order to avoid the "iron cage" of modernity. Whereas, prior to the 1960s, this kind of quest for actualization of a sacred self was limited to small numbers of cultural sophisticates (Heelas mentions literary figures like Rousseau, Goethe, Whitman, and Emerson), it then began to enter popular culture and subsequently spread through the agency of therapists, counsellors, healers in alternative medicine, management trainers (especially in Human Resource Management), educationalists, and some of the authors addressing feminist and environmentalist issues. The persuasiveness of self-religiosity may owe much to the failure of the ideology of progress to produce collectivist solutions by way of reforming institutions, leaving people to seek perfection and utopia within themselves. If this also serves to motivate them to perform their work and other institutional roles more effectively, then institutional encouragement is likely to be forthcoming. Large companies in Britain, America, and other countries have been prepared to spend considerable sums of money on training courses based on techniques deriving from the early self-religionist Gurdjieff, or contemporary gurus such as Erhard's Seminars Training (EST). Perhaps the fears of Daniel Bell about "a disjunction between the kind of organization and the norms demanded in the economic realm, and the norms of self-realization that are now central in the culture" (Bell, 1976, p. 15) will be dispelled by the New Age religionists. Alternatively, future economic crises may force a reversion to materialistic concerns at the expense of the quest for actualization of the sacred self: New Age religion may then be revealed as a temporary "yuppie religion."

Let us take another example: the televangelists that Hebdige mentions. They are part of an upsurge of fundamentalist and charismatic religious movements that have appeared across the globe and across religious boundaries – not only across Christian denominational boundaries, but also other religions such as Islam and Judaism. They accept and use many of the techniques and facilities made possible by modernity, while rejecting various aspects of modernist ideology. According to the secularization thesis and theories of social deprivation, such movements should have been diminishing and have had a residual appeal confined to the poor. But, as an article on the televangelists Jim and Tammy Bakker pointed out, this was not the case:

> Many, if not most, academic discussions of fundamentalist religion or televangelism in the nineteen-eighties rested on the premise that fundamentalism was a reaction against modernity on the part of the dispossessed, the uneducated, the minority of Americans left behind by the modern world. To theorists of fundamentalism, the donors to a televangelist such as Bakker had to be poor rural folk, elderly women living on Social Security: people outside the mainstream of middle-class American society. How a minority of poor rural folk managed to contribute such huge sums to the telepreachers – the total had risen to a billion five hundred million dollars annually by 1986 – was a question that most theorists never bothered to address. Of course, anyone who actually looked at Bakker's audiences in his high-tech television studios would see hundreds of well-dressed and extremely respectable looking people of all ages: a cross-section one might imagine of the American middle class.
> (Fitzgerald, 1990, p. 48)

Nor were these involvements merely transitory and limited to passive television viewing. Over a hundred thousand of Bakker's supporters contributed a thousand dollars each for "lifetime partnerships" in his community/theme park called Heritage USA. Other televangelists built universities, hospitals, hotels, television studios, and community centers. One of them, Pat Robertson, campaigned unsuccessfully in 1988 for the Presidency of the United States and was even thought at one stage to be a serious threat to the eventual winner, George Bush. There are many explanations offered to account for this upsurge of fundamentalism, and its attractiveness to a wide cross-section of people. (Some of these explanations were referred to in chapter 12, when the secularization thesis was discussed.) The point being made here is that it represents one of the forms taken by constructive post-modernism, combining elements of modernity with values that seemed to be excluded in the ideology of modernism.

The two concepts in classical sociology that might have been usefully developed to account for these trends – charisma and the sacred – were thought to refer to fringe phenomena destined to decline under the impact of science and the process of rationalization. Even Max Weber and Émile Durkheim, who developed the concepts, tended to think of them as being undercut by modernity.

Weber limited the concept of charisma to the relationship between outstanding leaders and their followers; and he said the opportunities for leaders to exercise a charismatic sway over their followers were destined to decline under the deadening force of rationalization and bureaucracy. Durkheim did not use the term charisma, but he attributed a kind of charismatic force to the sacred, which was a quality of the suprapersonal community: the sense of the social as timeless, all-encompassing, vital, emotionally compelling, evoking deep commitment and a sense of surpassing value. Durkheim saw such experiences of self-transcendence as being engendered by emotionally charged group rituals, and these were less likely to occur in modern society. However, he believed they had to occur to some extent in all societies, and the lack of such opportunities in his own time could only be because it was a "transitional era." Since Durkheim's lifetime (he died in 1917) there has been a significant development that he could not have foreseen: the growth of the mass media, which made possible a new sense of "collective effervescence" and imagined community. However, it is also the case that the apparent pluralization of sources of identity and imagined communities owes much to mass media representations or simulations. It is one of the strengths of theories of post-modernity that they emphasize these processes, as we saw in our discussions of Jameson, Baudrillard, and Hebdige.

Even mundane areas of life can give a mild taste of the collective effervescence and social communion offered by charisma. Identification with local or national sports teams, or with entertainment idols and their styles, can function in that way. Another alternative to membership of charismatic movements with an explicitly religious nature is found in the strong attachment fostered between individuals and the nation. In times of national crisis, this attachment may be strengthened by the rise of a charismatic leader who is thought to embody the potent characteristic of the threatened sacred nation. In the culture of everyday life, even the act of buying can be an exercise in community, as the shopping mall becomes an arena in which to congregate with others and to enjoy a pleasurable disjuncture of ordinary awareness within a group (Jacobs, 1984). In the shopping mall the personalized images that have been connected to the products – images of sexual power, glamour, or national pride – serve to convince shoppers that while purchasing goods they are simultaneously participating together in a shared experience of a more vital and sensual world (Lindholm, 1990).

However, it can be argued that in contemporary western societies, the major alternative forms of charisma are found not in public, secular realms of capitalist consumption, or in the worship of the nation, or in entertainment, or in religion, either orthodox or magical. Instead, people experience merger and self-loss, fundamental meaning and identity, in more intimate circumstances. For example, it is in the supposedly private community of the family or home, whatever form or regime it takes, that people look for a "haven in a heartless world" (Lasch, 1977). But because so much is now required of the family in terms of personal fulfillment, and because the social pressures on the family are so great (the need for two incomes, housing shortages, social mobility, low status of housework), many are disappointed at what is actually delivered. Lindholm, in his study of charismatic communities and movements, suggests that it is for this reason that many counter-cultural communes, such as the Manson group who committed several brutal murders in California in 1969, call themselves "families" and attempt to live out in the commune a fantasy of what they believe families ought to be (Lindholm, 1990, p. 182).

The challenge that "reconstructive post-modernists" face is to develop a sociological paradigm, developing further ideas that were only touched on by earlier theorists such as Weber and Durkheim, which will do justice to the non-rational aspects of the social. Concepts such as charisma and the sacred point to the fact that society is based on a deeply evocative communion of self and other, and the Enlightenment privileging of reason has distracted sociological attention from that fundamental dimension of social life. Such a paradigm also has political and policy implications because it focuses not merely on the ownership and distribution of wealth, but also on the conditions which would permit a pluralistic and multiplex society to tolerate and even promote numerous middle-level communal groups offering a satisfying sense of commitment and emotional gratification.

# 8  Conclusion

It is difficult to make an overall assessment of the many and diverse elements that have been included under the label of post-modernity or post-modernism. To some extent this may be because it is not yet established as a distinct period or a single tendency. In many respects the label is more usefully seen as indicating a number of developments that do not seem to fit in with the Enlightenment's metanarratives about progress, rationalization, and secularization, which were continued in sociological convergence theories of modernity and modernization maintaining that all societies were evolving in the same direction, and in Marxist scientific materialist theories of increasing class polarization and class consciousness.

Post-modernism, as it relates to aesthetics, supports this reading, as it refers to a tendency towards pastiches of incongruent cultural codes, without any single articulating principle or theoretical foundation. It is very much a question of indiscriminate populism: "anything goes" or "whatever turns you on." Of course, there are limits to this apparent free-for-all – not least the fact that things are seldom free; indeed, culture is increasingly commodified. In that respect there are definite ties between culture and economic developments. However, capitalism as an economic system is now so firmly established, despite its cycles of booms and slumps, that it can afford to allow a high level of social and cultural pluralism. If anything, it is in the interests of capitalism to foster the dynamic tendencies of social and cultural pluralism because they encourage innovation and develop more niche markets and flexible specialization. As we have seen, even socially innovative phenomena such as Band Aid and New Age religion, which are motivated by autonomous moral principles that may appear to be antithetical to materialistic and commercial values, may be reconciled with and even co-opted into the economic system. This may be viewed negatively, or it can be interpreted more positively as indicating that there is scope within late capitalism for increased social and cultural variety and pluralism. Consequently, there are different views about how post-modernism should be judged in political terms. If, as Jameson and others believe, post-modernism indicates that we are in a transitional phase before the emergence of a new epoch, then it is too soon to make a final judgment about its potentially progressive or reactionary qualities. There is still room for debate, and that may be the best thing to come out of the current fascination with post-modernism and post-modernity. This is the conclusion of some (though not all) feminists, for example Janet Flax, who welcome the space opened up for new and partial standpoints:

> Feminist theories, like other forms of postmodernism, should encourage us to tolerate and interpret ambivalence, ambiguity, and multiplicity as well as to expose the roots of our needs for imposing order and structure no matter how arbitrary and oppressive these needs may be. If we do our work well, "reality" will appear even more unstable, complex, and disorderly than it does now.
> (Flax, 1987, p. 643)

# References

Baudrillard, J. (1968) *Le Système des Objets*, Paris, Gallimard.

Baudrillard, J. (1970) *La Société de Consommation*, Paris, Gallimard.

Baudrillard, J. (1981) *Simulacres et Simulations*, Paris, Galilee, part translated as *Simulations*, New York, Semiotext(e), 1983.

Baudrillard, J. (1988a) *America*, London, Verso. Original published in French, 1986.

Baudrillard, J. (1988b) *Jean Baudrillard: Selected works* (ed. M. Poster), Cambridge, England, Polity Press.

Bell, D. (1973) *The Coming of Post-Industrial Society*, New York, Basic Books.

Bell, D. (1976) *The Cultural Contradictions of Capitalism*, London, Heinemann.

Bocock, R. and Thompson, K. (eds) (1992) *Social and Cultural Forms of Modernity*, Cambridge, England, Polity Press.

Callinicos, A. (1989) *Against Post-modernism: a Marxist Critique*, Cambridge, England, Polity Press.

Connor, S. (1989) *Post-modernist Culture*, Oxford, Basil Blackwell.

Fitzgerald, F. (1990) "Reflections: Jim and Tammy," *The New Yorker*, April, 1990, pp. 45–87.

Flax, J. (1987) "Post-modernism and gender relations in feminist theory," *Signs: Journal of Women in Culture and Society*, vol. 12, no. 4, pp. 621–43.

Gott, R. (1986) "Modernism and post-modernism: the crisis of contemporary culture," *The Guardian*, December 1, p. 10.

Harvey, D. (1989) *The Condition of Postmodernity*, Oxford, Basil Blackwell.

Hebdige, D. (1989) "After the masses," in Hall, S. and Jacques, M. (eds) *New Times*, London, Lawrence and Wishart.

Heelas, P. (1991) "The sacralization of the self and new age capitalism," in Abercrombie, N. and Warde, A. (eds) *Social Change in Contemporary Britain*, Cambridge, England, Polity Press.

Jacobs, J. (1984) *The Mall*, Prospect Heights, IL, Waveland.

Jameson, F. (1984) "Post-modernism or the cultural logic of late capitalism," *New Left Review*, no. 146, pp. 53–92.

Jameson, F. (1991) *Postmodernism or The Cultural Logic of Late Capitalism*, London, Verso.

Kellner, D. (1989) *Jean Baudrillard: From Marxism to Postmodernism and Beyond*, Cambridge, England, Polity Press.

Laclau, E. and Mouffe, C. (1985) *Hegemony and Socialist Strategy*, London, Verso.

Lasch, C. (1977) *Haven in a Heartless World*, New York, Basic Books.

Lindholm, C. (1990) *Charisma*, Oxford, Basil Blackwell.

*Marxism Today* (1988) October.

Parsons, T. (1975) *The Educational and Expressive Revolutions*, London, London School of Economics.

Simmel, G. (1900) *Die Philosophie des Geldes*, Leipzig: Duncker and Humblot, translated as *The Philosophy of Money*, London, Routledge, 1978.

Stacey, J. (1990) *Brave New Families*, New York, Basic Books.

Venturi, R. et al. (1977) *Learning from Las Vegas*, revised edn, Cambridge, MA, MIT Press.

# 18 The Question of Cultural Identity

Stuart Hall

## Contents

| | | |
|---|---|---|
| 1 | Introduction: Identity in Question | 596 |
| 1.1 | Three concepts of identity | 597 |
| 1.2 | The character of change in late-modernity | 598 |
| 1.3 | What is at stake in the question of identities? | 600 |
| 2 | The Birth and Death of the Modern Subject | 601 |
| 2.1 | De-centering the subject | 606 |
| 3 | National Cultures as "Imagined Communities" | 611 |
| 3.1 | Narrating the nation: an imagined community | 613 |
| 3.2 | Deconstructing the "national culture": identity and difference | 615 |
| 4 | Globalization | 618 |
| 4.1 | Time–space compression and identity | 619 |
| 4.2 | Towards the global post-modern? | 621 |
| 5 | The Global, the Local, and the Return of Ethnicity | 623 |
| 5.1 | "The Rest" in "the West" | 626 |
| 5.2 | The dialectic of identities | 627 |
| 6 | Fundamentalism, Diaspora, and Hybridity | 629 |
| | References | 632 |

# 1    Introduction: Identity in Question

The question of "identity" is being vigorously debated in social theory. In essence, the argument is that the old identities which stabilized the social world for so long are in decline, giving rise to new identities and fragmenting the modern individual as a unified subject. This so-called "crisis of identity" is seen as part of a wider process of change which is dislocating the central structures and processes of modern societies and undermining the frameworks which gave individuals stable anchorage in the social world.

The aim of this chapter is to explore some of these questions about cultural identity in late-modernity and to assess whether a "crisis of identities" exists, what it consists of, and in which directions it is moving. The chapter addresses such questions as: What do we mean by a "crisis of identity"? What recent developments in modern societies have precipitated it? What form does it take? What are its potential consequences? The first part of this chapter (sections 1–2) deals with shifts in the concepts of identity and the subject. The second part (sections 3–6) develops this argument with respect to *cultural identities* – those aspects of our identities which arise from our "belonging" to distinctive ethnic, racial, linguistic, religious, and, above all, national cultures.

Several of the chapters in part III approach their central concern from a number of different positions, framing it within a debate, as if between different protagonists. This chapter works somewhat differently. It is written from a position basically sympathetic to the claim that modern identities are being "de-centered"; that is, dislocated or fragmented. Its aim is to explore this claim, to see what it entails, to qualify it, and to discuss what may be its likely consequences. In the course of the argument, this chapter modifies the claim by introducing certain complexities and examining some contradictory features which the "de-centering" claim, in its simpler forms, neglects.

Accordingly, the formulations in this chapter are provisional and open to contestation. Opinion within the sociological fraternity is still deeply divided about these issues. The trends are too recent and too ambiguous, and the very concept we are dealing with – identity – too complex, too under-developed, and too little understood in contemporary social science to be definitively tested. As with many of the other phenomena examined in this volume, it is impossible to offer conclusive statements or to make secure judgments about the theoretical claims and propositions being advanced. You should bear this in mind as you read the rest of the chapter.

For those theorists who believe that modern identities are breaking up, the argument runs something like this. A distinctive type of structural change is transforming modern societies in the late twentieth century. This is fragmenting the cultural landscapes of class, gender, sexuality, ethnicity, race, and nationality which gave us firm locations as social individuals. These transformations are also shifting our personal identities, undermining our sense of ourselves as integrated subjects. This loss of a stable "sense of self" is sometimes called the dislocation or de-centering of the subject. This set of double displacements – de-centering individuals both from their place in the social and cultural world, and from themselves – constitutes a "crisis of identity" for the individual. As the cultural critic, Kobena Mercer, observes, "identity only becomes an issue when it is in crisis, when something assumed to be fixed, coherent and stable is displaced by the experience of doubt and uncertainty" (Mercer, 1990, p. 43).

Many of these processes of change have been discussed at length in earlier chapters. Taken together, they represent a process of transformation so fundamental and wide-ranging that we are bound to ask if it is not modernity itself which is being transformed. This chapter adds a new dimension to the argument: the claim that, in what is sometimes described as our post-modern world, we are also "post" any fixed or essentialist conception of identity – something which, since the Enlightenment, has been taken to define the very core or essence of our being, and to ground our existence as human subjects. In order to explore this claim, I shall look first at definitions of identity and at the character of change in late-modernity.

## 1.1  Three concepts of identity

For the purposes of exposition, I shall distinguish three very different conceptions of identity: those of the (a) Enlightenment subject, (b) sociological subject, and (c) post-modern subject. The Enlightenment subject was based on a conception of the human person as a fully centered, unified individual, endowed with the capacities of reason, consciousness, and action, whose "center" consisted of an inner core which first emerged when the subject was born, and unfolded with it, while remaining essentially the same – continuous or "identical" with itself – throughout the individual's existence. The essential center of the self was a person's identity. I shall say more about this in a moment, but you can see that this was a very "individualist" conception of the subject and "his" (for Enlightenment subjects were usually described as male) identity.

The notion of the sociological subject reflected the growing complexity of the modern world and the awareness that this inner core of the subject was not autonomous and self-sufficient, but was formed in relation to "significant others," who mediated to the subject the values, meanings, and symbols – the culture – of the worlds he/she inhabited. G.H. Mead, C.H. Cooley, and the symbolic interactionists are the key figures in sociology who elaborated this "interactive" conception of identity and the self. According to this view, which has become the classic sociological conception of the issue, identity is formed in the "interaction" between self and society. The subject still has an inner core or essence that is "the real me," but this is formed and modified in a continuous dialogue with the cultural worlds "outside" and the identities which they offer.

Identity, in this sociological conception, bridges the gap between the "inside" and the "outside" – between the personal and the public worlds. The fact that we project "ourselves" into these cultural identities, at the same time internalizing their meanings and values, making them "part of us," helps to align our subjective feelings with the objective places we occupy in the social and cultural world. Identity thus stitches (or, to use a current medical metaphor, "sutures") the subject into the structure. It stabilizes both subjects and the cultural worlds they inhabit, making both reciprocally more unified and predictable.

Yet these are exactly what are now said to be "shifting." The subject, previously experienced as having a unified and stable identity, is becoming fragmented; composed, not of a single, but of several, sometimes contradictory or unresolved, identities. Correspondingly, the identities which composed the social landscapes "out there," and which ensured our subjective conformity with the objective "needs" of the culture, are breaking up as a result of structural and institutional change. The very process of identification, through which we project ourselves into our cultural identities, has become more open-ended, variable, and problematic.

This produces the post-modern subject, conceptualized as having no fixed, essential, or permanent identity. Identity becomes a "moveable feast": formed and transformed continuously in relation to the ways we are represented or addressed in the cultural systems which surround us (Hall, 1987). It is historically, not biologically, defined. The subject assumes different identities at different times, identities which are not unified around a coherent "self." Within us are contradictory identities, pulling in different directions, so that our identifications are continuously being shifted about. If we feel we have a unified identity from birth to death, it is only because we construct a comforting story or "narrative of the self" about ourselves (see Hall, 1990). The fully unified, completed, secure, and coherent identity is a fantasy. Instead, as the systems of meaning and cultural representation multiply, we are confronted by a bewildering, fleeting multiplicity of possible identities, any one of which we could identify with – at least temporarily.

You should bear in mind that the above three conceptions of the subject are, to some extent, simplifications. As the argument develops, they will become more complex and qualified. Nevertheless, they are worth holding on to as crude pegs around which to develop the argument of this chapter.

## 1.2   The character of change in late-modernity

A further aspect of the issue of identity relates to the character of change in late-modernity; in particular, to that process of change known as "globalization" (discussed in earlier chapters, especially chapter 14), and its impact on cultural identity.

In essence, the argument here is that change in late-modernity has a very specific character. As Marx said about modernity, "[it is a] constant revolutionizing of production, uninterrupted disturbance of all social relations, everlasting uncertainty and agitation. . . . All fixed, fast-frozen relationships, with their train of venerable ideas and opinions, are swept away, all new-formed ones become obsolete before they can ossify. All that is solid melts into air. . . ." (Marx and Engels, 1973, p. 70).

Modern societies are therefore by definition societies of constant, rapid, and permanent change. This is the principal distinction between "traditional" and "modern" societies. Anthony Giddens argues that "In traditional societies, the past is honoured and symbols are valued because they contain and perpetuate the experience of generations. Tradition is a means of handling time and space, which inserts any particular activity or experience within the continuity of past, present and future, these in turn being structured by recurrent social practices" (Giddens, 1990, pp. 37–8). Modernity, by contrast, is not only defined as the experience of living with rapid, extensive, and continuous change, but is a highly reflexive form of life in which "social practices are constantly examined and reformed in the light of incoming information about those very practices, thus constitutively altering their character" (Giddens, 1990, pp. 37–8).

Giddens cites in particular the *pace of change* and the *scope of change* – "as different areas of the globe are drawn into interconnection with one another, waves of social transformation crash across virtually the whole of the earth's surface" – and the *nature of modern institutions* (Giddens, 1990, p. 6). The latter are either radically new compared with traditional societies (e.g. the nation-state or the commodification of products and wage labor), or have a specious continuity with earlier forms (e.g. the city) but are organized on quite different principles. More significant are the transformations of time and space, and what he calls the "disembedding of the social system" – "the 'lifting out' of social relations from local contexts of interaction and their restructuring across indefinite spans of time–space" (1990, p. 21). We will take up all these themes later. However, the general point we would stress is that of *discontinuities*.

> The modes of life brought into being by modernity have swept us away from all traditional types of social order in quite unprecedented fashion. In both their extensionality ["external aspects"] and their intensionality ["internal aspects"] the transformations involved in modernity are more profound than most sorts of change characteristic of prior periods. On the extensional plane they have served to establish forms of social interconnection which span the globe; in intensional terms they have come to alter some of the most intimate and personal features of our day-to-day existence.
> (Giddens, 1990, p. 21)

David Harvey speaks of modernity as not only entailing "a ruthless break with any or all preceding conditions," but as "characterized by a never-ending process of internal ruptures and fragmentations within itself" (1989, p. 12). Ernesto Laclau (1990) uses the concept of "dislocation." A dislocated structure is one whose center is displaced and not replaced by another, but by "a plurality of power centers." Modern societies, Laclau argues, have no center, no single articulating or organizing principle, and do not develop according to the unfolding of a single "cause" or "law." Society is not, as sociologists often thought, a unified and well-bounded whole, a totality, producing itself through evolutionary change from within itself, like the unfolding of a daffodil from its bulb. It is constantly being "de-centered" or dislocated by forces outside itself.

Late-modern societies, he argues, are characterized by "difference"; they are cut through by different social divisions and social antagonisms which produce a variety of different "subject positions" – i.e. identities – for individuals. If such societies hold together at all, it is not because they are unified, but because their different elements and identities can, under certain circumstances, be articulated together. But this articulation is always partial: the structure of identity remains open. Without this, Laclau argues, there would be no history.

This is a very different, and far more troubled and provisional, conception of identity than the earlier two (see section 1.1). We should add that, far from being dismayed by all this, Laclau argues that dislocation has positive features. It unhinges the stable identities of the past, but it also opens up the possibility of new articulations – the forging of new identities, the production of new subjects, and what he calls the "recomposition of the structure around particular nodal points of articulation" (Laclau, 1990, p. 40).

Giddens, Harvey, and Laclau offer somewhat different readings of the nature of change in the post-modern world, but their emphasis on discontinuity, fragmentation, rupture, and dislocation contains a common thread. You should bear this in mind when we come to consider what some theorists claim to be the impact of the contemporary change that is known as "globalization."

## 1.3   What is at stake in the question of identities?

So far the arguments may seem rather abstract. To give you some sense of how they apply to a concrete situation, and what is "at stake" in these contested definitions of identity and change, let us take an example which highlights the *political* consequences of the fragmentation or "pluralization" of identities.

In 1991, President Bush, anxious to restore a conservative majority to the US Supreme Court, nominated Clarence Thomas, a black judge of conservative political views. In Bush's judgment, white voters were likely to support Thomas because he was conservative on equal-rights legislation, and black voters would support Thomas because he was black. In short, the President was "playing the identities game."

During the Senate "hearings" on the appointment, Judge Thomas was accused of sexual harassment by a black woman, Anita Hill, a former junior colleague of Thomas's. The hearings caused a public scandal and polarized American society. Some blacks supported Thomas on racial grounds; others opposed him on sexual grounds. Black women were divided, depending on whether their "identities" as blacks or as women prevailed. Black men were also divided, depending on whether their sexism overrode their liberalism. White men were divided, depending not only on their politics, but on how they identified themselves with respect to racism and sexism. White conservative women supported Thomas not only on political grounds, but because of their opposition to feminism. White feminists, often liberal on race, opposed Thomas on sexual grounds. And because Judge Thomas is a member of the judicial elite and Anita Hall, at the time of the alleged incident, was a junior employee, there were issues of social class position at work in these arguments too.

The question of Judge Thomas's guilt or innocence is not at issue here; what is, is the "play of identities" and its political consequences. Consider:

- The identities were contradictory. They cross-cut or "dislocated" each other.

- The contradictions operated both "outside," in society, cutting across settled constituencies, *and* "inside" the heads of each individual.

- No single identity – e.g. that of social class – could align all the different identities into one, overarching "master identity," on which a politics could be securely grounded. People no longer identify their social interests exclusively in class terms; class cannot serve as a discursive device or mobilizing category through which all the diverse social interests and identities of people can be reconciled and represented.

- Increasingly, the political landscapes of the modern world are fractured in this way by competing and dislocating identifications – arising, especially, from the erosion of the "master identity" of class and the emerging identities belonging to the new political ground defined by the new social movements: feminism, black struggles, national liberation, anti-nuclear, and ecological movements (Mercer, 1990).

- Since identity shifts according to how the subject is addressed or represented, identification is not automatic, but can be won or lost. It has become politicized. This is sometimes described as a shift from a politics of (class) identity to a politics of *difference*.

I can now briefly outline the shape of the rest of the chapter. First, I shall look in somewhat more depth at how the concept of identity is said to have shifted, from that of the Enlightenment subject to that of the sociological and then the "post-modern" subject. Thereafter, the chapter will explore that aspect of modern cultural identity which is formed through one's membership of a *national* culture – and how the processes of dislocating change, encapsulated by the concept of "globalization," are affecting it.

# 2  The Birth and Death of the Modern Subject

In this section I shall outline the account offered by some contemporary theorists of the main shifts that have occurred in the way the subject and identity are conceptualized in modern thought. My aim is to trace the stages through which a particular version of "the human subject" – with certain fixed human capacities and a stable sense of its own identity and place in the order of things – first emerged in the modern age; how it became "centered" in the discourses and practices which shaped modern societies; how it acquired a more sociological or interactive definition; and how it is being "de-centered" in late-modernity. The main focus of this section is conceptual. It is concerned with *changing conceptions* of the human subject as a discursive figure, whose unified form and rational identity, I shall argue, were presupposed by, and essential to, both the discourses of modern thought and the processes which shaped modernity.

To try to map the history of the notion of the modern subject is an exceedingly difficult exercise. The idea that identities were fully unified and coherent, and have now become totally dislocated, is a highly simplistic way of telling the story of the modern subject, and I adopt it here as a device entirely for the purpose of convenient exposition. Even those who hold broadly to the notion of a de-centering of identity would not subscribe to it in this simplified form, and you should bear this qualification in mind as you read this section. However, this simple formulation does have the advantage of enabling me (in the brief space of this chapter) to sketch a crude picture of how, according to the proponents of the de-centering view, the conceptualization of the modern subject has shifted at *three* strategic points during modernity. These shifts underline the basic claim that conceptualizations of the subject change, and therefore have a history. Since the modern subject emerged at a particular time (its "birth") and has a history, it follows that it can also change and, indeed, that under certain circumstances we can even contemplate its "death."

It is now commonplace to say that the modern age gave rise to a new and decisive form of *individualism*, at the center of which stood a new conception of the individual subject and its identity. This does not mean that people were not individuals in pre-modern times, but that individuality was "lived," "experienced," and "conceptualized" differently. The transformations (discussed in earlier volumes in this series) which ushered in modernity tore the individual free from its stable moorings in traditions and structures. Since these were believed to be divinely ordained, they were held not to be subject to fundamental change. One's status, rank, and position in the "great chain of being" – the secular and divine order of things – overshadowed any sense that one was a sovereign individual. The birth of the "sovereign individual" between the Renaissance humanism of the sixteenth century and the Enlightenment of the eighteenth century represented a significant break with the past. Some argue that it was the engine which set the whole social system of "modernity" in motion.

Raymond Williams notes that the modern history of the individual subject brings together two distinct meanings: on the one hand, the subject is "indivisible" – an entity which is unified within itself and cannot be further divided; on the other, it is also an entity which is "singular, distinctive, unique" (see Williams, 1976, pp. 133–5). Many

major movements in western thought and culture contributed to the
emergence of this new conception: the Reformation and Protestantism,
which set the individual conscience free from the religious institutions
of the Church and exposed it directly to the eye of God; Renaissance
humanism, which placed Man (*sic*) at the center of the universe; the
scientific revolutions, which endowed Man with the faculty and
capacities to inquire into, investigate, and unravel the mysteries of
Nature; and the Enlightenment, centered on the image of rational,
scientific Man, freed from dogma and intolerance, before whom the
whole of human history was laid out for understanding and mastery.

Much of the history of western philosophy consists of reflections on,
or refinements of, this conception of the subject, its powers and
capacities. One major figure who gave this conception its primary
formulation was the French philosopher René Descartes (1596–1650).
Sometimes seen as "the father of modern philosophy," Descartes was a
mathematician and scientist, the founder of analytic geometry and
optics, and deeply influenced by the "new science" of the seventeenth
century. He was afflicted by that profound doubt which followed the
displacement of God from the center of the universe; and the fact that
the modern subject was "born" amidst metaphysical doubt and
skepticism reminds us that it was *never* as settled and unified as this
way of describing it suggests (see Forester, 1987). Descartes settled
accounts with God by making him the Prime Mover of all creation;
thereafter he explained the rest of the material world entirely in
mechanical and mathematical terms.

Descartes postulated two distinct substances – spatial substance
(matter) and thinking substance (mind). He thus re-focused that great
*dualism* between "mind" and "matter" which has troubled western
philosophy ever since. Things must be explained, he believed, by
reducing them to their essentials – the fewest possible, ultimately,
irreducible elements. At the center of "mind" he placed the individual
subject, constituted by its capacity to reason and think. "Cogito, ergo
sum" was Descartes' watchword: "I *think*, therefore I am" (my
emphasis). Ever since, this conception of the rational, cogitative, and
conscious subject at the center of knowledge has been known as "the
Cartesian subject."

Another critical contribution was made by John Locke, who, in his
*Essay Concerning Human Understanding*, defined the individual in
terms of "the sameness of a rational being" – that is, an identity which
remained the same and which was continuous with its subject: "as far
as this consciousness can be extended backwards to any past action or
thought, so far reaches the identity of that person" (Locke, 1967, pp.
212–13). This conceptual figure or discursive device – the "sovereign
individual" – was embedded in each of the key processes and practices
which made the modern world. He (*sic*) was the "subject" of modernity
in two senses: the origin or "subject" of reason, knowledge, and
practice; and the one who bore the consequences of these practices –
who was "subjected to" them (see Foucault, 1986).

Some have questioned whether capitalism actually required a
conception of sovereign individuals of this kind (Abercrombie et al.,

1986). Nevertheless, the rise of a more individualist conception of the subject is widely accepted. Raymond Williams summarizes this embedding of the modern subject in the practices and discourses of modernity in the following passage:

> The emergence of notions of **individuality**, in the modern sense, can be related to the break-up of the medieval social, economic and religious order. In the general movement against feudalism there was a new stress on a man's personal existence over and above his place or function in a rigid hierarchical society. There was a related stress, in Protestantism, on a man's direct and individual relation to God, as opposed to this relation mediated by the Church. But it was not until the late seventeenth and eighteenth centuries that a new mode of analysis, in logic and mathematics, postulated the individual as the substantial entity (cf. Leibniz's "monads"), from which other categories and especially collective categories were derived. The political thought of the Enlightenment mainly followed this model. Argument began from individuals, who had an initial and primary existence, and laws and forms of society were derived from them: by submission, as in Hobbes; by contract or consent, or by the new version of natural law, in liberal thought. In classical economics, trade was described in a model which postulated separate individuals who [possessed property and] decided, at some starting point, to enter into economic or commercial relations. In utilitarian ethics, separate individuals calculated the consequences of this or that action which they might undertake.
> (Williams, 1976, pp. 135–6)

It was just possible in the eighteenth century to imagine the great processes of modern life as centered on the individual subject-of-reason. But as modern societies grew more complex, they acquired a more collective and social form. Classic liberal theories of government based on individual rights and consent were obliged to come to terms with the structures of the nation-state and the great masses which make up a modern democracy. The classic laws of political economy, property, contract, and exchange had to operate, after industrialization, amidst the great class formations of modern capitalism. The individual entrepreneur of Adam Smith's *Wealth of Nations* or even of Marx's *Capital* was transformed into the corporate conglomerates of the modern economy. The individual citizen became enmeshed in the bureaucratic administrative machineries of the modern state.

A more *social* conception of the subject then emerged. The individual came to be seen as more located and "placed" within these great supporting structures and formations of modern society. Two major developments contributed to articulating a broader set of conceptual foundations for the modern subject. The first was Darwinian biology. The human subject was "biologized" – reason was given a basis in Nature, and mind a "ground" in the physical development of the human brain.

The second development emerged with the rise of new social

sciences. However, the transformations which this set in motion were uneven. These were:

1   The "sovereign individual," with "his" wants, needs, desires, and interests, remained the pivotal figure in the discourses of both modern economics and the law.

2   The dualism typical of Cartesian thought was institutionalized in the split in the social sciences between psychology and the other disciplines. The study of the individual and its mental processes became psychology's special and privileged object of study.

3   Sociology, however, provided a critique of the "rational individualism" of the Cartesian subject. It located the individual in group processes and the collective norms which, it argued, underpin any contract between individual subjects. It therefore developed an alternative account of how individuals are formed subjectively through their membership of, and participation in, wider social relationships; and, conversely, how processes and structures are sustained by the roles which individuals play in them. This "internalizing" of the outside in the subject, and "externalizing" of the inside through action in the social world (as discussed earlier), is the primary sociological account of the modern subject, and is encapsulated in the theory of socialization. As was noted above, G.H. Mead and the symbolic interactionists adopted a radically interactive view of this process. The integration of the individual into society has been a long-term concern of sociology. Theorists like Goffman were highly attentive to the way "the self" is presented in different social situations, and how conflicts between these different social roles are negotiated. At a more macro-sociological level, Parsons studied the "fit" or complementarity between "the self" and the social system. Nevertheless, some critics would claim that mainstream sociology has retained something of Descartes' dualism, especially in its tendency to construct the problem as a relation between two connected, but separate, entities: here, "the individual *and* society."

This interactive sociological model, with its stable reciprocity between "inside" and "outside," is very much a product of the first half of the twentieth century, when the social sciences assumed their current disciplinary form. However, in the very same period, a more disturbed and disturbing picture of the subject and identity was beginning to emerge in the aesthetic and intellectual movements associated with the rise of modernism.

Here we find the figure of the isolated, exiled, or estranged individual, framed against the background of the anonymous and impersonal crowd or metropolis. Examples include the poet Baudelaire's famous portrait of the "Painter of Modern Life," who sets up his house "in the heart of the multitude, amid the ebb and flow of motion, in the midst of the fugitive and the infinite" and who "becomes one flesh with the crowd," enters into the crowd "as though it were an immense reservoir of electrical energy"; the *flaneur* (or "idle stroller"), who wanders amid the new shopping arcades watching the passing spectacle of the metropolis, whom Walter Benjamin celebrated in his essay on Baudelaire's Paris, and whose counterpart in late-modernity is probably the tourist (cf. Urry, 1990); "K," the anonymous victim confronted by a faceless bureaucracy in Kafka's novel *The Trial*; and that host of estranged figures in twentieth-century literature and social criticism who are meant to represent the unique experience of modernity. Several such "exemplary instances of modernity," as Frisby calls them, people the pages of major turn-of-the-century social theorists like George Simmel, Alfred Schutz, and Siegfried Kracauer (all of whom tried to capture the essential features of modernity in famous essays on "The Stranger" or "Outsider") (see Frisby, 1985, p. 109). These images proved prophetic of what was to befall the Cartesian and sociological subjects in late-modernity.

## 2.1   De-centering the subject

Those who hold that modern identities are being fragmented argue that what has happened in late-modernity to the conception of the modern subject is not simply its estrangement, but its dislocation. They trace this dislocation through a series of ruptures in the discourses of modern knowledge. In this section, I shall offer a brief sketch of five great advances in social theory and the human sciences which have occurred in, or had their major impact upon, thought in the period of late-modernity (the second half of the twentieth century), and whose main effect, it is argued, has been the final de-centering of the Cartesian subject.

The first major de-centering concerns the traditions of Marxist thinking. Marx's writing belongs, of course, to the nineteenth and not the twentieth century. But one of the ways in which his work was recovered and re-read in the 1960s was in the light of his argument that "men (*sic*) make history, but only on the basis of conditions which are not of their own making." His re-readers interpreted this to mean that individuals could not in any true sense be the "authors" or agents of history since they could only act on the basis of the historical conditions made by others into which they were born, and using the resources (material and culture) provided to them from previous generations.

Marxism, properly understood, they argued, displaced any notion of individual agency. The Marxist structuralist Louis Althusser (1918–89) (whose theories of ideology are discussed by Kenneth Thompson in chapter 12) argued that, by putting social relations (modes of production, exploitation of labor power, the circuits of capital) rather than an abstract notion of Man at the center of his theoretical system, Marx displaced two key propositions of modern philosophy: "(1) that there is a universal essence of man; (2) that this essence is the attribute of 'each single individual' who is its real subject":

> These two postulates are complementary and indissoluble. But their existence and their unity presuppose a whole empiricist–idealist world outlook. By rejecting the essence of man as his theoretical basis, Marx rejected the whole of this organic system of

postulates. He drove the philosophical category of *the subject*, of
*empiricism*, of the *ideal essence* from all the domains in which
they had been supreme. Not only from political economy
(rejection of the myth of *homo economicus*, that is, of the
individual with definite faculties and needs as the subject of the
classical economy); not just from history; . . . not just from ethics
(rejection of the Kantian ethical idea); but also from philosophy
itself.
(Althusser, 1966, p. 228)

This "total theoretical revolution" was, of course, fiercely contested by
many humanistic theorists who give greater weight in historical
explanation to human agency. We need not argue here about whether
Althusser was wholly or partly right, or entirely wrong. The fact is that,
though his work has been extensively criticized, his "theoretical anti-
humanism" (that is, a way of thinking opposed to theories which derive
their argument from some notion of a universal essence of Man lodged
in each individual subject) has had considerable impact on many
branches of modern thought.

The second of the great "de-centerings" in twentieth-century western
thought comes from Freud's "discovery" of the unconscious. Freud's
theory that our identities, our sexuality, and the structure of our desires
are formed on the basis of the psychic and symbolic processes of the
unconscious, which function according to a "logic" very different from
that of Reason, plays havoc with the concept of the knowing and
rational subject with a fixed and unified identity – the subject of
Descartes' "I think, therefore I am." This aspect of Freud's work has
also had a profound impact on modern thought in the last three
decades. Psychoanalytic thinkers like Jacques Lacan, for example
(whose work on the unconscious foundations of femininity is discussed
by Helen Crowley: see chapter 10), read Freud as saying that the image
of the self as "whole" and unified is something which the infant only
gradually, partially, and with great difficulty, *learns*. It does not grow
naturally from inside the core of the infant's being, but is formed in
relation to others; especially in the complex unconscious psychic
negotiations in early childhood between the child and the powerful
fantasies which it has of its parental figures. In what Lacan calls the
"mirror phase" of development, the infant who is not yet coordinated,
and possesses no self image as a "whole" person, sees or "imagines"
itself reflected – either literally in the mirror, or figuratively, in the
"mirror" of the other's look – as a "whole person" (Lacan, 1977).
(Incidentally, Althusser borrowed this metaphor from Lacan, when
trying to describe the operation of ideology; see chapter 12.) This is
close in some ways to Mead's and Cooley's "looking glass" conception
of the interactive self; except that for them socialization was a matter of
conscious learning, whereas for Freud subjectivity was the product of
unconscious psychic processes.

This formation of the self in the "look" of the Other, according to
Lacan, opens the child's relation with symbolic systems outside itself,
and is thus the moment of the child's entry into the various systems of

symbolic representation – including language, culture, and sexual difference. The contradictory and unresolved feelings which accompany this difficult entry – the splitting of love and hate for the father, the conflict between the wish to please and the impulse to reject the mother, the division of the self into its "good" and "bad" parts, the disavowal of the masculine/feminine parts of oneself, and so on – which are key aspects of this "unconscious formation of the subject," and which leave the subject "divided," remain with one for life. However, though the subject is always split or divided it experiences its own identity as being held together and "resolved," or unified, as a result of the fantasy of itself as a unified "person" which it formed in the mirror phase. This, according to this kind of psychoanalytic thinking, is the contradictory origin of "identity."

Thus, identity is actually something formed through unconscious processes over time, rather than being innate in consciousness at birth. There is always something "imaginary" or fantasized about its unity. It always remains incomplete, is always "in process," always "being formed." The "feminine" parts of the male self, for example, which are disavowed, remain with him and find unconscious expressions in many unacknowledged ways in adult life. Thus, rather than speaking of identity as a finished thing, we should speak of *identification*, and see it as an on-going process. Identity arises, not so much from the fullness of identity which is already inside us as individuals, but from a *lack* of wholeness which is "filled" from *outside us*, by the ways we imagine ourselves to be seen by *others*. Psychoanalytically, the reason why we continually search for "identity," constructing biographies which knit together the different parts of our divided selves into a unity, is to recapture this fantasized pleasure of fullness (plenitude).

Again, Freud's work, and that of the psychoanalytic thinkers like Lacan who read him in this way, has been widely contested. By definition, unconscious processes cannot be easily seen or examined. They have to be inferred by the elaborate psychoanalytic techniques of reconstruction and interpretation and are not easily amenable to "proof." Nevertheless, their general impact on modern ways of thought has been very considerable. Much modern thinking about subjective and psychic life is "post-Freudian," in the sense that it takes Freud's work on the unconscious for granted, even when it rejects some of his specific hypotheses. Again, you can appreciate the damage which this way of thinking does to notions of the rational subject and identity as fixed and stable.

The third de-centering I shall examine is associated with the work of the structural linguist Ferdinand de Saussure (see chapter 5 for a discussion of his theories of language). Saussure argued that we are not in any absolute sense the "authors" of the statements we make or of the meanings we express in language. We can only use language to produce meanings by positioning ourselves within the rules of language and the systems of meaning of our culture. Language is a social, not an individual system. It pre-exists us. We cannot in any simple sense be its authors. To speak a language is not only to express our innermost, original thoughts, it is also to activate the vast range of meanings which are already embedded in our language and cultural systems.

Further, the meanings of words are not fixed in a one-to-one relation to objects or events in the world outside language. Meaning arises in the relations of similarity and difference which words have to other words within the language code. We know what "night" is because it is *not* "day." Notice the analogy here between language and identity. I know who "I" am in relation to "the other" (e.g. my mother) whom I cannot be. As Lacan would say, identity, like the unconscious, "is structured like language." What modern philosophers of language, like Jacques Derrida, who have been influenced by Saussure and the "linguistic turn," argue is that, despite his/her best efforts the individual speaker can never finally fix meaning – including the meaning of his or her identity. Words are "multi-accentual." They always carry echoes of other meanings which they trigger off, despite one's best efforts to close meaning down. Our statements are underpinned by propositions and premises of which we are not aware, but which are, so to speak, carried along in the bloodstream of our language. Everything we say has a "before" and an "after" – a "margin" in which others may write. Meaning is inherently unstable: it aims for closure (identity), but is constantly disrupted (by difference). It is constantly sliding away from us. There are always supplementary meanings over which we have no control, which will arise and subvert our attempts to create fixed and stable worlds (see Derrida, 1981).

The fourth major de-centering of identity and the subject occurs in the work of the French philosopher and historian Michel Foucault. In a series of studies (some of which have been referred to in chapters 6 and 11), Foucault has produced a sort of "genealogy of the modern subject." Foucault isolates a new type of power, evolving through the nineteenth century, and coming to full flower at the beginning of this century, which he calls "disciplinary power." Disciplinary power is concerned with the regulation, surveillance, and government of, first, the human species or whole populations, and secondly, the individual and the body. Its sites are those new institutions which developed throughout the nineteenth century and which "police" and discipline modern populations – in workshops, barracks, schools, prisons, hospitals, clinics, and so on (see, for example, *Madness and Civilization* (1967), *Birth of the Clinic* (1973), and *Discipline and Punish* (1975)).

The aim of "disciplinary power" is to bring "the lives, deaths, activities, work, miseries and joys of the individual," as well as his/her moral and physical health, sexual practices, and family life under stricter discipline and control; bringing to bear on them the power of administrative regimes, the expertise of the professional, and the knowledge provided by the "disciplines" of the social sciences. Its basic object is to produce "a human being who can be treated as a 'docile body' " (Dreyfus and Rabinow, 1982, p. 135).

What is particularly interesting from the point of view of the history of the modern subject is that, though Foucault's disciplinary power is the product of the new large-scale regulating *collective* institutions of late-modernity, its techniques involve an application of power and knowledge which further "individualizes" the subject and bears down more intensely on his/her body:

> In a disciplinary regime, individualization is descending. Through surveillance, constant observation, all those subject to control are individualized. . . . Not only has power now brought individuality into the field of observation, but power fixes that objective individuality in the field of writing. A vast, meticulous documentary apparatus becomes an essential component of the growth of power [in modern societies]. This accumulation of individual documentation in a systematic ordering makes "possible the measurement of overall phenomena, the description of groups, the characterization of collective facts, the calculation of gaps between individuals, their distribution in a given population."
> (Dreyfus and Rabinow, 1982, p. 159, quoting Foucault)

It is not necessary to accept every detail of Foucault's picture of the all-encompassing character of the "disciplinary regimes" of modern administrative power to understand the paradox that, the more collective and organized is the nature of the institutions of late-modernity, the greater the isolation, surveillance, and individuation of the individual subject.

The fifth de-centering which proponents of this position cite is the impact of feminism, both as theoretical critique and as a social movement. Feminism belongs with that company of "new social movements," all of which surfaced during the 1960s – the great watershed of late-modernity – alongside the student upheavals, the anti-war and counter-cultural youth movements, the civil-rights struggles, the "Third World" revolutionary movements, the peace movements, and the rest associated with "1968." What is important about this historical moment is that:

- These movements were opposed to the corporate liberal politics of the West as well as the "Stalinist" politics of the East.
- They affirmed the "subjective" as well as the "objective" dimensions of politics.
- They were suspicious of all bureaucratic forms of organization and favored spontaneity and acts of political will.
- As argued earlier, all these movements had a powerful *cultural* emphasis and form. They espoused the "theater" of revolution.
- They reflected the weakening or break-up of class politics, and the mass political organizations associated with it, and their fragmentation into various and separate social movements.
- Each movement appealed to the social *identity* of its supporters. Thus feminism appealed to women, sexual politics to gays and lesbians, racial struggles to blacks, anti-war to peaceniks, and so on. This is the historical birth of what came to be know as *identity politics* – one identity per movement.

But feminism also had a more direct relation to the conceptual de-centering of the Cartesian and the sociological subject:

- It questioned the classic distinction between "inside" and "outside," "private" and "public." Feminism's slogan was "the personal is political."
- It therefore opened up to political contestation whole new arenas of social life – the family, sexuality, housework, the domestic division of labor, child-rearing, etc.
- It also exposed, as a political and social question, the issue of how we are formed and produced as gendered subjects. That is to say, it politicized subjectivity, identity, and the process of identification (as men/women, mothers/fathers, sons/daughters).
- What began as a movement directed at challenging the social *position* of women expanded to include the *formation* of sexual and gendered identities.
- Feminism challenged the notion that men and women were part of the same identity – "Mankind" – replacing it with *the question of sexual difference*.

In this section, then, I have tried to map the conceptual shifts by which, according to some theorists, the Enlightenment "subject," with a fixed and stable identity, was de-centered into the open, contradictory, unfinished, fragmented identities of the post-modern subject. I have traced this through five great de-centerings. Let me remind you again that a great many social scientists and intellectuals do not accept the conceptual or intellectual implications (as outlined above) of these developments in modern thought. However, few would now deny their deeply unsettling effects on late-modern ideas and, particularly, on how the subject and the issue of identity have come to be conceptualized.

# 3 National Cultures as "Imagined Communities"

Having traced the conceptual shifts by which the late-modern or post-modern conceptions of the subject and identity have emerged, I shall now turn to the question of how this "fragmented subject" is placed in terms of its *cultural* identities. The particular cultural identity I am concerned with is that of *national* identity (though other aspects are implicated in the story). What is happening to cultural identity in late-modernity? Specifically, how are national cultural identities being affected or displaced by the process of globalization?

In the modern world, the national cultures into which we are born are one of the principal sources of cultural identity. In defining ourselves we sometimes say we are English or Welsh or Indian or Jamaican. Of course, this is to speak metaphorically. These identities are not literally imprinted in our genes. However, we do think of them as if they are part of our essential natures. The conservative philosopher Roger Scruton argues that:

> The condition of man [sic] requires that the individual, while he exists and acts as an autonomous being, does so only because he can first identify himself as something greater – as a member of a society, group, class, state or nation, of some arrangement to which he may not attach a name, but which he recognizes instinctively as home.
> (Scruton, 1986, p. 156)

Ernest Gellner, from a more liberal position, also believes that without a sense of national identification the modern subject would experience a deep sense of subjective loss:

> The idea of a man [sic] without a nation seems to impose a [great] strain on the modern imagination. A man must have a nationality as he must have a nose and two ears. All this seems obvious, though, alas, it is not true. But that it should have come to seem so very obviously true is indeed an aspect, perhaps the very core, of the problem of nationalism. Having a nation is not an inherent attribute of humanity, but it has now come to appear as such.
> (Gellner, 1983, p. 6)

The argument we will be considering here is that, in fact, national identities are not things we are born with, but are formed and transformed within and in relation to *representation*. We only know what it is to be "English" because of the way "Englishness" has come to be represented, as a set of meanings, by English national culture. It follows that a nation is not only a political entity but something which produces meanings – *a system of cultural representation*. People are not only legal citizens of a nation; they participate in the *idea* of the nation as represented in its national culture. A nation is a symbolic community and it is this which accounts for its "power to generate a sense of identity and allegiance" (Schwarz, 1986, p. 106).

National cultures are a distinctly modern form. The allegiance and identification which, in a pre-modern age or in more traditional societies, were given to tribe, people, religion, and region, came gradually in western societies to be transferred to the *national* culture. Regional and ethnic differences were gradually subsumed beneath what Gellner calls the "political roof" of the nation-state, which thus became a powerful source of meanings for modern cultural identities.

The formation of a national culture helped to create standards of universal literacy, generalized a single vernacular language as the dominant medium of communication throughout the nation, created a homogeneous culture and maintained national cultural institutions, such as a national education system. In these and other ways, national culture became a key feature of industrialization and an engine of modernity. Nevertheless, there are other aspects of a national culture which pull it in a different direction, bringing to the fore what Homi Bhabha calls "the particular ambivalence that haunts the idea of the nation" (Bhabha, 1990, p. 1). Some of these ambiguities are explored in section 4. First, section 3.1 will consider how a national culture functions as a system of representation, and section 3.2, whether national identities are really as unified and homogeneous as they represent themselves to be. It is only when these two questions have been answered that we can properly consider the claim that national identities were once centered, coherent, and whole, but are now being dislocated by the processes of globalization.

## 3.1 Narrating the nation: an imagined community

National cultures are composed not only of cultural institutions, but of symbols and representations. A national culture is a *discourse* – a way of constructing meanings which influences and organizes both our actions and our conception of ourselves (see chapter 6). National cultures construct identities by producing meanings about "the nation" with which we can *identify*; these are contained in the stories which are told about it, memories which connect its present with its past, and images which are constructed of it. As Benedict Anderson (1983) has argued, national identity is an "imagined community" (see the discussion of this idea by Kenneth Thompson in chapter 12).

Anderson argues that the differences between nations lie in the different ways in which they are imagined. Or, as Enoch Powell put it, "the life of nations no less than that of men is lived largely in the imagination" (Powell, 1969, p. 245). But how is the modern nation imagined? What representational strategies are deployed to construct our common-sense views of national belonging or identity? What are the representations of, say, "England" which win the identifications and define the identities of "English" people? "Nations," Homi Bhabha has remarked, "like narratives, lose their origins in the myths of time and only fully realize their horizons in the mind's eye" (Bhabha, 1990, p. 1). How is the narrative of the national culture told?

Of the many aspects which a comprehensive answer to that question would include, I have selected *five* main elements.

1 First, there is the *narrative of the nation*, as it is told and retold in national histories, literatures, the media, and popular culture. These provide a set of stories, images, landscapes, scenarios, historical events, national symbols, and rituals which stand for, or *represent*, the shared experiences, sorrows, and triumphs and disasters which give meaning to the nation. As members of such an "imagined community," we see ourselves in our mind's eye sharing in this narrative. It lends significance and importance to our humdrum existence, connecting our everyday lives with a national destiny that pre-existed us and will outlive us. From England's green and pleasant land, its gentle, rolling countryside, rose-trellised cottages and country-house gardens – Shakespeare's "sceptered isle" – to public ceremonials like Royal weddings, the discourse of "Englishness" represents what "England" *is*, gives meaning to the identity of "being English," and fixes "England" as a focus of identification in English (and Anglophile) hearts. As Bill Schwarz observes:

These make up the threads that bind us invisibly to the past. Just as English nationalism is denied, so is the fact of its turbulent and contested history. What we get instead . . . is an emphasis on tradition and heritage, above all on *continuity* so that our present political culture is seen as the flowering of a long organic evolution.
(Schwarz, 1986, p. 155)

2　Secondly, there is the emphasis on *origins, continuity, tradition, and timelessness*. National identity is represented as primordial – "there, in the very nature of things," sometimes slumbering, but ever ready to be "awoken" from its "long, persistent and mysterious somnolence" to resume its unbroken existence (Gellner, 1983, p. 48). The essentials of the national character remain unchanged through all the vicissitudes of history. It is there from birth, unified and continuous, "changeless" throughout all the changes, eternal. Prime Minister Margaret Thatcher remarked at the time of the Falklands War that there were some people "who thought we could no longer do the great things which we once did . . . that Britain was no longer the nation that had built an Empire and ruled a quarter of the world. . . . Well they were wrong . . . Britain has not changed" (quoted in Barnett, 1982, p. 63).

3　A third discursive strategy is what Hobsbawm and Ranger call *the invention of tradition*: "Traditions which appear or claim to be old are often quite recent in origin and sometimes invented. . . . 'Invented tradition' [means] a set of practices, . . . of a ritual or symbolic nature which seek to inculcate certain values and norms of behaviours by repetition which automatically implies continuity with a suitable historical past." For example, "Nothing appears more ancient, and linked to an immemorial past, than the pageantry which surrounds British monarchy and its public ceremonial manifestations. Yet . . . in its modern form it is the product of the late nineteenth and twentieth centuries" (Hobsbawm and Ranger, 1983, p. 1).

4　A fourth example of the narrative of national culture is that of a *foundational myth*: a story which locates the origin of the nation, the people, and their national character so early that they are lost in the mists of, not "real," but "mythic" time. Invented traditions make the confusions and disasters of history intelligible, converting disarray into "community" and disasters into triumphs. Myths of origin also help disenfranchised peoples to "conceive and express their resentment and its contents in intelligible terms" (Hobsbawm and Ranger, 1983, p. 1). They provide a narrative in terms of which an alternative history or counter-narrative, which pre-dates the ruptures of colonization, can be constructed (e.g. Rastafarianism for the dispossessed poor of Kingston, Jamaica; see Hall, 1985). New nations are then founded on these myths. (I say "myths" because, as was the case with many African nations which emerged after decolonization, what preceded colonization was not "one nation, one people," but many different tribal cultures and societies.)

5 National identity is also often symbolically grounded on the idea of a *pure, original people or "folk."* But, in the realities of national development, it is rarely this primordial folk who persist or exercise power. As Gellner wryly observes, "When [simple people] donned folk costume and trekked over the hills, composing poems in the forest clearings, they did not also dream of one day becoming powerful bureaucrats, ambassadors and ministers" (1983, p. 61).

The discourse of national culture is thus not as modern as it appears to be. It constructs identities which are ambiguously placed between past and future. It straddles the temptation to return to former glories and the drive to go forwards ever deeper into modernity. Sometimes national cultures are tempted to turn the clock back, to retreat defensively to that "lost time" when the nation was "great," and to restore past identities. This is the regressive, the anachronistic, element in the national cultural story. But often this very return to the past conceals a struggle to mobilize "the people" to purify their ranks, to expel the "others" who threaten their identity, and to gird their loins for a new march forwards. In Britain during the 1980s, the rhetoric of Thatcherism sometimes inhabited both these aspects of what Tom Nairn calls the "Janus-face" of nationalism (Nairn, 1977): looking back to past imperial glories and "Victorian values" while simultaneously undertaking a kind of modernization in preparation for a new stage of global capitalist competition. Something of the same kind may be going on now in Eastern Europe. Areas breaking away from the old Soviet Union reaffirm their essential ethnic identities and claim nationhood, buttressed by (sometimes extremely dubious) "stories" of mythic origins, religious orthodoxy, and racial purity. Yet they may be also using the nation as the form in which to compete with other ethnic "nations," and so to gain entry to the rich "club" of the West. As Immanuel Wallerstein has acutely observed, "the nationalisms of the modern world are the ambiguous expression [of a desire] for . . . assimilation into the universal . . . and simultaneously for . . . adhering to the particular, the reinvention of differences. Indeed it is a universalism through particularism and particularism through universalism" (Wallerstein, 1984, pp. 166–7).

## 3.2 Deconstructing the "national culture": identity and difference

Section 3.1 considered how a national culture functions as a source of cultural meanings, a focus of identification, and a system of representation. This section now turns to the question of whether national cultures and the national identities they construct are actually *unified*. In his famous essay on the topic, Ernest Renan said that three things constitute the spiritual principle of the unity of a nation: ". . . the possession in common of a rich legacy of memories, . . . the desire to live together, [and] the will to perpetuate the heritage that one has received in an undivided form" (Renan, 1990, p. 19). You should bear in mind these three resonant concepts of what constitutes a national culture as an "imagined community": *memories* from the past; the *desire* to live together; the perpetuation of the *heritage*.

Timothy Brennan reminds us that the word *nation* refers "both to the modern nation-state and to something more ancient and nebulous – the *natio* – a local community, domicile, family, condition of belonging" (Brennan, 1990, p. 45). National identities represented precisely the result of bringing these two halves of the national equation together – offering both membership of the political nation-state and identification with the national culture: "to make culture and polity congruent" and to endow "reasonably homogeneous cultures, each with its own political roof" (Gellner, 1983, p. 43). Gellner clearly establishes this impulse to *unify* in national cultures.

> . . . culture is now the necessary shared medium, the life-blood, or perhaps rather the minimal shared atmosphere, within which alone the members of the society can breathe and survive and produce. For a given society it must be one in which they can all breathe and speak and produce; so it must be the *same* culture. (Gellner, 1983, pp. 37–8)

To put it crudely, however different its members may be in terms of class, gender, or race, a national culture seeks to unify them into one cultural identity, to represent them all as belonging to the same great national family. But is national identity a unifying identity of this kind, which cancels or subsumes cultural difference?

Such an idea is open to doubt, for several reasons. A national culture has never been simply a point of allegiance, bonding and symbolic identification. It is also a structure of cultural power. Consider the following points:

1   Most modern nations consist of disparate cultures which were only unified by a lengthy process of violent conquest – that is, by the forcible suppression of cultural difference. "The British people" are the product of a series of such conquests – Celtic, Roman, Saxon, Viking, and Norman. Throughout Europe the story is repeated *ad nauseam*. Each conquest subjugated conquered peoples and their cultures, customs, languages, and traditions and tried to impose a more unified cultural hegemony. As Ernest Renan has remarked, these violent beginnings which stand at the origins of modern nations have first to be "forgotten" before allegiance to a more unified, homogeneous national identity could begin to be forged. Thus "British" culture still does not consist of an equal partnership between the component cultures of the UK, but of the effective hegemony of "English," a southern-based culture which represents itself as the essential British culture, over Scottish, Welsh, and Irish and, indeed, other regional cultures. Matthew Arnold, who tried to fix the essential character of the English people from their literature, claimed when considering the Celts that such "provincial nationalisms had to be swallowed up at the level of the political and licensed as cultural contributors to English culture" (Dodd, 1986, p. 12).

2   Secondly, nations are always composed of different social classes, and gender and ethnic groups. Modern British nationalism was the product of a very concerted effort, in the late Victorian and high imperial period, to unify the classes across social divisions by providing them with an alternative point of identification – common membership of "the family of the nation." The same point can be made about gender. National identities are strongly gendered. The meanings and values of "Englishness" have powerful masculine associations. Women play a secondary role as guardians of hearth, kith, and kin, and as "mothers" of the nation's "sons."

3   Thirdly, modern western nations were also the centers of empires or of neo-imperial spheres of influence, exercising cultural hegemony over the cultures of the colonized. Some historians now argue that it was in this process of comparison between the "virtues" of "Englishness" and the negative features of other cultures that many of the distinctive characteristics of English identities were first defined (see C. Hall, 1992).

Instead of thinking of national cultures as unified, we should think of them as constituting a *discursive device* which represents difference as unity or identity. They are cross-cut by deep internal divisions and differences, and "unified" only through the exercise of different forms of cultural power. Yet – as in the fantasies of the "whole" self of which Lacanian psychoanalysis speaks – national identities continue to be represented as *unified*.

One way of unifying them has been to represent them as the expression of the underlying culture of "one people." Ethnicity is the term we give to cultural features – language, religion, custom, traditions, feeling for "place" – which are shared by a people. It is therefore tempting to try to use ethnicity in this "foundational" way. But this belief turns out, in the modern world, to be a myth. Western Europe has no nations which are composed of only one people, one culture or ethnicity. *Modern nations are all cultural hybrids.*

It is even more difficult to try to unify national identity around race; first, because – contrary to widespread belief – race is not a biological or genetic category with any scientific validity. There are different genetic strains and "pools," but they are as widely dispersed *within* what are called "races" as they are *between* one "race" and another. Genetic difference – the last refuge of racist ideologies – cannot be used to distinguish one people from another. Race is a *discursive*, not a biological category. That is to say, it is the organizing category of those ways of speaking, systems of representation, and social practices (discourses) which utilize a loose, often unspecified set of differences in physical characteristics – skin color, hair texture, physical and bodily features, etc. – as *symbolic markers* in order to differentiate one group socially from another.

Of course the unscientific character of the term "race" does not undermine "how racial logics and racial frames of reference are articulated and deployed, and with what consequences" (Donald and Rattansi, 1992, p. 1). In recent years, biological notions of races as a

distinct species (notions which underpinned extreme forms of
nationalist ideology and discourse in earlier periods: Victorian
eugenics, European race theories, fascism) have been replaced by
*cultural* definitions of race, which allow race to play a significant role
in discourses about the nation and national identity. Paul Gilroy has
commented on the links between "cultural racism" and "the idea of
race and the ideas of nation, nationality, and national belonging":

> We increasingly face a racism which avoids being recognized as
> such because it is able to line up "race" with nationhood,
> patriotism and nationalism. A racism which has taken a necessary
> distance from crude ideas of biological inferiority and superiority
> now seeks to present an imaginary definition of the nation as a
> unified *cultural* community. It constructs and defends an image of
> national culture – homogeneous in its whiteness yet precarious
> and perpetually vulnerable to attack from enemies within and
> without. . . . This is a racism that answers the social and political
> turbulence of crisis and crisis management by the recovery of
> national greatness in the imagination. Its dream-like construction
> of our sceptered isle as an ethnically purified one provides special
> comfort against the ravages of [national] decline.
> (Gilroy, 1992, p. 87)

But even when "race" is used in this broader discursive way, modern
nations stubbornly refuse to be resolved into it. As Renan observed,
"the leading nations of Europe are nations of essentially mixed blood":
"France is [at once] Celtic, Iberic and Germanic. Germany is Germanic,
Celtic and Slav. Italy is the country where . . . Gauls, Etruscans,
Pelagians and Greeks, not to mention many other elements, intersect in
an indecipherable mixture. The British Isles, considered as a whole,
present a mixture of Celtic and Germanic blood, the proportions of
which are singularly difficult to define" (Renan, 1990, pp. 14–15). And
these are relatively simple "mixtures" as compared with those to be
found in Central and Eastern Europe.

This brief examination undermines the idea of the nation as a
unified cultural identity. National identities do not subsume all other
forms of difference into themselves and are not free of the play of
power, internal divisions and contradictions, cross-cutting allegiances
and difference. So when we come to consider whether national
identities are being dislocated, we must bear in mind the way national
cultures help to "stitch up" differences into one identity.

# 4   Globalization

The previous section qualified the idea that national identities have
ever been as unified or homogeneous as they are represented to be.
Nevertheless, in modern history, national cultures have dominated
"modernity" and national identities have tended to win out over other,
more particularistic sources of cultural identification.

What, then, is so powerfully dislocating national cultural identities now, at the end of the twentieth century? The answer is a complex of processes and forces of change, which for convenience can be summed up under the term "globalization." This concept was extensively discussed by Anthony McGrew in chapter 14. As he argued, "globalization" refers to those processes, operating on a global scale, which cut across national boundaries, integrating and connecting communities and organizations in new space–time combinations, making the world in reality and in experience more interconnected. Globalization implies a movement away from the classical sociological idea of a "society" as a well-bounded system, and its replacement by a perspective which concentrates on "how social life is ordered across time and space" (Giddens, 1990, p. 64). These new temporal and spatial features, resulting in the compression of distances and time-scales, are among the most significant aspects of globalization affecting cultural identities, and they are discussed in greater detail below.

Remember that globalization is not a recent phenomenon: "Modernity is inherently globalizing" (Giddens, 1990, p. 63). As David Held argued in chapter 2, nation-states were never as autonomous or as sovereign as they claimed to be. And, as Wallerstein reminds us, capitalism "was from the beginning an affair of the world economy and not of nation states. Capital has never allowed its aspirations to be determined by national boundaries" (Wallerstein, 1979, p. 19). So *both* the trend towards national autonomy and the trend towards globalization are deeply rooted in modernity (see Wallerstein, 1991, p. 98).

You should bear in mind these two contradictory tendencies within globalization. Nevertheless, it is generally agreed that, since the 1970s, both the scope and pace of global integration have greatly increased, accelerating the flows and linkages between nations. In this and the next section, I shall attempt to track the consequences of these aspects of globalization on cultural identities, examining *three* possible consequences:

1  National identities are being *eroded* as a result of the growth of cultural homogenization and "the global post-modern."

2  National and other "local" or particularistic identities are being *strengthened* by the resistance to globalization.

3  National identities are declining but *new* identities of hybridity are taking their place.


## 4.1  Time–space compression and identity

What impact has the latest phase of globalization had on national identities? You will remember from chapter 14 that one of its main features is "time–space compression" – the speeding up of global processes, so that the world feels smaller and distances shorter, so that events in one place impact immediately on people and places a very long distance away. David Harvey argues that:

> As space appears to shrink to a "global" village of
> telecommunications and a "spaceship earth" of economic and
> ecological inter-dependencies – to use just two familiar and
> everyday images – and as time horizons shorten to the point
> where the present is all there is, so we have to learn to cope with
> an overwhelming sense of compression of our spatial and
> temporal worlds.
> (Harvey, 1989, p. 240)

What is important for our argument about the impact of globalization
on identity is that time and space are also the basic coordinates
of all systems of *representation*. Every medium of representation –
writing, drawing, painting, photography, figuring through art, or the
telecommunications systems – must translate its subject into
spatial and temporal dimensions. Thus, narrative translates events
into a beginning–middle–end time sequence; and visual systems of
representation translate three-dimensional objects into two
dimensions. Different cultural epochs have different ways of
combining these time–space coordinates. Harvey contrasts the
rational ordering of space and time of the Enlightenment (with its
regular sense of order, symmetry, and balance) with the broken and
fragmented time–space coordinates of the Modernist movements of the
late nineteenth and early twentieth centuries. We can see new space–
time relationships being defined in developments as different as
Einstein's theory of relativity, the cubist paintings of Picasso and
Braque, the works of the Surrealists and Dadaists, the experiments with
time and narrative in the novels of Marcel Proust and James Joyce, and
the use of montage techniques in the early cinema of Vertov and
Eisenstein.

Section 3 argued that identity is deeply implicated in representation.
Thus, the shaping and reshaping of time–space relationships within
different systems of representation have profound effects on how
identities are located and represented. The male subject, represented in
eighteenth-century paintings surveying his property, in the form of the
well-regulated and controlled classical spatial forms of the Georgian
crescent or English country residence, or seeing himself located in the
spacious, controlled forms of Nature of a formal garden or parkland,
has a very different sense of cultural identity from the subject who sees
"himself/herself" mirrored in the fragmented, fractured "faces" which
look out from the broken planes and surfaces of one of Picasso's cubist
canvases. All identities are located in symbolic space and time. They
have what Edward Said calls their "imaginary geographies" (Said,
1990): their characteristic "landscapes," their sense of "place," "home,"
or *heimat*, as well as their placings in time – in invented traditions
which bind past and present, in myths of origin which project the
present back into the past, and in the narratives of the nation which
connect the individual to larger, more significant national historic
events.

Another way of thinking about this is in terms of what Giddens
(1990) calls the separation of space from place. "Place" is specific,

concrete, known, familiar, bounded: the site of specific social practices which have shaped and formed us, and with which our identities are closely bound up.

> In premodern societies, space and place largely coincided, since the spatial dimensions of social life are, for most of the population . . . dominated by "presence" – by localised activity. . . . Modernity increasingly tears space away from place by fostering relations between "absent" others, locationally distant from any given situation of face-to-face interaction. In conditions of modernity . . . locales are thoroughly penetrated by and shaped in terms of social influences quite distant from them. What structures the locale is not simply that which is present on the scene; the "visible form" of the locale conceals the distanced relations which determine its nature.
> (Giddens, 1990, p. 18)

Places remain fixed; they are where we have "roots." Yet space can be "crossed" in the twinkling of an eye – by jet, fax, or satellite. Harvey calls this "the annihilation of space through time" (1989, p. 205).

## 4.2 Towards the global post-modern?

Some theorists argue that the general effect of these globalizing processes has been to weaken or undermine national forms of cultural identity. They argue that there is evidence of a loosening of strong identifications with the national culture, and a strengthening of other cultural ties and allegiances, "above" and "below" the level of the nation-state. National identities remain strong, especially with respect to such things as legal and citizenship rights, but local, regional, and community identities have become more significant. Above the level of the national culture, "global" identifications begin to displace, and sometimes over-ride, national ones.

Some cultural theorists argue that the trend towards greater global interdependence is leading to the breakdown of *all* strong cultural identities and is producing that fragmentation of cultural codes, that multiplicity of styles, emphasis on the ephemeral, the fleeting, the impermanent, and on difference and cultural pluralism which Kenneth Thompson described in chapter 17, but on a global scale – what we might call *the global post-modern*. Cultural flows and global consumerism between nations create the possibilities of "shared identities" – as "customers" for the same goods, "clients" for the same services, "audiences" for the same messages and images – between people who are far removed from one another in time and space. As national cultures become more exposed to outside influences it is difficult to preserve cultural identities intact, or to prevent them from becoming weakened through cultural bombardment and infiltration.

People in small, apparently remote villages in poor, "Third World" countries can receive in the privacy of their homes the messages and images of the rich, consumer cultures of the West, purveyed through TV sets or the transistor radio, which bind them into the "global village" of the new communications networks. Jeans and tennis shoes – the "uniform" of the young in western youth culture – are as ubiquitous in South-East Asia as the US or Europe, not only because of the growth of the world-wide marketing of the youth consumer image, but because they are often actually produced in Taiwan or Hong Kong or South Korea for the New York, Los Angeles, London, or Rome store.

The more social life becomes mediated by the global marketing of styles, places, and images, by international travel, and by globally networked media images and communications systems, the more *identities* become detached – disembedded – from specific times, places, histories, and traditions, and appear "free-floating." We are confronted by a range of different identities, each appealing to us, or rather to different parts of ourselves, from which it seems possible to choose. It is the spread of consumerism, whether as reality or dream, which has contributed to this "cultural supermarket" effect. Within the discourse of global consumerism, differences and cultural distinctions which hitherto defined *identity* become reducible to a sort of international *lingua franca* or global currency into which all specific traditions and distinct identities can be translated. This phenomenon is known as "cultural homogenization."

> What is being created is a new electronic cultural space, a "placeless" geography of image and simulation. . . . This new global arena of culture is a world of instantaneous and depthless communication, a world in which space and time horizons have become compressed and collapsed. . . .
>
> Globalization is about the compression of time and space horizons and the creation of a world of instantaneity and depthlessness. Global space is a space of flows, an electronic space, a decentred space, a space in which frontiers and boundaries have become permeable. Within this global arena, economies and cultures are thrown into intense and immediate contact with each other – with each "Other" (an "Other" that is no longer simply "out there", but also within).
>
> I have argued that this is the force shaping our times. Many commentators, however, suggest that something quite different is happening: that the new geographies are, in fact, about the renaissance of locality and region. There has been a great surge of interest recently in local economies and local economic strategies. The case for the local or regional economy as the key unit of production has been forcefully made by the "flexible specialization" thesis. . . . This perspective stresses the central and prefigurative importance of localized production complexes. Crucial to their success, it is suggested, are strong local institutions and infrastructures: relations of trust based on face-to-face contact; a "productive community" historically rooted in a particular place; a strong sense of local pride and attachment. . . .
>
> Whilst globalization may be the prevailing force of our times, this does not mean that localism is without significance. If I have emphasized processes of de-localization, associated especially

with the development of new information and communications networks, this should not be seen as an absolute tendency. The particularity of place and culture can never be done away with, can never be absolutely transcended. Globalization is, in fact, also associated with new dynamics of *re*-localization. It is about the achievement of a new global–local nexus, about new and intricate relations between global space and local space. Globalization is like putting together a jigsaw puzzle: it is a matter of inserting a multiplicity of localities into the overall picture of a new global system.

(Robins, 1991, pp. 28–31, 33–6)

To some extent, what is being debated is the tension between the "global" and the "local" in the transformation of identities. National identities, as we have seen, represent attachment to particular places, events, symbols, histories. They represent what is sometimes called a *particularistic* form of attachment or belonging. There has always been a tension between these and more *universalistic* identifications – for example, to "humanity" rather than to "Englishness." This tension has persisted throughout modernity: the growth of nation-states, national economies, and national cultures continuing to provide a focus for the first; the expansion of the world market and modernity as a global system providing the focus for the second. In reading section 5, which examines how globalization in its most recent forms impacts on identities, you may find it helpful to think of such impact in terms of new ways of articulating the particularistic and the universalistic aspects of identity, or new ways of negotiating the tension between the two.


# 5   The Global, the Local, and the Return of Ethnicity

Are national identities being "homogenized"? Cultural homogenization is the anguished cry of those who are convinced that globalization threatens to undermine national identities and the "unity" of national cultures. However, as a view of the future of identities in a post-modern world this picture is too simplistic, exaggerated and one-sided as it stands.

We can pick up at least three major qualifications or counter-tendencies. The first arises from the observation that alongside the tendency towards global homogenization, there is also a fascination with *difference* and the marketing of ethnicity and "otherness." There is a new interest in "the local" together with the impact of "the global." Globalization (in the form of flexible specialization and "niche" marketing) actually exploits local differentiation. Thus, instead of thinking of the global *replacing* the local, it would be more accurate to think of a new articulation between "the global" and "the local." This "local" is not, of course, to be confused with older identities, firmly rooted in well-bounded localities. Rather, it operates within the logic of globalization. However, it seems unlikely that globalization will simply destroy national identities. It is more likely to produce, simultaneously *new* "global" and *new* "local" identifications.

The second qualification to the argument about the global homogenization of identities is that globalization is very unevenly distributed around the globe, between regions and between different strata of the population *within* regions. This is what Doreen Massey calls globalization's "power geometry":

> . . . I want to make one simple point here, and that is about what one might call the *power-geometry* of it all; the power-geometry of time–space compression. For different social groups, and different individuals, are placed in very distinct ways in relation to these flows and interconnections. This point concerns not merely the issue of who moves and who doesn't, although that is an important element of it; it is also about power in relation *to* the flows and the movement. Different social groups have distinct relationships to this anyway differentiated mobility: some people are more in charge of it than others; some initiate flows and movement, others don't; some are more on the receiving-end of it than others; some are effectively imprisoned by it.
>
> In a sense, at the end of all the spectra are those who are both doing the moving and the communicating and who are in some way in a position of control in relation to it – the jet-setters, the ones sending and receiving the faxes and the e-mail, holding the international conference calls, the ones distributing the films, controlling the news, organising the investments and the international currency transactions. These are the groups who are really in a sense in charge of time–space compression, who can really use it and turn it to advantage, whose power and influence it very definitely increases. On its more prosaic fringes this group probably includes a fair number of Western academics and journalists – those, in other words, who write most about it.
>
> But there are also groups who are also doing a lot of physical moving, but who are not "in charge" of the process in the same way at all. The refugees from El Salvador or Guatemala and the undocumented migrant workers from Michoacán in Mexico, crowding into Tijuana to make a perhaps fatal dash for it across the border into the US to grab a chance of a new life. Here the experience of movement, and indeed of a confusing plurality of cultures, is very different. . . .
>
> Or – one final example to illustrate a different kind of complexity – there are the people who live in the *favelas* of Rio, who know global soccer like the back of their hand, and have produced some of its players; who have contributed massively to global music, who gave us the samba and produced the lambada that everyone was dancing to last year in the clubs of Paris and

London; and who have never, or hardly ever, been to downtown
Rio. At one level they have been tremendous contributors to what
we call time–space compression; and at another level they are
imprisoned in it.

This is, in other words, a highly complex social differentiation.
There are differences in the degree of movement and
communication, but also in the degree of control and of initiation.
The ways in which people are placed within "time–space
compression" are highly complicated and extremely varied.
(Massey, 1991, pp. 25–6)

The third point in the critique of cultural homogenization is the
question of who is most affected by it. Since there is an uneven
direction to the flow, and since unequal relations of cultural power
between "the West" and "the Rest" persist, globalization – though by
definition something which affects the whole globe – may appear to be
essentially a western phenomenon.

Kevin Robins reminds us:

For all that it has projected itself as transhistorical and
transnational, as the transcendent and universalizing force of
modernization and modernity, global capitalism has in reality
been about westernization – the export of western commodities,
values, priorities, ways of life. In a process of unequal cultural
encounter, "foreign" populations have been compelled to be the
subjects and subalterns of western empire, while, no less
significantly, the west has come face to face with the "alien" and
"exotic" culture of its "Other." Globalization, as it dissolves the
barriers of distance, makes the encounter of colonial centre and
colonized periphery immediate and intense.
(Robins, 1991, p. 25)

In the latest form of globalization, it is still the images, artefacts, and
identities of western modernity, produced by the cultural industries of
"western" societies (including Japan) which dominate the global
networks. The proliferation of identity choices is more extensive at the
"center" of the global system than at its peripheries. The patterns of
unequal cultural exchange, familiar from earlier phases of globalization,
persist into late-modernity. If you want to sample the exotic cuisines of
other cultures in one place, it would be better to eat in Manhattan,
Paris, or London than in Calcutta or Delhi.

On the other hand, societies of the periphery have *always* been open
to western cultural influences and are now more so. The idea that these
are "closed" places – ethnically pure, culturally traditional,
undisturbed until yesterday by the ruptures of modernity – is a western
fantasy about "otherness": a "colonial fantasy" maintained *about* the
periphery *by* the West, which tends to like its natives "pure" and its
exotic places "untouched." Nevertheless, the evidence suggests that
globalization is impacting everywhere, including the West, and the
"periphery" is experiencing its pluralizing impact too, though at a
slower, more uneven pace.

## 5.1  "The Rest" in "the West"

The preceding pages have presented three qualifications to the first of the three possible consequences of globalization: i.e. the homogenization of global identities. These are that:

1   Globalization can go hand in hand with a strengthening of local identities, though this is still within the logic of time–space compression;

2   Globalization is an uneven process and has its own "power geometry";

3   Globalization retains some aspects of western global domination, but cultural identities everywhere are being relativized by the impact of time–space compression.

Perhaps the most striking example of this third point is the phenomenon of migration. After World War II, the decolonizing European powers thought they could pull out of their colonial spheres of influence, leaving the consequences of imperialism behind them. But global interdependence now works both ways. The movements of western styles, images, commodities, and consumer identities outwards has been matched by a momentous movement of peoples from the peripheries to the center in one of the largest and most sustained periods of "unplanned" migration in recent history. Driven by poverty, drought, famine, economic under-development and crop failure, civil war and political unrest, regional conflict and arbitrary changes of political regime, the accumulating foreign indebtedness of their governments to western banks, very large numbers of the poorer peoples of the globe have taken the "message" of global consumerism at face value, and moved towards the places where "the goodies" come from and where the chances of survival are higher. In the era of global communications, the West is only a one-way airline charter ticket away.

There have been continuous, large-scale, legal and "illegal" migrations into the US from many poor countries of Latin America and the Caribbean basin (Cuba, Haiti, Puerto Rico, the Dominican Republic, the islands of the British Caribbean), as well as substantial numbers of "economic migrants" and political refugees from South-East Asia and the Far East – Chinese, Koreans, Vietnamese, Cambodians, Indians, Pakistanis, Japanese. Canada has a substantial minority Caribbean population. One consequence is a dramatic shift in the "ethnic mix" of the US population – the first since the mass migrations of the early part of this century. In 1980, one in every five Americans came from an African-American, Asian-American, or American-Indian background. In 1990, the figure was one in four. In many major cities (including Los Angeles, San Francisco, New York, Chicago, and Miami), whites are now a minority. In the 1980s, the population of California grew by 5.6 million, 43 percent of which were people of color – that is, including Hispanics and Asians, as well as African-Americans (compared to 33 percent in 1980) – and one-fifth are foreign born. By 1995 one-third of

American public school students were expected to be "non-white" (US Census, 1991, quoted in Platt, 1991).

Over the same period, there has been a parallel "migration" into Europe of Arabs from the Maghreb (Morocco, Algeria, Tunisia), and Africans from Senegal and Zaire into France and Belgium; of Turks and North Africans into Germany; of Asians from the ex-Dutch East and West Indies and Surinam into the Netherlands; of North Africans into Italy; and, of course, of people from the Caribbean and from India, Pakistan, Bangladesh, Kenya, Uganda, and Sri Lanka into the United Kingdom. There are political refugees from Somalia, Ethiopia, the Sudan, and Sri Lanka and other places in small numbers everywhere.

This formation of ethnic-minority "enclaves" within the nation-states of the West has led to a "pluralization" of national cultures and national identities.

## 5.2   The dialectic of identities

We can look at how this situation has played itself out in Britain in terms of identity. The first effect has been to contest the settled contours of national identity, and to expose its closures to the pressures of difference, "otherness," and cultural diversity. This is happening, to different degrees, in all the western national cultures and as a consequence it has brought the whole issue of national identity and the cultural "centeredness" of the West into the open.

> Older certainties and hierarchies of British identity have been called into question in a world of dissolving boundaries and disrupted continuities. In a country that it is now a container of African and Asian cultures, the sense of what it is to be British can never again have the old confidence and surety. Other sources of identity are no less fragile. What does it mean to be European in a continent coloured not only by the cultures of its former colonies, but also by American and now Japanese cultures? Is not the very category of identity itself problematical? Is it at all possible, in global times, to regain a coherent and integral sense of identity? Continuity and historicity of identity are challenged by the immediacy and intensity of global cultural confrontations. The comforts of Tradition are fundamentally challenged by the imperative to forge a new self-interpretation based upon the responsibilities of cultural Translation.
> (Robins, 1991, p. 41)

Another effect has been to trigger a widening of the field of identities, and a proliferation of new identity-positions together with a degree of polarization among and between them. These developments constitute the second and third possible consequences of globalization I referred to earlier (section 4) – the possibility that globalization might lead to a *strengthening* of local identities, or to the production of *new identities*.

The strengthening of local identities can be seen in the strong defensive reaction of those members of dominant ethnic groups who feel threatened by the presence of other cultures. In the UK, for example, such defensiveness has produced a revamped Englishness, and a retreat to ethnic absolutism in an attempt to shore up the nation and rebuild "an identity that coheres, is unified and filters out threats in social experience" (Sennett, 1971, p. 15). This is often grounded in what I have earlier called "cultural racism," and is evident now in legitimate political parties of both Left and Right, and in more extremist political movements throughout Western Europe.

It is sometimes matched by a strategic retreat to more defensive identities among the minority communities themselves in response to the experience of cultural racism and exclusion. Such strategies include re-identification with cultures of origin (in the Caribbean, India, Bangladesh, Pakistan); the construction of strong counter-ethnicities – as in the symbolic identification of second-generation Afro-Caribbean youth, through the symbols and motifs of Rastafarianism, with their African origin and heritage; or the revival of cultural traditionalism, religious orthodoxy, and political separatism, for example, among *some* sections of the Muslim community.

There is also some evidence of the third possible consequence of globalization – the production of *new* identities. A good example is those new identities which have emerged in the 1970s, grouped around the signifier "black," which in the British context provides a new focus of identification for *both* Afro-Caribbean and Asian communities. What these communities have in common, which they represent through taking on the "black" identity, is not that they are culturally, ethnically, linguistically, or even physically the same, but that they are seen and treated as "the same" (i.e. non-white, "other") by the dominant culture. It is their exclusion which provides what Laclau and Mouffe call the common "axis of equivalence" of this new identity. However, despite the fact that efforts are made to give this "black" identity a single or unified content, it continues to exist as an identity *alongside a wide range of other differences*. Afro-Caribbean and Indian people continue to maintain different cultural traditions. "Black" is thus an example, not only of the *political* character of new identities – i.e. their *positional* and conjunctural character (their formation in and for specific times and places) – but also of the way identity and difference are inextricably articulated or knitted together in different identities, the one never wholly obliterating the other.

As a tentative conclusion it would appear, then, that globalization *does* have the effect of contesting and dislocating the centered and "closed" identities of a national culture. It does have a pluralizing impact on identities, producing a variety of possibilities and new positions of identification, and making identities more positional, more political, more plural and diverse; less fixed, unified or trans-historical. However, its general impact remains contradictory. Some identities gravitate towards what Robins calls "Tradition," attempting to restore their former purity and recover the unities and certainties which are felt as being lost. Others accept that identity is subject to the play of history, politics, representation, and difference, so that they are unlikely ever again to be unitary or "pure"; and these consequently gravitate towards what Robins (following Homi Bhabha) calls "Translation."

Section 6 will now briefly sketch this contradictory movement between Tradition and Translation on a wider, global canvas and ask what it tells us about the way identities need to be conceptualized in relation to modernity's futures.


# 6  Fundamentalism, Diaspora, and Hybridity

Where identities are concerned, this oscillation between Tradition and Translation (which was briefly traced above in relation to Britain) is becoming more evident on a global canvas. Everywhere, cultural identities are emerging which are not fixed, but poised, *in transition*, between different positions; which draw on different cultural traditions at the same time; and which are the product of those complicated cross-overs and cultural mixes which are increasingly common in a globalized world. It may be tempting to think of identity in the age of globalization as destined to end up in one place or another: either returning to its "roots" or disappearing through assimilation and homogenization. But this may be a false dilemma.

For there is another possibility: that of "Translation." This describes those identity formations which cut across and intersect natural frontiers, and which are composed of people who have been *dispersed* forever from their homelands. Such people retain strong links with their places of origin and their traditions, but they are without the illusion of a return to the past. They are obliged to come to terms with the new cultures they inhabit, without simply assimilating to them and losing their identities completely. They bear upon them the traces of the particular cultures, traditions, languages, and histories by which they were shaped. The difference is that they are not and will never be *unified* in the old sense, because they are irrevocably the product of several interlocking histories and cultures, belong at one and the same time to several "homes" (and to no one particular "home"). People belonging to such *cultures of hybridity* have had to renounce the dream or ambition of rediscovering any kind of "lost" cultural purity, or ethnic absolutism. They are irrevocably *translated*. The word "translation," Salman Rushdie notes, "comes etymologically from the Latin for 'bearing across'." Migrant writers like him, who belong to two worlds at once, "having been borne across the world . . . are translated men" (Rushdie, 1991). They are the products of the new *diasporas* created by the post-colonial migrations. They must learn to inhabit at least two identities, to speak two cultural languages, to translate and negotiate between them. Cultures of hybridity are one of the distinctly novel types of identity produced in the era of late-modernity, and there are more and more examples of them to be discovered.

Some people argue that "hybridity" and syncretism – the fusion between different cultural traditions – is a powerful creative source, creating new forms that are more appropriate to late-modernity than the old, embattled national identities of the past. Others, however, argue that hybridity, with the indeterminacy, "double consciousness," and relativism it implies, also has its costs and dangers. Salman Rushdie's novel about migration, Islam, and the prophet Mohammed, *The Satanic Verses*, with its deep immersion in Islamic culture *and* its secular consciousness of the exiled "translated man," so offended the Iranian fundamentalists that they passed sentence of death on him for blasphemy. In defending his novel, Rushdie offered a strong and compelling defense of "hybridity":

> Standing at the centre of the novel is a group of characters most of whom are British Muslims, or not particularly religious persons of Muslim background, struggling with just the sort of great problems that have arisen to surround the book, problems of hybridization and ghettoization, of reconciling the old and the new. Those who oppose the novel most vociferously today are of the opinion that intermingling with different cultures will inevitably weaken and ruin their own. I am of the opposite opinion. *The Satanic Verses* celebrates hybridity, impurity, intermingling, the transformation that comes of new and unexpected combinations of human beings, cultures, ideas, politics, movies, songs. It rejoices in mongrelization and fears the absolutism of the Pure. *Mélange*, hotchpotch, a bit of this and a bit of that is *how newness enters the world*. It is the great possibility that mass migration gives the world, and I have tried to embrace it. *The Satanic Verses* is for change-by-fusion, change-by-conjoining. It is a love-song to our mongrel selves.
> (Rushdie, 1991, p. 394)

On the other hand, there are equally powerful attempts to reconstruct purified identities, to restore coherence, "closure," and Tradition, in the face of hybridity and diversity. Two examples are the resurgence of nationalism in Eastern Europe and the rise of fundamentalism.

In an era when regional integration in the economic and political fields, and the breaking down of national sovereignty, are moving very rapidly in Western Europe, the collapse of the communist regimes in Eastern Europe and the break-up of the old Soviet Union have been followed by a powerful revival of ethnic nationalism, fuelled by ideas of both racial purity and religious orthodoxy. The ambition to create new, culturally and ethnically unified nation-states (which I have suggested above never really existed in western national cultures) was the driving force behind the break-away movements in the Baltic states of Estonia, Latvia, and Lithuania, the disintegration of Yugoslavia and the move to independence of many former Soviet Republics, from Georgia, the Ukraine, Russia, and Armenia to Kurdistan, Uzbekistan, and the "Muslim" Asian republics of the old Soviet state. Much the same process has been taking place in the "nations" of Central Europe which were carved out of the disintegration of the Austro-Hungarian and Ottoman Empires at the end of World War I.

These new would-be "nations" try to construct states that are unified in both ethnic and religious terms, and to create political entities around homogeneous cultural identities. The problem is that they contain within their "borders" minorities who identify themselves with different cultures. Thus, for example, there are "ethnic" Russian minorities in the Baltic Republics and the Ukraine, ethnic Poles in Lithuania, an Armenian enclave (Nagorno-Karabakh) in Azerbaijan, Turkic-Christian minorities among the Russian majorities of Moldavia, and large numbers of Muslims in the southern republics of the old Soviet Union who share more, in cultural and religious terms, with their Middle-Eastern Islamic neighbors than with many of their "countrymen."

The other significant form of the revival of particularistic nationalism and ethnic and religious absolutism is, of course, the phenomenon of "fundamentalism." This is evident everywhere, though its most striking example is to be found in some Islamic states in the Middle East. Beginning with the Iranian Revolution, fundamentalist Islamic movements, which seek to create religious states in which the political principles of organization are aligned with the religious doctrines and laws of the *Koran*, have arisen in many hitherto secular Islamic societies. In fact, this trend is difficult to interpret. Some analysts see it as a reaction to the "forced" character of western modernization; certainly, Iranian fundamentalism was a direct response to the efforts of the Shah in the 1970s to adopt western models and cultural values wholesale. Some interpret it as a response to being left out of "globalization." The reaffirmation of cultural "roots" and the return to orthodoxy has long been one of the most powerful sources of counter-identification among many Third World and post-colonial societies and regions (one thinks here of the roles of nationalism and national culture in the Indian, African, and Asian independence movements). Others see the roots of Islamic fundamentalism in the failure of Islamic states to throw up successful and effective "modernizing" leaderships or secular, modern parties. In conditions of extensive poverty and relative economic under-development (fundamentalism is stronger in the poorer Islamic states of the region), a restoration of the Islamic faith is a powerful mobilizing and binding political and ideological force, especially where democratic traditions are weak.

The trend towards "global homogenization," then, is matched by a powerful revival of "ethnicity," sometimes of the more hybrid or symbolic varieties, but also frequently of the exclusive or "essentialist" varieties cited above. Bauman has referred to this "resurgence of ethnicity" as one of the main reasons why the more extreme, free-ranging or indeterminate versions of what happens to identity under the impact of the "global post-modern" requires serious qualification.

> The "resurgence of ethnicity" ... puts in the forefront the unanticipated flourishing of ethnic loyalties inside national minorities. By the same token, it casts a shadow on what seems to be the deep cause of the phenomenon: the growing separation between the membership of body politic and ethnic membership (or more generally, cultural conformity) which removes much of

its original attraction from the programme of cultural assimilation. . . . Ethnicity has become one of the many categories or tokens, or "tribal poles," around which flexible and sanction-free communities are formed and in reference to which individual identities are constructed and asserted. There are now, therefore, [many] fewer centrifugal forces which once weakened ethnic integrity. There is instead a powerful demand for pronounced, though symbolic rather than institutionalized, ethnic distinctiveness.

(Bauman, 1990, p. 167)

The resurgence of nationalism and other forms of particularism at the end of the twentieth century, alongside and intimately linked to globalization, is of course a remarkable reversal, a most unexpected turn of events. Nothing in the modernizing Enlightenment perspectives or ideologies of the West – neither liberalism nor indeed Marxism, which for all its opposition to liberalism also saw capitalism as the unwitting agent of "modernity" – foresaw such an outcome.

Both liberalism and Marxism, in their different ways, implied that the attachment to the local and the particular would gradually give way to more universalistic and cosmopolitan or international values and identities; that nationalism and ethnicity were archaic forms of attachment – the sorts of thing which would be "melted away" by the revolutionizing force of modernity. According to these "metanarratives" of modernity, the irrational attachments to the local and the particular, to tradition and roots, to national myths and "imagined communities," would gradually be replaced by more rational and universalistic identities. Yet globalization seems to be producing neither simply the triumph of "the global" nor the persistence, in its old nationalistic form, of "the local." The displacements or distractions of globalization turn out to be more varied and more contradictory than either its protagonists or opponents suggest. However, this also suggests that, though powered in many ways by the West, globalization may turn out to be part of that slow and uneven but continuing story of the decentering of the West.

# References

Abercrombie, N., Hill, S., and Turner, B. (1986) *Sovereign Individuals of Capitalism*, London, Allen & Unwin.

Althusser, L. (1966) *For Marx*, London, Verso.

Anderson, B. (1983) *Imagined Communities*, London, Verso.

Barnett, A. (1982) *Iron Britannia*, London, Allison and Busby.

Bauman, Z. (1990) "Modernity and ambivalence," in Featherstone, M. (ed.) *Global Culture*, London, Sage.

Bhabha, H. (ed.) (1990) *Narrating the Nation*, London, Routledge.

Brennan, T. (1990) "The national longing for form," in Bhabha, H. (ed.) (1990).

Derrida, J. (1981) *Writing and Difference*, London, Routledge.

Dodd, P. (1986) "Englishness and the national culture," in Colls, R. and Dodd, P. (eds) *Englishness: Politics and Culture, 1880–1920*, London, Croom Helm.

Donald, J. and Rattansi, A. (eds) (1992) *"Race," Culture and Difference*, London, Sage.

Dreyfus, H. and Rabinow, P. (1982) *Michel Foucault: Beyond Structuralism and Hermeneutics*, Brighton, England, Harvester.

Forester, J. (1987) "A brief history of the subject," in *Identity: The Real Me*, ICA Document 6, London, Institute for Contemporary Arts.

Foucault, M. (1967) *Madness and Civilization*, London, Tavistock.

Foucault, M. (1973) *Birth of the Clinic*, London, Tavistock.

Foucault, M. (1975) *Discipline and Punish*, London, Allen Lane.

Foucault, M. (1986) "The subject and power," in Dreyfus, J. and Rabinow, P., *Michel Foucault: Beyond Structuralism and Hermeneutics*, Brighton, England, Harvester.

Frisby, D. (1985) *Fragments of Modernity*, Cambridge, England, Polity Press.

Gellner, E. (1983) *Nations and Nationalism*, Oxford, Basil Blackwell.

Giddens, A. (1990) *The Consequences of Modernity*, Cambridge, England, Polity Press.

Gilroy, P. (1987) *There ain't no Black in the Union Jack*, London, Hutchinson.

Gilroy, P. (1992) "The end of anti-racism," in Donald, J. and Rattansi, A. (eds) (1992).

Hall, C. (1992) *White, Male and Middle Class: Explorations in Feminism and History*, Cambridge, England, Polity Press.

Hall, S. (1985) "Religious cults and social movements in Jamaica," in Bocock, R. and Thompson, K. (eds) *Religion and Ideology*, Manchester, England, Manchester University Press.

Hall, S. (1987) "Minimal Selves," in *Identity: The Real Me*, ICA Document 6, London, Institute for Contemporary Arts.

Hall, S. (1990) "Cultural identity and diaspora," in Rutherford, J. (ed.) *Identity*, London, Lawrence and Wishart.

Harvey, D. (1989) *The Condition of Postmodernity*, Oxford, Basil Blackwell.

Hobsbawm, E. and Ranger, T. (eds) (1983) *The Invention of Tradition*, Cambridge, England, Cambridge University Press.

Lacan, J. (1977) "The mirror stage as formative of the function of the I," in *Écrits*, London, Tavistock.

Laclau, E. (1990) *New Reflections on the Revolution of our Time*, London, Verso.

Locke, J. (1967) *An Essay Concerning Human Understanding*, London, Fontana.

Marx, K. and Engels, F. (1973) *The Communist Manifesto*, in *Revolutions of 1848*, Harmondsworth, England, Penguin.

Massey, D. (1991) "A global sense of place," *Marxism Today*, June.

Mercer, K. (1990) "Welcome to the jungle," in Rutherford, J. (ed.) *Identity*, London, Lawrence and Wishart.

Nairn, T. (1977) *The Break-up of Britain*, London, Verso.

Parekh, B. (1989) "Between holy text and moral void," *New Statesman and Society*, March 23.

Platt, A. (1991) *Defending the Canon*, Fernand Braudel Center and Institute of Global Studies, Binghamton, State University of New York.

Powell, E. (1969) *Freedom and Reality*, Farnham, England, Elliot Right Way Books.

Renan, E. (1990) "What is a nation?," in Bhabha, H. (ed.) (1990).

Robins, K. (1991) "Tradition and translation: national culture in its global context," in Corner, J. and Harvey, S. (eds) *Enterprise and Heritage: Crosscurrents of National Culture*, London, Routledge.

Rushdie, S. (1991) *Imaginary Homelands*, London, Granta Books.

Said, E. (1990) "Narrative and geography," *New Left Review*, no. 180, March/April, pp. 81–100.

Schwarz, B. (1986) "Conservatism, nationalism and imperialism," in Donald, J. and Hall, S. (eds) *Politics and Ideology*, Milton Keynes, England, Open University Press.

Scruton, R. (1986) "Authority and allegiance," in Donald, J. and Hall, S. (eds) *Politics and Ideology*, Milton Keynes, England, Open University Press.

Sennett, R. (1971) *The Ideas of Disorder*, Harmondsworth, England, Penguin.

Urry, J. (1990) *The Tourist Gaze*, London, Sage.

Wallerstein, I. (1979) *The Capitalist Economy*, Cambridge, England, Cambridge University Press.

Wallerstein, I. (1984) *The Politics of the World Economy*, Cambridge, England, Cambridge University Press.

Wallerstein, I. (1991) "The national and the universal," in King, A. (ed.) *Culture, Globalization and the World System*, London, Macmillan.

Williams, R. (1976) *Keywords*, London, Fontana.

# The Enlightenment Project Revisited

Gregor McLennan

## Contents

| | | |
|---|---|---|
| 1 | Introduction: The Post-Modern Condition | 636 |
| 2 | A Debate: Post-Modernity versus Enlightenment | 638 |
| 3 | Lyotard: Abandoning the Metanarratives of Modernity | 639 |
| 4 | Habermas: Defending Modernity and Enlightenment | 642 |
| 5 | A Problem with Post-Modernism: Its Relativism | 644 |
| 6 | A Problem with Enlightenment: Its Hubris | 648 |
| 7 | Post-Modernity as "Reflexivity" | 651 |
| 8 | Overview | 654 |
| 8.1 | The Marxist resolution | 656 |
| 8.2 | Feminist dilemmas | 659 |
| 9 | Conclusion | 661 |
| | References | 663 |

# 1   Introduction: The Post-Modern Condition

The previous chapters have outlined a series of debates about the changing structures and dynamics of modern (mainly western) society. Sometimes these debates are about social processes such as market diversification, occupational restructuring, and economic or political "globalization." Sometimes the focus appears to be rather more political, cultural, and experiential: our changing sense of personal identity and political allegiance, for example. Of course, the overall key question has been whether "modernity" is passing, or has already passed, into a state of "post-modernity."

This chapter is about the changing nature of modern social thought. An examination of this topic confirms, perhaps even more than in other topic areas, how radical the challenge of "post-modernity" is. This is because the crisis and (supposed) surpassing of modernity is not merely a matter of economic, political, and cultural *processes*; it is also the crisis of a whole way of *understanding* the social world, a long-established way of "knowing" society. Post-modern theorists say that a changing social world requires an entirely different way of reflecting on our existence today. In other words, they argue that, just as social conditions change, so too do the concepts and categories that we use to make sense of society. As social scientists, we thus need to fundamentally "deconstruct" the way we habitually look at the social world. This means examining and perhaps even discarding some of the basic ideas and aspirations of social science, ideas which go back to the Enlightenment of the eighteenth century. That is why the title of this chapter invites us to "revisit" the whole Enlightenment project for social science.

Notice that in speaking of an "Enlightenment project" we are not implying a totally unified theory or organized intellectual movement, though it is true that the phrase does tend to suggest something very deliberate and coherent. Such a degree of unity and purpose did not exist even among the original *philosophes*; and today those who share a desire to preserve something of the Enlightenment heritage do not necessarily share a particular belief system or an "ism" in the way, for example, that Marxists or feminists do. So there is something slightly misleading about the term "Enlightenment project."

And yet it is also undeniable that there is a cluster of underlying assumptions and expectations about the nature of modern social theory which are shared by a significant number of social scientists and which stem from classical eighteenth- and nineteenth-century scientific aspirations. Today, these assumptions are being put under the theoretical microscope, and whether the decision is finally to preserve or reject them, one thing is clear: that they form a very strong and distinctive cluster of beliefs and expectations about the role of knowledge in the improvement of the human condition. In that sense, the idea of a "project" – a general aspiration – seems a more appropriate label to use for the Enlightenment heritage than a blander term such as "outlook" or "perspective."

But in what sense are the ideas of the "Enlightenment project" coming under attack? Take, for example, one manifestly central idea: the scientific study of something called "society." From the outset, this proposition implies that a fairly coherent and uniform set of interrelated phenomena, one which exists "out there," as it were, is readily amenable to sociological reflection "in here." In sociological knowledge, therefore, the real state of a singular being (society) gets mentally appropriated by means of abstract sociological concepts and appropriate methods of investigation.

But, at this point, the post-modernist comes along and says: Wait a minute, are we really sure that we can make even this initial distinction between what is "out there" and what is "in here"? Moreover, what gives us the right, he or she asks, to see society as a totality, as a unified and coherent being? Why isn't it just a collection of unrelated bits and pieces? And how can we ever tell if our concepts genuinely do "grasp" or "reflect" this thing called society accurately? Indeed, who is to say what "knowledge" of society really amounts to?

Such a provocative trail of questions is not exclusive to post-modernists — many other social scientists have posed them too. But post-modernists are especially convinced that now more than ever before we need to be openly *un*certain about the status of all the concepts and results of social science. This concern to unsettle the basic concepts of sociology explains why one of the key texts for this chapter, Lyotard's *The Postmodern Condition*, is actually subtitled "A report on *knowledge*" rather than, say, "a report on social change." To truly begin to understand post-modern society, in other words, it is not enough to register and reflect on changes in social conditions: the very form and content of sociological reflection itself must be fundamentally reoriented.

It is important at this point to clarify the relation between social science and philosophy or epistemology (i.e. the theory of knowledge). You could say, to begin with, that only philosophers are interested *primarily* in epistemological questions such as "what is knowledge?" or "what is truth?" Social scientists, by contrast, are primarily interested in finding out about human society and in developing theories about its structure and dynamics. However, social scientists do become embroiled in philosophical questions as a "secondary" pursuit. This is because it is impossible to understand society by merely looking and seeing what is there. We need *theories* of society for deep understanding. And yet, as is well known, very *different* theories and interpretations are usually available to be drawn on in any sociological area; and these different theories often present us with very different "facts," different "pictures," and different *versions* of what society is really all about.

So although social scientists are interested primarily in *society*, they become interested in questions about truth, knowledge, and validity because theories must be judged between and *justified*. And the process of justification inevitably raises the question about how we *know* one theory or version of society is better or truer than another. Moreover, when it is realized that many of the apparently "hard" terms of sociology – such as "class," "social action" or "interaction," and even "society" itself – are organizing *concepts* as much as palpable entities, then once again social science is plunged into a secondary concern with epistemology. We want to ask: Why *that* concept rather than some other? What *is* the relation between sociological concepts and social reality? – and so on.

# 2   A Debate: Post-Modernity versus Enlightenment

The Enlightenment occurred at the threshold of typically modern western society, and it gave a definitive shape to many of the ideas and procedures of modern western social science (see chapter 1). The post-modernist challenge to the Enlightenment model of social knowledge involves either rejecting entirely, or at least seriously questioning, the following typical Enlightenment tenets:

- The view that our knowledge of society, like society itself, is *holistic*, *cumulative*, and broadly *progressive* in character.
- That we can attain *rational* knowledge of society.
- That such knowledge is *universal* and thus *objective*.
- That sociological knowledge is both *different* from, and *superior* to, "distorted" forms of thought, such as ideology, religion, common sense, superstition, and prejudice.
- That social scientific knowledge, once validated and acted on, can lead to mental liberation and social betterment among humanity generally.

In sum, the post-modernist thesis is that, not only have the structures of modern *society* begun to change dramatically, but also that the foundations of modern social *thought* have become obsolete and dogmatic.

There are three main possible responses to that critical thesis. One is to accept it as valid and consequently to embark on a search for a distinctly "non-Enlightenment" rationale for sociological inquiry. The second response is to try to refute the post-modernist challenge and in various ways defend the Enlightenment project. A third response is to attempt something of a compromise; for example, we might accept that, as a result of post-modernist criticisms, the Enlightenment project now looks rather weak or dogmatic or in crisis; we may also perhaps feel that post-modernism itself has few *constructive* answers to the sorts of difficult questions it raises.

The pattern of this chapter follows the logic of the debate as just sketched out. The next two sections present brief discussions of Lyotard and Habermas, respectively. Then I look at responses to the debate between these two which are, broadly speaking, pro-Habermas, pro-Lyotard, and neutral.

# 3  Lyotard: Abandoning the Metanarratives of Modernity

Let us begin by analyzing a short quotation from a key figure in the anti-Enlightenment camp, Jean-François Lyotard. Lyotard's book *The Postmodern Condition* was first published in France in 1979 and translated into English in 1984, causing something of a sensation within social philosophy. Here is how that book opens:

> The object of this study is the condition of knowledge in the most highly developed societies. I have decided to use the word *postmodern* to describe that condition. The word is in current use on the American continent among sociologists and critics; it designates the state of our culture following the transformations which, since the end of the nineteenth century, have altered the game rules for science, literature, and the arts. The present study will place these transformations in the context of the crisis of narratives.
>
> Science has always been in conflict with narratives. Judged by the yardstick of science, the majority of them prove to be fables. But to the extent that science does not restrict itself to stating useful regularities and seeks the truth, it is obliged to legitimate the rules of its own game. It then produces a discourse of legitimation with respect to its own status, a discourse called philosophy. I will use the term *modern* to designate any science that legitimates itself with reference to a metadiscourse of this kind making an explicit appeal to some grand narrative, such as the dialectics of Spirit, the hermeneutics of meaning, the emancipation of the rational or working subject, or the creation of wealth. For example, the rule of consensus between the sender and addressee of a statement with truth-value is deemed acceptable if it is cast in terms of a possible unanimity between rational minds: this is the Enlightenment narrative, in which the hero of knowledge works towards a good ethico-political end – universal peace. As can be seen from this example, if a metanarrative implying a philosophy of history is used to legitimate knowledge, questions are raised concerning the validity of the institutions governing the social bond: these must be legitimated as well. Thus justice is consigned to the grand narrative in the same way as truth.
>
> Simplifying to the extreme, I define *postmodern* as incredulity toward metanarratives. This incredulity is undoubtedly a product of progress in the sciences: but that progress in turn presupposes it. To the obsolescence of the metanarrative apparatus of legitimation corresponds, most notably, the crisis of metaphysical philosophy and of the university institution which in the past relied on it. The narrative function is losing its functors, its great hero, its great dangers, its great voyages, its great goal. It is being dispersed in clouds of narrative language elements – narrative, but also denotative, prescriptive, descriptive, and so on. Conveyed

within each cloud are pragmatic valencies specific to its kind.
Each of us lives at the intersection of many of these. However, we
do not necessarily establish stable language combinations, and the
properties of the ones we do establish are not necessarily
communicable. . . .

. . . Where, after the metanarratives, can legitimacy reside? The
operativity criterion is technological; it has no relevance for
judging what is true or just. Is legitimacy to be found in consensus
obtained through discussion, as Jürgen Habermas thinks? Such
consensus does violence to the heterogeneity of language games.
And invention is always born of dissension. Postmodern
knowledge is not simply a tool of the authorities; it refines our
sensitivity to differences and reinforces our ability to tolerate the
incommensurable.
(Lyotard, 1984, pp. 3–11)

For Lyotard, the "postmodern condition" refers to the status of
*knowledge* about society; knowledge of ourselves in the post-modern
age. It thus concerns the basic conceptual frameworks that we adopt in
order to understand modern life. This focus on knowledge involves
developing an *epistemological* rather than a substantive slant on the
issue of whether modernity is passing (has passed) into post-modernity.
(Epistemological = concerning concepts of knowledge; substantive =
concerning matters of empirical substance.)

Lyotard asserts that the main feature of the Enlightenment approach
to knowledge is its concern to be scientifically legitimate. Science in
this sense implies "objective" and "impartial" knowledge of the world,
and stands in sharp contrast to what Lyotard terms "narratives"; that is,
the myriad *stories* or "fables" that we invent in order to give meaning
and significance to our lives. These stories or narratives may be
personal, political, moral, mythical, religious, or whatever. But the
point, as far as the Enlightenment view of knowledge is concerned, is
that narratives as such do not deliver *real* knowledge (i.e. universally
valid principles or laws), be they laws of nature or laws of society.
Rather, narratives exist to provide existential or ideological comforts to
us as we go through life, and they are irremediably tainted – as
compared with scientific truths – by their essentially local, social, and
personal contexts. The governing assumption of Enlightenment thought,
for Lyotard, is altogether loftier than this, namely that society "out
there" can be progressively "captured" by social scientific knowledge
without any recourse whatsoever to the taints and comforts of personal
and social narratives.

However, the dramatic assertion which Lyotard then makes is that
this whole Enlightenment picture of "pure" knowledge is itself nothing
but a very powerful *myth*: in effect precisely a narrative of sorts. Now,
while the scientific concern with objective knowledge may not, as such,
be a comforting story, nevertheless that concern is invariably justified
or "legitimated" by reference to higher-level storylines, and these
Lyotard terms "metanarratives." Among the main influential
metanarratives of the last 200 years which have served to legitimate the

myth of objective Science, Lyotard mentions the heroic legends of "the creation of wealth," the "working subject," and "the dialectics of Spirit."

What Lyotard is getting at here is that aspirations to scientific knowledge are never quite as pure as Enlightenment thought makes out. Scientific progress, for example, is often seen as a necessary and crucial part of the drive for industrial and commercial growth ("the creation of wealth"). And economic growth is often in turn seen as the precondition of human well-being and civilization. Marxist theorists would present a somewhat different metanarrative, saying that science ultimately serves, or ought to serve, the liberation of humanity (i.e. "the working subject") from exploitation, labor, and toil. Other philosophers have conceived of human progress in terms of the progress of *ideas themselves*, forming a potential spiral of spiritual emancipation ("the dialectics of Spirit").

So it seems after all that many supposedly objective aspirations to science inevitably tend to be framed by some kind of metanarrative involving distinctly value-laden notions of social progress and human emancipation. Emancipation here is, if you like, the end of the story, and it is science that enables us to clearly perceive the essence of that story of humanity's progress.

Science alone, however, cannot provide the whole of the metanarrative, for that, according to Lyotard, is the job of the discourse known as *philosophy*. It is philosophy rather than science as such which decides what is to be classed as "real" science and what is to be stigmatized as "mere" narrative; it is philosophy which exists to inform us of what the true essence and end points of the story of human Progress and Knowledge are; and it is philosophy which judges what counts as true and what does not.

Now, Lyotard proposes further that this modernist conception of knowledge, which features such a cosy partnership between the pursuit of science and the legitimating discourse of philosophy, should be abandoned completely. Instead of pursuing the truth, we should openly embrace the post-modern condition of uncertainty and "agonistics" (i.e. rhetorical jousting). There are two prongs to Lyotard's attack.

One is really a point of logic, and is already implicit in what I have said so far. If the objective grandeur of "science" actually always turns out to rest on some sort of metanarrative or other – none of which can be "objectively" proved or refuted, but each acting as the philosophical rationalization of human ideologies – then the very claim to objectivity and value-neutrality is spurious, deceitful, and self-cancelling. Further, if the mantle of "objectivity" is simply unavailable, then no one metanarrative is inherently "privileged" over any other. But if *this is* so, then we need to be very skeptical about the ultimate truth-claims of *all* metanarratives. Lyotard thus defines the condition of post-modernity as "incredulity toward metanarratives," whether the latter are to do with the historical march of Reason, Civilization, Wealth, or the Proletariat.

Lyotard's second prong of argumentation is more sociological than philosophical. He points to the significant changes going on in the whole mode of collecting and communicating social information. And ultimately "knowledge" is about just that: the storage of, and "aura" surrounding, certain kinds of discourse and information. If this is so, he then implies, there is simply no place today for a view of knowledge which sees it as a privileged unified body of mental "thought" which exists in the collective Mind, and which is guarded preciously by an elite of scientists, philosophers, and academics. Rather, the reality of knowledge today is a huge array of "moves" within pragmatic "discourses" or "language games," all targeted towards very specific audiences, each having its own criterion of accreditation and each increasingly treated in practice as an economic *commodity* to be bought and sold according to its market demand.

Moreover, the advanced technology of computerized information storage encourages us to treat knowledge as a set of resources and services which we can draw on, and pass on, for particular social purposes. To view knowledge pragmatically and realistically in this way is virtually to destroy the sacred "aura" of modernist conceptions of knowledge and science. But note also that to "deconstruct" knowledge, to de-sanctify it, to remove it from the hereditary possession of philosophers, scholars, and scientists, is not necessarily to wholly *devalue* it, in Lyotard's eyes. On the contrary, by adopting the post-modern view of knowledge as a kaleidoscopic array of limited and transient language games, we can see how deep at the heart of post-modern society, knowledges (in the plural, not the singular) actually lie. The control of information, for example, is quite central nowadays to economic production, political opinion-forming, and military control alike. Nothing could be more significant than that.

# 4  Habermas: Defending Modernity and Enlightenment

Lyotard has cited Jürgen Habermas as someone still very much concerned to "legitimate" knowledge in the classical Enlightenment sense (Lyotard, 1984). Habermas has been developing over the decades, and in great volume, a defense of "the Enlightenment project" as he understands it. While much of this intellectual labor pre-dates Lyotard's broadside, it is useful here to see Habermas's views as a kind of *response* to post-modernists like Lyotard:

> The project of modernity formulated in the 18th century by the philosophers of the Enlightenment consisted in their efforts to develop objective science, universal morality and law, and autonomous art according to their inner logic. At the same time, this project intended to release the cognitive potentials of each of these domains from their esoteric forms. The Enlightenment philosophers wanted to utilize this accumulation of specialized culture for the enrichment of everyday life – that is to say, for the rational organization of everyday social life.
>
> Enlightenment thinkers of the cast of mind of Condorcet still

had the extravagant expectation that the arts and sciences would promote not only the control of natural forces but also understanding of the world and of the self, moral progress, the justice of institutions and even the happiness of human beings. The 20th century has shattered this optimism. The differentiation of science, morality and art has come to mean the autonomy of the segments treated by the specialist and their separation from the hermeneutics of everyday communication. This splitting off is the problem that has given rise to efforts to "negate" the culture of expertise. But the problem won't go away: should we try to hold on to the *intentions* of the Enlightenment, feeble as they may be, or should we declare the entire project of modernity a lost cause? . . .

   I think that instead of giving up modernity and its project as a lost cause, we should learn from the mistakes of those extravagant programs which have tried to negate modernity.
   (Habermas, 1985, pp. 8–15)

In this quotation, Habermas elaborates a little further than Lyotard on the origins of Enlightenment aspirations. He reminds us that part of the Enlightenment project was the separating out of three main forms of human thinking – science, morality, and art – forms which had previously been rolled up together as a whole world-view under the hegemony of religious or metaphysical principles. In that sense, the Enlightenment project was far less "holistic" than Lyotard and post-modernists frequently imply.

   Habermas sees three different types of rationality developing according to that separation of cognitive spheres. "Experts" in each sphere come to dominate access to it, and serve to protect specialist knowledge from the clutches of the wider public. In a sense, Habermas is admitting that the Enlightenment project was only ever an *ideal*, not a reality, because from the outset a kind of "separatist" culture evolved which compartmentalized and professionalized the different spheres of knowledge. Indeed, Habermas goes as far as to suggest that the original fragmentation ("splitting off") of rationality does tend to lead to the kind of atomized, pragmatic forms of knowledge that are highlighted by post-modernists such as Lyotard. To that extent, Habermas does not dispute that the use of knowledge *has* become computerized, compartmentalized, commodified, and fragmented. Nor does he have any innocent faith in the actual prospects for pure Enlightenment. As he says, the brutal history of the twentieth century has shattered such optimism.

   What, then, *is* the dispute between these two thinkers? Firstly, Habermas wants to emphasize the relative narrow-mindedness and backwardness of the epoch of *pre-modernity*. In that context, he pleads, we should remember the positive role of the original Enlightenment epoch.

   Secondly, Habermas feels that we have met the likes of Lyotard before in the history of modern philosophy and modern art. Indeed, the history of modernity in its widest sense must be conceived as *including*

"those extravagant programs which have tried to negate modernity."
While agreeing to learn something from anti-modernist movements
(such as Lyotard now offers and such as the German philosopher
Friedrich Nietzsche offered in the nineteenth century), Habermas
believes that such movements have "failed" intellectually. Habermas
basically accuses the "radical critique of reason" or "Nietzscheanism"
of throwing the baby out with the bath water: so totally negative is this
critique that its proponents forget the many ambivalent aspects of
modernity, and indeed forget about its positive connotations, notably
"the prospect of a self-conscious practice, in which the solidary self-
determination of all was to be joined with the self-realization of each."

Thirdly, such a (misplaced) total critique of Enlightenment and
modernity inevitably results, politically speaking, in disillusionment
and conservatism. By contrast, if we hold on to the original *intentions*
of the Enlightenment, then the search for some degree of universality
and objectivity remains wedded to the hope that knowledge might
"promote . . . the justice of institutions and even the happiness of
human beings." Habermas believes that we can retain the hope without
falling prey to naïve expectations; and in any case, he thinks, the
alternative seems to be nothing less than despair. In that sense alone,
the Enlightenment project has some running left in it yet.

But true to his dislike of purely negative critique, Habermas does not
rest his case for upholding the Enlightenment project solely on the (in
his view) demerits of post-modernist arguments. In addition, and at
great length, he has constructed a theory of what he calls
*communicative action* or *communicative reason*. This theory (elements
of which I shall return to) is designed to be both analytically valid as
an account of the conditions of meaningful social interaction, and
politically progressive as a yardstick for emancipated relationships.

*The story so far*   Lyotard has criticized both the logical inconsistency
and the sociological *naïveté* of Enlightenment or modernist
epistemology. Instead, he articulates a post-modernist conception of
local pragmatic language games and incredulity towards all
metanarratives. In response, Habermas accepts the failures of the
original Enlightenment project and the precise way in which the
Enlightenment belief in science was presented. Nevertheless, he sees
the Enlightenment project as historically progressive vis-à-vis pre-
modernity, and regards its intentions as still progressive today given
the prospect of post-modernist conservatism. In that belief he has
attempted to construct a positive theory of communicative reason, one
in which an ideal of egalitarian, rational, and undistorted interaction
between social agents is preserved and promoted.

# 5   A Problem with Post-Modernism: Its Relativism

It could be argued that the central issue of the whole debate about the
fate of the Enlightenment project hangs on the question of relativism.

Today, many would accept the idea that the morals and manners of a society are very much specific to that particular type of society. In that sense, cultural relativism seems a sound basis from which to conduct social investigations. However, whether the adoption of *cultural relativism* as a sensible basis for social observation necessarily requires the acceptance of *cognitive relativism* (i.e. the view that there can be no such things as universal principles of validity, truth, or rationality) is hotly disputed. Critics of the Enlightenment project are convinced that the connection between the two types of relativism cannot be broken, and that a more genuine enlightenment is created by simply accepting relativism right across the board. Against this, defenders of the Enlightenment project feel that cultural relativism does not necessarily entail cognitive relativism, for otherwise we would have to renounce any commitment to principled intellectual inquiry.

Peter Dews (1986) claims that, for Lyotard and Nietzsche, the world is conceived of as a "plurality" – a vast array of very different people, ideas, beliefs, and standards, of judgment. He further suggests that, for Lyotard, this plurality is irreducible; that is to say, any attempt to give it some kind of hidden unity or ultimate meaning is really to "violate" that plurality. Lyotard's own version of plurality-in-the-world, as we have already seen, involves treating the social world as an almost infinite series of small-scale discourses or "language games." The latter are very definitely "heterogeneous" – that is, intrinsically different and non-comparable – so almost by definition they cannot be boxed up together as if they have exactly the same or even a similar purpose or meaning.

Habermas, however (according to Lyotard), tries to do precisely this: he tries to "enforce" the myriad local language-games into a similar mold, whereby they all reveal the same hidden meaning. This, for Lyotard, is Habermas's cardinal "error."

Dews's response identifies "three distinct levels" of counter-critique, by means of which Lyotard's case can be dismissed. One, he states, is philosophical. (When writers refer to an argument as being philosophical, they usually mean that there is some point of logic to be made, or that there is something to do with the very definitions of the concepts used by another writer which renders the theory under review flawed or perhaps even self-contradictory.)

In this instance, Dews takes Lyotard to task for creating a "chronic confusion" between two distinct ideas. From the fact that there exist a great many different discourses or "language games," Lyotard wrongly infers that there can be no possible common standards of consistency or validity which cut across all discourses, *in spite of* the notable differences between them. But Dews contends that this is a false inference – that the second idea does not logically follow from the first.

Dews further contends that, contrary to what Lyotard asserts, Habermas is perfectly willing to accept that multiple discourses exist in complex modern societies. Habermas himself, of course, tends to emphasize just three main types of discourse (science, art, and morality), but we can readily think of many other language games in society, each governed by conventions and terms which are rather peculiar to itself. Commerce, for example, might involve a distinct species of language game, as might sport, work, leisure, shopping, love, and war. And each of these "games" will probably vary with different socio-cultural contexts (e.g. "East" and "West"), thus adding a further layer to the complexity of discourses within society.

All the same, Habermas and Dews want to hold on to the possibility that all that complexity does not obliterate the need for some overarching notions of validity which govern all mini-discourses. This does *not* mean that all discourses appeal to exactly the same criterion of validity. Each language game permits very different sorts of valid "moves." But still, within *any* language game, all participants must be equally clear about the governing rules, and must in a sense "agree" to abide by them, even if only to register further disagreement. For Habermas, all linguistic communication implies an "agreement" of this sort. When two speakers engage with one another, even if only to disagree, they *take for granted* certain assumptions about the organization of speech, and necessarily assume that they could reach an agreement, if they were to debate specific issues with one another under conditions free of distorting factors (i.e. free of domination). This notion is the core of what Habermas calls "the ideal of rational discourse" embedded in communicative action; and it is at the core of his positive theory. (For a fuller account, see Bernstein, 1985.)

Dews terms his second set of arguments "political," in that he accuses Lyotard of political complacency and conservatism by his very use of the term "language game." A language game is never just a matter of mere talk or specialist terminology. Rather, "games" are spheres of action involving the exchange of attitudes, values, behavior, and strategy. Games thus also give rise to *conflict*. For example, although young boys frequently play "war games," war itself is a kind of "game" – that is, a pattern of structured interaction between people with its own rules of cooperation and conflict (the "first strikes," the "retaliation," the "truce," the "lull in the fighting," etc.). War, then, is a game like many other forms of social interaction, but a game which is not at all "in pretense"; it is very much for real.

Dews seems to believe that something as grave as, say, war should not really be termed a "game" at all, nor that such literally action-packed games should be reduced to their *linguistic* element. So he objects to the very idea of society as made up entirely of language games. He prefers the term "social practice," which has a ring of gravity about it. Of course, social practices still very much involve language, but they are not *reducible* to their linguistic aspect. Lyotard's usage, for Dews, has more than a hint of liberal complacency about it, almost as though a cosy chat or an "agonistic" dispute about semantics were a sufficient response to such vital social "language games" as dealing with pollution, de-industrialization, or alcoholism.

The second part of Dews's "political" objection is, in fact, an extension of his earlier "philosophical" point, and it is here that Dews most fully raises the question of relativism. Dews starts this point by asserting that Lyotard's position *is* in effect a relativist one; he then lodges the charge that Lyotard's position is invalid because it shares the pitfall of all relativism: self-contradiction.

Let us probe these objections more closely. The first step arises because Lyotard claims that all language games are intrinsically separate from one another – they all have different underlying rules, logics, and motivations which absolutely cannot be reduced to one another, nor can they all be subsumed under some higher abstract idea such as "truth." It would seem to follow from this that no discourse, or human participant within it, can genuinely *communicate* with any other. Discourses are "incommensurable" in that sense – they simply cannot be compared or judged against one another. It would seem that, as participants within discourses, we must be "locked" inside them, forever debarred from saying anything "objective" at all about whether one discourse is better or worse than any other; or whether anything is right or wrong, period.

A classic example of this relativist dilemma is the debate about "other cultures." Here the question is: How *can* a modern, western, scientific culture (discourse) judge – or even properly understand – a so-called "alien" or "primitive" tribal culture, when the standards and meanings prevalent within the one discourse simply do not have any direct equivalents within the other? It would be better, then, say the relativists, just to accept such interesting differences between cultures/ discourses and try our best to understand them in a sympathetic, non-judgmental way. What we *cannot* do is match them against fictitious abstract notions such as Truth, Beauty, etc., since each culture has its own standards in these matters. It follows that no one is ever in a position to assert the truth and validity of any particular set of "universal" principles with which to make comparative judgments across societies. And from this it follows that no culture is truly universal: all of us are, always, "locked" into the norms of our own very transient and specific "slot" located within space and history. To imagine otherwise, say the relativists, is mere illusion, a wholly false bid by mere humans to attain the impossible "God's eye view" of the world.

For "objectivists," however, this relativist argument is specious, and its conclusion is an unnecessary caricature. For one thing, to recognize that we can come to understand something of another culture/discourse immediately is, paradoxically, to accept that some things can be asserted as meaningful across very different cultures. And, secondly, if meanings and concepts *can* come to be shared, then perhaps so can some cross-cultural concepts of truth and validity, however difficult and complex those inevitably must be. Thirdly, to say that discursive values are always radically and necessarily unmatchable itself looks suspiciously like an *absolute* claim to validity, and this is something which relativists hold to be impossible. But in that case, relativism becomes self-contradictory and therefore unpersuasive.

This introduction to the relativism versus objectivism debate was indispensable, since Dews relishes finding the "nemesis of all relativism" in Lyotard's specific version of it. The latter says that any attempt to impose "homogeneity" on the infinity of "heteromorphous" language games is both impossible and "terroristic." Dews replies that this itself is an absolute and terroristic claim which must apply to all language games. Therefore, some principles of verbal and intellectual exchange are universal after all. But this is just the conclusion Lyotard was most concerned to avoid!

Dews's third argument is "historical" in focus. Lyotard's position seems to imply that in post-modern times we are moving out of an age of uniformity, collectivity, and universality and into one characterized by individuation, fragmentation, and difference. In response, Dews wants to avoid any sharp contrast between these clusters of concepts, pointing out that, in fact, the whole period of modernity has witnessed *both* individualization and universality. Indeed, he thinks (along with Habermas) that the more separate from one another people or societies or language games become, the *more* they tend to rely on abstract general principles, and the explicit formalization of social rules. Lyotard's vision of pluralism has no place for this important phenomenon of increasing abstract universality. As a result, his post-modern world looks merely "particularistic"; that is, one in which people are simply atomized and fragmented. Dews implies that this is not a very good or very "emancipated" condition to advocate. Further, Dews says, relativism encourages intellectual and human indifference: if all cognitive and moral values are relative to specific discourses/language/cultures, then why make any big claims at all about what is right, just, or true? Why bother to hold any views about anything?

Throughout this line of thought, Dews (and Habermas), though not seeking to find a grandiose "God's eye view" of society, do nevertheless seem to believe that arguments about what is true and good *can* be productively engaged in, within and across cultures. They also believe that some important measure of agreement can be reached about how to decide what is true and good. For the moment, Lyotard looks like he is in trouble.

# 6  A Problem with Enlightenment: Its Hubris

In the last section, you probably felt that the weight of argument was swinging towards Dews and Habermas and against Lyotard. This is partly because we took as our starting point Dews's own summary of Lyotard, and such summaries in academic and political debate often have distinctly unfavorable "conclusions" already written between the lines.

So now we need to put the shoe on the other foot. What if Dews is caricaturing Lyotard and post-modernism every bit as much as he claims Lyotard caricatures Habermas? And what if some parallel undesirable political conclusion can be seen to follow from the adoption of hardline "objectivist" arguments against relativism?

Zygmunt Bauman contrasts strongly with Peter Dews in being broadly pro-Lyotard:

> How can one argue the case for or against a form of life, for or against a version of truth, when one feels that one's argument

cannot any more legislate, that there are powers behind the *plural* forms of life and plural versions of truth which would not be *made* inferior, and hence would not surrender to the argument of their inferiority? Suddenly, the two-centuries-old philosophical voyage to certainty and universal criteria of perfection and "good life" seems to be a wasted effort. This does not necessarily mean that we do not like the terrains to which it has brought us; on the contrary, it is the refusal of others to admire them and to follow us there which makes us worry and prompts us to look for a new, stronger tune for the praise we still wish to sing. If we wish to defend the direction our journey took us, we need to redefine, retrospectively, its sense.

Ernest Gellner is arguably the staunchest and the most profound defender of the peculiar form of life born in the north-western tip of the European peninsula four centuries ago which has subordinated all other forms of life for the last two hundred years. His is perhaps the most convincing plea on its behalf:

> On balance, one option – a society with cognitive growth based on a roughly atomistic strategy – seems to us superior, for various reasons, which are assembled without elegance; this kind of society alone can keep alive the large numbers to which humanity has grown, and thereby avoid a really ferocious struggle for survival among us; it alone can keep us at the standard to which we are becoming accustomed; it, more than its predecessors, *probably* favours a liberal and tolerant social organization . . . This type of society also has many unattractive traits, and its virtues are open to doubt. On balance, and with misgivings, we opt for it; but there is no question of an elegant, clear-cut choice. We are half pressurised by necessity (fear of famine, etc.), half-persuaded by a promise of liberal affluence (which we do not fully trust). There it is: lacking better reasons we will have to make do with these.
> (1984, p. 258)

This statement is modest – and, in a sense, apologetic. It is self-conscious of its inadequacy in terms of the extant criteria of the elegance of philosophical proof. It justifies the *raison d'être* of the philosophical tradition, which devoted its life and energy to exorcizing the ghost of pragmatic relativism, in pragmatic terms – an ultimate irony, as it were. And the argument it employs (again self-consciously, I am sure) is circular: this system is better because it caters for the things which it taught us to like better – like that "standard to which we are becoming accustomed." There is nothing intrinsically wrong with such an argument. On the contrary, it seems much more human and realistic than the philosophical elegance it proposes to replace. That is, if we first agree to abandon philosophical pretensions to universality.

Gellner's reasoning has a decisive advantage over many other arguments, similar in their self-inflicted modesty, pragmatism and circularity. It is honest about its own purpose, which is the

defence of the world which we, the intellectuals of the West,
shaped by the two centuries of recent Western history we
collectively helped to shape, find to approximate closer than any
other world we know to the standards we set for a good society.
To phrase it differently, Gellner's argument makes explicit a case
for the kind of world which may provide (and has been providing,
with qualifications, for some time) a suitable setting for the
Western intellectual mode of life; and may also create a demand
for the traditional (legislating) role that Western intellectuals have
learned to perform best. This makes Gellner's argument
particularly interesting; it demonstrates how difficult, if not
downright impossible, it is to argue the superiority of the Western
type of society in objective, absolute or universal terms. At its
best, the argument must be self-constrained, pragmatic and,
indeed, unashamedly circular.
(Bauman, 1988, pp. 140–4)

Bauman's place in the debate over the Enlightenment project is not
immediately obvious, due to his refusal to endorse, or even discuss at
length, the opposite "extremes" of outright Enlightenment or outright
relativism. His very starting point is that "the two-centuries-old
philosophical voyage to certainty and universal criteria of perfection
and 'good life' seems to be a wasted effort." In a sense he is ruling out
right from the beginning those elements in Dews's and Habermas's
argument which continue to suggest that a "God's eye view" of the
world remains feasible. The chief flaw in all modernist philosophy and
social theory is its *hubris*: the western "pretensions to universality."
   As a sociologist, Bauman cannot take these philosophical pretensions
at face value. Behind all attempts to "legislate" what is eternally true,
universal, and rational, he implies, lies an ideological drive, whether
consciously followed or not: the need constantly to rationalize and
elevate the norms of our own type of society. In other words, while
philosophers and scientists, often in good faith, have striven after
disembodied truth and rationality, it is the *culture* and *society* of
western science and philosophy that is ultimately being defended, not
timeless mental values. To that extent, Bauman accepts Lyotard's claim
that science and truth are always embedded in ideological
metanarratives. The "unstoppable march of Reason" is thus really only
a front for cultural imperialism, and the hubristic seeking-after-truth in
western philosophy is geared to producing the "comforting" mirage of
universality, not its reality. Reason could therefore be seen as merely
one form of distinguishing "the West" from "the Rest" (see chapter 6).
   Bauman makes it clear that he sees the *attraction* of the search for
pure Reason, but the rationalist philosophers he most respects are those
like Ernest Gellner, who is cited and discussed. Gellner is thought to be
at least open to the idea that all that searching is inevitably in vain, and
that its best rationale is *not* Truth in the end but a half-hearted belief
that modern western society – for all its crimes and faults – contains
more potential for ultimate good than other alternatives. In other words,
the best objectivists, for Bauman, are those who concede that "science"

rests on a moral metanarrative which cannot be finally demonstrated as valid for all times and places.

Bauman further sees the traditional identity of the western intellectual as today entering a stage of terminal crisis. His/her role as "legislator" for scientific truth and the good society must therefore be abandoned in the face of the manifest failure of intellectuals to be successful legislators in practice: history simply does not follow any single pattern or intellectually-derived blueprint. Instead, we are witnessing an increasing *pluralization* of the life-world (to use a favorite term of Habermas). In that "irreversibly plural" world, the proper role for intellectuals, Bauman feels, is the appropriately humble one of *interpreting* different cultural traditions and the linkages between them.

Notice here that, in espousing relativism and in debunking the hubris of western universalist philosophy, Bauman makes clear his dissatisfaction with some expressions of a similar stance – Lyotard is not mentioned but he is surely in Bauman's sights here. The problems with outright post-modernism, he implies, are threefold. It is too vociferously stated to make a proper impact on serious but hesitant "legislators"; it is self-defeating in that the dream of the non-absolute is stated in "absolutist terms"; and any role for the intellectual seems rather futile if we are confronted by a "hopelessly plural" world that we can do nothing with.

Bauman's "interpreter" figure is modest, but not self-negating. Indeed, by retaining an important, if greatly reduced role for intellectuals, Bauman concedes that he too may be engaged in nothing more than a subtle defense of the western intellectual mode. Moreover, the importance of that role is thought to consist of promoting understanding between different cultures and traditions, an understanding which will "urgently" contribute to a better life in common among the peoples of the world. In that sense, even the figure of the interpreter holds on to aspects of the Enlightenment project.

Having said that, the brunt of Bauman's discussion is clearly aimed *towards* an acceptance of a post-modern conception of social knowledge and simultaneously it is aimed mostly *against* the kind of objectivism which "refuse[s] to admit realities" which strongly support relativism.

# 7 Post-Modernity as "Reflexivity"

At this point in these deliberations, a summary would perhaps be welcome, especially one which is neither particularly pro-Enlightenment nor particularly enamored of post-modernism. Such a standpoint can be found in the writings of Anthony Giddens, the British social theorist. Giddens encapsulates the debate in a clear and helpful way, and manages to throw in one or two points which we have not considered much so far (Giddens, 1990).

First of all, Giddens has three very brief, but quite decisively phrased, criticisms of post-modernism *à la* Lyotard. He wants to dismiss outright as "unworthy of serious intellectual consideration" the idea that with the coming of post-modernism we must relinquish any claim to proper *knowledge* of society, and claim instead merely fragmentary opinions, insights, or language games. If this really were true, Giddens wagers, then books like *The Postmodern Condition* would just not get written, and their authors would be out jogging rather than engaging in philosophical argumentation.

Giddens further comments that to see society and social knowledge as moving from modernity to post-modernity is, whether we like it or not, to give the history of society a recognizable "shape" or intellectual storyline – even if the current phase of that overall shape is held to be pretty shapeless. In other words, while post-modernism seems to celebrate intellectual and social indeterminacy, its very self-definition inevitably confers a degree of unity and coherence on social evolution – yet unity, coherence, and evolution are just the sort of values post-modernism wants to abandon. The post-modern perspective thus seems rather contradictory.

Giddens's third point against post-modernism is that it advocates nothing that was not already present in Nietzsche's work written over a hundred years ago; so it cannot be said to be new. But in that case, he goes on, we have to admit either that post-modernism has (paradoxically) been around for a very long time, or (more plausibly) that modernism for that length of time has contained *within itself* a post-modern "moment" or aspect. Either way, modernity is more complex than post-modernists make out.

These are emphatic arguments, lucidly stated. However, for all that, Giddens does not end up wholeheartedly backing the Enlightenment project. Like Zygmunt Bauman, Giddens is highly suspicious of "foundationalism"; that is, the philosophical attempt to find and exhibit the essential foundations of our knowledge of the world, thus grounding it in a set of indubitable truths and methods. He points to a number of such foundationalist ventures: for example, some philosophers (rationalists) have tried to invoke the power of reason itself, while others ("logical positivists") have appealed to the certainty of empirical sense-perception in an effort to "stabilize" scientific and social scientific categories. But these categories, Giddens implies, and indeed the very business of scientific inquiry, are always changing, are never stable. There is simply no point in chasing after epistemological certainty in this way. There are no indubitable "foundations" to be discovered in humanity's quest for understanding.

Nor is there any necessary "progress," whether in knowledge or in society. Giddens dislikes the very idea that history has a hidden essential meaning and *direction* (he calls this "teleology"). He insists that we need to start feeling more comfortable with the fact that there are *always* going to be conflicting views of progress, that there are always going to be different ways of construing the essence and goal of history in the first place. If the Enlightenment was really only about substituting for religious certainty the belief in a sort of secular "providence," then it cannot be accepted as a "reasonable" project at all.

This brings us to Giddens's own way of conceiving of "post-modernism." In fact, he declares, the Enlightenment is *not* best regarded as supplying a new "providential view of history." From the very beginning, Giddens asserts, any tendency for the appeal to reason to become itself dogmatic and faith-like, was sure to be rigorously questioned in the very name of reason. In a sense, critical reason involves questioning *all* faiths, all pre-given "foundations" for knowledge and society. This is the critical "voice" or "moment" *within* modern thought itself, a voice which is suspicious of reason and progress and which has become louder and more persistent through the nineteenth and twentieth centuries. The label that Giddens gives to this inherently self-critical aspect of the Enlightenment project, and of the experience of modernity more generally, is "reflexivity."

To be typically modern, Giddens reckons, is not so much to be convinced of rational progress as to be thoroughly "unsettled" by the way in which reason and progress can be used for very different political and social purposes. The experience of modernity is thus as much about intellectual puzzlement and existential doubt as it is about intellectual conviction in the powers of reason. Such self-questioning, or *reflexivity*, is *inherent* in modernity, Giddens maintains, as indeed can be seen by the very endlessness of debates about whether knowledge has any foundations or not!

Note here that, by introducing the concept of "reflexivity," Giddens aims to widen the debate, to take it outside of the limited academic sphere. That is because he is sure that reflexivity (i.e. increasing self-questioning, together with proliferating sources of *information*) also bears on the thinking and everyday lives of most "modern" people. In the streets as well as in the seminar rooms, he implies, people are increasingly self-aware rather than playing fixed roles, are troubled rather than certain, are aware that there may be *many* certainties within and across cultures, not just a few. Later in his book, he compares the experience of modernity to that of riding a scarcely controllable juggernaut. This is a far cry from taking our place aboard the "A train" of history, guaranteed of controlled progress.

Overall, Giddens thinks that post-modernism, minus the sensationalism, is getting at *something* important in contemporary experience and intellectual reflection. However, he thinks that that "something" is best understood as "radicalized modernity," modernity coming to terms with its own intrinsic reflexivity, rather than being a new phase of post-modernity as such.

Finally, Giddens touches on another crucial issue in our debate which Bauman also raised. He connects the rise and fall of Enlightened reason with the rise and decline of western civilization more generally. After all, when we speak of Enlightenment society and thought, we are normally referring to the product of only a handful of modern nation-states in North-west Europe – nations which also first discovered the powers of capitalist industrialization. So, for all its emphasis on the "higher" pursuits of philosophy and culture, the Enlightenment project can also be seen sociologically as the inner conscience of the wider *western, industrial, capitalist* project.

The march of reason is thus also the march of this particular type of society, its intellectual "reflection" if you like. Such societies depend absolutely on technological advance which, in turn, thrives on unfettered competition and exchange in the realm of scientific ideas and inventions. Arguably, these cultural "needs" or reflections of modern industrial society also, in turn, tend to generate an underlying *philosophical* rationale: hence the Enlightenment project, characterized by reason, progress, and historical advance. These intellectual "tools" are of course also very much a part of what distinguishes the "West" from "the Rest" and sets it *above* other cultures.

Such a view of Enlightenment should not be seen as straightforward cynicism. It is a way of saying that *all* intellectual works are cultural products; that *all* cultural products inevitably reflect something of the type of material society which gives them birth; and that western thought and society are no exception. How vain, when you come to think about it, is the claim to have "unlocked" the secret of universal reason, a claim made by a tiny handful of people and states among the vastness of the world's peoples and cultures? What about Chinese science and culture? What about Eastern ways of knowing? What about peasant practical wisdom? Why should western "scientific" ideas automatically be granted *cultural* dominance? Just because the West has often sought to impose itself on the rest of humanity does not mean that its core ideas have universal validity. Looked at in this way, the increasing *questioning* of modernist ideas from within a "radicalized modernity" parallels the more general weakening of western imperialism. The cultural decline of these "advanced" nations means that a correspondingly more significant place must be taken by other peoples, other cultures and other philosophical ideas than "western" ones – whether these others are conceived of as "Eastern," "Southern," "non-white," "Third World," "peripheral," or whatever.

# 8   Overview

In Giddens's hands, we seem to have struck a happy compromise between Enlightenment and post-modernism. The "extremes" of both apparent alternatives have been debunked, and the problem area has been more subtly redefined so as to include the good parts of both poles of opinion. What more, we might ask, needs to be said? Isn't that simply the end of the story? However, before accepting Giddens's views as the last word on the matter, we should at least make an effort to pose some tricky questions for him as well: for example, isn't Giddens in the end just trying to have his cake and eat it too?

In taking a little from each camp and in giving nothing away, isn't Giddens himself displaying signs of indecisive *ambivalence* or even confusion in his own mind? Such a line of suspicious questioning seems justified in the light of Giddens's presentation of the intellectual history of modernity as constantly oscillating between the poles or "voices" of Enlightenment and anti-Enlightenment. This is after all a predicament which he feels has today reached an all-time degree of intensity, and which he affirms is shared by philosophers and lay actors alike (which presumably includes himself). In that sense, the intractability of the Enlightenment debate is not *resolved* by Giddens at all; instead, he seems to be proposing that we should come to *accept* it as part of the fabric of life in "radicalized modernity."

So, while some readers will be attracted to Giddens's way of handling the post-modernity/Enlightenment debate, others may find it somewhat indecisive and unsatisfactory, and will be the more eager to press for definite intellectual commitment one way or the other. "Which side are you on?," we might want to ask. As an alternative conclusion, one could perhaps return here to Dews and Habermas, on the one hand, or Lyotard and Bauman on the other. The former pair shares Giddens's suspicion of post-modernism and his concern to preserve something of modernity and something of the classical sociological project. But why, then, Dews might ask, is Giddens so hesitant – here and in his other work – to specify some basic "foundations" for social theory? And why is he so vehemently opposed (as Habermas is not) to some kind of evolutionary perspective on society?

Post-modernists, of course, would merely reverse the weighting of these critical questions. If Giddens is so against objectivists and evolutionism, how can he claim to stage even a partial defense of modernist thought, since objectivism and evolutionism are widely acknowledged to be at the heart of classical Enlightenment social theory? Again, while Giddens appears wholly committed to reflexivity, he never fully tackles the crucial issue of relativism, to which it is closely related. At least the post-modernists grab the bull by the horns on this matter.

Looked at in this way, you could reasonably maintain that Giddens does not so much "advance" the debate as cloud it; and the original positions he appeared to have moved "beyond" can themselves be made to look, on reflection, more principled and honorable by comparison. This sequence of criticism might also note with disapproval that Giddens's subtle "middle way" leaves the political ramifications of the debate rather unclear also. Theoretical views certainly tend to reflect more general ideological themes; but they also surely exist to enhance and articulate them in an influential way. By that criterion, Giddens's thinking on post-modernity – whether for good or ill – does not pack much of a punch.

In other words, Giddens's approach will, for some readers, shine through as a sensitive synthesis with little political dogma coming along as baggage; whereas, for others, it will merely express vacillation and ambivalence. The influence of our own *prior* theoretical and ideological leanings in assessing a position is clearly pertinent here. Those who are already committed to a theoretical tradition or stance are likely to be predisposed towards the side of a debate which tends to confirm that allegiance; whereas wholly "open-minded" readers are perhaps liable to be a little naïve and impressionable.

Before concluding, therefore, let us look at two possible responses to the Enlightenment debate which are certainly anchored more firmly within particular traditions of theory and politics than that of Giddens:

namely, Marxism and feminism. The strengths and weaknesses of such "committed" responses should leave us more aware of the range of available evaluative options.

## 8.1   The Marxist resolution

Theoretically, Marxism is chiefly about the *class analysis* of modern capitalist societies. Essentially, for Marxists, capitalism exists and thrives on the basis of the exploitation of labor by capital, of workers by capitalists. The dynamics of technological growth can generally be explained by reference to the labor–capital relation and the ceaseless drive for profits that is built into the structure of economic calculation. That economic structure broadly determines the social priorities, political formations, and ideological ambience of capitalist society.

More generally, Marxist theory sees human history as a succession of social formations, each governed by its dominant mode of economic production. In successive modes of production, masters have exploited slaves, feudal lords have exploited peasants, and nowadays capitalists exploit workers. Further, each mode of production "governs" the social, political, and cultural character of its epoch and also the character of social *transitions* between successive modes of production. Marx held that each mode of production could expand and subsist only so far, technologically and socially speaking, before severe and inbuilt "contradictions" arose. Such contradictions and the social crises they encourage impel society into revolutionary change towards some other, historically more appropriate, economic and social structure.

Understood thus, classical Marxism is an Enlightenment project in three main senses. Firstly, class analysis strives to be "objective" in some sense. Whatever the social and intellectual beliefs of the epoch happen to be, Marx argued, the ultimate rationale for what we do and how we think stems from the logic of the mode of production and from the social relations or class struggles which characterize that mode. The salient "subjective" aspects of social life in any epoch can thus generally be related to more objective socio-economic factors. Marxist analysis in that sense seeks to be "scientific" and is committed to the project of rationally unmasking the various ideological "distortions" which cloud the real driving forces in modern society.

Secondly, when we widen the picture to cover human history in its entirety, it is clear that, for Marxists, history is seen as having an inner logic and dynamic which impels it forward. History is thus assumed to have a significant evolutionary shape; it is relatively coherent, unified, progressive, and rational – not in the sense of *reasonable*, given its frightful record of oppression, but certainly in terms of having an *explicable rationale*.

Thirdly, in Marxism, as in the original Enlightenment idea, scientific knowledge of human society is thought capable of leading to social and spiritual *emancipation* if used correctly. Now the initial impulse in Marxism, which sets its whole *intellectual* endeavor into motion, is in fact a profound sense of the human waste and injustice of class exploitation. Marxism thus begins with a strong commitment to right the wrongs of capitalist and other class-based societies, to help workers and other oppressed groups free themselves so that they can aspire to a better, individually fulfilling, peaceful, and cooperative society. From this ethical impulse grows Marxist "scientific" analysis, which, in turn, confers an "objective" status on Marxist political practice.

It now appears evident why post-modernism is anathema to traditional Marxism. Post-modernism "deconstructs" and even mocks the notions of science, objectivity, progress, and emancipation that Marxism requires in some version or other. Post-modernism is skeptical of metanarratives, whereas the Marxist "story" of the liberation of humanity from oppression and ignorance *via* the class struggle provides just such a powerful tale. Post-modernism dissolves the idea of society as possessing some kind of hidden core of meaning into the "play" of innumerable language games; whereas the category of "mode of production" provides a clear core concept for seeing society as a totality in spite of its many complex facets. Post-modernism (its opponents feel) can lead to liberal complacency or (worse still) to ultra-conservative nihilism, whereas Marxism must retain a firm sense of (faith in) socialist hope.

In fact, given this antagonism, Marxists would not be altogether happy about Habermas himself being taken to be the prime defender of Enlightenment. Here it needs to be remembered that Habermas regards (regarded) himself as a sort of Marxist. Over the years, however, he has come to share some standard reservations about classical Marxism and has given these a distinctive twist of his own. In particular, Habermas doubts whether the Marxist focus on labor and production can be broad enough to encompass the special features of cultural and political life. The state, for example, has become so enmeshed in economic life that to see the state as a "mere" superstructure of the economic base is dangerously schematic. Indeed, for Habermas, the whole sphere of moral and political discourse, the sphere which crucially *legitimates* dominant socio-economic structures, possesses today an autonomy and force which traditional Marxism cannot really come to terms with. This argument places not only the state, but also science and technology and the whole apparatus of discourse, argument, and proof, at the leading edge of social development.

These very substantial "revisions" of Marxism prompt Habermas to recast the whole trajectory of social evolution as an ongoing social *learning* process, rather than simply as a succession of class societies or as the historical development of productive *labor*. All this helps explain why a theory of "communicative reason" has become crucial to Habermas's thinking. In a sense, Habermas reworks the Marxist story of human development (that of the logic, fettering, and emancipation of labor) into a story about the logic, distortion, and (potential) fulfillment of communicative reason.

By way of response to this critique, orthodox Marxists would first probably want to accuse Habermas of exaggerating the autonomy of reason, morality, and the process of communicative interaction. Indeed, in Habermas's hands these aspects of society almost lose all anchorage in the material structures and class relationships of modern life. In that respect, Habermas might be seen as being almost as "idealist" and as "superstructuralist" as the post-modernists he opposes.

Secondly, in spite of Habermas's desire to rescue the Enlightenment notions of validity, rationality, and truth, he himself operates with a "pragmatist" concept of truth. In other words, he sees truth and validity as being the *product* of interactive communication between social actors. He does not see truth in absolute terms, as something inherent in the world which human discourse strives to capture; instead, truth is what human beings, in the process of everyday communicative exchange, come to agree on. But here it appears that Habermas once again shares a great deal (i.e. relativism) with the post-modernists. And once again, because classical Marxism is firmly anti-relativist in flavor, it seems that the latter, and not Habermas, is the more committed defender of Enlightenment values.

All in all, the classical Marxist would strive to adjudicate the debate between Habermas and Lyotard along the lines of "a plague on both your houses" – though with the moral points definitely going to Habermas. Furthermore, Marxists are liable to see non-Marxist attempts to transcend this debate (such as that of Giddens) as being a kind of fudging or abstention from the serious issues that the debate does succeed in posing. Not surprisingly, the conclusion would be that Marxism should be respected as the most developed and clear defense of "radical Enlightenment" (see Callinicos, 1990).

But wait a minute. What of the fact – often cited in social science texts – that there are several variants of Marxism? And is not the entire Marxist tradition in the throes of a major crisis, both theoretically and politically? Politically speaking, the period since the mid-1980s has witnessed the most dramatic collapse of regimes which have claimed to be based on Marxist ideas. Furthermore, many on the Left as well as the Right have long felt that the characteristics and complexities of advanced capitalist society itself are no longer best or exclusively understood in classical Marxist terms. Even Marxism's most fruitful analytical category – "mode of production" – is regarded by many neo-Marxists as being only one of *several* necessary concepts for comprehending human interaction and struggle. (The others might include gender relations, ethnicity, generation, culture, etc.)

The "classical" or "fundamentalist" Marxist would no doubt seek to come back on these apparent weaknesses in Marxism, seeking to show the misplacedness or irrelevance of such "revisions." However, as a matter of fact it is clear that Marxism does admit to many variations, some of which entertain serious doubts, not only about the comprehensiveness and validity of classical Marxism, but also about the Enlightenment form in which classical Marxism is undoubtedly cast. These quasi-Marxists feel that Marxism itself has to become more *pluralistic* in its analytic strategy because society and politics themselves are more multi-levelled or pluralistic than Marxists traditionally concede. Such "revisionist" Marxists will thus accept a great deal of the post-modernist critique of Enlightenment. They will find themselves asking: Who is to say, in the end, which "grand narrative" is "objectively" correct? And why continually strive to present Marxism itself as scientific and objectively true, with other views cast in the role of "distorted" and "ideological" thought? Is this not indeed precisely *replacing* real science – which ought to be open, relativistic, and hesitant – with a blind *faith* in (Marxist) reason? The vulnerable world of the late twentieth century would seem to be too important a context for Marxists to persist in elevating themselves into omniscient "legislators" (in Bauman's terms).

According to this train of thought, the initial *firmness* of the Marxist "line" on our debate can fairly quickly be seen to crumble into a series of dilemmas and problems for Marxism itself. If nothing else, this testifies to the vitality and importance of the "fate of Enlightenment" debate. No sooner has it been resolved than it breaks out again. A similar message can emerge from a consideration of the stance of another radical tradition, namely feminism.

## 8.2   Feminist dilemmas

In some ways, we might expect feminism to provide the most decisive of interventions in the kind of debate we have been following. For one thing, feminism is a confident, committed, and historically ascendant perspective; it therefore remains unsullied (as Marxism is not) by the historical record, and is continually fired (as liberalism is not) by the strength of male resistance to feminist claims and insights.

From the point of view of this chapter, the feminist critique of the philosophical *style* of reasoning is particularly notable. The point here is that, on the surface, it is philosophy's concern for very *abstract* debate, for purely *logical* forms of demonstration and proof, that distinguishes it from other disciplines. Philosophers deal not in people or things, but in ideas and disembodied argument. In that sense, nothing could seem further removed from the biases of gender, class, or whatever. Moreover, it is presumed from the outset in philosophical discussion, as part of the occupational culture, so to speak, that the participants in philosophical inquiry will, on entering its lofty portals, willingly *shed* their worldly characteristics in order to engage in a pure meeting of minds. These minds may well happen to be predominantly male, but they might also happen to be female: their being male or female is really quite *incidental* to the process of rational inquiry that they embark on.

However, feminists above all have come to challenge this picture of the philosophical realm as a depersonalized sphere of reason. On the contrary, they ask, is it not *precisely* characteristic of the strivings of a typically *male* outlook to try desperately to shake off worldly connections and responsibilities so as to presume to speak in the name of reason itself?

The ideal of scientific rationality (as espoused in many versions of the Enlightenment project) is but one expression of this male striving for pure reason. Such an ideal stems in the first place from a sharp contrast between, on the one hand, the individual mind or pure ego and, on the other hand, the messy, living world of nature and society. Through a process of interrogation (scientific research) and reflection (philosophy), the pure ego comes to *comprehend* and then *control* nature. The process of intellectual and physical "mastery" is then complete, and the philosopher-king can congratulate himself on his absolute powers of reason and technique. He has come to *know* and indeed even to *possess* the previously mysterious and threatening "other" – the concrete, intuitive world of nature.

In short, from a feminist characterization, the austere business of philosophical inquiry *could* be made out as nothing more or less than the very grandest of Boy's Games. Far from being disinterested and cooperative, philosophical debate is often nit-picking, egoistic, and competitive. The picture of pure reason it depicts reveals a world of isolated man, the hunter after truth, "probing," "interrogating," and finally "possessing" the secrets of nature (where nature is usually described in female terms). And the overall aim is ultimately *control*; that is, power. Such a picture of rationality, far from being presuppositionless (as philosophers have always supposed), is arguably teeming with unquestioned assumptions, assumptions which are essentially "masculinist."

This interpretation of philosophical endeavor is undoubtedly insightful and hard-hitting. However, if all claims to "truth" and "reason" are part of the great Boy's Game that we know as philosophy, then what of the arguments of feminism itself: are they *not* to be judged as fair, good, forceful, reasonable, and true in something like the normal (male?) meanings of those terms?

In the following excerpt by Margareta Halberg, this pressing question for feminist philosophy is explored further. She identifies a number of tensions in feminist theorizing:

> The tension between objectivism and relativism is inherent in the feminist standpoint epistemology [that is, in the view that women have a privileged access to knowledge] and cannot be overcome. Either there is a feminist objectivist standpoint, grounded in women's position in society, or there is no such standpoint. If it is recognized that there are many various, and sometimes necessarily contradictory, "women's standpoints", there is no possible way of deciding which one is the objective one.
>
> Furthermore, . . . . "experience" when used as a basis for knowledge is an extremely vague term. Experiences are always influenced by the contexts surrounding them, and therefore never coherent or identical for all women. Even if all women shared certain "determining" experiences, it is by no means obvious that this would give rise to the same kind of knowledge.
>
> I reject experience as a grounding for feminist epistemologies, and I oppose the proposals that men and women do have different ways to knowledge. I also reject the idea that philosophical and scientific concepts are totally genderized. Feminist philosophical challenges to science are in my view very important and valuable, in so far as they identify and contribute to a recognition of

> formerly ignored groups and problems; in the process feminists
> thus highlight new and important areas where research is needed.
> (Halberg, 1989, p. 6)

Halberg gives an admirably concise résumé of the dilemmas for
feminist philosophy. It is also a very honest résumé. Indeed, although
she cannot see any feasible way of "grounding" feminist epistemology
(thus sharing the post-modern gripe against Enlightenment), she is also
manifestly reluctant to give up altogether the objectivist Enlightenment
goal of *progressively* enlarging our shared total knowledge, of
*demonstrating* rather than merely asserting better arguments, and of
holding that good arguments of any kind tell us something positive
about the real world "outside" of the speaker's chosen discourse.

Thus, the author concludes that the problems she raises cannot be
resolved at the theoretical level alone. Moreover, Halberg accepts that
the most obvious *practical* concept which might be thought to help
resolve the issue, namely the common *experience* of women, is just too
vague and questionable to bear the theoretical burden placed upon it.
As in the case of Marxism – though with different theoretical bearings –
an apparently firm and holistic resolution of the Enlightenment debate
becomes once again entangled in complications.

# 9 Conclusion

In this chapter I have presented a range of commentaries on the
Enlightenment project revisited. In each case the aim has been not only
to give you an understanding of the key themes, but also to give you
access to a number of evaluative options. The idea is that you will at
least feel you have seriously engaged in an intriguing but sometimes
complex theoretical exchange. Additionally, it is hoped that you will
by now feel in a position to decide whether, for example, you would
defend something like the Enlightenment ideal of social science; or
whether you are a relativist or not; or whether or not you favor a
holistic social theory (such as Marxism).

However, one of the things which emerges from debates such as this
is that the way in which issues are initially framed and subsequently
conducted strongly influences how we finally judge them; and, as I
mentioned earlier, none of us comes to these debates entirely free of
value commitments, stylistic and political preferences, and so on.
Given that, it seems appropriate to finish by making two sets of points
about my own way of framing issues. In making these points, the idea
is that you are encouraged even further to ask yourself "What do I
really make of all this?" – and then, crucially, to try to *answer* that
question.

One point concerns the style in which the chapter has been couched,
namely that of a "debate." Now, in a sense this rhetorical strategy might
already be thought to favor an Enlightenment rather than a post-modern
perspective. This is because post-modernists might say that a debate

format, rather like a law court, encourages spectators to be *judges*, rationally weighing up the pros and cons, in the light of the evidence, and then deciding who has the *truth* of the matter. But post-modernists would prefer to bracket off the whole question of "truth" and "rationality" altogether, and choose to speak instead of various rhetorical exchanges, contributions, and discussions. Furthermore, they would say that we choose among these various strategies as much on aesthetic and emotive grounds as on purely intellectual ones (and that these latter in any pure sense are really just a figment of the academic imagination).

So one conclusion which is available, but which I have not seriously opened up to you, is that the whole "debate" format is a bit of a trick, an academic rhetorical ploy which you need not feel obliged to follow. However, such a conclusion is acceptable, paradoxically, only on condition that it is thoroughly *argued through*, and not merely *asserted*. Also, as long as we are *aware* that we are deploying a particular rhetorical format (in this case the debate format), then arguably we have met the minimum condition for "reflexivity" in this area.

The second point has to do with my own favored position within the debate. Here again it is possible that I have maneuvered the discussion in a direction that I personally favor; and so, if I am to be truly fair to the reader, I should at least declare my hand – if only to offer a conclusion that you can "bounce off" in forming your own.

Of the options posed, my own view comes closest to that of Dews. In other words, I favor a broadly pro-Enlightenment perspective, mainly because, like many closet objectivists, I too am perturbed at the prospect of full-scale relativism. It seems to me that without some universal concepts, without some attempt to see the social world as an evolving totality, without some aspiration to better humanity through improving knowledge, I see no purpose whatever in doing social science at all. Indeed, in a back-handed way, I think many avowed post-modernists are themselves actually in the business of seeking to improve our self-critical faculties and thus contributing to a better totalizing perspective on the nature and direction of society.

In favoring this broadly Enlightenment stance, I should add that much of the original motivation for this came from a general allegiance to Marxism as, in my view, the best available theoretical and political tradition. Like many other quasi-Marxists, I would now want to qualify this as follows:

1   The pro-Enlightenment stance can and should be defended *independently* of any preference for particular social theories (including Marxism).

2   The attraction of Marxism today lies as much in the fact that it is an Enlightenment *type* of theory as it does in its particular substantive or theoretical claims. In other words, the *form* of Marxism as a totalizing, determinate social theory seems to me as important as its specific claims about class struggle or the influence of the modes of production at any given time.

By focusing on the type of theory Marxism is, modern Marxists allow themselves an "escape clause" which enables them to embrace in principle the contributions of other traditions (for instance feminism) in the hope that a new "synthesis" can emerge to satisfy the continuing Enlightenment cravings of many social scientists. I choose these emotive words (embrace, hope, satisfy, craving) deliberately: for one central lesson Enlighteners have learned from post-modernists (and I am no exception) is that the ultimate motivation for "rational" progress in knowledge and society is as much emotive, linguistic, and social as it is purely cognitive. How else could it be where engaged human beings are the subject as well as the object of knowledge? In that sense, the strategy of the chapter has not been to steer you unilaterally down the Enlightenment road; rather it has been to highlight the mixed blessings of all the various options. My main intention will have been fulfilled, in other words, if I have made you feel something of the intellectual and moral *ambivalence* that is a central element of the experience of (post-)modernity.

# References

Bauman, Z. (1988) *Legislators and Interpreters*, Cambridge, England, Polity Press.

Bernstein, R. (ed.) (1985) *Habermas and Modernity*, Cambridge, England, Polity Press.

Callinicos, A. (1990) "Reactionary postmodernism," in Boyne, R. and Rattansi, A. (eds) *Postmodernism and Society*, London, Macmillan.

Dews, P. (1986) *Habermas: Autonomy and Solidarity*, London, Verso.

Gellner, E. (1984) "Tractatus Sociologico-Philosophicus," in Brown, S.L. (ed.) *Objectivity and Cultural Divergence*, Royal Institute of Philosophy, Lecture Series, 17.

Giddens, A. (1990) *The Consequences of Modernity*, Cambridge, England, Polity Press.

Habermas, J. (1985) "Modernity: an incomplete project," in Foster, H. (ed.) *Postmodern Culture*, London, Pluto.

Habermas, J. (1987) "The normative content of modernity," in *The Philosophical Discourse of Modernity*, Cambridge, England, Polity Press.

Halberg, M. (1989) "Feminist epistemology: an impossible project?," *Radical Philosophy*, no. 53, Autumn, pp. 3–7.

Lyotard, J.-F. (1984) *The Postmodern Condition: A Report on Knowledge*, Manchester, England, Manchester University Press.

# Index

Abercrombie, N.  310, 314, 413, 415, 416, 418, 603–4
absolute monarchy  31, 43, 45, 47, 66–70
absolutism: ethnic  628; France  47; and modern state
    70–1, 72; sexuality  388–9; states  66–70
acid rain  508–9, 527
Adams, Richard  523
Adorno, T.  178, 180–1, 437
advanced capitalist state  240, 243–9, 261–3, 275–6;
    autonomy and power  271–2, 492; diversity/uniformity
    242  3; formation  249–61; globalization  273–6;
    industrial output  288–9; interconnectedness  272–3;
    Marxism  265–6; neo-Marxism  269; New Right
    266–7; policy communities  263; society-centered
    approaches  263–6, 272; state-centered approaches
    266–71, 272; trade unions  267–8; war  241; welfare
    241, 244–6, 259–61
advertising  94–5, 96–7; see also consumerism; marketing
Aglietta, Michel  547–8, 553–4, 555
agriculture: changing methods  82, 103, 130; dominance
    64, 101, 103, 537; and manufacturing  116, 119; output
    share  103, 104–5; pre-industrial society  124; workers
    134
AIDS  391–2
Alber, J.  246, 261, 262, 267, 270, 273
Alembert, Jean d'  26, 28
alienation  176–7, 179, 398
Allen, R.  522
Althusser, Louis  13, 413–14, 606–7
ambition  112, 116–17
American Revolution  see USA
Americas, explored  192–3; see also New World; USA
Amos, V.  379
Anderson, B.  11, 33–4, 35, 402, 413, 414, 613
Anderson, P.  13, 63, 68
Andreski, S.  78
Andrews, S.  415
anomie  177, 401
anthropology  152, 208
Archer, M. S.  469, 498–9
architecture, post-modern  569, 573–5
Arendt, H.  463
Arens, W.  214
Aristotle  206, 403
arms race  441
Armstrong, P.  288
Arnold, Matthew  616
Aron, R.  481
asceticism  164, 166, 168, 173, 174
astronomy  30
Atkinson, M. M.  272
Austria, state expenditure  76
authority  63–5, 222, 492, 496
automobile industry  see car industry
autonomy  see state autonomy

Bacon, Francis  37, 151
Bahro, R.  526, 527
Barnett, A.  614
Barrett, M.  352, 354
Barron, R.  321
Baudelaire, C.  605–6
Baudrillard, J.  567–8, 582, 583–6
Bauman, Z.  468, 482, 495, 497–8, 631–2, 648–51
Beaglehole, J. C.  210, 218
Beckford, J. A.  407, 408
Beechey, V.  320
Beetham, D.  447
Behn, Aphra  218
Beitz, C.  70, 495
Bell, D.  319, 488, 537, 539–40, 544, 556–7, 558, 559, 589
Benjamin, W.  11, 605–6
Benn, S. I.  67
Bennett, J.  454
Berger, J.  247
Berger, P.  407, 527
Berkhofer, R.  212
Berlin, I.  445
Bernal, M.  58

Bernstein, R.  646
Bertramsen, R. B.  269, 271, 272
Beynon, H.  335
Bhabha, Homi  612–13
binary oppositions  160, 162, 164, 167, 168, 413, 478–80
Birnbaum, N.  416
birth control  375, 376, 391
bisexuality  381
Black, J.  27
Blackburn, R.  313
Blumler, J. G.  416
Bobbio, N.  57, 447–8
body  364–5, 368–72; see also sexuality
Böhning, W.  324–5, 326
Borbón, Josefa Amar y  35
Bosquet, M.  525
Bossuet, J. B.  30
Bougainville, L. A. de  207, 218
bourgeoisie  134–9
Boyer, R.  549
Bozeman, A.  479
Braudel, F.  81, 558
Braverman, H.  333, 335
Brennan, T.  616
Breuilly, J.  79
Brinton, C.  21–2
Britain  93–106, 124–5, 194–5; employment  310–11,
    318–19; industry  133–43, 289, 293–5, 311, 325, 336;
    politics  74–5, 263–4, 266, 286; society  175–8, 265,
    414–15, 417–18
Brown, V.  114
Bruce, S.  406, 407
Bry, T. de  209, 212
Bull, H.  63, 65, 467, 479, 493, 496, 497
bureaucracy  144–5, 171, 233, 267
bureaucratization  246
Burke, Edmund  45, 219, 415
Burman, S.  326
Burton, J.  481, 492
Butt, R.  390

Callinicos, A.  658; collective goals  458; critical response
    to  449–52; Eastern Europe  439–40; liberal democracy
    447–9, 451; post-modernism  567, 568, 578–80
Campbell, T. D.  108, 110
cannibalism  213, 214
capital  137, 256–61, 270, 656
capitalism: class  427; exploitation  113; globalization  190,
    474; ideology  410; modern state  79–84; modernity  5,
    12, 452; politics  109; power  264; production  134;
    religion  164–7; resource depletion  515; sexuality
    369; state  79–84, 269, 448–9, 456–7; technology  541;
    warfare  249–50; see also advanced capitalist state
capitalism, types: adventurer  164; bourgeois  164, 166;
    global  482; industrial  144, 177; laissez-faire  109, 312;
    late  568, 571, 572–8, 592; liberal  108, 110; managed
    256, 257, 258–9, 268, 273–4; rational  164–5, 169;
    restless  555; state  448–9
capitalist world society  482–3
capitalists  102, 130, 135–9
car industry: Britain  289–90, 293; Germany  323–4;
    Japan  336, 337
Carnoy, M.  269, 270
Cartesian dualism  603, 605
Cassese, A.  69
Castells, M.  540–1, 544–5, 557–8, 559, 561
Castles, S.  323, 326
Catherine II, the Great, empress of Russia  44–5
Catholic Church  64–5, 411–12
centralization/decentralization  479
Cerny, P.  276, 495
Chambers, Ephraim  28
Chaney, D.  418
change  558–60; consumption  552; culture  150, 155–6;
    economics  303, 535–6, 555–60; employment  288–9,
    313–14, 382; family  381–2, 383, 390–1; and knowledge
    42; occupational  312–13; political  552; production
    552; social  110, 133–4, 163–71, 233

charisma 402, 590–1
childcare 141, 350–1, 352
China, population policy 350
choice 427; *see also* consumerism
Christendom 64, 197, 200
Christianity 199, 200–1, 396–7, 399; Catholic Church
64–5, 411–12; Methodism 414–15; Protestantism 399,
406, 603; Puritanism 173, 174, 199; televangelism 582,
589–90
citizenship 78, 84, 240, 245, 253, 463
city-state 59
civil rights 83–4
civil society 52, 57, 243; fragmentation 492; post-modern
580; and state 82–3, 262, 459–63
civilization: costs 171–81; discontents 178–80;
evolution of 219, 221; global 480–2; stages 49–50,
52, 163
Clark, A. 127, 129, 139
class 13, 66, 135, 138–9, 265; capitalism 427;
fragmentation 137–8, 431; industrialism 134–9;
Marxism 113, 221–3, 409, 463, 656; pre-industrial
society 129–30; sexuality 375–6; state 83–4; welfare
provision 258; *see also* bourgeoisie; middle class;
working class
class conflicts 84, 137–8, 221–3, 577, 656
class politics 568, 575–8, 579
classification systems 159–62, 372
Cliff, T. 448
cliometrics 99–100, 106
Cloward, R. 258
Cobbe, F. P. 145
Cockburn, C. 313
coercion 71, 241
Cohen, B. 325–6
Cohen, R. 308, 323, 327
Cole, W. A. 105
Coleman, W. D. 272
Coleridge, Samuel Taylor 175–6, 415
collective bargaining 295
collective identities 402, 582
collective representations 157–9, 413, 416
colonization 190, 224
Columbus, Christopher 193, 204, 212, 214
commerce 93–100, 105–6
commodification: culture 540, 572–3, 584, 592;
information 540, 541–2
communication technology 542, 544, 622, 624
community: affective 582; good 495; ideological 398,
412–20; imagined 402, 413, 414, 420, 611–13; political
495–7; secularization 403–7; stateless 56–7; universal
467
competitive advantage 285, 311
Comte, Auguste 22, 49–51, 52–3, 484
Condorcet, Marquis de 26, 34–5, 642–3
confession 408–9
conflict: class 84, 137–8, 221–3, 577, 656; games 646;
ideological 400, 437, 442–4, 446–7; *see also* war
Connor, S. 573
constitutionalism 36, 68, 72
consumerism: advertising 94–5, 96–7; changes 552;
choice 427; global 622; green 523–6; as luxury
117–18, 119; positional goods 112; post-modern
583–6; and production 552; resource depletion 513; as
social system 400; and underconsumption 286
Cook, Captain James 210, 212
Cook, W. 496
Cooley, C. H. 586, 597, 607
corporatism 268–9
cosmology 30
Cotgrove, S. 521
Cousins, M. 201
Coward, R. 359–60, 378, 392
Cox, R. 490
Crafts, N. F. R. 99
critical thinking 29
cultural homogenization 407–9, 622, 623–5
cultural identity 7, 8–9, 596, 611–13
cultural persuaders 418–19
cultural processes 15, 419–20
cultural racism 618, 628
cultural relativism 42–3, 645, 647
cultural revolutions 405
culture 151–4, 178, 565; aesthetic/erotic 173–4;
analyzed 150, 154–62; changes 150, 155–6; collective
representations 157–9; commodified 540, 572–3, 584,
592; and economy 572–5; Enlightenment 152;

globalization 477; hybridity 617, 619, 629–32; and
ideology 419; masculinity/femininity 358, 359, 370–2;
national 188, 611–18; politics 572–8; and science
169–71; secularized 163, 165; sexuality 370–2, 374;
social change 163–71, 233; societies 396, 418
Cunningham, H. 410–11

Dahl, R. 78, 79, 263, 264, 445, 446
Daniel, W. 326
Darnton, R. 32
Deane, P. 74, 105
deconstructionism 13–14, 435, 570
defense 251, 255; *see also* military spending
degradation rituals 213–15
deindustrialization 105
democracy 78, 448, 458–9, 461–2; *see also* liberal
democracy; social democracy
democratization 86, 253
depression, economic 260, 285
Derrida, J. 13, 570, 609
Descartes, René 603
desire, and meaning 359–60, 371
deskilling 316, 320–1, 333, 334, 335–6, 551–2
despotism 31, 69
Deutsch, K. 495
development theories 223, 537
Dews, P. 645–8
Dex, S. 317, 318
Diderot, Denis 25, 26, 28, 31, 32, 33, 42, 45, 218
difference: identity 615–18; meaning 187–8;
mis-recognized 211–13; politics of 601; sexual 345,
355, 356–7, 360, 377, 611
discourse 14–16, 201–5, 225, 407–9
discrimination, in employment 325–6, 327
dislocation 599–600, 606
divine right of kings 67
division of labor 110–12, 312; cottage industry 115; and
flexible specialization 332–7; gendered 345–6, 348;
global 557; migrant workers 321–7; new international
327–32; sectoral 308–9, 544; sexual 127–8, 141–2,
344–8; social 50, 351–2
Dobbelaere, K. 403
Dobson, A. 515–18, 524, 525, 526–7, 528
Dodd, P. 616
domesticity: gendered 344, 345, 354; ideology 140–1,
145; modern society 391; and paid work 320, 352
Domhoff, G. 265
Donald, J. 617
Douglas, Mary 162
Doyle, W. 27, 28, 29, 39, 40, 45, 46
Dreyfus, H. 609
Dryden, John 217
dualism 215, 216, 603, 605
Duff, A. 521
Dunleavy, P. 267, 269
Dunn, J. 445
Durkheim, Émile 21, 50–1; *anomie* 177, 401;
classification systems 159; collective representations
157–9; institutions 233–4; religion 50–1, 161, 199,
412–13; sacred 160, 398, 590; society 123;
structuralism 155–6; women 345
Dutch explorers 195

Eccleston, B. 264, 265, 268
ecologism 515–18
ecology 430; *see also* environmentalism
economic history 97–101
economics 97–101; changes 303, 535–6, 555–60; crises
260–1; dominance 558; externalities 512; growth
106, 256, 286–7, 294–6, 302, 524, 528;
interconnectedness 488–9, 536; 'invisible hand' 108,
109; and modernity 91–3, 555; neo-Marxism 232–3;
professionalization 112–13; regulation 547–8;
religion 413
economies of scale 102, 285, 333
*Economist, The* 326
economy: culture 572–5; free market 108–10; global
274, 561–2; harmony of interests 108; modern 101,
114–18; multinational corporations 305; national 305;
sectoral divisions 104–5; self-regulating 109–10;
wealth generation 302
education: and Enlightenment 46, 48, 52; women 145,
349
Ehrenreich, B. 128, 143
Elias, N. 163, 180
Eliot, S. 32

elites 264–5; communications 624; knowledge 431, 527, 538, 544; land-owning 129–30; professional 538, 544, 557–8
Elliot, F. R. 349, 351
Ellis, Havelock 366–7, 378, 382–3
Elster, J. 72
Elsworth, S. 507, 508, 510
emotivism 403
empires 62–3, 190–1, 224
empiricism 23, 36, 37, 158
employment: changing patterns 288–9, 313–14, 382; discrimination 325–6, 327; flexibility 314–16; managed capital 256; part- /full-time 308–9, 315, 320
Employment Gazette 317, 318
Encyclopédie 27–9
Engels, Friedrich 13, 399, 409, 599
English, D. 128, 143
Enlightenment 20, 22–5, 221, 636–8, 640–1; critical thinking 29; culture 152; Encyclopédie 27–9, environmental challenges 529–30; equality 33; feminism 659–61; Frankfurt school 178, 180–1; and Green politics 516–18; hubris 648–51; intellectual society 38–40; living conditions 93; locations 25–7; Marxism 656–9, 662–3; and modernity 30–1, 35–7, 398–403, 642–4; morality 42, 403; opposed 584; and post-modernism 638, 642–4, 654–6; public/private sphere 397, 399; publishing 39–40; reflexivity 652–5; religion 30–1, 36, 173; revolution 44–8; salons 33–5; science 23, 28, 30, 37–40, 173, 640–1; social science 4, 40–4, 118–20, 221; society 31–3, 51–2, 53; sociology 21–2; totalitarianism 180, 437; tradition 30–1; universal community 467; universality of reason 498–9; West 185–9; women's status 29, 33–5, 42; see also France, Enlightenment; philosophes; Scottish Enlightenment
entrepreneurs 130; see also capitalists
environmentalism 505–7, 522; Enlightenment 529–30; and industrialism 524–5; interdependence 528; pollution 507–14, 526; pressure groups 514, 521–3; see also Green politics
epistemology 637, 640; see also knowledge
equality 33
Eratosthenes 206
Erikson, E. 386
erotic 173
Esping-Andersen, G. 257
essentialism: ethnicity 631–2; power 347; sexual 366, 368, 369, 386
estates, polity of 65–6, 70
ethics, and rationality 181
ethnic minorities 316
ethnicity 615, 617, 631–2
ethnography 208
eugenics 374–5, 378
Euro-centrism 26, 152, 200–1
Europe 8–9, 32, 63–4; agriculture 82; authority systems 63–5; and Christendom 64, 197, 200–1; conceptual barriers 191–2, 196–7; environmental reform 523; expansion 80, 82–3, 189–97, 199, 204; globalization 80–1; government departmental growth 246; Green parties 519–20; inferiority/superiority 212–13; modern state 70–3; modernity 231–2; New World 192–3, 211–13, 215–16; and Others 204–5; physical barriers 195–6; post-war reconstruction 266; social structure 32, 198; state systems 58–62; territorial boundaries 62, 70–1, 185; travellers' tales 157; welfare state 244–6
Europe, Central and Eastern 439–42, 457–8, 459
exploitation 113, 131, 135–6, 190, 317
explorations 189–97, 207, 218

Faderman, L. 385
Falk, R. 69
family: changes 381–2, 383, 390–1; industrialization effects 139–40, 142; legislation 349; patriarchal 142; post-modern 587–8; sexuality 390–2; and state 349–51
fascism 180
femininity 356–7, 358, 359–60, 370–2, 381
feminism 610–11; and Enlightenment 659–61; industrial society 143–6; post-modernism 592; rationalism 659–60; sexual segregation 145–6; sexuality 379
feminist philosophy 660
Ferguson, Adam 20, 26, 52, 220
fertility 382

feudalism 10, 63–4, 125, 131–2
finance: global 472; innovation 553; US hegemony 291–2
Financial Times 330, 331
Firestone, S. 126
Fishman, W. 317
Fitzgerald, F. 589
Flax, J. 592
flexibility: employment 314–16; labor process 550–1; migrant workers 321, 323–4
flexible specialization 328–9, 332–7, 622
Flynn, A. 515, 521–2
Ford, Henry 282, 283–5
Fordism 281–2, 296–7, 546–7; dominance 292–7; global 555; hegemonic 287; as industrial era 285–92; and post-Fordism 546–55; regulationist 547–53; turnover 284; wage system 284
Forester, J. 603
fossil fuels 508, 510
Foucault, Michel: de-centered subject 603, 606 10; discourse 201–3, 204–5, 407–9; dispersion system 214, 301; post-modernism 570; sexuality 368, 369, 372–3, 375–6, 380
foundationalism 652, 655
Fox, A. 313
Fox, D. M. 255
fragmentation: civil society 492; class 137–8, 431; and integration 478–9, 483
France: ancien régime 45; educational system 46; Enlightenment 39, 220; explorations 195, 207, 218; French Revolution 44–7, 399; monarchy 68; regulationists 547–8; Republic 47; three Estates 32–3
franchise 73, 459
Frankfurt school 178, 180–1
free market economy 108–10
freedom 23, 447
Freud, Sigmund: sexuality 355–6, 358, 368, 369–70; unconscious 179–80, 358, 369–70, 607–8; warfare 178–9
Frieden, J. 491, 493
Friedman, A. 335
Friends of the Earth 507, 508, 514, 515, 523
Frisby, D. 606
Fröbel, F. 328, 329–30, 331, 332, 333, 338
Fukuyama, F.: critical response to 445–7; democracy 458–9, 480; ideological conflict 400, 437, 442–4; modernity 452, 463
fundamentalism 630–1

Gadamer, H.-G. 438
Gagnon, J. 369
games, and conflict 646
garment industry 331
Garrett, G. 491
Gay, P. 25, 26, 28, 31–2, 38
Gellner, E. 612, 614, 615, 616, 649–50
gender 367; division of labor 345–6, 348; domesticity 344, 345, 354; hierarchies 146–7; and labor market segmentation 317–21; separate spheres 140, 143; sexuality 376–8; stereotyping 318, 320
gender identity 354–5
George, S. 454
Germany: flexible specialization 335; Fordism 293–4; Green party 519–20; mass production 295; migrant workers 323–5, 327
Gershuny, J. 311, 556
Gibbon, Edward 26, 31
Giddens, A.: advanced capitalist state 249, 273, 276; capitalism 82, 83; citizenship 78; critical response to 455–7; globalization 273, 470–3, 476–7, 478, 619; militarism 252, 255–6; modernity 433, 452–5; post-modernism 459, 651–6; society 497–8; states system 68, 69, 71; technology 560–1; territorial boundaries 62, 72, 470–3; time–space distanciation 17, 471, 498, 619, 620–1; tradition 599; welfare 257; working class 144
Gill, P. 483
Gilman, S. 216
Gilpin, R. 473, 475–6, 485–7, 493, 494
Gilroy, P. 618
Ginsburg, N. 258
Girardet, H. 506–7
global warming 492, 508, 510–11, 527, 528–9
globalization 428, 429–30, 467, 478–80, 482; advanced capitalist state 273–6; capitalism 190, 474; changing

globalization (*cont.*):
world 487; compliance and authority 492; culture 477; economic life 561–2; European 80–1; identity 628; and industry 304–5; interconnectedness 272–3, 470, 472–3, 476; labor 483; logics 473–8; modern economic life 561–2; and modernity 455, 469–73; and nation-state 488–93; and national identities 618–19; politics 45–6; post-modernity 621–3; power geometry 624; sociology 468–9; technology 474–5, 484; time–space compression 571, 619–21, 622, 624–5; time–space distanciation 17, 471, 498, 619, 620–1; universalism 497–9
Goffman, Erving 386, 605
Goldthorpe, J. 316
Gordon, D. 494, 495, 560
Gorz, A. 542–3, 544, 551, 558–9
Gott, R. 565, 568
Gough, I. 258
Gourevitch, P. 256, 257, 260, 261, 271, 490
Gramsci, Antonio 398, 410–12, 419, 547
Green politics: consumerism 523–6; and Enlightenment 516–18; in parliament 518–21; *see also* environmentalism
Green/green politics 515–18, 520–1, 522, 530
Greenpeace 514
group identity 577
*Guardian, The* 445, 523, 565
Gummett, P. 251
gynocentrism 128

Haakonssen, K. 114
Habermas, J. 586, 642–4, 645–6, 657–8
Hakim, C. 309, 315, 316, 336
Halberg, M. 660
Hale, J. R. 194, 204
Hall, C. 217, 617
Hall, S. 389, 598, 614
Hampson, N. 46, 47, 516
Hannerz, U. 478
Hanreider, W. 494
Hartmann, G. 335, 336
Hartmann, H. 126, 142, 143
Harvey, D.: capitalism 482; globalization 478, 479, 557–9; modernity 599; post-modernism 552–3, 555, 567, 569–72; time–space compression 17, 471–2, 571, 619–21
Harvey, J. 321
Hayter, T. 528
health policy 263–4
Hebdige, D. 567, 568, 580–3, 586
Heelas, P. 588
hegemony 412; Fordism 287; Islamic 80, 196, 197; military 476; western 194; US 291–2, 442
Held, D.: democracy 79, 451, 461; social movements 456; socialism 452; sovereignty 495, 496; state/civil society 72, 265, 463
Herder, J. G. 152
hermaphroditism 372–4
Herodotus 207
Hertz, J. 488
Hertzman, R. 496
heterosexuality 357, 380–2, 391
Hillier, J. 350
Himmelfarb, G. 447
Hintze, O. 74, 84
Hippel, Theodor von 35
history 9–13, 21, 443, 447
HIV virus 364, 391–2
Hobbes, Thomas 155, 219, 604
Hobsbawm, E. 133, 614
Hoffman, K. 332, 334, 336
Holcombe, L. 143
Holy Roman Empire 64–5
home 127, 130, 141, 352; *see also* domesticity
homogenization, and differentiation 478
homosexuality 357, 375, 380–1, 382–5, 391–2
Honour, H. 209, 213, 215, 217, 218
Hont, I. 114
Horace 207
Horkheimer, M. 178, 180–1, 437
Hounshell, A. 283, 285
household, as work-unit 101–2, 104, 107, 124–5, 130, 236
Hudson, R. 316
Hulme, P. 197, 210, 214, 215–16
human nature, uniformity 23, 36–7, 152, 216–17

human subject *see* subject
Hume, David 20, 26, 36
Hussain, A. 201
hybridity 617, 619, 629–32
hyperreality 571, 584, 585

idealization 209–10, 215
identity 386–7, 627–9; and difference 615–18; and ideology 412–13; globalization 628; psychoanalytical approach 608; time–space compression 619–21; *see also* subject
identity, types: collective 402, 582; cultural 7, 8–9, 596, 611–13; de-centered 596–7, 602; dislocated 599–600, 606; ethnic 615; gender 354–5; group 577; national 65, 79, 416, 613–14, 616, 618–19; pluralized 600–1; sexual 372–4, 380–8, 385–8; social 8, 610–11
identity politics 610–11
ideological community 398, 412–20
ideology: capitalism 410; conflicting 400, 437, 442–4, 446–7; cultural 419; discourse 202–3; domesticity 140–1, 145; dominant 415–16; history 443; identity 412–13; political 419; religion 411; scientific 202–3; symbolism 413; unity 412; of West 186
Ignatieff, M. 114
*Illuminati* 45
ILO (1984) 317
imagined communities 402, 413, 414, 420, 611–13
imperialism 62–3, 190–1, 224
income distribution 113, 123
individual: estranged 605–6; public/private sphere 408; rights 72; self-restraint 371, 374; social space 159, 353, 385, 610; sovereign 603–4, 605; state legitimacy 71; *see also* subject
individualism 23, 53, 399, 415, 602, 604, 605
individuation 353–5, 358
industrial production *see* production
industrialism: class structure 134–9; and environmentalism 524–5; feminism 143–6; in modernity 452; to post-industrialism 536–46; poverty 137
industrialization: family life 139–40, 142; social change 110, 133–5; of warfare 250–1, 252–3; women 127, 128–9, 139–43
industrially advanced country 308; employment upgrades 313–14; industry location 328–9; labor shortage 323; manufacturing/service economy 309–12; meritocracy 313; productivity/employment statistics 289; unemployment 316–17
industry: discourse of 301–4; eighteenth century 102; globalization 304–5; growth rates 103–5; proto-industry 130; state intervention 252
inequality, economic/social 543–4, 561
information 537–8, 540, 541–2, 544
information occupations 540, 542, 544; *see also* communication technology
information society 539, 540–1
institutionalization 256, 264–8
institutions: collective 609–10; discourse 202; modernity 427, 433–4, 452–3, 454, 456, 457; pillarization 407; public 242; and regulation 548; social representations 233–4; welfare state 256, 266
instrumentalism, and structuralism 266
integration, and fragmentation 478–9, 483
intellectuals 38–40, 53, 172
interconnectedness: economic 488–9, 536; global 272–3, 470, 472–3, 476; and interdependence 494–5; states system 455–6
interdependence: environmental 528; global 274–5, 467, 489; and interconnectedness 494–5; technological 474
international law 69–70
international regimes 275, 483, 489–90, 494
interpellation 413, 417, 418
investment flows 332
Islam: fundamentalism 630–1; hegemony 80, 196, 197; Ottoman Empire 58, 196; social development 222

Jackson, M. 382
Jackson, R. V. 98, 99, 100
Jacobs, J. 591
Jacobsen, J. 317
Jameson, F.: capitalism 482, 488; culture 572–8; globalization 479; post-modernism 498, 567, 570–1
Janowitz, M. 78
Japan 264, 266, 268, 336, 337
Jenkins, R. 331

Jenner, P. 325–6
Jerusalem, as world center 197, 200, 207
Jervis, R. 489
Jessop, B. 270, 271, 292, 294, 296, 456, 552
jobs see work
Jones, H. G. 74
Jones, J. 522
juxtaposition, and syncretization 479, 482

Kafka, Franz 606
Kaiser, K. 490
Kames, Henry 220
Kant, Immanuel 26–7, 28, 52
Kaplinsky, R. 332, 334, 336, 337
Keane, J. 57, 463
Keely, C. 322
Kellner, D. 585
Kennedy, P. 42
Keohane, R. 274, 442, 490, 494
Kertbeny, K. 380
Keynes, J. M. 113
Kindleberger, C. 323
King, A. 483
King, G. 124
kingship 65, 67; see also monarchy
Kinsey, A. 376, 387
kinship classifications 159
knowledge: as agent of change 42; classical 206–7;
    closing-off 25; contextual 100–1; deconstructed 642;
    descriptive/predictive 581–2; discourse 201–2;
    idealization 209–10, 215; information 537–8, 544;
    justification process 637–8; legitimacy 640–1, 642;
    materialist 36; modernity 8; power 194, 557–8;
    rationalism 642–3, 652; religious/biblical 207; of
    society 637, 638, 640, 652; specialization 643;
    technology 538, 560–1; western concept 187
knowledge elites 431, 527, 538, 544
knowledge theory of value 540
Kosack, G. 326
Krafft-Ebing, R. von 365–6, 380, 382
Krasner, S. 271, 494–5

labor: alienated 176–7; capital 656; gendered division
    345–6, 348; globalization 483; mobility potential
    324–5; productive/reproductive 346, 351–3;
    subdivision 134; see also division of labor; work
labor aristocracy 144
labor force: disposability 329–30, 338; feminization
    318–19; hierarchy 144; migrant workers 329–30,
    337–8; routinization 333–4; unrest 549–50; women
    126, 140–1, 316–18, 330–1, 337–8, 344; see also
    workers
labor laws 141, 142–3, 349
labor market: core/periphery 308–9; dual 314, 316, 337;
    gender/ethnic segregation 236, 317–21; homogenized
    313–14; segmentation 312–17; sexual segregation
    141–2, 318, 319; and technology 335; women 308–9,
    317–21
labor process 548, 549, 550–1
labor reserve 338
Lacan, Jacques 354–5, 607
Laclau, E. 567, 568, 577, 579, 599–600
laissez-faire capitalism 109, 312
land-ownership 124, 129–30
Lane, C. 334, 335, 336
Lange, P. 491
Langford, P. 94, 106
language: langue/parole 156; meaning 359, 609; and
    narrative 13–14; post-modernism 570; and religion
    50; sexuality 366–7; social factor 153, 156, 608–9; and
    truth 203
language games, and discourse 645–6
Laqueur, T. 370, 377
Las Casas, Bartolomé de 217
Lasch, C. 591
Lash, S. 274
Laski, H. 16
Laslett, P. 124, 125–6
late capitalism 568, 571, 572–8, 592
late-modernity 432, 434, 598–600
Latham, R. 196
Law, D. 483
lead industries 559, 560
Lechner, F. 477, 497
Lee, C. H. 289, 298–9

Leggett, J. 508
legislation: labor laws 141, 142–3, 349; sexuality 380;
    state's role 242–3; women's rights 145–6
legitimacy: democracy 459; knowledge 640–1, 642;
    modern state 71, 85, 86; state 420
Lehmbruch, G. 269
Leninism 448
lesbianism 384–5, 386
Lévi-Strauss, C. 152, 155, 156, 159–60, 162
Lewis, F. 483
Lewis, P. 440
liberal democracy 72–3, 263, 437, 445, 447–8, 462
liberalism 442–6, 449–50, 460–1
Lijphart, A. 243, 445
Lindblom, C. 263, 264
Lindholm, C. 591
linguistics 608–9
Lipietz, A. 327, 330, 331, 551, 554–5, 557
Locke, John 26, 36–7, 72, 109, 219, 603
Louis XV, King of France 67
Loveridge, R. 315, 331
Lovering, J. 251
Lowe, P. 515, 521–2
Luckmann, T. 407
Luhmann, N. 391
Lukes, S. 265
Lyotard, J.-F. 540, 570, 579, 637, 639–42, 645, 647–8

McDowell, L. 318
Macfarlane, A. 125
McGrew, A. 476
McIntosh, M. 352, 354
MacIntyre, A. 397, 403
MacIver, R. M. 396
McKendrick, N. 94
MacKenzie, G. 252
McKibben, B. 506
McLaren, A. 376
McLennan, G. 272
McNeill, N. 252, 254
McNeill, W. 198
Macpherson, C. B. 73
Malcolmson, Robert 129–30
managed capitalism see capitalism, types
Mandeville, Bernard 118, 219
Mandeville, Sir John 207–8
Mann, M.: absolutism/constitutionalism 66–7, 68, 69, 72;
    advanced capitalist state 249; capitalism 84, 261;
    citizenship 78; European expansion 80, 82–3, 190,
    197, 199; history and social science 10; militarism 251,
    252, 261; military expenditure 74–6; society 497–8;
    state intervention 240, 241, 271
Mann, N. 313
manufacturing 297–9; flexible 551–2; globalization
    472; household work-unit 102, 104, 107, 124–5, 130,
    236; job worth 303; and service industries 297,
    298–303, 309–12; and war 253–4
maps, as fiction 200–1
Marcuse, H. 178, 180–1
marketing 581–2
markets: competitive 108, 109, 198, 490–1; free market
    economy 108–10; international 274; laissez-faire
    445–6
Marshall, P. 219
Marshall, T. H. 83
Marx, Karl: alienation 176–7, 179, 398; Asiatic mode of
    production 223; class struggle 113, 221–3, 409, 463;
    Das Kapital 135; exploitation 131; industrialization
    134–5; modernity 11–12, 17, 598–9; pre-industrial
    society 130–2; religion 399, 401, 413; social practices
    15; working class and revolution 136, 139
Marxism 11, 232, 450; advanced capitalist state 265–6;
    class struggle 221–3, 656; collective goals 458;
    de-centering of subject 606–7; delegitimizing of politics
    451; and democracy 450–1; as Enlightenment project
    656–9, 662–3; labor–capital relationship 656; and
    liberalism 449–50, 460–1; post-modernism 567, 657;
    power 453; production 221, 223; ruling class 265; and
    Stalinism 448, 451–2; welfare 258–9; see also
    neo-Marxism
Marxism Today 579
masculinity 358, 359, 370–2, 381
mass media 566, 568, 583–4
mass production 281, 283–5, 294–5, 296–7, 332, 534
Massey, D. 312, 624

Mathias, P. 133
Mead, G. H. 586, 597, 605, 607
meaning: contextual 14; desire 359–60, 371; and difference 187–8; from words 153; and language 359, 609; social practices 15–16, 158, 201–2
mechanization 115, 289
medievalism, new 496–7
Meegan, R. 334–5
Meek, R. 218–19, 220
mercantilism 109, 117
Mercer, K. 597, 601
meritocracy 312–13
Methodism 414–15
Mexican workers in USA 321–2
middle class: Enlightenment 40; environmentalism 527; French 32, 134–9; industrial society 144–5; new 136; pre-industrial 130
migrant workers 308–9, 316, 321–7, 624
migration 626–7
Miles, I. 311
Miliband, R. 265
militarism 74–9, 250–6, 261, 476
military-industrial-bureaucratic-techno-complex 251–2
military spending 74–6, 243–4, 248–9
Millar, J. 220
Miller, D. 446
Millett, K. 126
Mills, C. W. 251–2, 264, 265
Milward, A. 254–5
Mitchell, B. R. 74
Mitchell, J. 354, 356–8, 359
Mitchell, T. 243
Modelski, G. 80, 469, 479–80, 481, 487, 493
modern state 57, 70–3, 86–7; capitalism 79–84; civilianization 248, 250; legitimacy 71, 85, 86; and society 240; see also nation-state; state
modernism 17, 432, 569
modernity 3–7, 8–9, 400–1, 426–8; capitalism 5, 12, 452; economic foundation 91–3, 555; and Enlightenment 30–1, 35–7, 398–403, 642–4; as European phenomenon 231–2; globalization 455, 469–73; industrialism 427, 433–4, 452–3, 454, 456, 457; late-modernity 432, 434, 598–600; Marxism 11–12, 17, 598–9; metanarratives 639–42; pluralism 432; and post-modernity 452–7; power 452–3; secularization 175, 237, 398, 401–2; social movements 453–4, 456; and tradition 30–1; women's role 345, 346
modernization theory 11–12
Molyneux, M. 350
monarchy 65; absolute 31, 43, 47, 66–70; administration 68; centralized 190; constitutional 66, 69
Montaigne, M. E. de 218
Montesquieu, Baron de 20, 26, 31, 43, 46
Moorhead, A. 210, 218
Moral Majority 396, 405, 406
moral sciences 36
morality 42, 397, 403, 416
Morse, E. 274, 489
Mortimer, E. 442
motherhood 354–8, 360–1
Mouffe, C. 567, 568, 577, 579
multinational corporations 304–5, 308, 327–8, 331–2, 483
Murgatroyd, L. 352
Murray, R. 290, 293, 483, 552, 553–4, 555
mysticism 168
myths 157, 207, 614

Nairn, T. 615
narrative 13–14, 620, 639
nation 219–21, 613–14, 616, 617
nation-state 7, 71–4, 85, 453, 488–95; culture 612; globalization 488–93; society 468–9; warfare 77–8, 84–5, 86; see also modern state; state
national culture 188, 611–18
national identity 65, 79, 416, 613–14, 616, 618–19
nationalism 72, 78–9, 414, 493–4, 632
naturalism 41–2
nature, marginalized 506–7
nature conservation 513–14
neo-Fordism 550–1, 553–4
neo-Marxism 258–9; advanced capitalist state 269; economics 232–3; environmentalism 525; globalization 482; instrumentalism/structuralism 266;

late capitalism 568; post-modernism 566–7; welfare 258–9
neo-pluralism 264
neo-realism 486–7
Netherlands 407
Neumann, F. 57
neutrality 203–5
New Age movements 568–9, 588–9
New Christian Right 405, 406
new international division of labor 327–32
New Right 240, 266–7, 419
New Times 567, 568, 578–9, 580–3
New World 192–3, 211–17
Newby, E. 191, 207, 212
newly industrialized countries (NICs) 308, 312, 551
Newton, Isaac 26, 37, 38, 41
Nietzsche, F. 170–1, 177, 644
nihilism 170–1, 177
Nisbet, R. 22
Nordlinger, E. 262, 263, 266, 268, 271
Norris, C. 14
Norris, E. 321
North, D. 322
nostalgia 17–18, 410–11, 574
nuclear weapons 255
Nye, J. 489, 490

O'Leary, B. 267, 269
objectivism 647–8, 651, 660, 662
occupational change 312–13
Oedipus complex 355–6, 357
Offe, C. 258–9, 270, 274, 313
oligopolies 290–1, 295, 550
one-party polity 73
Open University (1981) 411
organicism 53
Orientalism (Said) 205–6, 209, 211
Other 7; as dark side 221; representations 204–16; and self 607–8; sexuality 378–9; stereotypes 216
Ottoman Empire 58, 196
Ovid 207
ownership 431, 446; land 124, 129–30
ozone layer 508, 509

Paine, Thomas 45
Panitch, L. 268
Parkinson, F. 475, 484
Parmar, P. 379
Parsons, T. 353–4, 416, 588, 605
particularization/universalization 478, 498, 623, 648
pastiche 574, 592
Pateman, C. 346
patriarchy 125–9, 142, 346–8
peace dividend 251
Pearce, D. 512, 525
Pearton, M. 250, 252, 253, 254
Peasants' Revolt 132
Pełczynski, Z. A. 57
Perkins, T. 320
Perlmutter, H. V. 479, 480, 481
Peters, R. S. 67
philosophes 4, 21–2, 23–7, 31–2; American 44; modes of thought 35–7; religion 30–1, 36, 173; revolution 44–5; science 41–3; see also Enlightenment
philosophy 637, 641, 660–1
Phizacklea, A. 316, 331
physiocrats 302
Pierson, C. 248, 253, 258–9, 260, 267, 274
Piore, M. 321, 332, 333, 334, 335
Piven, F. 258
Plato 206
Pliny 207
Plummer, K. 384, 386
pluralism 263–4; lifeworld 645, 651; post-modern 498, 565–6, 568; social 432, 575, 579, 592
Poggi, G. 63, 64, 66, 67, 68, 76, 79, 83
Polan, A. J. 451
Poland 441–2
policy process 264–5
polis 59
political good 438, 458–9
political rights 83–4
politics: capitalism 109; changes 552; culture 572–8; of difference 601; globalization 475–6; ideologies 419; Marxism 451; modern societies 233; post-international

politics (*cont.*):
  485; sexuality 370, 388–92; sovereignty 495–7
polity of estates 65–6, 70
pollution 507–14, 526
Polo, Marco 196, 204, 207–8
Ponting, C. 507
Poole, R. 154
Poor Law 133, 244
population growth 93–4, 133
population policies 350
populism 592
Porat, M. 540
Porritt, Jonathon 514–15, 524
Porter, M. 311, 332
Porter, R. 25, 26, 43, 93, 94–8, 101–2, 106
Portuguese expansion 191–2, 193–4, 195
positivism 22, 41, 155, 652
post-Fordism 546, 551–4, 556–7
post-industrial economy 310, 311–12
post-industrial society 105, 324–5, 542–3
post-industrialism 484, 534–46, 556, 557, 559
post-Marxism 579
post-modernism 17, 569–72, 637, 638; constructive
  580–3, 586–91; consumerism 583–6; and
  Enlightenment 638, 642–4, 654–6; and feminism 592;
  global 621–3; identity 597–8; language 570; and
  Marxism 567, 657; modernity 452–7; narratives
  639–40, 641; neo-Marxism 566–7; pluralism 498,
  565–6, 568; reflexivity 653–5; rejected 578–80;
  relativism 644–8, 651, 655, 658, 660, 662;
  schizophrenia 574
Poulantzas, N. 265–6
poverty: feminization 351; industrialism 137; Third
  World 528; urban/rural 133; welfare 244; women
  141, 142
Powell, Enoch 613
power 493, 609; autonomy 271–2; capitalist societies
  264; essentialism 347; global 486, 489, 624; of
  knowledge 194, 557–8; Marxism 453; men/women
  126; modernity 452–3; pre-industrial society 129–30;
  private 243; public 242–3, 462; sexuality 367,
  375–80; state 71, 271–2, 462
power politics 427, 486
Pratten, C. F. 115
pre-industrial society 124–33
pressure groups 514, 521–3; *see also* social movements
prices 108–9, 117, 550
private sphere *see* public/private spheres
production 107, 115, 300–1; Asiatic 223; capitalism
  134; changes 552; cooperative 139; craft 283, 284–5;
  decentralized 551; ecology 526; fragmented 328;
  geographical divide 557; labour-/capital-intensive 325;
  Marxism 221, 223; mechanization 115, 289; relocation
  326–7, 329, 331; *see also* mass production
productivity 110–11, 115, 288–9
products, standardization 285
progress 23, 36, 37–8, 237–8
proletariat 130, 134–9
prostitution 374
Protestant ethic 132, 165–6, 166–7, 172
Protestantism 399, 406, 603
Proust, Marcel 383–4
psychoanalytic theory 354–5, 358, 369–70, 608
psychographics 581
Ptolemy 206
public/private spheres 344–5, 346, 349–50, 353–4, 397,
  399, 408, 427, 597–8
public expenditure 247, 248, 259–60, 261
public goods 109
Puritanism 173, 174, 199

Rabinow, P. 609
race: as category 617–18; and sexuality 378–80, 387–8;
  *see also* cultural racism
Ramazanoglu, C. 346
Ranger, T. 614
Rasler, K. 249
rationalism 23, 158, 171–5, 199; capitalism 164–6, 169;
  critical 22, 180–1; ethics 181; and feminism 659–60;
  and knowledge 642–3, 652; scientific 170; and truth
  662
Rattansi, A. 617
realism 454, 485–7
reason, universality 498–9
reciprocity 68, 212–13, 605

reflexivity 14, 434, 653–5
regulation 199–201, 294–6, 547–9
Reich, Wilhelm 369
Reisler, M. 321
relativism: cultural 42–3, 645, 647; Foucault 205;
  post-modernism 644–8, 651, 655, 658, 660, 662
religion 167–9, 396–9, 403–5; capitalism 164–7;
  economics 413; ideology 411; knowledge 207;
  language 50; *philosophes* 30–1, 36, 173;
  pre-Reformation 175; public role 407; Reformation
  603; ritual 161; sects 404–5; and secular world 6,
  401; social cement 50; televangelism 582, 589–90;
  Weber 132; *see also* Christianity; Islam; New Age
Renan, E. 615, 616, 618
Reppy, J. 251
representations 201, 620; collective 157–9, 413, 416;
  cultural 612; Other 204–16; social 233–4; symbolic
  157; West 186–7, 188
repression, political 441
resource depletion 512–13, 515, 529
revolution 44–8, 439–40
rhetoric 419
Ricardo, David 113
Rich, A. 382
rights 72, 83–4, 145–6
ritual 160, 161; degradation 213–15; national 415–16,
  417
Roberts, B. 314
Roberts, C. 320
Roberts, J. 185, 187, 189, 194, 196, 197, 200–1
Robertson, R. 477, 478, 497, 498
Robertson, William 219–20
Robins, K. 623, 625, 627, 628-9
Roman Empire 58
Rorty, R. 435
Rose, R. 240, 246
Rosecrance, R. 489
Rosenau, R. 467, 473, 474–5, 479, 484–5, 487, 492
Rosenbrock, H. 333
Rostow, W. 11–12
Rousseau, Jean-Jacques 26, 31, 41, 43, 47, 218
Rüdig, W. 521
Ruggie, J. 495
ruling class 66, 265
Rushdie, Salman 629, 630
Ruskin, John 140
Rustin, M. 557

Sabel, C. 332, 333, 334, 335
Sachs, Jonathan 400–1, 403
sacred 160, 174, 398, 402, 590
Said, Edward 205–6, 209, 211, 620
Saint-Simon, Henri de 22, 48–9, 52–3
Saussure, Ferdinand de 155, 156, 187, 608–9
savages, noble/ignoble 43, 217–19, 378
Sayer, A. 286, 292, 297, 557
scale economies 102, 285, 333
Schama, S. 67, 195
Scharpf, F. 495
Schmitter, P. 267, 268
Schwarz, B. 612–13
science 41–2; and cultural values 169–71;
  Enlightenment 23, 28, 30, 37–40, 173, 640–1; and
  ideology 202–3; knowledge 170; and legend 208
Scott, A. 522, 526–7
Scott, H. 351
Scott, J. 265
Scottish Enlightenment 4, 27, 42–3, 50, 52, 219–20
Scruton, R. 419, 612
Searle, G. 528
secularism 24, 53
secularization: and community 403–7; culture 163, 165;
  modernity 175, 237, 398, 401–2; moral values 397,
  416
security *see* state security
seduction 584
Seear, N. 313
segregation, sexual 123, 141–2, 145–6, 318, 319
Seidel, G. 419
self-determination 459
self-interest 112, 165
self-reflection 460
self-restraint 163
Sennett, R. 628
service industries: Britain 311; and manufacturing 297,

service industries (*cont.*):
298–303, 309–12; post-industrial 537–8, 556–7;
women workers 319
sewage 511
sex 365–8; essential element 366, 368, 369, 386; instinct
365–6; pleasure 382
sexology 365–6, 368, 380–1
sexual difference 345, 355, 356–7, 360, 377, 611
sexual identities 372–4, 380–8
sexuality 236–7, 364, 368–9, 372–4, 380–1; absolutist
approach 388–9; capitalism 369; class 375–6; as
construct 210, 365, 367, 369; culture 370–2, 374;
division of labor 127–8, 141–2, 344–8; in family
390–2; feminism 379; gender 376–8; language
366–7; legislation 380; Other 378–9; permissiveness
388–90; politics of 370, 388–92; power 367, 375–80;
race 378–80, 387–8; and sin 383; social factors
374–5; stigmatization 383–4, 387; as taboo 173–4;
Victorian 374–5
sexuality, types: bisexuality 381; hermaphroditism
372–4; heterosexuality 357, 380–2, 391; homosexuality
357, 375, 380–1, 382–5, 391–2; infantile 355–6, 357;
lesbianism 384–5, 386; transvestism 383
Seymour, J. 506–7
Shaw, C. 318
Shaw, M. 489
Shils, E. 415–16
Shorter, E. 127, 129
signs 153
Simmel, G. 572
Simon, W. 369
skills: enskilling 552; labor force 320–1; and status
314; and technology 336–7; and wages 331; women
313, 320–1; *see also* deskilling
Skinner, Q. 57, 71
Sklair, L. 483
Skocpol, T. 84, 271
slavery 44, 192, 217
Smith, Adam 5, 26, 92–3, 107–9, 110–18, 220, 302
Smith, H. L. 253
social class *see* class
social constructionism 368, 370–1
social democracy 256–8, 427–8
social history 97–8, 370
social identity 8, 610–11
social movements 453–4, 456, 539, 576–7
social practices 15–16, 153, 158, 201–2, 373–4, 646
social science 4, 40–4, 118–20, 221, 433–4, 637, 638
social security 258
social structure 31–3, 123, 581
socialism 427, 437–8, 449, 451–2
societies 497–8; collective representations 159;
commercial 93–100; core/peripheral 625; cultural
bonds 396, 418; environmental threats 506–14; Law of
Human Progress 49–50; modern 8–9, 123; nation-state
468–9; post-industrial divisions 105, 324–5, 542–3;
post-modern 637, 638; public/private spheres 344–5,
346, 349–50, 353–4, 397, 399, 408, 427, 597–8; state/
stateless 57; western/non-western 186
sociology 4–5, 21–4, 40–51, 53, 396; of aspiration 581;
charisma/sacred 590; globalization 468–9; identity
597–8; moral sciences 36; positivism 155; Western
concepts 221–4
soldier, subject/citizen 78
Sontag, S. 364
Sorel, A. 45–6
sovereignty: advanced capitalist state 275; and autonomy
491; kingship 67–8; modern state 86–7; political
community 495–7; state 69, 491; subject 603–4,
605
Spanish exploration 192–3, 194, 195
spending, and production 290
Springborg, P. 58
Stacey, J. 568, 583, 587–8
Stafford, W. 415
Stalinism 448, 451–2
state 5, 56, 76, 241; absolutist 66–70; capitalism
79–84, 269, 456–7; citizens 240; civil society 82–3,
262, 459–63; class 83–4; economic growth 106, 256,
286–7; as employer 248; European 58–62; and
family 349–51; as government 242; internationalized
490; intervention 240, 241, 252, 271; legislation
242–3; legitimacy 420; military spending 74–5;
paternalism 110; *polis* 59; power 71, 271–2, 462;
welfare 361; *see also* advanced capitalist state; modern
state; nation-state
state autonomy 259, 266, 268–70, 271–2, 491–2, 494
state formation 5, 76, 85–6
state security 76, 250, 489
state socialism 427, 451–2, 525
states system: European 58–62, 68, 71; global 252, 475,
485–7, 493; interconnectedness 455–6; security
dilemma 76, 250, 489; Westphalian model 69–70
*Statistical Abstract of US* (1994) 322
stereotyping 127–8, 214, 215–16, 318, 320, 344–5, 379
Stern, B. 32
stigmatization, sexual 383–4, 387
Stoicism 117, 119
structural linguistics 608–9
structuralism 161–2; cultural change 150, 155–6;
instrumentalism 266; synchronic/diachronic analysis
156–7, 163
sub-groupism 492–3
subcontracting 316, 337
subject: biological concept 604–5; birth and death of
601–6; Cartesian 603; de-centered 517, 602, 603,
606–11; gendered 611; social concept 604; sovereignty
603–4, 605; *see also* individual
subscription libraries 39–40
subsistence, modes 221
suffrage 145–6
Sweden 256–7, 268, 271
symbolic interactionism 586, 597–8, 605
symbolism 162; civic 417; ideology 413; representation
157; as social activity 153; unconscious 356–7

taboos 173–4
Tahiti 210, 212, 218
Taylor, Frederick W. 283–4
Taylor, K. 48
Taylorism 333, 334
technology 36; capitalism 541; computer numerical
control 335; elites 538; globalization 474–5, 484;
innovations 102, 290; interdependence 474; knowledge
538, 560–1; skills 336–7
Teichgraeber, R. F. 114
Teilhard de Chardin, P. 481
teleology 652
televangelism 582, 589–90
territorial boundaries 62, 70–1, 72, 470–3
textile industry 102–3, 325
Thatcherism 270, 419
Thee, M. 251
theodicy 171–2
*Theory of Moral Sentiments* (Smith) 107, 112, 116–17,
220
Therborn, G. 78, 248, 256, 257, 259
Third World 11–12, 527–9
Thomas, K. 507
Thomas, W. I. 579
Thompson, E. P. 138–9
Thompson, J. B. 446
Thompson, K. 49, 415
Thompson, N. R. 249
Thrift, N. 331
Tilly, C.: absolutism 68; capitalism 82, 241; class conflict
84; Europe 59, 80; modern state 248, 249, 250;
nation-state 71, 76–7, 85
time–space compression 571–5, 619–21, 622, 624–5
time–space distanciation 17, 471, 498, 619, 620–1
Tocqueville, Alexis de 399, 401
toleration 23
Tolliday, S. 293
totalitarianism 180, 437
totems 154, 159, 162, 413
Touraine, A. 538–9, 554
trade 212, 303–4
trade unions: advanced capitalist state 267–8; labor
aristocracy 144; labor market 314; war 254; women
workers 141
tradition 30–1, 418, 599, 614, 628–9
translation and tradition 629
transnational corporation *see* multinational corporation
transport infrastructure 94, 101, 102
transvestism 383
travellers' tales 207
tribute system 63
Trotskyist tradition 448
Trumbach, R. 383
truth 203, 205, 208, 409, 662

Turgot, Anne Robert  26
Turner, B. S.  17, 78, 222, 223, 370, 396, 468

UK *see* Britain
unconscious: Freudian  179–80, 358, 369–70, 607–8;
  individuation  354–5; symbolism  356–7
UNCTC (1988)  304
unemployment  113, 285, 316–17, 327, 527, 542
uniformity of human nature  23, 36–7, 152, 216–17
universalism  23, 25, 26, 480, 497–9, 649–50
universalization/particularization  478, 498, 623, 648
urban growth  133
Urry, J.  274
Urwin, D.  520
USA: American Revolution  44; autonomy  492; loss of
  hegemony  442; migrant labor  321–2, 326; New Deal
  258, 286; *philosophes*  44; welfare provisions  256–7;
  *see also* Americas; New World utopia

value-neutrality  180–1, 182
Vance, C.  364–5, 370, 371
Venturi, R.  573
Vespucci, Amerigo  193, 210, 213
Vicinus, M.  385
Vigée-Lebrun, Elizabeth  35
violence  145, 163–4, 233; *see also* coercion
Voltaire, F. M. A. de  20, 26; anticlericalism  36;
  monarchy  34; revolution  45; scientific knowledge
  37–8, 41, 42; social system  32–3

Wachter, C.  322
wage-workers  82, 127, 135–6, 548
wages  284, 286, 290, 317, 331, 561
Walby, S.  142, 347–8
Walker, R.  480
Wallerstein, I.  81–2, 473–4, 478, 479, 480, 615, 619
Wallis, R.  406, 407
Waltz, K.  493
war  646; advanced capitalist state 241; capitalism
  249–50; in democracy  78; Freud  178–9;
  industrialization of  250–1, 252–3; loyalty  63;
  manufacturing  253–4; nation-state  77–8, 84–5, 86;
  nuclear  255; welfare  253–4; *see also* militarism;
  military spending
Ward, A.  324
Warde, A.  310
waste: disposal costs  512; earthbound  511–12; gaseous
  508, 510; nuclear  512
wealth distribution  123
*Wealth of Nations, The* (Smith)  107–8, 110–12, 113–14,
  115–16, 118, 119–20
Webb, M. C.  489, 491
Weber, Max  132–3; asceticism  173; capitalism  83,
  164–5, 169, 401; charisma  402, 590–1; class system
  136–7, 144–5; elective affinity  172; Islam and Western
  Europe  222; patriarchy  125; Protestant ethic  400;
  rationalism  171–5, 199; religion  150, 163–4, 165–9,
  404; science  169–70; social practices  15; society  53;
  theodicy  171–2; violence control  233
Weeks, J.  369, 370, 376, 388, 391
welfare politics, eugenics  374–5
welfare state  259–60, 361; advanced capitalist state  241,

244–6, 259–61; autonomy  259; class  258–9;
  institutionalized  256, 266; poverty  244, 351; social
  democratic account 257; universal nature  256–61; war
  253–4
Werneke, D.  319
West: as global story  187; hegemony  194; as historical
  construct  185–9; internal differences  188–9; and
  Islam  197; as representation  186–7, 188; and rest
  186, 626–7; sociology  221–4; and Third World  446
westernization  625
Westphalian model, state systems  69–70
White, H.  13
White, John  209
Wilde, Oscar  384
Wilkinson, F.  314, 327, 338
Williams, G.  219
Williams, K.  293
Williams, R.  16, 150, 151, 152, 176, 410, 602, 604
Wilson, B.  403, 404–5
Winch, D.  114
Withey, L.  208
Wollstonecraft, Mary  34
women: domestic tasks  127, 128; Enlightenment  29,
  33–5, 42; and family  127, 145, 348–9; industrialization
  127, 128–9, 139–43; inferiorized psychology  356; in
  labor force  126, 140–1, 316–18, 330–1, 337–8, 344; in
  labor market  308–9, 317–21; as labor reserve  319–20;
  legal position  142, 145–6; modernity  345, 346;
  mothering  346–7, 354–8, 360–1; poverty  141, 142,
  351; separate spheres  140, 143, 353–4; sexuality  374;
  skills  313, 320–1; stereotypes  127–8, 344–5; wages
  317, 561; working class  139–43
Wood, S.  557
work: achievement principle  313; changes  312–13;
  creativity denied  334; and non-work time  431–2;
  part-time  308–9, 315, 320; servile  561; sexual
  stereotyping  127–8; temporary  315; transformation
  538, 542; and wages  303; *see also* division of labor
workers  130; agricultural  134; core/peripheral  309, 314,
  316; creativity denied  334; female  126, 140–1,
  316–18, 330–1, 337–8, 344; flexibility  314–16; illegal
  322; specialization  285; *see also* wage-workers
working class: and capitalism  135–9; culture  144;
  dual consciousness  410, 411; emancipated  449;
  embourgeoisement  123; fragmented  431; revolution
  136, 139; welfare state  257; women  139–43
workplace: home  127, 130, 141, 352; scientific
  management  283–4, 557
World War I  253–4, 402
World War II  254–5, 437, 440
world-systems  81–2
Worsley, P.  312, 468, 481, 484–5; *see also* globalization
writers  32

Yearley, S.  507, 514, 518, 521, 522, 525
Yeatman, A.  353
Young, Arthur  105
Young, M.  415–16
Young, R.  14

Zinsser, J.  33–4, 35